Adobe Photoshop

2021 release

P9-DGU-186

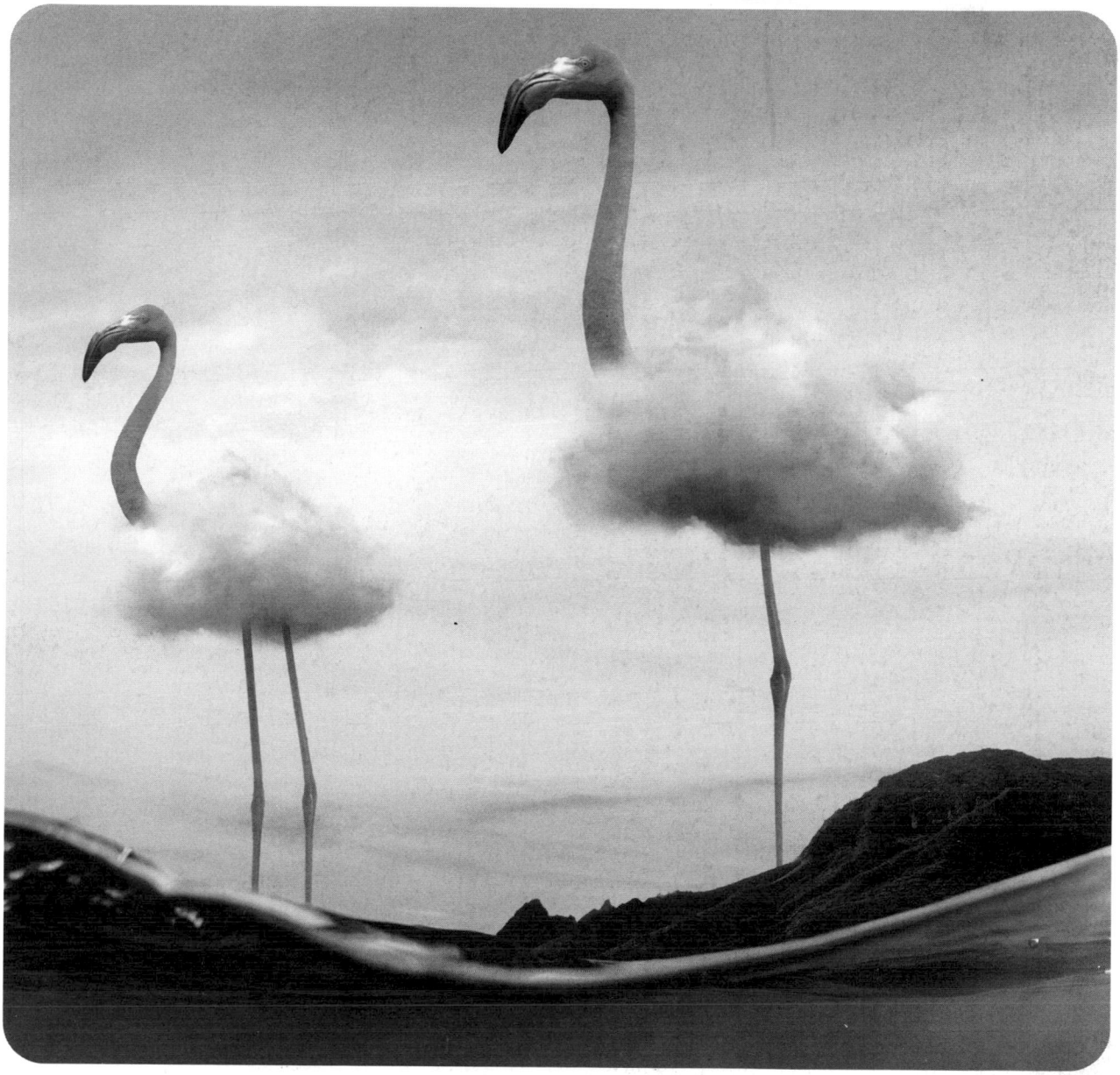

Classroom in a Book®

The official training workbook from Adobe

Andrew Faulkner & Conrad Chavez

Adobe Photoshop Classroom in a Book (2021 release)

© 2021 Adobe. All rights reserved.

Adobe Press is an imprint of Pearson Education, Inc. For the latest on Adobe Press books, go to www.adobepress.com. To report errors, please send a note to errata@peachpit.com. For information regarding permissions, request forms and the appropriate contacts within the Pearson Education Global Rights & Permissions department, please visit www.pearson.com/permissions.

If this guide is distributed with software that includes an end user license agreement, this guide, as well as the software described in it, is furnished under license and may be used or copied only in accordance with the terms of such license. Except as permitted by any such license, no part of this guide may be reproduced, stored in a retrieval system, or transmitted, in any form or by any means, electronic, mechanical, recording, or otherwise, without the prior written permission of Adobe. Please note that the content in this guide is protected under copyright law even if it is not distributed with software that includes an end user license agreement.

The content of this guide is furnished for informational use only, is subject to change without notice, and should not be construed as a commitment by Adobe. Adobe assumes no responsibility or liability for any errors or inaccuracies that may appear in the informational content contained in this guide.

Please remember that existing artwork or images that you may want to include in your project may be protected under copyright law. The unauthorized incorporation of such material into your new work could be a violation of the rights of the copyright owner. Please be sure to obtain any permission required from the copyright owner.

Any references to company names in sample files are for demonstration purposes only and are not intended to refer to any actual organization. Adobe, the Adobe logo, Adobe Fonts, Adobe Premiere, Adobe Stock, After Effects, Behance, Classroom in a Book, Creative Cloud, Creative Cloud logo, Illustrator, InDesign, Lightroom, Photoshop, and PostScript are either registered trademarks or trademarks of Adobe in the United States and/or other countries. Adobe product screenshots reprinted with permission from Adobe.

Apple, Mac OS, macOS, and Macintosh are trademarks of Apple, registered in the U.S. and other countries. Microsoft and Windows are either registered trademarks or trademarks of Microsoft Corporation in the U.S. and/or other countries. All other trademarks are the property of their respective owners.

Unless otherwise indicated herein, any third party trademarks that may appear in this work are the property of their respective owners and any references to third party trademarks, logos or other trade dress are for demonstrative or descriptive purposes only. Such references are not intended to imply any sponsorship, endorsement, authorization, or promotion of Pearson Education, Inc. products by the owners of such marks, or any relationship between the owner and Pearson Education, Inc. or its affiliates, authors, licensees or distributors.

Adobe Inc., 345 Park Avenue, San Jose, California 95110-2704, USA

Notice to U.S. Government End Users. The Software and Documentation are "Commercial Items," as that term is defined at 48 C.F.R. §2.101, consisting of "Commercial Computer Software" and "Commercial Computer Software Documentation," as such terms are used in 48 C.F.R. §12.212 or 48 C.F.R. §227.7202, as applicable. Consistent with 48 C.F.R. §12.212 or 48 C.F.R. §§227.7202-1 through 227.7202-4, as applicable, the Commercial Computer Software and Commercial Computer Software Documentation are being licensed to U.S. Government end users (a) only as Commercial Items and (b) with only those rights as are granted to all other end users pursuant to the terms and conditions herein. Unpublished-rights reserved under the copyright laws of the United States. Adobe Inc., 345 Park Avenue, San Jose, CA 95110-2704, USA. For U.S. Government End Users, Adobe agrees to comply with all applicable equal opportunity laws including, if appropriate, the provisions of Executive Order 11246, as amended, Section 402 of the Vietnam Era Veterans Readjustment Assistance Act of 1974 (38 USC 4212), and Section 503 of the Rehabilitation Act of 1973, as amended, and the regulations at 41 CFR Parts 60-1 through 60-60, 60-250, and 60-741. The affirmative action clause and regulations contained in the preceding sentence shall be incorporated by reference.

Cover Illustration: Ted Chin

ISBN-13: 978-0-13-690473-1
ISBN-10: 0-13-690473-4

3 2021

WHERE ARE THE LESSON FILES?

Purchase of this Classroom in a Book in any format gives you access to the lesson files you'll need to complete the exercises in the book.

1 Go to www.adobepress.com/PhotoshopCIB2021.

2 Sign in or create a new account.

3 Click Submit.

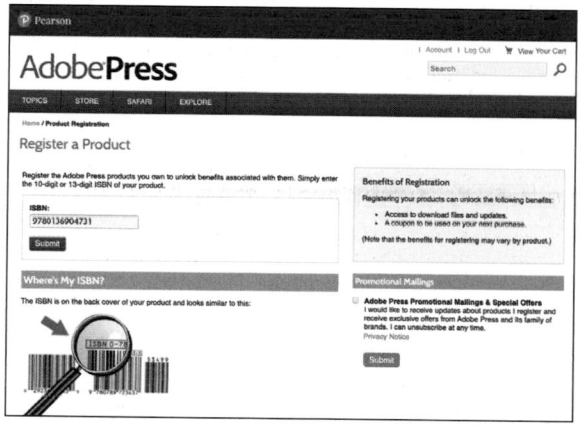

Note: If you encounter problems registering your product or accessing the lesson files or web edition, go to www.adobepress.com/support for assistance.

4 Answer the questions as proof of purchase.

5 The lesson files can be accessed through the Registered Products tab on your Account page.

6 Click the Access Bonus Content link below the title of your product to proceed to the download page. Click the lesson file links to download them to your computer.

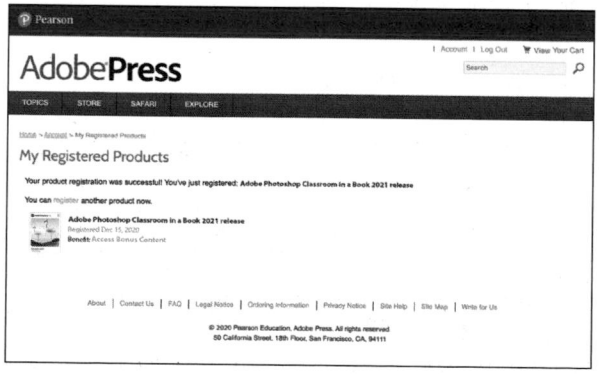

Note: If you purchased a digital product directly from www.adobepress.com or www.peachpit.com, your product will already be registered. However, you still need to follow the registration steps and answer the proof of purchase question before the Access Bonus Content link will appear under the product on your Registered Products tab.

CONTENTS

GETTING STARTED 1

About Classroom in a Book 1

What's new in this edition 2

Prerequisites 2

Installing Adobe Photoshop, Adobe Bridge, and Adobe Camera Raw 3

Installing fonts 4

Starting Adobe Photoshop 4

Online content 4

Restoring default preferences 5

Additional resources 6

Adobe Authorized Training Centers 7

1 GETTING TO KNOW THE WORK AREA 8

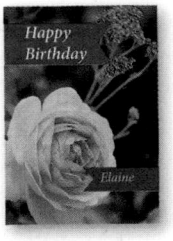

Starting to work in Adobe Photoshop 10

Using the tools 13

Sampling a color 18

Working with tools and tool properties 19

Undoing actions in Photoshop 25

More about panels and panel locations 27

2 BASIC PHOTO CORRECTIONS 32

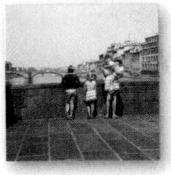

Strategy for retouching 34

Resolution and image size 35

Opening a file with Adobe Bridge 36

Straightening and cropping the image in Photoshop 38

Adjusting the color and tone 40

Using the Spot Healing Brush tool 44
Applying a content-aware patch..... 45
Repairing areas with the Clone Stamp tool 46
Sharpening the image 48

3 WORKING WITH SELECTIONS **52**

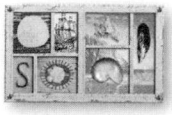

About selecting and selection tools 54
Getting started 55
Using Cloud Documents 55
Using the Magic Wand tool..... 57
Using the Quick Selection tool 59
Moving a selected area 60
Using the Object Selection tool 61
Manipulating selections 61
Selecting with the lasso tools 65
Rotating a selection..... 66
Selecting with the Magnetic Lasso tool 67
Selecting from a center point 68
Resizing and copying a selection 69
Cropping an image 72

4 LAYER BASICS **74**

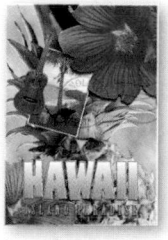

About layers..... 76
Getting started 76
Using the Layers panel..... 77
Rearranging layers..... 82
Applying a gradient to a layer 92
Applying a layer style 94
Adding an adjustment layer..... 99
Updating layer effects 102
Adding a border 103
Flattening and saving files 105

5 QUICK FIXES 110

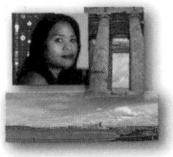

Getting started 112
Improving a snapshot 112
Adjusting facial features with Liquify 116
Blurring a background 118
Creating a panorama 122
Filling empty areas when cropping 126
Correcting image distortion 129
Extending depth of field 132
Removing objects using Content-Aware Fill 135
Adjusting perspective in an image 141

6 MASKS AND CHANNELS 146

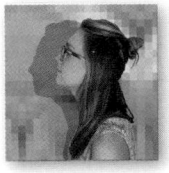

Working with masks and channels 148
Getting started 148
Using Select and Mask and Select Subject 149
Creating a quick mask 160
Manipulating an image with Puppet Warp 162
Using an alpha channel to create a shadow 163

7 TYPOGRAPHIC DESIGN 168

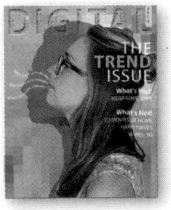

About type 170
Getting started 170
Creating a clipping mask from type 171
Creating type on a path 178
Warping point type 181
Designing paragraphs of type 182
Adding a rounded rectangle 186
Adding vertical text 187

8 VECTOR DRAWING TECHNIQUES **192**

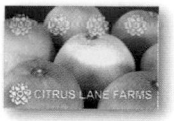

About bitmap images and vector graphics....194
About paths and the Pen tool....195
Getting started....195
Drawing a shape with the Pen tool....196
Drawing a path traced from a photo....202
Converting a path to a selection and a layer mask....206
Creating a logo with text and a custom shape....207

9 ADVANCED COMPOSITING **216**

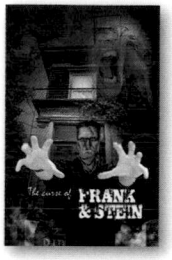

Getting started....218
Arranging layers....219
Using Smart Filters....222
Painting a layer....228
Adding a background....230
Using the History panel to undo edits....231
Upscaling a low-resolution image....237

10 PAINTING WITH THE MIXER BRUSH **240**

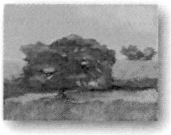

About the Mixer Brush....242
Getting started....242
Selecting brush settings....243
Mixing colors....246
Mixing colors with a photograph....249
Painting and mixing colors with brush presets....252

11 EDITING VIDEO **260**

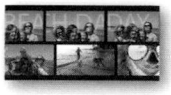

Getting started....262
About the Timeline panel....263
Creating a new video project....264
Animating text with keyframes....268
Creating effects....270
Adding transitions....274
Adding audio....275
Muting unwanted audio....276
Rendering video....277

12 WORKING WITH CAMERA RAW **280**

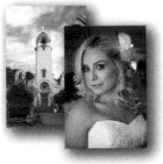

Getting started 282
About camera raw files 283
Processing files in Camera Raw 284
Applying advanced color correction 303

13 PREPARING FILES FOR THE WEB **318**

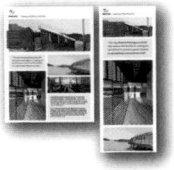

Getting started 320
Creating placeholders with the Frame tool 321
Using layer groups to create button graphics 326
Automating a multistep task 334
Designing with artboards 340

14 PRODUCING AND PRINTING CONSISTENT COLOR **352**

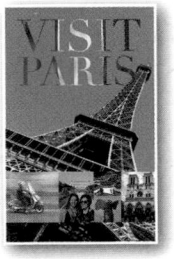

Preparing files for printing 354
Getting started 355
Performing a "zoom test" 356
About color management 360
Specifying color-management settings 361
Identifying out-of-gamut colors 362
Proofing document colors on a monitor 363
Bringing colors into the output gamut 365
Converting an image to CMYK 367
Saving the image as a CMYK EPS file 369
Printing a CMYK image from Photoshop 370

15 EXPLORING NEURAL FILTERS **376**

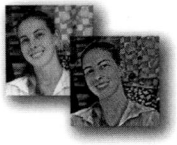

Understanding Neural Filters 378
Getting started 378
Exploring the Neural Filters workspace 379
Improving complexion with Skin Smoothing 380
Combining Neural Filters 381

APPENDIXES **388**

INDEX **396**

GETTING STARTED

Adobe® Photoshop®, the benchmark for digital imaging excellence, provides strong performance, powerful image editing features, and an intuitive interface. Adobe Camera Raw, included with Photoshop, offers flexibility and control as you work with raw images as well as TIFF and JPEG images. Photoshop gives you the digital editing tools you need to transform images more easily than ever before.

About Classroom in a Book

Adobe Photoshop Classroom in a Book® (2021 release) is part of the official training series for Adobe graphics and publishing software, developed with the support of Adobe product experts. The lessons are designed to let you learn at your own pace. If you're new to Adobe Photoshop, you'll learn the fundamental concepts and features you'll need to master the program. And if you've been using Adobe Photoshop for a while, you'll find that Classroom in a Book teaches many advanced features, including tips and techniques for using the latest version of the application and preparing images for the web.

Although each lesson provides step-by-step instructions for creating a specific project, there's room for exploration and experimentation. You can follow the book from start to finish or do only the lessons that match your interests and needs. Each lesson concludes with a review section summarizing what you've covered.

What's new in this edition

This edition covers new features in Adobe Photoshop, such as the improved Search feature integrated with tutorials, Pattern Preview, Sky Replacement, and the Neural Filters.

This edition is also chock-full of extra information on Photoshop features and how to work effectively with this robust and professional application. You'll learn best practices for organizing, managing, and showcasing your photos, as well as how to optimize images for the web. And throughout this edition, look for tips and techniques from one of Adobe's own experts, Photoshop evangelist Julieanne Kost.

Prerequisites

Before you begin to use *Adobe Photoshop Classroom in a Book (2021 release)*, you should have a working knowledge of your computer and its operating system. Make sure that you know how to use the mouse and standard menus and commands, and also how to open, save, and close files. If you need to review these techniques, see the documentation for your Microsoft® Windows® PC or Apple® Mac® computer.

Note: The official version numbers of Adobe applications don't align with years because many existed before the year was part of the name. For example, Photoshop was released in 1990 as version 1, and the year did not appear in the name until Photoshop CC 2014, which was officially version 15.

To complete the lessons in this book, you'll need to have Adobe Photoshop (2021 release) and Adobe Bridge 2021 installed on your computer. The exact version number of the software is different than the year in the application name; this book was specifically tested using Photoshop version 22.0, Bridge version 11.0, and Camera Raw 13.0:

- To find the version of Photoshop that you are running, choose Help > System Info and look at the first line (Adobe Photoshop Version).
- To find the version of Bridge that you are running, choose Help > About Bridge (Windows) or Adobe Bridge > About Bridge (Mac) and look at the first line in the window that opens.
- To find the version of Camera Raw that you are running, look in the Camera Raw window title bar when Camera Raw is open.

If a software version you are using is visibly different from what is shown in this book, you may be able to install a version matching this book; see "Installing a different version."

Installing Adobe Photoshop, Adobe Bridge, and Adobe Camera Raw

Before you begin using *Adobe Photoshop Classroom in a Book (2021 release)*, make sure that your system is set up correctly and that you've installed the required software and hardware. You must license the Adobe Photoshop software separately. For system requirements and complete instructions on installing the software, visit helpx.adobe.com/photoshop/system-requirements.html.

Note that some Photoshop features require at least 512MB of VRAM (graphics memory), and in Windows a 64-bit operating system is required. Photoshop can use the *integrated graphics* found in many lower-cost computers and commonly found in laptop computers; discrete graphics hardware (also called a *dedicated GPU* or *video card*) will perform better but is not required. If your computer uses integrated graphics, the amount of VRAM available to it may depend on how much RAM is installed; for more information see the documentation for your computer.

Many of the lessons in this book use Adobe Bridge, and one lesson uses Adobe Camera Raw. You install Photoshop and Bridge on your computer using the Adobe Creative Cloud desktop application, available at adobe.com/creativecloud/desktop-app.html; follow the onscreen instructions. Adobe Camera Raw is automatically installed when you install Photoshop.

Installing a different version

Adobe may update applications and services several times a year, or you might be using an older version than this book uses. If the current version of Photoshop or Bridge no longer matches this edition of Classroom in a Book (and if a newer edition is not yet available), you can install a different version of the Adobe software using the Creative Cloud desktop application:

Note: You can use the Creative Cloud desktop application to install the two most recent major versions of an application; for example, if the current version is 22, you can install version 22 or 21.

1 Start the Creative Cloud desktop application, and in the All Apps section, click the ... menu and choose Other Versions.

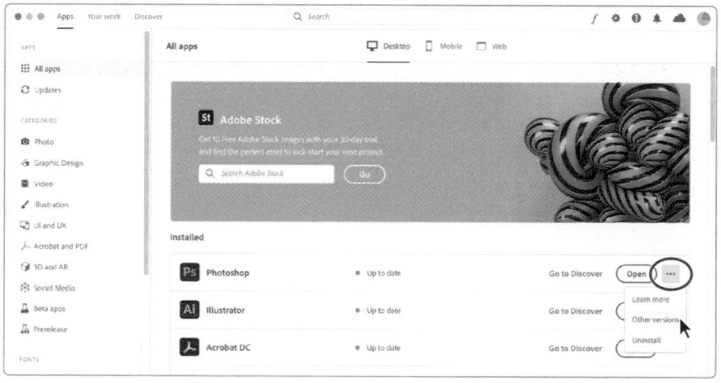

2 Find the versions of the software listed in "Prerequisites," and click Install for each of those versions.

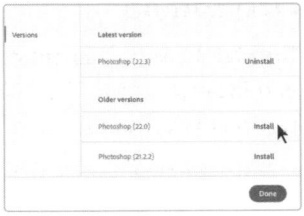

The Creative Cloud desktop application offers only the current version of Adobe Camera Raw. To install a different version of Camera Raw, find and download its installer from:

helpx.adobe.com/camera-raw/kb/camera-raw-plug-in-installer.html

Installing fonts

Some lessons in this book may refer to specific fonts. If a font is not installed on your computer, you may be able to sync it to your computer using Adobe Fonts, which is part of a personal Creative Cloud subscription. (Adobe Fonts might not be included in some educational or organizational subscriptions.) To activate a font from Adobe Fonts and sync it to your computer while in Photoshop, choose Type > More from Adobe Fonts and follow the directions.

Starting Adobe Photoshop

You start Photoshop just as you do most software applications.

To start Adobe Photoshop in Windows: Click the Start button in the taskbar, and in the alphabetical list under A, click Adobe Photoshop 2021.

To start Adobe Photoshop on a Mac: Click the Adobe Photoshop 2021 icon in the Launchpad or Dock.

If you don't see Adobe Photoshop, type **Photoshop** into the search box in the taskbar (Windows) or in Spotlight (Mac), and when the Adobe Photoshop 2021 application icon appears, select it, and press Enter or Return.

Online content

Your purchase of this Classroom in a Book includes online materials provided by way of your Account page on adobepress.com. These include:

Lesson files

To work through the projects in this book, you will need to download the lesson files by following the instructions on the next page.

Web Edition

The Web Edition is an online interactive version of the book providing an enhanced learning experience. Your Web Edition can be accessed from any device with a connection to the Internet, and it contains:

- The complete text of the book
- Hours of instructional video keyed to the text
- Interactive quizzes

Accessing the lesson files and Web Edition

You must register your purchase on adobepress.com to access the online content:

1 Go to www.adobepress.com/PhotoshopCIB2021.

2 Sign in or create a new account.

3 Click Submit.

4 Answer the question as proof of purchase.

5 The lesson files can be accessed from the Registered Products tab on your Account page. Click the Access Bonus Content link below the title of your product to proceed to the download page. Click the lesson file link(s) to download them to your computer.

The Web Edition can be accessed from the Digital Purchases tab on your Account page. Click the Launch link to access the product.

Note: If you purchased a digital product directly from www.adobepress.com or www.peachpit.com, your product will already be registered. However, you still need to follow the registration steps and answer the proof of purchase question before the Access Bonus Content link will appear under the product on your Registered Products tab.

Restoring default preferences

Like many applications, Adobe Photoshop stores various general settings in a document called a *preferences file*. Each time you quit Photoshop, certain workspace settings (such as the last-used options for some tools and commands) are recorded in the preferences file. Any changes you make in the Preferences dialog box are also saved in the preferences file.

To ensure that what you see onscreen matches the images and instructions in this book, you should restore the default preferences as described at the beginning of each lesson. If you choose to not reset your preferences, be aware that the tools, panels, and other settings in Photoshop may not match those described in this book.

If you have changed the settings in the Edit > Color Settings dialog box, those settings are saved in a different location than the Preferences file, so use the following procedure to save them as a preset before you start work in this book. When you want to restore your color settings, you can simply select the preset you created.

Tip: Color Settings can affect whether you see color profile alert messages when you open a document or paste content in Photoshop. One clue that color settings were altered is that profile alerts appear when they previously didn't, or they no longer appear when they used to.

To save your current color settings:

1 Start Adobe Photoshop.

2 Choose Edit > Color Settings.

3 Note what is selected in the Settings menu:

- If it is anything other than Custom, write down the name of the settings file, and click OK to close the dialog box. You do not need to perform steps 4–6 of this procedure.
- If Custom is selected in the Settings menu, click Save (*not* OK).

The Save dialog box opens. The default location is the Settings folder, which is where you want to save your file. The default filename extension is .csf (color settings file).

4 In the File Name field (Windows) or Save As field (Mac), type a descriptive name for your color settings, preserving the .csf file extension. Then click Save.

5 In the Color Settings Comment dialog box, type any descriptive text that will help you identify the color settings later, such as the date, specific settings, or your workgroup.

6 Click OK to close the Color Settings Comment dialog box, and again to close the Color Settings dialog box.

To restore your color settings:

1 Start Adobe Photoshop.

2 Choose Edit > Color Settings.

3 From the Settings menu in the Color Settings dialog box, choose the settings file you noted or saved in the previous procedure, and click OK.

Additional resources

Adobe Photoshop Classroom in a Book (2021 release) is not meant to replace documentation that comes with the program or to be a comprehensive reference for every feature. Only the commands and options used in the lessons are explained in this book. For comprehensive information about program features and tutorials, refer to these resources:

Home screen: In Photoshop, the top of the Home screen may suggest tutorials.

Search command: Choose Edit > Search to open the Discover panel, which offers a wealth of tutorials, suggestions, and links before you even enter a search term. If you enter a term (such as "crop"), the Discover panel can highlight relevant Photoshop tools and commands for you and provides links to more information.

▶ **Tip:** If you find that the Discover panel (Edit > Search) is useful, consider memorizing its keyboard shortcut in Photoshop: Press Ctrl+F (Windows) or Command+F (Mac). To close the panel, press the shortcut again.

Adobe Photoshop Help and Support: Choose Help > Photoshop Help to open the Discover panel with a list of online help resources including the User Guide and Support Community. You can also use your web browser to go to helpx.adobe.com/support/photoshop.html to find Help and Support content on Adobe.com.

Photoshop tutorials: Choose Help > Hands-On Tutorials to learn from guided lessons by following along in Photoshop with provided sample documents. To find more tutorials online, go to helpx.adobe.com/photoshop/tutorials.html.

Photoshop blog: theblog.adobe.com/creative-cloud/photoshop/ brings you tutorials, product news, and inspirational articles about using Photoshop.

Julieanne Kost's blog: jkost.com/blog/ is where veteran Adobe product evangelist Julieanne Kost posts useful tips and videos that introduce and provide valuable insights on the latest Photoshop features.

Adobe Support Community: community.adobe.com lets you tap into user forums where you can ask questions about Photoshop and other Adobe applications.

Adobe Photoshop product home page: adobe.com/products/photoshop.html

Plug-ins menu: To find add-on "plug-in" software modules to extend and add features to your Creative Cloud tools, in Photoshop choose Plug-ins > Browse Plug-ins.

Creative Cloud desktop application: Click Discover to see tutorials, online streaming video, inspirational examples of creative work, and other links and resources for Photoshop and other Adobe applications you have installed.

Resources for educators: adobe.com/education and edex.adobe.com offer a treasure trove of information for instructors who teach classes on Adobe software. Find solutions for education at all levels, including free curricula that use an integrated approach to teaching Adobe software and can be used to prepare for the Adobe Certified Associate exams.

▶ **Tip:** You'll see the same Creative Cloud learning resources (and access to your work stored on Creative Cloud servers) when you use the Creative Cloud mobile app or when you're signed into creative.adobe.com.

Adobe Authorized Training Centers

Adobe Authorized Training Centers offer instructor-led courses and training on Adobe products.

A directory of AATCs is available at learning.adobe.com/partner-finder.html.

1 GETTING TO KNOW THE WORK AREA

Lesson overview

In this lesson, you'll learn how to do the following:

- Open image files in Adobe Photoshop.
- Select and use tools in the Tools panel.
- Set options for a selected tool using the options bar.
- Use various methods to zoom in to and out from an image.
- Select, rearrange, and use panels.
- Choose commands in panel and context menus.
- Open and use a panel in the panel dock.
- Undo actions to correct mistakes or to make different choices.

This lesson will take about an hour to complete. To get the lesson files used in this chapter, download them from the web page for this book at www.adobepress.com/PhotoshopCIB2021. For more information, see "Accessing the lesson files and Web Edition" in the Getting Started section at the beginning of this book.

As you work on this lesson, you'll preserve the start files. If you need to restore the start files, download them from your Account page.

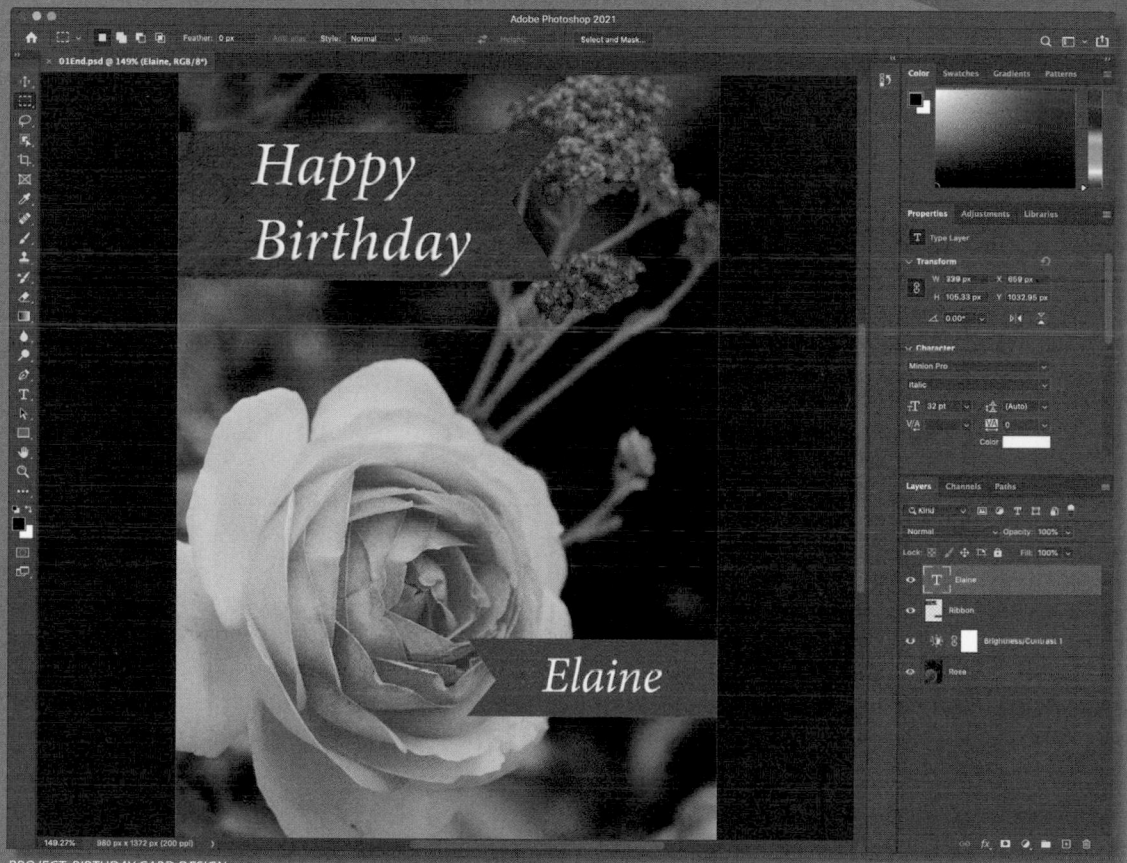

PROJECT: BIRTHDAY CARD DESIGN

As you work with Adobe Photoshop, you'll discover that you can often accomplish the same task in several ways. To make the best use of the extensive editing capabilities in Photoshop, you must first learn to navigate the work area.

Starting to work in Adobe Photoshop

The Adobe Photoshop work area includes menus, toolbars, and panels that give you quick access to a variety of tools and options for editing and adding elements to your image. You can also add commands and filters to the menus by installing third-party software known as *plug-ins*.

In Photoshop, you primarily work with bitmapped digital images: continuous-tone images that have been converted into a series of small squares, or picture elements, called *pixels*. You can also work with vector graphics, which are drawings made of smooth lines that retain their crispness when scaled. You can create original artwork in Photoshop, or you can import images from many sources, such as:

- Photographs from a digital camera or mobile phone
- Stock photography, such as images from the Adobe Stock service
- Scans of photographs, transparencies, negatives, graphics, or other documents
- Captured video images
- Artwork created in drawing or painting programs

Starting Photoshop

Note: Typically, you won't need to reset defaults when you're working on your own projects. However, you'll reset the preferences before working on most lessons in this book to ensure that what you see onscreen matches the descriptions in the lessons. For more information, see "Restoring default preferences" on page 5.

To begin, you'll start Adobe Photoshop and reset the default preferences.

1 Click the Adobe Photoshop 2021 icon in your Start menu (Windows) or the Launchpad or Dock (Mac), and then simultaneously hold down Ctrl+Alt+Shift (Windows) or Command+Option+Shift (Mac) to reset the default settings.

If you don't see Adobe Photoshop 2021, type **Photoshop** into the search box in the taskbar (Windows) or in Spotlight (Mac), and when the Adobe Photoshop 2021 application icon appears, select it, and press Enter or Return.

2 When prompted, click Yes to confirm that you want to delete the Adobe Photoshop Settings file.

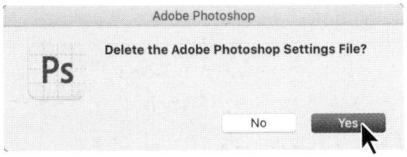

Using the Home screen

After starting Photoshop, the first thing you see is the Home screen, which gives you a number of ways to get started. The Home screen appears as shown in the following illustration.

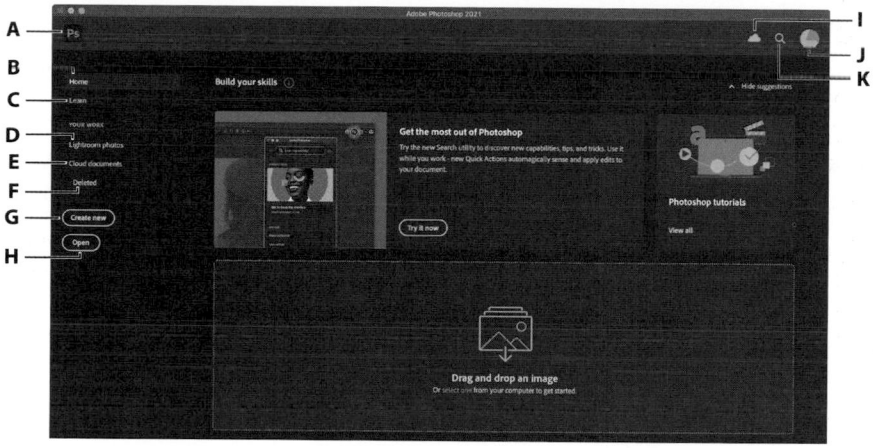

A. *Exit to Photoshop*
B. *Home screen content and recently opened local documents*
C. *Learn tutorials*
D. *Lightroom cloud photos*
E. *Cloud Documents*
F. *Deleted Cloud Documents*
G. *Create new document*
H. *Open document*
I. *Cloud storage sync status*
J. *Creative Cloud profile*
K. *Search, Help, and Learn*

On the left you see a list of view options, divided into upper and lower sections. In the upper section:

- **Home** helps you use and learn about the current version and includes a tour. When you upgrade to a new version of Photoshop, the Home screen may include information about new features and changes. After you've opened at least one locally stored document, a Recent section of previously opened documents will appear at the bottom of the Home screen.
- **Learn** presents links to a range of tutorials that open in Photoshop, where the Learn panel leads you through the steps for each lesson using actual Photoshop controls.

▶ **Tip:** To skip past the Home screen and go straight to the Photoshop application workspace, click the Photoshop icon in the upper-left corner.

The lower section of the list on the left lets you use Photoshop to work with files you've stored on some Creative Cloud online services:

- **Lightroom Photos** lists images synced to your Creative Cloud account's Lightroom online photo storage.
- **Cloud Documents** lists any Photoshop document stored in Adobe Cloud Documents, including those you saved to Cloud Documents from other devices. You'll learn more about Cloud Documents in Chapter 3.
- **Deleted** lists Cloud Documents you've deleted, in case you change your mind and want to recover them (similar to the Recycle Bin or Trash on your computer desktop). This list includes Cloud Documents only, not files you deleted from Lightroom Photos or from your computer's local storage.

▶ **Tip:** To manage files in the Deleted list, click the ellipsis (...) button next to a file, and choose Restore or Permanently Delete.

When you click the Search icon in the upper-right corner and enter text, Photoshop looks for matching content in the Learn tutorials about Photoshop, and in Adobe Stock images. When a document is open, the Search icon can also find specific commands and tools in Photoshop and can find content in your cloud-synced Lightroom images. For example, enter "bird" to find your Lightroom cloud photos that contain birds.

The Home screen automatically hides when you open a document, which is what you're going to do next. You can return to the Home screen by clicking the Home icon in the upper-left corner of the application window.

Open a document

Photoshop provides a number of ways to open documents. For this lesson, you'll use the traditional Open command, which works like the Open command you've probably used in other applications.

▶ **Tip:** If you drag and drop a compatible file anywhere on the Home screen, Photoshop will open it.

1 Choose File > Open. If a dialog box appears that says Cloud Documents at the top, click On Your Computer at the bottom of the dialog box.

2 Navigate to the Lessons/Lesson01 folder that you copied to your hard drive from the peachpit.com website. (If you haven't downloaded the files, see "Accessing the lesson files and Web Edition" on page 4.)

3 Select the 01End.psd file, and click Open. Click OK if the Embedded Profile Mismatch dialog box appears, and click No if a message about updating text layers appears.

The 01End.psd file opens in its own window, in the default Photoshop workspace. The end files in this book show you what you are creating in each project. In this project, you'll create a birthday card.

A. *Options bar*
B. *Exit to Home screen*
C. *Tools panel*
D. *Search, Help, and Learn*
E. *Workspaces menu*
F. *Share an Image button*
G. *Panels*

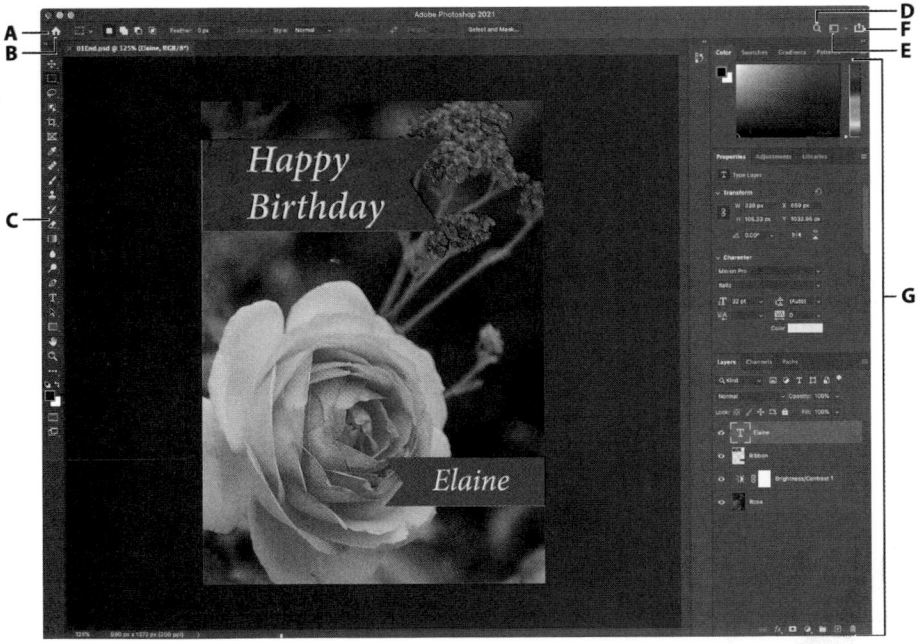

● **Note:** This illustration shows the Mac version of Photoshop. The arrangement is similar on Windows, but operating system styles may vary.

The default workspace in Photoshop consists of the menu bar and options bar at the top of the screen, the Tools panel on the left, and several open panels in the panel dock on the right. When you have documents open, one or more image windows also appear, and you can display them at the same time using the tabbed interface. The Photoshop user interface is similar to the one in Adobe Illustrator® and Adobe InDesign®, so learning how to use the tools and panels in one application makes it easier to learn and use the other applications.

There is one main difference between the Photoshop work area on Windows and that on the Mac: Windows always presents Photoshop in a contained window. On the Mac, you can choose whether to work with an *application frame*, which contains the Photoshop document windows and panels within a frame that is distinct from other applications you may have open; only the menu bar is outside the application frame. The application frame is enabled by default; to disable the application frame, choose Window > Application Frame, but note that the illustrations in this book are created with the application frame enabled.

Tip: When you open multiple documents in Photoshop, each is identified by a tab at the top of its document windows, similar to the tabbed windows in a web browser.

4 Choose File > Close, or click the close button (the x next to the filename) on the tab of the document window. Do not close Photoshop, and don't save changes to the document. The filename is added to the Recent list on the Home screen.

Using the tools

Photoshop provides an integrated set of tools for producing sophisticated graphics for print, web, and mobile viewing. We could easily fill the entire book with details about the wealth of Photoshop tools and tool configurations, but that's not the goal of this book. Instead, you'll gain experience by configuring and using a few tools on a sample project. Every lesson will introduce you to more tools and ways to use them. By the time you finish all the lessons in this book, you'll have a solid foundation for exploring the Photoshop toolset.

Selecting and using a tool from the Tools panel

The Tools panel is the long, narrow panel on the far-left side of the work area. It contains selection tools, painting and editing tools, foreground- and background-color selection boxes, and viewing tools.

Note: For a complete list of the tools in the Tools panel, see the appendix "Tools panel overview."

You'll start by using the Zoom tool, which also appears in many other Adobe applications, including Illustrator, InDesign, and Acrobat.

1 Choose File > Open, navigate to the Lessons/Lesson01 folder, and double-click the 01Start.psd file to open it.

The 01Start.psd file contains the background image and a ribbon graphic that you'll use to create the birthday card that you viewed in the end file.

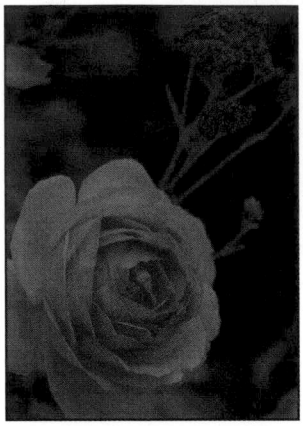

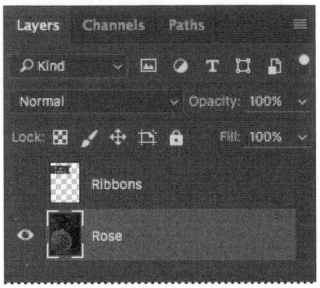

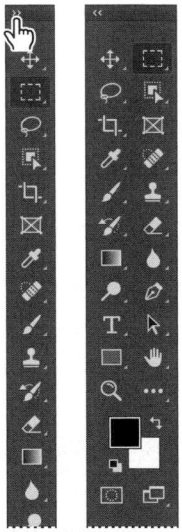

▶ **Tip:** You can customize the Tools panel by arranging, removing, and adding tools. To do this, hold down the Edit Toolbar icon (•••) that appears after the Zoom tool, and choose Edit Toolbar.

2 Click the double arrows just above the Tools panel to toggle to a double-column view. Click the double arrows again to return to a single-column Tools panel and use your screen space more efficiently.

3 Examine the status bar at the bottom of the work area (Windows) or image window (Mac), and notice the percentage that appears on the far left. This represents the current enlargement view of the image, or zoom level.

4 Move the pointer over the Tools panel, and hover it over the magnifying-glass icon until a tool tip appears. The tool tip displays the tool's name (Zoom tool) and keyboard shortcut (Z).

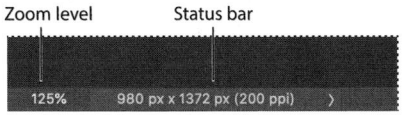

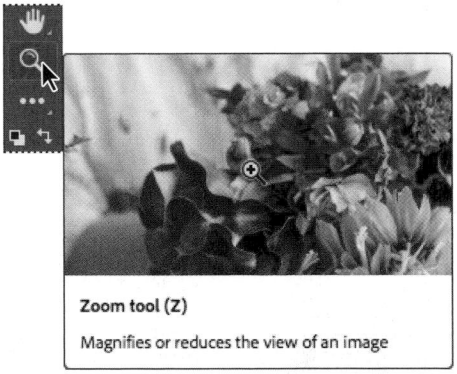

▶ **Tip:** To select the Zoom tool using a keyboard shortcut, press the Z key. Tool shortcuts are single-key (do not press modifier keys such as Ctrl or Command). If a tool has a keyboard shortcut, you'll see it in the pop-up tool tip.

5 Click the Zoom tool icon (🔍) in the Tools panel to select it.

6 Move the pointer over the image window. The pointer now looks like a tiny magnifying glass with a plus sign in the center of the glass (⊕).

7 Click anywhere in the image window.

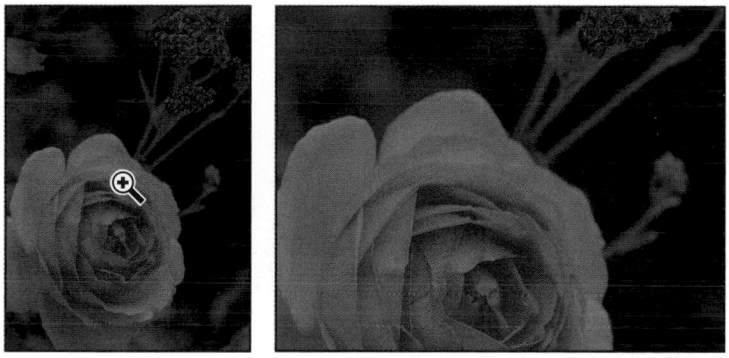

The image enlarges to a preset percentage level, which replaces the previous value in the status bar. If you click again, the zoom advances to the next preset level, up to a maximum of 12800%.

8 Hold down the Alt key (Windows) or Option key (Mac) so that the Zoom tool pointer appears with a minus sign in the center of the magnifying glass (🔍), and then click anywhere in the image. Then release the Alt or Option key.

Now the view zooms out to a lower preset magnification, so you can see more of the image, but in less detail.

9 If Scrubby Zoom is selected in the options bar, click anywhere on the image and drag the Zoom tool to the right. The image enlarges. Drag the Zoom tool to the left to zoom out.

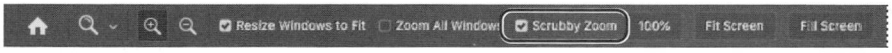

10 Deselect Scrubby Zoom in the options bar if it's selected. Then, using the Zoom tool, drag a rectangle to enclose part of the rose blossom.

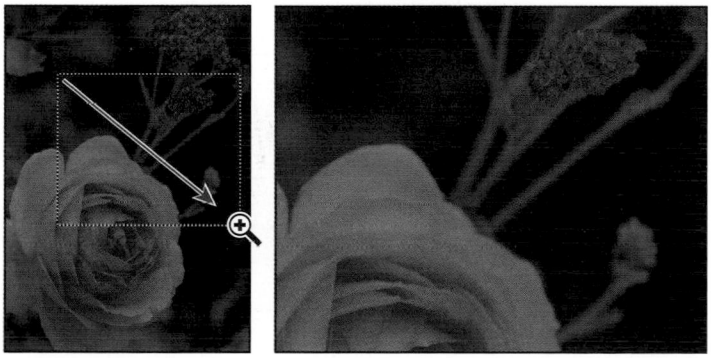

The image enlarges so that the area you enclosed in your rectangle now fills the entire image window.

Note: You can use other methods to zoom in and out. For example, when the Zoom tool is selected, you can select the Zoom In or Zoom Out mode on the options bar. You can choose View > Zoom In or View > Zoom Out. Or, you can type a new percentage in the status bar and press Enter or Return.

11 Click Fit Screen in the options bar to see the entire image again.

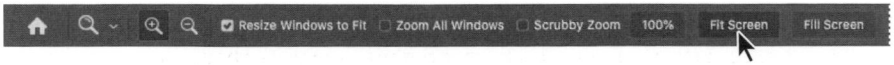

You have used the Zoom tool in four different ways to change the magnification in the image window: clicking, holding down a keyboard modifier while clicking, dragging to zoom in and out, and dragging to define a magnification area. Many of the other tools in the Tools panel can be used with keyboard combinations and options as well. You'll have opportunities to use these techniques as you work through the lessons in this book.

Zooming and scrolling with the Navigator panel

The Navigator panel is another speedy way to make large changes in the zoom level, especially when the exact percentage of magnification is unimportant. It's also a great way to scroll around in an image, because the thumbnail shows you exactly what part of the image appears in the image window. To open the Navigator panel, choose Window > Navigator.

The slider under the image thumbnail in the Navigator panel enlarges the image when you drag to the right (toward the large mountain icon) and reduces it when you drag to the left.

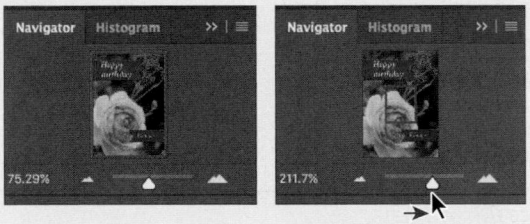

The red rectangular outline represents the area of the image that appears in the image window. When you zoom in far enough that the image window shows only part of the image, you can drag the red outline around the thumbnail area to see other areas of the image. This is also an excellent way to verify which part of an image you're working on when you work at very high zoom levels.

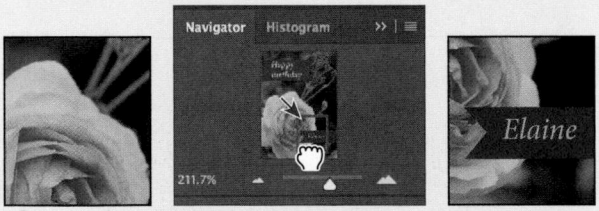

Brightening an image

One of the most common edits you're likely to make is to brighten an image taken with a digital camera or phone. You'll brighten this image by changing its brightness and contrast values.

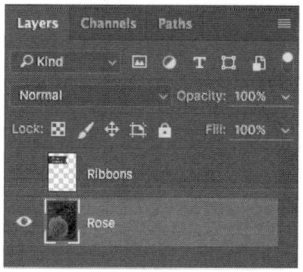

1 In the Layers panel, on the right side of the workspace, make sure the Rose layer is selected.

2 In the Adjustments panel, which is above the Layers panel in the panel dock, click the Brightness/Contrast icon (☀) to add a Brightness/Contrast adjustment layer. The Properties panel opens, displaying the Brightness/Contrast settings.

3 In the Properties panel, move the Brightness slider to **98** and the Contrast slider to **18**.

The image of the rose brightens.

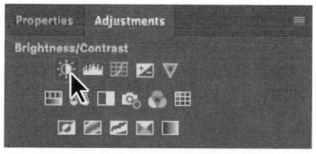

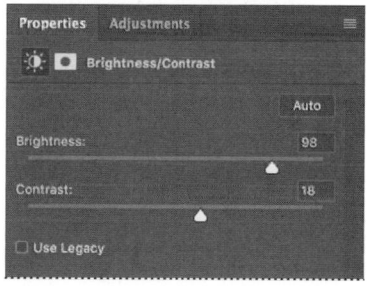

In these lessons, we'll often instruct you to enter specific numbers in panels and dialog boxes to achieve particular effects. When you're working on your own projects, experiment with different values to see how they affect your image. There is no right or wrong setting; the values you should use depend on the results you want.

4 In the Layers panel, click the eye icon for the Brightness/Contrast adjustment layer to hide its effect, and then click the eye icon again to show the effect.

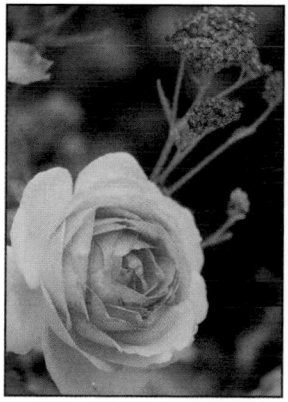

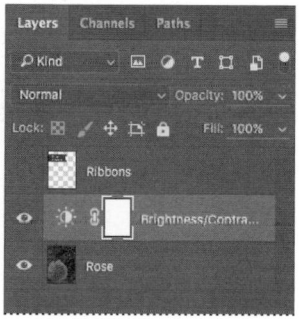

Adjustment layers let you make changes to your image, such as adjusting the brightness of the rose, without permanently altering the actual pixels. Because you've used an adjustment layer, you can always disable the edit by hiding or deleting the adjustment layer—and you can edit the adjustment layer at any time. You'll use adjustment layers in several lessons in this book.

Layering is one of the fundamental and most powerful features in Photoshop. Photoshop includes many kinds of layers, some of which contain images, text, or solid colors, and others that simply interact with layers below them. You'll learn more about layers in Lesson 4, "Layer Basics," and throughout the book.

Note: If Photoshop displays a dialog box telling you about the difference between saving to Cloud Documents and Your Computer, click Save On Your Computer. You can also select Don't Show Again, but that setting will deselect after you reset Photoshop preferences.

5 Double-click the Properties panel tab to collapse it.

6 Choose File > Save As, name the file **01Working.psd**, and click OK or Save.

7 Click OK in the Photoshop Format Options dialog box.

Saving the file with a different name ensures that the original file (01Start.psd) remains unchanged. That way, you can return to it if you want to start over.

You've just completed your first task in Photoshop. Your image is bright and punchy and ready for a birthday card.

Sampling a color

Note: When a layer mask is selected, the default foreground color is white and the default background color is black. You'll learn more about layer masks in Chapter 6.

Photoshop uses a *foreground color* and *background color* when you paint on a layer. Most of the time you'll pay attention to the foreground color, such as the color loaded for a brush. By default, the foreground color is black and the background color is white. You can change the foreground and background colors in several ways. One way is to use the Eyedropper tool to sample a color from the image. You'll use the Eyedropper tool to sample the blue of one ribbon so that you can match that color when you create another ribbon.

First you'll display the Ribbons layer so you can see the color you want to sample.

1 In the Layers panel, click the Visibility column for the Ribbons layer to make the layer visible. When a layer is visible, an eye icon (👁) appears in that column.

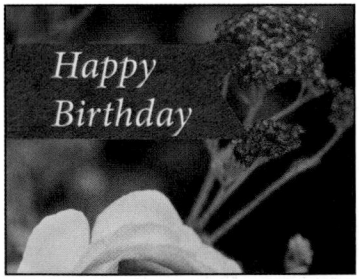

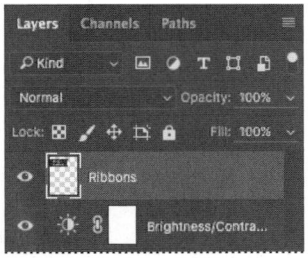

A ribbon with "Happy Birthday" written on it appears in the image window.

2 Select the Ribbons layer in the Layers panel so that it's the active layer.

3 Select the Eyedropper tool (🧪) in the Tools panel.

4 Click the blue area in the Happy Birthday ribbon to sample a blue color.

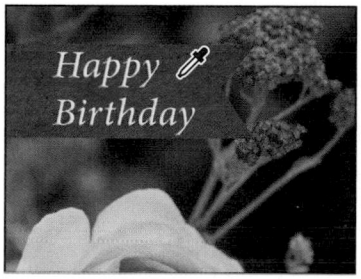

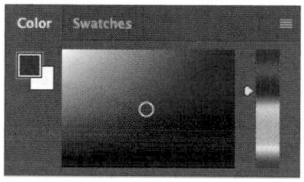

Note: If you have trouble finding the Eyedropper tool, click the Search icon near the top-right corner of the workspace, and type **eyedropper**. Click Eyedropper Tool in the search results; the tool will be selected in the Tools panel for you.

The foreground color changes in the Tools panel and the Color panel. Anything you draw will be this color until you change the foreground color again.

Working with tools and tool properties

When you selected the Zoom tool in the previous exercise, you saw that the options bar provided ways for you to change the view of the current image window. Now you'll learn more about setting tool properties using context menus, the options bar, panels, and panel menus. You'll use all of these methods as you work with tools to add the second ribbon to your birthday card.

Setting the unit of measure

You can change the unit of measure you use to work in Photoshop. This greeting card will be printed, so you'll work in inches.

1 Choose Edit > Preferences > Units & Rulers (Windows) or Photoshop > Preferences > Units & Rulers (Mac).

2 In the Units section, choose Inches from the Rulers menu, and click OK.

Tip: When rulers are displayed (View > Rulers), you can change the unit of measure by right-clicking (Windows) or Control-clicking (Mac) a ruler.

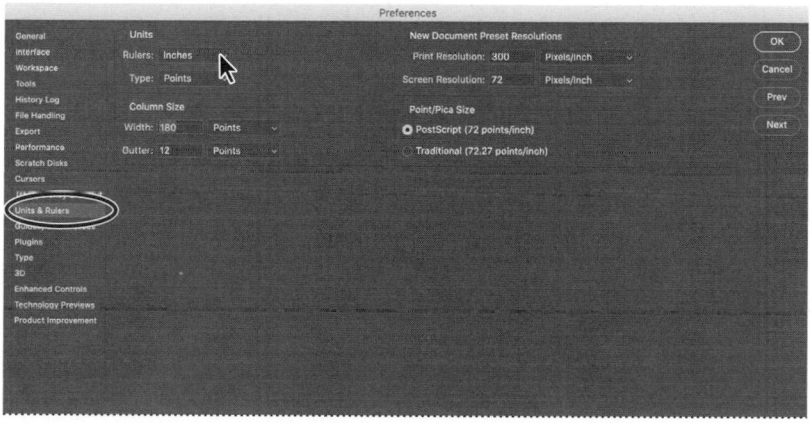

Using context menus

Context menus contain commands and options appropriate to specific elements in the work area. They are sometimes called "right-click" or "shortcut" menus. Usually, the commands on a context menu are also available in the menu bar or panel menus, but using the context menu is more immediate and can save time.

1 Change the view as needed (zoom or scroll) so that you can clearly see the lower third of the card.

2 Select the Rectangular Marquee tool (⬚) in the Tools panel.

The Rectangular Marquee tool selects rectangular areas. You'll learn more about selection tools in Lesson 3, "Working with Selections."

3 Drag the Rectangular Marquee tool to create a selection about 0.75 inches tall and 2.5 inches wide, ending at the right edge of the card. (See the illustration.) As you drag the tool, Photoshop displays the width and height of the selected area. It's okay if the size of your selection is a little different from ours.

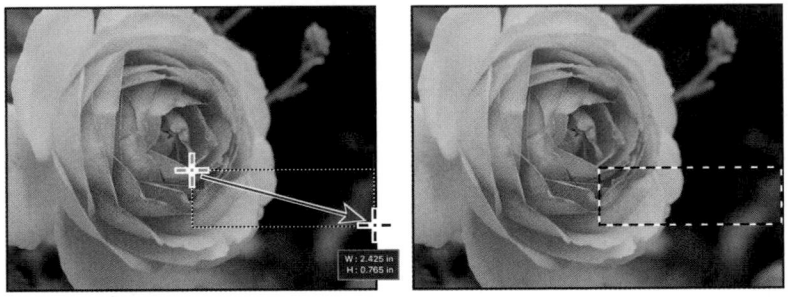

A selection border is indicated by a dashed line called a *selection marquee* (also called *marching ants*), which is animated so that you can see it more easily.

4 Select the Brush tool (🖌) in the Tools panel.

5 In the image window, right-click (Windows) or Control-click (Mac) anywhere in the image to open the Brush tool context menu.

Context menus usually show a list of commands, but in this case, it's a pop-up panel with options for the Brush tool.

6 Click the arrow next to the General Brushes preset group (folder) to expand it, select the first brush (Soft Round), and change the size to **65** pixels.

7 Press Enter or Return to close the context menu.

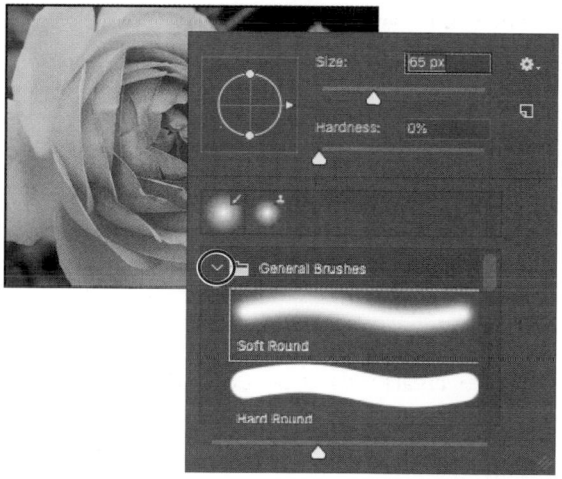

▶ **Tip:** You can also close a context menu by clicking outside it. Be careful when you click, so that you don't paint an unwanted stroke or accidentally change a setting or selection.

8 Make sure the Ribbons layer is still selected in the Layers panel; then drag the Brush tool across the selected area until it's fully painted blue. Don't worry about staying within the selection; you can't affect anything outside the selection as you paint.

9 When the bar is colored in, choose Select > Deselect so that nothing is selected.

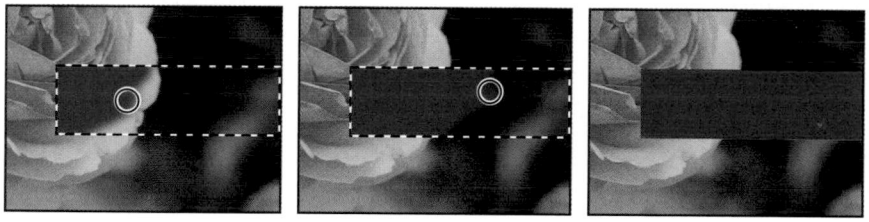

The selection is gone, but the blue bar remains on the Ribbons layer.

Selecting and using a hidden tool

To save space on your screen, the Tools panel arranges some of the tools in groups, with only one tool shown for each group. The other tools in the group are hidden behind that tool. A small triangle in the lower-right corner of a button is your clue that other tools are available but hidden under that tool.

You'll use the Polygonal Lasso tool to remove a triangular notch from the color bar so that it matches the ribbon at the top of the card.

1 Position the pointer over the third tool from the top in the Tools panel until the tool tip appears. The tool tip identifies the Lasso tool (), with the keyboard shortcut L.

2 Select the Polygonal Lasso tool (), which is hidden behind the Lasso tool, using one of the following methods:

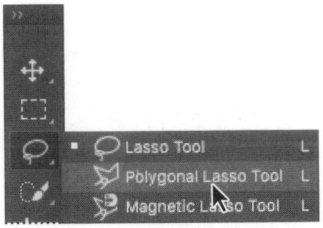

- Press and hold the mouse button over the Lasso tool to open the pop-up list of hidden tools, and select the Polygonal Lasso tool.
- Alt-click (Windows) or Option-click (Mac) the tool button in the Tools panel to cycle through the hidden tools until the Polygonal Lasso tool is selected.
- Press Shift+L, which cycles between the tools in the group (the Lasso, Polygonal Lasso, and Magnetic Lasso tools).

With the Lasso tool, you can draw free-form selections; the Polygonal Lasso tool makes it easier to draw straight-edged sections of a selection border. You'll learn more about selection tools, making selections, and adjusting the selection contents in Lesson 3, "Working with Selections."

3 Move the pointer over the left edge of the blue color bar that you just painted. Click just to the left of the upper-left corner of the bar to start your selection. You should begin your selection just outside the colored area.

4 Move the cursor to the right a little more than ¼ inch, and click about halfway between the top and bottom of the bar. You're creating the first side of the triangle. It doesn't need to be perfect.

5 Click just to the left of the bottom-left corner of the bar to create the second side of the triangle.

6 Click the point where you started to finish the triangle.

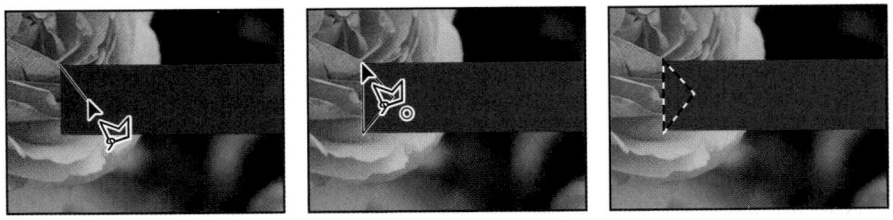

7 Press the Delete key on your keyboard to delete the selected area from the colored bar, creating a notch for your ribbon.

8 Choose Select > Deselect to deselect the area you deleted.

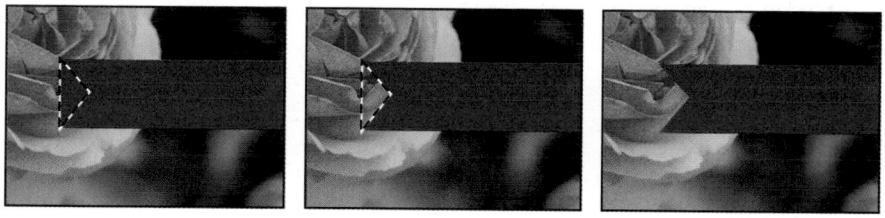

Note: The Select menu contains Deselect and Deselect Layers commands; be mindful of which one you need to choose.

The ribbon is ready. Now you can add a name to your birthday card.

Setting tool properties in the options bar

Next, you'll use the options bar to select the text properties and then type the name.

1 In the Tools panel, select the Horizontal Type tool (**T**).

The buttons and menus in the options bar now relate to the Type tool.

2 In the options bar, select a font you like from the first pop-up menu. (We used Minion Pro Italic, but you can use another font if you prefer.)

3 Specify **32 pt** for the font size.

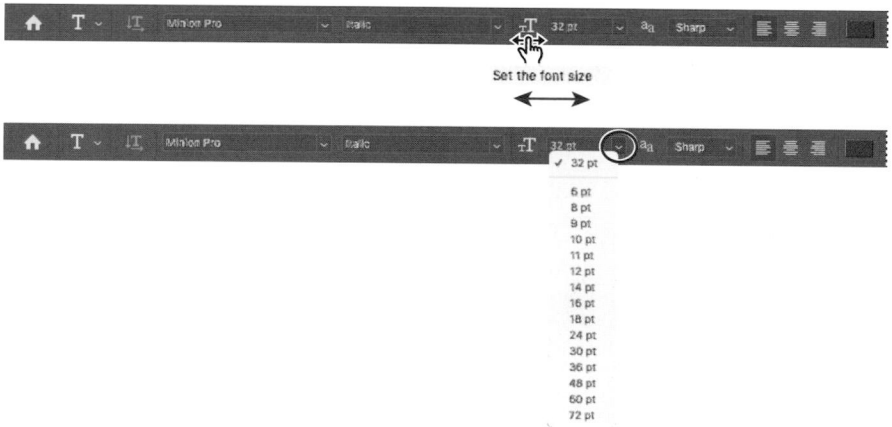

Tip: You can position the pointer over the labels of most numeric settings in the tool options bar, in panels, and in dialog boxes in Photoshop to display a "scrubby slider." Dragging the pointing-finger slider to the right increases the value; dragging to the left decreases the value. Alt-dragging (Windows) or Option-dragging (Mac) changes the values in smaller increments; Shift-dragging changes them in larger increments.

You can specify 32 points by typing directly in the font-size text box and pressing Enter or Return or by *scrubbing* the font-size menu label (see the tip in the margin). You can also choose a standard font size from the font-size pop-up menu.

4 Click the Swatches tab to bring that panel forward, if it's not already visible, then click the triangle next to the Pastel preset group to expand it, and select any light-colored swatch. (We chose Pastel Yellow.)

▶ **Tip:** When you move the pointer over the swatches, it temporarily changes into an eyedropper. Position the tip of the eyedropper over the swatch you want, and click to select it.

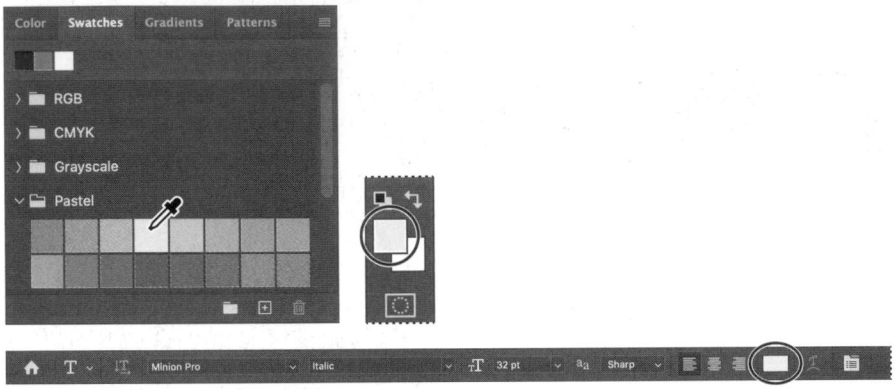

The color you select appears in two places: as the Foreground Color in the Tools panel and in the text color swatch in the options bar. The Swatches panel is one easy way to select a color; later you'll learn other ways to select a color in Photoshop.

5 Click the Horizontal Type tool once anywhere on the left side of the colored bar. "Lorem Ipsum" placeholder text appears as a sample of the current type specifications. It's selected by default so that you can immediately type over it.

6 Type a name; we typed Elaine. It replaces the placeholder text. Don't worry if the text isn't positioned well; you'll correct that later.

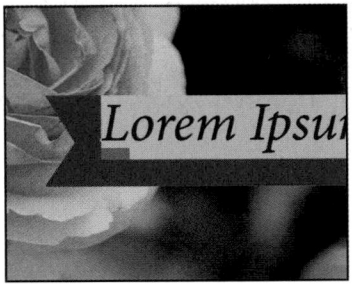

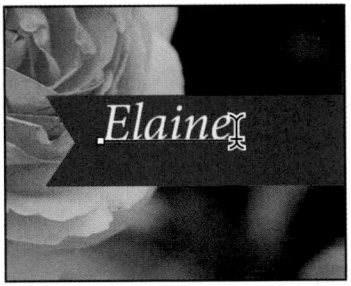

7 Click the check mark icon in the options bar (✓) to commit the text.

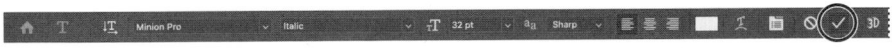

While the pastel yellow looks OK, you'll now use a specific color that matches the text in the other ribbon. It's easier to find it if you change the Swatches panel display.

8 Click the menu button (≡) on the Swatches panel to open the panel menu, and choose Small List.

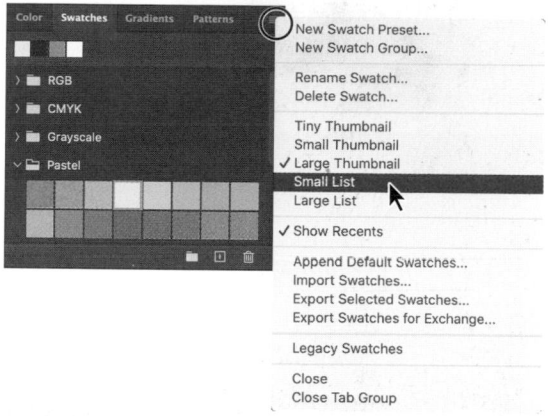

9 With the Horizontal Type tool, double-click the text. The text becomes selected.

10 In the Swatches panel, click the triangle next to the Light group of swatch presets to expand it, and then select the Light Yellow Orange swatch.

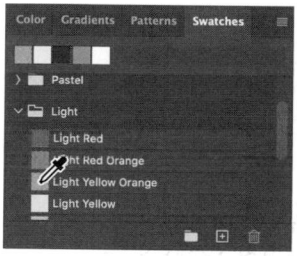

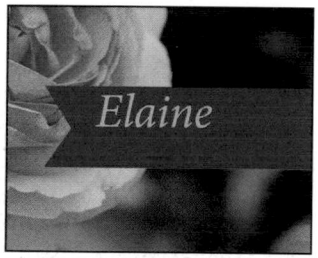

11 Click the check mark button (✓) to commit and deselect the text.

Now the text appears in the orange color.

▶ **Tip:** If you want to select just some of the text in a layer, drag the Horizontal Type tool over a range of characters instead of double-clicking.

▶ **Tip:** After you select a different color swatch, you can see the change in the foreground color swatch in the Tools panel, and in the color swatch in the options bar for the Horizontal Type tool.

▶ **Tip:** You can also commit text edits by clicking outside the text layer.

Undoing actions in Photoshop

In a perfect world, you'd never make a mistake. You'd never click the wrong object. You'd always correctly anticipate how specific actions would bring your design ideas to life exactly as you imagined them. You'd never have to backtrack.

For the real world, Photoshop gives you the power to step back and undo actions so that you can try other options. You can experiment freely, knowing that you can reverse the process.

Even beginning computer users quickly come to appreciate the familiar Undo command. You'll use it to move back one step and then step further backward. In this case, you'll go back to the light color that you originally chose for the name.

1 Choose Edit > Undo Edit Type Layer, or press Ctrl+Z (Windows) or Command+Z (Mac) to undo your last action.

The name returns to its previous color.

2 Choose Edit > Redo Edit Type Layer, or press Ctrl+Shift+Z (Windows) or Command+Shift+Z (Mac) to reapply the orange color to the name.

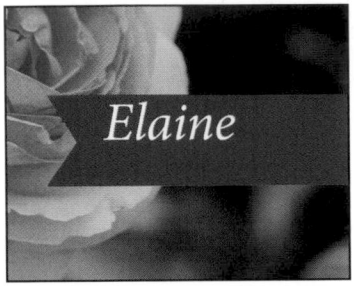

Undo reverses the last step.

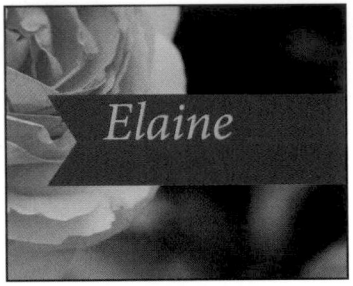

Redo restores the undone step.

▶ **Tip:** To see the steps you can undo and redo, look at the History panel (Window > History).

Each time you use the Undo command it reverses one more step, so if you want to undo five steps, you can apply the Undo command (or its keyboard shortcut) five times. The Redo command works the same way.

If you want to switch back and forth between the current and previous steps you did, choose Edit > Toggle Last State or press Ctrl+Alt+Z (Windows) or Command+Option+Z (Mac) to go back, and then choose the same command again to go forward. Applying Toggle Last State multiple times is a great way to see a before/after comparison of your last edit.

▶ **Tip:** As you drag, magenta lines called *Smart Guides* may appear. They help align the edges and centers of dragged content to other objects and guides. If they are getting in your way, you can disable them by deselecting the View > Show > Smart Guides command or by holding down the Control key as you drag.

3 Once the name is back to the color you'd like it to be, use the Move tool (✥) to drag the name so it's centered in the blue bar.

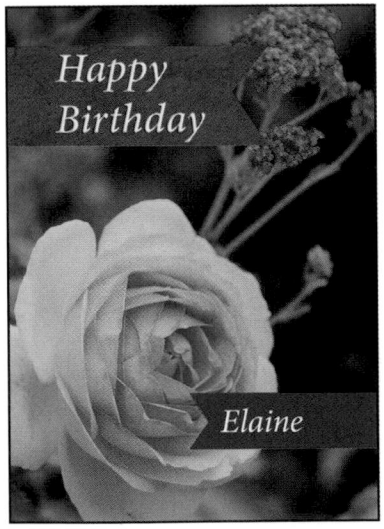

4 Save the file. Your birthday card is done!

More about panels and panel locations

Photoshop panels are powerful and varied. Rarely would you need to see all panels simultaneously. That's why they're in panel groups and why the default configurations leave many panels unopened.

The complete list of panels appears in the Window menu. Check marks appear next to the names of the panels that are open and active in their panel groups. You can open a closed panel or close an open one by selecting the panel name in the Window menu.

You can hide all panels at once—including the options bar and Tools panel—by pressing the Tab key. To reopen them, press Tab again.

Note: When panels are hidden, a thin vertical strip is visible at the left or right edge of the application frame. Hover the pointer over the strip to temporarily reveal the panels docked along that edge.

You already used panels in the panel dock when you used the Layers and Swatches panels. You can drag panels to or from the panel dock. This is convenient for bulky panels or ones that you use only occasionally but want to keep handy.

You can arrange panels in other ways as well:

- To move an entire panel group, drag the title bar to another location in the work area.
- To move a panel to another group, drag the panel tab into that panel group so that a blue highlight appears inside the group, and then release the mouse button.

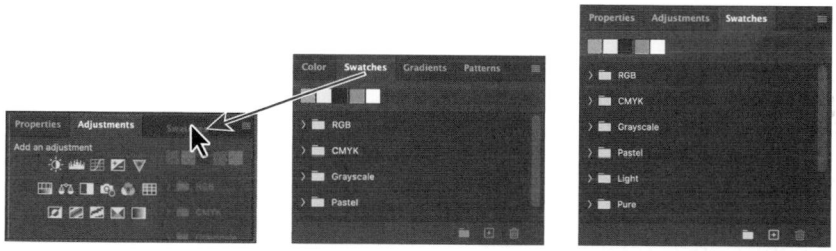

- To dock a panel or panel group, drag the title bar or panel tab onto the top of the dock.

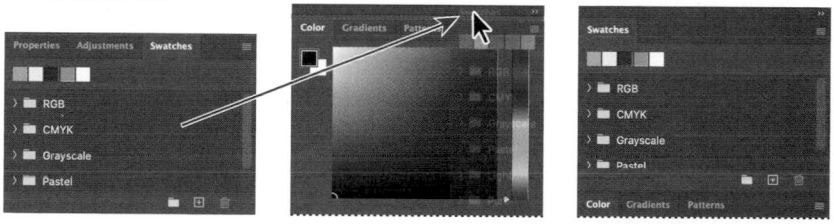

- To undock a panel or panel group so that it becomes a floating panel or panel group, drag its title bar or panel tab away from the dock.

Expanding and collapsing panels

You can resize panels to use screen space more efficiently and to see fewer or more panel options, either by dragging or by clicking to toggle between preset sizes:

- To collapse open panels to icons, click the double arrow in the title bar of the dock or panel group. To expand a panel, click its icon or the double arrow.

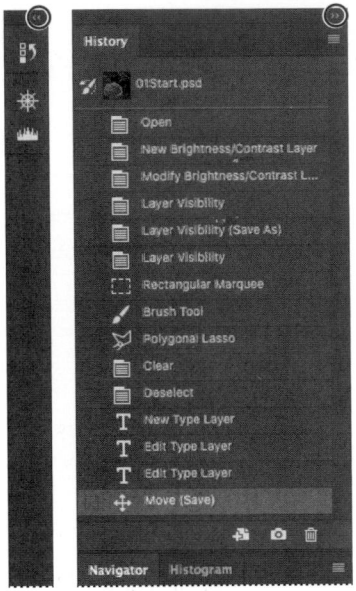

- To change the height of a panel, drag its bottom edge.
- To change the width of a dock, position the pointer on the left edge of the dock until it becomes a double-headed arrow, and then drag to the left to widen the dock, or to the right to narrow it.
- To resize a floating panel, move the pointer over the right, left, or bottom edge of the panel until it becomes a double-headed arrow, and then drag the edge in or out. You can also pull the lower-right corner in or out.
- To collapse a panel group so that only the dock header bar and tabs are visible, double-click a panel tab or panel title bar. Double-click again to restore it to the expanded view. You can open the panel menu even when the panel is collapsed.

Note: Some panels cannot be resized, such as the Character and Paragraph panels, but you can still collapse them.

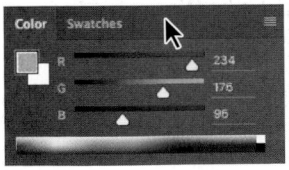

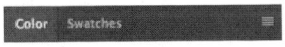

Notice that the tabs for the panels in the panel group and the button for the panel menu remain visible after you collapse a panel.

Special notes about the Tools panel and options bar

The Tools panel and the options bar share some characteristics with other panels:

- You can drag the Tools panel by its title bar to a different location in the work area. You can move the options bar to another location by dragging the grab bar at the far-left end of the panel.
- You can hide the Tools panel and options bar.

However, some panel features are not available or don't apply to the Tools panel or options bar:

- You cannot group the Tools panel or options bar with other panels.
- You cannot resize the Tools panel or options bar.
- You cannot stack the Tools panel or options bar in the panel dock.
- The Tools panel and options bar do not have panel menus.

▶ **Tip:** To restore the default Essentials workspace, click the workspace icon at the top-right corner of the application window, and choose Reset Essentials.

Simplifying edits with the Properties panel

The number of panels in Photoshop can be overwhelming at times. As you gain experience with Photoshop, consider using the Properties panel for much of your work. As you select different kinds of objects, the Properties panel changes to show the options most relevant to the selected object. When nothing is selected, the Properties panel shows options about the document. This can save you time.

For example, if you select a type layer, the Properties panel shows you Transform options (in case you want to move or rotate the layer), and Character options (so you can change more type specifications than will fit in the options bar). This saves you time because you probably won't have to open the Transform or Character panel. If you want to use a more obscure option, you may need to open a more specialized panel, but for many common tasks, what you want to do may already be presented to you in the Properties panel. If you have the space, it's a good idea to leave the Properties panel open all the time.

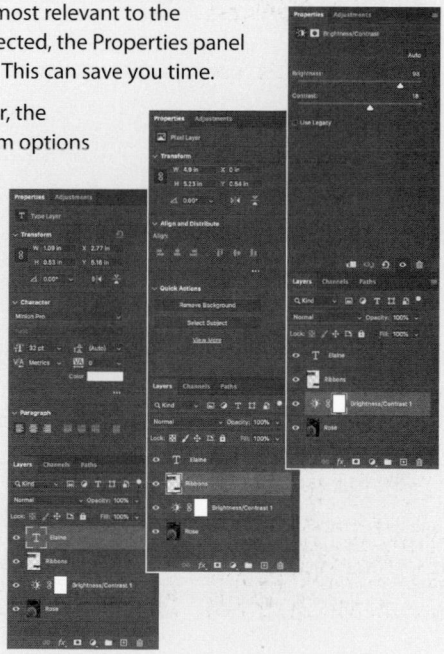

Changing interface settings

By default, the panels, dialog boxes, and background in Photoshop are dark. You can lighten the interface or make other changes in the Photoshop Preferences dialog box:

1 Choose Edit > Preferences > Interface (Windows) or Photoshop > Preferences > Interface (Mac).

2 Select a different color theme, or make other changes.

When you select a different theme, you can see the changes immediately. You can also select specific colors for different screen modes and change other interface settings in this dialog box.

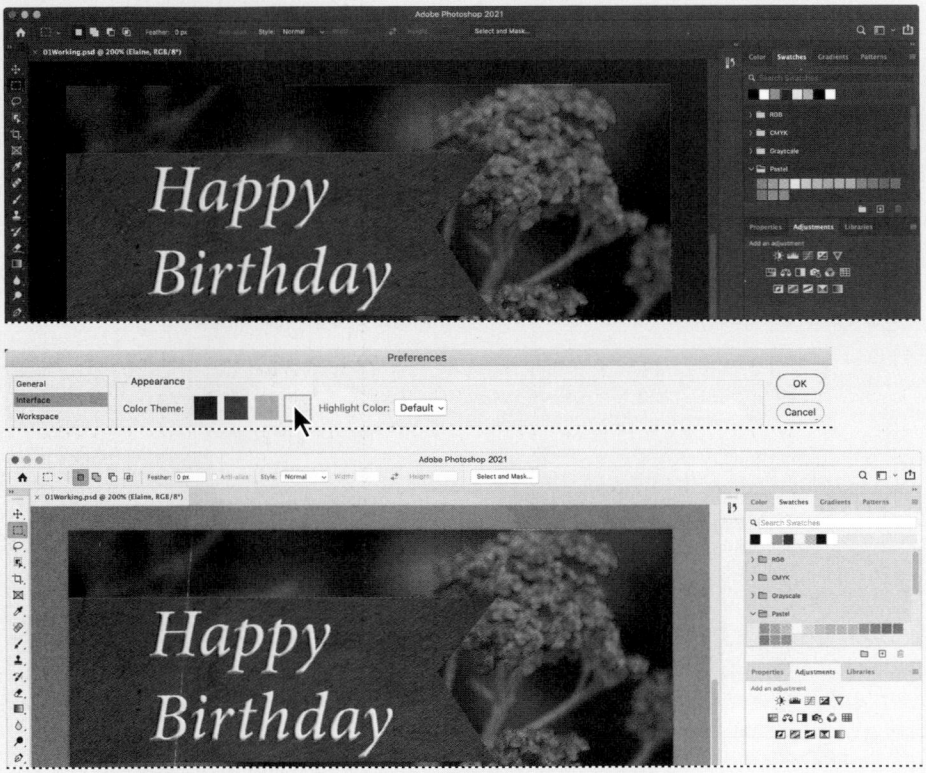

3 When you're satisfied with the changes, click OK.

Review questions

1 Describe at least two types of images you can open in Photoshop.

2 How do you select tools in Photoshop?

3 Describe two ways to zoom in to or out from an image.

Review answers

1 You can open a photograph from a digital camera. You can also open a scanned image of a photographic print, a transparency or negative film frame, or a graphic. You can open images downloaded from the Internet such as photography from Adobe Stock, or images uploaded to your Cloud Documents or your Lightroom photos.

2 To select a tool in Photoshop, click its icon in the Tools panel, or press the tool's keyboard shortcut. A selected tool remains active until you select a different tool. To select a hidden tool, either use a keyboard shortcut to toggle through the tools or click and hold the tool in the Tools panel to open a pop-up menu of the hidden tools.

3 Choose commands from the View menu to zoom in on or out from an image, or to fit it onscreen, or use the zoom tools and click or drag over an image to enlarge or reduce the view. You can also use keyboard shortcuts or the Navigator panel to control the display of an image.

2 BASIC PHOTO CORRECTIONS

Lesson overview

In this lesson, you'll learn how to do the following:

- Understand image resolution and size.
- View and access files in Adobe Bridge.
- Straighten and crop an image.
- Adjust the tonal range of an image.
- Use the Spot Healing Brush tool to repair part of an image.
- Use the content-aware Patch tool to remove or replace objects.
- Use the Clone Stamp tool to touch up areas.
- Remove digital artifacts from an image.
- Apply the Smart Sharpen filter to finish retouching photos.

This lesson will take about an hour to complete. To get the lesson files used in this chapter, download them from the web page for this book at www.adobepress.com/PhotoshopCIB2021. For more information, see "Accessing the lesson files and Web Edition" in the Getting Started section at the beginning of this book.

As you work on this lesson, you'll preserve the start files. If you need to restore the start files, download them from your Account page.

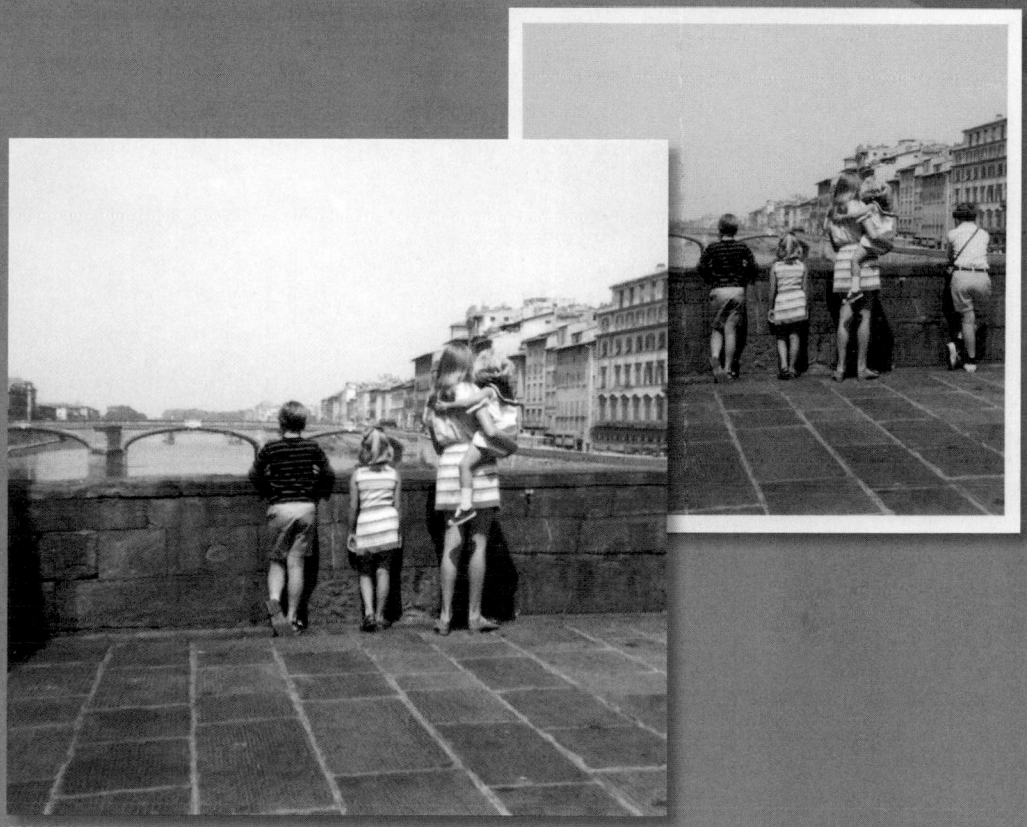

PROJECT: VINTAGE PHOTOGRAPH RESTORATION

Photoshop includes a variety of tools and commands for improving the quality of a photographic image. This lesson steps you through the process of acquiring, resizing, and retouching a vintage photograph.

Strategy for retouching

Note: In this lesson, you retouch an image using Photoshop. For some images, such as those saved in camera raw format, it may be more efficient to work in Adobe Camera Raw, which is installed with Photoshop. You'll learn about the tools Camera Raw has to offer in Lesson 12, "Working with Camera Raw."

How much retouching you do depends on the image you're working on and your goals for it. For many images, you may need only to adjust its lightness or color, or repair a minor blemish. For others, you may need to perform several tasks and employ more advanced tools and techniques.

Organizing an efficient sequence of tasks

Most retouching procedures follow these general steps, which you'll learn about in this chapter:

- Duplicating the original image; working in a copy of the image makes it easier to recover the original later if necessary
- Ensuring that the resolution is appropriate for the way you'll use the image
- Cropping the image to its final size and orientation
- Adjusting the overall contrast or tonal range of the image
- Removing a color cast, such as correcting an image that is too bluish
- Repairing flaws in scans of damaged photographs (such as rips, dust, or stains)
- Adjusting the color and tone in specific parts of the image to bring out highlights, midtones, shadows, and desaturated colors
- Sharpening the image

The order of the tasks may vary depending on the project, and not every task may be necessary for all projects. In a basic workflow, correcting tones and color are early steps, and the last steps typically include adjusting the pixel dimensions and sharpening for the final delivery medium.

Adjusting your process for different intended uses

The decisions you make for retouching an image depend in part on how you'll use the image. For example, if an image is intended for black-and-white publication on newsprint, you might make different cropping and sharpening choices than if the image is intended for a full-color web page. Photoshop supports RGB color mode for web and mobile device authoring and desktop photo printing, CMYK color mode for preparing an image for printing using process colors, Grayscale mode for black-and-white printing, and other color modes for more specialized purposes. You can also use Photoshop to adjust image pixel dimensions or resolution. In general, plan to do most edits on a full-resolution high-quality master image, and then for specific uses such as print or the web, make copies adjusted for the special requirements of each of those media.

Resolution and image size

When you edit an image in Photoshop for a specific use, you need to make sure the image contains an appropriate number of *pixels*, the small squares that describe an image and establish the degree of detail it contains. You can work this out from the *pixel dimensions*, or the number of pixels along an image's width and height.

Note: In Photoshop and many other image editors, 100 percent magnification does not preview the image's ppi value (resolution); the image is shown at the ppi value of your display. In other words, 100% zoom means one display pixel shows one image pixel. So 100% zoom looks smaller on displays with higher ppi values.

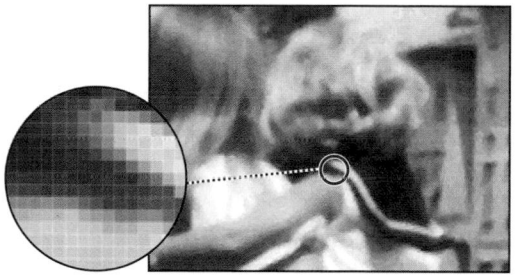

Pixels in a photographic image

When you multiply an image's width by its height in pixels, you find out how many pixels are in the image. For example, a 1000 × 1000 pixel image has 1,000,000 pixels (one megapixel), and a 2000 × 2000 pixel image has 4,000,000 pixels (four megapixels). Pixel dimensions affect file size and upload/download time.

Note: For computer displays and televisions, the term *resolution* often describes only the pixel dimensions (such as 1920 × 1080 pixels) instead of a pixel density ratio (300 pixels per inch). In Photoshop, resolution is the pixels per inch value, not the pixel dimensions.

In Photoshop, *resolution* means the number of pixels per unit of physical length, such as pixels per inch (ppi).

Does changing resolution affect file size? Only when the pixel dimensions change. For example, a 7 × 7 inch image at 300 ppi is 2100 × 2100 pixels; if you change either the size in inches or the ppi value (resolution) while keeping the pixel dimensions at 2100 × 2100 pixels, the file size does not change. But if you change the size in inches without changing the ppi value (or vice versa), the pixel dimensions must change, and so will the file size. For example, if the image in the previous example is changed to 72 ppi while maintaining 7 × 7 inches, the pixel dimensions must change to 504 × 504 pixels, and the file size decreases accordingly.

Resolution requirements vary depending on the intended output. An image might be considered *low resolution* when its ppi value is below 150 to 200 ppi. An image with a ppi value above 200 ppi is generally considered *high resolution* because it can contain enough detail to take advantage of the device resolution offered by commercial or fine-art printers and high-resolution (Retina/HiDPI) device displays.

Tip: To determine the resolution needed for an image you'll print on a press, follow this industry guideline: Edit the image to a ppi value that is 1.5 to 2 times the halftone screen frequency (in lines per inch, or lpi) used by the printer. For example, if the image will be printed using a screen frequency of 133 lpi, the image should be 200 ppi (133 × 1.5).

Factors such as viewing distance and output technology influence the resolution our eyes actually perceive, and this affects resolution requirements too. A 220-ppi laptop display may appear to have the same high resolution as a 360-ppi smartphone, because the laptop is viewed farther away. But 220 ppi might not be enough resolution for a high-end printing press or fine-art inkjet printer, which might reproduce the most detail at 300 ppi and up. At the same time, a 50-ppi image can appear perfectly sharp on a highway billboard because it's seen from hundreds of feet away.

Because of the way display and output technologies work, your images may not need to match the device resolution of high-resolution printers. For example, while some commercial printing platesetters and photo-quality inkjet printers have a device resolution of 2400 dots per inch (dpi) or more, the appropriate image resolution to send to those devices may be only 200 to 360 ppi for photos. This is because the device dots are grouped into larger halftone cells or inkjet dot patterns that build tones and colors. Similarly, a 500-ppi smartphone display may not necessarily require 500-ppi images. Whatever your medium, ask your production team or output service provider to verify the pixel dimensions or ppi value they require in the final images you deliver.

Opening a file with Adobe Bridge

In this book, you'll work with different start files in each lesson. You may make copies of these files and save them under different names or locations, or you may work from the original start files and then download them from the peachpit.com website again if you want a fresh start.

In this lesson, you'll retouch a scan of a damaged and discolored vintage photograph so it can be shared or printed. The final image size will be 7 × 7 inches.

In Lesson 1, you used the Open command to open a file. You'll start this lesson by comparing the original scan to the finished image in Adobe Bridge, a visual file browser that helps take the guesswork out of finding the image file that you need.

Note: If Bridge isn't installed, the File > Browse in Bridge command in Photoshop will start the Creative Cloud desktop app, which will download and install Bridge. After installation completes, you can start Bridge.

Note: If Bridge asks you if you want to import preferences from a previous version of Bridge, select Don't Show Again, and click No.

1. Start Photoshop, and then simultaneously hold down Ctrl+Alt+Shift (Windows) or Command+Option+Shift (Mac) to reset the default settings.
2. When prompted, click Yes to confirm that you want to delete the Adobe Photoshop Settings file.
3. Choose File > Browse In Bridge. If you're prompted to enable the Photoshop extension in Bridge, click Yes or OK.

Adobe Bridge opens, displaying a collection of panels, menus, and buttons.

4. Select the Folders tab in the upper-left corner, and then browse to the Lessons folder you downloaded onto your hard disk so that the lessons in the Lessons folder appear in the Content panel.

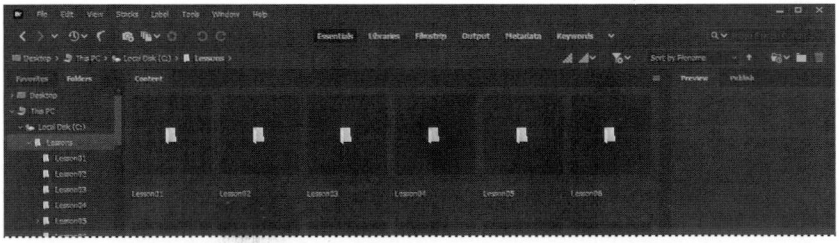

5 With the Lessons folder still selected in the Folders panel, choose File > Add To Favorites.

The Favorites panel lets you quickly access files, folders, applications, and other assets that you frequently use.

6 Click the Favorites tab to open the panel, and click the Lessons folder to open it. Then, in the Content panel, double-click the Lesson02 folder.

Thumbnail previews of the folder contents appear in the Content panel.

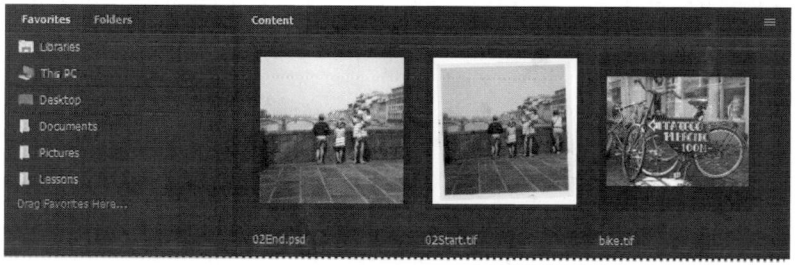

▶ **Tip:** If the Favorites panel list and a folder you want to add to Favorites are both visible, you can drag the folder and drop it in the Favorites panel. You can even drag and drop to add a folder from your computer desktop to the Favorites panel.

7 Compare the 02Start.tif and 02End.psd files. To enlarge the thumbnails in the Content panel, drag the thumbnail slider at the bottom of the Bridge window to the right.

In the 02Start.tif file, notice that the image is crooked, the colors are relatively dull, and the image has a green color cast and a distracting crease. You'll fix all of these problems in this lesson, and a few others. You'll start by cropping and straightening the image.

8 Double-click the 02Start.tif thumbnail to open the file in Photoshop. Click OK if you see the Embedded Profile Mismatch dialog box.

9 In Photoshop, choose File > Save As. Choose Photoshop from the Format menu, and name the file **02Working.psd**. Then click Save.

▶ **Tip:** In Bridge, you can see a larger preview of a selected item by using the Preview panel (choose Window > Preview Panel). If that's not big enough, you can resize the Preview panel. Or, press the spacebar to see a full-screen preview of the selected item.

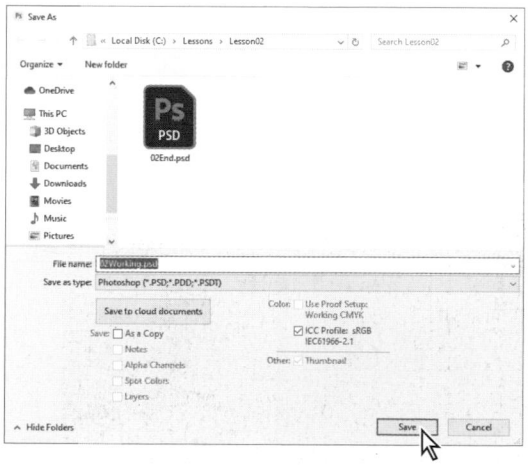

● **Note:** If Photoshop displays a dialog box about the difference between saving to Cloud Documents and Your Computer, click Save On Your Computer. You can also select Don't Show Again, but that setting will deselect after you reset Photoshop preferences.

Straightening and cropping the image in Photoshop

You'll use the Crop tool to straighten, trim, and scale the photograph. By default, cropping deletes cropped pixels.

1 In the Tools panel, select the Crop tool (⌗).

Crop handles appear, and a *crop shield* covers the area outside the cropping region to help focus your attention on the cropped area.

▶ **Tip:** If you need to see crop edges more closely, it's OK to change the view magnification while the crop rectangle is active.

2 In the options bar, choose W × H × Resolution from the Select A Preset Aspect Ratio or Crop Size menu. (Ratio is the default value.) A crop overlay appears.

3 In the options bar, type **7 in** for the width, **7 in** for the height, and **200** px/in for the resolution.

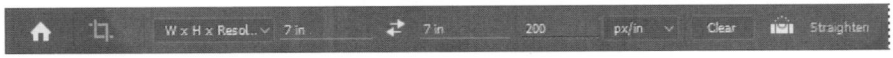

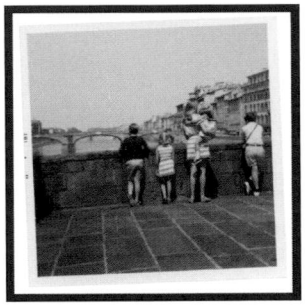

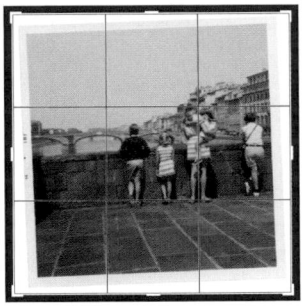

First, you'll straighten the image.

▶ **Tip:** Deselect the Delete Cropped Pixels option if you want the document to keep the pixels outside the crop area. You'll be able to reveal previously cropped areas by enlarging the Crop tool rectangle, which is useful if you change your mind later.

4 Click the Straighten icon in the options bar. The pointer changes to the Straighten tool.

5 Click the top-left corner of the image (where the sky ends), press the mouse button as you drag a straight line across the top edge, and then release.

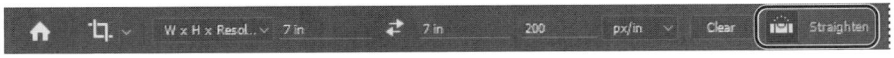

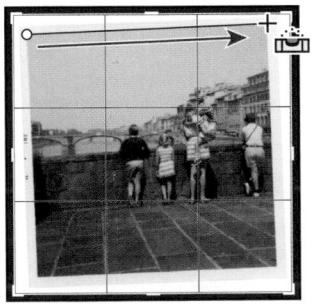

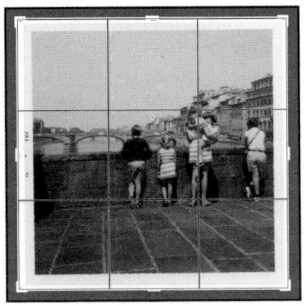

Photoshop straightens the image so that the line you drew is parallel with the top of the image area. You drew a line across the top of the photo, but you can also draw it along anything in the image that should be perfectly vertical or horizontal.

Now, you'll trim the white border and scale the image.

6 Drag the corners of the crop rectangle inward to crop out the white border. If you need to adjust the position of the photo inside the crop, position the pointer within the crop rectangle and drag the photo.

7 Press Enter or Return to accept the crop.

The image is now cropped, straightened, sized, and positioned according to the Crop tool options you used.

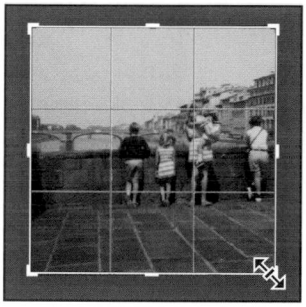

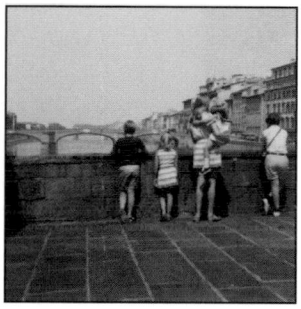

8 If the image dimensions are not already displayed in the status area at the bottom of the application window, click the arrow there and choose Document Dimensions from the pop-up menu that appears.

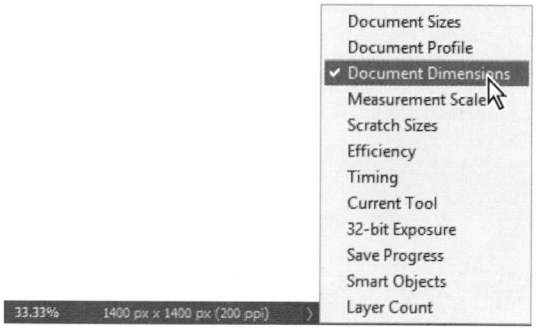

You can use the status bar display to monitor various aspects of Photoshop or the current document. Before cropping, the image was 2160 × 2160 pixels at 240 ppi. After cropping to the dimensions and resolution specified in step 3, Document Dimensions shows that the image is now 1400 × 1400 pixels at 200 ppi.

9 Choose File > Save to save your work. Click OK if you see the Photoshop Format Options dialog box.

▶ **Tip:** The Crop tool will continue to create a 7 × 7 inch, 200 ppi crop as long as the current options bar settings are applied. If you want to crop with total freedom, click the Clear button in the Crop tool options bar.

▶ **Tip:** If you need to adjust the crop after the crop rectangle disappears, choose Edit > Undo, and try again.

▶ **Tip:** The units in the status bar (pixels, inches, etc.) match the units display set in the Photoshop Preferences dialog box, in the Units & Rulers pane.

▶ **Tip:** To straighten a photo and crop out the scanned background in a single step, choose File > Automate > Crop And Straighten Photos. It can also automatically separate multiple photos scanned as one document.

Adjusting the color and tone

You'll use Curves and Levels adjustment layers to remove the color cast and adjust the color and tone in the image. The Curves or Levels options may look complex, but don't be intimidated. You'll work with them more in later lessons; for now, you'll take advantage of their tools to quickly brighten and adjust the tone of the image.

▶ **Tip:** If the Libraries panel is open and taking up a lot of screen space, go ahead and collapse or close it, because it won't be used in this lesson.

1 In the Adjustments panel, click the Curves icon (first row, third button). This adds a Curves adjustment layer; its controls appear in the Properties panel.

2 Select the White Point tool on the left side of the Properties panel.

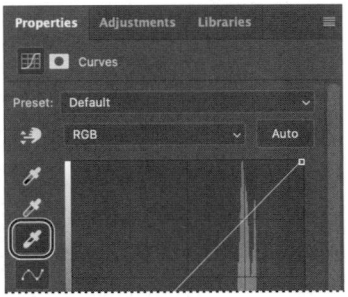

The White Point tool defines what color value should be made a neutral white. Once defined, all other colors and tones shift accordingly. When done correctly, this is a quick way to remove a color cast and correct image brightness. To set an accurate white point, click an area of the image that should be the brightest neutral area of the image that contains detail—not a blown-out area like the sun or a lamp, and not a specular highlight such as a reflection of sunlight on chrome.

3 Click a white stripe on the girl's dress.

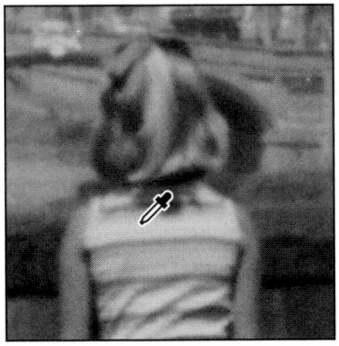

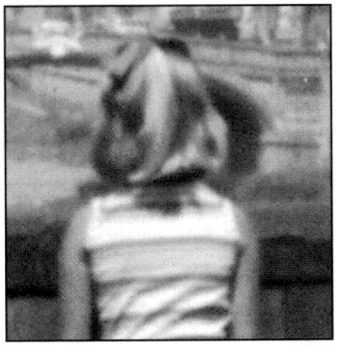

▶ **Tip:** If you want to know the color values of the pixels that the pointer is positioned over, they're displayed in the Info panel (Window > Info).

The white stripe has a warm color cast that affects the entire image, and it's darker than it should be. Clicking it removes the color cast and lightens it, dramatically improving image contrast and color. Try clicking different white areas, such as the child's sailor dress, a stripe on the woman's dress, or the child's sock, to see how the color values at each location change the result.

Now you'll use a Levels adjustment layer to fine-tune the tonal range of the image.

4 In the Adjustments panel (if needed, click its tab to make it visible), click the Levels icon (▲) (first row, second button) to add a Levels adjustment layer.

For both Curves and Levels, the Properties panel displays a *histogram*—a graph displaying the distribution of tonal values in the image, from black on the left to white on the right. For Levels, the left triangle under the histogram represents the black point (the tonal level you want to set as the darkest in the image), the right triangle represents the white point (the tonal level you want to set as the lightest in the image), and the middle triangle represents the midtones.

5 Drag the left triangle (black point) under the histogram to the right, where significant shadow tones start to appear. Our value was **15**. All tones less than 15 become black.

6 Drag the middle triangle a little to the right to adjust the midtones. Our value was **.90**.

Note: The color and tone edits in this section are relatively basic; it's possible to do them all using only Levels or Curves. Typically, Curves is used for edits that are more specialized or complex.

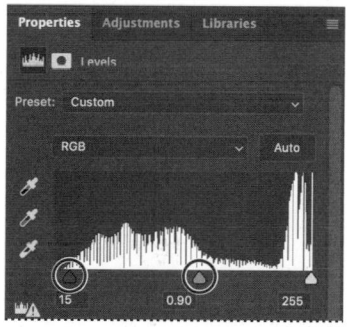

Now you'll *flatten* the image so it's easier to work with while you touch it up. Flattening an image merges all of its layers into the Background layer. Flatten only if you no longer need the flexibility of adjusting the edits you previously made using separate layers.

7 Choose Layer > Flatten Image.

The adjustment layers merge with the Background layer.

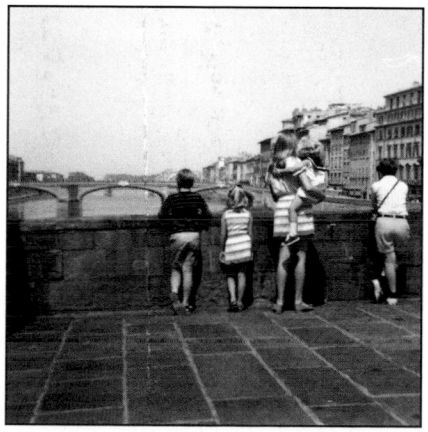

Note: Flattening also removes content hidden beyond the visible edge of the canvas. For example, if you used the Crop tool with the Delete Cropped Pixels option disabled, flattening removes the hidden pixels that the Crop tool preserved.

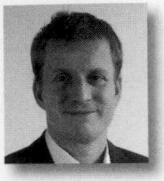

As owner of Gawain Weaver Art Conservation, Gawain Weaver has conserved and restored original works by artists ranging from Eadweard Muybridge to Man Ray, and from Ansel Adams to Cindy Sherman. He teaches workshops internationally as well as online on the care and identification of photographs.

Find out more at gawainweaver.com.

Real-world photo restoration

The tools in Photoshop make restoration of old or damaged photographs seem like magic, giving virtually anyone the power to scan, retouch, print, and frame their photo collections.

However, when dealing with works by famous artists, museums, galleries, and collectors need to preserve original objects to the greatest degree possible despite deterioration or accidental damage. Professional art conservators are called upon to clean dust and soiling from print surfaces, remove discoloration and staining, repair tears, stabilize prints to prevent future damage, and even paint in missing areas of a work.

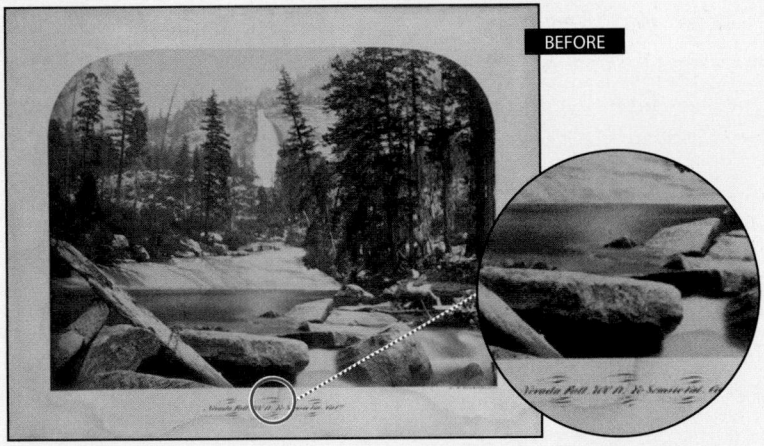

Carleton E. Watkins, Nevada Fall, 700 FT, Yosemite Valley, CA, mammoth albumen print, 15⅝"×20¾". This print was removed from its mount to remove the stains and then remounted.

"Photograph conservation is both a science and an art," says Weaver. "We must apply what we know about the chemistry of the photograph, its mount, and any varnishes or other coatings in order to safely clean, preserve, and enhance the image. Since we cannot quickly 'undo' a step in a conservation treatment, we must always proceed with great caution and a healthy respect for the fragility of the photographic object, whether it's a 160-year-old salt print of Notre Dame or gelatin silver print of Half Dome from the 1970s."

Many of the manual tools of an art conservator have analogous digital versions in Photoshop:

An art conservator might wash a photograph to remove the discolored components of the paper, or even use a mild bleaching process known as light-bleaching to oxidize and remove the colored components of a stain or overall discoloration. In Photoshop, you can use a Curves adjustment layer to remove the color cast from an image.

A conservator working on a fine-art photograph might use special paints and fine brushes to manually "in-paint" damaged areas of a photograph. Likewise, you can use the Spot Healing Brush tool in Photoshop to spot out specks of dust or dirt on a scanned image.

A conservator might use Japanese papers and wheat-starch paste to carefully repair and rebuild torn paper before finalizing the repair with some skillful in-painting. In Photoshop, you can remove a crease or repair a tear in a scanned image with a few clicks of the Clone Stamp tool.

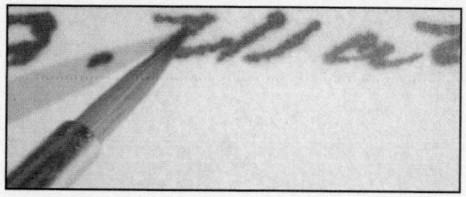

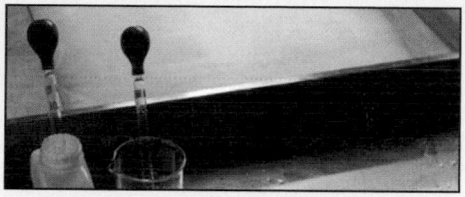

A fixative was applied to the artist's signature with a small brush to protect it when the mount was washed.

"Although our work has always been first and foremost about the preservation and restoration of the original photographic object, there are instances, especially with family photographs, where the use of Photoshop is more appropriate," says Weaver. "More dramatic results can be achieved in far less time. After digitization, the original print can be safely stored away, while the digital version can be copied or printed for many family members. Often, we first clean or unfold family photographs to safely reveal as much of the original image as possible, and then we repair the remaining discoloration, stains, and tears on the computer after digitization."

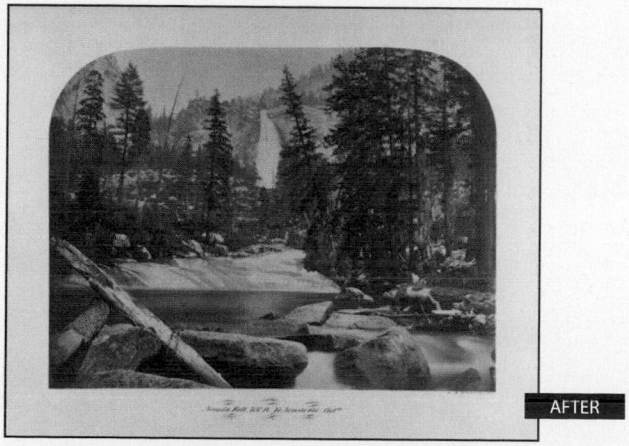

Using the Spot Healing Brush tool

Note: The Healing Brush tool works similarly to the Spot Healing Brush tool, except that it requires you to sample source pixels before retouching an area.

The next task is to remove the crease in the photo. You'll use the Spot Healing Brush to erase the crease. While you're at it, you'll use it to address a few other issues.

The Spot Healing Brush tool quickly removes blemishes and other imperfections. It samples pixels around the retouched area and matches the texture, lighting, transparency, and shading of the sampled pixels to the pixels being healed.

The Spot Healing Brush is excellent for retouching blemishes in portraits, but also works nicely wherever there's a uniform appearance near the areas you want to retouch.

1 Zoom in to see the crease clearly.

2 In the Tools panel, select the Spot Healing Brush tool (✎).

3 In the options bar, open the Brush pop-up panel, and specify a brush with a Size of about **25** px and **100%** Hardness. Make sure Content-Aware is selected in the options bar.

Tip: To avoid creating obvious new seams or patterns, paint the Spot Healing Brush closely around the area you're repairing. Don't cover more area than necessary; make the brush size only slightly larger than the blemish.

4 In the image window, drag the Spot Healing Brush down from the top of the crease. You can probably repair the entire crease with four to six neat downward strokes. As you drag, the stroke at first appears black, but when you release the mouse, the painted area is "healed."

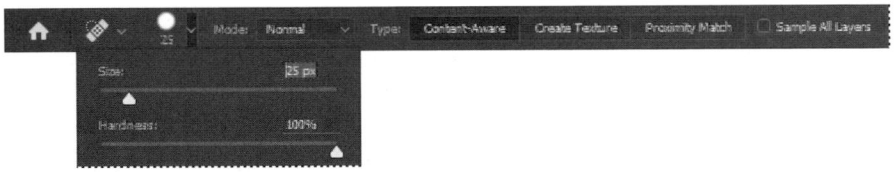

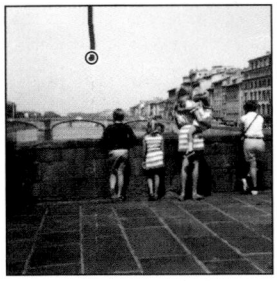

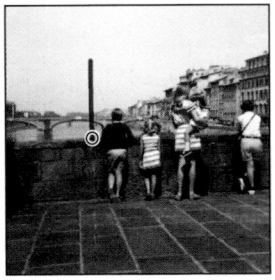

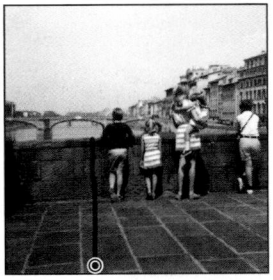

Tip: You may not be able to see the entire crease when you're zoomed in, but you can reposition the view as you work, without switching tools. Use the scroll bars, or hold down the spacebar to temporarily use the Hand tool.

5 Zoom in to see the white hair in the upper right area of the image. Then use the Spot Healing Brush to paint over the hair.

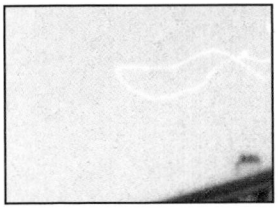

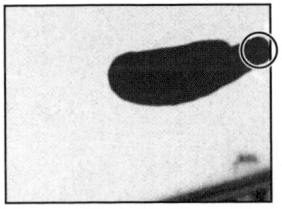

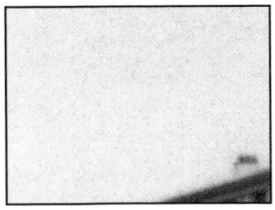

6 Zoom out, if necessary, to see the full sky. Then click the Spot Healing Brush wherever there are unwanted spots you want to heal.

7 Save your work so far.

Applying a content-aware patch

Use the Patch tool to remove larger unwanted elements from an image. You'll use a content-aware patch to remove an unrelated person from the right side of the photo. In Content-Aware mode, the Patch tool creates nearly seamless blending with the nearby content.

1 In the Tools panel, select the Patch tool (), hidden under the Spot Healing Brush tool ().

2 In the options bar, choose Content-Aware from the Patch menu. Type **4** into the Structure slider.

The Structure menu determines how closely the patch reflects the existing image patterns. You can choose from 1 to 7, with 1 allowing the loosest adherence to the source structure and 7 requiring the strictest.

3 Drag the Patch tool around the boy and his shadow. It isn't necessary to be exact, but draw a tight selection. You may want to zoom in to see him more clearly.

4 Position the pointer within the area you've just selected, and drag the selection to the left. Photoshop displays a preview of the content that will replace the boy. Position the dragged area so that the preview area no longer overlaps the area occupied by the boy, but also doesn't overlap the woman or the girl she's holding. Release the mouse button when the patch is positioned where you want it.

Note: The healing and content-aware tools may produce results that still need a small amount of manual touch-up. It isn't realistic to expect them to be perfect every time; the point of the tools is to reduce the total amount of retouching time.

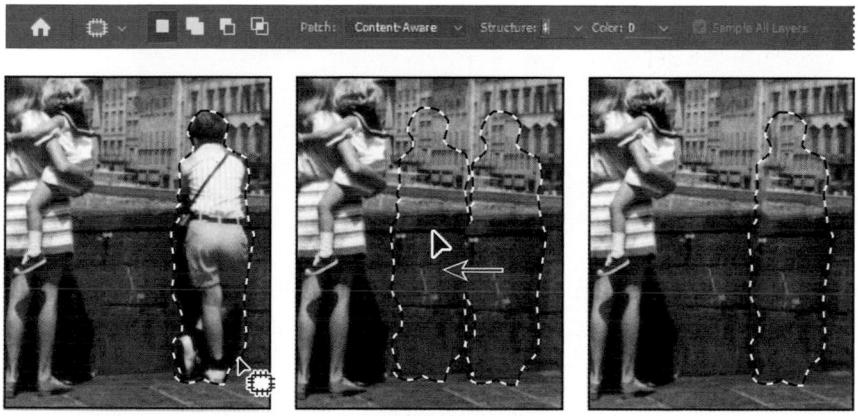

The selection changes to better match the area around it. The boy is gone, and where he stood is a section of the bridge wall and of a building.

5 Choose Select > Deselect.

The effect is impressive, but not quite perfect. You'll touch up the results next.

Repairing areas with the Clone Stamp tool

The Clone Stamp tool uses pixels from one area of an image to replace the pixels in another part of the image. Using this tool, not only can you remove unwanted objects from your images, but you can also fill in missing areas in photographs you scan from damaged originals.

You'll use the Clone Stamp tool to smooth out some irregularities in the height of the bridge wall and the windows on the building.

▶ **Tip:** You may need to set a larger brush size when editing higher resolution images.

1 Select the Clone Stamp tool (🖃) in the Tools panel, and select a **60**-px brush with **30**% Hardness. Make sure that the Aligned option is selected.

2 Move the Clone Stamp tool to an area where the top of the bridge wall is smooth. That's the area you want to copy to smooth out the area that was patched.

3 Alt-click (Windows) or Option-click (Mac) to sample that part of the image as a source point. (When you press Alt or Option, the pointer appears as target crosshairs.)

4 Drag the Clone Stamp tool across the top of the bridge wall in the patched area to even it out, and then release the mouse button.

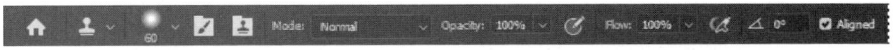

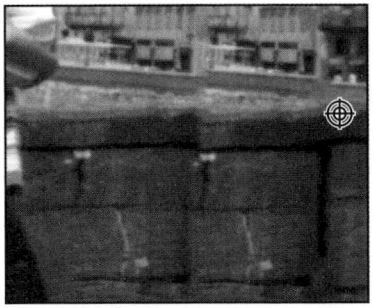

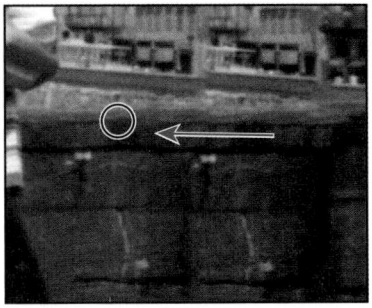

▶ **Tip:** Unlike the Spot Healing Brush and Patch tools you used earlier, the Clone Stamp tool doesn't try to make edits seamless. It simply copies pixels from the source point to where you drag, so it may take more manual work to make an edit look good.

Each time you click the Clone Stamp tool, it begins again with a new source point, in the same relationship to the tool as the first stroke you made. That is, if you begin painting farther right, it samples from stone that is farther right than the original source point. That's because Aligned is selected in the options bar. Deselect Aligned if you want to start from the same source point each time.

5 Select a source point where the bottom of the bridge wall is even, and then drag the Clone Stamp tool across the bottom of the wall where you patched it.

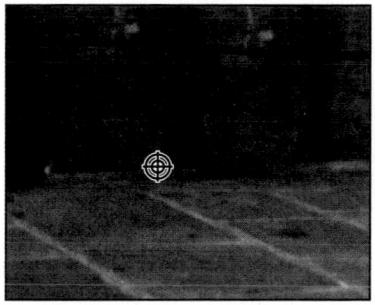

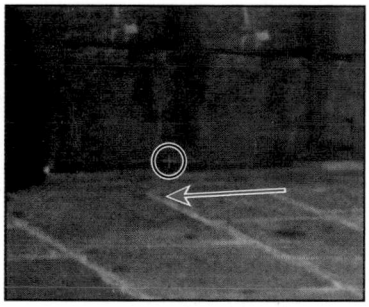

6 Select a smaller brush size, and deselect Aligned. Then select a source point over the rightmost windows in the lowest row on the building you patched. Click across to create accurate windows there.

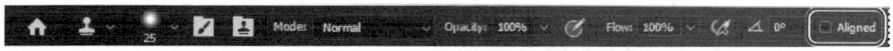

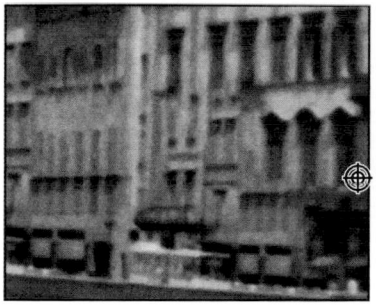

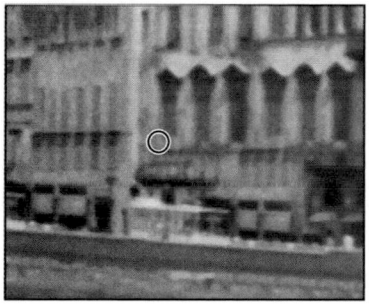

7 Repeat step 6 to make any adjustments you want to apply to the lowest area of the building and the wall that runs in front of it. Look carefully for areas that obviously repeat as a result of the cloning, and retouch them.

8 If you like, you can use a smaller brush size to touch up the stones in the patched portion of the wall.

9 Save your work.

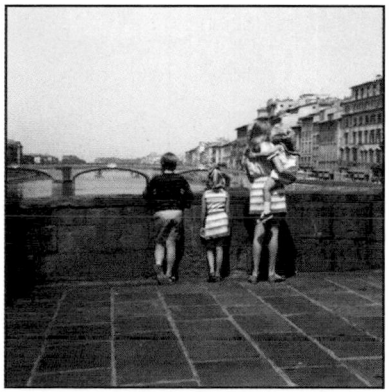

Sharpening the image

The last task you might want to do when retouching a photo is to sharpen the image. There are several ways to sharpen an image in Photoshop, but the Smart Sharpen filter gives you the most control. Because sharpening can emphasize artifacts, you'll remove those first.

1 Zoom in to about **400%** to see the boy's shirt clearly. The colored dots you see are artifacts of the scanning process.

2 Choose Filter > Noise > Dust & Scratches.

3 In the Dust & Scratches dialog box, leave the default settings with a Radius of **1** pixel and Threshold at **0**, and click OK.

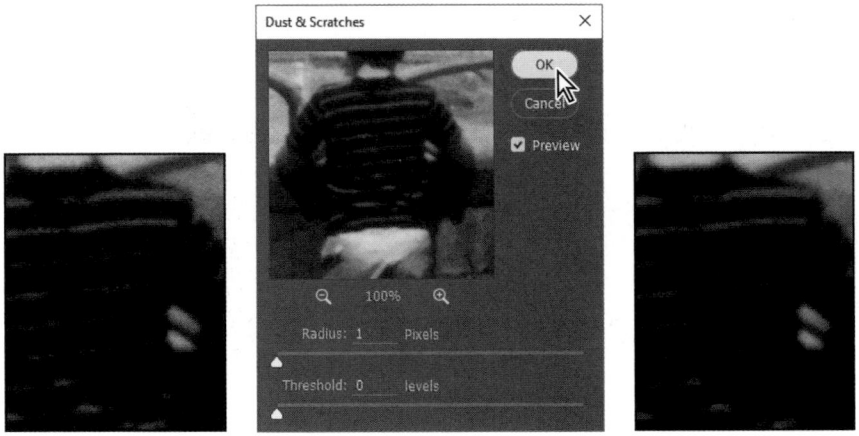

The Threshold value determines how dissimilar the pixels should be before they are eliminated. The Radius value determines the size of the area searched for dissimilar pixels. The default values are great for tiny dots of color like the ones in this image.

Now that the artifacts are gone, you can sharpen the image.

4 Choose Filter > Sharpen > Smart Sharpen.

5 In the Smart Sharpen dialog box, make sure that Preview is selected, so you can see the effect of settings you adjust in the document window.

You can drag inside the preview window in the dialog box to see different parts of the image, or you can use the magnification buttons below the thumbnail to zoom in and out.

6 Make sure Lens Blur is chosen in the Remove menu.

You can choose to remove Lens Blur, Gaussian Blur, or Motion Blur in the Smart Sharpen dialog box. Lens Blur provides finer sharpening of detail and reduced sharpening halos. Gaussian Blur increases contrast along the edges in an image. Motion Blur reduces the effects of blur that resulted from the camera or the subject moving when the photo was taken.

7 Drag the Amount slider to about **60**% to sharpen the image.

8 Drag the Radius slider to about **1.5**.

The Radius value determines the number of pixels surrounding the edge pixels that affect the sharpening. The higher the resolution, the higher the Radius setting should usually be.

9 When you're satisfied with the results, click OK to apply the Smart Sharpen filter.

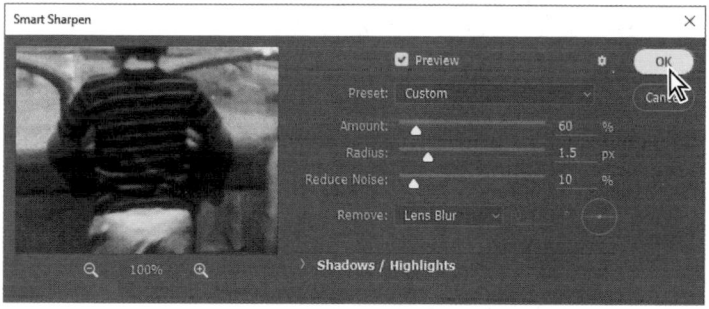

10 Choose File > Save, and then close the project file.

Your image is ready to share or print!

▶ **Tip:** When using a dialog box such as Smart Sharpen, remember that clicking the Preview option lets you compare before-and-after views of the settings you're applying.

Extra credit

Converting a color image to black and white

You can get great results converting a color image to black and white (with or without a tint) in Photoshop.

1 Choose File > Open, and navigate to the bike.tif file in the Lesson02 folder. Click Open.

2 In the Adjustments panel, click the Black & White button to add a Black & White adjustment layer.

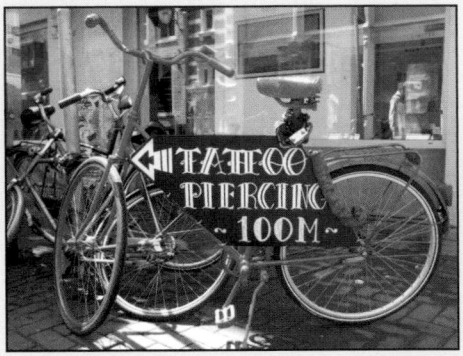

3 Adjust the color sliders to change the lightness of different colors, similar to the effects of using color filters with black-and-white film but with more control. You can also experiment with options from the preset menu, such as Darker or Infrared. Or, select the targeted adjustment tool ( ) in the upper-left corner of the Properties panel, position it over a color you want to adjust, and drag horizontally. The tool moves the sliders associated with the original color of the pixels where you started dragging; for example, dragging on the red bike frame adjusts the lightness of all red areas. We darkened the bike and made the background areas lighter.

4 If you want to colorize the entire photo with a single hue, select Tint in the Properties panel. Then, click the color swatch, and select a tint color (we used R=227, G=209, B=198).

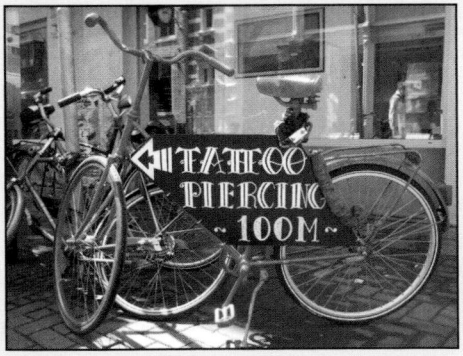

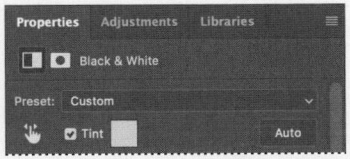

Review questions

1 What does *resolution* mean in Photoshop?

2 What are some ways to use the Crop tool to improve an image?

3 How can you adjust the tone and color of an image in Photoshop?

4 What tools can you use to remove blemishes in an image?

5 How can you remove artifacts such as colored pixels and scanned dust from an image?

Review answers

1 The term *resolution* refers to the number of pixels per unit of physical length in an image, such as pixels per inch (ppi). Printer resolution may be expressed in dots per inch (dpi), because device dots do not always correspond to image pixels. For web and video, resolution typically refers to pixel dimensions, not pixels per inch.

2 You can use the Crop tool to trim, straighten, resize, or change the resolution of an image.

3 You can adjust the tone and color of an image in Photoshop using the Curves and Levels adjustment layers.

4 In this lesson, you used the Spot Healing Brush to remove blemishes from an image. (You can also use other tools such as the Healing Brush, Patch, and Clone Stamp, but they are not covered in this lesson.)

5 The Dust & Scratches filter removes artifacts from an image.

3 WORKING WITH SELECTIONS

Lesson overview

In this lesson, you'll learn how to do the following:

- Make specific areas of an image active using selection tools.
- Reposition a selection marquee.
- Move and duplicate the contents of a selection.
- Use keyboard-mouse combinations that save time and hand motions.
- Deselect a selection.
- Constrain the movement of a selected area.
- Adjust the position of a selected area using the arrow keys.
- Add to and subtract from a selection.
- Rotate a selection.
- Use multiple selection tools to make a complex selection.

This lesson will take about an hour to complete. To get the lesson files used in this chapter, download them from the web page for this book at www.adobepress.com/PhotoshopCIB2021. For more information, see "Accessing the lesson files and Web Edition" in the Getting Started section at the beginning of this book.

As you work on this lesson, you'll preserve the start files. If you need to restore the start files, download them from your Account page.

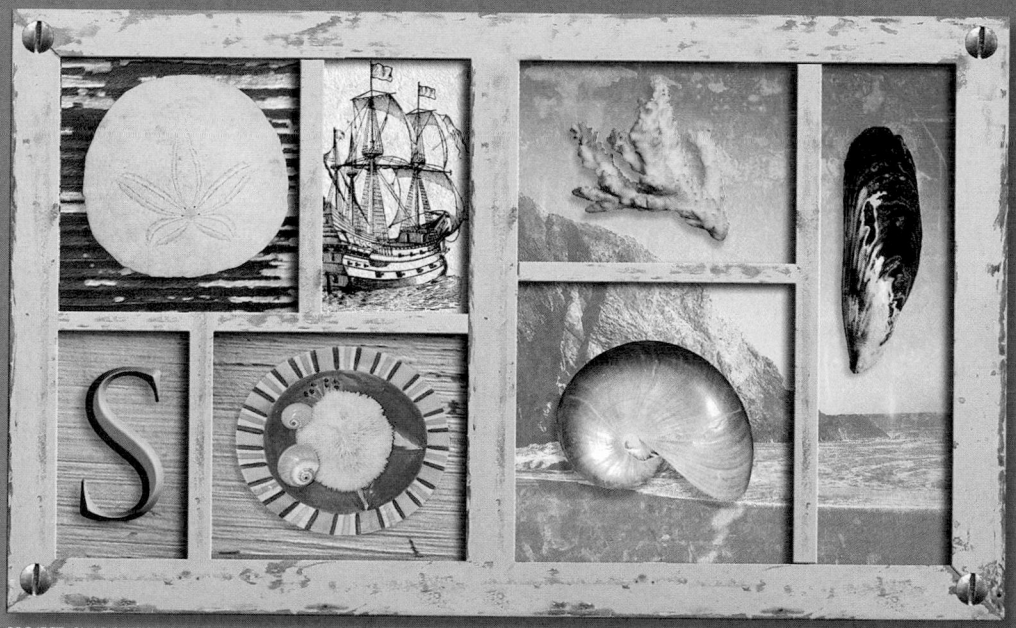

PROJECT: SHADOWBOX COLLAGE

Learning how to select areas of an image is of primary importance—you must first select what you want to affect. As long as a selection is active, only the area within the selection can be edited.

About selecting and selection tools

▶ **Tip:** The concept of selecting the content you want to change is common across many image-editing applications. As soon as you understand how selections work in one application, you can use that knowledge in other similar applications.

Making changes to an area within an image in Photoshop is a two-step process. You first use one of the selection tools to select the part of an image you want to change. Then you use another tool, filter, or other feature to make changes, such as moving the selected pixels to another location or applying a filter to the selected area. You can make selections based on size, shape, and color. When a selection is active, changes you make apply only to the selected area; other areas are unaffected.

The best selection tool for a specific area often depends on the characteristics of that area, such as shape or color. There are four primary types of selections:

Geometric selections The Rectangular Marquee tool (⬚) selects a rectangular area in an image. The Elliptical Marquee tool (◯), which is hidden under the Rectangular Marquee tool, selects elliptical areas. The Single Row Marquee tool (▭) and Single Column Marquee tool (▯) select either a 1-pixel-high row or a 1-pixel-wide column, respectively.

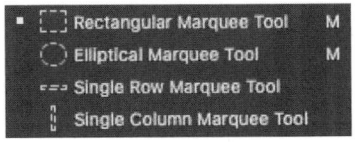

Freehand selections The Lasso tool (ʃ) traces a freehand selection around an area. The Polygonal Lasso tool (⊿) sets anchor points in straight-line segments around an area. The Magnetic Lasso tool (⊿) works something like a combination of the other two lasso tools, and gives the best results when good contrast exists between the area you want to select and its surroundings.

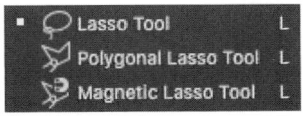

Edge-based selections The Quick Selection tool (⬚) quickly "paints" a selection by automatically finding and following defined edges in the image. The Object Selection tool (⬚) identifies and selects a subject within an approximate area that you define.

Color-based selections The Magic Wand tool (✨) selects parts of an image based on the similarity in pixel color. It is useful for selecting odd-shaped areas that share a specific range of colors.

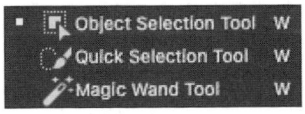

Getting started

First, you'll look at the image you will create as you explore the selection tools in Photoshop.

1 Start Photoshop, and then simultaneously hold down Ctrl+Alt+Shift (Windows) or Command+Option+Shift (Mac) to restore the default preferences. (See "Restoring default preferences" on page 5.)

2 When prompted, click Yes to confirm that you want to delete the Adobe Photoshop Settings file.

3 Choose File > Browse In Bridge to open Adobe Bridge.

4 In the Favorites panel, click the Lessons folder. Then double-click the Lesson03 folder in the Content panel to see its contents.

5 Study the 03End.psd file. Move the thumbnail slider to the right if you want to see the image in more detail.

Note: If Bridge isn't installed, the File > Browse In Bridge command in Photoshop will start the Creative Cloud desktop app, which will download and install Bridge. After installation completes, you can start Bridge.

Note: If Bridge asks you if you want to import preferences from a previous version of Bridge, click No.

The project is a shadowbox that includes a piece of coral, a sand dollar, a mussel, a nautilus, and a plate of small shells. The challenge in this lesson is to arrange these elements, which were scanned together on the single page you see in the 03Start.psd file.

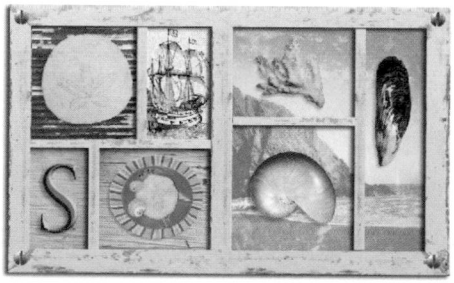

Using Cloud Documents

Photoshop document sizes can become large, especially for high-resolution images that use many layers. When you work with documents stored online, large file sizes upload and download more slowly; on a limited mobile data plan you may reach the data limit more quickly. Adobe Cloud Documents help you edit online documents efficiently by using file formats optimized for networks. For example, editing a Photoshop file as a Cloud Document means only the parts affected by an edit are transmitted, instead of the entire file. If you use Photoshop on both a computer and on an Apple iPad and you save an image as a Cloud Document, you'll find it in the Photoshop Home screen on both devices, always updated with your latest changes.

Tip: Using Cloud Documents can be more efficient than putting a Photoshop file on a cloud-based file sharing service. A Cloud Document transfers only the parts of a file that change, and you can open it in one click on the Photoshop Home screen.

Using Cloud Documents is easy; the only thing you have to do is save it to Cloud Documents. After you do this, your Photoshop document filename will have a .psdc filename extension to indicate that it's now a Cloud Document, and you will now find it listed in the Cloud Documents section in the Photoshop Home screen. The conversion to the PSDC format is automatic, so you don't have to think about it.

1 In Bridge, double-click the 03Start.psd thumbnail to open the image file in Photoshop. You've opened the document from your local storage.

2 Choose File > Save As. If you see the conventional Save As dialog box, click the Save To Cloud Documents button.

Note: If Photoshop displays a dialog box about the difference between saving to Cloud Documents and Your Computer, click Save To Cloud Documents. You can also select Don't Show Again, but that setting will deselect after you reset Photoshop preferences.

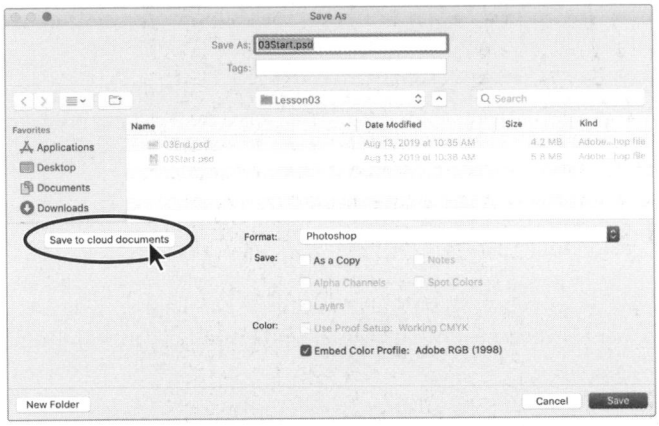

3 Rename the file **03WorkingCloud**, and click Save. The file is uploaded to Cloud Documents. In the document window tab, you can see a cloud icon before the filename, and the filename now ends in .psdc.

Tip: You can also find your Cloud Documents in the Creative Cloud app (mobile or desktop) and website, in the Your Work tab in the Cloud Documents panel. The list may also contain Cloud Documents from other Adobe applications.

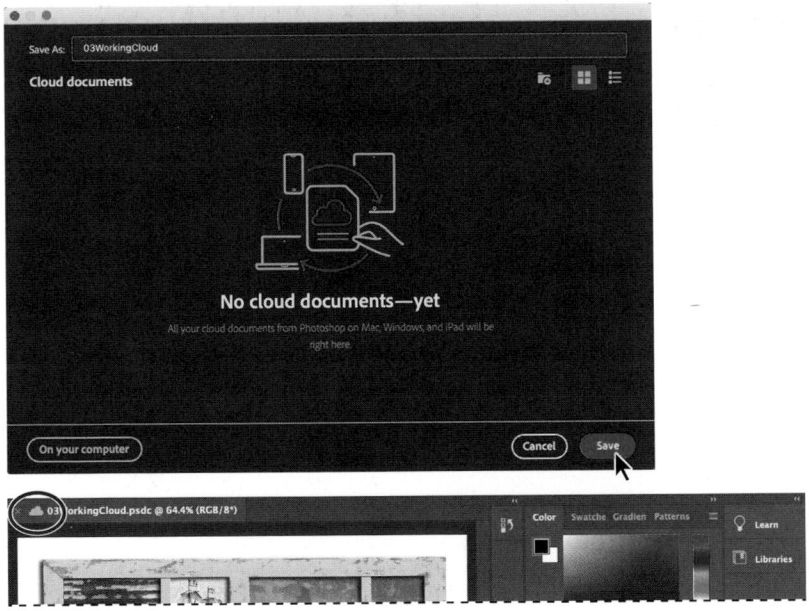

Note: Adobe Cloud Documents are stored in a different online area than Creative Cloud Files or Creative Cloud Libraries.

4 Close the document.

Now you'll open the Cloud Document. Again, this will be slightly different than opening a document from local storage.

1 In the Photoshop Home screen, make sure Cloud Documents is selected on the left side. The Cloud Documents list shows all Cloud Documents you have uploaded using your Adobe ID. You'll see your Cloud Documents list in Photoshop on any device when you're signed in with your Adobe ID.

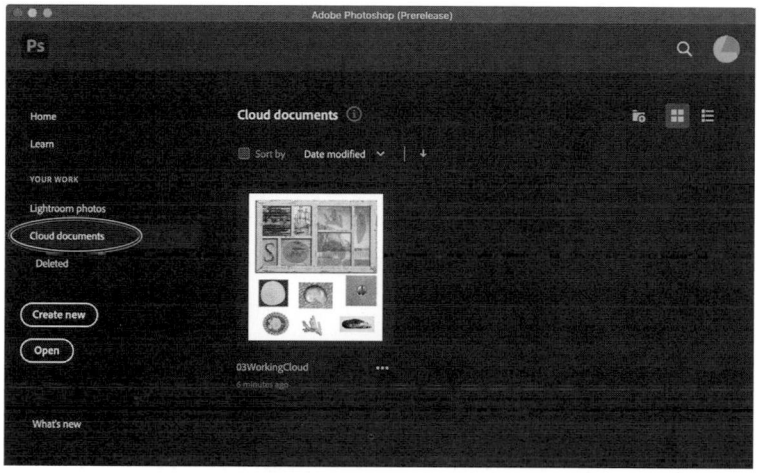

2 Click 03WorkingCloud, the file you just saved. This downloads the file to your computer and opens it in Photoshop.

If you're editing a Photoshop Cloud (PSDC) Document, how can you provide that file to a client who requires a PSD file? By saving the Cloud Document to your own local storage. Again, the conversion is automatic, so it's easy and seamless.

1 Choose File > Save As. If you see the Cloud Documents dialog box, click Save On Your Computer at the bottom to see the conventional Save As dialog box. Notice that the filename extension is now .psd, because you are now saving this document to your local storage, not Cloud Documents.

2 Name the document **03Working.psd**, and save it into the Lesson03 folder. Now you have your own local PSD format copy that you can distribute to others and back up, like any other local document.

For this lesson, you can continue with your local copy (03Working.psd), or you can close the local PSD copy and instead open and work with your Cloud Documents copy (03WorkingCloud.psdc).

▶ **Tip:** You can organize your Cloud Documents in folders. When viewing Cloud Documents on the Photoshop Home screen, click the folder icon near the top to create and name a new folder within Cloud Documents.

▶ **Tip:** If you want to manage or delete a Cloud Document, click the ellipsis (...) button for the document in the Cloud Documents list on the Photoshop Home screen, and choose Open, Rename, Delete, or Move To.

● **Note:** You can't find a Cloud Document on your computer by looking through folders on your desktop; you see Cloud Documents in the Home screen in Photoshop. A Cloud Document is stored on Adobe servers and only cached to your local storage. If you need a local copy of a Cloud Document, choose File > Save As and save it to your computer as described to the left.

Using the Magic Wand tool

The Magic Wand tool selects all the pixels of a particular color or color range. It's most useful for selecting an area of similar colors surrounded by areas of very different colors. As with many of the selection tools, after you make the initial selection, you can improve it by adding to or subtracting from the selection.

The Tolerance option sets the sensitivity of the Magic Wand tool. This value limits or extends the range of pixel similarity. The default tolerance value of 32 selects the color you click plus 32 lighter and 32 darker tones of that color. You may need to adjust the tolerance level up or down depending on the color ranges and variations in the image.

1 Select the Zoom tool in the Tools panel, and then zoom in so that you can see the entire sand dollar in detail.

2 Select the Magic Wand tool (), hidden under the Object Selection tool ().

3 In the options bar, confirm that the Tolerance value is **32**. This value determines the range of colors the wand selects.

4 Position the Magic Wand tool over the red background outside the sand dollar, and click.

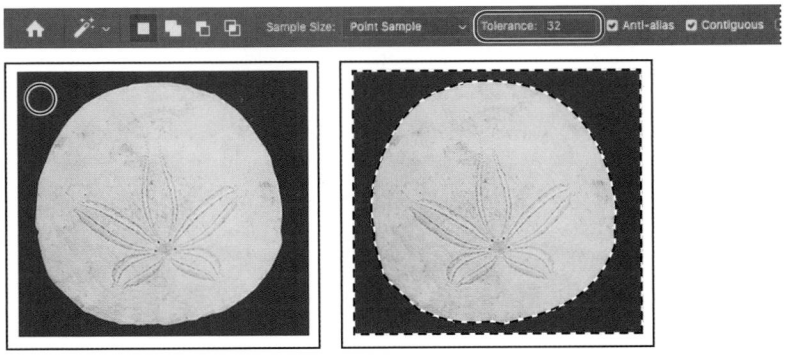

The Magic Wand tool perfectly selected the red background, because all of the colors in the background are similar enough to the position where you clicked (within the 32 levels specified in the Tolerance setting). But it's the shell we want, so let's start over.

5 Choose Select > Deselect.

6 Position the Magic Wand tool over the sand dollar, and click.

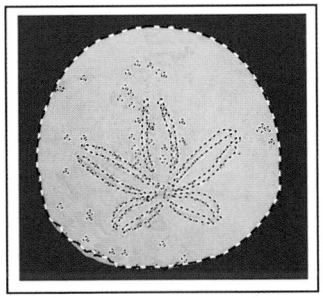

Look carefully at the animated selection marquee that appears over the sand dollar. If this was a perfect selection, the selection marquee would tightly follow the outer edge of the sand dollar. But notice that some interior areas of the sand dollar show selection marquees, because their colors differ from the color you clicked by more than 32 levels (the Tolerance setting). That means the current selection isn't ideal, because it doesn't include all interior areas.

When you want to select a subject that is mostly the same color and value, against a relatively solid background, you can often solve this by increasing the Tolerance value. But the more complex the subject or background, the more likely a wide Tolerance value will also select unwanted parts of the background. In that case, it's usually better to use a different selection tool, such as the Quick Selection tool. You'll do that next, but first let's deselect the current selection.

7 Choose Select > Deselect.

Using the Quick Selection tool

The Quick Selection tool is one of the easier ways to make a selection. You simply click or drag it within a subject, and the tool automatically finds the edges. You can add or subtract areas of the selection until you have exactly the area you want. This works better than the Magic Wand tool because the Quick Selection tool is more aware of image content, instead of relying on color similarity alone. Let's see if the Quick Selection tool does a better job selecting the sand dollar.

1 Select the Quick Selection tool ( ) in the Tools panel. It may be hidden under the Magic Wand tool ( ).

2 Select Enhance Edge in the options bar.

When Enhance Edge is selected, the Quick Selection tool creates better quality selections, with edges that are truer to the object. The selection process is slightly slower than using the Quick Selection tool without Enhance Edge, but the results are superior.

3 Click or drag within the sand dollar (do not cross over into the background).

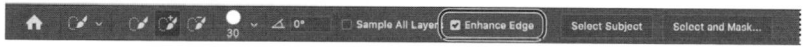

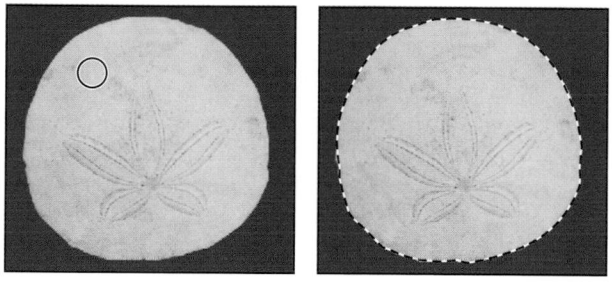

The Quick Selection tool looks at what content is probably connected to the area where you clicked or dragged and finds the full edge automatically, selecting the entire sand dollar. The sand dollar is simple enough that the Quick Selection tool can isolate it easily. When the Quick Selection tool doesn't complete the selection initially, click or drag over areas you want to add to the selection.

Leave the selection active so that you can use it in the next exercise.

▶ **Tip:** If the Quick Selection tool includes areas outside the subject, you can remove unwanted areas from the selection by clicking or dragging over them while holding down the Alt (Windows) or Option (Mac) key. That's the shortcut for selecting the Subtract From Selection icon in the options bar.

Moving a selected area

Once you've made a selection, any changes you make apply exclusively to the pixels within the selection. The rest of the image is not affected by those changes.

To move the selected area to another part of the composition, you use the Move tool. This image has only one layer, so the pixels you move will replace the pixels beneath them. This change is not permanent until you deselect the moved pixels, so you can try different locations for the selection you're moving before you make a commitment.

▶ **Tip:** If you deselect an area by accident, you may be able to restore the selection by choosing Edit > Undo or Select > Reselect.

1 If the sand dollar is not still selected, repeat the previous exercise to select it.

2 Zoom out so you can see both the shadowbox and the sand dollar.

3 Select the Move tool (✣). Notice that the sand dollar remains selected.

4 Drag the selected area (the sand dollar) to the upper-left area of the frame, which is labeled "A." Position it over the silhouette in the frame, leaving the lower-left part of the silhouette showing as a shadow.

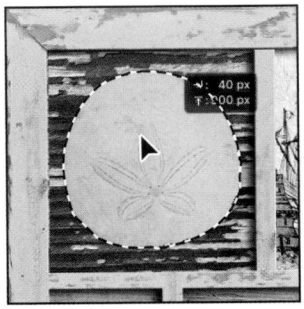

5 Choose Select > Deselect, and then choose File > Save.

In Photoshop, it's not easy to lose a selection. Unless a selection tool is active, clicking elsewhere in the image will not deselect the active area. To deliberately deselect a selection, you can choose Select > Deselect, press Ctrl+D (Windows) or Command+D (Mac), or click outside the selection with any selection tool.

Julieanne Kost is an official Adobe Photoshop evangelist.

Tool tips from the Photoshop evangelist

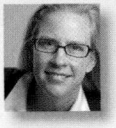

Move tool tip

If you're moving objects in a multilayer file with the Move tool and you need to select one of the layers, try this: With the Move tool selected, position the pointer over any area of an image, and right-click (Windows) or Control-click (Mac). The context menu that appears lists all layers where content exists under the pointer so that you can select a different layer.

Using the Object Selection tool

The Object Selection tool is similar to the Quick Selection tool, but it's a little smarter. All you have to do is draw a rough selection around the object you want to select, and the Object Selection tool identifies and selects the object. The Object Selection tool can save you the most time with an object that has a complicated outline that would take a lot of time to select by hand, such as the coral.

1 Select the Object Selection tool (), hidden under the Quick Selection tool ().

2 Drag a selection around the piece of coral. It doesn't have to be precise or centered. What's important is that it's a relatively tight selection with a small amount of space between the coral and the edges of the selection marquee. You're simply showing Photoshop which object you want to select.

▶ **Tip:** The Object Selection tool works best on a simple background. On a busy background its selection may not be perfect, but you'll probably be able to clean it up with the Quick Selection tool faster than drawing your own manual selection from scratch.

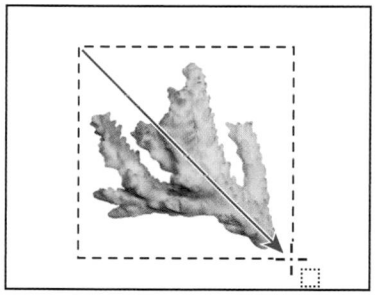

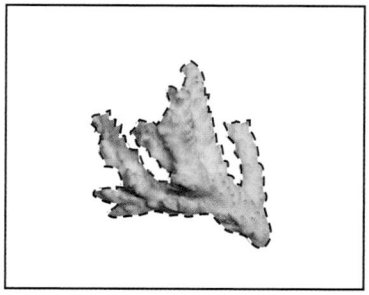

The Object Selection tool analyzes the area inside the rectangular selection, finds the object, and creates a selection marquee along its complicated edge.

3 Select the Move tool (), and drag the coral to the area of the shadowbox labeled "B," positioning it so that a shadow appears to the left of and below the coral.

4 Choose Select > Deselect, and then save your work.

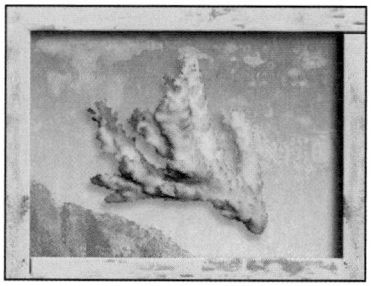

▶ **Tip:** In a busy image, drawing a rectangular area with the Object Selection tool might include other objects or background patterns, making it hard to isolate the object you want. To more precisely indicate the object you want, choose Lasso from the Mode menu in the options bar, and drag the Object Selection tool more closely along the object's outline. Again, it doesn't have to be exact.

Manipulating selections

You can move selections, reposition them as you create them, and even duplicate them. In this section, you'll learn several ways to manipulate selections. Most of these methods work with any selection; you'll use them here with the Elliptical Marquee tool, which lets you select ovals or perfect circles.

One of the most useful things you may find in this section is the introduction of keyboard shortcuts that can save you time and arm motions.

Repositioning a selection marquee while creating it

Selecting ovals and circles can be tricky. It's not always obvious where you should start dragging, so sometimes the selection will be off-center, or the ratio of width to height won't match what you need. In this exercise, you'll learn techniques for managing those problems, including two important keyboard-mouse combinations that can make your Photoshop work much easier.

As you perform this exercise, be careful to follow the directions about keeping the mouse button or specific keys pressed. If you accidentally release the mouse button at the wrong time, simply start the exercise again from step 1.

1 Select the Zoom tool (🔍), and click the plate of shells at the bottom of the image window to zoom in to at least 100% view (use 200% view if the entire plate of shells will still fit in the image window on your screen).

2 Select the Elliptical Marquee tool (◯), hidden under the Rectangular Marquee tool (⬚).

3 Move the pointer over the plate of shells, and drag diagonally across the oval plate to create a selection, but *do not release the mouse button*. It's OK if your selection does not match the plate shape yet.

Note: You don't have to include every pixel in the plate of shells, but the selection should be the shape of the plate, and should contain the shells comfortably.

If you accidentally release the mouse button, draw the selection again. In most cases—including this one—the new selection replaces the previous one.

4 Still holding down the mouse button, press the spacebar, and continue to drag the selection. Instead of resizing the selection, now you're moving it. Position it so that it more closely aligns with the plate.

5 Carefully release the spacebar (but not the mouse button) and continue to drag, trying to make the size and shape of the selection match the oval plate of shells as closely as possible. If necessary, hold down the spacebar again, and drag to move the selection marquee into position around the plate of shells.

Tip: The technique of holding down the spacebar to reposition as you draw also works with other drawing tools in Photoshop, such as the shape tools and the Pen tool.

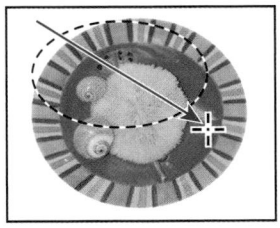

Begin dragging a selection.

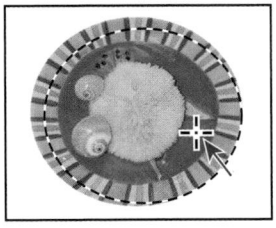

Press the spacebar to move it.

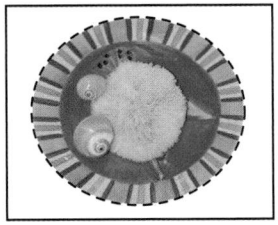

Complete the selection.

6 When the selection border is positioned appropriately, release the mouse button.

7 Choose View > Fit On Screen or use the slider in the Navigator panel to reduce the zoom view so that you can see all of the objects in the image window.

Tip: If you want to resize a selection after you've drawn it (after releasing the mouse button), choose Select > Transform Selection.

Leave the Elliptical Marquee tool and the selection active for the next exercise.

Moving selected pixels with a keyboard shortcut

Now you'll use a keyboard shortcut to move the selected pixels onto the shadowbox. The shortcut temporarily switches the active tool to the Move tool, so you don't need to select it from the Tools panel.

Note: If you try to move the pixels but Photoshop displays an alert saying "Could not use the Move tool because the layer is locked," make sure you start dragging by positioning the pointer inside the selection.

1 If the plate of shells is not still selected, repeat the previous exercise to select it.

2 With the Elliptical Marquee tool (◌) selected in the Tools panel, press Ctrl (Windows) or Command (Mac), and hover the pointer within the selection. Continue to hold down the key for the next step.

The pointer icon now includes a pair of scissors (▶✂), indicating that the selection will be cut from its current location.

3 While continuing to hold down the Ctrl or Command key, drag the plate of shells onto the area of the shadowbox labeled "C." (You'll use another technique to nudge the oval plate into the exact position in a minute.)

Note: You can release the Ctrl or Command key after you start dragging, and the Move tool remains active. Photoshop reverts to the previously selected tool when you deselect, whether you click outside the selection or use the Deselect command.

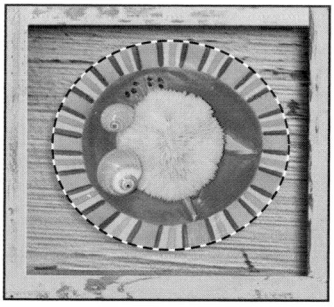

4 Release the mouse button and the key, but don't deselect the plate of shells.

Moving a selection with the arrow keys

You can make minor adjustments to the position of selected pixels by using the arrow keys. You can nudge the selection in increments of either one pixel or ten pixels.

When a selection tool is active in the Tools panel, the arrow keys nudge the selection border, but not the contents. When the Move tool is active, the arrow keys move both the selection border and its contents.

You'll use the arrow keys to nudge the plate of shells. Before you begin, make sure that the plate of shells is still selected in the image window.

1 Select the Move tool (✥), and press the Up Arrow key (↑) on your keyboard a few times to move the oval upward.

Notice that each time you press the arrow key, the plate of shells moves one pixel. Experiment by pressing the other arrow keys to see how they affect the selection.

Softening the edges of a selection

To smooth the hard edges of a selection, you can apply anti-aliasing or feathering or use the Select and Mask option.

Anti-aliasing smooths the jagged edges of a selection by softening the color transition between edge pixels and background pixels. Since only the edge pixels change, no detail is lost. Anti-aliasing is useful when you cut, copy, and paste selections to create composite images.

Anti-aliasing is available for the Lasso, Polygonal Lasso, Magnetic Lasso, Elliptical Marquee, and Magic Wand tools. (Select the tool to display its options in the options bar.) To apply anti-aliasing, you must select the option before making the selection. Once a selection is made, you cannot add anti-aliasing to it.

Feathering blurs edges by building a transition boundary between the selection and its surrounding pixels. This blurring can cause some loss of detail at the edge of the selection.

You can define feathering for the marquee and lasso tools as you use them, or you can add feathering to an existing selection. Feathering effects become apparent when you move, cut, or copy the selection.

- To feather a selection edge using the Select and Mask option, make a selection, and then click Select and Mask in the options bar to open its dialog box. In there you can smooth the outline, feather it, or contract or expand it.
- To anti-alias a selection edge, select a lasso tool, or the Elliptical Marquee or Magic Wand tool, and select Anti-alias in the options bar.
- To define a feathered edge for a selection you're about to draw, select any of the lasso or marquee tools. Enter a Feather value in the options bar. This value defines the width of the feathered edge and can range from 1 to 250 pixels.
- To define a feathered edge for an existing selection, choose Select > Modify > Feather. Enter a value for the Feather Radius, and click OK.

2 Hold down the Shift key as you press an arrow key.

When you hold down the Shift key, the selected pixels move ten pixels every time you press an arrow key.

▶ **Tip:** Selection edges, guidelines, and other visible items that aren't actual objects are called *extras*, so another way to hide the selection edges is to deselect the View > Extras command or press its keyboard shortcut, Ctrl+H (Windows) or Command+H (Mac).

Sometimes the selection marquee can distract you as you make adjustments. You can hide the edges of a selection temporarily without actually deselecting and then display the selection border once you've completed the adjustments.

3 Choose View > Show > Selection Edges to deselect the command, hiding the selection border around the plate of shells.

4 Use the arrow keys to nudge the plate of shells until it's positioned over the silhouette so that there's a shadow on the left and bottom of the plate. Then choose View > Show > Selection Edges to reveal the selection border again.

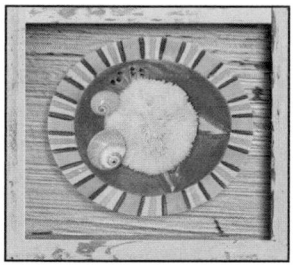

Hidden selection edges

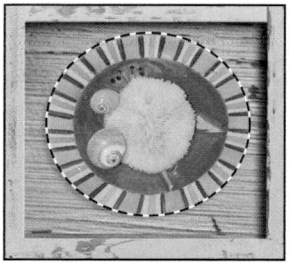

Visible selection edges

5 Choose Select > Deselect, or press Ctrl+D (Windows) or Command+D (Mac).

6 Choose File > Save to save your work so far.

Selecting with the lasso tools

As we mentioned earlier, Photoshop includes three lasso tools: the Lasso tool, the Polygonal Lasso tool, and the Magnetic Lasso tool. You can use the Lasso tool to make selections that require both freehand and straight lines, using keyboard shortcuts to move back and forth between the Lasso tool and the Polygonal Lasso tool. You'll use the Lasso tool to select the mussel. It takes a bit of practice to alternate between straight-line and freehand selections—if you make a mistake while you're selecting the mussel, simply deselect and start again.

▶ **Tip:** Because the lasso tools are manual, they can be the most time-consuming way to create a selection. They are typically most useful for selecting simple shapes or adjusting an existing selection.

1 If the window magnification is below 100%, select the Zoom tool (🔍), and click the mussel to zoom in to at least 100%.

2 Select the Lasso tool (). Starting at the lower-left section of the mussel, drag around the rounded end of the mussel, tracing the shape as accurately as possible. *Do not release the mouse button.*

3 When you reach a corner or straight part of the edge, press the Alt (Windows) or Option (Mac) key, and then release the mouse button so that the lasso pointer changes to the polygonal lasso shape (). *Do not release the Alt or Option key.*

▶ **Tip:** Go slowly until you become comfortable with the Lasso tool. If you make a mistake or accidentally release the mouse button during steps 2–8, choose Edit > Undo, and start again at step 2.

4 Begin clicking along the end of the mussel to place anchor points, following the contours of the mussel. Be sure to hold down the Alt or Option key throughout this process. This lets you create perfectly straight segments along the selection.

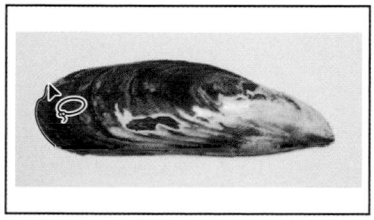

Drag with the Lasso tool.

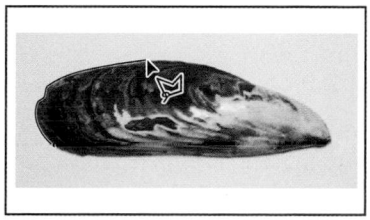

Click with the Polygonal Lasso tool.

The selection border automatically stretches like a rubber band between anchor points.

5 When you reach the tip of the mussel, hold down the mouse button as you release the Alt or Option key. The pointer again appears as the lasso icon.

6 Carefully drag around the tip of the mussel, holding down the mouse button.

7 When you finish tracing the tip and reach the straight segments along the lower side of the mussel, first press Alt or Option again, and then release the mouse button. Click along the straight segments of the lower side of the mussel as needed. Continue to trace the straight and curved mussel edges until you arrive back at the starting point of your selection at the left end of the mussel.

8 Click the starting point of the selection, and then release Alt or Option. The mussel is now entirely selected. Leave the mussel selected for the next exercise.

Note: To make sure that the selection is the shape you want when you use the Lasso tool, end the selection by dragging across the starting point of the selection. If you start and stop the selection at different points, Photoshop draws a straight line between the start and end points of the selection.

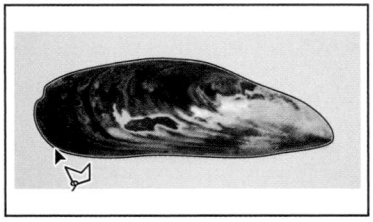

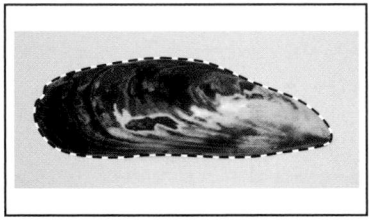

Rotating a selection

Now you'll rotate the mussel.

Before you begin, make sure that the mussel is still selected.

1 Choose View > Fit On Screen to resize the image window to fit on your screen.

2 Press Ctrl (Windows) or Command (Mac) as you drag the selected mussel to the section of the shadowbox labeled "D."

The pointer changes to the Move tool icon when you press Ctrl or Command.

3 Choose Edit > Transform > Rotate.

The mussel and selection marquee are enclosed in a bounding box.

Tip: You can constrain rotation to common angles such as 90 degrees by holding down the Shift key as you drag the bounding box.

4 Move the pointer outside the bounding box so that it becomes a curved, two-headed arrow (↻). Drag to rotate the mussel to a 90-degree angle. You can verify the angle in the transformation values display next to the pointer, or in the Rotate box in the options bar. Press Enter or Return to commit the transformation.

5 If necessary, select the Move tool (✥), and drag to reposition the mussel, leaving a shadow to match the others. When you're satisfied, choose Select > Deselect.

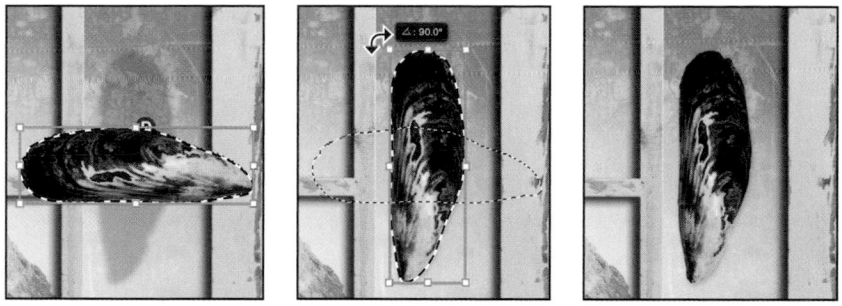

6 Choose File > Save.

Selecting with the Magnetic Lasso tool

You can use the Magnetic Lasso tool to make freehand selections of areas with high-contrast edges. When you draw with the Magnetic Lasso tool, the selection border automatically snaps to the edge between areas of contrast. You can also control the selection path by occasionally clicking the mouse to place anchor points in the selection border.

You'll use the Magnetic Lasso tool to select the nautilus so that you can move it to the shadowbox.

1 Select the Zoom tool (🔍), and click the nautilus to zoom in to at least 100%.

2 Select the Magnetic Lasso tool (), hidden under the Lasso tool ().

3 Click once along the left edge of the nautilus, and then move the Magnetic Lasso tool along the edge to trace its outline.

▶ **Tip:** In low-contrast areas, you may want to click to place your own fastening points. You can add as many as you need. To remove the most recent fastening point, press Delete, and then move the mouse back to the remaining fastening point and continue selecting.

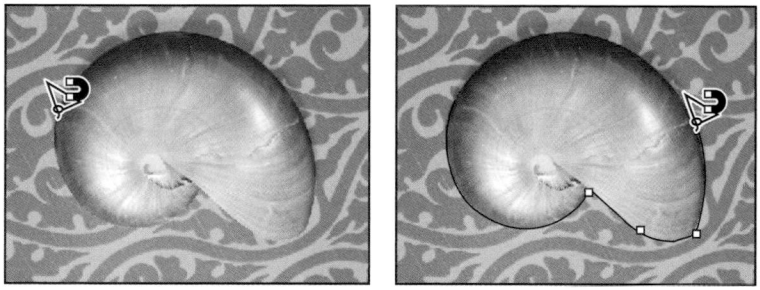

Even though you're not holding down the mouse button, the tool snaps to the edge of the nautilus and automatically adds fastening points.

4 When you reach the left side of the nautilus again, double-click to return the Magnetic Lasso tool to the starting point, closing the selection. Or you can move the Magnetic Lasso tool over the starting point and click once.

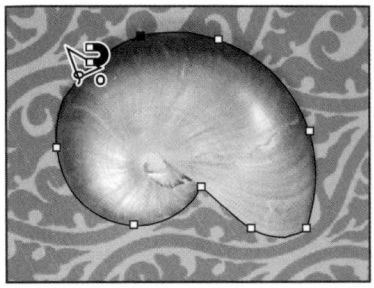

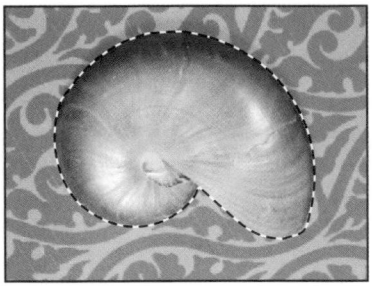

5 Double-click the Hand tool (✋) to fit the entire image in the window.

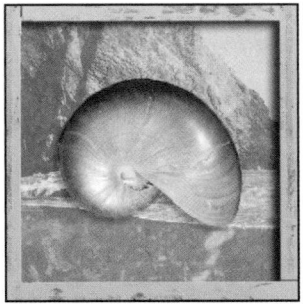

6 Select the Move tool (✥), and drag the nautilus onto its silhouette in the section of the frame labeled "E," leaving a shadow below it and on the left side.

7 Choose Select > Deselect, and then choose File > Save.

Selecting from a center point

In some cases, it's easier to make elliptical or rectangular selections by drawing a selection from an object's center point. You'll use this technique to select the head of the screw for the shadowbox corners.

1 Select the Zoom tool (🔍), and zoom in on the screw to a magnification of about 300%. Make sure that you can see the entire screw head in your image window.

2 Select the Elliptical Marquee tool (◌) in the Tools panel.

3 Move the pointer to the approximate center of the screw.

4 Click and begin dragging. Then, without releasing the mouse button, press Alt (Windows) or Option (Mac) as you continue dragging the selection to the outer edge of the screw.

The selection is centered over its starting point.

5 When you have the entire screw head selected, release the mouse button first, and then release Alt or Option (and the Shift key if you used it). Do not deselect, because you'll use this selection in the next exercise.

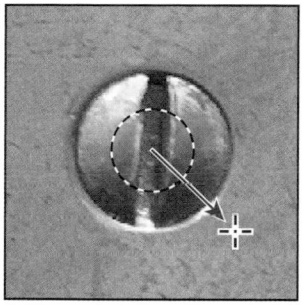

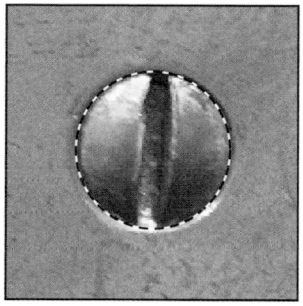

6 If necessary, reposition the selection border using one of the methods you learned earlier. If you accidentally released the Alt or Option key before you released the mouse button, select the screw again.

▶ **Tip:** To select a perfect circle, press Shift as you drag. Hold down Shift while dragging the Rectangular Marquee tool to select a perfect square.

Resizing and copying a selection

Now you'll move the screw to the lower-right corner of the wooden shadowbox and then duplicate it for the other corners.

Resizing the contents of a selection

You'll start by moving the screw, but it's too large for the space. You'll need to resize it as well.

Before you begin, make sure that the screw is still selected. If it's not, reselect it by completing the previous exercise.

1 Choose View > Fit On Screen so that the entire image fits within the image window.

2 Select the Move tool (✥) in the Tools panel.

3 Position the pointer within the screw selection.

The pointer becomes an arrow with a pair of scissors (▸✂), indicating that dragging the selection will cut it from its current location and move it to the new location.

4 Drag the screw onto the lower-right corner of the shadowbox.

▶ **Tip:** If the screw won't move or resize smoothly, as if it gets "stuck," hold down the Control key to temporarily disable snapping to magenta Smart Guides as you drag. Or permanently disable them by deselecting the View > Show > Smart Guides command.

5 Choose Edit > Transform > Scale. A bounding box appears around the selection.

6 Drag one of the corner points inward to reduce the screw to about 40% of its original size or until it is small enough to sit on the shadowbox frame.

As you resize the object, the selection marquee resizes, too. Both resize proportionally by default.

7 Press Enter or Return to commit the change and remove the transformation bounding box.

8 Use the Move tool to reposition the screw after resizing it so that it is centered in the corner of the shadowbox frame.

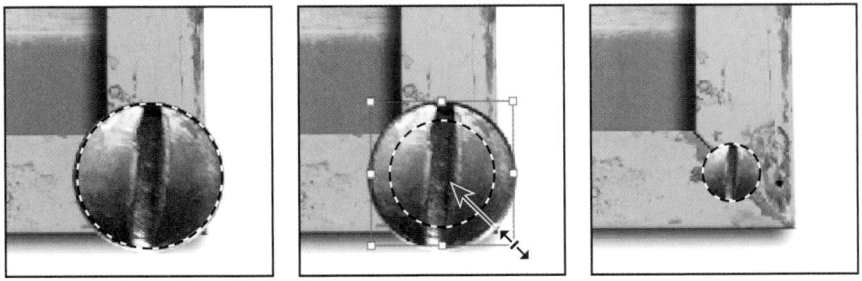

▶ **Tip:** If you don't want to maintain original proportions while resizing, press the Shift key as you drag a corner handle of a transformation bounding box.

9 Leaving the screw selected, choose File > Save to save your work.

Moving and duplicating a selection simultaneously

You can move and duplicate a selection at the same time. You'll copy the screw for the other three corners of the frame. If the screw is no longer selected, reselect it now, using the techniques you learned earlier.

1 With the Move tool (✥) selected, press Alt (Windows) or Option (Mac) as you position the pointer inside the screw selection.

The pointer changes, displaying the usual black arrow and an additional white arrow, which indicates that a duplicate will be made when you move the selection.

2 Continue holding down the Alt or Option key as you drag a duplicate of the screw straight up to the top-right corner of the frame. Release the mouse button and the Alt or Option key, but don't deselect the duplicate image.

3 Hold down Alt+Shift (Windows) or Option+Shift (Mac), and drag a new copy of the screw straight left to the upper-left corner of the frame.

Pressing the Shift key as you move a selection constrains the movement horizontally or vertically in 45-degree increments.

4 Repeat step 3 to drag a fourth screw to the lower-left corner of the frame.

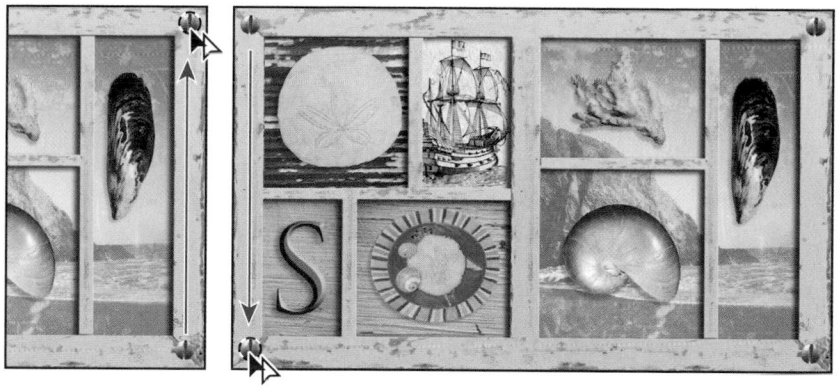

5 When you're satisfied with the position of the fourth screw, choose Select > Deselect, and then choose File > Save.

Copying selections

You can use the Move tool to copy selections as you drag them within or between images, or you can copy and move selections using commands on the Edit menu. The Move tool uses less memory, because it doesn't use the clipboard.

Photoshop has several copy and paste commands on the Edit menu:

- **Copy** takes the selected area on the active layer and puts it on the clipboard.
- **Copy Merged** creates a merged copy of all the visible layers in the selected area.
- **Paste** inserts the clipboard contents at the center of the image. If you paste into another image, the pasted content becomes a new layer.

On the Edit > Paste Special submenu, Photoshop also provides specialized pasting commands to give you more options in certain situations:

- **Paste without Formatting** pastes text without the formatting it may have been copied with, such as font and size. It helps ensure that text pasted from another document or application matches the formatting of a Photoshop text layer.
- **Paste in Place** pastes clipboard content at the location it had in the original image, instead of at the center of the document.
- **Paste Into** pastes clipboard content inside the active selection in the same or a different image. The source selection is pasted onto a new layer, and the area outside the selection is converted into a layer mask.
- **Paste Outside** is the same as Paste Into except that Photoshop pastes the content outside the active selection and converts the area inside the selection to a layer mask.

If two documents have different pixel dimensions, content you paste between them may appear to change size. This is because content maintains its pixel dimensions when pasted into a document with different pixel dimensions. You can resize a pasted selection, but the image quality of the selection may decrease if enlarged.

Cropping an image

Now that your composition is in place, you'll crop the image to a final size. You can use either the Crop tool or the Crop command to crop an image.

1 Select the Crop tool (⌗), or press C to switch from the current tool to the Crop tool. Photoshop displays a crop boundary around the entire image.

2 In the options bar, make sure Ratio is selected in the Preset pop-up menu and that there are no ratio values specified. (If there are, click Clear.) Then confirm that Delete Cropped Pixels is selected.

When Ratio is selected but no ratio values are specified, you can freely crop the image to any proportions.

▶ **Tip:** To crop an image with its original proportions intact, choose Original Ratio from the Preset pop-up menu in the options bar.

3 Drag the crop handles so that the shadowbox is in the highlighted area, omitting the backgrounds from the original objects at the bottom of the image. Crop the frame so that there's an even area of white around it.

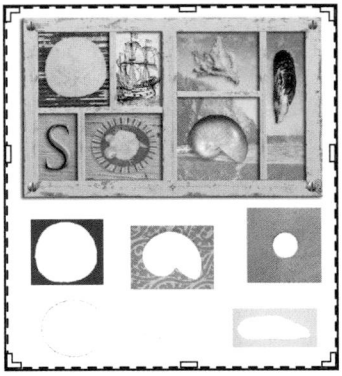

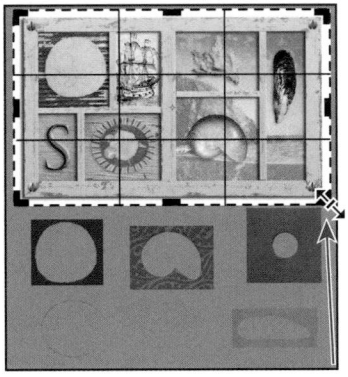

4 When you're satisfied with the position of the crop area, click the Commit Current Crop Operation button (✓) in the options bar.

5 Choose File > Save to save your work.

You've used several different selection tools to move all the seashells into place. The shadowbox is complete!

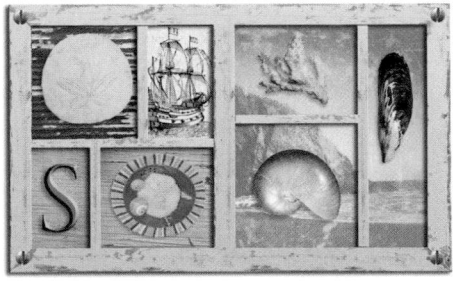

Review questions

1 Once you've made a selection, what area of the image can be edited?

2 How do you add to and subtract from a selection when using a tool such as the Quick Selection tool?

3 How can you move a selection while you're creating it?

4 What does the Quick Selection tool do?

5 How does the Magic Wand tool determine which areas of an image to select? What is tolerance, and how does it affect a selection?

Review answers

1 Only the area within an active selection can be edited.

2 To add to a selection, click the Add To Selection button in the options bar, and then click the area you want to add. To subtract from a selection, click the Subtract From Selection button in the options bar, and then click the area you want to subtract. You can also add to a selection by pressing Shift as you drag or click; to subtract, press Alt (Windows) or Option (Mac) as you drag or click.

3 To reposition a selection as you're creating it, keep holding down the mouse button as you also hold down the spacebar and drag.

4 The Quick Selection tool expands outward from where you click to automatically find and follow defined edges in the image.

5 The Magic Wand tool selects adjacent pixels based on their similarity in color. The Tolerance value determines how many color tones the Magic Wand tool will select. The higher the tolerance setting, the more tones are selected.

4 LAYER BASICS

Lesson overview

In this lesson, you'll learn how to do the following:

- Organize artwork on layers.
- Create, view, hide, and select layers.
- Rearrange layers to change the stacking order of artwork.
- Apply blending modes to layers.
- Resize and rotate layers.
- Apply a gradient to a layer.
- Apply a filter to a layer.
- Add text and layer effects to a layer.
- Add an adjustment layer.
- Save a copy of the file with the layers flattened.

This lesson will take less than an hour to complete. To get the lesson files used in this chapter, download them from the web page for this book at www.adobepress.com/PhotoshopCIB2021. For more information, see "Accessing the lesson files and Web Edition" in the Getting Started section at the beginning of this book.

As you work on this lesson, you'll preserve the start files. If you need to restore the start files, download them from your Account page.

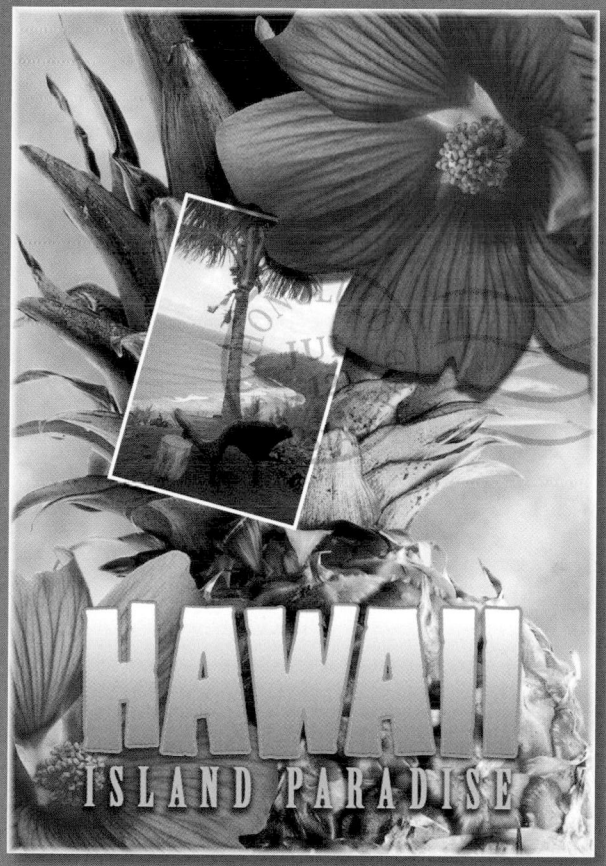

Pineapple and flower photography © Image Source, www.imagesource.com

PROJECT: TRAVEL POSTCARD

In Photoshop, you can isolate different parts of an image on layers. Each layer can then be edited as discrete artwork, giving you tremendous flexibility as you compose and revise an image.

About layers

Every Photoshop file contains one or more *layers*. All new layers in an image are transparent until you add text or artwork. Working with layers is analogous to placing portions of a drawing on clear sheets of film, such as those viewed with an overhead projector: Individual sheets may be edited, repositioned, and deleted without affecting the other sheets. When the sheets are stacked, the entire composition is visible.

Many of the lesson files for this book have a *background layer*, a layer behind all others that is always completely opaque. Photoshop documents intended for print, digital camera images, and scanned images typically have a background layer. Photoshop documents created for mobile devices and websites might not have a background layer; for example, website graphics may need transparent areas that won't block a web page's background or other elements. To learn more about the background layer, see "About the background layer" on page 78.

Note: Some file formats, such as JPEG and GIF, don't support layers. To save those images with layers, you must save them in Photoshop or TIFF format. Also, some color modes (on the Image > Mode submenu), such as Bitmap and Indexed Color, don't support layers. The lesson files in this chapter are Photoshop documents in RGB color mode.

Getting started

You'll start the lesson by viewing an image of the final composition.

1 Start Photoshop, and then simultaneously hold down Ctrl+Alt+Shift (Windows) or Command+Option+Shift (Mac) to restore the default preferences. (See "Restoring default preferences" on page 5.)

2 When prompted, click Yes to delete the Adobe Photoshop Settings file.

3 Choose File > Browse In Bridge to open Adobe Bridge.

4 In the Favorites panel, click the Lessons folder. Then double-click the Lesson04 folder in the Content panel to see its contents.

5 Study the 04End.psd file. Move the thumbnail slider to the right if you want to see the image in more detail.

Note: If Bridge isn't installed, you'll be prompted to install it. For more information, see page 3.

This layered composite represents a postcard. You will assemble it in this lesson as you learn how to create, edit, and manage layers.

6 Double-click the 04Start.psd file to open it in Photoshop.

7 Choose File > Save As, rename the file **04Working.psd**, and click Save. Click OK if you see the Photoshop Format Options dialog box.

Note: If Photoshop displays a dialog box telling you about the difference between saving to Cloud Documents and Your Computer, click Save On Your Computer. You can also select Don't Show Again, but that setting will deselect after you reset Photoshop preferences.

Saving another version of the start file frees you to make changes without worrying about overwriting the original.

Using the Layers panel

The Layers panel lists all the layers in an image, displaying the layer names and thumbnails of the content on each layer. You can use the Layers panel to hide, view, reposition, delete, rename, and merge layers. The layer thumbnails are automatically updated as you edit the layers.

1 If the Layers panel is not visible in the work area, choose Window > Layers.

The Layers panel lists five layers for the 04Working.psd file (from top to bottom): Postage, HAWAII, Flower, Pineapple, and Background.

2 Select the Background layer to make it active (if it's not already selected). Notice the layer thumbnail and the icons shown for the Background layer:

- The lock icon (🔒) indicates that the layer is protected from layer changes. That's why the options above the layer list are unavailable. However, it's still possible to edit the layer content itself, such as painting on it.
- The eye icon (👁) indicates that the layer is visible in the document window. If you click the eye, the document window no longer displays that layer.

▶ **Tip:** Use the context menu to hide or resize the layer thumbnail. Right-click (Windows) or Control-click (Mac) a thumbnail in the Layers panel to open the context menu, and then choose a thumbnail size.

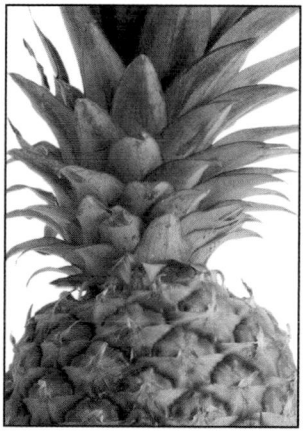

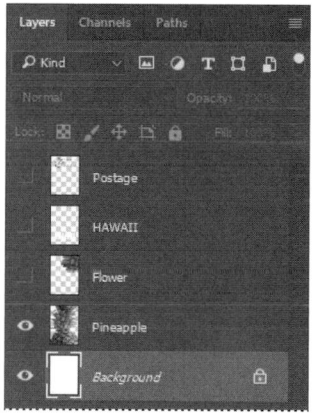

The first task for this project is to add a photo of the beach to the postcard. First, you'll open the beach image in Photoshop.

3 In Photoshop, choose File > Open, navigate to the Lesson04 folder, and then double-click the Beach.psd file to open it.

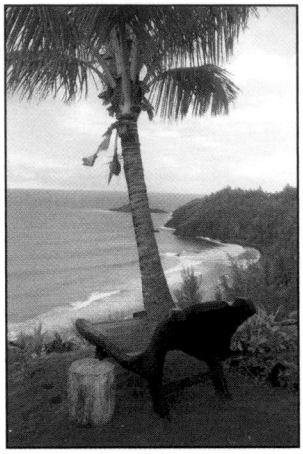

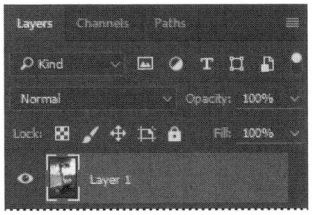

The Layers panel changes to display the layer information for the active Beach.psd file. Notice that only one layer appears in the Beach.psd image: Layer 1. It's not a Background layer, so it can use layer features such as transparency.

About the background layer

If you see a layer named Background at the bottom of the Layers panel and it displays a lock icon, it's a *background layer*. You can't change a background layer's position in the stacking order, it can't have a mask, and it's always opaque. When you flatten the layers of a Photoshop document, the document contains only a background layer.

You can convert a background layer to a regular layer or create a document without a background layer. When a Photoshop document has no background layer, any pixels that don't contain content in any layer are fully transparent. That makes it possible for the content in a Photoshop document to have a non-rectangular shape when placed over another background in Photoshop or in other applications.

To convert a background layer into a regular layer:

1 Click the lock icon next to the layer name. The layer name changes to a numbered default layer name.

2 Rename the layer.

To convert a regular layer into a background layer:

1 Select a layer in the Layers panel.

2 Choose Layer > New > Background From Layer.

Renaming and copying a layer

To add content and simultaneously create a new layer for it, drag and drop one or more files or Photoshop layers into a Photoshop document window. You can drag layers from a source document window or from the Layers panel.

You'll drag the Beach.psd image onto the 04Working.psd file. Before you begin, make sure that both the 04Working.psd and Beach.psd files are open and that the Beach.psd file is selected.

First, you'll give Layer 1 a more descriptive name.

1 In the Layers panel, double-click the name Layer 1, type **Beach**, and then press Enter or Return. Keep the layer selected.

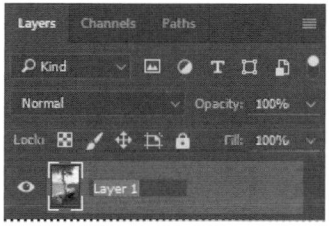

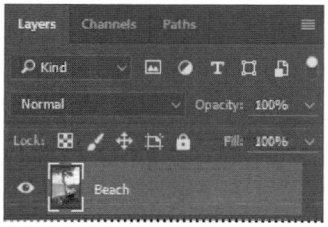

2 Choose Window > Arrange > 2-Up Vertical. Photoshop displays both of the open image files. Select the Beach.psd image so that it is the active file.

3 Select the Move tool (✣), and use it to drag the Beach.psd image onto the 04Working.psd document window.

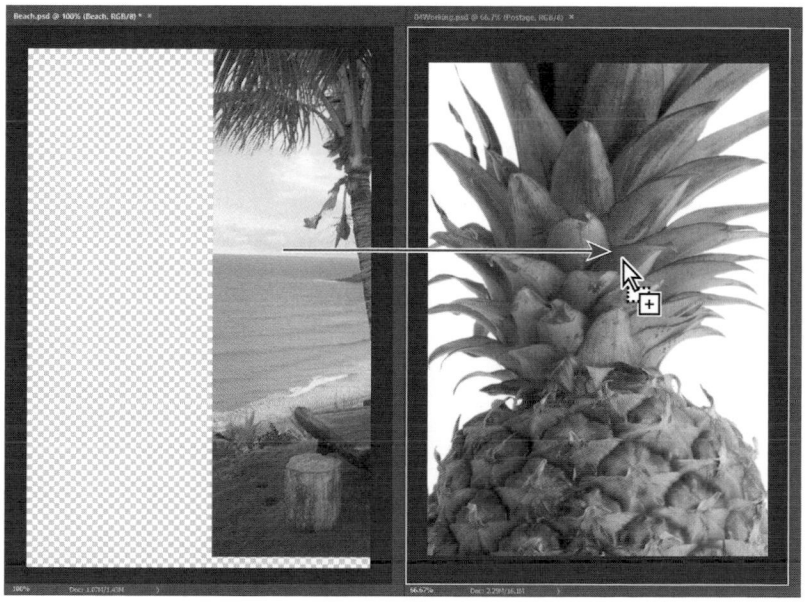

▶ **Tip:** Dragging many layers to another document can be easier if you combine them into a layer group first. Select them in the Layers panel, and then choose Layer > Group Layers. Now you have only one thing to drag: the layer group (which looks like a folder).

Note: When you rename a layer, make sure you double-click the layer name text. If you double-click outside the name, other layer options may appear instead.

▶ **Tip:** If you hold down Shift as you drag an image from one file into another, the dragged image automatically centers itself in the target image window.

▶ **Tip:** You can also transfer layers between documents by copying and pasting: Select layers in the Layers panel, choose Edit > Copy, switch to another document, and choose Edit > Paste.

▶ **Tip:** Need images for a project like this one? In Photoshop, choose File > Search Adobe Stock to download low-resolution placeholder images from the Adobe Stock online photo library. If you license the images, Photoshop replaces the placeholders with high-resolution images.

The Beach layer now appears in the 04Working.psd file document window and its Layers panel, between the Background and Pineapple layers. Photoshop always adds new layers directly above the selected layer; you selected the Background layer earlier.

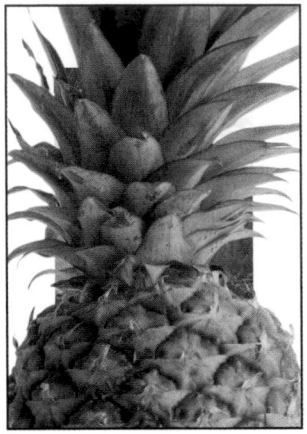

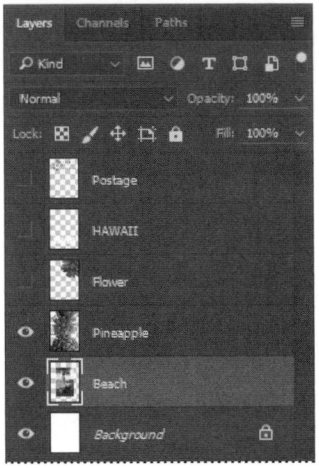

4 Close the Beach.psd file without saving changes to it.

Viewing individual layers

▶ **Tip:** If you need to center the Beach layer, select the Beach layer in the Layers panel, choose Select > All, and then choose Layer > Align Layers to Selection > Horizontal Centers (or Vertical Centers, as needed). Then choose Select > Deselect.

The 04Working.psd file now contains six layers. Some of the layers are visible, and some are hidden. The eye icon (👁) next to a layer thumbnail in the Layers panel indicates that the layer is visible.

1 Click the eye icon (👁) next to the Pineapple layer to hide the image of the pineapple.

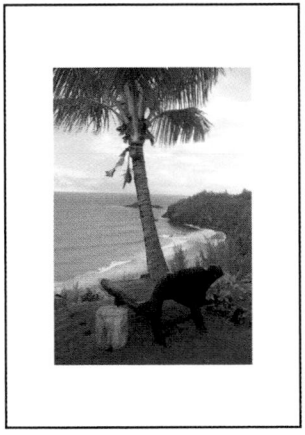

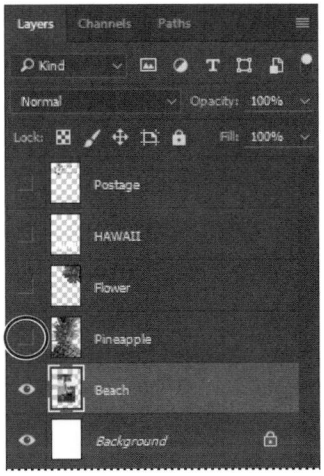

You can hide or show a layer by clicking this icon or clicking in its column, also called the Show/Hide Visibility column.

2 Click again in the Show/Hide Visibility column to display the pineapple.

Adding a border to a layer

Now you'll add a white border around the Beach layer to create the impression that it's an old photograph.

1 Select the Beach layer. (To select the layer, click the layer name in the Layers panel.)

The layer is highlighted, indicating that it is active. Changes you make in the document window affect the active layer.

2 To make the opaque areas on this layer more obvious, hide all layers except the Beach layer: Press Alt (Windows) or Option (Mac) as you click the eye icon (👁) next to the Beach layer.

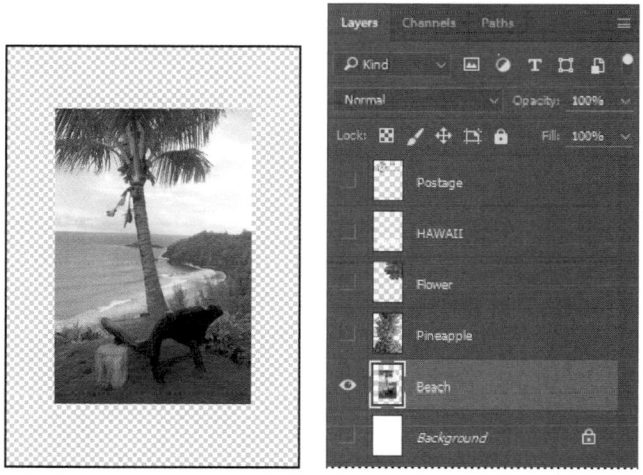

The white background and other objects in the image disappear, leaving only the beach image against a checkerboard background. The checkerboard indicates transparent areas of the active layer.

3 Choose Layer > Layer Style > Stroke.

The Layer Style dialog box opens. Now you'll select the options for the white stroke around the beach image.

4 Specify the following settings:

- Size: **5** px
- Position: Inside
- Blend Mode: Normal
- Opacity: **100**%
- Color: White (Click the Color box, and select white in the Color Picker.)

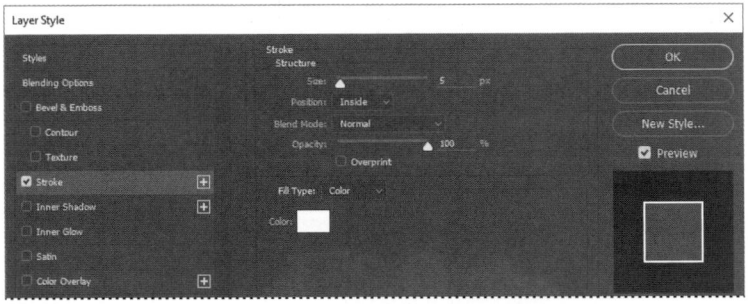

5 Click OK. A white border appears around the beach photo.

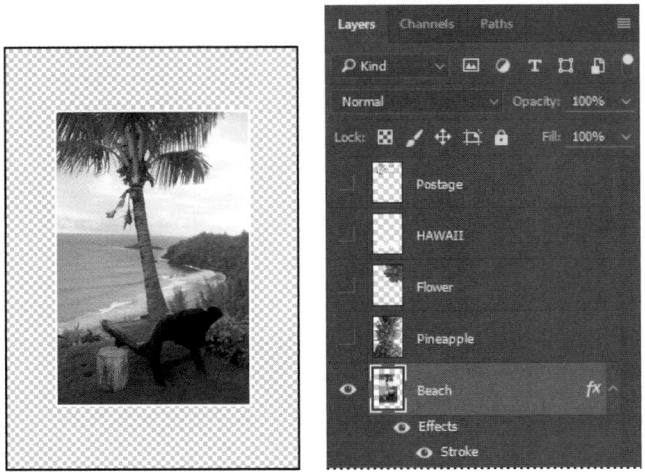

Rearranging layers

The order in which the layers of an image are organized is called the *stacking order*. The stacking order determines how the image is viewed—you can change the order to make certain parts of the image appear in front of or behind other layers.

You'll rearrange the layers so that the beach image is in front of another image that is currently hidden in the file.

1 Make the Postage, HAWAII, Flower, Pineapple, and Background layers visible by clicking the Show/Hide Visibility column next to their layer names.

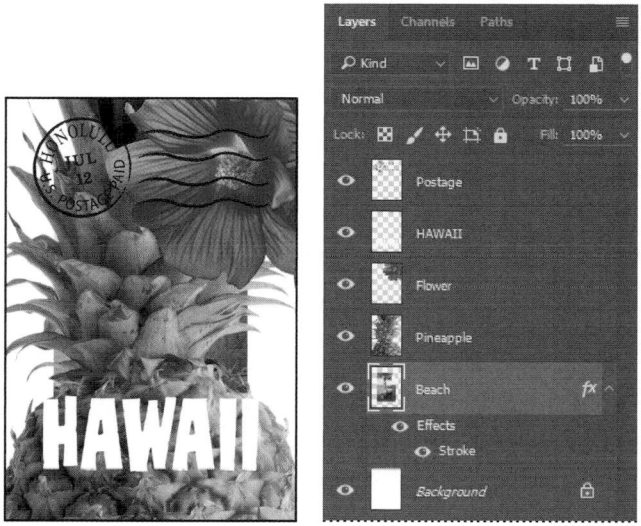

▶ **Tip:** When you want to hide or show a continuous series of layers, you can also drag through their eye icons in the Show/Hide Visibility column, instead of clicking each eye icon separately.

The beach image is almost entirely blocked by images on other layers.

2 In the Layers panel, drag the Beach layer up so that it is positioned between the Pineapple and Flower layers—when you've positioned it correctly, you'll see a double blue line between the layers in the panel—and then release the mouse button.

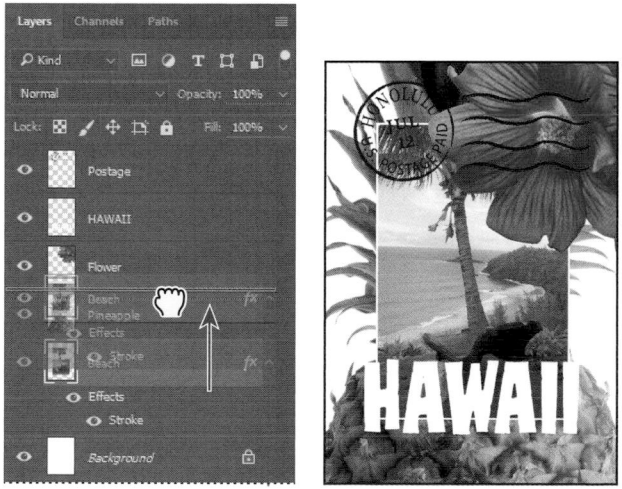

The Beach layer moves up one level in the stacking order, and the beach image appears on top of the pineapple and background images but under the postmark, flower, and the word "HAWAII."

▶ **Tip:** You can also control the stacking order of layered images by selecting them in the Layers panel and choosing Layer > Arrange, and then choosing Bring To Front, Bring Forward, Send Backward, or Send To Back.

Changing the opacity of a layer

You can reduce the opacity of any layer to reveal the layers below it. In this case, the postmark is too dark on the flower. You'll edit the opacity of the Postage layer to let the flower and other images show through.

1 Select the Postage layer, and then click the arrow next to the Opacity field to display the Opacity slider. Drag the slider to 25%. You can also type **25** in the Opacity box or scrub the Opacity label.

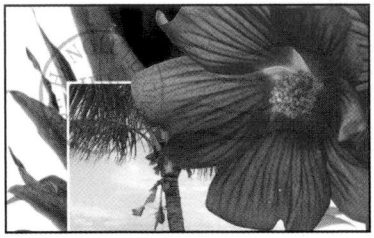

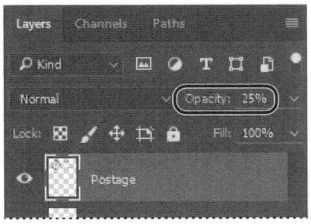

The Postage layer becomes partially transparent so you can better see the layers underneath. Notice that the change in opacity affects only the content of the Postage layer. The Pineapple, Beach, Flower, and HAWAII layers remain opaque.

2 Choose File > Save to save your work.

Duplicating a layer and changing the blending mode

You can apply different blending modes to a layer. *Blending modes* affect how the color pixels on one layer blend with pixels on the layers behind it (see the "Blending Modes" sidebar on page 86). First you'll use blending modes to increase the intensity of the image on the Pineapple layer so that it doesn't look so dull. Then you'll change the blending mode on the Postage layer. (Currently, the blending mode for both layers is Normal.)

1 Click the eye icons next to the HAWAII, Flower, and Beach layers to hide them.

2 Right-click or Control-click the Pineapple layer, and choose Duplicate Layer from the context menu. (Make sure you click the layer name, not its thumbnail, or you'll see the wrong context menu.) Click OK in the Duplicate Layer dialog box.

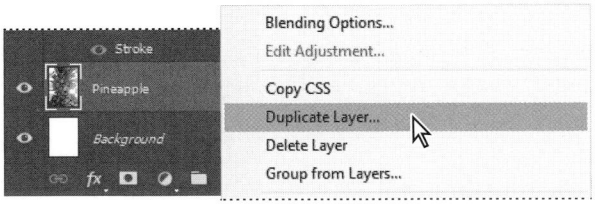

A layer called "Pineapple copy" appears above the Pineapple layer in the Layers panel.

3 With the Pineapple copy layer selected, choose Overlay from the Blending Modes menu in the Layers panel.

▶ **Tip:** Notice that the image changes as you move the mouse over the options in the Blending Modes menu. This is a quick way to preview the effect of each blending mode.

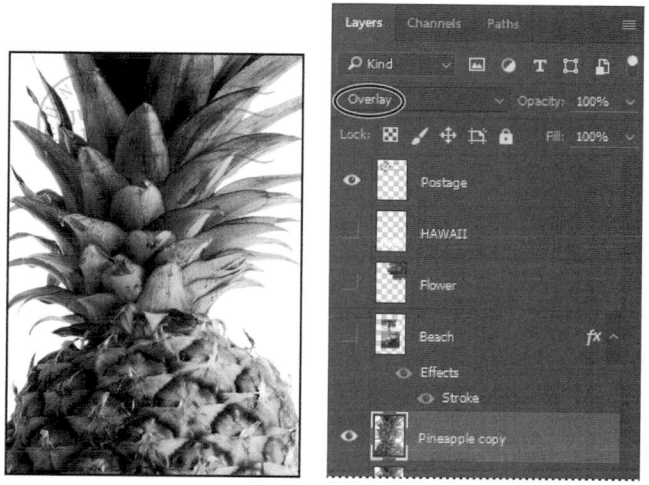

The Overlay blending mode blends the Pineapple copy layer with the Pineapple layer beneath it to create a vibrant, more colorful pineapple with deeper shadows and brighter highlights.

4 Select the Postage layer, and choose Multiply from the Blending Modes menu.

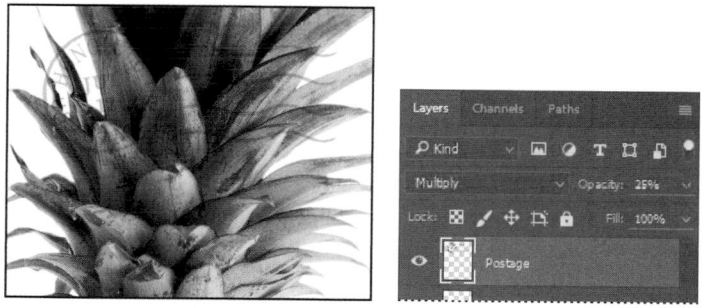

The Multiply blending mode multiplies the color values of its layer with those of the underlying layers. In this example, areas of the postmark that are over the pineapple are darkened using the tonal values of the pineapple.

Each blending mode uses different math to combine a layer with the layers behind it. Overlay tends to increase contrast; Multiply tends to darken its layer.

5 Choose File > Save to save your work.

Blending modes

Blending modes affect how the color pixels on a layer blend with pixels on the layers beneath them. The default blending mode, Normal, hides pixels beneath the top layer unless the top layer is partially or completely transparent. Each of the other blending modes lets you control the way the pixels in the layers interact with each other.

Often, the best way to see how a blending mode affects your image is simply to try it. You can easily experiment with different blending modes in the Layers panel, watching the image change as you move the mouse over different options in the Blending Modes menu. As you experiment, keep in mind how different groups of blending modes affect an image. Generally, if you want to:

- Darken underlying layers, try Darken, Multiply, Color Burn, Linear Burn, or Darker Color.
- Lighten underlying layers, try Lighten, Screen, Color Dodge, Linear Dodge, or Lighter Color.
- Increase the contrast between layers, try Overlay, Soft Light, Hard Light, Vivid Light, Linear Light, Pin Light, or Hard Mix.
- Change the color values of the image, try Hue, Saturation, Color, or Luminosity.
- Create an inversion effect, try Difference or Exclusion.

The following blending modes often come in handy and can be good places to start experimenting:

- **Multiply** does what the name implies: It multiplies the selected layer's color values with the color values of underlying layers.
- **Lighten** replaces pixels in underlying layers when the selected layer's pixel color values are lighter.
- **Overlay** multiplies either the colors or the inverse of the colors, depending on the underlying layers. Patterns or colors overlay the existing pixels while preserving the highlights and shadows of the underlying layers.
- **Luminosity** replaces the luminance of underlying pixels, using the selected layer.

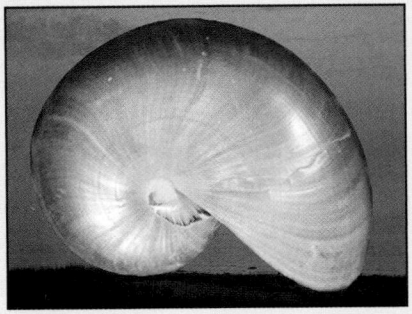

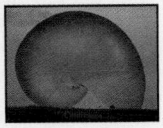

Multiply

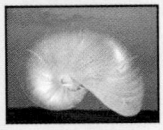

Lighten

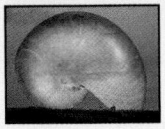

Overlay

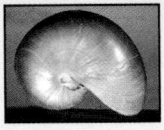

Luminosity

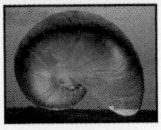

Difference

- **Difference** subtracts darker colors from lighter ones. It's a great way to visually identify the differences between two nearly identical images on different layers.

When you apply different blending modes to multiple layers, you can change the effect by applying the blending modes in a different order in the layer stack. Also, applying a blending mode to a layer group gives you a different result than applying the same blending mode to each layer in the group.

Resizing and rotating layers

Changing the position, size, and angle of layers gives you many creative possibilities. In Photoshop, these kinds of edits are called *transformations*. You performed transformations in Chapter 3 with selections, and they also apply to layers.

1 Click the Visibility column on the Beach layer to make the layer visible.

2 Select the Beach layer in the Layers panel, and choose Edit > Free Transform.

A Transform bounding box appears around the beach image. The bounding box has handles on each corner and each side.

First, you'll resize and angle the layer.

3 Drag a corner handle inward to scale the beach photo down by about 50%. (Watch the Width and Height percentages in the options bar.)

4 With the bounding box still active, position the pointer just outside the bounding box until the pointer becomes a curved double arrow. Drag clockwise to rotate the beach image approximately 15 degrees. You can also enter **15** in the Set Rotation box in the options bar.

▶ **Tip:** The Edit > Free Transform command is so useful that you may want to memorize its keyboard shortcut: Ctrl-T (Windows) or Command-T (Mac).

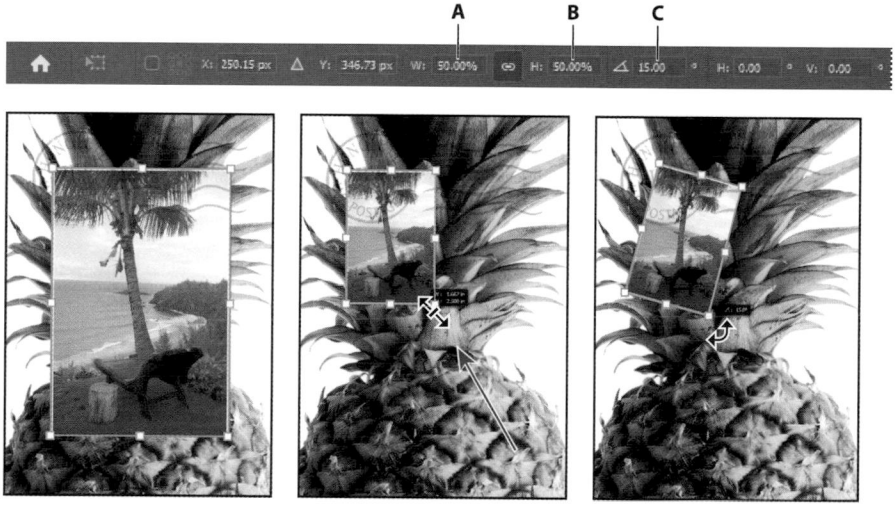

A. *Width value*
B. *Height value*
C. *Set Rotation box*

5 Click the Commit Transform button (✓) in the options bar.

6 Make the Flower layer visible. Then select the Move tool (✥), and drag the beach photo so that its corner is tucked neatly beneath the flower, as in the illustration.

▶ **Tip:** You can also commit a transformation by clicking far outside the transform bounding box. Just make sure you aren't clicking somewhere that will alter a setting or layer accidentally.

7 Choose File > Save.

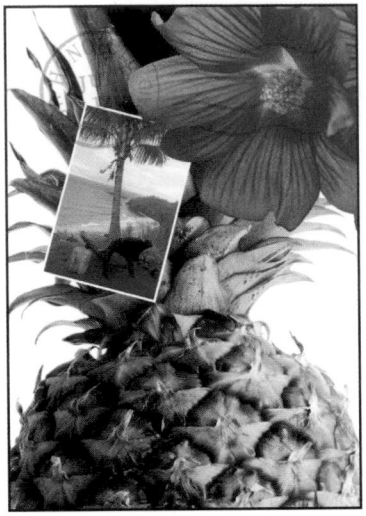

Using a filter to create artwork

Next, you'll create a new layer with no artwork on it. (Adding empty layers to a file is comparable to adding blank sheets of film to a stack of images.) You'll use this layer to add realistic-looking clouds to the sky with a Photoshop filter.

1 In the Layers panel, select the Background layer to make it active, and then click the Create A New Layer button (⊞) at the bottom of the Layers panel.

A new layer, named Layer 1, appears between the Background and Pineapple layers. The layer has no content, so it has no effect on the image.

Note: You can also create a new layer by choosing Layer > New > Layer or by choosing New Layer from the Layers panel menu.

2 Double-click the name Layer 1, type **Clouds**, and press Enter or Return to rename the layer.

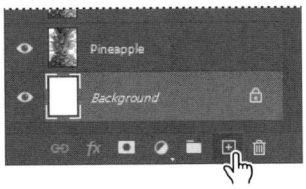

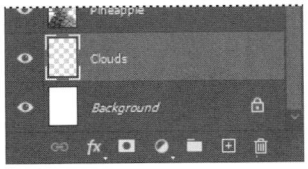

3 In the Tools panel, click the foreground color swatch, select a sky blue color from the Color Picker, and click OK. We selected a color with the following values: R=48, G=138, B=174. The Background Color remains white.

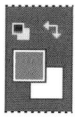

▶ **Tip:** If you expect to use a certain color frequently in multiple documents, add it to your Creative Cloud Libraries. Create a swatch of the color in the Swatches panel, and then drag the swatch to a library in the Libraries panel. Now that color is available to any Photoshop document that you open.

4 With the Clouds layer still active, choose Filter > Render > Clouds.

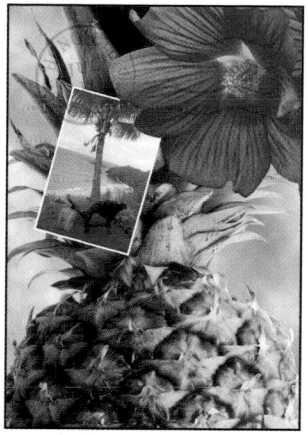

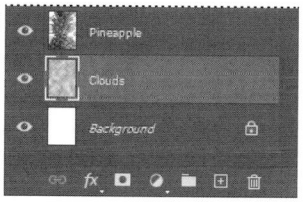

Realistic-looking clouds appear behind the image.

5 Choose File > Save.

Dragging to add a new layer

You can add a layer to an image by dragging an image file from Bridge or from the desktop in Explorer (Windows) or the Finder (Mac). You'll add another flower to the postcard now.

▶ **Tip:** If you're adding artwork from a Creative Cloud library, you can simply drag and drop it from the Libraries panel into a Photoshop document. You can also do this with Adobe Stock images stored in your Creative Cloud Libraries.

1 If Photoshop fills your monitor, reduce the size of the Photoshop window:

- On Windows, click the Restore button (⧉) in the upper-right corner, and then drag any corner of the Photoshop window to make it smaller.
- On a Mac, click the green Maximize/Restore button (●) in the upper-left corner of the document window, or drag any corner of the Photoshop window to make it smaller.

2 In Photoshop, select the Pineapple copy layer in the Layers panel to make it the active layer.

3 In Explorer (Windows) or the Finder (Mac), navigate to the Lessons folder you downloaded from the peachpit.com website. Then navigate to the Lesson04 folder.

4 Select Flower2.psd, and drag it from Explorer or the Finder onto your image.

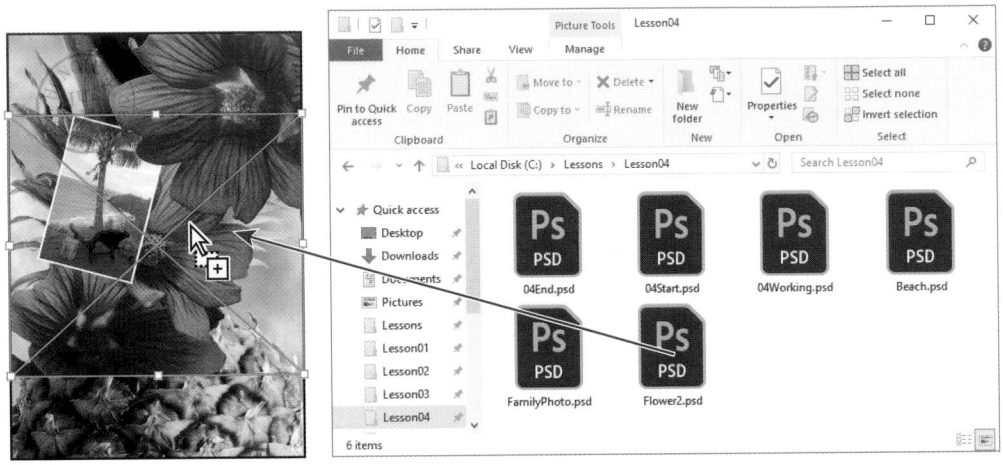

▶ **Tip:** You can drag images from a Bridge window to Photoshop as easily as you can drag from the Windows or Mac desktop.

The Flower2 layer appears in the Layers panel, directly above the Pineapple copy layer. Photoshop places the image as a Smart Object, which is a layer you can edit without making permanent changes. You'll work more extensively with Smart Objects in Lesson 5.

5 Position the Flower2 layer in the lower-left corner of the postcard so that about half of the top flower is visible.

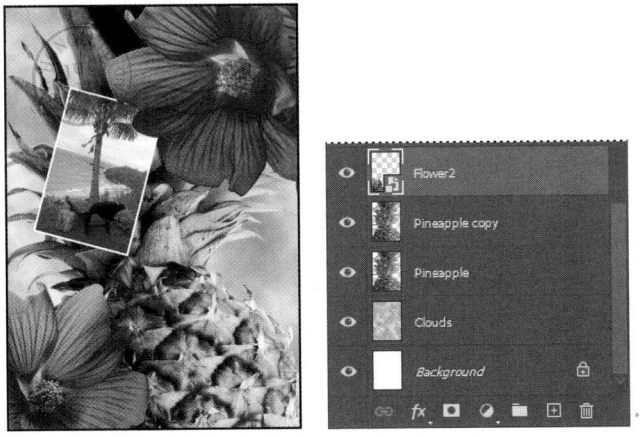

▶ **Tip:** You can also commit a transformation by pressing Enter or Return.

6 Click the Commit Transform button (✓) in the options bar to accept the layer.

7 If you want, make the Photoshop application window larger again if it will give you more room to work comfortably.

Adding text

Now you're ready to create some type using the Horizontal Type tool, which places the text on its own type layer. You'll then edit the text and apply a special effect.

1 Make the HAWAII layer visible. You'll add text just below this layer and apply special effects to both layers.

2 Choose Select > Deselect Layers to ensure that no layers are selected.

3 In the Tools panel, select the Horizontal Type tool (T). Then choose Window > Character to open the Character panel. Do the following in the Character panel:

- Select a condensed font (we used Birch Std, which you can add from Adobe Fonts; if you use a different font, adjust other settings accordingly).
- Select a font style (we used Regular).
- Select a large font size (we used 36 points).
- Select a large tracking value (VA) (we used 250).
- Click the color swatch, select a shade of grassy green in the Color Picker, and click OK to close the Color Picker.
- If the font does not have a bold variant, click the Faux Bold button (T).
- Click the All Caps button (TT).
- Select Crisp from the Anti-aliasing menu (aa).

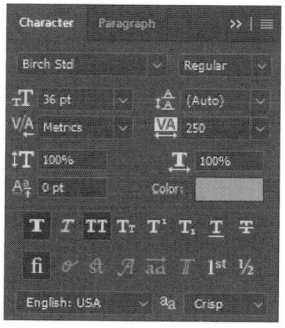

4 Click just below the "H" in the word "HAWAII," and type **Island Paradise**, replacing the selected placeholder text that appears. Then click the Commit Any Current Edits button (✓) in the options bar.

The Layers panel now includes a layer named Island Paradise with a "T" thumbnail, indicating that it is a type layer. This layer is at the top of the layer stack because no layers were selected when it was created.

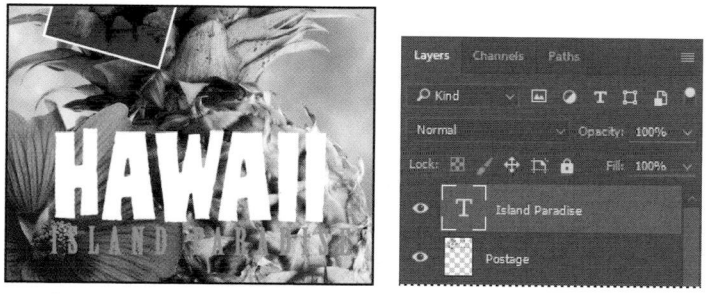

The text appears where you clicked, which probably isn't exactly where you want it to be positioned.

5 Select the Move tool (✣), and drag the "Island Paradise" text so that it is centered below "HAWAII."

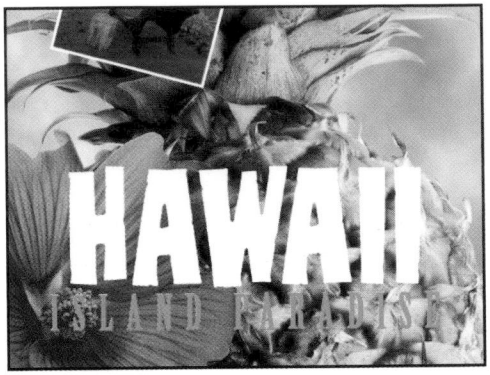

Applying a gradient to a layer

You can apply a color gradient to all or part of a layer. In this example, you'll apply a gradient to the word "HAWAII" to make it more colorful. First you'll select the letters, and then you'll apply the gradient.

1 Select the HAWAII layer in the Layers panel to make it active.

2 Right-click or Control-click the thumbnail in the HAWAII layer, and choose Select Pixels.

Note: Make sure you click the thumbnail, rather than the layer name, or you'll see a different context menu.

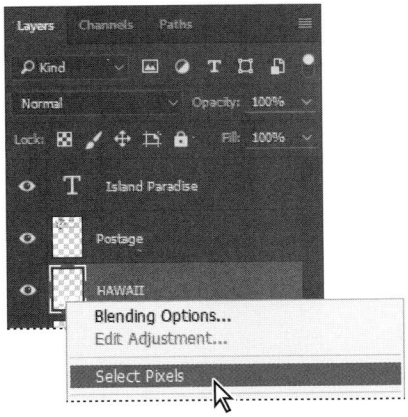

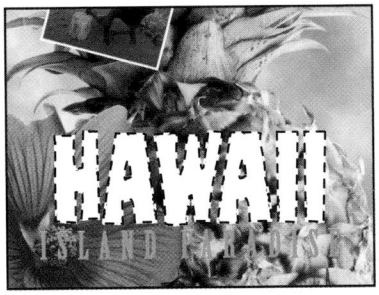

Everything on the HAWAII layer (the white lettering) is selected. Now that you've selected the area to fill, you'll apply a gradient.

Note: Though the layer contains the word "HAWAII," it is not an editable type layer. The text has been rasterized (converted to pixels).

3 In the Tools panel, select the Gradient tool (▣).

4 Click the Foreground Color swatch in the Tools panel, select a bright shade of orange in the Color Picker, and click OK. The Background Color should still be white.

5 In the options bar, make sure that Linear Gradient (▣) is selected.

6 In the options bar, click the arrow next to the Gradient Editor box to open the Gradient Picker. Select the Foreground To Background swatch (it's the first one in the Basics group), and then click anywhere outside the gradient picker to close it.

Tip: To list the gradient options by name rather than by sample, click the menu button in the gradient picker, and choose either Small List or Large List. Or, hover the pointer over a thumbnail until a tool tip appears, showing the gradient name.

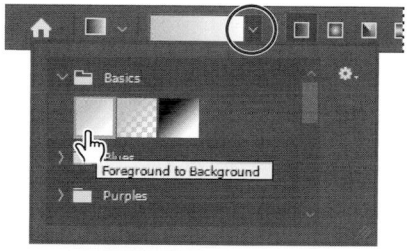

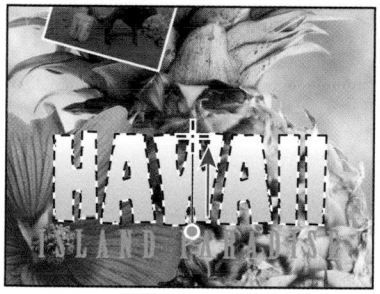

7 With the selection still active, drag the Gradient tool from the bottom to the top of the letters. If you want to be sure you drag straight up, hold down the Shift key and then drag. When the pointer reaches the top of the letters, release the mouse button.

The gradient extends across the type, starting with orange at the bottom and gradually blending to white at the top.

8 Choose Select > Deselect to deselect the "HAWAII" type.

9 Save the work you've done so far.

Applying a layer style

You can enhance a layer by adding a shadow, stroke, satin sheen, or other special effect from a collection of automated and editable layer styles. These styles are easy to apply, and they link directly to the layer you specify.

Like layers, layer styles can be hidden by clicking their eye icons (👁) in the Layers panel. Layer styles are nondestructive, so you can edit or remove them at any time.

Earlier, you used a layer style to add a stroke to the beach photo. Now, you'll add drop shadows to the text to make it stand out.

▶ **Tip:** You can also open the Layer Style dialog box by clicking the Add A Layer Style button at the bottom of the Layers panel and then choosing a layer style, such as Bevel & Emboss, from the pop-up menu.

1 Select the Island Paradise layer, and then choose Layer > Layer Style > Drop Shadow.

2 In the Layer Style dialog box, make sure that the Preview option is selected, and then, if necessary, move the dialog box so that you can see the Island Paradise text in the image window. A drop shadow is now applied.

3 In the Structure area, select Use Global Light, and then specify the following settings:

- Blend Mode: Multiply
- Opacity: **75**%
- Angle: **78** degrees
- Distance: **5** px
- Spread: **30**%
- Size: **10** px

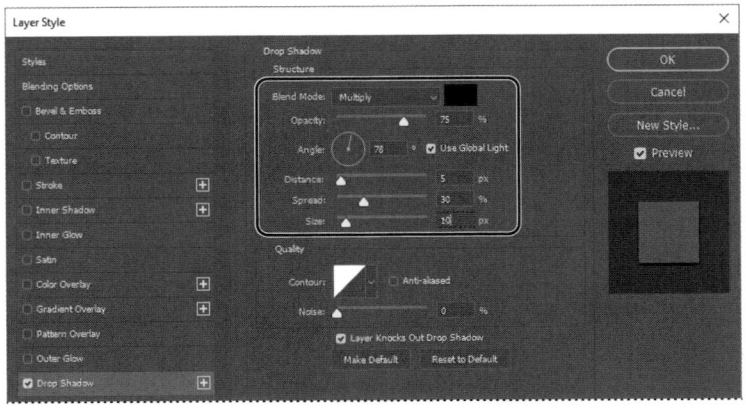

▶ **Tip:** To change the Global Light settings, choose Layer > Layer Style > Global Light.

When Use Global Light is selected, one "master" lighting angle is available in all the layer effects that use shading. If you set a lighting angle in one of these effects, every other effect with Use Global Light selected inherits the same angle setting.

Angle determines the lighting angle at which the effect is applied to the layer. Distance determines the offset distance for a shadow or satin effect. Spread determines how gradually the shadow fades toward the edges. Size determines how far the shadow extends.

Because the Preview option is selected, as you make changes Photoshop updates the drop shadow preview in the document window.

4 Click OK to accept the settings and close the Layer Style dialog box.

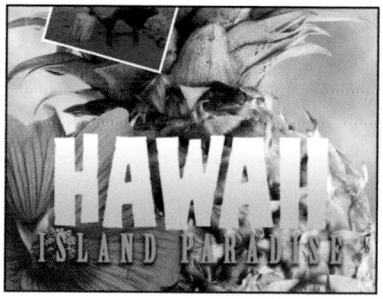

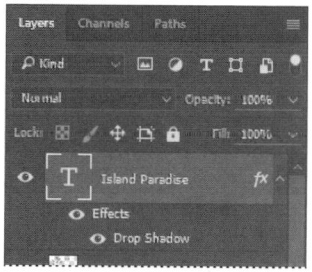

In the Layers panel, the layer style appears nested in the Island Paradise layer. An Effects heading is listed first, and under that, the layer styles applied to the layer. An eye icon (👁) appears next to the effect category and next to each effect. To turn off an effect, click its eye icon. Click the visibility column again to restore the effect. To hide all layer styles for that layer, click the eye icon next to Effects. To collapse the list of effects, click the arrow to the right of the layer name.

5 Make sure that eye icons appear for both items nested in the Island Paradise layer.

6 Press Alt (Windows) or Option (Mac), and in the Layers panel, drag the Effects listing or the fx symbol (*fx*) for the Island Paradise layer onto the HAWAII layer.

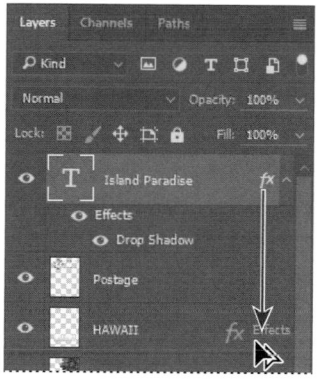

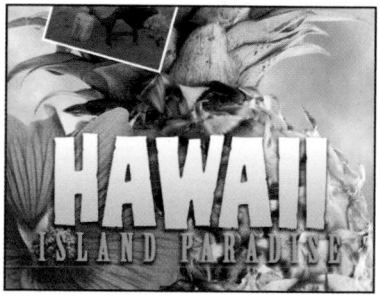

The Drop Shadow layer style is applied to the HAWAII layer, copying the settings you applied to the Island Paradise layer. Now you'll add a green stroke around the word "HAWAII."

▶ **Tip:** If you expect to use a layer style frequently in multiple documents, add it to your Creative Cloud Libraries. Select a layer using the style, click the Add Content button (+.) at the bottom of the Libraries panel, make sure Layer Style is selected, and then click Add. Now that style is available to any open Photoshop document.

7 Select the HAWAII layer in the Layers panel, click the Add A Layer Style button (*fx*) at the bottom of the panel, and then choose Stroke from the pop-up menu.

8 In the Structure area of the Layer Style dialog box, specify the following settings:

- Size: **4** px
- Position: Outside
- Blend Mode: Normal
- Opacity: **100**%
- Color: Green (Select a shade that goes well with the one you used for the "Island Paradise" text.)

▶ **Tip:** Here's a quick way to match the color of the Island Paradise text. When the Color Picker is open for the Stroke Color, position the pointer outside the Color Picker dialog box so that it changes into an eyedropper icon. Click the Island Paradise to sample its green color, loading it into the Color Picker.

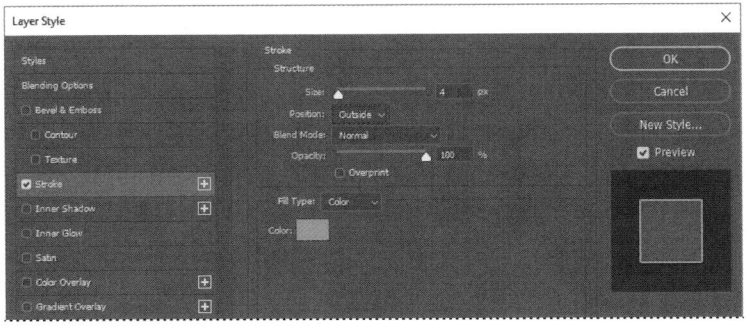

9 Click OK to apply the stroke.

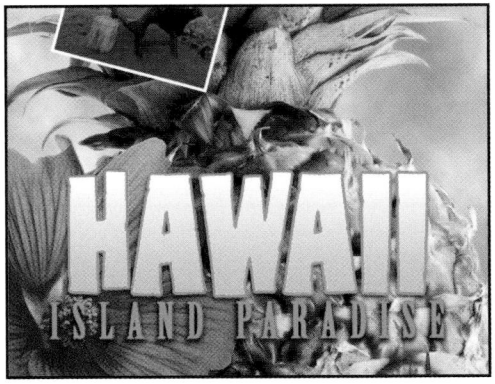

Now you'll add a drop shadow and a satin sheen to the flower.

Using the Gradients panel

Earlier in this chapter, you applied a gradient to the "HAWAII" text in the lesson file by dragging the Gradient tool, which creates a gradient based on the settings in the options bar for the Gradient tool. That's a good way to do it if you want to adjust gradient settings before you apply it.

You can also apply a gradient to a selected layer by using the Gradients panel. Simply display the Gradients panel (Window > Gradients) and click the one you want. The presets you saw in the options bar for the Gradient tool are the same ones listed in the Gradients panel.

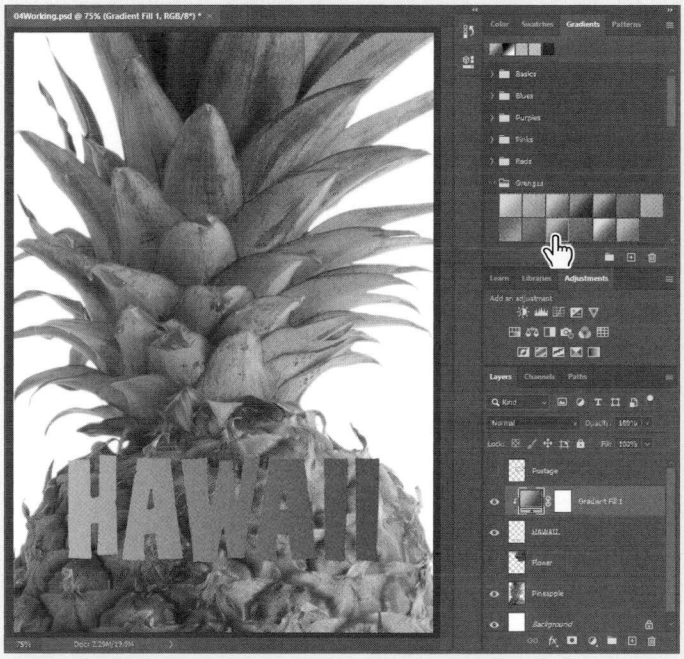

Instead of applying a gradient to a layer as pixels, the Gradients panel applies a Gradient Fill layer, using the selected layer as a clipping mask (for more about clipping masks, see page 100). A Gradient Fill layer is a nondestructive adjustment; you can easily edit it (by double-clicking) or remove it without damaging the layer it's applied to. If you apply another gradient, it's applied as another Gradient Fill layer, so you can compare them by hiding and showing them and then decide which to keep.

For a text layer, the gradient is applied as a Gradient Overlay effect, and applying another gradient updates the Gradient Overlay effect settings.

Other types of Photoshop presets are organized in similar panels. In the Gradients, Swatches, Patterns, or Shapes panel, click any preset to apply it to a selected layer. You can manage the presets in those panels using the buttons along the bottom of the panel or the commands on the panel menu.

10 Select the Flower layer, and choose Layer > Layer Style > Drop Shadow. Then change the following settings in the Structure area:

- Opacity: **60**%
- Distance: **13** px
- Spread: **9**%
- Make sure Use Global Light is selected and that the Blend Mode is Multiply. Do not click OK.

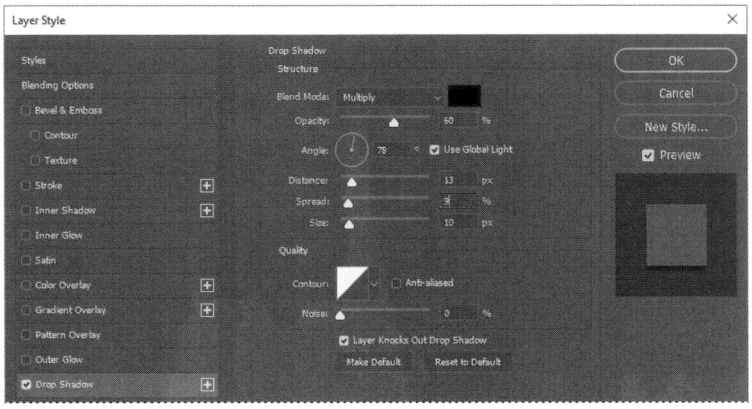

Note: Be sure to click the word Satin. If you click only the check box, Photoshop applies the layer style with its default settings, but you won't see the options.

11 With the Layer Style dialog box still open, click the word Satin on the left to select it and display its options. Then make sure Invert is selected, and apply the following settings:

- Color (next to Blend Mode): Choose a color that enhances the flower color, such as a fuschia hue
- Opacity: **20**%
- Distance: **22** px

The Satin layer effect applies interior shading to create a satiny finish. The contour controls the shape of the effect; Invert flips the contour curve.

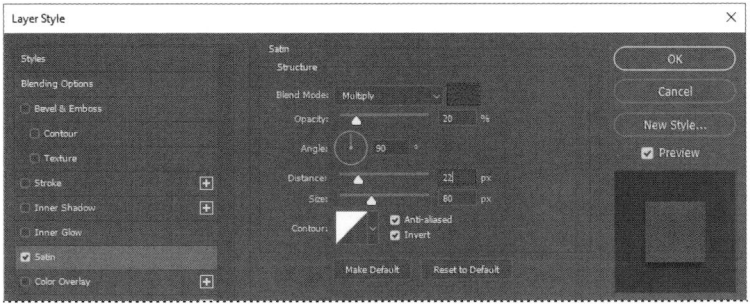

12 Click OK to apply both layer styles. In the Layers panel you can see the two layer styles applied to the Flower layer, and you can use the eye icons to see what the Flower layer looks like with and without the layer styles applied.

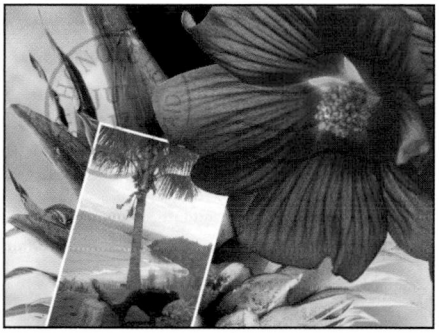

Before applying layer styles

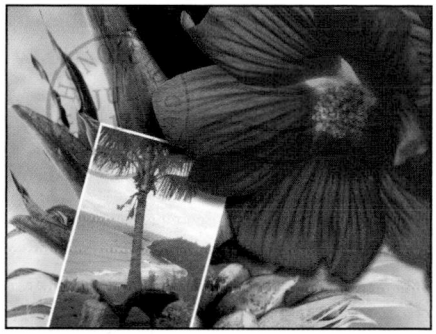

The flower with the drop shadow and satin layer styles applied

Adding an adjustment layer

You can add adjustment layers to an image to apply color and tonal adjustments without permanently changing the pixel values in the image. For example, if you add a Color Balance adjustment layer to an image, you can experiment with different colors repeatedly, because the change occurs only on the adjustment layer. If you decide to return to the original pixel values, you can hide or delete the adjustment layer.

You've used adjustment layers in other lessons. Here, you'll add a Hue/Saturation adjustment layer to change the color of the purple flower. An adjustment layer affects all layers below it in the image's stacking order unless a selection is active when you create it or you create a clipping mask.

1 Select the Flower2 layer in the Layers panel.

2 Click the Hue/Saturation icon in the Adjustments panel to add a Hue/Saturation adjustment layer.

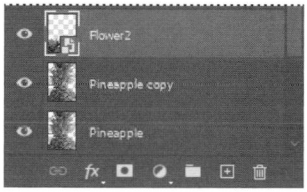

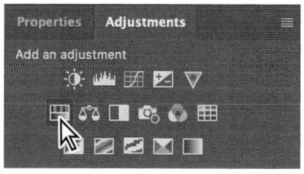

3 In the Properties panel, apply the following settings:

- Hue: **43**
- Saturation: **19**
- Lightness: **0**

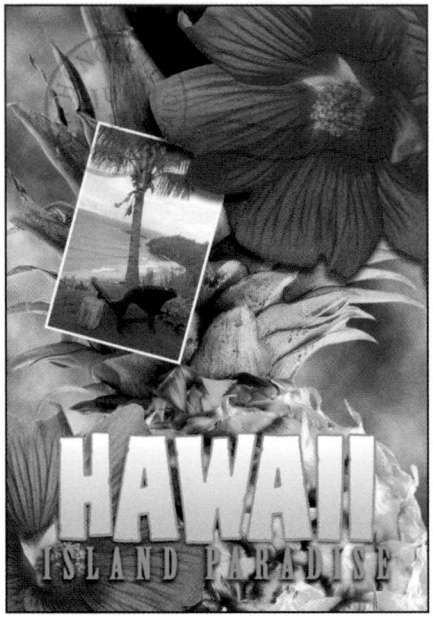

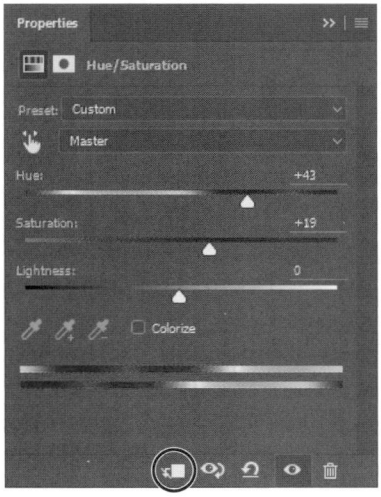

The changes affect the Flower2, Pineapple Copy, Pineapple, Clouds, and Background layers. The effect is interesting, but you want to change only the Flower2 layer.

4 In the Properties panel, click the Create Clipping Mask button (). It's the first button along the bottom of the panel, and you see it when the Properties panel displays options for a layer that can become a clipping mask, such as an adjustment layer.

▶ **Tip:** You can also find the Create Clipping Mask and Release Clipping Mask commands (and their keyboard shortcut) on the Layer menu, on the Layers panel menu, and by right-clicking the layer name. You can also create a clipping mask by Alt-clicking (Windows) or Option-clicking (Mac) the line under a layer in the Layers panel.

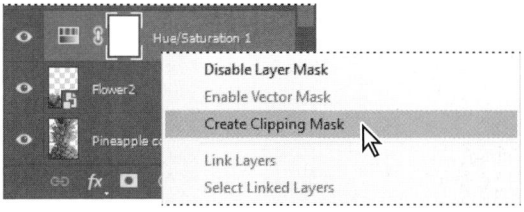

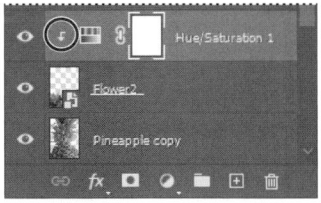

An arrow appears in the Layers panel, indicating that the adjustment layer applies only to the Flower2 layer. You'll learn more about clipping masks in Lessons 6 and 7.

Extra credit

Using an effect more than once in a layer style

A great way to add visual impact to a design element is to apply multiple instances of effects such as strokes, glows, or shadows. You don't have to duplicate layers to do this, because you can apply multiple instances of an effect inside the Layer Style dialog box.

1 Open 04End.psd in your Lesson04 folder.

2 In the Layers panel, double-click the Drop Shadow effect applied to the HAWAII layer.

3 In the effects list on the left side of the Layer Style dialog box, click the + button to the right of the Drop Shadow effect, and select the second Drop Shadow effect.

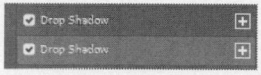

Now for the fun part! You can adjust your second drop shadow to change options such as color, size, and opacity.

4 In the Drop Shadow options area, click the color swatch, move the pointer outside the Layer Style dialog box so that the pointer changes into an eyedropper, and click the bottom flower to sample its purplish color. Then match the Drop Shadow settings as shown here, and click OK.

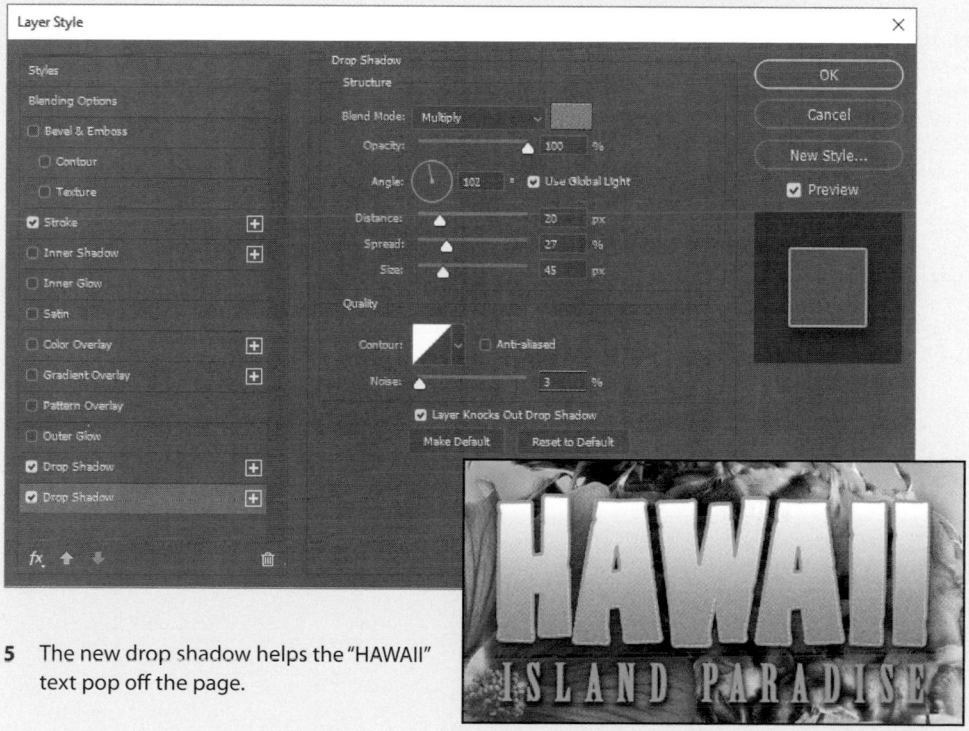

5 The new drop shadow helps the "HAWAII" text pop off the page.

Updating layer effects

Layer effects are automatically updated when you make changes to a layer. You can edit the text and watch how the layer effect tracks the change.

▶ **Tip:** You can search and filter for layers in the Layers panel by attributes such as layer kind, layer name, effect, and more. You can also display only the selected layers: Choose Select > Isolate Layers. When you do this, you see a red filter switch in the Layers panel to let you know some layers are hidden in the list.

1 Select the Island Paradise layer in the Layers panel.

2 In the Tools panel, select the Horizontal Type tool (T).

3 In the options bar, change the Size by a few points, and press Enter or Return.

You were able to change the settings for the entire type layer, even though you didn't select the text by highlighting the characters (as you would have to do in a word processing program). This worked because in Photoshop, you can change settings for an entire type layer by selecting it in the Layers panel, as long as a type tool is selected.

4 Using the Horizontal Type tool, click between "Island" and "Paradise," and type **of**.

As you edit the text, the layer styles are applied to the new text.

5 You don't actually need the word "of," so delete it.

6 Select the Move tool (✣), and drag "Island Paradise" to center it beneath the word "HAWAII."

● **Note:** You don't have to click the Commit Any Current Edits button after making the text edits, because selecting the Move tool has the same effect.

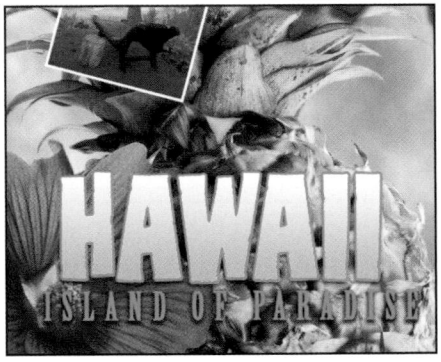

When you add text, layer effects are automatically applied.

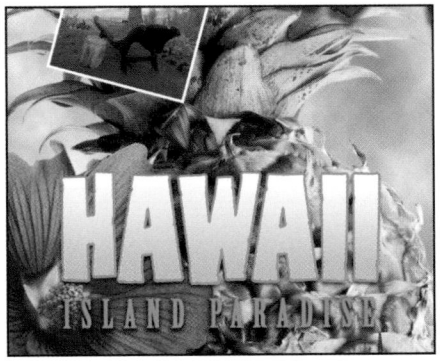

Center the text beneath the word "HAWAII."

7 Choose File > Save.

Adding a border

The Hawaii postcard is nearly done. The elements are almost all arranged correctly in the composition. You'll finish up by positioning the postmark and then adding a white postcard border.

1 Select the Move tool, and in the options bar, make sure Auto-Select is disabled.

2 Select the Postage layer, and then use the Move tool (✣) to drag it to the middle right of the image, as in the illustration.

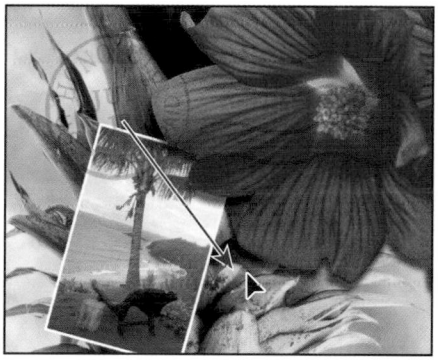

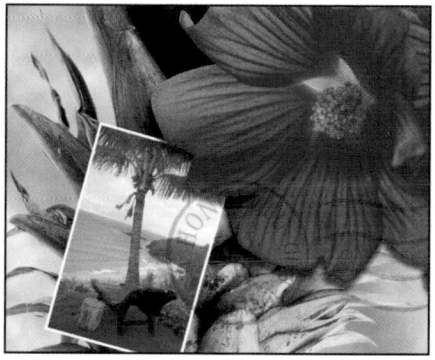

3 Select the Island Paradise layer in the Layers panel, and then click the Create A New Layer button (⊞) at the bottom of the panel.

4 Choose Select > All.

5 Choose Select > Modify > Border. In the Border Selection dialog box, type **10** pixels for the Width, and click OK.

A 10-pixel border is selected around the entire image. Now, you'll fill it with white.

6 Select white for the Foreground Color, and then choose Edit > Fill.

7 In the Fill dialog box, choose Foreground Color from the Contents menu, and click OK.

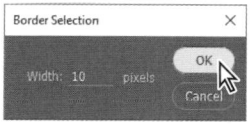

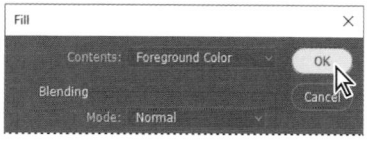

8 Choose Select > Deselect.

Note: The Auto-Select option can save time by letting you select a layer by clicking it with the Move tool, instead of having to select it in the Layers panel. But in documents where many layers overlap, if clicking keeps selecting the wrong layer, try turning off Auto-Select.

9 Double-click the Layer 1 name in the Layers panel, and rename the layer **Border**.

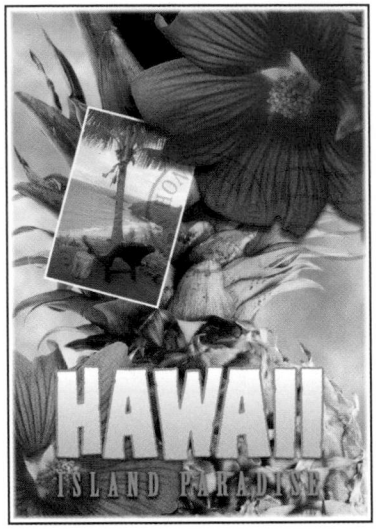

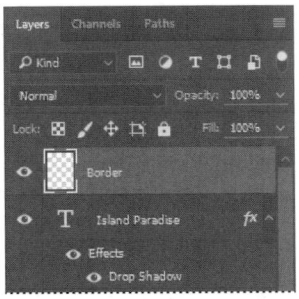

Use layer comps to store and switch among design ideas

The Layer Comps panel (choose Window > Layer Comps) provides one-click flexibility in switching between different views of a multilayered image file. A layer comp is simply a saved state of the settings in the Layers panel. Whenever you want to preserve a specific combination of layer properties, create a new layer comp. Then, by switching from one layer comp to another, you can quickly review the two designs. The beauty of layer comps becomes apparent when you want to demonstrate a number of possible design arrangements. When you've created a few layer comps, you can review the design variations without having to tediously select and deselect eye icons or change settings in the Layers panel.

Say, for example, that you are designing a brochure, and you're producing a version in English as well as in French. You might have the French text on one layer, and the English text on another in the same image file. To create two different layer comps, you would simply turn on visibility for the French layer and turn off visibility for the English layer, and then click the Create New Layer Comp button in the Layer Comps panel. Then you'd do the inverse—turn on visibility for the English layer and turn off visibility for the French layer, and click the Create New Layer Comp button—to create an English layer comp. To view the different layer comps, click the Layer Comp box for each comp in the Layer Comps panel in turn.

Layer comps can be an especially valuable feature when the design is in flux or when you need to create multiple versions of the same image file. If some aspects need to stay consistent among layer comps, you can change the visibility, position, or appearance of one layer in a layer comp and then sync it to see that change reflected in all the other layer comps.

Flattening and saving files

When you finish editing all the layers in your image, you can merge or *flatten* layers to reduce the file size. Flattening combines all the layers into a single background layer. However, you cannot edit layers once you've flattened them, so you shouldn't flatten an image until you are certain that you're satisfied with all your design decisions. Rather than flattening your original PSD files, it's a good idea to save a copy of the file with its layers intact, in case you need to edit a layer later.

To appreciate what flattening does, notice the two numbers for the file size in the status bar at the bottom of the document window. The first number represents what the file size would be if you flattened the image. The second number represents the file size without flattening. This lesson file, if flattened, would be 2–3MB, but the current file is much larger. So flattening is well worth it in this case.

Note: If the sizes do not appear in the status bar, click the status bar pop-up menu arrow, and choose Document Sizes.

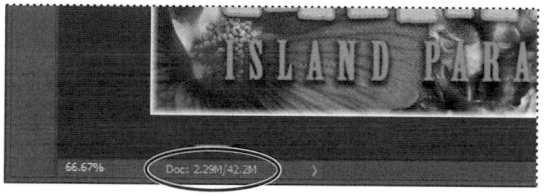

1 Select any tool but the Type tool (**T**), to be sure that you're not in text-editing mode. Then choose File > Save (if it is available) to be sure that all your changes have been saved in the file.

2 Choose Image > Duplicate.

3 In the Duplicate Image dialog box, name the file **04Flat.psd**, and click OK.

4 Leave the 04Flat.psd file open, but close the 04Working.psd file.

5 Choose Flatten Image from the Layers panel menu.

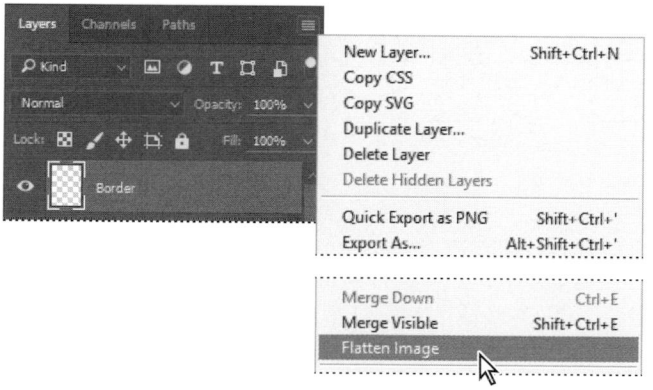

Tip: The Flatten Image command is also on the Layer menu, and on the context menu when you right-click/Control-click a layer name.

Only one layer, named Background, remains in the Layers panel.

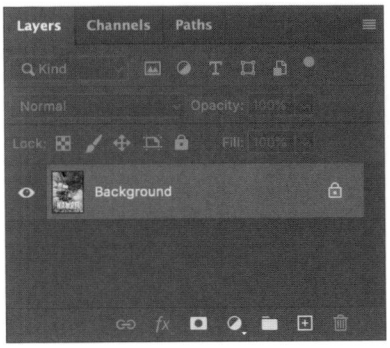

6 Choose File > Save. Even though you chose Save rather than Save As, the Save As dialog box appears, because this document has not yet been saved to storage.

7 Make sure the location is the Lessons/Lesson04 folder, and then click Save to accept the default settings and save the flattened file.

You have saved two versions of the file: a one-layer, flattened copy as well as the original file, in which all the layers remain intact.

You've created a colorful, attractive postcard. This lesson only begins to explore the vast possibilities and the flexibility you gain when you master the art of using Photoshop layers. You'll get more experience and try out different techniques for layers in almost every chapter as you move forward in this book.

▶ **Tip:** If you want to flatten only some of the layers in a file, click the eye icons to hide the layers you don't want to flatten, and then choose Merge Visible from the Layers panel menu.

Extra credit

Creating a pattern

Photoshop offers several features that work together to help you make patterns quickly and easily. You'll create a pattern for a new border around the artwork you created in this lesson.

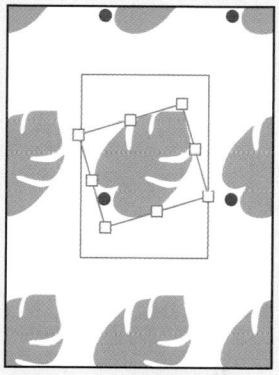

Pattern Preview helps you visualize a pattern you create.

1 In the Lesson04 folder, open 04End.psd, save it as **04End_Pattern.psd**, and then choose Layer > Flatten Image.

2 Choose Layer > New Fill Layer > Solid Color, name it Pattern Background, click OK, use the Color Picker to specify white, and click OK.

3 Choose File > Place Linked; in the Lesson04 folder, select PalmLeaf.ai and click Place; click OK in the Open as Smart Object dialog box; and then when the graphic appears in the document, press Return or Enter. This is vector art from Adobe Illustrator, but you can create a pattern using only Photoshop layers.

4 Zoom out to at 30% magnification or less, and then choose View > Pattern Preview. If an alert message appears, click OK. Pattern Preview simulates what the document would look like if tiled as a pattern, by repeating it outside the canvas.

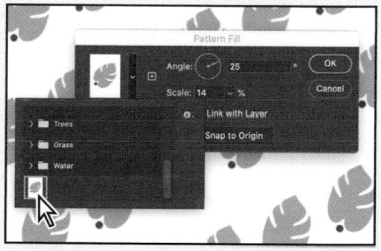

You can adjust pattern fill layer settings.

5 Draw a colored dot with the Ellipse tool to add another element to the pattern.

6 Refine your pattern by moving, rotating, or scaling the leaf and dot layers until you're happy with the pattern preview. Feel free to add more layers to the pattern.

7 Select the layers that make up your pattern, choose Edit > Define Pattern, name it **Leaf**, and click OK.

8 Choose View > Pattern Preview to deselect it, and hide the layers that make up your pattern.

9 Select only the Pattern Background layer, choose Layer > New Fill Layer > Pattern, name it Border, and click OK. In the Pattern Fill dialog box, select your new pattern from the pop-up menu of thumbnail previews. Reduce the Scale and adjust the Angle until it looks good, then click OK.

10 Unlock the Background layer by clicking its lock icon, and drag to stack it above the Border layer. Choose Edit > Free Transform, and scale it down to reveal the new border.

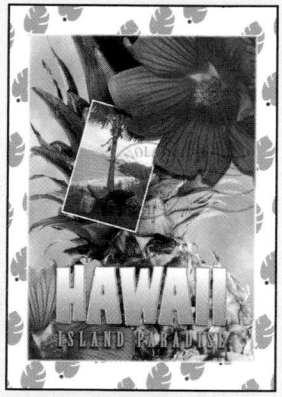

Scale down the design to reveal the pattern fill layer behind it.

Your new pattern is added to the Patterns panel, and you can edit the Leaf layer at any time by double-clicking it in the Layers panel.

Extra credit

Exploring design options with Adobe Stock

Visualizing different ideas for a design project is easier when you can experiment with images. The Libraries panel in Photoshop gives you direct access to millions of Adobe Stock images. We'll add a stock image of a ukulele to this lesson's composition.

1 In the Lesson04 folder, open 04End.psd. Save it as **04End_Working**.

2 In the Layers panel, select the Beach layer.

3 In the Libraries panel, type **ukulele** into the search field, make sure the search field menu (⌄) is set to Adobe Stock, and locate any vertical image of a ukulele on a white background.

4 Drag the ukulele image into the document. Drag a corner handle to proportionally scale the image to about 25% of its original size. Apply the changes to finish importing the image.

5 Choose Current Library from the search field menu (⌄). The image was added to your library. Click the ⊗ to clear the search.

6 Now remove the background. With the ukulele layer selected, choose the Magic Wand tool (🪄)in the Tools panel, and click anywhere within the white background. If the image you picked has an ID number in a corner, Shift-drag around the numbers with the Rectangular Marquee tool to include them in the selection. Alt/Option-click the Add Layer Mask button (◘) at the bottom of the Layers panel.

7 With the Move tool, drag the ukulele to the upper-left corner so that it partially overlaps the small photo of the beach view. You've just added an Adobe Stock photo to your postcard image!

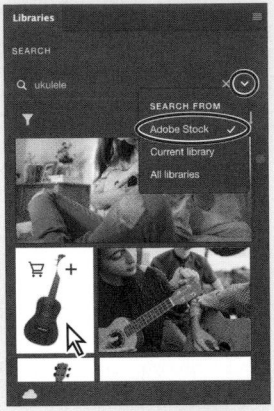

Adobe Stock search results

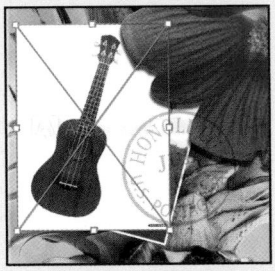

Stock image in document

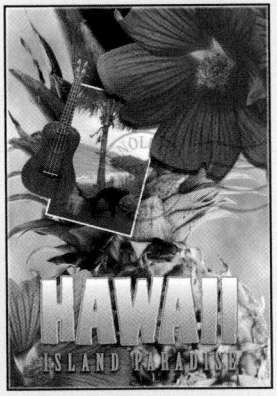

You've added a new element to your postcard using Adobe Stock!

Licensing an image

Until it's licensed, the ukulele image is a low-resolution version with an Adobe Stock watermark. You don't have to license the ukulele image used here, but you must license images used in a final project. With the ukulele layer (not mask) selected, click License Asset in the Properties panel and follow the prompts. After licensing, the image is automatically replaced with a high-resolution version without a watermark. If you plan to license many images, consider an Adobe Stock monthly plan or a pack of credits.

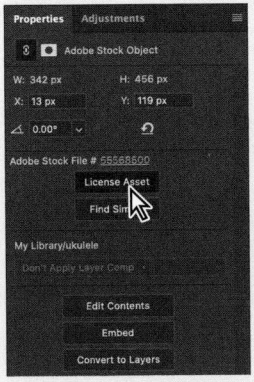

Review questions

1 What is the advantage of using layers?

2 When you create a new layer, where does it appear in the Layers panel stack?

3 How can you make artwork on one layer appear in front of artwork on another layer?

4 How can you apply a layer style?

5 When you've completed your artwork, what can you do with layers to minimize the file size without changing the quality, dimensions, or compression?

Review answers

1 Layers let you move and edit different parts of an image as discrete objects. You can also hide individual layers as you work on other layers.

2 A new layer always appears immediately above the active layer. If no layers are active, a new layer appears at the top of the layer list.

3 You can make artwork on one layer appear in front of artwork on another layer by dragging layers up or down the stacking order in the Layers panel or by using the Layer > Arrange commands—Bring To Front, Bring Forward, Send Backward, and Send To Back. However, you can't change the layer position of a background layer unless you convert it to a regular layer (unlock it or double-click to rename it).

4 To apply a layer style, select the layer, and then click the Add A Layer Style button in the Layers panel, or choose Layer > Layer Style > [style].

5 To minimize file size, you can flatten the image, which merges all the layers onto a single background. It's a good idea to keep a duplicate with layers intact before you flatten the document, in case you have to make changes to a layer later.

5 QUICK FIXES

Lesson overview

In this lesson, you'll learn how to do the following:

- Remove red eye.
- Brighten an image.
- Adjust the features of a face.
- Combine images to create a panorama.
- Crop and straighten an image and fill in any resulting empty areas.
- Blur the background of an image using Iris Blur.
- Merge two images to extend depth of field.
- Apply optical lens correction to a distorted image.
- Remove an object and seamlessly fill the empty space.
- Adjust the perspective of an image to match another image.

This lesson will take about an hour to complete. To get the lesson files used in this chapter, download them from the web page for this book at www.adobepress.com/PhotoshopCIB2021. For more information, see "Accessing the lesson files and Web Edition" in the Getting Started section at the beginning of this book.

As you work on this lesson, you'll preserve the start files. If you need to restore the start files, download them from your Account page.

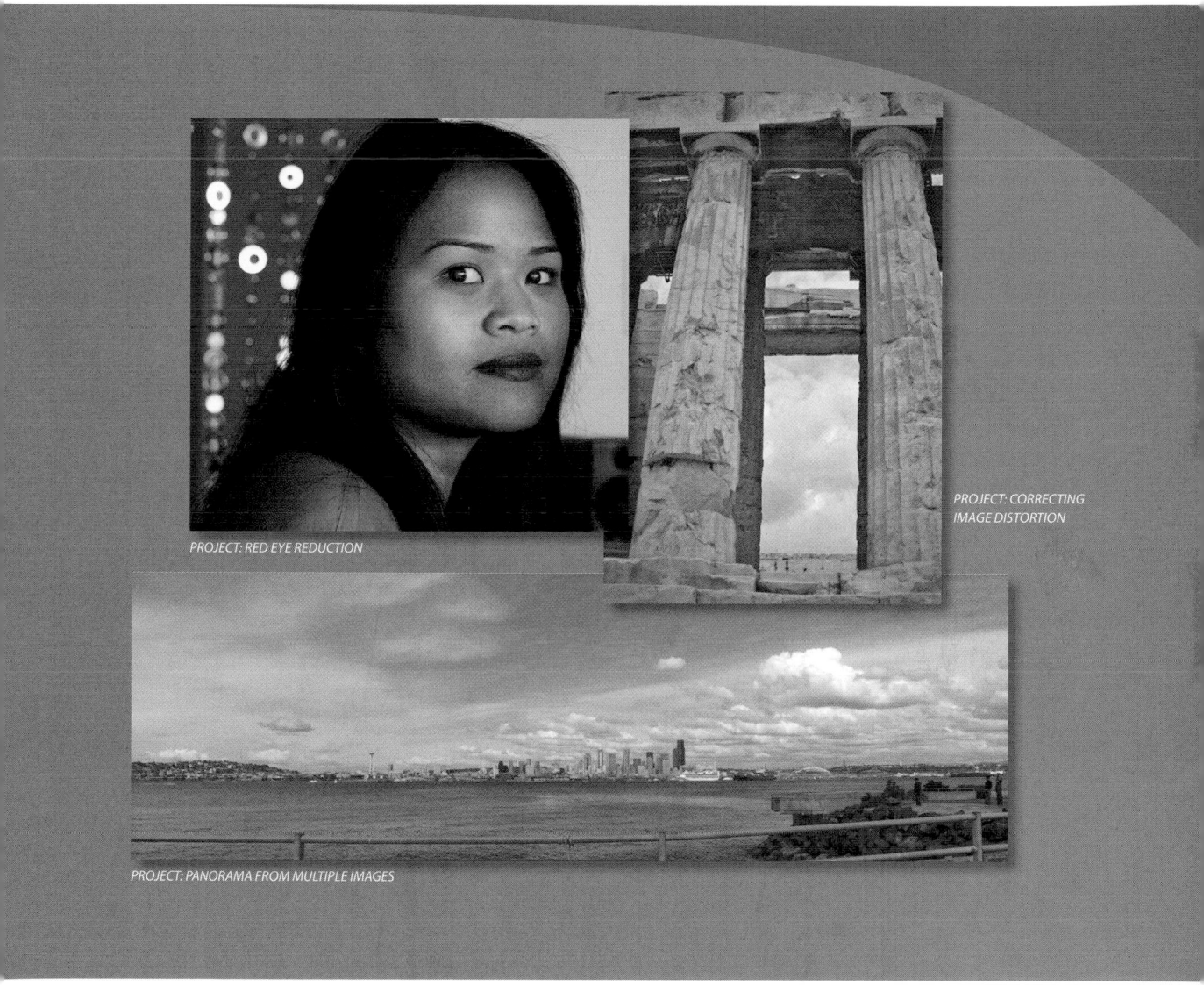

PROJECT: RED EYE REDUCTION

PROJECT: CORRECTING IMAGE DISTORTION

PROJECT: PANORAMA FROM MULTIPLE IMAGES

Sometimes just one or two clicks in Photoshop can turn an image from so-so (or worse) to awesome. Quick fixes get you the results you want without a lot of fuss.

Getting started

Not every image requires a complicated makeover using advanced features in Photoshop. In fact, once you're familiar with Photoshop, you can often improve an image quickly. The trick is to know what's possible and how to find what you need.

In this lesson, you'll make quick fixes to several images using a variety of tools and techniques. You can use these techniques individually or team them up when you're working with an image that needs just a little more help.

1 Start Photoshop, and then immediately hold down Ctrl+Alt+Shift (Windows) or Command+Option+Shift (Mac) to restore the default preferences. (See "Restoring default preferences" on page 5.)

2 When prompted, click Yes to delete the Adobe Photoshop Settings file.

Improving a snapshot

If you're sharing a snapshot with family and friends, you may not need it to look professional. But you probably don't want glowing eyes, and it would be good if the picture isn't too dark to show important detail. Photoshop gives you the tools to make quick changes to a snapshot.

Correcting red eye

Red eye occurs when the retina of a subject's eye is reflected by the camera flash. It commonly occurs in photographs taken in a dark room, because the subject's irises are wide open. Fortunately, red eye is easy to fix in Photoshop. In this exercise, you will remove the red eye from the woman's eyes in the portrait.

Note: If you haven't installed Bridge, you'll be prompted to do so when you choose Browse In Bridge. For more information, see page 3.

You'll start by viewing the before and after images in Adobe Bridge.

1 Choose File > Browse In Bridge to open Adobe Bridge.

Note: If Bridge asks you if you want to import preferences from a previous version of Bridge, click No.

2 In the Favorites panel in Bridge, click the Lessons folder. Then, in the Content panel, double-click the Lesson05 folder to open it.

3 Adjust the thumbnail slider, if necessary, so that you can see the thumbnail previews clearly. Then look at the RedEye_Start.jpg and RedEye_End.psd files.

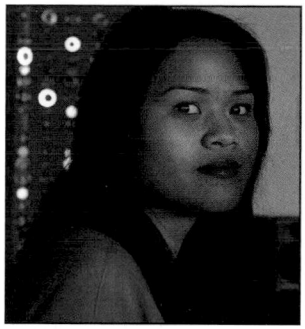

RedEye_Start.jpg

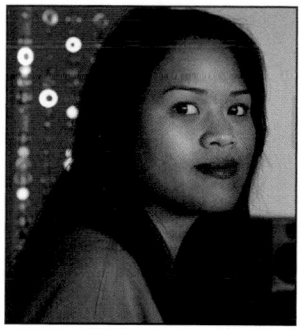

RedEye_End.psd

Not only does red eye make an ordinary person or animal appear unusual, but it can distract from the subject of the image. It's easy to correct red eye in Photoshop, and you'll quickly lighten this image too.

4 Double-click the RedEye_Start.jpg file to open it in Photoshop.

5 Choose File > Save As, choose Photoshop for the Format, name the file **RedEye_Working.psd**, and click Save.

6 Select the Zoom tool (🔍), and then drag to zoom in to see the woman's eyes. If Scrubby Zoom isn't selected, drag a marquee around the eyes to zoom in.

7 Select the Red Eye tool (+👁), hidden under the Spot Healing Brush tool (🩹).

8 In the options bar, reduce the Pupil Size to **23%** and the Darken Amount to **62%**.

The Darken Amount specifies how dark the pupil should be.

9 Click the pupil in the woman's left eye. The red reflection disappears.

10 Click the pupil in the woman's right eye to remove the red reflection there, too.

Note: If Photoshop displays a dialog box telling you about the difference between saving to Cloud Documents and Your Computer, click Save On Your Computer. You can also select Don't Show Again, but that setting will deselect after you reset Photoshop preferences.

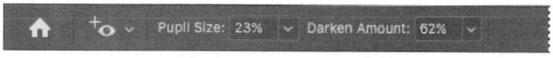

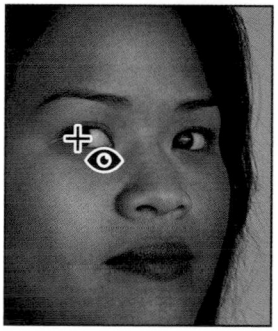

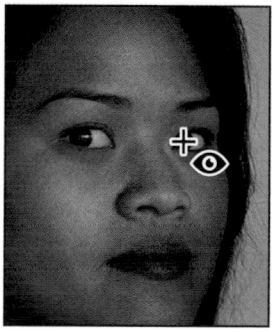

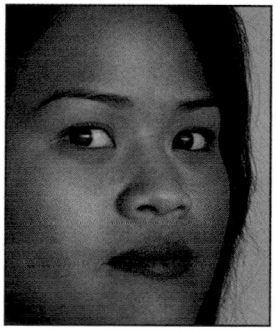

If the red reflection is directly over the pupil, clicking the pupil usually removes it. If it doesn't, you can try clicking the highlight, or try dragging the Red Eye tool around the entire pupil.

11 Choose View > Fit On Screen to see the entire image, and save your work.

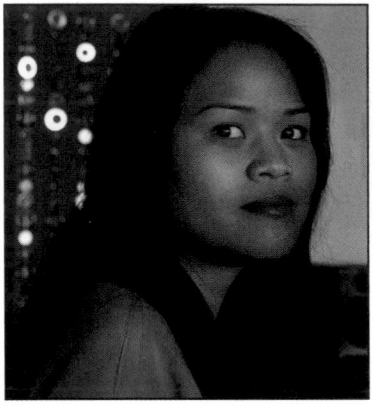

Brightening an image

The woman's eyes no longer glow red, but the overall image is a bit dark. You can brighten an image in several different ways, as you've already seen. You can try adding adjustment layers for Brightness/Contrast, Levels, and Curves, depending on the degree of adjustment you want to make. For a quick fix or a good starting point, try the Auto button or the presets, which are available in both the Levels and Curves adjustments. Let's try a Curves adjustment layer for this image.

1 Click Curves in the Adjustments panel.

2 Click Auto. In this example, the automatic correction adds a midpoint on the curve and raises its value, lightening the image mostly around the midtones.

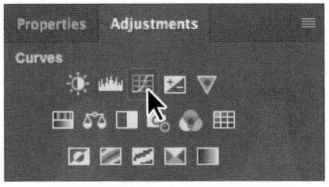

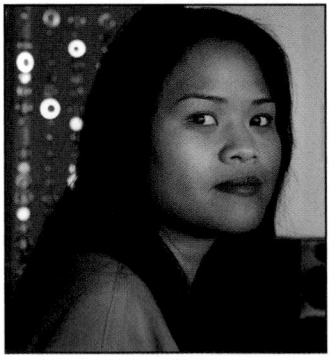

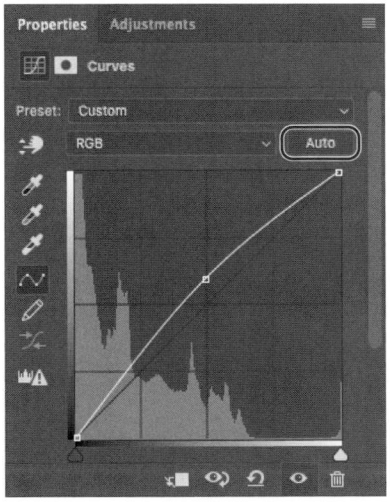

3 Choose Lighter (RGB) from the Preset menu. The curve changes slightly. The difference is that a preset applies the same curve to every image, while Auto analyzes the layer and creates a curve customized for it.

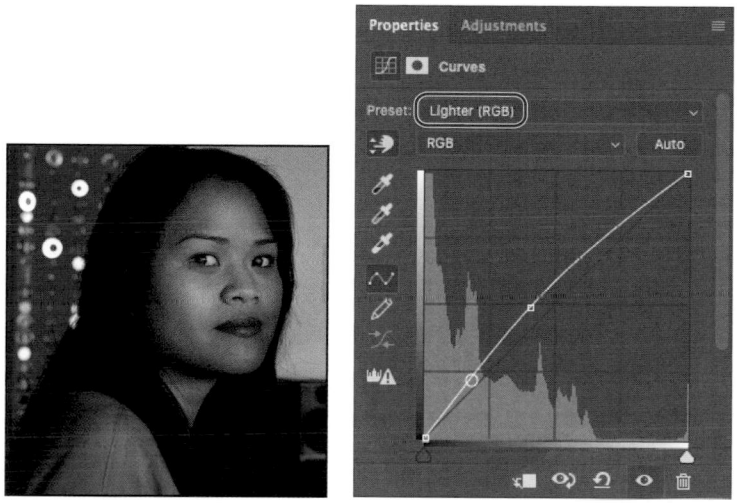

4 Click the Reset To Adjustment Defaults button (↺) at the bottom of the Properties panel to revert to the unadjusted image.

5 Select the on-image adjustment tool (⊕) in the Curves panel, and then click the center of the forehead and drag up. Clicking with that tool adds a curve point that corresponds to the tonal level you clicked in the image. When you drag up, you raise that point and the curve, brightening the image from that tonal level.

▶ **Tip:** If you want to use the Auto button or the white point or black point samplers (eyedropper icons) in the Curves or Levels adjustments, use them before applying manual adjustments. Like presets, adjustments by those tools replace manual adjustments.

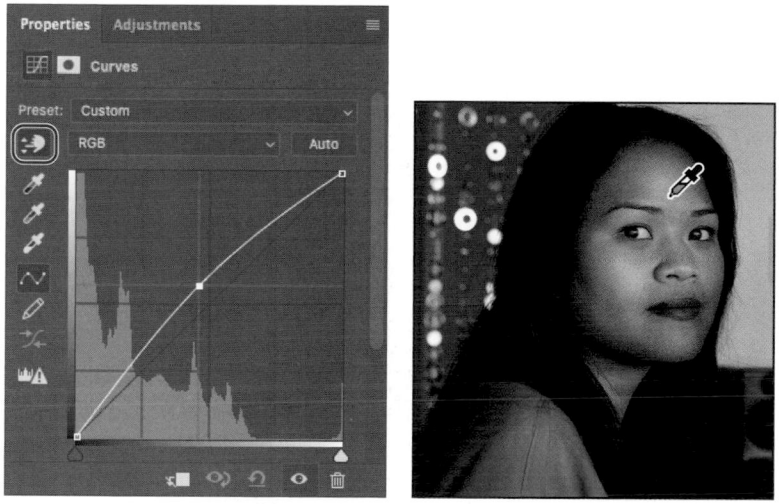

▶ **Tip:** To see how much you've brightened the image, hide the Curves layer, and then show it again.

6 Choose Layer > Flatten Image.

7 Save the file.

Adjusting facial features with Liquify

The Liquify filter is useful when you want to distort only part of an image. It includes Face-Aware Liquify options that can automatically recognize faces in images and then lets you easily adjust facial features such as the eyes, nose, and mouth. For example, you can adjust the size of or distance between the eyes. Being able to adjust facial features can be useful for photos used in advertising and fashion, when portraying a certain look or expression may be more important than faithfully representing a specific person.

1 With RedEye_Working.psd still open, choose Filter > Liquify.

2 In the Properties panel, if the Face-Aware Liquify options are collapsed (hidden), expand them.

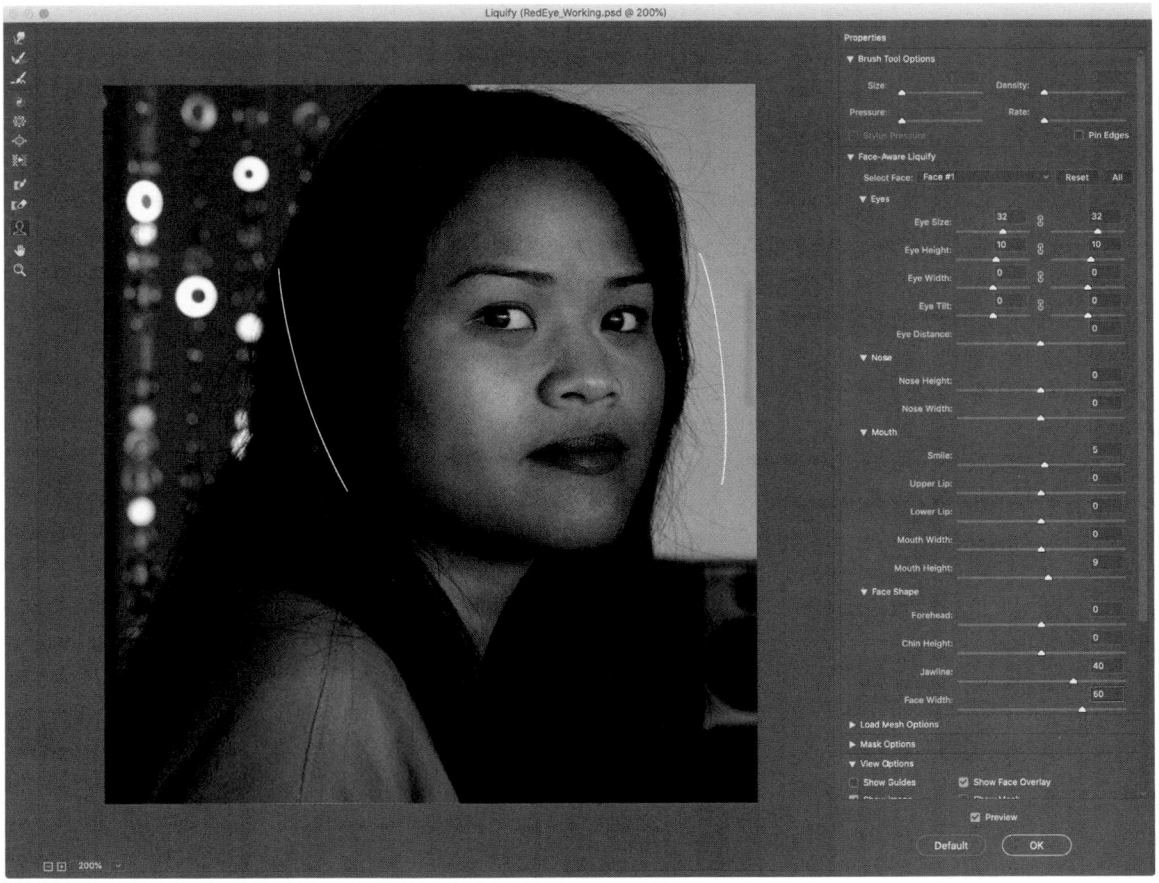

▶ **Tip:** When the Face tool ( ) is selected in the Liquify toolbar, handles appear as you hover the pointer over different parts of the face. You can drag those handles to adjust different parts of the face directly, as an alternative to dragging the Face-Aware Liquify sliders.

3 Make sure the Eyes section is expanded and that the link icon is selected for both Eye Size and Eye Height; then enter **32** for Eye Size and **10** for Eye Height.

When the link icon is not selected for an Eyes option, you can set different values for the left and right eyes.

4 Make sure the Mouth section is expanded, and then enter **5** for Smile and **9** for Mouth Height.

5 Make sure the Face Shape section is expanded, and then enter **40** for Jawline and **50** for Face Width.

6 Deselect and reselect the Preview option to compare the image before and after your changes.

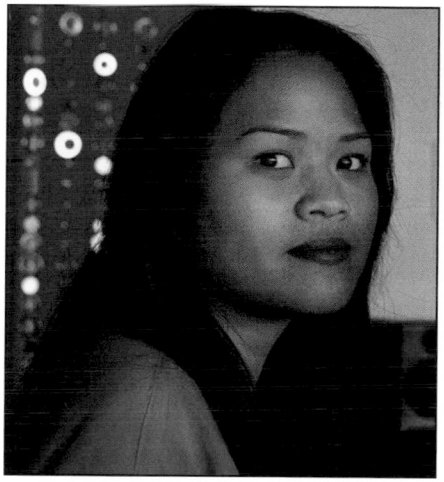

Before Face-Aware Liquify

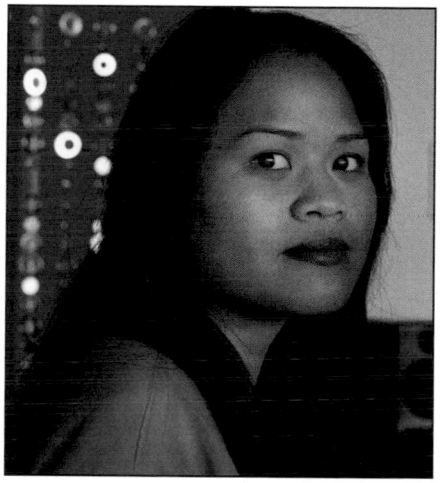

After Face-Aware Liquify

▶ **Tip:** The Face-Aware Liquify options have a limited range because they're designed for subtle, believable distortions. If you want to exaggerate faces into caricatures or extreme expressions, you may want to use the more advanced manual tools along the left side of the Liquify dialog box. Or try the face-altering filters in Filter > Neural Filters, which you'll explore in Lesson 15.

Feel free to experiment with any of the Face-Aware Liquify options to get a better sense of the possibilities for quick, easy alterations.

7 Click OK to exit Liquify. Close the document and save your changes.

The Face-Aware Liquify features are available only when Photoshop recognizes a face in an image. It may not recognize a face that is turned too far away from the camera or partially covered by hair, sunglasses, or a hat shadow.

Blurring a background

The interactive blurs in the Blur Gallery let you customize a blur as you preview it on your image. You'll use an iris blur to blur the background in an image, focusing the viewer's attention on the main attraction—in this case, the egret. You'll apply the blur as a Smart Filter so that you have the option of changing it later.

You'll start by looking at the start and end files in Bridge.

1 Choose File > Browse In Bridge to open Adobe Bridge.

2 In the Favorites panel in Bridge, click the Lessons folder. Then, in the Content panel, double-click the Lesson05 folder to open it.

3 Compare the Egret_Start.jpg and Egret_End.psd thumbnail previews.

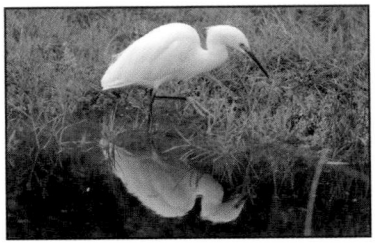

Egret_Start.jpg

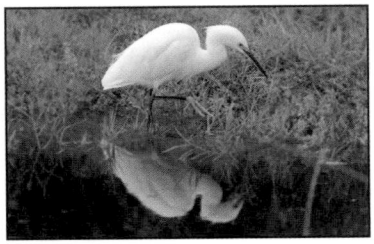

Egret_End.psd

In the final image, the egret appears sharper, as its reflection and the grass around it have been blurred. Iris Blur, one of the interactive blurs in the Blur Gallery, makes the task an easy one—no masking required.

4 Choose File > Return To Adobe Photoshop, and choose File > Open As Smart Object.

5 Select the Egret_Start.jpg file in the Lesson05 folder, and click OK or Open.

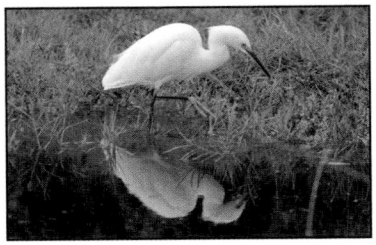

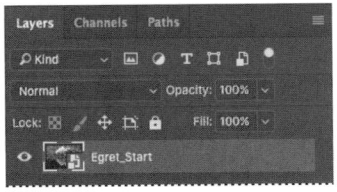

Photoshop opens the image. There is one layer in the Layers panel, and it's a Smart Object, as indicated by the badge on the layer thumbnail icon.

6 Choose File > Save As, choose Photoshop for the Format, name the file **Egret_Working.psd**, and click Save. Click OK in the Photoshop Format Options dialog box.

7 Choose Filter > Blur Gallery > Iris Blur.

A blur ellipse is centered on your image. You can adjust the location and scope of the blur by moving the center pin, feather handles, and ellipse handles. At the top-right corner of the Blur Gallery task space, you also see the expandable Field Blur, Tilt-Shift Blur, Path Blur, and Spin Blur panels; those are additional types of blur you can apply.

8 Drag the center pin so that it's at the bottom of the bird's body.

9 Click the ellipse, and drag inward to tighten the focus around the bird.

▶ **Tip:** If you have a newer iPhone camera that can save an HEIF depth map with a photo, you can create a more realistic background blur effect by loading the depth map into the Lens Blur filter (choose Filter > Blur > Lens Blur).

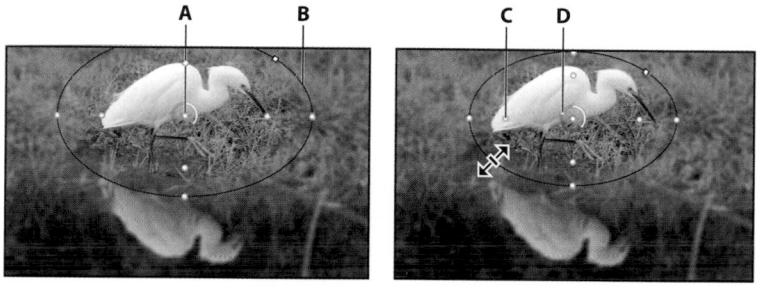

A. *Center* **B.** *Ellipse* **C.** *Feather handle* **D.** *Blur*

10 Press Alt (Windows) or Option (Mac) as you click and drag the feather handles to match those in the first image below. Pressing Alt or Option lets you drag each handle separately.

11 Click and drag on the Blur ring to reduce the amount of blur to **5** px, creating a gradual but noticeable blur. You can also change the same value by moving the Blur slider in the Iris Blur area of the Blur Tools panel.

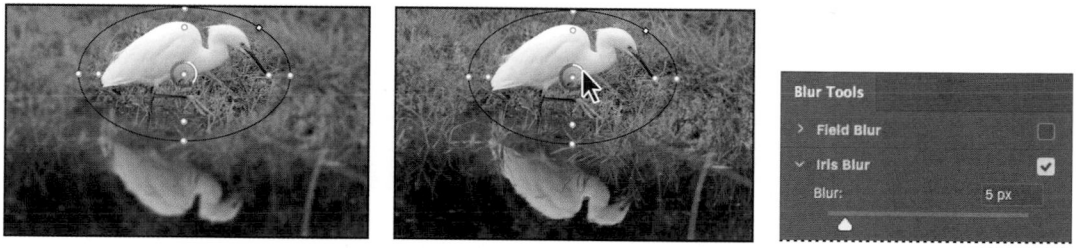

12 Click OK in the options bar to apply the blur.

The blur may be a little too subtle. You'll edit the blur to increase it slightly.

13 Double-click Blur Gallery in the Egret layer in the Layers panel to open it again. Adjust the blur to **6** px, and click OK in the options bar to apply it.

The egret is accentuated by blurring the rest of the image. Because you applied the filter to a Smart Object, you can hide or edit the effect without altering the original image.

14 Save the file, and then close it.

Blur Gallery

The Blur Gallery includes five interactive blurs: Field Blur, Iris Blur, Tilt-Shift, Path Blur, and Spin Blur. Each gives you on-image selective motion blur tools, with an initial blur pin. You can create additional blur pins by clicking on the image. You can apply a single blur or a combination of blurs, and you can create a strobe effect for path and spin blurs.

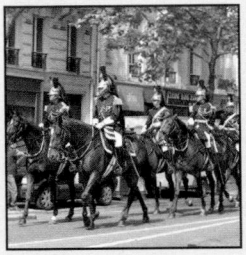

Before

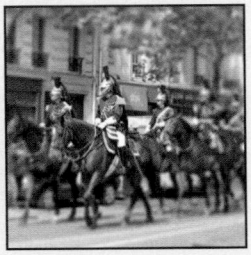

After

Field Blur applies a gradient blur to areas of the image, defined by pins you create and settings you specify for each. When you first apply Field Blur, a pin is placed in the center of the image. You can adjust the blur relative to that point by dragging the blur handle or specifying a value in the Blur Tools panel; you can also drag the pin to a different location.

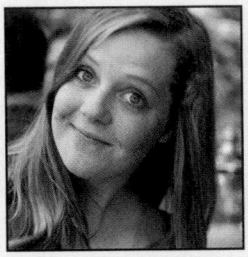

Before

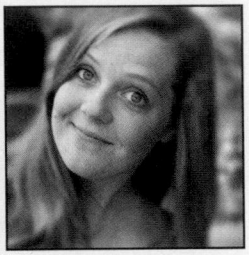

After

Iris Blur simulates a shallow depth-of-field effect, gradually blurring everything outside the focus ring. Adjust the ellipse handles, feather handles, and blur amount to customize the iris blur.

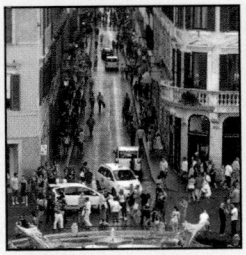

Before

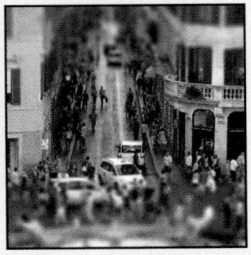

After

Tilt-Shift simulates an image taken with a tilt-shift lens, where the image has very shallow depth of field with the focus point in the distance. This blur defines a plane of sharpness and then fades outward to a blur. You can use this effect to simulate photos of miniature objects.

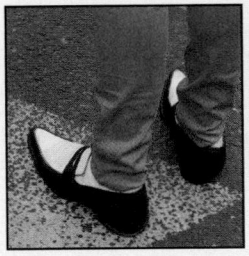

Before

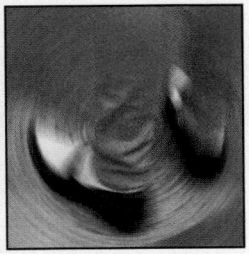

After

Spin Blur is a radial-style blur measured in degrees. You can change the size and shape of the ellipse, re-center the rotation point by pressing Alt or Option as you click and drag, and adjust the blur angle. You can also specify the blur angle in the Blur Tools panel. Multiple spin blurs can overlap. This blur can be useful for illustrating the rotation of propellers, wheels, or gears.

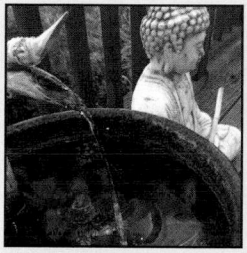

Before

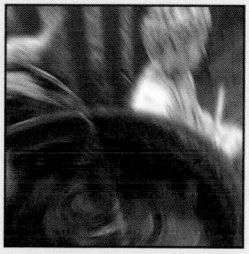

After

Path Blur creates motion blurs along paths you draw. You control the shape and amount of the blur.

When you first apply a Path Blur, a default path appears. Drag the end point to reposition it. Click the center point and drag to change the curve. Click to add additional curve points. The arrow on the path indicates the blur's direction.

You can also create a multiple-point path or a shape. Blur shapes describe the local motion blurs, similar to camera shake (see "Camera Shake Reduction" on page 144). The Speed slider in the Blur Tools panel determines the speed for all the path blurs. The Centered Blur option ensures that the blur shape for any pixel is centered on that pixel, resulting in more stable-feeling motion blurs; to make the motion appear more fluid, deselect this option.

If you wanted to illustrate the blurs of individual animal legs moving in different directions, you could add a separate instance of Path Blur to each leg.

Some blur types provide additional options in the **Effects** tab, where you specify the bokeh parameters to control the appearance of blurred areas. Light Bokeh brightens the blurred areas; Bokeh Color adds more vivid colors to lightened areas that aren't blown out to white; Light Range determines the range of tones that the settings affect.

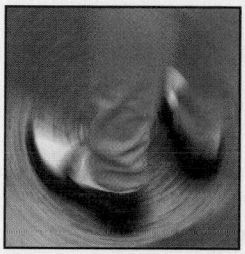

Before

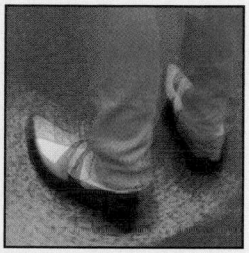

After

You can add a **strobe effect** to spin and path blurs. Select the **Motion Effects** tab to bring its panel forward. The Strobe Strength slider determines how much blur shows between flash exposures (0% gives no strobe effect; 100% gives full strobe effect with little blur between exposures). Strobe Flashes determines the number of exposures.

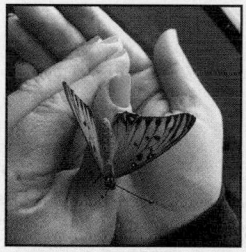

Before

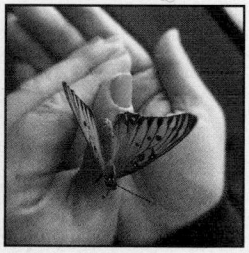

After

Applying a blur will smooth out visible digital image noise or film grain that's in the original image, and this mismatch between the original and blurred areas can make the blur appear artificial. You can use the **Noise** tab to restore noise or grain so that blurred areas match up with unblurred areas. Start with the Amount slider, and then use the other Noise options to match the character of the original grain. Increase the Color value if the original has visible color noise, and lower the Highlights value if you need to balance the noise level in the highlights compared to the shadows.

Creating a panorama

Sometimes a vista is just too large for a single shot. Photoshop makes it easy to combine multiple images into a panorama so that your viewers can get the full effect.

Once again, you'll take a look at the end file first, to see where you're going.

1 Choose File > Browse In Bridge.

2 Navigate to the Lesson05 folder, if you're not there already. Then, look at the Skyline_End.psd thumbnail preview.

▶ **Tip:** In Bridge, you can preview a selected image in full screen mode by pressing the spacebar. This is useful for previewing detailed or large images such as a panorama. Press the spacebar again to close the preview.

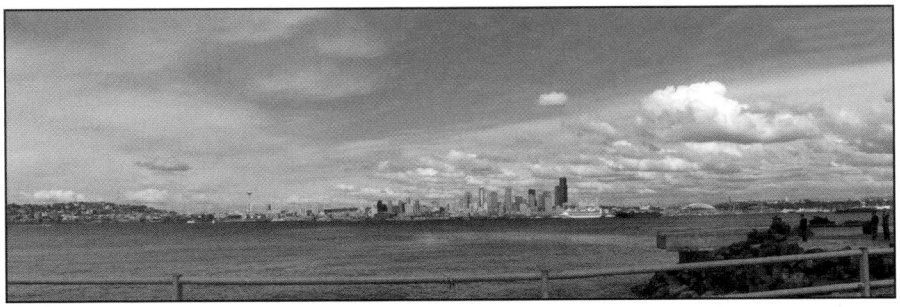

Skyline_End.psd

You'll combine four shots of the Seattle skyline into a single wide panorama image so that viewers get a sense of the whole scene. Creating a panorama from multiple images requires only a few clicks. Photoshop does the rest.

3 Return to Photoshop.

4 With no files open in Photoshop, choose File > Automate > Photomerge.

5 In the Source Files area, click Browse, and navigate to the Lesson05/Files For Panorama folder.

6 Shift-select all the images in the folder, and click OK or Open.

7 In the Layout area of the Photomerge dialog box, select Perspective.

▶ **Tip:** You can also open selected images from Bridge directly into Photomerge by choosing Tools > Photoshop > Photomerge.

The best option for merging photos isn't always Perspective; it depends on how the originals were photographed. If you're not completely happy with the result of a particular merge, you can always try again with a different Layout option. If you're not sure which one to use, you can simply click Auto.

8 At the bottom of the Photomerge dialog box, select Blend Images Together, Vignette Removal, Geometric Distortion Correction, and Content Aware Fill Transparent Areas. Then click OK.

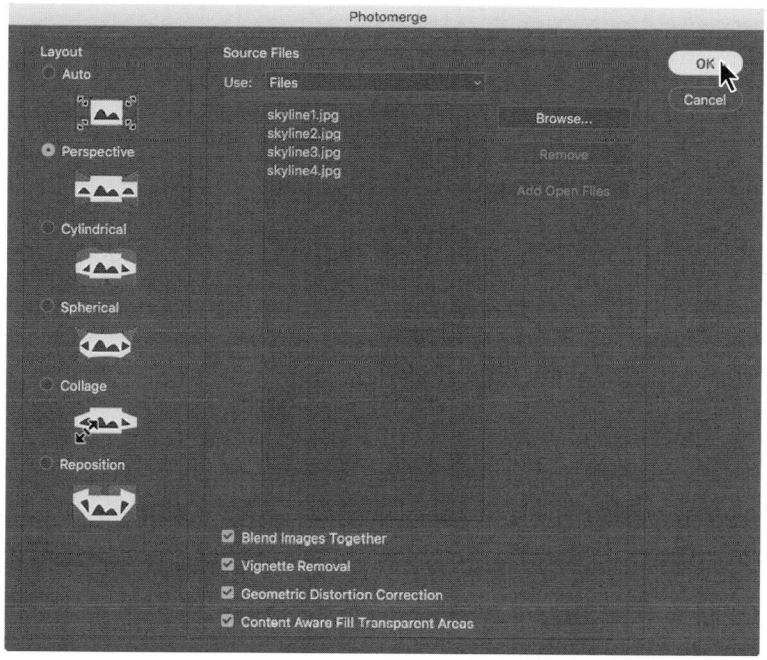

Blend Images Together blends images based on the optimal borders between them, instead of just creating a simple rectangular blend. Vignette Removal performs exposure compensation in images with darkened edges. Geometric Distortion Correction compensates for barrel, pincushion, or fisheye distortion. Content Aware Fill Transparent Areas automatically patches the empty areas between the merged image edges and the sides of the canvas.

Photoshop creates the panorama image. It's a complex process, so you may have to wait a few moments while Photoshop works. When it's finished, you'll see the full vista in the image window with five layers in the Layers panel. The bottom four layers are the original four images you selected. Photoshop identified the overlapping areas of the images and matched them, correcting any angular discrepancies. The top layer, containing "(merged)" in the layer name, is a single panorama image blended from all of the images you selected, combined with formerly empty areas filled in by Content Aware Fill. Those areas are indicated by the selection.

Note: Photomerge will require more time when you merge more images, or images with large pixel dimensions. Photomerge works faster on computers that are newer or that have more RAM.

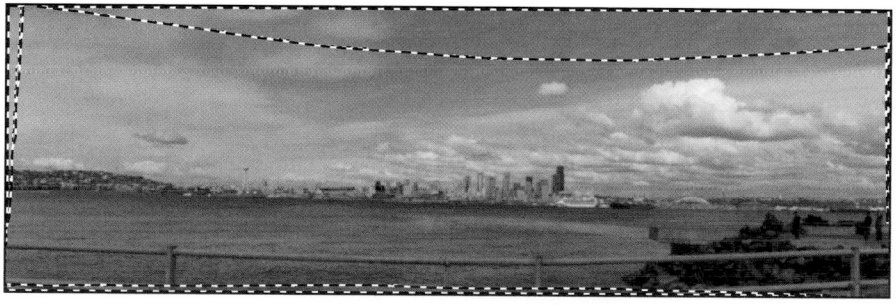

Tip: If you want to see how the panorama looks without the areas created by Content Aware Fill, hide the top layer.

Getting the best results with Photomerge

If you know you're going to create a panorama when you take your shots, keep the following guidelines in mind to get the best result.

Overlap images by 15% to 40% Sufficient overlap helps Photomerge blend edges seamlessly. Over 50% overlap won't help and makes you take too many images.

Use a consistent focal length If you use a zoom lens, keep the focal length the same for all the pictures in the panorama.

Stay level Keep the horizon at the same vertical position in each frame to avoid a tilted panorama. If your camera has a level indicator in the viewfinder, use it.

Use a tripod if possible You'll get the best results if the camera is at the same height for each shot. A tripod with a rotating head makes that easier.

Take the photos from the same position If you're not using a tripod with a rotating head, try to stay in the same position as you take the photos so that they are taken from the same viewpoint.

Avoid lenses that produce creative distortion They can interfere with Photomerge. (The Auto option does adjust for images you take with fisheye lenses.)

Use the same exposure The images will blend more gracefully if they all have the same exposure. For example, either use flash for all the images or for none of them.

Try different layout options If you don't like the results you get when you create the panorama, try again using a different layout option. Often, Auto selects the appropriate option, but sometimes you'll get a better image with one of the other options.

▶ **Tip:** If you plan to create panoramas of interiors or with objects close to the camera, rotating a camera by hand or on a tripod may introduce parallax errors where items don't line up. You can avoid such errors by using a tripod attachment (sometimes called a *nodal slide*) that precisely rotates the camera around the entrance pupil of the specific lens you use.

9 Choose Select > Deselect.

10 Choose Layer > Flatten Image.

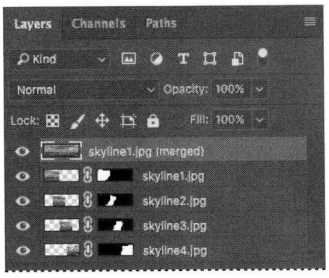

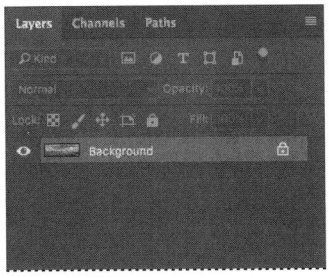

▶ **Tip:** In the finished panorama files, the layers created from the original images have masks. Photoshop created the masks to blend the edges where adjacent images match. You can edit those masks, but if you won't need to, flattening the image results in a smaller file size.

11 Choose File > Save As. Choose Photoshop for the Format, and name the file **Skyline_Working.psd**. Save the file in the Lesson05 folder. Click Save.

The panorama looks great, but it's a little dark. You'll add a Levels adjustment layer to brighten it a little bit.

12 Click the Levels icon in the Adjustments panel to add a Levels adjustment layer.

13 Select the White Point eyedropper in the Properties panel, and then click a white area of the clouds.

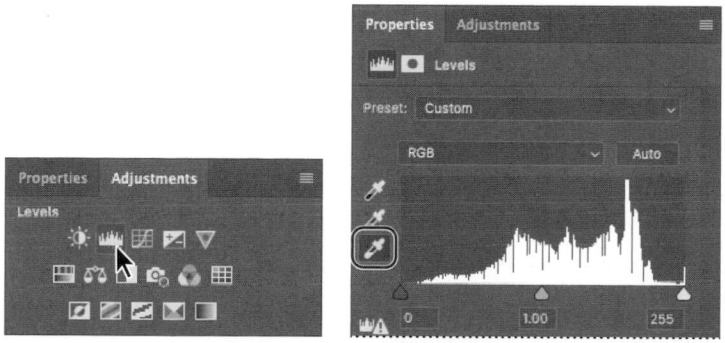

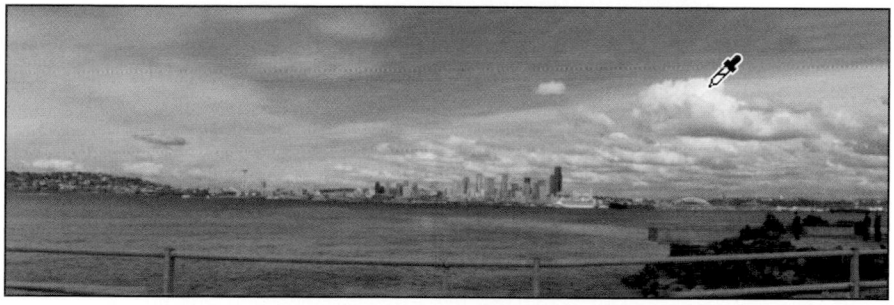

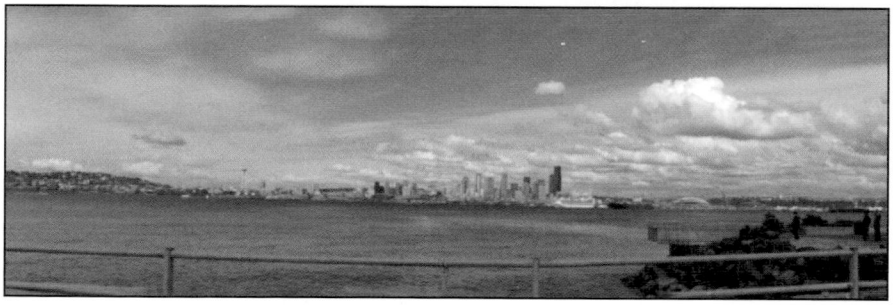

The entire image brightens. The sky appears more blue, because the image was originally a little warm. The White Point eyedropper neutralized the warm cast.

14 Save your work. Click OK in the Photoshop Format Options dialog box.

It's that easy to create a panorama!

Note: Step 13 works when you click an area that is close to, but not exactly, pure white. If an image doesn't change when you click it with the White Point eyedropper, you probably clicked an area that can't become any whiter and there is no color cast to correct. That happens when the pixel values where you clicked are already pure white in all color channels (such as RGB 255,255,255).

Note: In step 14, the Photoshop Format Options alert may appear because a layer was added. The Photoshop Format Options dialog box usually won't appear for Photoshop documents containing only a Background layer.

Filling empty areas when cropping

The panorama image looks great except for two things: The horizon is slightly tilted, and the lower handrail is incomplete where the rocks on the right descend into the water. If you were to rotate the image, empty areas might appear at the corners, requiring a tighter crop and losing parts of the image. Fortunately, the same Content-Aware technology that filled in empty areas resulting from the panorama merge can also fill in empty areas that can result from straightening and cropping.

1 Make sure **Skyline_Working.psd** is open, and make sure the Background layer is selected in the Layers panel.

2 Choose Layer > Flatten Image.

3 In the Tools panel, select the Crop tool. The crop rectangle and its handles appear around the image.

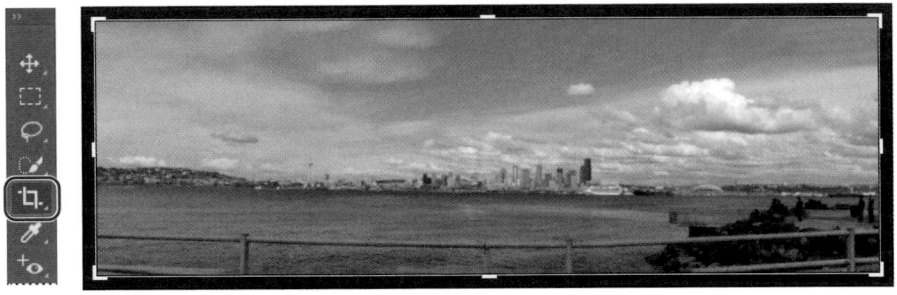

4 In the options bar, select the Straighten button (), and make sure Content-Aware is selected.

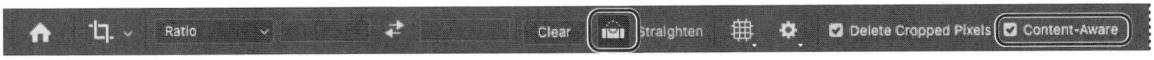

5 Position the Straighten pointer on the horizon at the left edge of the image, and drag to the right to create a Straighten line that's aligned with the horizon; release the mouse button when you reach the end of the horizon at the right edge of the image.

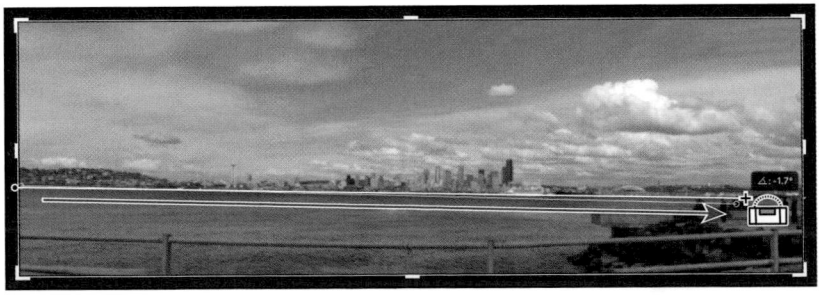

Notice there is now white space that needs to be filled near the corners.

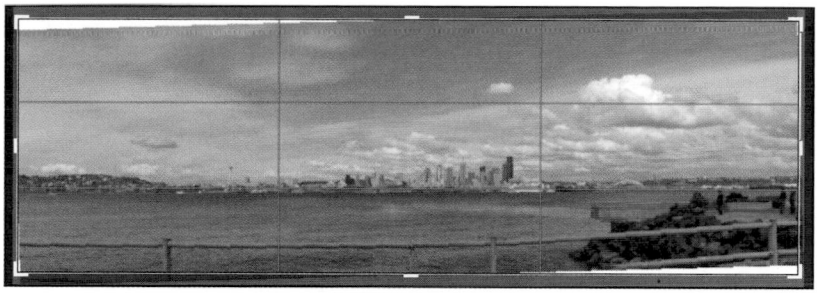

6 With the crop rectangle still active, drag the image down until the incomplete part of the lower guardrail is outside the crop rectangle.

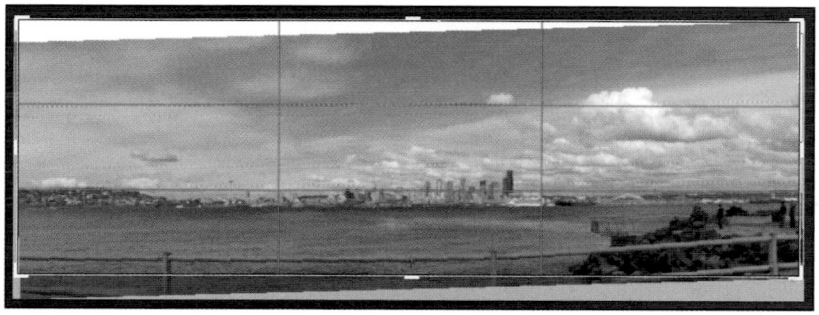

7 Click the Commit button in the options bar (✓) to apply the current crop settings. Content-Aware Crop fills in the empty areas at the top and sides of the image.

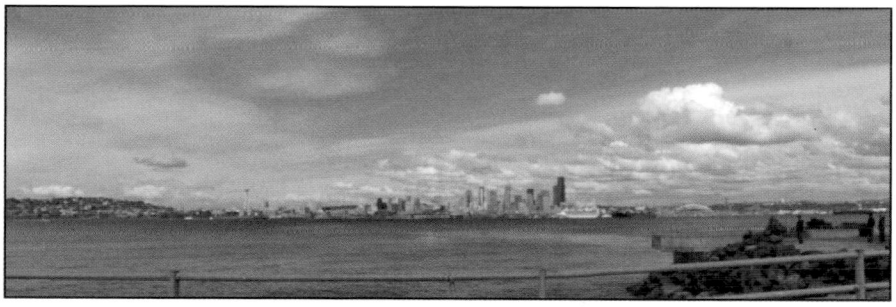

8 Save your changes, and close the document.

Replacing a sky

When you find the right subject for a photo illustration or composite, but it doesn't have quite the right sky to match the mood or time of day you want to convey, you can easily swap out the sky in Photoshop. Sky Replacement does many of the tough parts for you, such as creating a mask for the sky and making colors more consistent between the photo and the new sky.

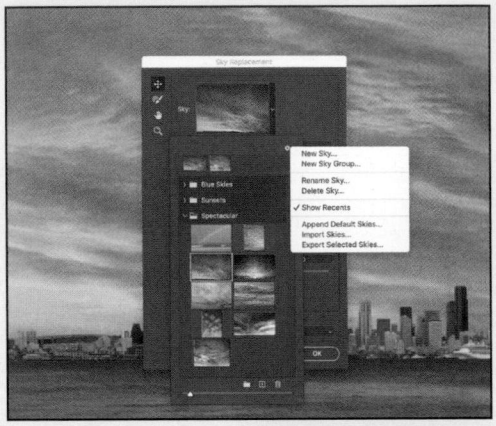

1 In the Lesson05 folder, open the document Skyline_End.psd, and then choose Edit > Sky Replacement.

2 Select an image from the Sky list. The sky updates in the document; you can compare the original and new sky by clicking the Preview option. To use your own sky image, click the gear icon in the Sky list and choose New Sky.

3 Check the quality of the automatically composited image. Are the colors of the two images consistent? Do you see any issues with the edge quality of the automatic sky mask? (Zoom in to check the edge.)

4 If you notice problems, use the Sky Replacement options. For example, you can reposition the sky image with the Sky Move tool, edit the mask edge with the Sky Brush tool, or change the Scale value in Sky Adjustments.

5 When you are satisfied with the Sky Replacement settings, make sure New Layers is selected in the Output To menu, and click OK.

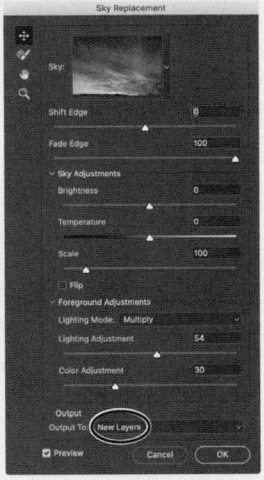

If Output is set to New Layers, notice in the Layers panel that Sky Replacement automatically created layers to add the new sky and adjustments separately from the original layer. After you click OK in Sky Replacement, you can edit the layers and masks it created (you'll learn more about layer masks in Lesson 6). Hiding the new layers reveals the original sky.

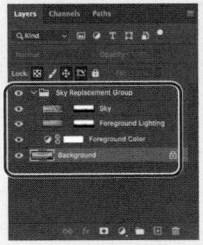

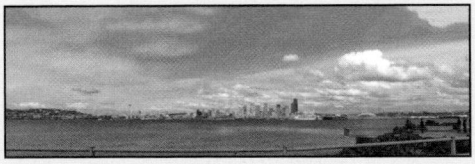

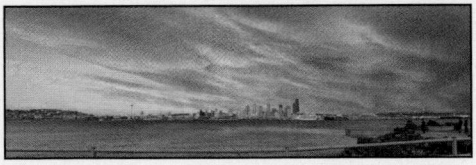

Correcting image distortion

The Lens Correction filter fixes common camera lens flaws, such as barrel and pincushion distortion, chromatic aberration, and vignetting. *Barrel distortion* is a lens defect that causes straight lines to bow out toward the edges of the image. *Pincushion distortion* is the opposite effect, causing straight lines to bend inward. *Chromatic aberration* appears as a color fringe along the edges of image objects. *Vignetting* occurs when the edges of an image, especially the corners, are darker than the center.

▶ **Tip:** If you capture photos with your camera set to save raw files, the Adobe Camera Raw plug-in module (for processing raw files in Photoshop and Bridge) has similar lens correction options in its Optics panel, including lens-specific correction profiles and chromatic aberration correction.

Some lenses exhibit these defects depending on the focal length or the f-stop used. The Lens Correction filter can apply settings based on the camera, lens, and focal length that were used to make the image. The filter can also rotate an image or fix image perspective caused by tilting a camera vertically or horizontally. The filter's image grid makes it easier and more accurate to make these adjustments than using the Transform command.

1 Choose File > Browse In Bridge.

2 Navigate to the Lesson05 folder if you're not already there, and then look at the Columns_Start.psd and Columns_End.psd thumbnail previews.

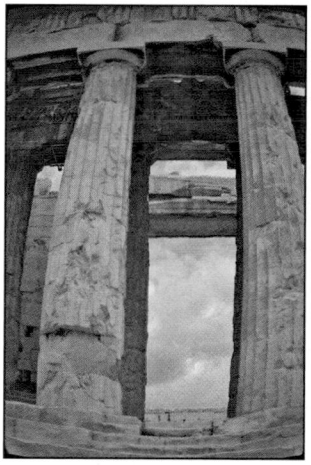

Columns_Start.psd

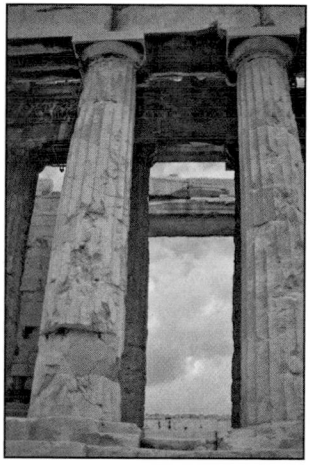

Columns_End.psd

In this case, the original image of a Greek temple is distorted, with the columns appearing to be bowed. This photo was shot at a range that was too close with a wide-angle lens. You'll quickly correct the lens barrel distortion.

▶ **Tip:** If the crop rectangle from the previous exercise is still visible and distracting, switch to a tool such as the Hand tool.

3 Double-click the Columns_Start.psd file to open it in Photoshop.

4 Choose File > Save As. In the Save As dialog box, name the file **Columns_Working.psd**, and save it in the Lesson05 folder. Click OK if the Photoshop Format Options dialog box appears.

5 Choose Filter > Lens Correction. The Lens Correction dialog box opens.

6 Select Show Grid at the bottom of the dialog box, if it's not already selected.

An alignment grid overlays the image. To the right are options for automatic corrections based on lens profiles. In the Custom tab are manual controls for correcting distortion, chromatic aberration, and perspective.

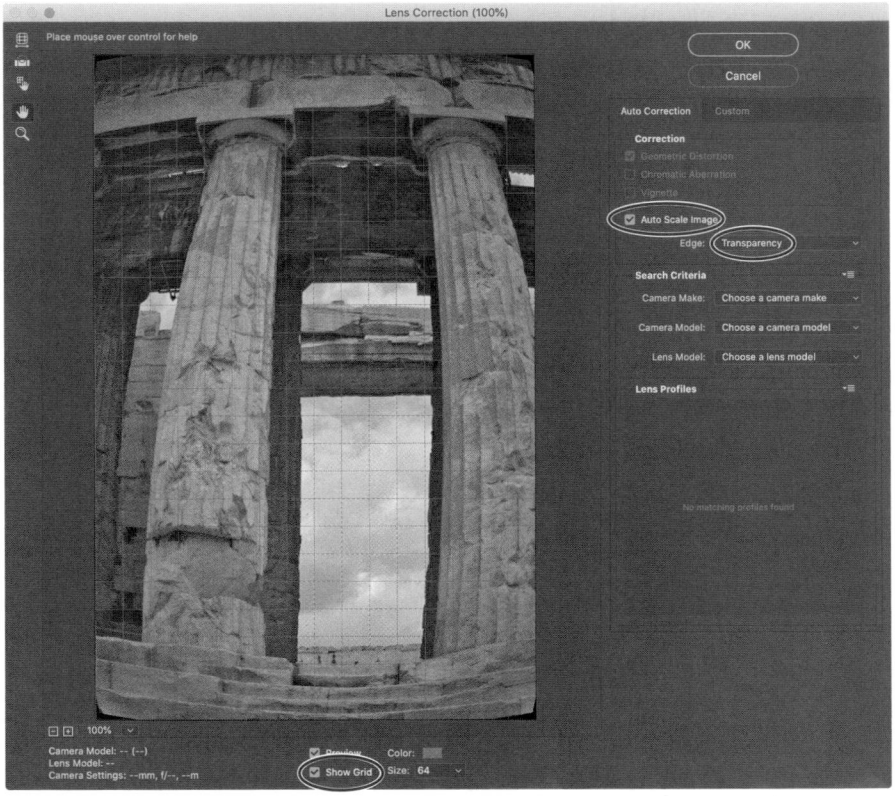

The Lens Correction dialog box includes auto-correction options. You'll adjust one setting in the Auto Correction tab and then customize the settings.

7 In the Correction area of the Auto Correction tab, make sure Auto Scale Image is selected and that Transparency is selected from the Edge menu.

8 Select the Custom tab.

9 In the Custom tab, drag the Remove Distortion slider to about **+52.00** to remove the barrel distortion in the image. Alternatively, you could select the Remove Distortion tool (⊞) and drag in the image preview area until the columns are straight. The adjustment causes the image borders to bow inward. However, because you selected Auto Scale Image, the Lens Correction filter automatically scales the image to adjust the borders.

▶ **Tip:** Watch the alignment grid as you make these changes so that you can see when the vertical columns are straightened in the image.

10 Click OK to apply your changes and close the Lens Correction dialog box.

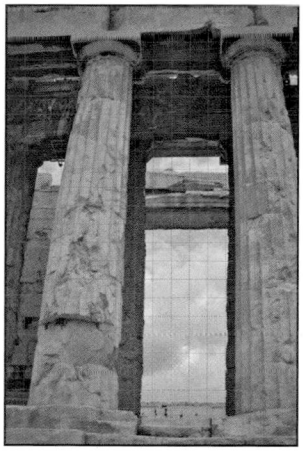

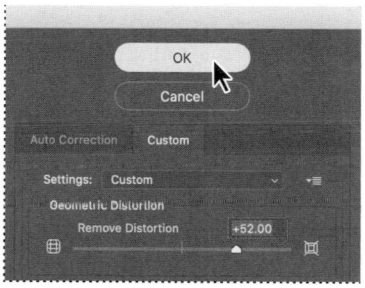

The curving distortion caused by the wide-angle lens and low shooting angle is reduced.

11 (Optional) To compare the image before and after the last change, press Ctrl+Alt+Z (Windows) or Command+Option+Z (Mac) to undo the filter, and then press the same keys to redo the filter. That's a keyboard shortcut for the Edit > Toggle Last State command, so you can press it repeatedly to go back and forth between the last two states of the document.

12 Choose File > Save to save your changes, click OK if the Photoshop Format Options dialog box appears, and then close the image.

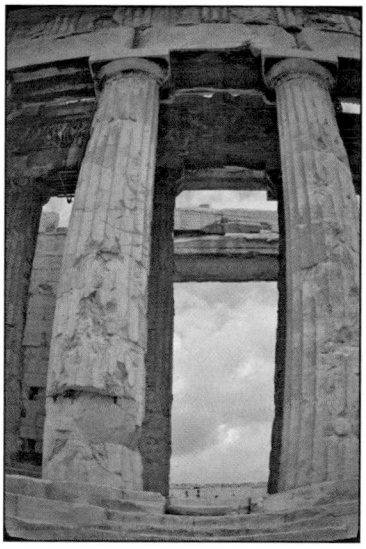

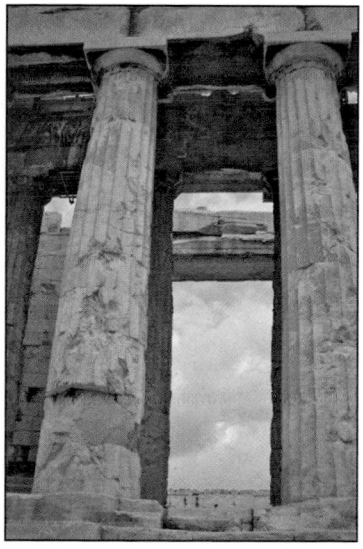

The temple looks much more stable now!

Extending depth of field

When you're shooting a photo, you often have to choose to focus on either the background or the foreground. If you want the entire image to be in focus, you can take two photos—one with the background in focus and one with the foreground in focus—and then merge the two in Photoshop.

Because you'll need to align the images exactly, it's helpful to use a tripod to keep the camera steady. However, you may be able to get good results with a handheld camera if you pay attention to framing and alignment. In this exercise, you'll add depth of field to an image of a wine glass in front of a beach.

1 Choose File > Browse In Bridge.

2 Navigate to the Lesson05 folder, if you're not there already, and then look at the Glass_Start.psd and Glass_End.psd thumbnail previews.

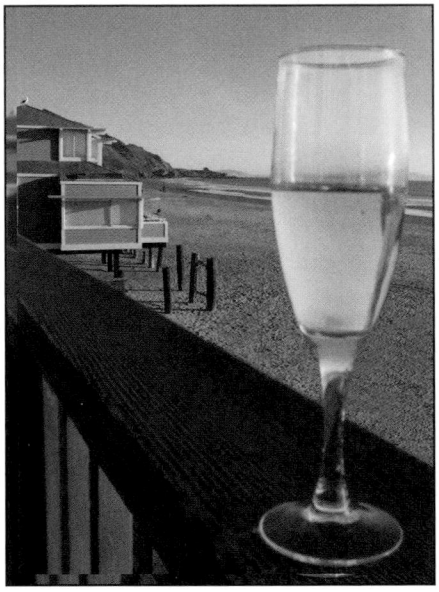

Glass_Start.psd

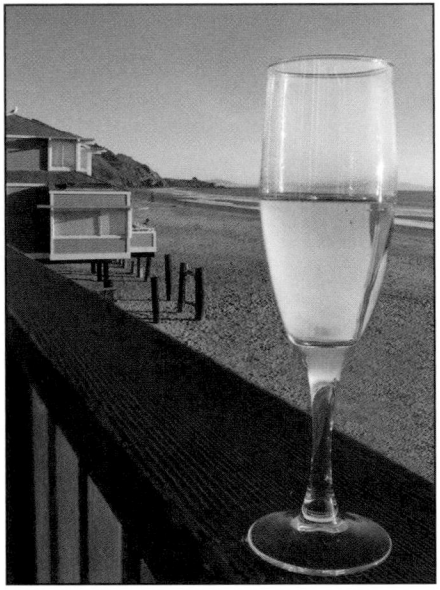

Glass_End.psd

The first image has two layers. Depending on which layer is visible, either the glass in the foreground or the beach in the background is in focus. You'll extend the depth of field to make both clear.

3 Double-click the Glass_Start.psd file to open it.

4 Choose File > Save As. Name the file **Glass_Working.psd**, and save it in the Lesson05 folder. Click OK if the Photoshop Format Options dialog box appears.

5 In the Layers panel, hide the Beach layer so that only the Glass layer is visible. The glass is in focus, but the background is blurred. Then, show the Beach layer again. Now the beach is in focus, but the glass is blurred.

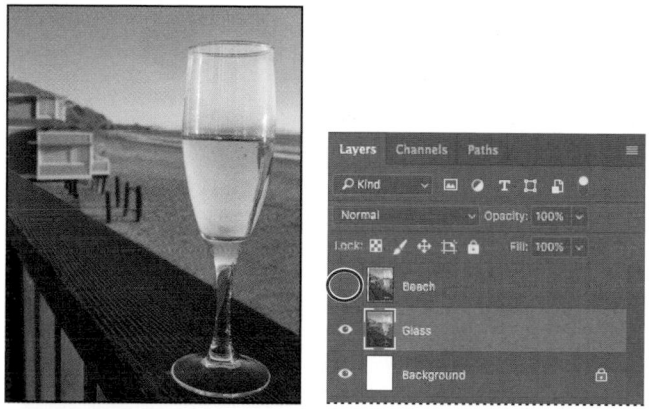

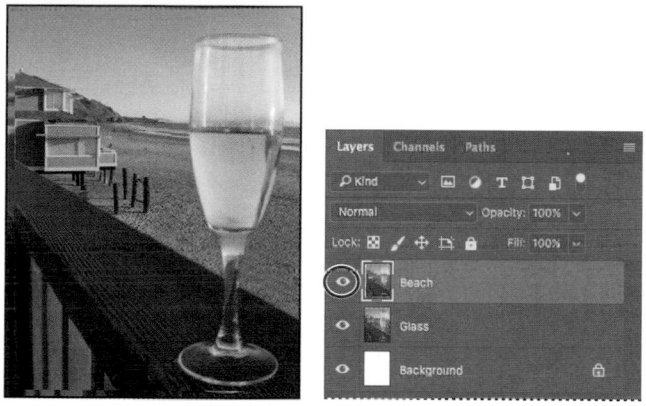

You'll merge the layers, using the part of each layer that is in focus. First, you need to align the layers.

6 Shift-click to select both of the layers.

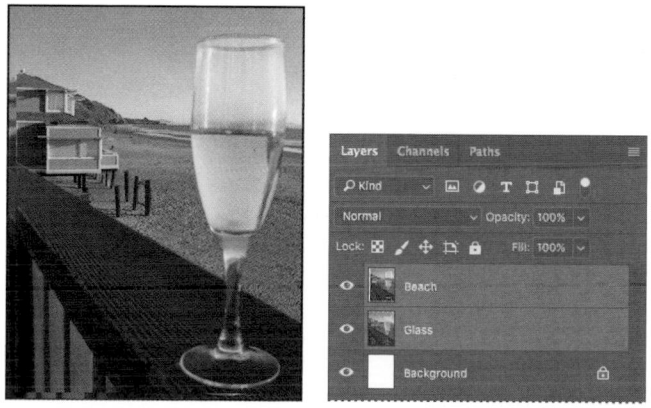

7 Choose Edit > Auto-Align Layers.

Because these images were shot from the same angle, Auto will work just fine.

▶ **Tip:** When aligning layers that are not involved in a panorama, Reposition is often the best alignment option to use. In this exercise, Reposition is the projection that the Auto option chose.

8 Select Auto, if it isn't already selected. Make sure neither Vignette Removal nor Geometric Distortion is selected. Then click OK to align the layers.

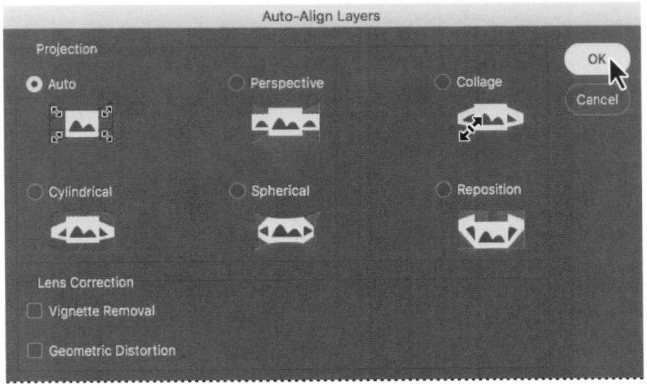

Now that the layers are perfectly aligned, you're ready to blend them.

9 Make sure both layers are still selected in the Layers panel. Then choose Edit > Auto-Blend Layers.

▶ **Tip:** The technique in this exercise, called *focus stacking*, is useful for macro photography, where depth of field is typically very shallow. Multiple images with shallow depth of field are shot at different focus distances and then merged.

10 Select Stack Images and Seamless Tones And Colors, if they aren't already selected. Make sure Content Aware Fill Transparent Areas is not selected, and then click OK.

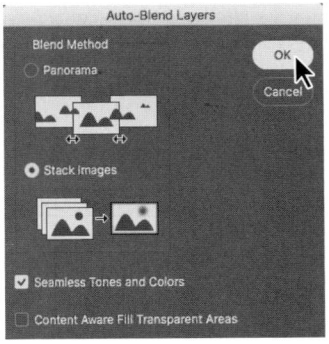

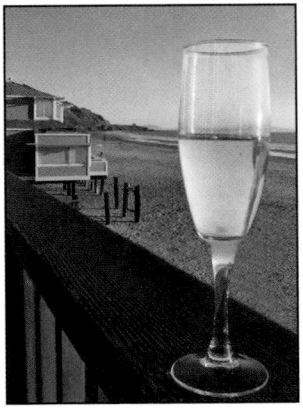

Both the wine glass and the beach behind it are in focus, because Auto-Blend Layers combined the sharpest parts of each image.

11 Save your work, and close the file.

Removing objects using Content-Aware Fill

You've used the content-aware features in some pretty impressive ways in earlier lessons and to fill in the sky in the panorama project in this lesson. Now you'll use Content-Aware Fill to remove an unwanted object and have Photoshop convincingly fill in the area instead of leaving a blank space.

1 Choose File > Browse In Bridge.

2 Navigate to the Lesson05 folder, if you're not there already, and then look at the JapaneseGarden_Start.jpg and JapaneseGarden_End.jpg thumbnail previews.

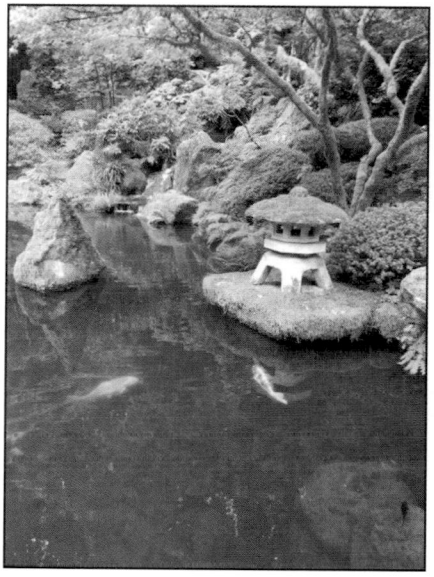

JapaneseGarden_Start.jpg

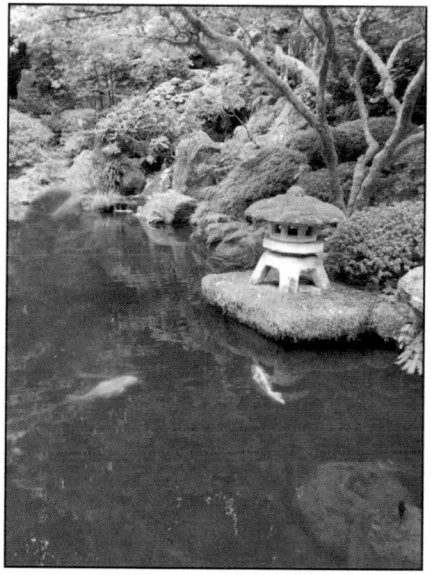

JapaneseGarden_End.jpg

You'll use the Content-Aware Fill tool to simplify the composition by removing the cone-shaped rock near the left edge of the photo, and its reflection.

3 Double-click the JapaneseGarden_Start.jpg file to open it in Photoshop.

4 Choose File > Save As, choose Photoshop for the format type, and name the new file **JapaneseGarden_Working.psd**. Click Save. Click OK if the Photoshop Format Options dialog box appears.

5 Select the Lasso tool (ꟷ).

6 Drag a selection marquee around the rock on the left and the rock's reflection below it, including some of the water around it. The selection can be approximate.

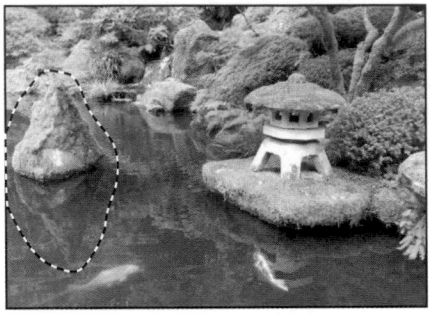

7 Choose Edit > Content-Aware Fill.

▶ **Tip:** Preview is a panel. You can drag the divider between the image and the Preview panel. You can drag the Preview panel tab to undock it, making Preview a floating panel. This Preview panel is available only when using Content-Aware Fill.

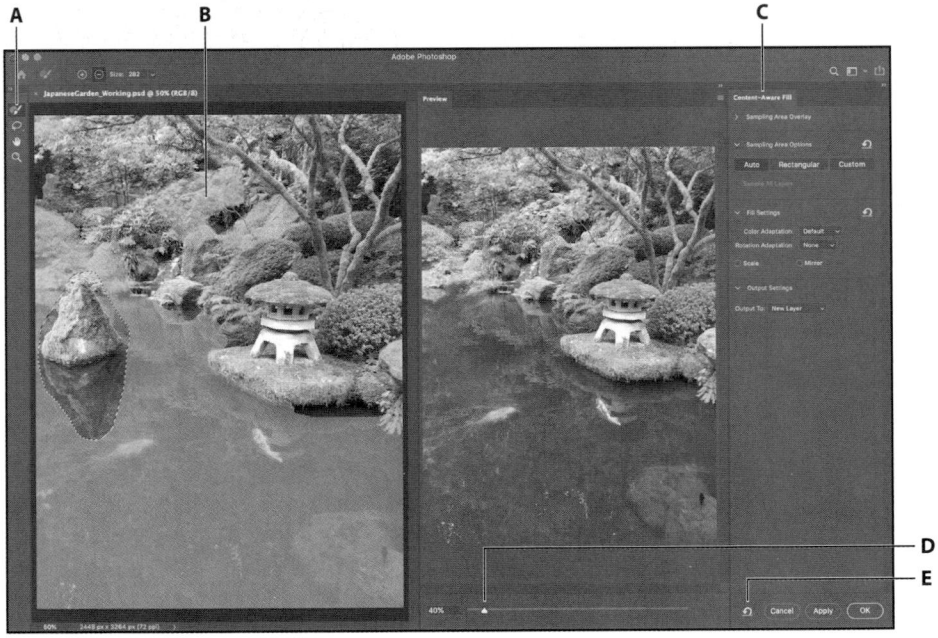

A. *Sampling Brush tool* **B.** *Sampling area* **C.** *Content-Aware Fill options* **D.** *Preview zoom* **E.** *Reset*

The left side of the Content-Aware Fill dialog box displays the image and the selection you made. The colored area (displayed in green by default) indicates areas Content-Aware Fill will sample (use as a source) for filling the removed area.

The right side previews the fill you get from the sampling area, combined with the settings in the Content-Aware Fill options panel. The most important settings to look at first are the Sampling Area Options.

- Auto is selected by default. It analyzes the image to improve the sampling area and excludes areas that it thinks are dissimilar to the area around the selection. Notice that the trees are not part of the sampling area; that's because Auto decided that tree areas are too dissimilar to the water you selected.
- Rectangular uses the entire image as the sampling area, except the selection.
- Custom doesn't apply an initial sampling area. You use the Sampling Brush tool to manually paint the parts you want Photoshop to use as the sampling area.

How do you choose which one to use? Start with Auto, because if it works well, it will require the least amount of manual retouching. Try the other options when the results of Auto are not easy to work with.

If the Preview panel shows parts of the selection that still aren't sufficiently convincing, you can use the Sampling Brush to customize the sampling area further. The Sampling Brush is the first tool in the toolbar along the left side of the Content-Aware Fill workspace. (If you think the image is already convincing enough, you can skip steps 8–10. Results can vary based on your initial selection.)

8 Press the [key to reduce the Sampling Brush tool until the options bar indicates that the brush size is around 175 pixels. The Sampling Brush tool is selected by default when you open the Content-Aware Fill dialog box.

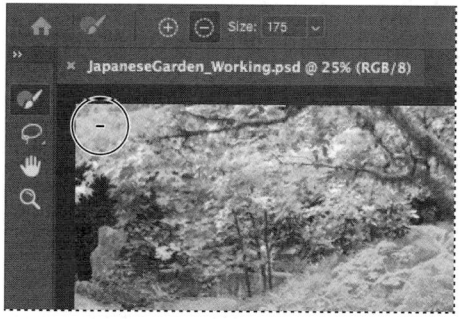

Notice that a minus sign (–) appears in the Sampling Brush pointer. This is because the tool is set to Subtract mode, which is indicated in the options bar.

9 Paint over unwanted areas (such as foliage, or the edge where the water meets the foliage) to exclude it from the sampling area. Areas you exclude no longer appear with the green sampling color. As you do this, the fill is recalculated, and you can evaluate the updated results in the Preview panel.

▶ **Tip:** If you need to make the selection larger or smaller by the same amount, use the Expand or Contract button, respectively, in the options bar.

10 As soon as the fill looks like it consists only of water and believable reflections, you can stop painting.

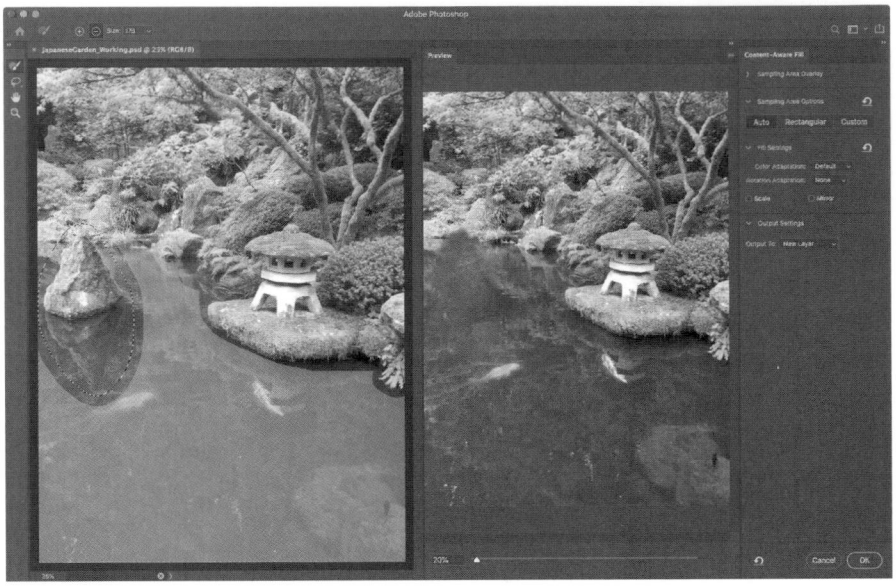

It may take some trial and error for the results to be successful. You may be able to improve the results using the following techniques:

- Use the Sampling Brush in Subtract mode to exclude more areas to stop them from contributing incorrect content to the fill. For example, it might help to also exclude the edges where the water meets the lantern base and other leaves.
- Use the Lasso tool to change the original selection. For example, try using the Lasso tool in Subtract mode to trim the selection where unwanted foliage is included, while still including all of the rock.
- Adjust the Fill Settings. For this exercise, adjusting the Color Adaptation setting should be the most useful. You probably won't use the other options, although they are useful in other situations. Rotation Adaptation is useful for re-creating missing areas of content that are radial (such as flower petals) or along an arc. Scale helps adapt a fill for patterned content. The Mirror option can be useful for symmetrical content.

▶ **Tip:** To quickly switch the Lasso tool between the Add and Subtract modes, press the E key.

11 If there are additional areas you want to fill, click Apply. The previous selection is committed, and now you can create a new selection to fill.

12 When you're finished, click OK, and then choose Select > Deselect.

In the Layers panel, notice that by default, the fill is created as a new layer named Background Copy. If you hide the new layer, you can see the entire original image in the Background layer.

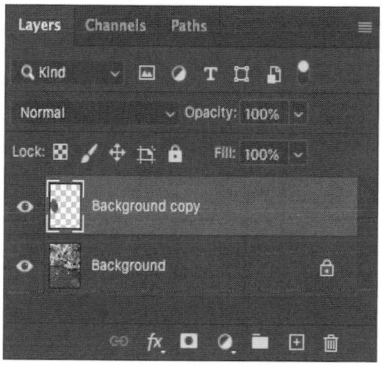

13 Save your work as a Photoshop document, and then close it.

▶ **Tip:** If you don't want Content-Aware Fill to create the fill as a new layer, before closing Content-Aware Fill, change the Output To option in Output Settings.

Tips for using the Content-Aware Move tool

The Content-Aware Move tool is very impressive when you're working with some images, and less impressive with others. For best results, use it when the background is consistent enough that Photoshop will be able to recognize and replicate a pattern, such as meadows, solid-colored walls, sky, wood grains, or water.

The Extend mode of the Content-Aware tool can be useful with architectural subjects, especially when they're shot on a plane parallel to the camera; it's less effective for subjects shot at an angle.

If you're working with an image that has multiple layers, select Sample All Layers in the options bar to include them all in the selection.

The Structure and Color options define how closely the results reflect the existing image patterns. In the Structure settings, 1 is the loosest and 5 the strictest. The Color settings range from 0 (no color adaptation) to 10 (matching the color as closely as possible). Experiment with the options while the object is still selected to see which give you the best results in a particular image. You may want to hide the selection edges (choose View > Show > Selection Edges or View > Extras) to see how the object integrates into its new position.

Extra credit

Transformations with the Content-Aware Move tool

With the Content-Aware Move tool, you need only a few quick steps to duplicate a thistle so that it combines seamlessly with the background and is also different enough that it doesn't look like an exact copy of the original.

1 Open Thistle.psd in your Lesson05/Extra Credit folder.

2 Select the Content-Aware Move tool (⤮) (grouped with the healing brush and Red Eye tools).

3 In the options bar, choose Extend from the Mode menu. Choosing Extend duplicates the thistle; if you just want to reposition the single thistle, you would choose Move.

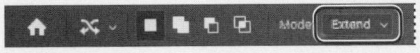

4 With the Content-Aware Move tool, draw a selection around the thistle, with a margin large enough to include a little of the grass around it.

5 Drag the selection to the left, and drop it in the empty area of grass.

6 Right-click (Windows) or Control-click (Mac) the dragged thistle, and choose Flip Horizontal.

7 Drag the top left transformation handle to make the thistle smaller. If you think the copy of the thistle should be farther from the original, position the pointer inside the transformation rectangle and drag the thistle copy slightly to the left.

8 Press Enter or Return to make the transformations permanent, leaving the content selected so you can adjust the Structure and Color options in the Options bar to improve how the new thistle blends with the background.

9 Choose Select > Deselect, and save your changes.

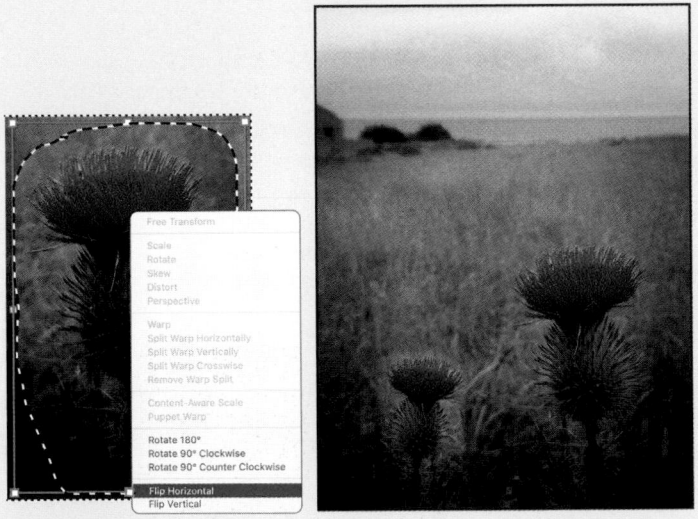

Adjusting perspective in an image

The Perspective Warp feature lets you adjust the way objects in your image relate to the scene. You can correct distortions, change the angle from which an object appears to be viewed, or shift the perspective of an object so that it merges smoothly with a new background.

Using the Perspective Warp feature is a two-step process: defining the planes and adjusting them. You start in Layout mode, drawing *quads* to define two or more planes; it's a good idea to align the edges of the quads so that they are parallel with the lines of the original object. Then you switch to Warp mode and manipulate the planes you defined.

You'll use Perspective Warp to merge images with different perspectives.

1 Choose File > Browse In Bridge.

2 Navigate to the Lesson05 folder, if you're not there already, and then look at the Bridge_Start.psd and Bridge_End.psd thumbnail previews.

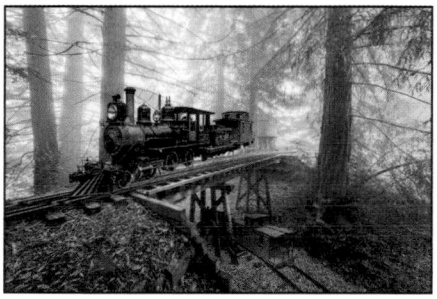

Bridge_Start.psd

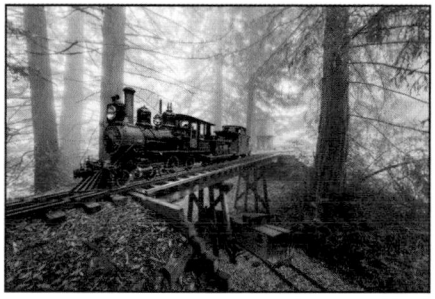

Bridge_End.psd

In the Bridge_Start.psd file, the image of the train has been combined with the image of a trestle bridge, but their perspectives don't match. If you're illustrating a story about a flying train that is making a landing on a trestle bridge, this might be perfect. But if you want a more realistic image, you'll need to adjust the perspective of the train to put it firmly on the tracks. You'll use Perspective Warp to do just that.

3 Double-click the Bridge_Start.psd file to open it in Photoshop.

4 Choose File > Save As, and rename the file **Bridge_Working.psd**. Click OK in the Photoshop Format Options dialog box.

5 Select the Train layer.

The tracks are on the Background layer. The train is on the Train layer. Because the Train layer is a Smart Object, you can apply Perspective Warp and then modify the results if you're not satisfied.

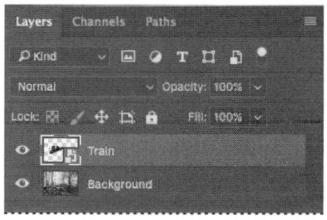

Note: Perspective Warp can work faster on a computer that qualifies for graphics acceleration. To see if your computer qualifies, see the "Getting Started" section for a link to the Photoshop system requirements.

6 Choose Edit > Perspective Warp.

A small animated tutorial appears, showing you how to draw a quad, which defines a plane.

7 Watch the animation, and then close it.

Now you'll create quads to define the planes of the train image.

8 Draw the quad for the side of the train: Click above the top of the smokestack, drag down to the railroad tie below the front wheel, and then drag across to the end of the caboose.

▶ **Tip:** Not sure if you've properly drawn the perspective of quads around a subject? They should look like a shipping container fitted to the subject.

9 Drag a second quad for the front of the train, dragging across the cowcatcher at the bottom and into the trees at the top. Drag it to the right until it attaches to the left edge of the first quad.

10 Drag the corners of the planes to match the angles of the train. The bottom line of the side plane should run along the bottom of the train wheels; the top edge should border the top of the caboose. The front plane should mirror the lines of the cowcatcher and the top of the light.

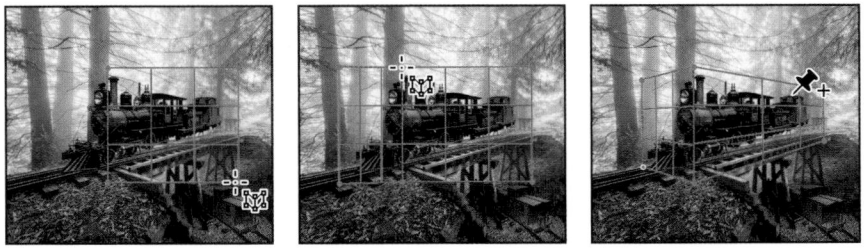

Now that the quads are drawn, you're ready for the second step: warping.

11 Click Warp in the options bar. Close the tutorial window that appears.

12 Click the Automatically Straighten Near Vertical Lines button, next to Warp in the options bar.

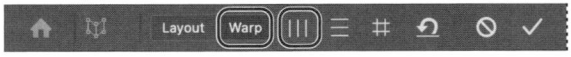

Lines close to vertical are made vertical, making it easier to adjust its perspective.

13 Drag the handles to manipulate the planes, moving the back end of the train down and into perspective with the tracks. Exaggerate the perspective toward the caboose for a more dramatic result.

14 Warp other parts of the train as needed. You may need to adjust the front of the train. Pay attention to the wheels; make sure you don't distort them as you warp the perspective.

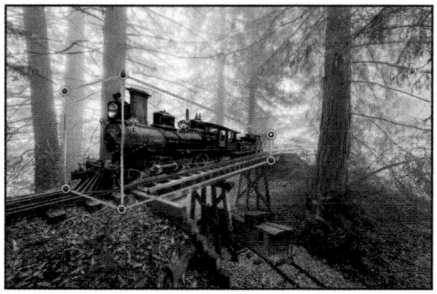

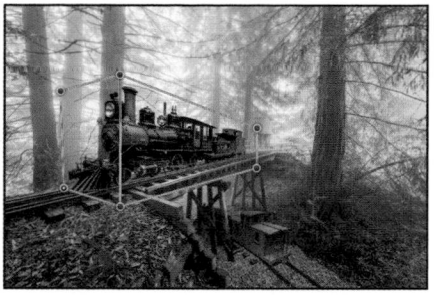

While there are precise ways to adjust perspective, in many cases you may need to trust your eyes to tell you when it looks right. Remember that you can return to tweak it again later, because you're applying Perspective Warp as a Smart Filter.

15 When you're satisfied with the perspective, click the Commit Perspective Warp button (✓) in the options bar.

16 To compare the changed image with the original, hide the Perspective Warp filter in the Layers panel. Then show the filter again.

If you want to make further adjustments, double-click the Perspective Warp filter in the Layers panel. You can continue to adjust the existing planes or click Layout in the options bar to reshape them. Remember to click the Commit Perspective Warp button to apply your changes.

17 Save your work, and close the file.

Changing the perspective of a building

In the exercise, you applied Perspective Warp to one layer to change its relationship with another. But you can also use Perspective Warp to change the perspective of an object in relationship to others in the same layer. For example, you can shift the angle from which you view a building.

In this case, you apply Perspective Warp the same way: In Layout mode, draw the planes of the object you want to affect. In Warp mode, manipulate those planes. Of course, because you're shifting angles within a layer, other objects on the layer will move too, so you need to watch for any irregularities.

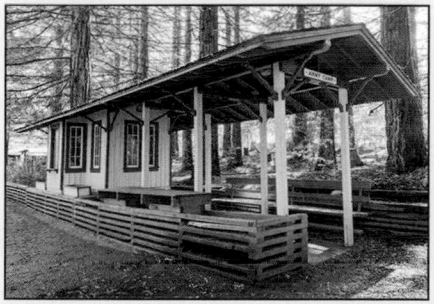

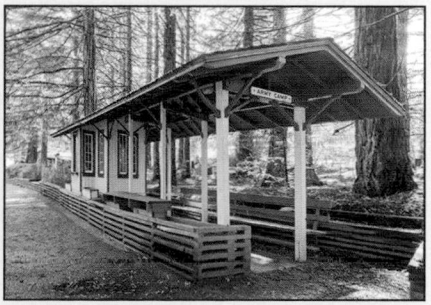

In this image, as the perspective of the building shifts, so does the perspective of the trees surrounding it.

Camera Shake Reduction

Even with a steady hand, unintended camera motion can occur with slow shutter speeds or long focal lengths. The Camera Shake Reduction filter reduces the resulting camera shake, giving you a sharper image.

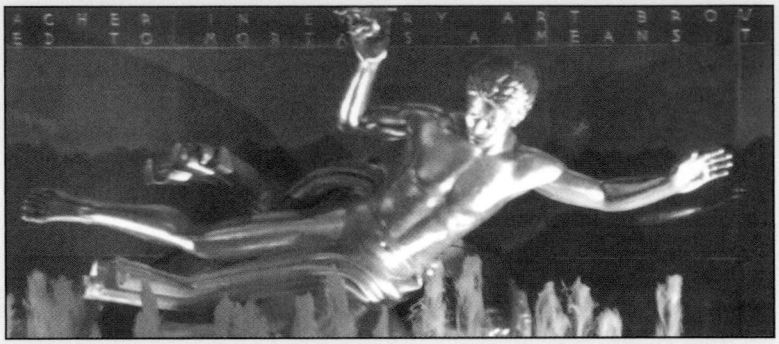

Before applying the Camera Shake Reduction filter

You'll get the best results if you apply the filter to a particular part of an image, rather than the entire image. It can be especially useful if text has become illegible due to camera shake.

To use the Camera Shake Reduction filter, open the image, and choose Filter > Sharpen > Shake Reduction. The filter automatically analyzes the image, selects a region of interest, and corrects the blur. Use the Detail loupe to examine the preview. That may be all you need to do. If so, click OK to close the Shake Reduction dialog box and apply the filter.

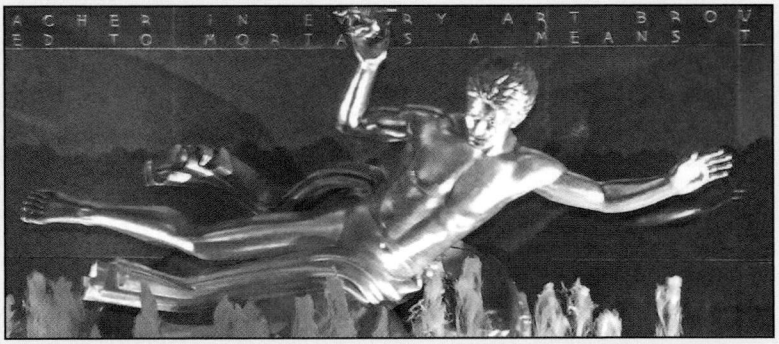

After applying the Camera Shake Reduction filter

You can adjust how Photoshop interprets the Blur Trace, which is the shape and size of the camera shake that Photoshop identified. You can change the region of interest or adjust its size, adjust the Smoothing and Artifact Suppression values, and more. For full information about the Camera Shake Reduction filter, see Photoshop Help.

Review questions

1 What is red eye, and how do you correct it in Photoshop?

2 How can you create a panorama from multiple images?

3 Describe how to fix common camera lens flaws in Photoshop. What causes these defects?

4 When you use Content-Aware Fill and the selection is filled with the wrong content, what are some of the first things you can try to correct this?

Review answers

1 Red eye occurs when a camera flash is reflected in the retinas of a subject's eyes. To correct red eye in Photoshop, zoom in to the subject's eyes, select the Red Eye tool, and then click or drag around each eye.

2 To blend multiple images into a panorama, choose File > Automate > Photomerge, select the files you want to combine, and click OK.

3 The Lens Correction filter fixes common camera lens flaws, such as barrel and pincushion distortion, in which straight lines bow out toward the edges of the image (barrel) or bend inward (pincushion); chromatic aberration, where a color fringe appears along the edges of image objects; and vignetting at the edges of an image, especially corners, that are darker than the center. Distortion can occur from choosing an inappropriate lens focal length, from using a lower-quality lens, or by tilting the camera vertically or horizontally.

4 When Content-Aware-Fill uses the wrong content in a fill, you can use the Sampling Brush or Lasso tools to exclude unwanted content from the sampled area, and you can try a different Sampling Area Option.

6 MASKS AND CHANNELS

Lesson overview

In this lesson, you'll learn how to do the following:

- Create a mask to remove a subject from a background.
- Refine a mask to include complex edges.
- Create a quick mask to make changes to a selected area.
- Edit a mask using the Properties panel.
- Manipulate an image using Puppet Warp.
- Save a selection as an alpha channel.
- View a mask using the Channels panel.
- Load a channel as a selection.

This lesson will take about an hour to complete. To get the lesson files used in this chapter, download them from the web page for this book at www.adobepress.com/PhotoshopCIB2021. For more information, see "Accessing the lesson files and Web Edition" in the Getting Started section at the beginning of this book.

As you work on this lesson, you'll preserve the start files. If you need to restore the start files, download them from your Account page.

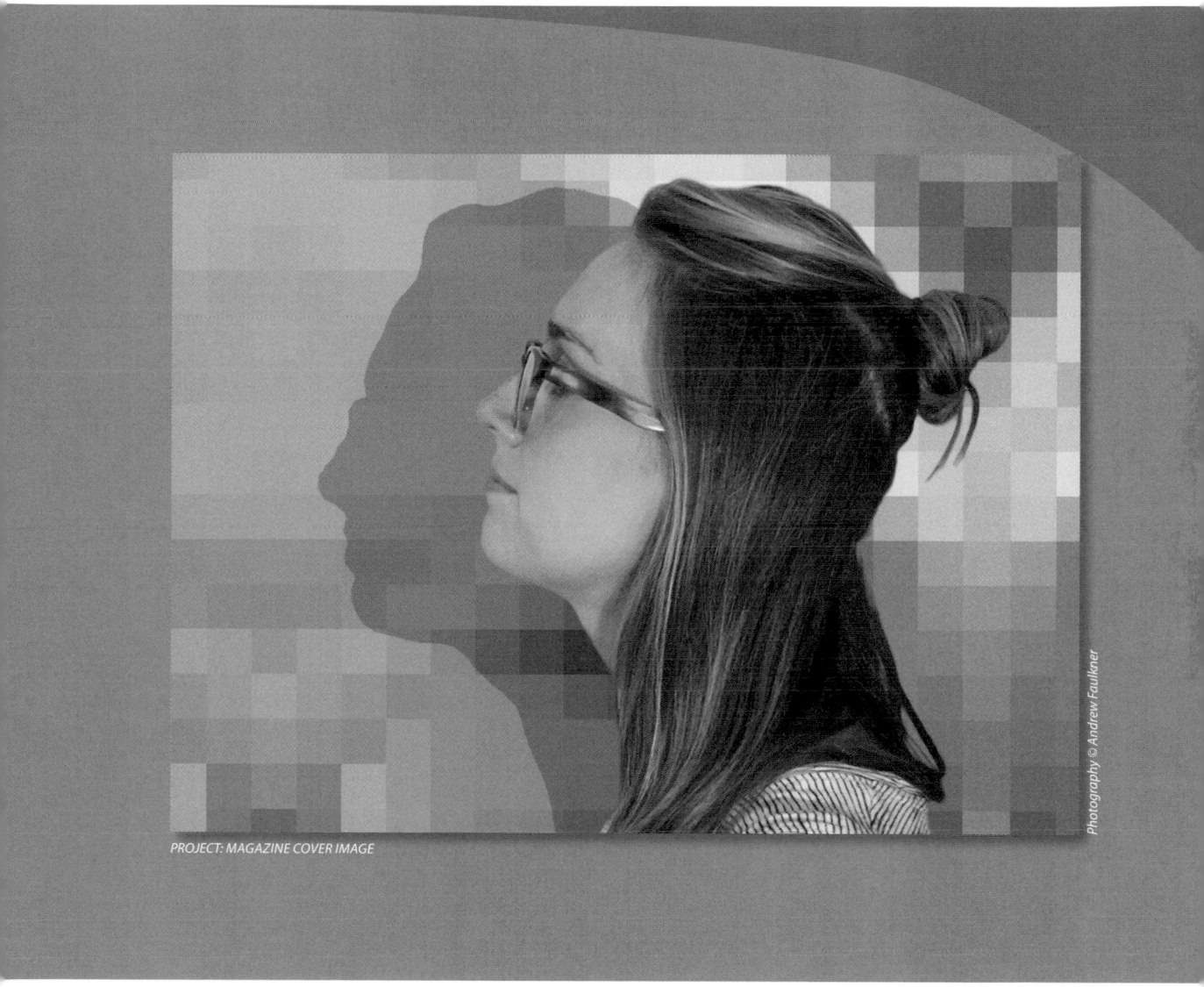

PROJECT: MAGAZINE COVER IMAGE

Photography © Andrew Faulkner

Use masks to isolate and manipulate specific parts of an image. The cutout portion of a mask can be altered, but the area surrounding the cutout is protected from change. You can create a temporary mask to use once, or you can save masks for repeated use.

▶ **Tip:** The way masks work is similar to applying masking tape to panes or wall trim before you paint a house: Masked areas are protected from being changed.

Working with masks and channels

When you want to edit a specific area of a layer, it can be difficult to keep edits from going past the precise edge you want. Or you might want to apply an adjustment layer or a filter to only part of a layer. Both are easier using a *mask*, a type of image overlay that controls which layer areas will be affected by edits.

You can also use a *layer mask* to mark transparent areas of a layer. Layer masks are essential for removing backgrounds, combining multiple images into a composite image, and controlling which areas are affected by adjustment layers. A layer mask is more useful than deleting unwanted areas of a layer, because it's reversible: By painting in a layer mask, you can make hidden areas visible again.

In addition to color channels, an image can contain *alpha channels*, useful for saving and reusing selections and marking transparent areas for an entire document.

● **Note:** Masks and alpha channels don't print and aren't visible; you see only their effects on visible layers.

It can be challenging to paint or draw a mask or channel edge that precisely follows a nonsharp border of a subject, such as fuzzy hair. Photoshop provides tools that use automation to help you quickly create complicated selections and masks.

Getting started

First, you'll view the image that you'll create using masks and channels.

1 Start Photoshop, and then simultaneously hold down Ctrl+Alt+Shift (Windows) or Command+Option+Shift (Mac) to restore the default preferences. (See "Restoring default preferences" on page 5.)

2 When prompted, click Yes to delete the Adobe Photoshop Settings file.

3 Choose File > Browse In Bridge to open Adobe Bridge.

● **Note:** If Bridge isn't installed, the File > Browse in Bridge command in Photoshop will start the Creative Cloud desktop app, which will download and install Bridge. After installation completes, you can start Bridge.

4 Click the Favorites tab on the left side of the Bridge window. Select the Lessons folder, and then double-click the Lesson06 folder in the Content panel.

5 Study the 06End.psd file. To enlarge the thumbnail so that you can see it more clearly, move the thumbnail slider at the bottom of the Bridge window to the right.

In this lesson, you'll create a magazine cover. The model for the cover was photographed in front of a different background, and the background isn't a single color, so it may be a challenge to mask. You'll use Select And Mask to quickly isolate the model over the final background. You'll also tilt the model's head up a little more.

6 Double-click the 06Start.psd thumbnail to open it in Photoshop. Click OK if you see an Embedded Profile Mismatch dialog box.

7 Choose File > Save As, rename the file to **06Working.psd**, and click Save. Click OK if the Photoshop Format Options dialog box appears.

● **Note:** If Photoshop displays a dialog box telling you about the difference between saving to Cloud Documents and Your Computer, click Save On Your Computer. You can also select Don't Show Again, but that setting will deselect after you reset Photoshop preferences.

Saving a working version of the file lets you return to the original if you need it.

About masks and alpha channels

Alpha channels, quick masks, clipping masks, layer masks, vector masks—what's the difference? They're all forms of the same idea: An image overlay that uses white, black, and gray areas to control which areas of a layer are visible or changed by edits. Choose the right one by understanding the following important differences:

- A **color channel** stores one of the visible components of a color image. For example, an RGB image has three color channels: red, green, and blue.
- An **alpha channel** stores a selection as a grayscale image. Alpha channels exist independently of layers and color channels. You can convert alpha channels to and from selections or paths. Some file formats can include an alpha channel that defines the transparent areas of an image.
- A **layer mask** is an alpha channel attached to a specific layer. A layer mask controls which parts of a layer are revealed or hidden. It appears as a white thumbnail next to the layer thumbnail in the Layers panel until you paint black in it; an outline around the layer mask thumbnail indicates that it's selected.
- A **vector mask** is a layer mask made of resolution-independent vector objects, not pixels, useful when precise mask edge control is more important than being able to edit a mask with a brush. You create vector masks using the commands on the Layer > Vector Mask submenu and using the pen or shape tools.
- A **clipping mask** is created when a layer masks another layer. The thumbnail preview of a clipped layer is indented in the layer list, with a right-angle arrow pointing to the layer below. The name of the clipped base layer is underlined.
- A **channel mask** defines areas based on the tonal contrast in a color channel, such as in the green channel in an RGB image. Channel masks are useful for advanced techniques for masking, color correction, and sharpening. For example, the edge between trees and sky may be clearest in the blue channel.
- A **quick mask** is a temporary mask you create to restrict painting or other edits to a specific area of a layer. It's a selection in pixel form; instead of editing the selection marquee, you edit a quick mask using painting tools.

Using Select And Mask and Select Subject

Photoshop provides a set of tools focused on creating and refining masks, collected in a task space called Select And Mask. Inside Select And Mask, you'll use the Select Subject tool to get a fast head start on the mask that will separate the model from the background. Then you'll refine the mask using other Select And Mask tools, such as the Quick Selection tool.

1 In the Layers panel, make sure both layers are visible and the Model layer is selected.

2 Choose Select > Select And Mask.

▶ **Tip:** When any selection tool is active, the Select And Mask button is available in the options bar. When the Select And Mask button is not available, you can still use the Select > Select And Mask command.

▶ **Tip:** The first time you use Select And Mask, a tutorial tip may pop up. You may view it before you continue with the lesson, or you can click Later or Close.

Select And Mask opens with the image. A semitransparent "onion skin" overlay indicates masked areas, which are represented by a checkerboard pattern. For now, the checkerboard pattern covers the entire image, because you haven't yet identified the areas to unmask.

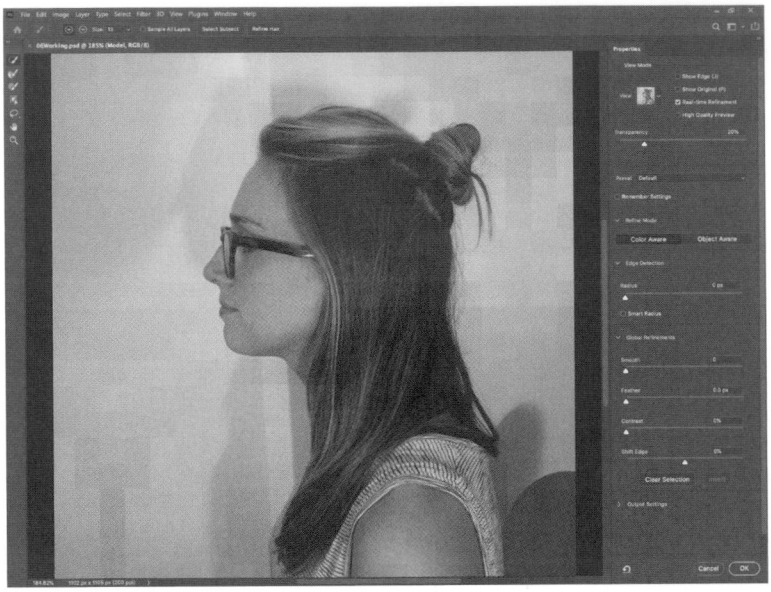

▶ **Tip:** For more help making selections, refer to Lesson 3, "Working with Selections."

▶ **Tip:** When a selection tool is active, you can enter Select And Mask by clicking the Select And Mask button in the options bar instead of having to find the command in the menus.

3 Click the View menu in the View Mode section of the Properties panel, and choose Overlay. The masked area is now shown as a semitransparent red color instead of the onion skin checkerboard. It's solid because nothing is masked yet.

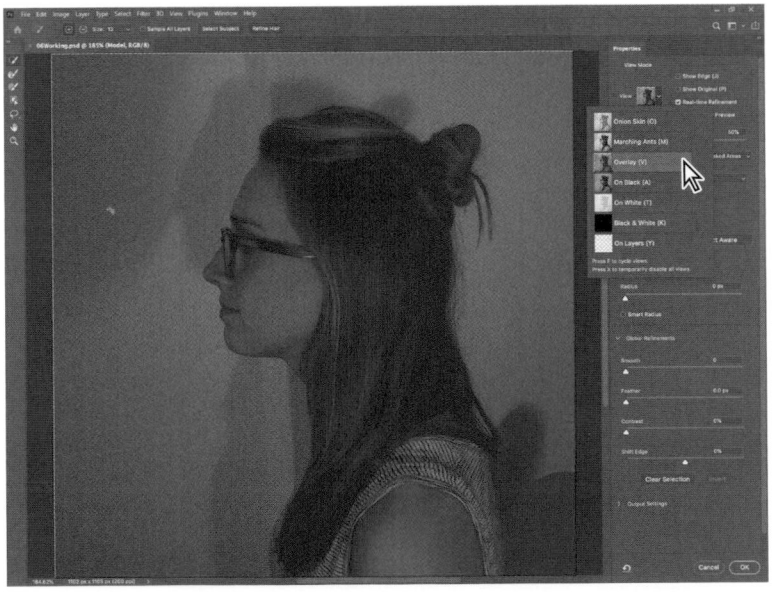

▶ **Tip:** Quickly cycle through the View Modes by pressing the F key. Viewing different modes helps you spot selection mistakes that might not be obvious in other modes.

The different View Modes are provided so that you can see the mask more easily over various backgrounds. In this case, the red overlay will make it easier to see missed areas and edges where loose hair isn't properly masked.

4 In the Options bar, click the Select Subject button (or choose Select > Subject).

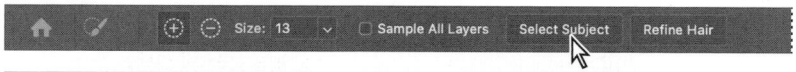

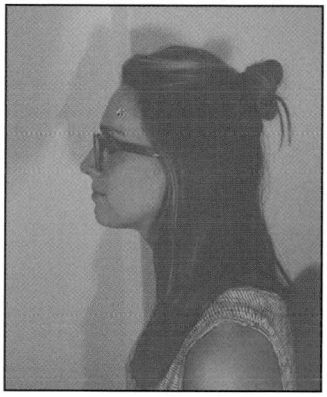

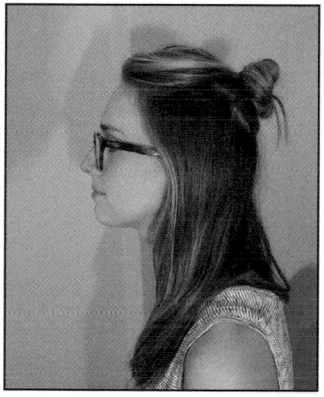

Using advanced machine learning technology, the Select Subject feature is trained to identify typical subjects of a photo, including people, animals, and objects, and then create a selection for them. The selection may not be perfect, but it's often close enough for you to refine easily and rapidly with other selection tools.

Notice that there are a few areas over the chest that were missed by Select Subject. You can easily add them to the selection using the Quick Selection tool.

5 Make sure the Quick Selection tool (🖌) is selected. In the options bar, set up a brush with a size of **15** px.

6 Drag the Quick Selection tool over the missed areas (without extending into the background) to add the missed areas to the selection. Notice that the Quick Selection tool fills in the selection as it detects content edges, so you don't have to be exact. It's OK if you release the mouse button and drag more than once.

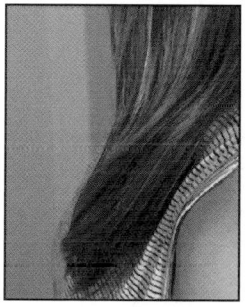

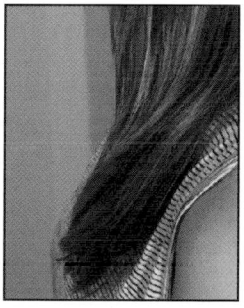

Note: If you don't see the Select Subject button in the Select And Mask task space, make sure the Quick Selection tool (the first one in the toolbox) is selected.

Tip: You don't have to be in the Select And Mask dialog box to use the Select > Subject command. It's available even when a selection tool is not active. Also, it's OK to Select Subject first and then enter Select And Mask to refine the selection.

Tip: When editing a selection, increase the magnification if it helps you see missed areas.

Where you drag teaches the Quick Selection tool which areas should be revealed and not part of the mask. Do not drag the Quick Selection tool over or past the model's edge to the background, because this teaches the Quick Selection tool to include part of the background in the mask, and you don't want that. If you accidentally add unwanted areas to the mask, either choose Edit > Undo or reverse the edit by painting over it with the Quick Selection tool in Subtract mode. To enable Subtract Mode for the Quick Selection tool, click the Subtract From Selection icon (⊖) in the options bar.

▶ **Tip:** You can adjust the opacity of the onion skin by dragging the Transparency slider under the View Mode options.

As you drag the Quick Selection tool over the model, the overlay disappears from the areas that you are marking to be revealed. Don't worry about total perfection at this stage.

7 Click the View menu in the View Mode section again, and choose On Layers. This shows you how the current Select And Mask settings look over any layers that are behind this layer. In this case, you're previewing how the current settings will mask the Model layer over the Magazine Background layer.

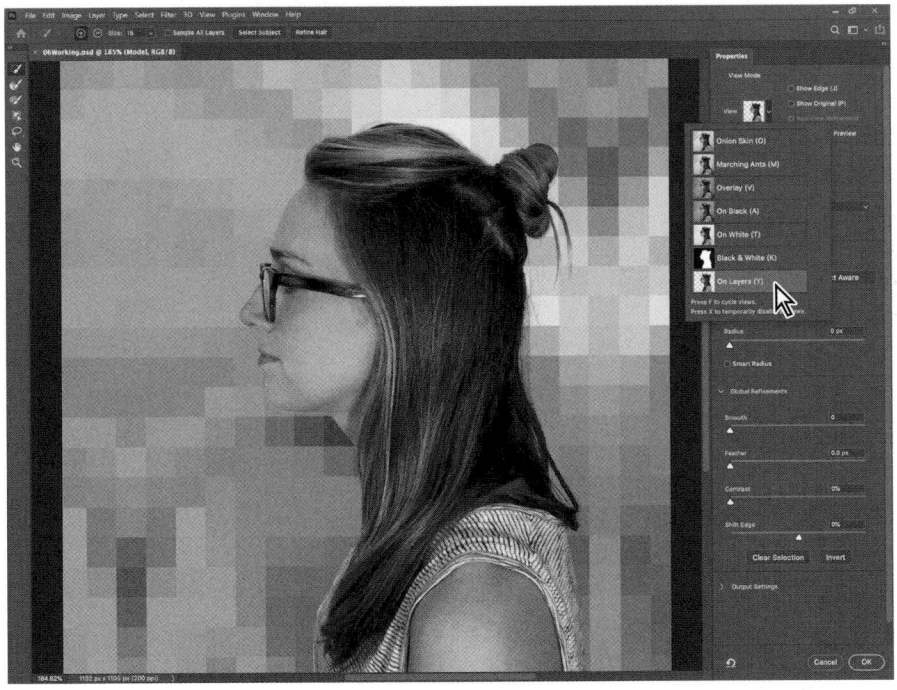

Inspect the edges around the model at a high magnification, such as 400%. Some of the original light background may still show between the model's edge and the magazine background, but overall the Select Subject and Quick Selection tools should have created clean edges for the shirt and face. Don't be concerned about edge gaps or imperfect hair edges, because you'll take care of those next.

Getting better and faster results with Select And Mask

When using Select And Mask, it's important to use different tools for image areas that should be fully revealed, for areas that should be fully masked, and for partially masked edges (such as fuzzy dog hair). Try these recommendations:

- The Select Subject button can be a fast way to create an initial selection.
- The Quick Selection tool is useful for rapidly touching up a selection produced by Select Subject or for creating an initial selection. As you drag it, it uses edge detection technology to find mask edges automatically. Don't drag it on or over a mask edge; keep it fully inside (in Add mode) or outside (in Subtract mode) the areas that should be revealed.
- To paint or draw solid mask edges manually (without using any automatic edge detection), use the Brush, Lasso, or Polygonal Lasso tool. These also have an Add mode for marking revealed areas and a Subtract mode for marking masked areas.
- Instead of having to switch between Add and Subtract modes with the toolbar, you can leave a tool in Add mode, and when you want to temporarily use the tool in Subtract mode, hold down the Alt (Windows) or Option (Mac) key.
- To improve the mask along edges containing complex transitions such as hair, drag the Refine Edge Brush along those edges. Do not drag the Refine Edge brush over areas that should be fully revealed or fully masked.
- You don't have to do all of your selecting inside Select And Mask. For example, if you've already created a selection with another tool such as Color Range, leave that selection active, and then click Select > Select And Mask in the options bar to clean up the mask.

▶ **Tip:** In Select And Mask, the Polygonal Lasso tool is grouped with the Lasso tool.

Refining a mask

The mask is pretty good so far, but Select Subject didn't quite capture all of the model's hair. For example, some of the strands coming off of the bun on the back of the model's head are discontinuous. In Select And Mask, the Refine Edge Brush tool is designed to mask edges with challenging details.

1 At a magnification of 300% or higher, inspect the hair edges at the back of the model's head.

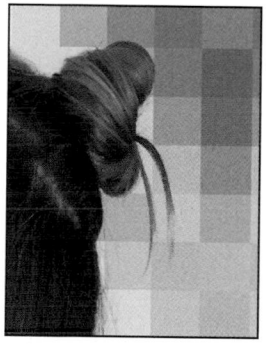

▶ **Tip:** The Refine Mode in Select And Mask Properties provides two ways to handle hair. Color Aware can work well on simple backgrounds like the one in this lesson. Object Aware may work better on more complex backgrounds.

2 Select the Refine Edge Brush tool (). In the options bar, set up a brush with a size of **20** px and Hardness of **100**%.

3 Choose Overlay from the View menu in the View Mode section so that the missing hair is visible.

4 Drag the Refine Edge Brush tool between the hair bun and the ends of the hair, where the selection needs to be improved. As you drag the Refine Edge Brush tool over the complex hair edge, you should see that the missing hair strands falling from the bun are now included in the visible areas.

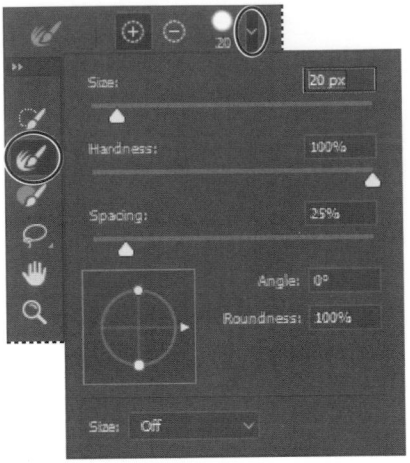

▶ **Tip:** If you use a tool to make the initial selection (instead of Select Subject), click the Refine Hair button. It should result in less manual brushing with the Refine Edge Brush tool.

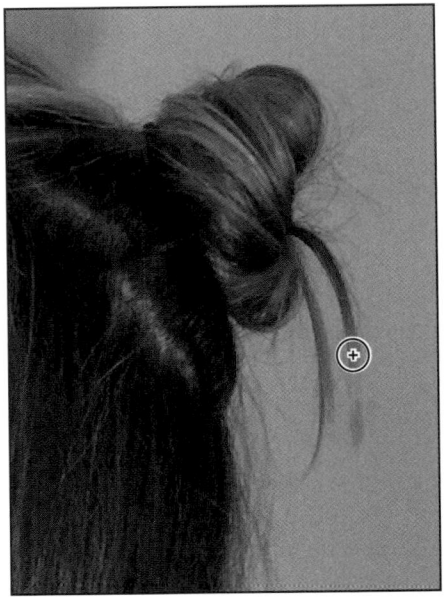

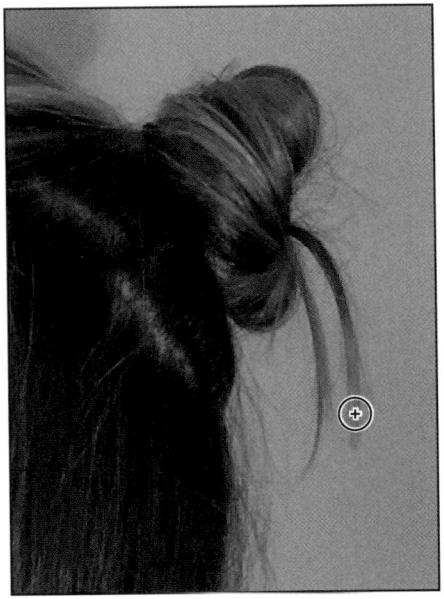

5 Scroll down to the loop of hair that falls over the back of the shirt.

Select Subject correctly masked the background inside the hair loop. However, a more subtle hole above still needs to reveal the orange magazine background, so you'll use the Refine Edge Brush to add that hole to the mask.

6 In the options bar, set up a Refine Edge brush with a size of **15** px, with a Hardness of **100**%.

Julieanne Kost is an official Adobe Photoshop evangelist.

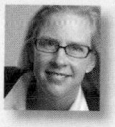

Tool tips from the Photoshop evangelist

Zoom tool shortcuts

Often when editing an image, you'll need to zoom in to work on a detail and then zoom out again to see the changes in context. Here are several keyboard shortcuts that make zooming faster and easier.

- With any tool selected, press Ctrl (Windows) or Command (Mac) with the plus sign (+) to zoom in, or with the minus sign (–) to zoom out.
- Double-click the Zoom tool in the Tools panel to return the image to 100% view.
- When Scrubby Zoom is selected in the options bar, just drag the Zoom tool to the left to zoom out or to the right to zoom in.
- Press Alt (Windows) or Option (Mac) to change the Zoom In tool to the Zoom Out tool, and click the image. Each Alt/Option-click reduces the image by the next preset increment, centering the image where you clicked.

7 Drag the Refine Edge Brush tool over the enclosed area that should be transparent. Gaps in the hair should become masked as transparent, and fine hairs are added to the visible edge.

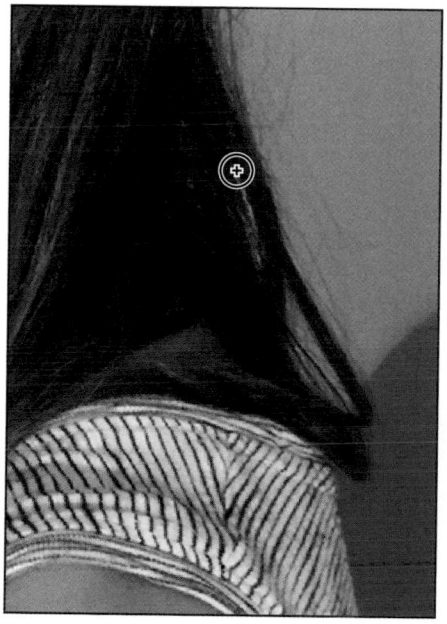

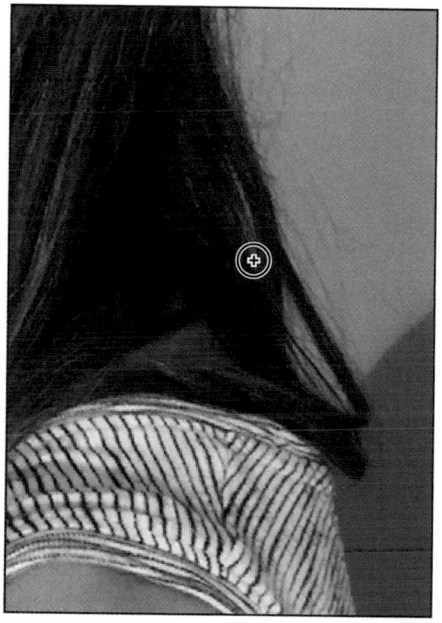

8 Click the View option, and choose Black & White. This is another good way to check your mask. Inspect the mask at different magnifications, and when you're done, choose View > Fit On Screen. Black areas indicate transparency.

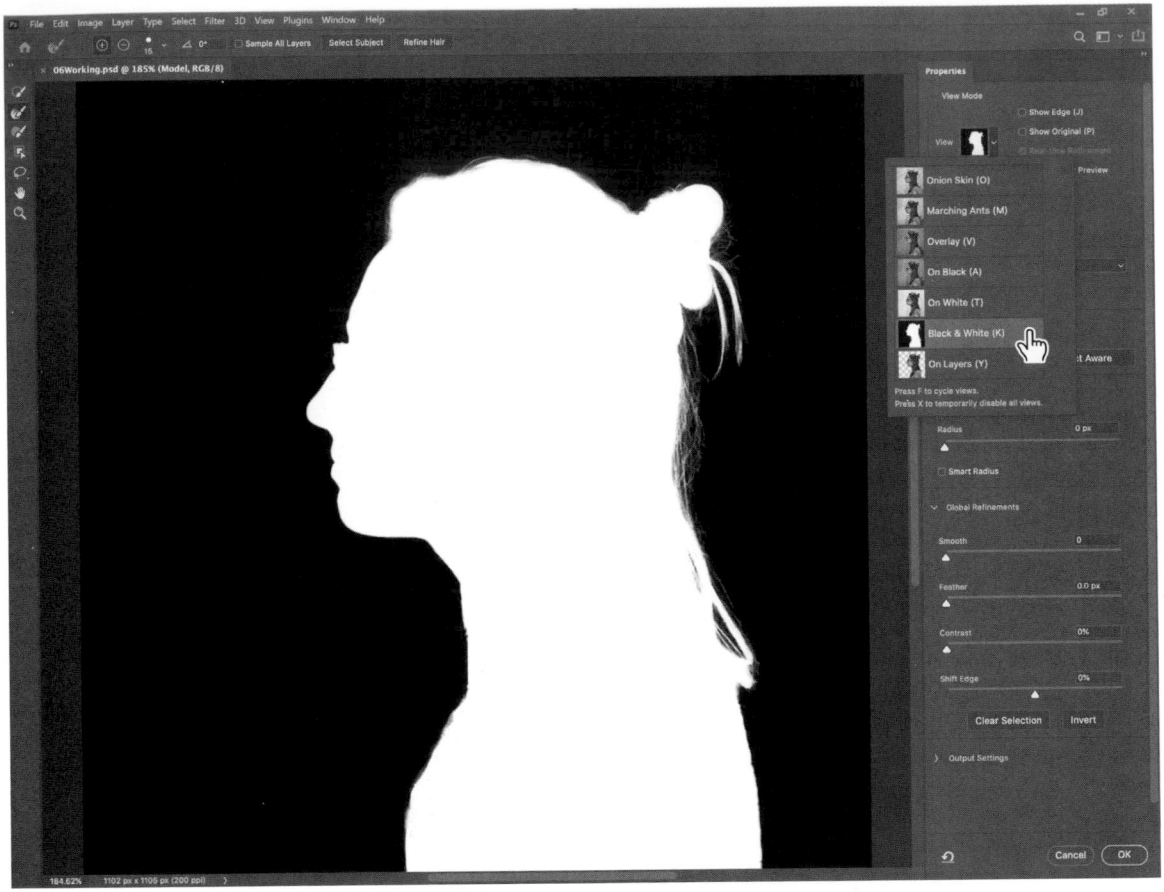

If you see hairs or other details that are masked but should be visible, drag the Refine Edge brush over them. The finer the details you want to mask, the smaller you should set the Refine Edge brush size. It's OK if the brush size is slightly larger than the details you want to mask, and you don't have to drag the Refine Edge Brush tool precisely.

If you see Refine Edge Brush tool mistakes that need to be erased, such as inner areas incorrectly added to the mask, drag the Refine Edge Brush tool over the mistakes while holding down the Alt (Windows) or Option (Mac) key.

▶ **Tip:** A quick way to remember what color to paint in a mask is the phrase "black conceals, white reveals."

If you see individual spots or discrete areas that need to be fully visible or fully transparent, you can paint them out using the Brush tool, the third one down in the toolbox. To make areas visible, paint them with white; to make areas hidden, paint them with black.

Adjusting Global Refinements

At this point the mask is in good shape, but needs to be tightened up a little. You can tune the overall appearance of the mask edge by adjusting the Global Refinements settings.

1 Click the View menu in the View Mode section of the Properties panel, and choose On Layers. This lets you preview adjustments over the Magazine Background layer, which is behind the Model layer.

2 In the Global Refinements section, move the sliders to create a smooth, unfeathered edge along the face. The optimal settings depend on the selection you created, but they'll probably be similar to ours. We moved the Smooth slider to 5 to reduce the roughness of the outline, Contrast to 20% to sharpen the transitions along the selection border, and Shift Edge to –15% to move the selection border inward and help remove unwanted background colors from selection edges. (Adjusting Shift Edge to a positive number would move the border outward.)

Note: Pay attention to details while using Global Refinements. For example, if you adjust Smooth and the mask edge starts to round corners or grind down important details, that means Smooth is set too high. Similarly, setting Feather too high can create unsightly halos along the edge.

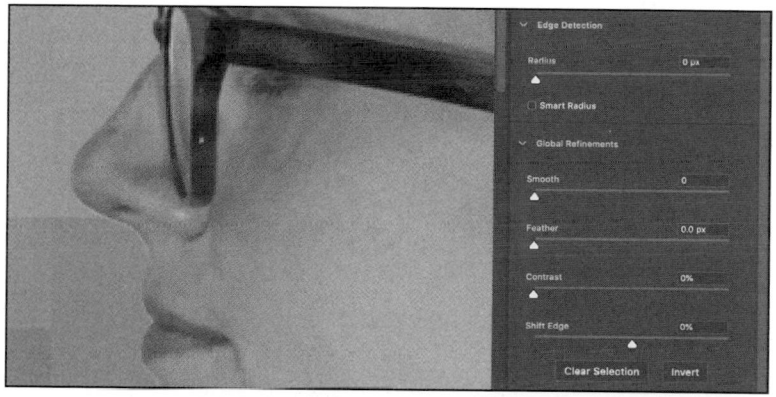

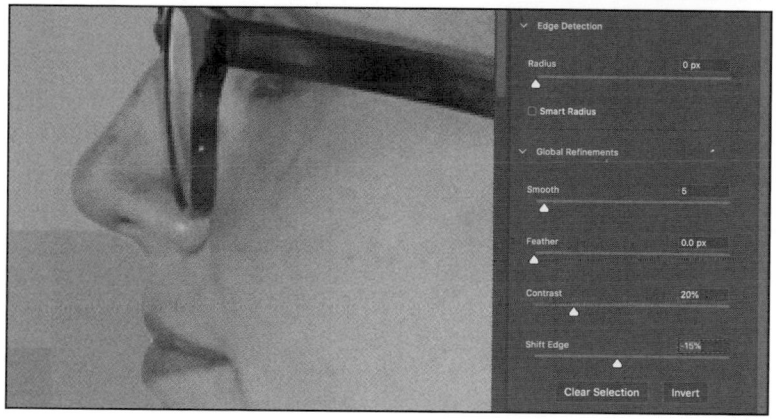

3 Take one more look at this preview of the current mask over the Magazine Background layer, and make any remaining corrections as needed.

Completing the mask

When you're satisfied with the mask preview, you can create its final output as a selection, a layer with transparency, a layer mask, or a new document. For this project, we want to use this as a layer mask on the Model layer, which was selected when you entered Select And Mask.

1 If the Output Settings are hidden, click the disclosure icon (›) to reveal them.

2 Zoom in to 200% or more so that you can more easily see the light fringing around the face edge that's due to the Model layer's original background color seeping in behind the mask.

3 Select Decontaminate Colors to suppress those color fringes. If Decontaminate Colors creates unwanted artifacts, reduce the Amount until the effect looks the way you want. We set Amount to 25%.

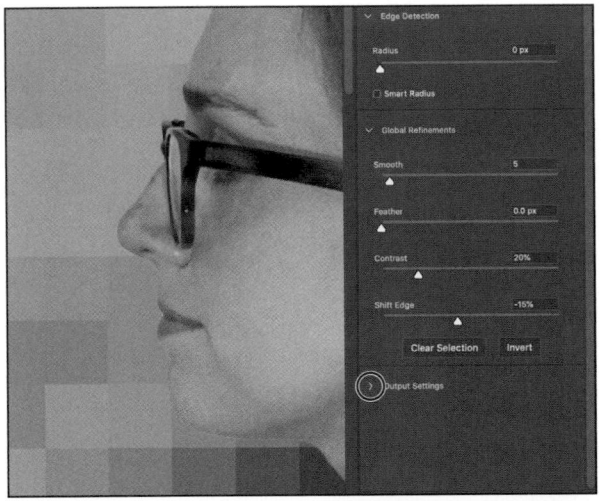

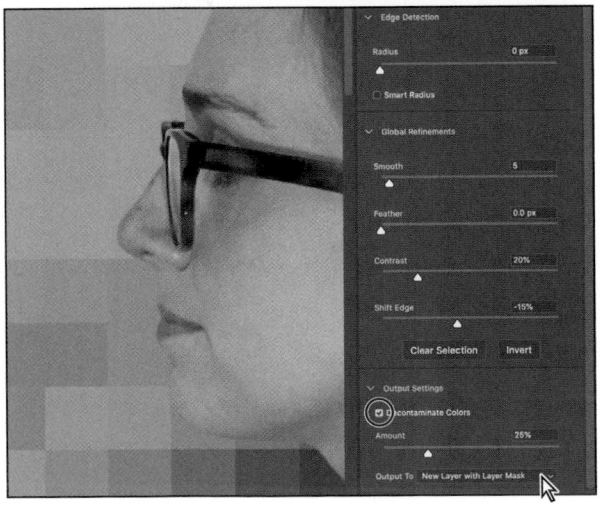

4 Choose New Layer With Layer Mask from the Output To menu. Then click OK.

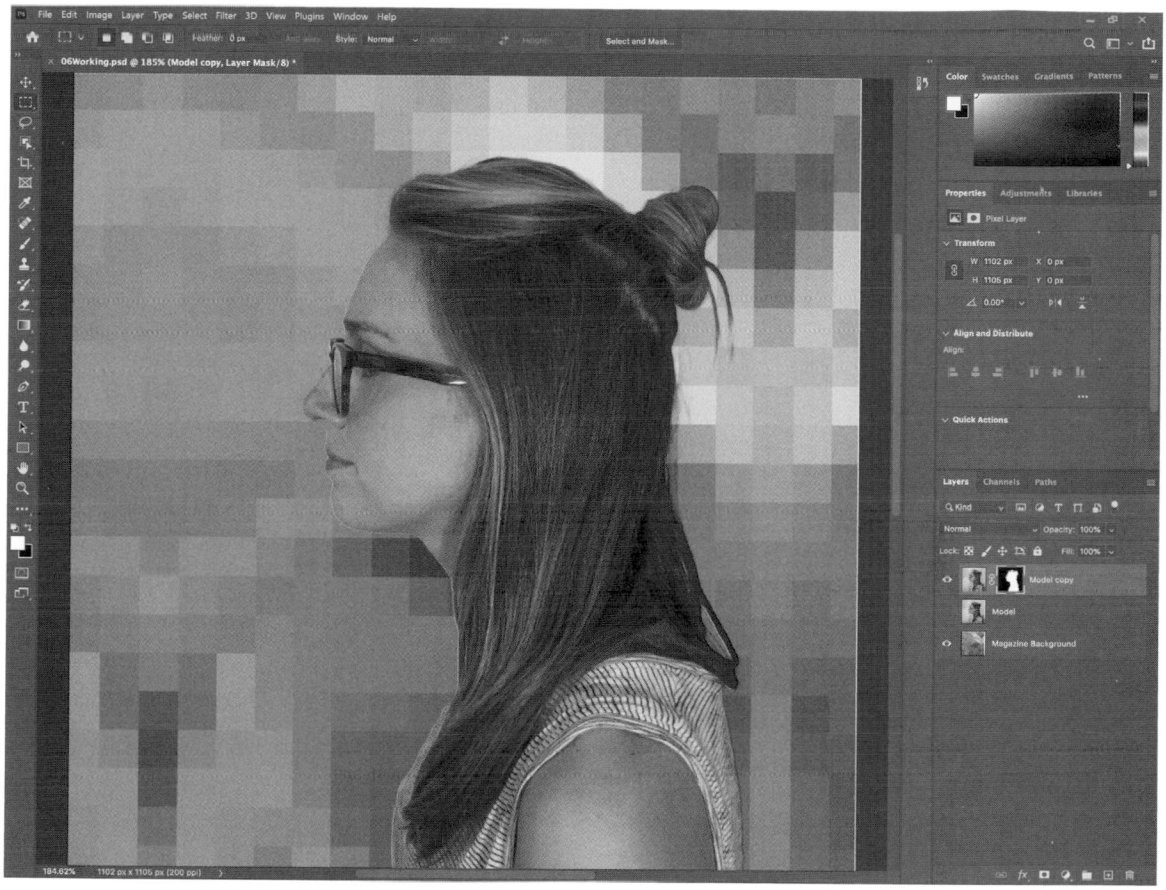

Clicking OK exits Select And Mask. In the Layers panel, the Model Copy layer now has a layer mask (pixel mask) that was generated by Select And Mask.

The layer was copied because using the Decontaminate Colors option requires generating new pixels. The original Model layer is preserved and automatically hidden. If you wanted to start over, you could delete the Model Copy layer, make the original Model layer visible again and selected, and open Select And Mask again.

If the mask isn't perfect, you can continue to edit it at any time. When a layer mask thumbnail is selected in the Layers panel, you can click the Select And Mask button in the Properties panel, click it in the options bar (if a selection tool is active), or choose Select > Select And Mask.

Note: If you had not selected Decontaminate Colors, it would have been possible to choose a Layer Mask output option that would have added a layer mask to the Model layer without copying it.

5 Save your work.

Creating a quick mask

To change the color of the glasses frames, you'll use a quick mask, because you won't need the mask after you're done with this one task and so that you can create the mask by painting. First, you'll clean up the Layers panel.

1 Hide the Magazine Background layer so you can concentrate on the model. Make sure the Model copy layer is selected.

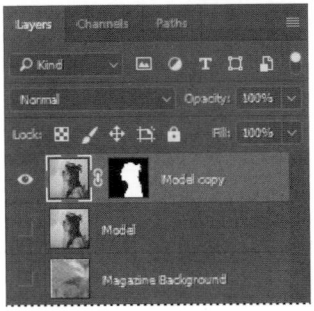

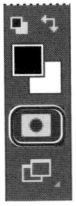

2 Click the Edit In Quick Mask Mode button near the bottom of the Tools panel. (Until now, you have been working in the default Standard mode.)

In Quick Mask mode, a red overlay appears as you make a selection, masking the area outside the selection the way a rubylith, or red acetate, was used to mask images in traditional print shops. (This idea is similar to the Overlay view mode you saw in Select And Mask.) You can apply changes only to the unprotected area that is visible and selected. Notice that the highlight color for the selected layer in the Layers panel is red, indicating you're in Quick Mask mode.

Note: If you are using a small display and the Tools panel is in single-column mode, the Quick Mask Mode button may be past the bottom of the screen. If the Tools panel is in two-column mode, the Quick Mask Mode button is at the bottom left corner of the panel.

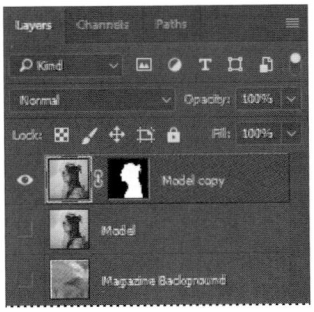

3 In the Tools panel, select the Brush tool (🖌).

4 In the options bar, make sure that the mode is Normal. Open the Brush pop-up panel, and select a small brush with a diameter of **13** px and a Hardness of **100**%. Click outside the panel to close it.

5 Paint the earpiece of the glasses frames. (Magnify the view if it helps you paint more precisely.) The area you paint will appear red, creating a mask.

6 Continue painting with the Brush tool to mask the earpiece of the frames and the frame around the lenses. Reduce the brush size to paint around the lenses. You can stop where the earpiece goes under the hair.

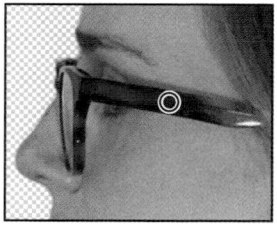

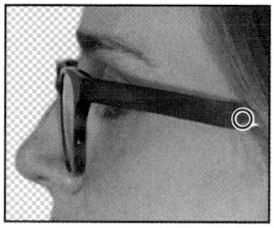

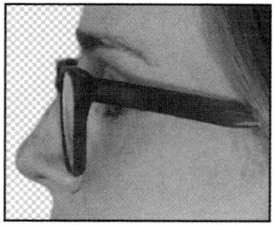

▶ **Tip:** Here, you're making a selection by painting the area you want to select. Compare this to Chapter 3, where you made selections using tools that create a selection marquee.

In Quick Mask mode, Photoshop treats the red overlay as a grayscale mask, where shades of gray correspond to degrees of mask transparency. When using a painting or editing tool in Quick Mask mode, keep these principles in mind:

- Painting with black adds to the mask (the red overlay), subtracting from the selected area.
- Painting with white erases the mask, adding to the selected area.
- Painting with gray or reduced opacity adds semitransparent areas to the mask, where darker shades are more transparent (more masked).

7 Click the Edit In Standard Mode button (), which is the same as the Enter Quick Mask Mode button.

Exiting Quick Mask mode converts the Quick Mask into a selection.

8 Choose Select > Inverse to select the area you originally masked.

9 Choose Image > Adjustments > Hue/Saturation. The selection is converted to a layer mask that restricts the Hue/Saturation adjustment to the unmasked area.

10 In the Hue/Saturation dialog box, change the Hue to **+70**. The new green color fills the glasses frame. Click OK.

▶ **Tip:** If you want to keep the selection for future use, save it as an alpha channel (Select > Save Selection); otherwise it will be lost as soon as the area is deselected.

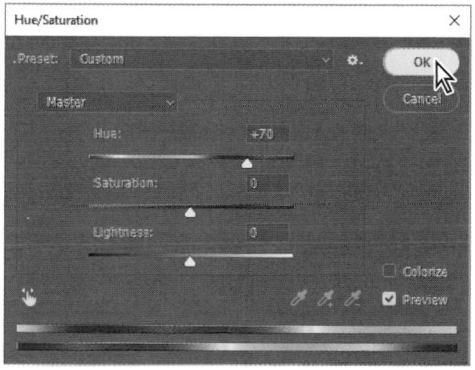

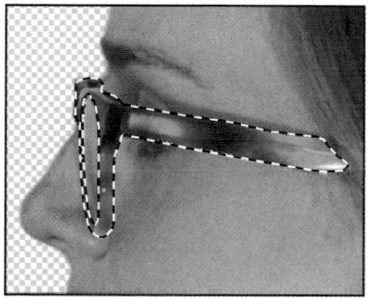

11 Choose Select > Deselect.

Manipulating an image with Puppet Warp

Note: Photoshop provides several different ways to warp a layer. You'll use Puppet Warp because it's the easiest way to pivot part of an image, such as tilting the head back in this example.

The Puppet Warp feature gives you flexibility in manipulating an image. You can reposition areas, such as hair or an arm, just as you might pull the strings on a puppet. Place pins wherever you want to control movement. You'll use Puppet Warp to tilt the model's head back so she appears to be looking up.

1 Zoom out so you can see the entire model.

2 With the Model Copy layer selected in the Layers panel, choose Edit > Puppet Warp.

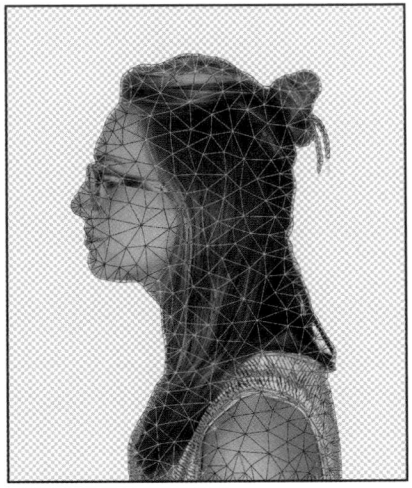

A mesh appears over the visible areas in the layer—in this case, the mesh appears over the model. You'll use the mesh to place pins where you want to control movement (or to ensure there is no movement).

3 Click to add pins around the body and along the base of the head, as shown below. Each time you click, Puppet Warp adds a pin. About 10 to 12 pins should work.

The pins you've added around the shirt will keep it in place as you tilt the head.

4 Select the pin at the nape of the neck. A blue dot appears in the center of the pin to indicate that it's selected.

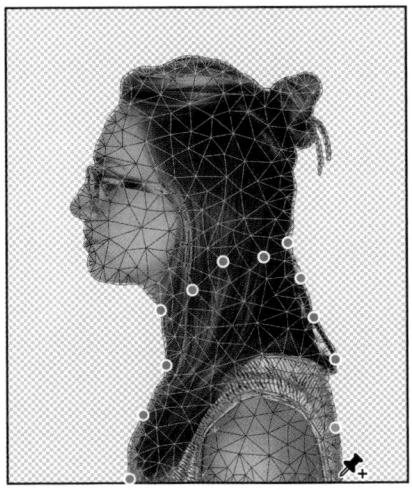

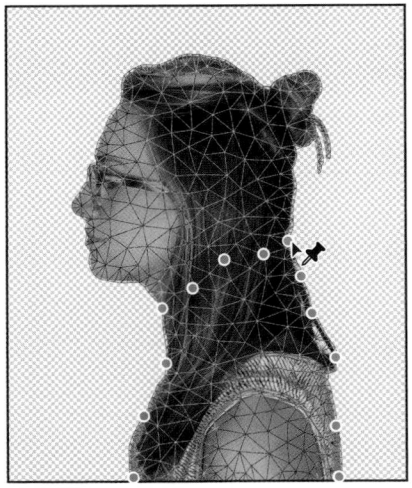

5 Press Alt (Windows) or Option (Mac). A larger circle appears around the pin, and a curved double arrow appears next to it. Continue pressing Alt or Option as you drag the pointer to rotate the head backwards. You can see the angle of rotation in the options bar; you can enter **170** there to rotate the head back.

6 When you're satisfied with the rotation, click the Commit Puppet Warp button (✓) in the options bar, or press Enter or Return.

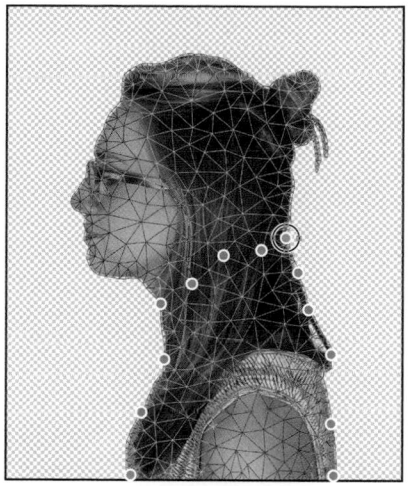

Note: Be careful not to Alt-click or Option-click the dot itself, or you'll delete the pin.

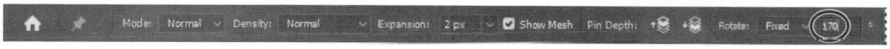

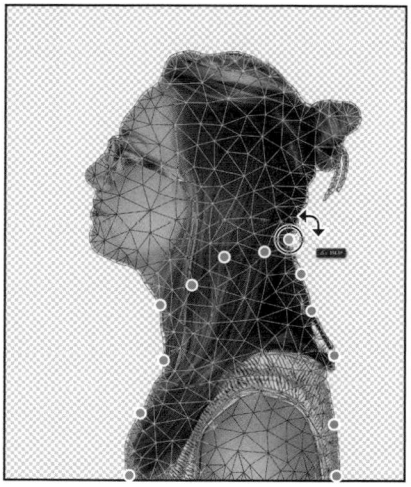

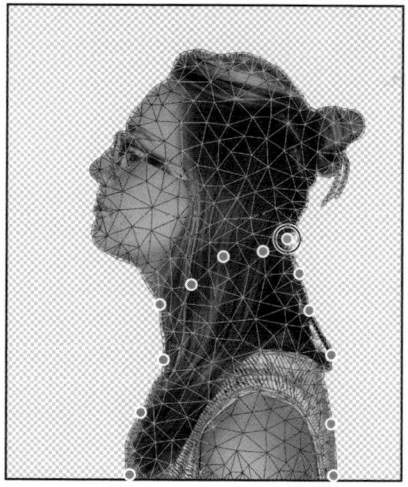

7 Save your work so far.

Using an alpha channel to create a shadow

Just as different information in an image is stored on different layers, channels also let you access specific kinds of information. Alpha channels store selections as grayscale images. Color information channels store information about each color in an image; for example, an RGB image automatically has red, green, blue, and composite channels.

To avoid confusing channels and layers, think of channels as containing an image's color and selection information, and think of layers as containing painting, shapes, text, and other content.

You'll first convert the transparent areas of the Model copy layer to a selection, and then fill it with black on another layer to create a shadow. Because the selection will be altered to make the shadow, you'll now save the current form of the selection as an alpha channel so that you can load it again later if needed.

1 In the Layers panel, Ctrl-click (Windows) or Command-click (Mac) the layer thumbnail icon for the Model Copy layer. The masked area is selected.

2 Choose Select > Save Selection. In the Save Selection dialog box, make sure New is chosen in the Channel menu. Then name the channel **Model Outline**, and click OK.

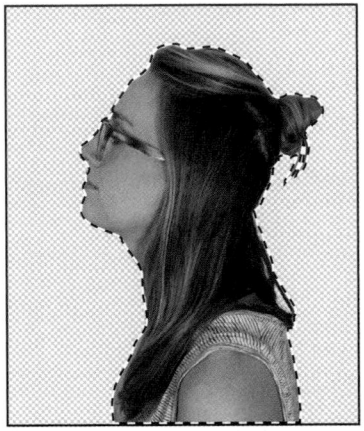

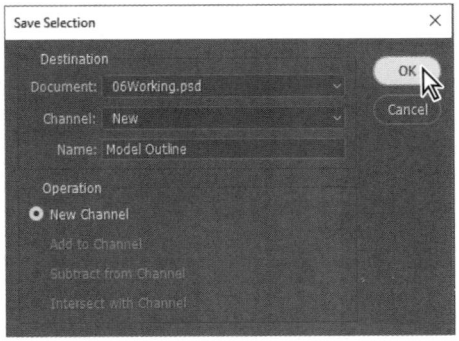

▶ **Tip:** Now that the original selection outline of the model is saved as an alpha channel, you can reuse that selection at any time, even from another Photoshop document, by choosing the Select > Load Selection command.

Nothing changes in the Layers panel or in the image window. However, a new channel named Model Outline has been added to the Channels panel. The selection is still active.

About alpha channels

As you work in Photoshop, you will eventually encounter alpha channels (saved selections). It's good to know a few things about them:

- An image can contain up to 56 channels, including all color and alpha channels.
- Alpha channels are 8-bit grayscale, storing 256 gray levels.
- You can specify a name, color, mask option, and opacity for each channel. (The opacity affects the preview of the channel, not the image.)
- All new channels have the same pixel dimensions as the containing document.
- You can edit an alpha channel mask using painting tools and filters.
- You can convert alpha channels to spot-color channels.
- The Select > Load Selection command lets you bring in an alpha channel from another document, as long as both documents have the same pixel dimensions.

3 Click the Create A New Layer icon (⊞) at the bottom of the Layers panel. Drag the new layer below the Model Copy layer so that the shadow will be below the image of the model. Double-click the new layer's name, and rename it **Shadow**.

4 With the Shadow layer selected, choose Select > Select And Mask. This loads the current selection into the Select And Mask task space.

5 Click the View menu in the View Mode section of the Properties panel, and choose On Black.

6 In Select And Mask, move the Shift Edge slider to **+36%**.

7 In the Output Settings section, make sure Selection is selected in the Output To menu, and then click OK.

Note: Some image file formats offer the option to save an alpha channel with the image document. If you use this option, Photoshop creates an alpha channel that includes all areas of the composite image that are not occupied by an opaque pixel.

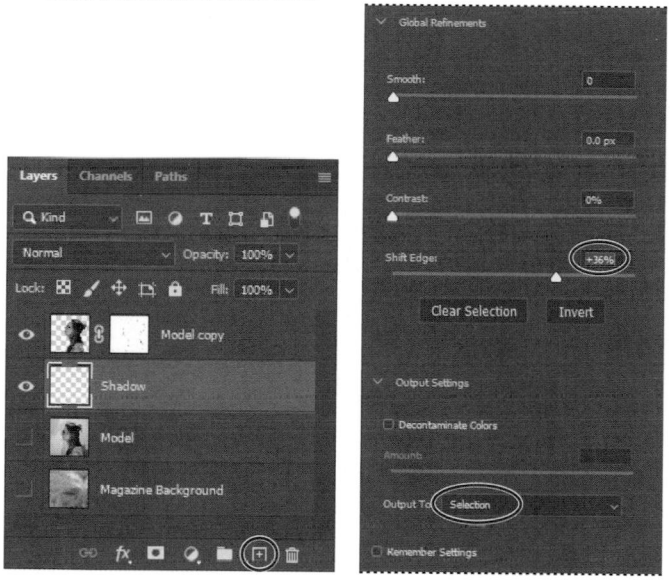

8 Choose Edit > Fill. In the Fill dialog box, choose Black from the Contents menu, and then click OK.

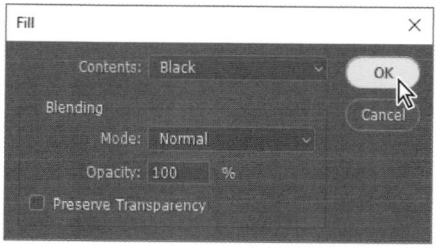

The Shadow layer displays a filled-in black outline of the model. Shadows aren't usually as dark as the person that casts them, so you'll reduce the layer opacity.

9 In the Layers panel, change the layer opacity to **30%**.

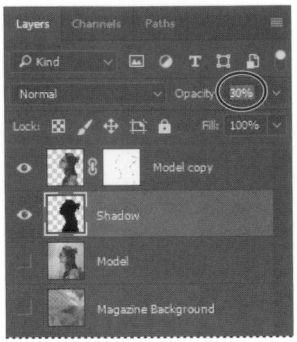

The shadow is in exactly the same position as the model, where it can't be seen. You'll shift it.

10 Choose Select > Deselect to remove the selection.

11 Choose Edit > Transform > Rotate. Rotate the shadow by hand, or enter **–15°** in the Rotate field in the options bar. Then drag the shadow to the left, or enter **545** in the X field in the options bar. Click the Commit Transform button (✓) in the options bar, or press Enter or Return, to accept the transformation.

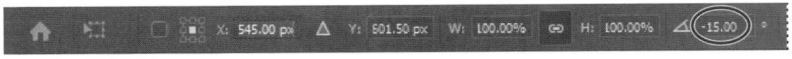

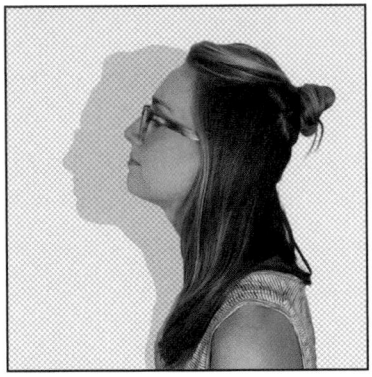

12 Click the eye icon for the Magazine Background layer to make it visible, and delete the Model layer (the one without the mask).

13 Choose File > Save to save your work so far.

Your magazine cover is ready to go!

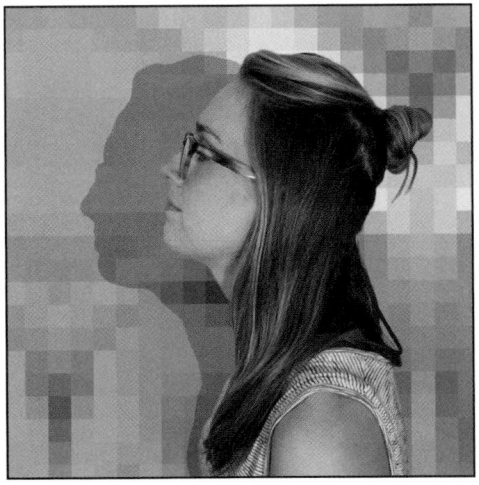

Review questions

1 What is the benefit of using a quick mask?

2 When you have a selection created by a quick mask, what happens when you deselect?

3 When you save a selection as an alpha channel, where is the alpha channel stored?

4 How can you edit a mask in a channel once you've saved it?

5 How do channels differ from layers?

Review answers

1 Quick masks are helpful for creating one-time selections. In addition, using a quick mask is an easy way to edit a selection using the painting tools.

2 As with any other selection, a quick mask selection disappears when you deselect it.

3 Alpha channels are stored in the Channels panel, along with the visible color channels.

4 You can paint in an alpha channel using black, white, and shades of gray.

5 Alpha channels are storage areas for saved selections. All layers set to be visible will be present in printed or exported output. But only the color channels are visible in printed or exported output; alpha channels are not. Layers contain information about image content, while alpha channels contain information about selections and masks.

7 TYPOGRAPHIC DESIGN

Lesson overview

In this lesson, you'll learn how to do the following:

- Use guides to position text in a composition.
- Make a clipping mask from type.
- Merge type with other layers.
- Preview fonts.
- Format text.
- Distribute text along a path.
- Control type and positioning using advanced features.

This lesson will take less than an hour to complete. To get the lesson files used in this chapter, download them from the web page for this book at www.adobepress.com/PhotoshopCIB2021. For more information, see "Accessing the lesson files and Web Edition" in the Getting Started section at the beginning of this book.

As you work on this lesson, you'll preserve the start files. If you need to restore the start files, download them from your Account page.

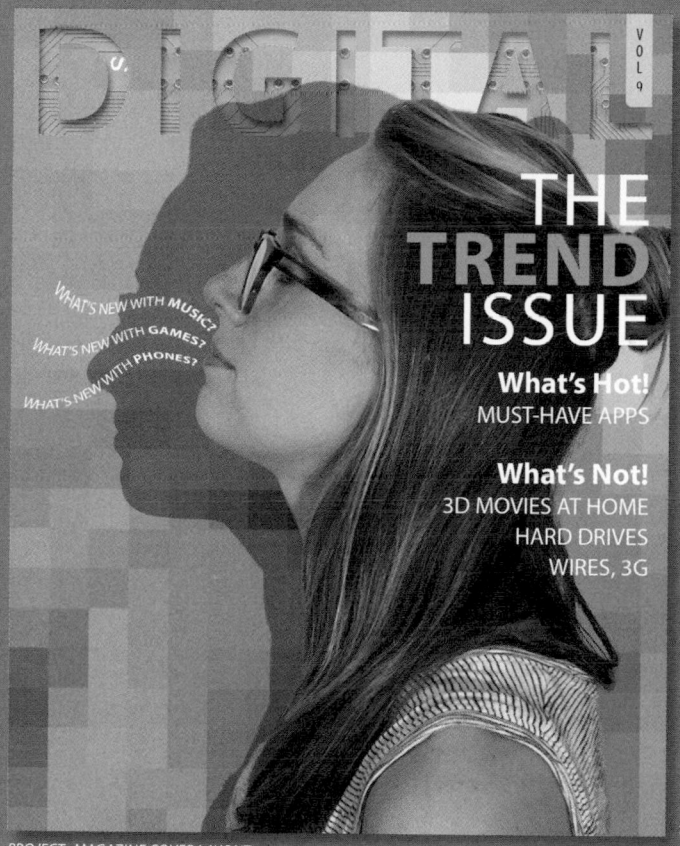

Photography © Andrew Faulkner

PROJECT: MAGAZINE COVER LAYOUT

Photoshop provides powerful, flexible text tools so you can add type to your images with great control and creativity.

About type

A Photoshop type layer consists of vector-based shapes that describe the letters, numbers, and symbols of a typeface. Many typefaces are available in more than one format. The TrueType format is widely used, and the OpenType format is preferred by professionals (see "OpenType in Photoshop" on page 185, later in this lesson). Type 1 or PostScript fonts are older font formats that are less commonly used today.

Photoshop preserves the vector-based character outlines, so type renders at the full resolution of the Photoshop document as you edit, scale, or resize type layers. However, the pixel dimensions of the document limit how sharp type can be. As you magnify a document, jagged type edges appear sooner in a document with smaller pixel dimensions, such as in low-resolution graphics designed for websites.

Getting started

Note: Though this lesson starts where Lesson 6 left off, use the 07Start.psd file. We've included a path and a sticky note in the start file that won't be in the 06Working.psd file you saved.

In this lesson, you'll work on the layout for the cover of a technology magazine. You'll start with the artwork you created in Lesson 6: The cover has a model, her shadow, and the orange background. You'll add and stylize type for the cover, including warping the text.

You'll start the lesson by viewing an image of the final composition.

1 Start Photoshop, and then simultaneously hold down Ctrl+Alt+Shift (Windows) or Command+Option+Shift (Mac) to restore the default preferences. (See "Restoring default preferences" on page 5.)

Note: If Bridge is not installed, you'll be prompted to download and install it. See page 3 for more information.

2 When prompted, click Yes to delete the Adobe Photoshop Settings file.

3 Choose File > Browse In Bridge to open Adobe Bridge.

4 In the Favorites panel on the left side of Bridge, click the Lessons folder, and then double-click the Lesson07 folder in the Content panel.

5 Select the 07End.psd file. Increase the thumbnail size to see the image clearly by dragging the thumbnail slider to the right.

You'll apply the type treatment in Photoshop to finish the magazine cover. All of the type controls you need are available in Photoshop, so you don't have to switch to another application to complete the project.

Note: If Photoshop displays a dialog box telling you about the difference between saving to Cloud Documents and Your Computer, click Save On Your Computer. You can also select Don't Show Again, but that setting will deselect after you reset Photoshop preferences.

6 Double-click the 07Start.psd file to open it in Photoshop.

7 Choose File > Save As, rename the file **07Working.psd**, and click Save.

8 Click OK in the Photoshop Format Options dialog box.

9 Choose Graphic and Web from the Workspace Switcher in the options bar.

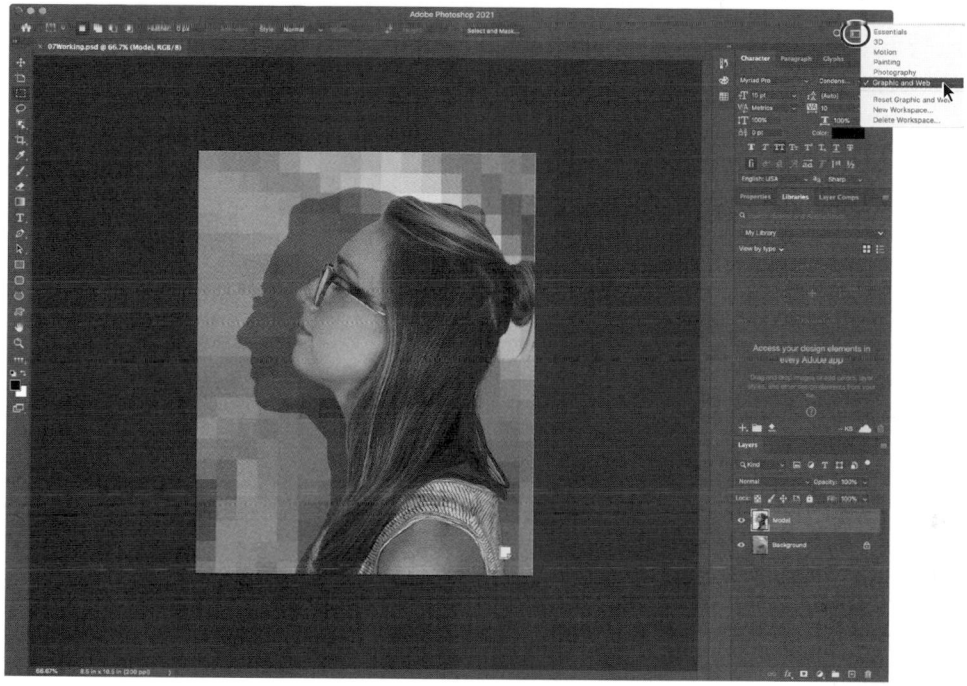

The Graphic and Web workspace displays the Character and Paragraph panels that you'll use in this lesson, along with the Glyphs and Layers panels.

Creating a clipping mask from type

A *clipping mask* is an object or a group of objects whose shape masks other artwork so that only areas within the clipping mask are visible. In effect, you are clipping the artwork to conform to the shape of the object (or mask). In Photoshop, you can create a clipping mask from shapes or letters. In this exercise, you'll use letters as a clipping mask to allow an image in another layer to show through.

Adding guides to position type

The 07Working.psd file includes a background layer, which will be the foundation for your typography. You'll start by zooming in on the work area and using ruler guides to help position the type.

▶ **Tip:** The View > Actual Size command makes the Photoshop ruler match a real world ruler. Actual Size works best with print documents, not documents measured in pixels.

1 Choose View > Fit On Screen to see the whole cover clearly.

2 Choose View > Rulers to display rulers along the left and top borders of the image window.

3 If the rulers aren't displaying in inches, right-click (Windows) or Control-click (macOS) the rulers, and choose Inches.

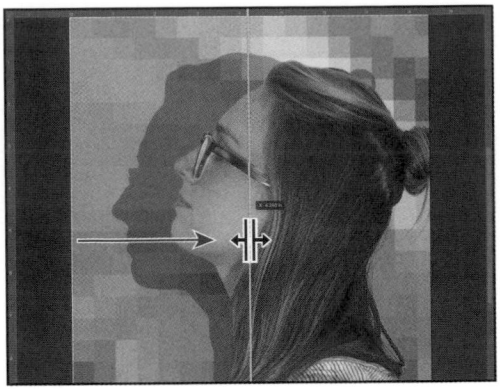

▶ **Tip:** If you find it difficult to position the vertical ruler guide exactly at 4.25", holding down Shift will snap the guide to the 4.25" ruler tick mark.

4 Drag a vertical guide from the left ruler to the center of the cover (4.25").

Adding point type

Now you're ready to add type to the composition. You can create horizontal or vertical type anywhere in an image. You can enter *point type* (a single letter, word, or line) or *paragraph type*. You will do both in this lesson. First, you'll create point type.

1 In the Layers panel, select the Background layer.

2 Select the Horizontal Type tool (**T**), and, in the options bar, do the following:

- Choose a serif typeface, such as Minion Pro Regular, from the Font Family pop-up menu.
- Type **144 pt** for the Size, and press Enter or Return.
- Click the Center Text button.

3 In the Character panel, change the Tracking value to **100**.

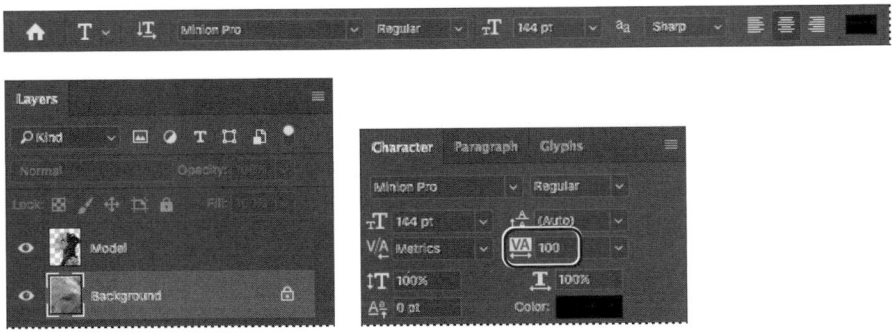

The Tracking value specifies the overall space between letters, which affects the density in a line of text.

4 Position the pointer over the center guide you added to set an insertion point, roughly where the guide crosses the edge of the model's forehead, click, and then type **DIGITAL** in all capital letters. Then click the Commit Any Current Edits button (✓) in the options bar.

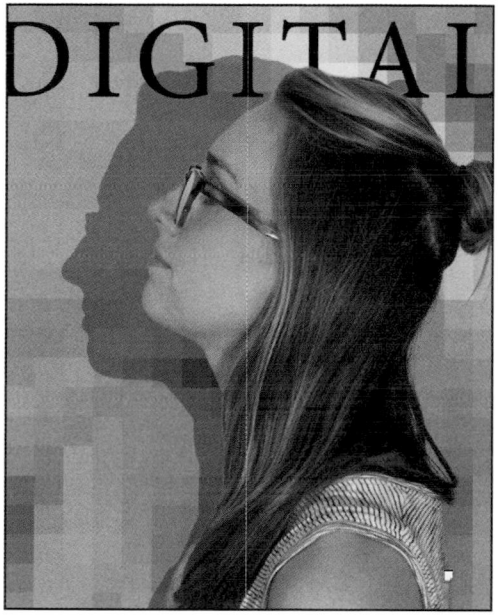

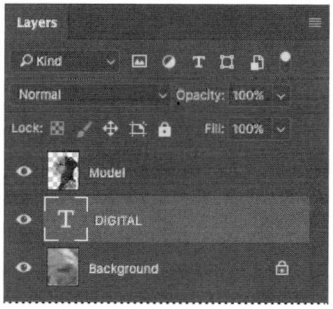

Note: After you type, you must commit your editing in the layer by clicking the Commit Any Current Edits button, switching to another tool or layer, or clicking away from the text layer. You cannot commit to current edits by pressing Enter or Return; doing so merely creates a new line of type.

The word "DIGITAL" is added to the cover, and it appears in the Layers panel as a new type layer named DIGITAL. You can edit and manage the type layer as you would any other layer. You can add or change the text, change the orientation of the type, apply anti-aliasing, apply layer styles and transformations, and create masks. You can move, restack, and copy a type layer, or edit its layer options, just as you would for any other layer.

The text is big enough, but not modern enough, for this magazine's style. You'll apply a different font.

5 Double-click the "DIGITAL" text to edit it.

6 Open the Font Family pop-up menu in the options bar. Move the cursor over the fonts, either with the mouse or using arrow keys.

When the cursor is over a font name, Photoshop temporarily applies that font to the selected text so you can preview the font in context.

Tip: When a type layer is selected in the Layers panel, the Properties panel displays type settings—another place you can change type options such as the font.

Note: If a lesson in this book uses a font that isn't installed on your system, you may be able to install it from Adobe Fonts as part of your Creative Cloud subscription: In Photoshop, choose Type > More from Adobe Fonts. (Some educational or organizational Creative Cloud plans might not include Adobe Fonts.)

7 Select Myriad Pro Semibold or a similar font, and then click the Commit Any Current Edits button (✓) in the options bar.

That's much more appropriate.

8 Select the Move tool, and drag the "DIGITAL" text to move it to the top of the cover, if it's not there already.

9 Choose File > Save to save your work so far.

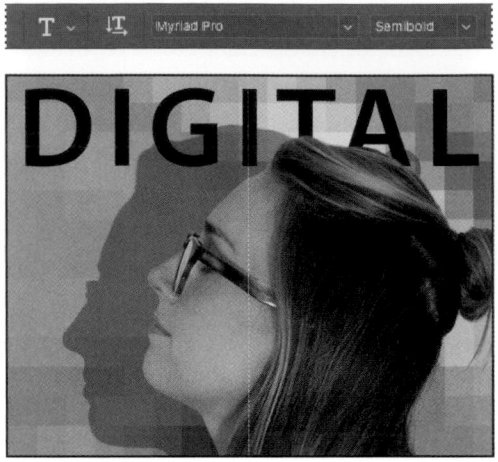

Making a clipping mask and applying a shadow

You added the letters in black, the default text color. However, you want the letters to appear to be filled with an image of a circuit board, so you'll use the letters to make a clipping mask that will allow another image layer to show through.

1 Choose File > Open, and open the circuit_board.tif file, which is in the Lesson07 folder.

2 Choose Window > Arrange > 2-Up Vertical. The circuit_board.tif and 07Working.psd files appear onscreen together. Click the circuit_board.tif file to ensure that it's the active window.

3 With the Move tool selected, hold down the Shift key as you drag the Background layer from the Layers panel in the circuit_board.tif file onto the center of the 07Working.psd file.

Pressing Shift as you drag centers the circuit_board.tif image in the composition.

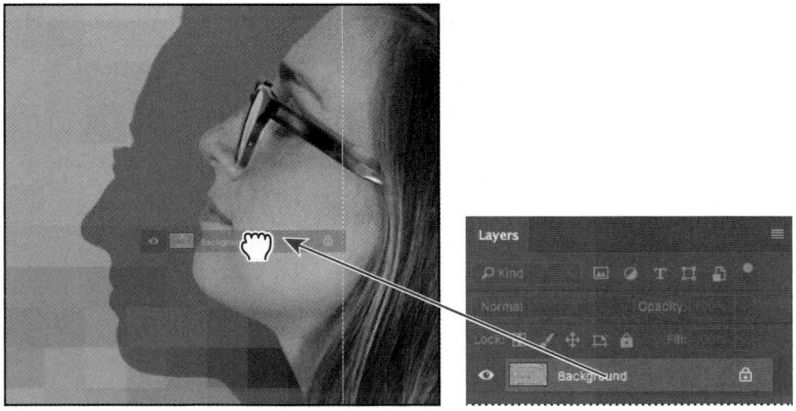

A new layer—Layer 1—appears in the Layers panel for the 07Working.psd file. This new layer contains the image of the circuit board, which will show through the type. But before you make the clipping mask, you'll resize the circuit board image, as it's currently too large for the composition.

4 Close the circuit_board.tif file without saving any changes to it.

5 In the 07Working.psd file, select Layer 1, and then choose Edit > Transform > Scale.

6 Hold down Alt (Windows) or Option (Mac) as you drag a corner handle on the bounding box for the circuit board, and resize it to approximately the same width as the area of text.

Pressing Alt or Option keeps it centered.

7 Reposition the circuit board so that the image covers the text, and commit the transformation by clicking away from the circuit board layer.

Note: If you click away from a layer and its bounding box doesn't deselect, move the pointer away from the bounding box until the rotation pointer becomes an arrow, and then click in the document window.

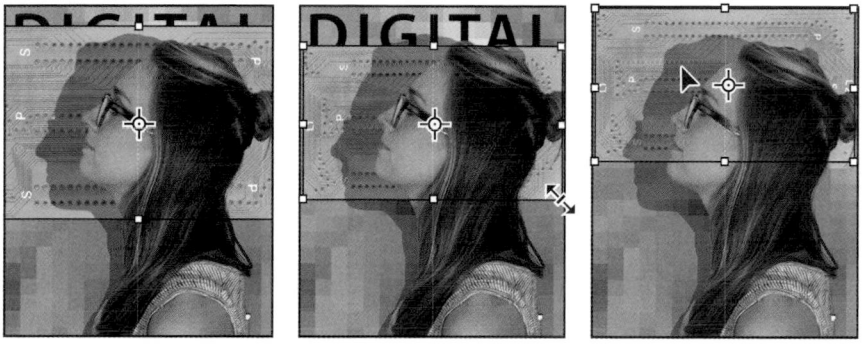

8 Double-click the Layer 1 name, and change it to **Circuit Board**. Then press Enter or Return, or click away from the name in the Layers panel, to apply the change.

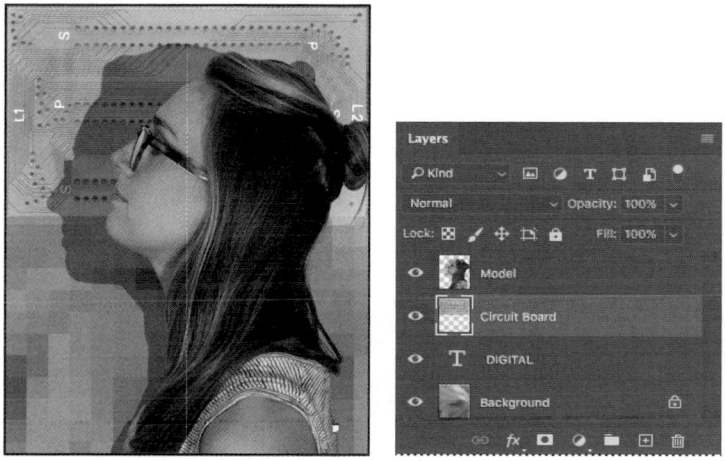

▶ **Tip:** You can also create a clipping mask by holding down the Alt (Windows) or Option (Mac) key and clicking between the Circuit Board and DIGITAL type layers. Or, choose Layer > Create Clipping Mask when the Circuit Board layer is selected.

9 Select the Circuit Board layer, if it isn't already selected, and choose Create Clipping Mask from the Layers panel menu (≡).

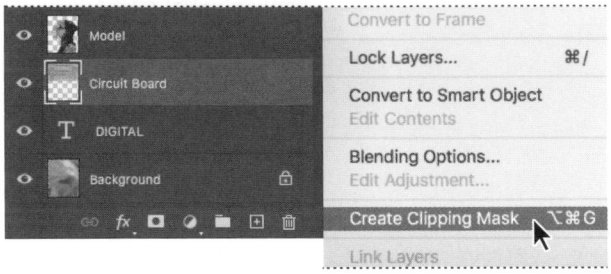

The circuit board now shows through the "DIGITAL" letters. A small arrow in the Circuit Board layer and the underlined type layer name indicate the clipping mask is applied. Next, you'll add an inner shadow to give the letters depth.

10 Select the DIGITAL layer to make it active. Then, click the Add A Layer Style button (*fx*) at the bottom of the Layers panel, and choose Inner Shadow from the pop-up menu.

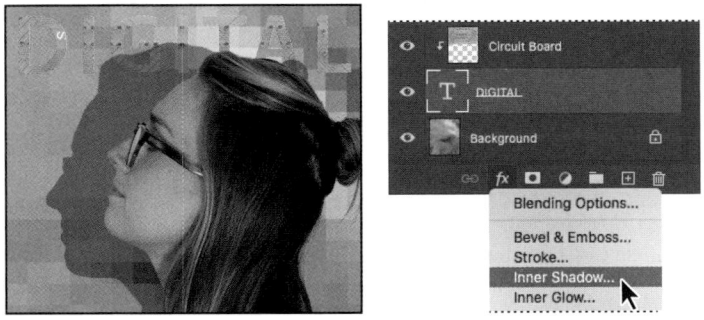

11 In the Layer Style dialog box, make sure the Blend Mode is set to Multiply, Opacity is set to **48**%, Distance to **18**, Choke to **0**, and Size to **16**. If the Preview option is enabled, you can see how changing the options affects the layer. Then click OK.

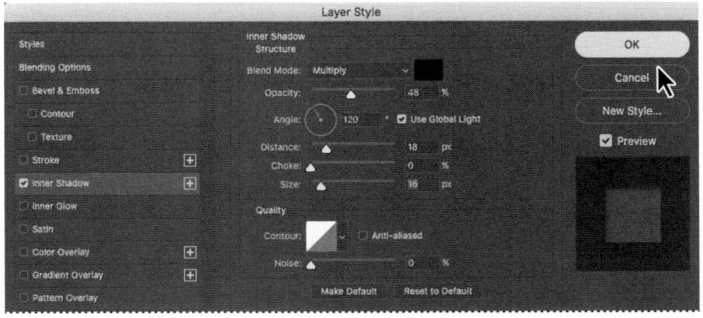

The Inner Shadow option adds a sense of dimension to the magazine title text.

12 Choose File > Save to save your work so far.

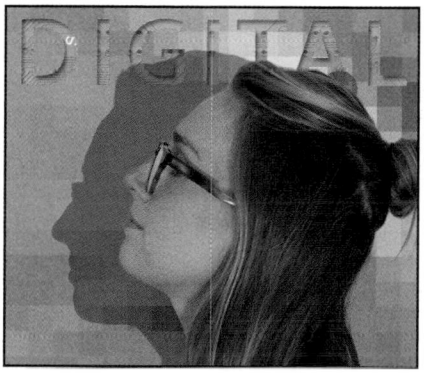

Paragraph and Character Styles

If you frequently work with type in Photoshop or if you need to consistently format a significant amount of type in an image, then paragraph and character styles can help you work more efficiently. A paragraph style is a collection of type attributes that you can apply to an entire paragraph with a single click. A character style is a collection of attributes that you can apply to individual characters. You can work with these styles by opening their panels: Choose Window > Paragraph Styles And Window > Character Styles.

The concept of type styles in Photoshop is similar to that in page layout applications such as Adobe InDesign and word-processing applications such as Microsoft Word. However, styles behave a little differently in Photoshop. For the best results working with type styles in Photoshop, keep the following in mind:

- By default, all text you create in Photoshop has the Basic Paragraph style applied. The Basic Paragraph style is defined by your text defaults, but you can change its attributes.
- Deselect all layers before you create a new style.
- If the selected text has been changed from the current paragraph style (usually the Basic Paragraph style), those changes (considered overrides) persist even when you apply a new style. To ensure that all the attributes of a paragraph style are applied to text, apply the style, and then click the Clear Override button in the Paragraph Styles panel.
- You can use the same paragraph and character styles across multiple files. To save the current styles as defaults for all new documents, choose Type > Save Default Type Styles. To use your default styles in an existing document, choose Type > Load Default Type Styles.

Creating type on a path

In Photoshop, you can create type that follows along a path that you create with a pen or shape tool. The direction the type flows depends on the order in which anchor points were added to the path. When you use the Horizontal Type tool to add text to a path, the letters are perpendicular to the baseline of the path. If you change the location or shape of the path, the type moves with it.

You'll create type on a path to make it look as if questions are coming from the model's mouth. We've already created the path for you; we stored it in the Paths panel.

1 In the Layers panel, select the Model layer.

2 Choose Window > Paths to show the Paths panel.

3 In the Paths panel, select Speech Path to make it active and visible.

The path appears to be coming out of the model's mouth.

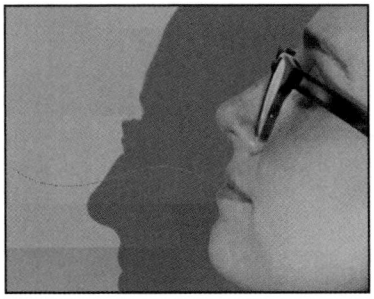

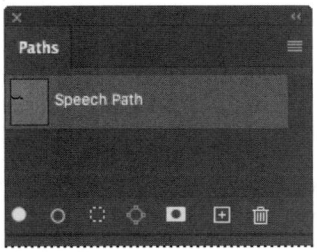

4 Select the Horizontal Type tool.

5 In the options bar, click the Right Align Text button.

Julieanne Kost is an official Adobe Photoshop evangelist.

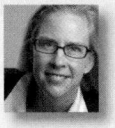

Tool tips from the Photoshop evangelist

Type tool tricks

- Shift-click in the image window with the Horizontal Type tool to create a new type layer—in case you're close to another block of type and Photoshop tries to select text on the existing type layer.
- Double-click the thumbnail icon of any type layer in the Layers panel to select all of the type on that layer.
- With any text selected, right-click (Windows) or Control-click (Mac) on the text to access the context menu. Choose Check Spelling to run a spell-check.

6 In the Character panel, select the following settings:

- Font Family: Myriad Pro Regular
- Font Style: Regular
- Font Size (TT): **14** pt
- Tracking (VA): **–10**
- Color: White
- All Caps (TT)

7 Move the Type tool over the path. When a small slanted line appears across the I-bar, click the end of the path closest to the model's mouth, and type **What's new with games?**.

Note: The path won't print or export because it isn't a shape layer—it exists only in the Paths panel. But the text on the path is a type layer, so the type will print and export.

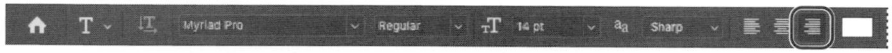

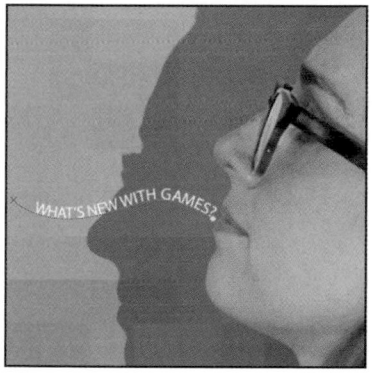

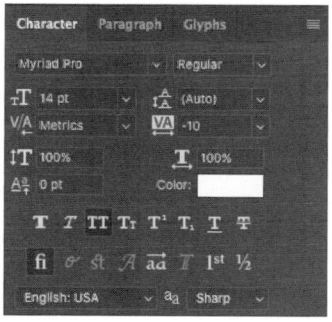

As you type on the path, the text is added from the right because Right Align Text was selected in step 5.

8 Select the word "GAMES?" and change its font style to Bold. Click the Commit Any Current Edits button (✓) in the options bar.

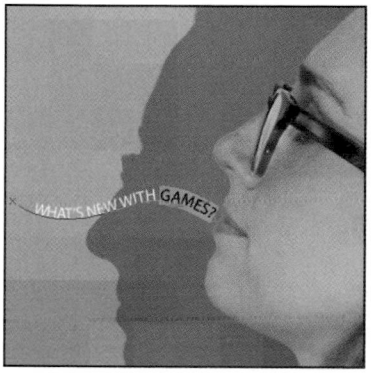

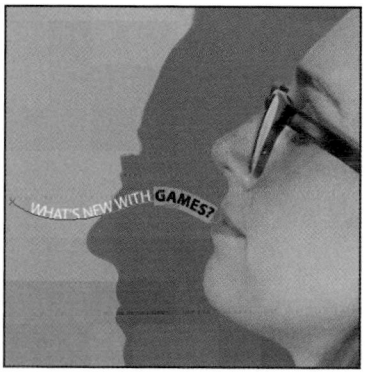

Note: When you position a type tool over a character that has alternate glyphs available, a grid may appear, containing alternates you can click to select from (see the sidebar on page 189). If the alternate glyphs get in your way, disable Enable Type Layer Glyph Alternates in the Type panel of the Preferences dialog box.

9 In the Layers panel, select the What's new with games? layer, and then choose Duplicate Layer from the Layers panel menu. Name the new layer **What's new with music?**, and click OK.

You can't see the duplicate text layer yet, because it's exactly on top of the original text layer.

10 With the Type tool, select "GAMES," and replace it with **music**. Click the Commit Any Current Edits button in the options bar.

Now that the two type layers have different text, it's easier to see that they're exactly on top of each other. You'll move one away from the other.

11 Choose Edit > Free Transform Path. Rotate the path approximately 15 degrees, and then shift the path up above the first path and a little to the right, as in the figure below. Click the Commit Transform button in the options bar.

Note: If you can't remember how to rotate using a transform bounding box, position the pointer just outside the transform bounding box until the pointer changes to a rotate icon (an arc with two arrows), and drag.

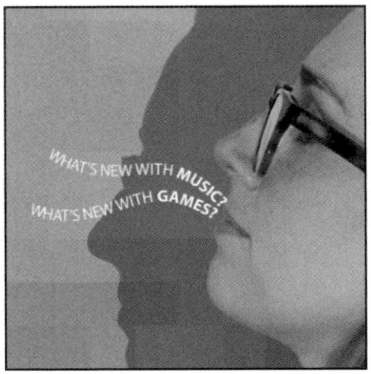

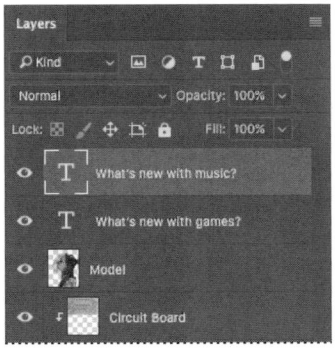

12 Repeat steps 9–11, replacing the word "GAMES" with **phones**. Rotate the left side of the path approximately –15 degrees, and move it below the original path.

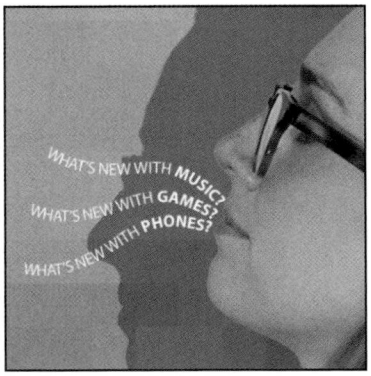

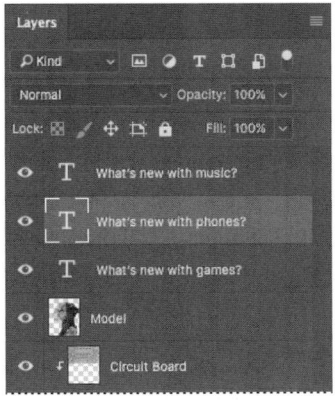

13 Choose File > Save to save your work so far.

Warping point type

The text on a curvy path is more interesting than straight lines would be, but you'll warp the text to make it more playful. *Warping* lets you distort type to conform to a variety of shapes, such as an arc or a wave. The warp style you select is an attribute of the type layer—you can change a layer's warp style at any time to change the overall shape of the warp. Warping options give you precise control over the orientation and perspective of the warp effect.

1 If necessary, zoom or scroll to move the visible area of the image window so that the sentences to the left of the model are in the center of the screen.

2 Right-click (Windows) or Control-click (Mac) the What's new with games? layer in the Layers panel, and choose Warp Text from the context menu.

Note: If you don't see the Warp Text command on the context menu, right-click/Control-click the layer or layer name, not the layer thumbnail.

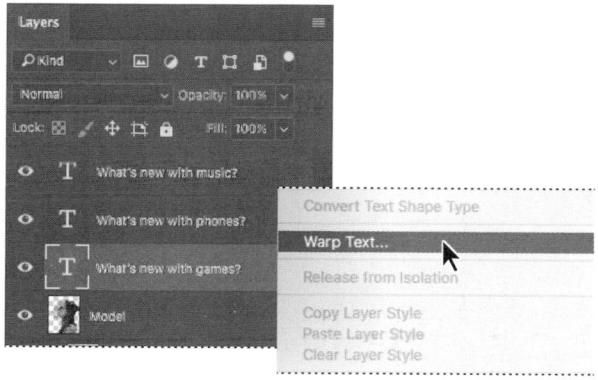

3 In the Warp Text dialog box, choose Wave from the Style menu, and select the Horizontal option. Specify the following values: Bend, +33%; Horizontal Distortion, −23%; and Vertical Distortion, +5%. Then click OK.

The Bend slider specifies how much warp is applied. Horizontal Distortion and Vertical Distortion determine the perspective of the warp.

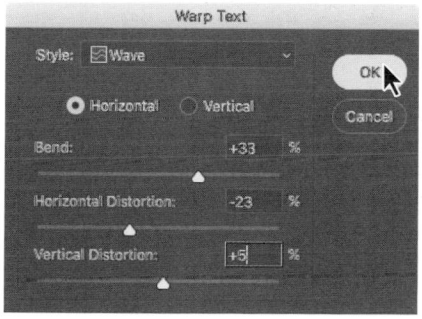

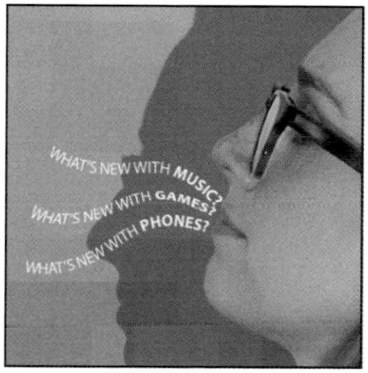

The words "What's new with games?" appear to float like a wave on the cover.

4 Repeat steps 2 and 3 to warp the other two text layers you typed on a path.

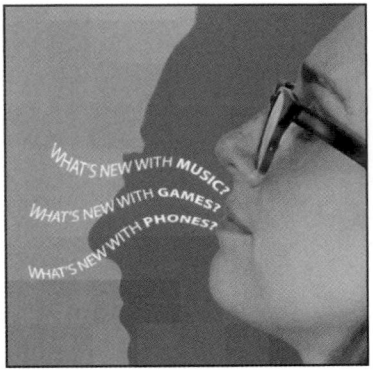

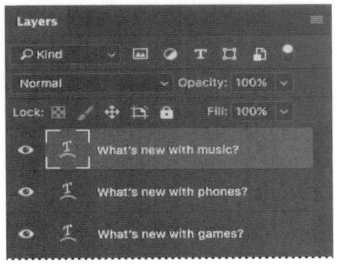

5 Save your work.

Designing paragraphs of type

All of the text you've written on this cover so far has been a few discrete words or lines—point type. However, many designs call for full paragraphs of text. You can design complete paragraphs of type in Photoshop; you can even apply paragraph styles. You don't have to switch to a dedicated page layout program for sophisticated paragraph type controls.

Using guides for positioning

You will add paragraphs to the cover in Photoshop. First, you'll add some guides to the work area to help you position the paragraphs.

1 If necessary, zoom or scroll so that you can see the entire top half of the document.

2 Drag a guide from the left vertical ruler, placing it approximately ¼" from the right side of the cover.

3 Drag a guide down from the top horizontal ruler, placing it approximately 2" from the top of the cover.

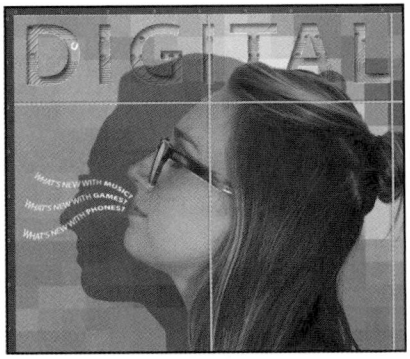

Adding paragraph type from a sticky note

You're ready to add the text. In a real world design environment, the text might be provided to you in a word-processing document or the body of an email message, which you could copy and paste into Photoshop. Or you might have to type it in. Another easy way to add a bit of text is for the copywriter to attach it to the image file in a sticky note, as we've done for you here.

1 Select the Move tool, and then double-click the yellow sticky note in the lower-right corner of the image window to open it in the Notes panel. Expand the Notes panel, if necessary, to see all the text.

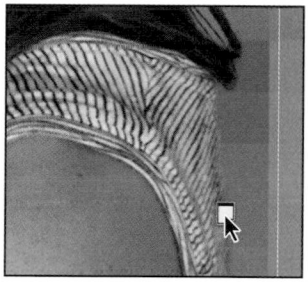

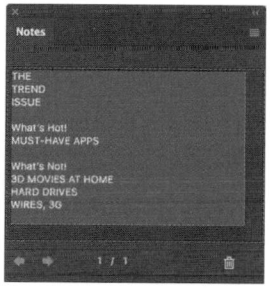

2 In the Notes panel, select all the text. Press Ctrl+C (Windows) or Command+C (Mac) to copy the text to the clipboard. Close the Notes panel.

3 Select the Model layer. Then, select the Horizontal Type tool (**T**).

4 Press Shift as you click where the guidelines intersect at about ¼" from the right edge and 2" from the top of the cover. Continue to hold the Shift key as you start to drag a text box down and to the left. Then release the Shift key, and continue dragging until the box is about 4 inches wide by 8 inches high, with the top and right edges aligned with the guides you just added.

5 Press Ctrl+V (Windows) or Command+V (Mac) to paste the text. The new text layer is at the top of the Layers panel, so the text appears in front of the model.

6 Select the first three lines ("The Trend Issue"), and then apply the following settings in the Character panel:

- Font Family: Myriad Pro (or another sans serif font)
- Font Style: Regular
- Font Size (T): **70** pt
- Leading (A/A): **55** pt
- Tracking (VA): **50**
- Color: White

7 With the text still selected, click the Right Align Text button in the options bar or Paragraph panel.

▶ **Tip:** In step 4, the reason you press Shift is to make sure you create a new type layer. If you don't press Shift, the Horizontal Type tool might instead select text in the nearby text layer containing the "DIGITAL" headline.

● **Note:** If the text isn't visible, make sure the new type layer is above the Model layer in the Layers panel.

▶ **Tip:** If you paste text and it includes unwanted formatting, you can instead choose the Edit > Paste Without Formatting command in Photoshop to remove all formatting from the pasted text.

● **Note:** *Leading* (pronounced "ledding") determines the vertical space between lines.

8 Select just the word "Trend," and change the Font Style to Bold.

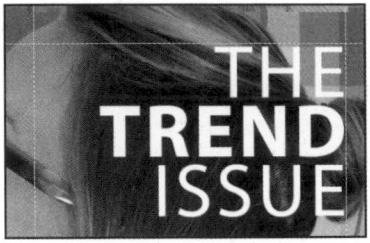

You've formatted the title. Now you'll format the rest of the text.

9 Select the rest of the text you pasted. In the Character panel, select the following:

- Font Family: Myriad Pro
- Font Style: Regular
- Font Size: **22** pt
- Leading: **28** pt
- Tracking: **0**
- Deselect All Caps (TT)

The text looks good, but it's all the same. You'll make the headlines stand out more.

10 Select the "What's Hot!" text, change the following in the Character panel, and then press Enter or Return:

- Font Style: Bold
- Font Size: **28** pt

11 Repeat step 10 for the "What's Not!" subhead.

12 Select the word "TREND." Then, in the Character panel, change the text color to green.

13 Click the Commit Any Current Edits button in the options bar.

14 Save your changes.

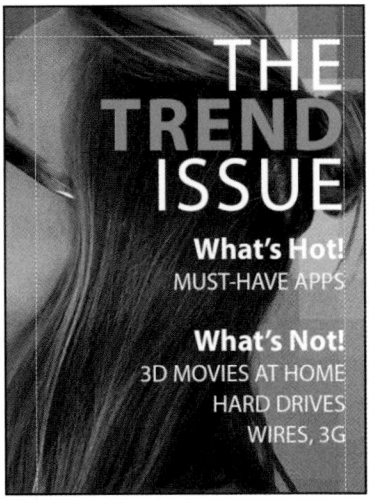

OpenType in Photoshop

OpenType is a cross-platform font file format developed jointly by Adobe and Microsoft. The format uses a single font file for both Mac and Windows, so you can move files from one platform to another without font substitution or reflowed text. OpenType offers expanded character sets and layout features, such as swashes and discretionary ligatures, that aren't available in traditional PostScript and TrueType fonts. This, in turn, provides richer linguistic support and advanced typography control. You can identify OpenType fonts in the Photoshop font menu because they appear with an OpenType icon (*O*). Here are some highlights of OpenType.

The OpenType menu. The Character panel menu includes an OpenType submenu that displays all available features for a selected OpenType font, including ligatures, alternates, and fractions. Dimmed features are unavailable for that typeface; check marks appear next to features that have been applied.

Discretionary ligatures. To add a discretionary ligature to two OpenType letters, such as to "th" in the Bickham Script Standard typeface, select them in the file, and choose OpenType > Discretionary Ligatures from the Character panel menu.

Swashes. Adding swashes or alternate characters works the same way as discretionary ligatures: Select the letter, such as a capital "T" in Bickham Script, and choose OpenType > Swash to change the ordinary capital into an ornate (swash) "T."

True fractions. To create true fractions, type the fraction's characters—for example, 1/2. Then, select the characters, and from the Character panel menu, choose OpenType > Fractions. Photoshop applies the true fraction (½).

Color fonts. While you can apply a color to a font in Photoshop, a format called OpenType-SVG allows multiple colors and gradients to be part of the font design itself. For example, a color font may provide the letter A in solid blue as well as solid red and in a blue-to-green gradient.

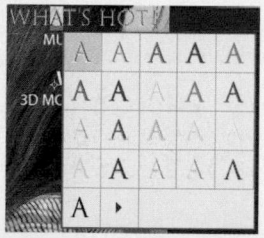

Emoji fonts. Another example of OpenType-SVG fonts are emoji fonts, made possible because OpenType-SVG allows vector graphics to be used as font characters. The Photoshop font family menu indicates color and emoji fonts with an OpenType SVG icon (SVG).

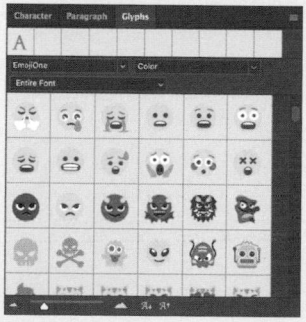

Variable fonts. When you want a certain font weight but Regular is too thin and Bold is too thick, you can use a variable font that lets you customize attributes such as weight, width, and slant in the Properties panel. The Photoshop font family menu indicates variable fonts with an OpenType VAR icon (VAR).

Note that some OpenType fonts have more options than others.

▶ **Tip:** Want to know if a character has OpenType alternates? Just select it. If a thick underline appears under a selected character, moving the pointer over that character reveals the alternate glyphs available for that character in the font applied to it. You can select from those glyphs just as you can in the Glyphs panel, or you can click a triangle to open the Glyphs panel.

Adding a rounded rectangle

You're almost done with the text for the magazine cover. All that remains is to add the volume number in the upper-right corner. First, you'll create a rectangle with rounded corners to serve as a background for the volume number.

1 Select the Rounded Rectangle tool (▢) in the Tools panel.

2 Draw a rectangle in the space above the letter "L" in the upper-right corner of the cover, placing its right edge along the guide. It should be about 0.34 in wide, according to the Properties panel.

3 Click the fill color swatch in the Properties panel, expand the Pastel presets group, and select the Pastel Yellow Orange swatch (the third one). Make sure the stroke is set to No Color.

By default, all the corners in the rectangle have the same radius, but you can adjust the radius for each corner separately. You can even return to edit the corners later if you want. You'll change the rectangle so that only the lower-left corner is rounded, changing the others to right angles.

4 At the bottom of the Properties panel, type **0** px in any of the corner radius values and press Enter or Return.

Because the Link Together Corner Radius Values icon (⛓) is selected (darker than the panel background), the corner radius is set to 0 on all four corners.

5 Click to deselect the Link Together Corner Radius Values icon, change the bottom-left corner to **16 px**, and press Enter or Return.

6 With the Move tool, drag the rectangle to the top of the image so it hangs down like a ribbon and its right edge is along the ruler guide.

7 Select Show Transform Controls in the options bar. Drag the bottom of the rectangle down so that it's near the letter "L." (If you're not sure how long to make it, refer to the 07End.psd file.) Then press Enter or Return.

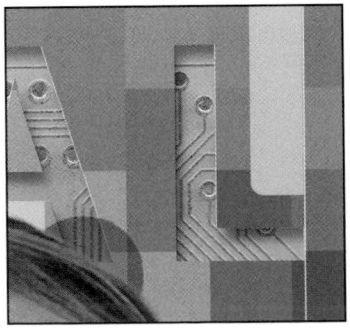

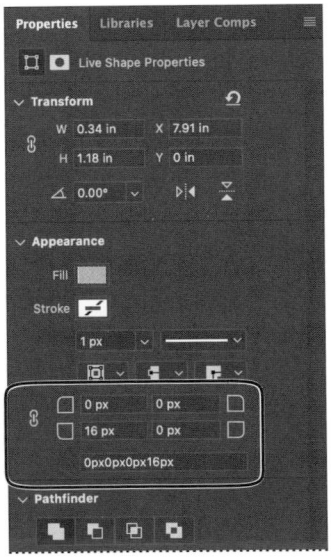

▶ **Tip:** You can also adjust the radius of shape corners by dragging the target icon near each corner. For the small rectangle in this lesson, you may have to zoom in to see the target icons. To adjust only one radius, Ctrl-drag (Windows) or Command-drag (Mac) a target icon.

● **Note:** The Properties panel has two link icons for a selected rectangle. The link icon near the top maintains the proportions of the object, and the link icon near the bottom changes all corner radius values when you edit any one of them.

Adding vertical text

You're ready to add the volume number on top of the ribbon.

1 Choose Select > Deselect Layers. Then select the Vertical Type tool (↓T), which is hidden under the Horizontal Type tool.

2 Press the Shift key, and click near the bottom of the rectangle you just created.

Pressing the Shift key as you click ensures that you create a new text box instead of selecting the title.

3 Type **VOL 9**.

The letters are too large to view. You'll need to change their size to see them.

4 Choose Select > All, and then, in the Character panel, select the following:

- Font Family: a sans-serif typeface, such as Myriad Pro
- Font Style: a light or narrow style, such as Condensed
- Font size: **15** pt
- Tracking: **10**
- Color: Black

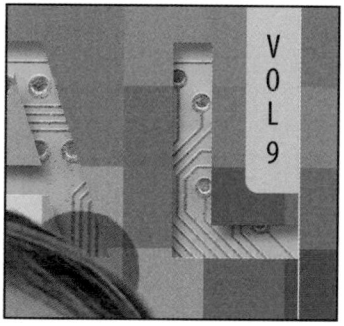

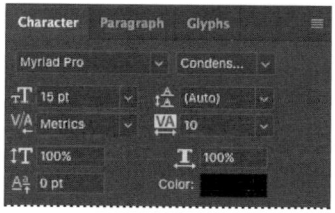

5 Click the Commit Any Current Edits button (✓) in the options bar. Your vertical text now appears as the layer named VOL 9. Use the Move tool (✥) to center it in the ribbon, if necessary.

Saving as Photoshop PDF

The type you've added consists of vector-based outlines, which remain crisp and clear as you zoom in or resize them. However, if you save the file as a JPEG or TIFF image, Photoshop rasterizes the type, so you lose that flexibility. When you save a Photoshop PDF file, vector type is preserved.

You can preserve other Photoshop editing capabilities in a Photoshop PDF file too. For example, you can retain layers, color information, and even notes.

To ensure you can edit the document later, select Preserve Photoshop Editing Capabilities in the Save Adobe PDF dialog box. This will result in a larger PDF file.

To preserve any notes in the file and convert them to Acrobat comments when you save to PDF, select Notes in the Save area of the Save As dialog box.

You can open a Photoshop PDF file in Acrobat or Photoshop, place it in another application, or print it. For more information about saving as Photoshop PDF, see Photoshop Help.

▶ **Tip:** Want a design to have a familiar look, but not with the exact font that look is known for? Try **Font Similarity**. Choose a font in the Font Family menu in either the Type tool options bar or the Character panel. You'll see options at the top of the font list; click the Show Similar Fonts button.

The font list will now show the 20 most similar fonts available either on your system or from Adobe Fonts.

Now, you'll clean up a bit.

6 With the Move tool, click the note to select it. Then right-click (Windows) or Control-click (Mac), and choose Delete Note from the context menu; click Yes to confirm that you want to delete the note.

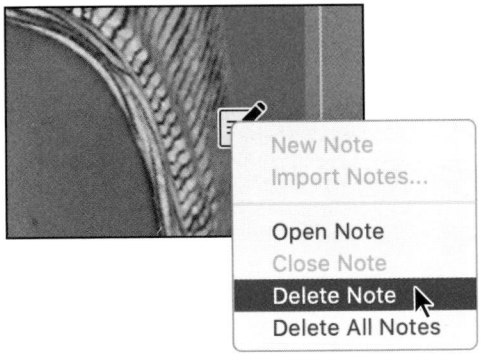

7 Hide the guides: Choose the Hand tool (✋), and then press Ctrl+; (Windows) or Command+; (Mac). Then zoom out to get a nice look at your work.

8 Choose File > Save to save your work.

Congratulations! You've added and stylized all of the type on the Digital magazine cover. Now that the magazine cover is ready to go, you'll flatten it and prepare it for printing.

The Glyphs panel

The Glyphs panel lists all characters available for a font, including specialized characters and alternate versions such as swashes. Above the font name and style menus is a row of recently used glyphs. It's blank if you haven't used any glyphs yet. A menu under the font name lets you display a writing system such as Arabic, or a category of characters such as punctuation or currency symbols. A black dot in the bottom-right corner of a character's box indicates that alternates are available for that character; click and hold the mouse on the character to view its alternate glyphs or to choose one to enter into a text layer.

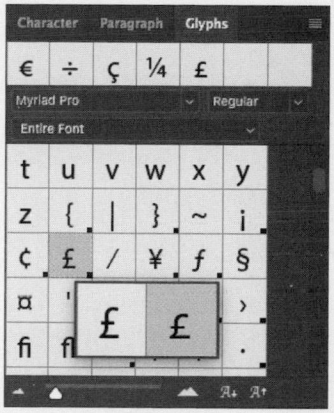

▶ **Tip:** Use the Glyphs panel (Window > Glyphs) to access the full range of alternate characters in OpenType fonts. When editing text, double-click a character in the Glyphs panel to add it to the text.

9 Choose File > Save As, rename the file **07Working_flattened**, and click Save. Click OK if you see the Photoshop Format Options dialog box.

Keeping a layered version lets you return to the 07Working.psd file in the future to edit it.

10 Choose Layer > Flatten Image.

11 Choose File > Save, and then close the document window.

▶ **Tip:** The Photoshop and TIFF file formats specify fixed pixel dimensions, which may limit the smoothness of text layers and vector shapes in a Photoshop document destined for high-resolution output, such as in an InDesign document intended for a printing press. Consult with your output service provider about the best format to use, such as non-flattened Photoshop PDF.

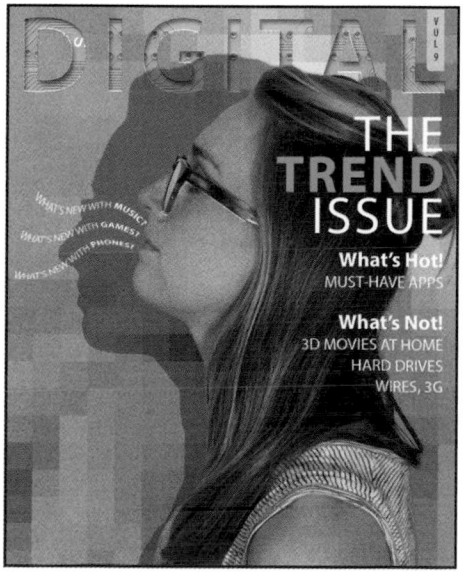

Extra credit

Using Match Fonts to keep your projects consistent

We want to identify a font that was used in an earlier issue, for text that says "Premiere Issue" (see the file MatchFont.psd in the Lesson07 folder). We'd like to use that font for other text inside the magazine. But the only available file is flattened, so the original type layer is lost. Because no type layer is available, it's impossible to select the text to find out which font was used. Fortunately, you don't have to guess which font is in the image because, in Photoshop, you can let the Match Font feature figure it out for you. Thanks to the magic of intelligent imaging analysis, using just a picture of a Latin font, Photoshop can use machine learning to detect which font it is. Match Font then shows you a list of similar fonts. Match Font is also useful for identifying fonts in photos, such as in the text on a sign in a street scene.

1 Open MatchFont.psd in the Lesson07 folder.

2 Select the area containing the mystery font. Keep the selection close to the text.

3 Choose Type > Match Font. Photoshop displays a list of fonts similar to the font in the image, including active fonts on your system and Adobe Fonts.

4 To list only the fonts on your computer, deselect Show Fonts Available To Activate From Adobe Fonts.

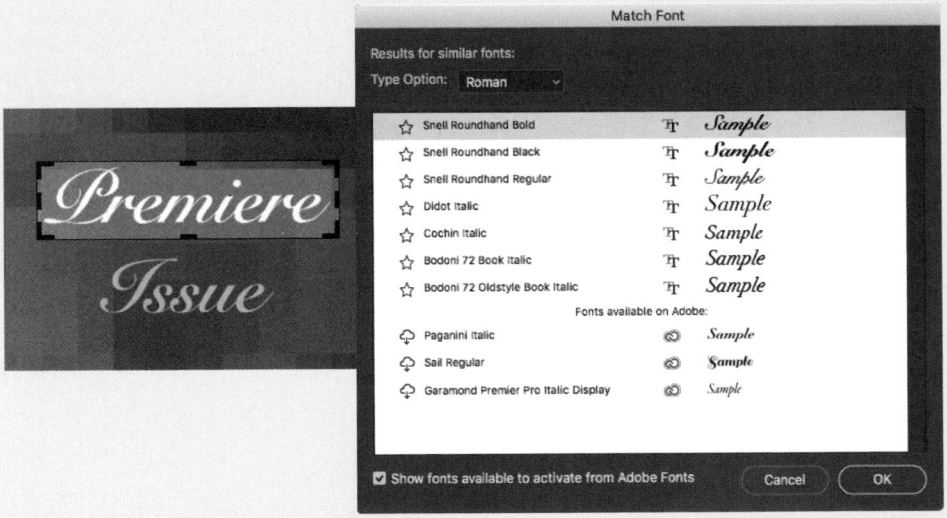

5 Select a script font that most closely resembles the font in the image from the list of fonts that Match Font determined to be similar. Your Match Font results may look different than ours.

6 Click OK. Photoshop selects the font you clicked, so you can now create new text with it.

Review questions

1 How does Photoshop treat type?

2 How is a text layer the same as or different from other layers in Photoshop?

3 What is a clipping mask, and how do you make one from type?

Review answers

1 Type in Photoshop consists of vector-based shapes that describe the letters, numbers, and symbols of a typeface. When you add type to an image in Photoshop, the characters appear on a text layer at the same resolution as the image file. As long as the type layer exists, Photoshop preserves the type outlines so that the text remains sharp when you scale or resize type, save a Photoshop PDF file, or print the image to a high-resolution printer.

2 Type that is added to an image appears in the Layers panel as a text layer that can be edited and managed in the same way as any other kind of layer. You can add to and edit the text, change the orientation of the type, and apply anti-aliasing as well as move, restack, copy, and change the options for layers.

3 A clipping mask is an object or group whose shape masks other artwork so that only areas that lie within the shape are visible. To use a text layer as a clipping mask, make sure the layer you want to reveal is directly above the text layer, select the layer you want to show through the letters, and apply the Create Clipping Mask command from the Layers panel menu (or from the Layer menu or from the layer's context menu).

8 VECTOR DRAWING TECHNIQUES

Lesson overview

In this lesson, you'll learn how to do the following:

- Differentiate between bitmap and vector graphics.
- Draw straight and curved paths using the Pen tool.
- Save paths.
- Draw and edit shape layers.
- Draw custom shapes.
- Use Smart Guides.

This lesson will take about 90 minutes to complete. Please log in to your account on peachpit.com to download the lesson files for this chapter, or go to the Getting Started section at the beginning of this book and follow the instructions under "Accessing the lesson files and Web Edition."

As you work on this lesson, you'll preserve the start files. If you need to restore the start files, download them from your Account page.

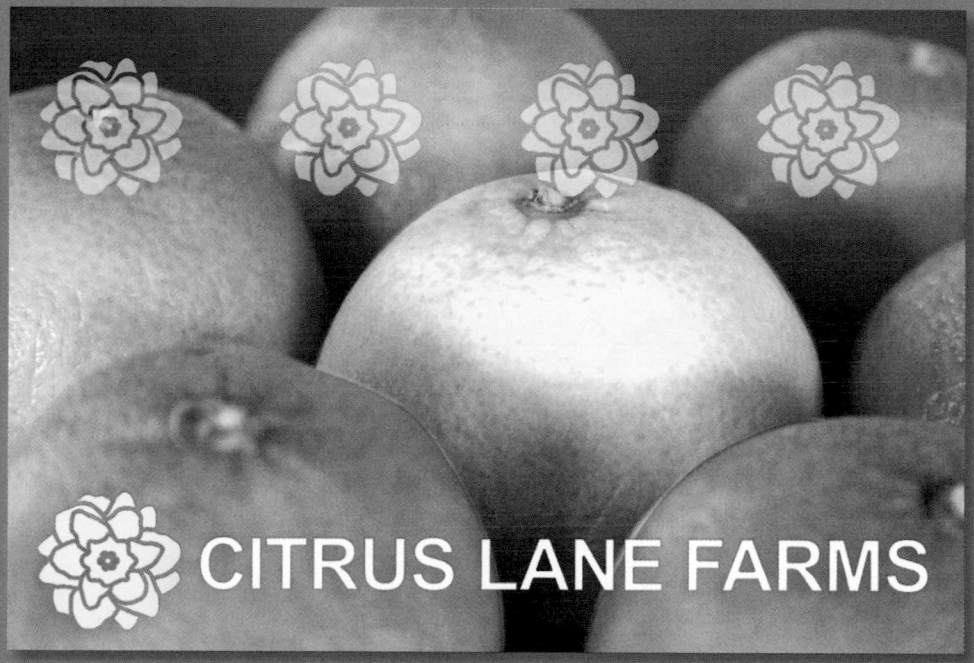

PROJECT: PROMOTIONAL POSTCARD

Unlike bitmap images, vector graphics retain their crisp edges when you enlarge them to any size. You can draw vector shapes and paths in your Photoshop images and add vector masks to control what is shown in an image.

About bitmap images and vector graphics

Before working with vector shapes and vector paths, it's important to understand the basic differences between the two main categories of computer graphics: *bitmap images* and *vector graphics*. You can use Photoshop to work with either kind of graphic; in fact, you can combine both bitmap and vector data in an individual Photoshop image file.

Bitmap images, technically called *raster images*, are based on a grid of dots known as *pixels*. Each pixel is assigned a specific location and color value. In working with bitmap images, you edit groups of pixels rather than objects or shapes. Because bitmap graphics can represent subtle gradations of shade and color, they are appropriate for continuous-tone images such as photographs or artwork created in painting programs. A disadvantage of bitmap graphics is that they contain a fixed number of pixels. As a result, they can lose detail and appear jagged when scaled up onscreen or printed at a lower resolution than they were created for.

Vector graphics are made up of lines and curves defined by mathematical objects called *vectors*. These graphics retain their crispness whether they are moved, resized, or have their color changed. Vector graphics are appropriate for illustrations, type, and graphics such as logos that may be scaled to different sizes.

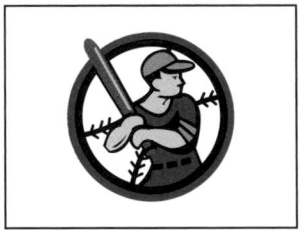

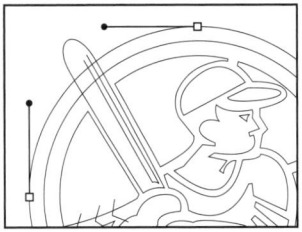

Logo drawn as vector art

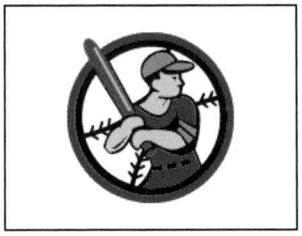

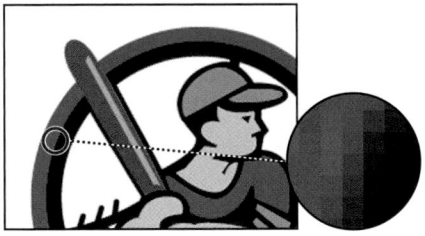

Logo rasterized as bitmap art

About paths and the Pen tool

In Photoshop, the outline of a vector shape is called a *path*. A path is a curved or straight line segment you draw using the Pen tool, the Freeform Pen tool, the Curvature Pen tool, or a shape tool. The Pen tool draws paths with the greatest precision; shape tools draw rectangles, ellipses, and other shape paths; the Freeform Pen tool draws paths as if you were drawing with a pencil on paper.

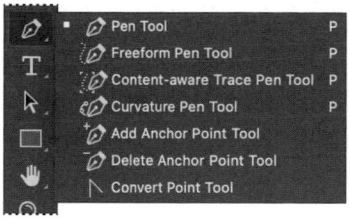

Julieanne Kost is an official Adobe Photoshop evangelist.

Tool tips from the Photoshop evangelist

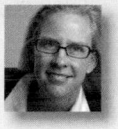

Accessing tools quickly

Each tool in the Tools panel has a single-letter keyboard shortcut. Type the letter, get the tool. Press Shift with the shortcut key to cycle through any nested tools in a group. For example, press P to select the Pen tool, and press Shift+P to toggle between the Pen and Freeform Pen tools.

Paths can be open or closed. An open path (such as a wavy line) has two distinct endpoints. A closed path (such as a circle) is continuous. The type of path you draw affects how it can be selected and adjusted.

Paths that have no fill or stroke do not print when you print your artwork. This is because paths are vector objects that contain no pixels, unlike the bitmap shapes drawn by the Pencil tool and other painting tools. If you want a path to have a fill or stroke, create it as a *shape*. A shape is a layer based on vector objects instead of pixels. Unlike a path, you can apply colors and effects to a shape layer.

Getting started

In this lesson, you'll create a postcard that will help promote a citrus fruit farm. You've been given an image of oranges, but because the farm wants to convey the idea that they grow more than just oranges, it's been decided that one of the oranges will be recolored to look like a lemon. Recoloring one item requires isolating it by creating a mask of its outline, and a quick way to create a clean outline of that item is using the Pen tool to draw a vector path.

Before you begin, view the image you'll be creating.

1 Start Photoshop, and then simultaneously hold down Ctrl+Alt+Shift (Windows) or Command+Option+Shift (Mac) to restore the default preferences. (See "Restoring default preferences" on page 5.)

2 When prompted, click Yes to delete the Adobe Photoshop Settings file.

3 Choose File > Browse In Bridge.

4 In the Favorites panel, click the Lessons folder, and then double-click the Lesson08 folder in the Content panel.

5 Select the 08End.psd file, and press the spacebar to see it in full-screen view.

To create this postcard, you'll trace an image and use that tracing to make a vector mask that lets you change the color of one of the oranges. First, you'll practice making paths and selections using the Pen tool.

6 When you've finished looking at the 08End.psd file, press the spacebar again. Then double-click the 08Practice_Start.psd file to open it in Photoshop.

7 Choose File > Save As, rename the file **08Practice_Working.psd**, and click Save. If the Photoshop Format Options dialog box appears, click OK.

Note: If Bridge isn't installed, the File > Browse In Bridge command in Photoshop will start the Creative Cloud desktop app, which will download and install Bridge. After installation completes, you can start Bridge. For more information, see page 3.

Note: If Photoshop displays a dialog box telling you about the difference between saving to Cloud Documents and Your Computer, click Save On Your Computer. You can also select Don't Show Again, but that setting will deselect after you reset Photoshop preferences.

Drawing a shape with the Pen tool

The Pen tool is one of the most commonly used tools for creating vector graphics on a personal computer. You find the Pen tool in many applications, including Adobe Illustrator (which first featured the Pen tool in 1987), Adobe Photoshop, and Adobe InDesign. Even video applications such as Adobe Premiere Pro and Adobe After Effects include the Pen tool because it provides such a high degree of control and precision when drawing many kind of lines, from shapes to masks to motion graphics paths. The Pen tool may not be easy to learn, but trust us: Knowing how to use the Pen tool is worth the effort and investment to master, partly because it's a marketable skill across many creative digital disciplines.

Tip: The Curvature Pen tool offers a potentially simpler way to draw precise vector paths; consider learning it if you find the Pen tool to be challenging to use. The Pen tool is taught in this chapter because it's a traditional and industry-standard tool for precisely drawing vector graphics.

The Pen tool works a little differently than a brush or pencil tool. We've created a practice file that you'll use to learn how to draw a straight path, a simple curve, and an S-curve with the Pen tool.

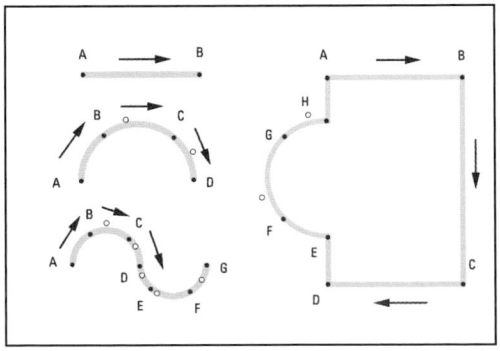

Creating paths with the Pen tool

You can use the Pen tool to create paths that are straight or curved, open or closed. If you're unfamiliar with the Pen tool, it can be confusing to use at first. Understanding the elements of a path and how to create those elements with the Pen tool makes paths much easier to draw.

To create a straight path, click the mouse button. The first time you click, you set the first *anchor point*. Each time that you click thereafter, a straight line is drawn between the previous anchor point and the current one. To draw complex straight-segment paths with the Pen tool, click each time you want to add a new segment.

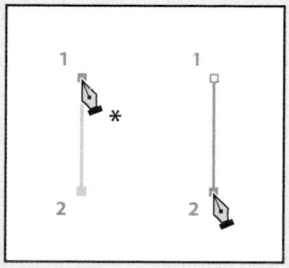

Creating a straight line

To create a curved path, click to place an anchor point, drag to create a direction line for that point, and then click to place the next anchor point. Each direction line ends in two direction points; the positions of direction lines and points determine the size and shape of the curved segment. Moving the direction lines and points reshapes the curves in a path.

Smooth curves are connected by anchor points called *smooth points*. Sharply curved paths are connected by *corner points*. When you move a direction line on a smooth point, the curved segments on both sides of the point adjust simultaneously, but when you move a direction line on a corner point, only the curve on the same side of the point as the direction line is adjusted.

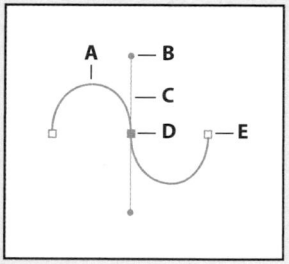

A. *Curved line segment*
B. *Direction point*
C. *Direction line*
D. *Selected anchor point*
E. *Unselected anchor point*

You can move path segments and anchor points, either individually or as a group. When a path contains multiple segments, you can drag individual anchor points to adjust individual segments of the path, or select all anchor points in a path to edit the entire path. Use the Direct Selection tool (⇖) to select and adjust an anchor point, a path segment, or an entire path.

Creating a closed path differs from creating an open path in the way that you end it. To end an open path, press Enter or Return. To create a closed path, position the Pen tool pointer over the starting point, and click. Closing a path automatically ends the path. After the path closes, the Pen tool pointer appears with a small *, indicating that your next click will start a new path.

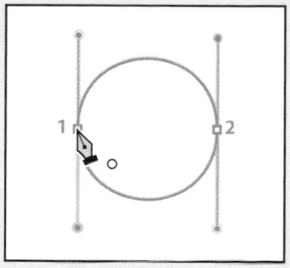

Creating a closed path

When you first draw a path, it appears in the Paths panel as a temporary object called Work Path. Save any work path you want to use again in the future, especially if you want to use multiple paths in the same document. To save a work path, double-click it in the Paths panel, type a name in the Save Path dialog box, and click OK. It's added as a new named path in the Paths panel and remains selected. If you don't save a work path, it's lost as soon as you deselect it and then start drawing again. (Saving the path isn't necessary when you draw a path as a shape, because a shape is created as a named layer.)

First, you'll configure the Pen tool options and the work area.

1 In the Tools panel, select the Pen tool (✎).

2 In the options bar, select or verify the following settings:

- Choose Shape from the Tool Mode pop-up menu.
- In the Path Options menu, make sure that Rubber Band is not selected.
- Make sure that Auto Add/Delete is selected.
- Choose No Color from the Fill pop-up menu.
- Choose a green color from the Stroke pop-up menu. We used the green swatch in the CMYK presets group.
- Enter **4 pt** for the stroke width.
- In the Stroke Options window, choose Center (the second option) from the Align menu.

▶ **Tip:** The Align stroke option controls whether the stroke width sits entirely to one side of a path or the other, or is centered over the path.

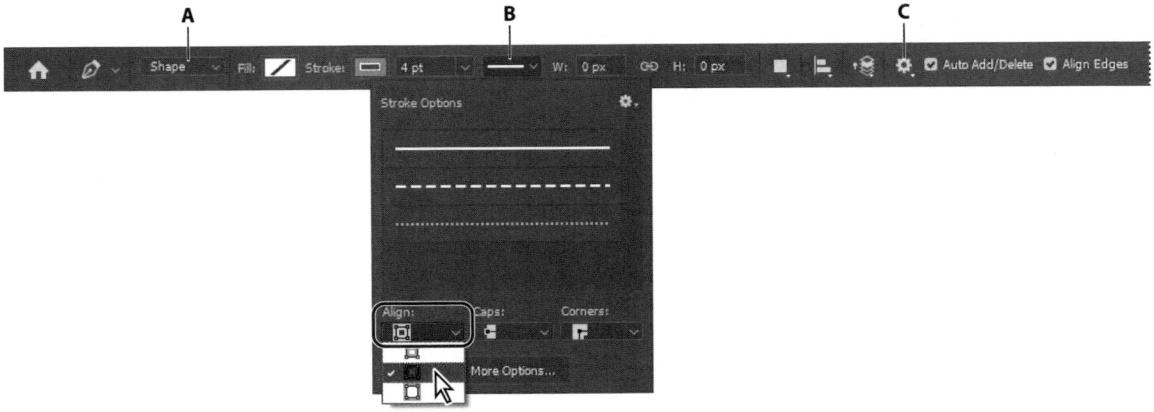

A. *Tool Mode menu* **B.** *Stroke Options menu* **C.** *Path Options menu*

Drawing a straight line

You'll start by drawing a straight line. Anchor points mark the ends of path segments; the straight line you'll draw is a single path segment with two anchor points.

1 Drag the Paths panel tab out of the Layers panel group so that you can see both it and the Layers panel at the same time. You can dock the Paths panel with another panel group.

The Paths panel displays thumbnail previews of the paths you draw. Currently, the panel is empty, because you haven't started drawing.

2 If necessary, zoom in so that you can easily see the lettered points and red circles on the shape template. Make sure you can see the whole template in the image window, and be sure to reselect the Pen tool after you zoom.

3 On the first shape, click point A, and release the mouse button. You've created an anchor point.

4 Click point B. You've created a straight line with two anchor points.

5 Press Enter or Return to stop drawing.

Note: If a tutorial pops up for the Curvature Pen tool, you don't need to read it at this time. It will probably close on its own, or you can close it.

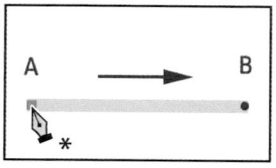

Create an anchor point.

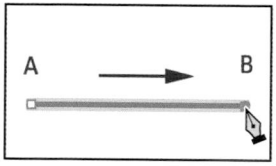

Click to create a straight line.

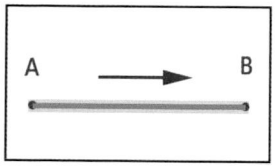

Complete the path.

The path you drew appears in the Paths panel, and as a new layer in the Layers panel.

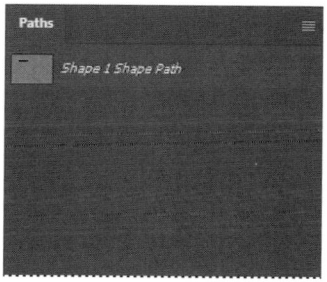

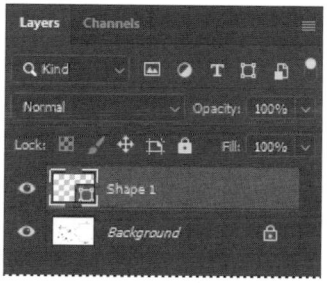

Note: The new path appears in both the Paths and Layers panels because the Tool Mode menu in the options bar is set to Shape, so drawing a new path also creates a new shape layer. If the Tool Mode menu was set to Path, the new path would be added to the Paths panel only.

Drawing curves

On curved segments, selecting an anchor point displays one or two direction lines, depending on the shapes of adjacent segments. You adjust the shape of a curved segment by dragging the direction point at the end of a direction line, and the direction line shapes the curve. You'll create curved lines, using smooth points.

1 Click A on the semicircle, and release the mouse to create the first anchor point.

2 Click point B, but don't release the mouse button. Instead, drag to the open red circle to the right of point B to create a curved path segment and a smooth anchor point. Then release the mouse button.

Tip: The red circles indicate where you should stop dragging an anchor point's direction point to form the desired shape of the curve. If you drag the direction point to a different location, the curve will have a different shape.

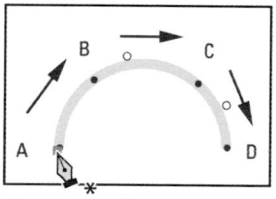

Create an anchor point.

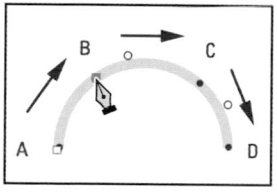

Click and hold.

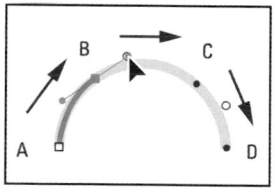

Drag to curve the path segment.

Smooth anchor points have two linked direction lines. When you move one, the curved segments on both sides of the path adjust simultaneously.

3 Position the pointer over point C, click and drag down to the open red circle below, and then release the mouse button. You've created a second curved path segment and another smooth point.

4 Click point D, and release the mouse to create the final anchor point. Press Enter or Return to complete the path.

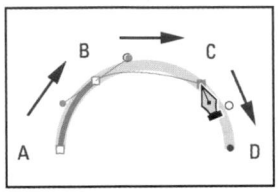

Click C to create a point.

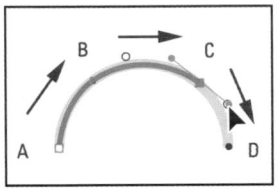

Drag to curve the segment.

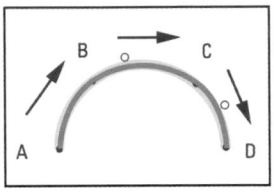

Click D to finish the semicircle.

▶ **Tip:** What's the advantage of drawing paths using points and handles, instead of drawing directly as with a real pen or pencil? For most people, it's difficult to draw curves and straight lines without bumps or other errors. Points and handles let you draw perfect curves and straight lines. If you prefer to draw normally, you can use the Freeform Pen tool.

When drawing a freehand path using the Pen tool, use as few points as possible to create the shape you want. The fewer points you use, the smoother the curves are—and the more efficient your file is.

Using the same techniques, you'll draw an S-shaped curve.

5 Click point A, and then click and drag from point B to its open red circle.

6 Continue with points C, D, E, and F, in each case clicking the point and then dragging to the corresponding open red circle.

7 Click point G to create the final anchor point, and then press Enter or Return to complete the path.

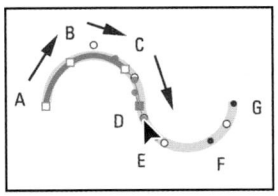

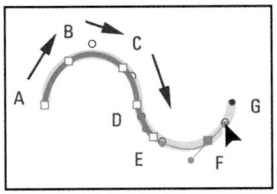

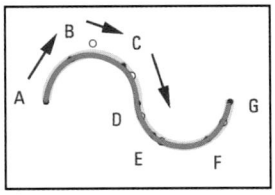

Each of the three shapes is on its own layer in the Layers panel. Only one path is in the Paths panel, because the Paths panel shows only the Shape Path for the layer that's currently selected in the Layers panel.

Notice that the curves you drew with the Pen tool are much smoother and easier to precisely control than if you had drawn them freehand.

Drawing a more complex shape

Now that you've got the idea, you'll have a chance to draw a more complex object.

1 Click point A on the shape on the right side to set the first anchor point.

2 Press the Shift key as you click point B. Pressing the Shift key constrains the line to 45-degree angles, which in this case ensures you'll get a horizontal line.

3 Press the Shift key as you click points C, D, and E to create straight path segments.

4 Click point F, and drag to the open red circle to create a curve. Then release the mouse button.

5 Click point G, and drag to the open red circle to create another curve. Then release the mouse button.

6 Click point H to create a corner point.

When you move a direction line on a corner point, only the curve on the same side of the point as the direction line is adjusted, so you can create a sharp transition between two segments.

7 Click point A to draw the final path segment and close the path. Closing a path automatically ends the drawing; you don't need to press Enter or Return.

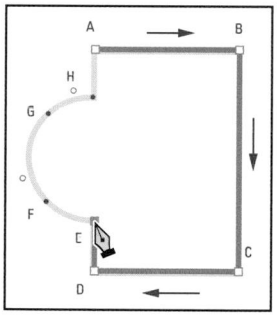

Start with straight segments.

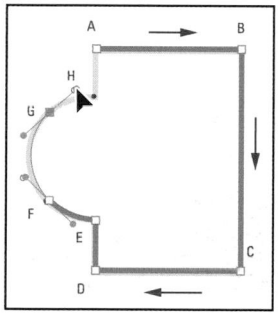

Drag to create a curve.

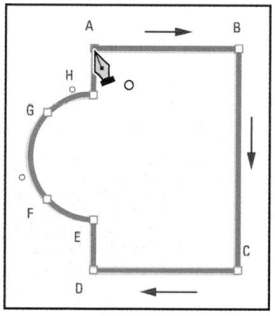

Close the path.

8 Close the file without saving changes. You have successfully used the Pen tool to draw both curves and straight lines.

▶ **Tip:** If you notice that you slightly missed the red dot on the template while dragging a curve point, you can reposition the point without starting over. Keeping the mouse button down, hold down the spacebar and drag until the point is in the right place. Then release the spacebar to continue dragging the direction lines of that anchor point.

Drawing a path traced from a photo

Now you're ready to draw a path around a real object. You'll use the techniques you've practiced to draw a path around the edge of one orange out of several. The path you draw will later be converted into a layer mask so that you can change the color of that orange. The orange is partially covered by surrounding oranges, so the path you draw will be a combination of curved and straight segments, like the shapes you've practiced on. Later, you'll combine the altered image with text and a shape layer to create a promotional postcard for a citrus farm.

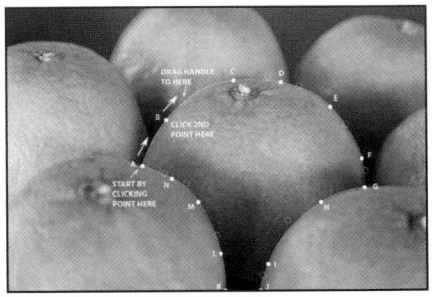

1 From Photoshop or Bridge, open the 08Start.psd file.

The image includes two layers: the background layer, and a template layer named Path Guide that you will trace to draw the path.

2 Choose File > Save As, rename the file **08Working.psd**, and click Save. If the Photoshop Format Options dialog box appears, click OK.

3 Select the Pen tool, and then, in the options bar, choose Path from the Tool Mode pop-up menu.

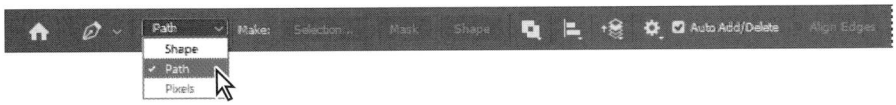

Because Path is now selected in the options bar instead of Shape, what you see when you draw will be different than in the practice exercise. You'll be drawing a path, not a shape. The path you draw will appear as a temporary work path in the Paths panel, and a shape layer won't be created.

The reason you're switching to a path is because you won't need to print or export the path you're about to draw. You'll be creating a mask from the path, so the path itself doesn't need to be a visible part of the final document. For more information about shapes and paths, see the sidebar "Comparing shapes, paths, and pixels."

Comparing shapes, paths, and pixels

When you use the Pen tool or the tools grouped with it, or the Rectangle tool or any of the tools grouped with it, a menu in the options bar lets you choose whether you want the tool to draw a shape, a path, or, in some cases, pixels.

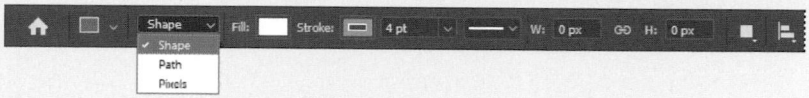

This is an important decision, because each option has different advantages:

Shape. A shape is a vector object created on its own layer in the Layers panel. You can apply the same layer effects, masks, and other properties that you would to a pixel layer. The difference is that you can continue to edit the shape as a vector path, using path editing tools such as the Pen tool and the Direct Selection tool. You can't edit a shape layer using pixel-based tools such as brushes.

Because a shape is a layer, it's always visible when its layer visibility is enabled, and it will print and export. When it's selected in the Layers panel, you can apply and change its fill and stroke color.

A selected shape layer also displays its path in the Paths panel.

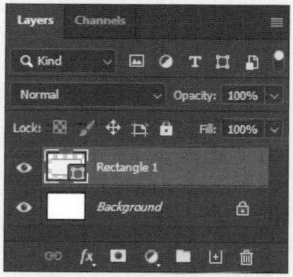

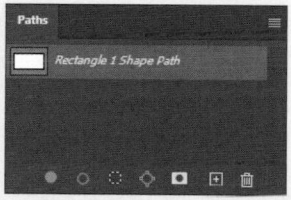

Path. A path is a vector object that doesn't display, print, or export, so it doesn't appear in the Layers panel. It lives only in the Paths panel. But the path is useful there, because you can use it as the basis for selections, clipping paths, type on a path, and other "backstage" roles.

Because a path is not a layer, it's visible in the document window only when it's selected in the Paths panel, and it can't have a stroke and fill. If it's hard to see, you can improve its visibility by clicking the Path Options menu (the gear) in the options bar and adjusting the path's Thickness and Color. Because a path isn't visible in a printed or exported image, those options affect only the visibility of the path while drawing in Photoshop.

Pixels. Some tools, such as the Rectangle tool and the tools grouped with it, also offer a Pixels option. Drawing with the Pixels option creates pixels on the currently selected layer, without creating a vector path or shape layer.

Because the Pixels option creates a pixel layer and not a vector path or shape, you won't be able to edit the resulting layer using path editing tools. You edit the layer using pixel-based tools such as the brushes, eraser, and selection tools.

4 With the Pen tool selected, click point A. A new temporary Work Path appears in the Paths panel.

5 Click point B, and drag to the open circle on the right to create the initial curve.

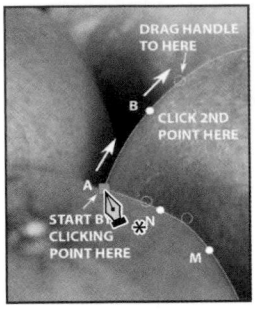

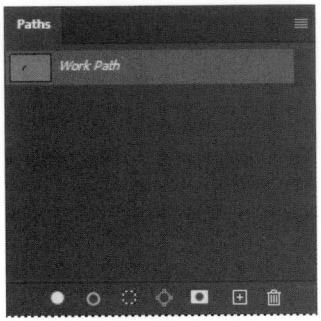

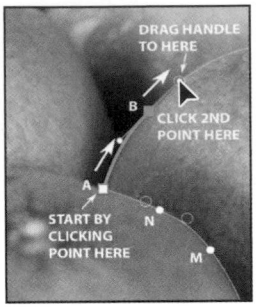

6 Click point C, and drag to the open circle to its right.

7 Continue tracing the orange, clicking and dragging curve segments for points D through F.

8 Click point G (do not drag). This creates the corner at point G.

9 At points H and I, click and drag to their corresponding open circles to create their curved segments.

▶ **Tip:** When tracing along a well-defined edge, the Pen tool is not the only useful tool. For some shapes and edges, you might find it easier to use the Magic Lasso tool, the Object Selection tool, or the Quick Selection tool.

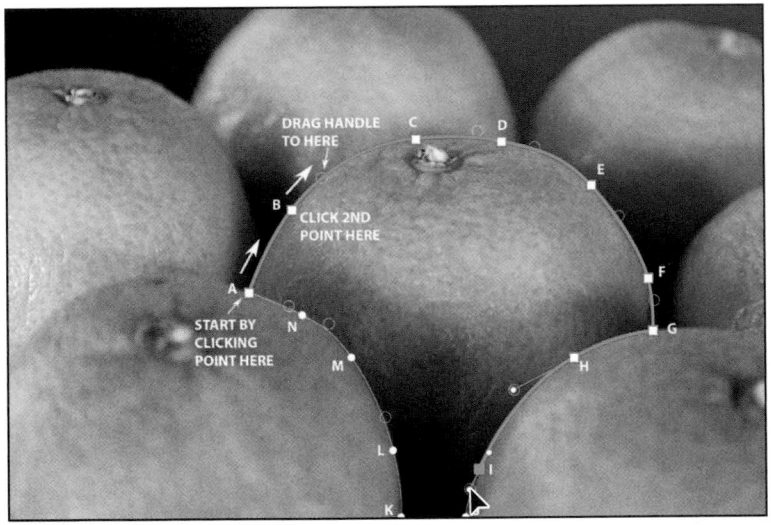

10 Click point J to create a corner.

11 Hold down Shift to create a perfectly level segment as you click point K.

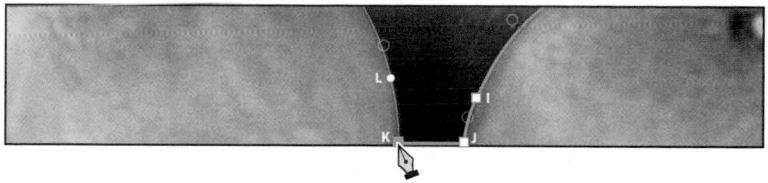

12 At points L, M, and N, click and drag to their corresponding open circles to create their curved segments.

13 Position the pointer over point A, and when you see a small circle by the Pen tool pointer, click to close the path. The circle indicates that the pointer is close enough to close the path.

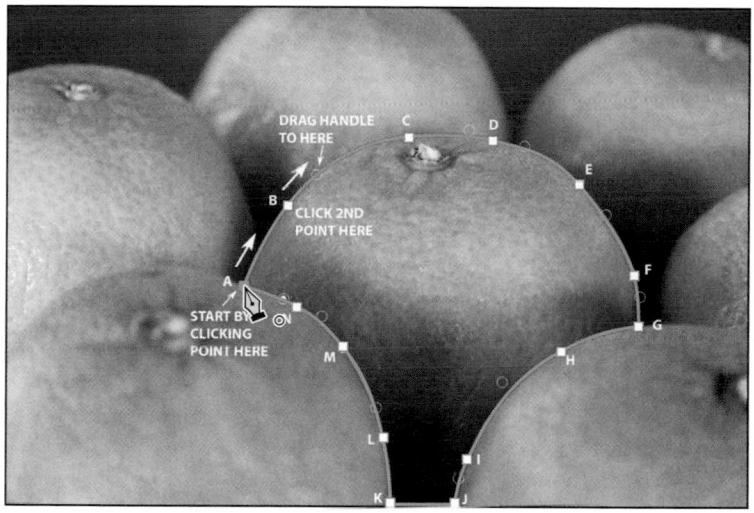

14 Evaluate your path. If you want to adjust any segments, do step 15; otherwise skip to step 16.

15 Select the Direct Selection tool (⇖) (grouped with the Path Selection tool (➚)), and then press the Esc key (or click in the document window away from the path) so that no points are selected, but you can still see the path. Then do any of the following with the Direct Selection tool as needed:

- To reposition a point or a straight segment, drag it.
- To change the shape of a curved segment between two points, drag the segment (not points).
- To change the shape of a curved segment extending from a point, drag its direction point to adjust the angle of that direction line.

16 When you're done, leave the path selected, and save your work so far.

▶ **Tip:** To move the entire path, drag it with the Path Selection tool, grouped with the Direct Selection tool.

Converting a path to a selection and a layer mask

▶ **Tip:** If you'd prefer to create a mask that you can always edit as a path, create a vector mask for the layer instead. Skip step 2, and then, in step 4, make sure the Lemon path is selected in the Paths panel when you add the new Hue/Saturation adjustment layer.

Using the Pen tool made it easy to create a precise outline of the orange in the center of the image. But the goal is to change the color of that orange without changing the others, through a layer mask. Creating the layer mask requires making a selection. Fortunately, it's easy to convert a path to a selection.

The path was a work path, which is temporary; it will be replaced if you draw another path. You can still create a selection from a work path, but first, it's a good practice to save any path you might want to use again in the future.

1 In the Paths panel, double-click Work Path. In the Save Path dialog box, type **Lemon** for the name, and click OK.

2 Make sure the Lemon path is selected in the Paths panel, and then click the Load Path as a Selection button (⬚) at the bottom of the Paths panel.

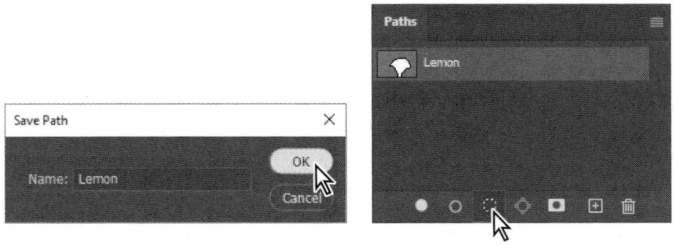

You're going to change the color of the selected orange to lemon yellow, using a Hue/Saturation adjustment layer through a layer mask of the orange. You currently have an active selection for this orange. That will make it quick and easy to create the layer mask, because an active selection is automatically converted to a layer mask when you add an adjustment layer.

▶ **Tip:** It's just as easy to convert a selection to a path. When a selection is active, click the Make Work Path from Selection button in the Paths panel; it's the button to the right of the one you clicked in step 2.

3 In the Layers panel, hide the Path Guide layer, because you no longer need it, and select the Background layer.

4 In the Adjustments panel, click the Hue/Saturation button (▦) to add a new Hue/Saturation adjustment layer in the Layers panel. It automatically includes a layer mask, created from your selection.

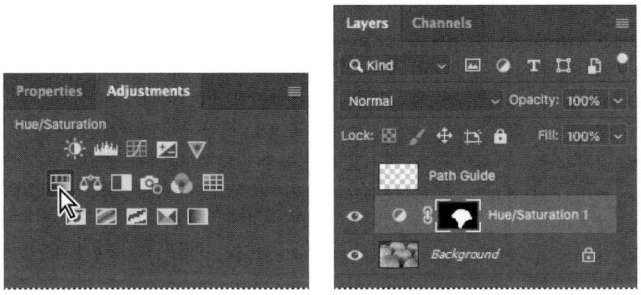

5 In the Properties panel, change the Hue setting so that the orange in the center changes to a lemon yellow color. We entered a Hue value of +17.

6 Save the document.

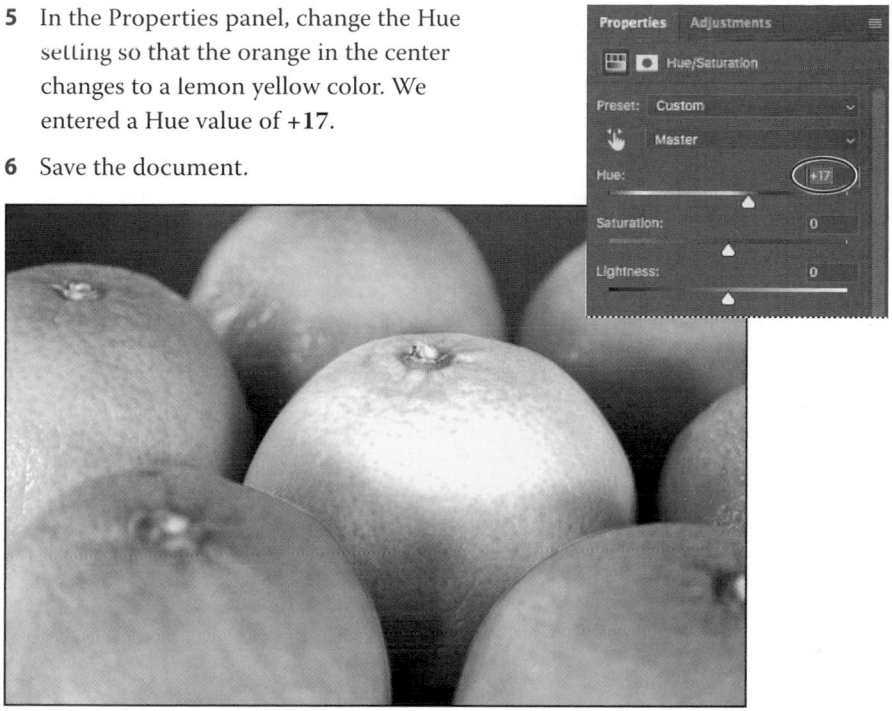

▶ **Tip:** After you change the color of the center orange, you may notice minor errors along the edges of the layer mask. Remember that you can edit a layer mask: Click the layer mask thumbnail in the Layers panel to select it, and then use the Brush tool to paint white where you want the color applied by the adjustment layer to be visible, or paint black where you want the color of the Background layer to be visible. (If it was a vector mask, you would edit it using the Direct Selection tool and Pen tool.)

You used the Pen tool to quickly and precisely draw a path that traces the outline of an object in an image (the orange that now looks like a lemon), you converted the path into a selection and used that selection to create a layer mask that isolates the subject when applying an adjustment layer.

Creating a logo with text and a custom shape

Now you'll create a logo that will overlay the image, using text and a shape layer.

1 If the rulers aren't visible, choose View > Rulers to display them.

2 Right-click (Windows) or Control-click (Mac) the rulers, and if they are currently displaying in pixels, choose Inches. This document will become a printed postcard, and Inches is an appropriate unit of measure for print.

3 In the Layers panel, make sure the Hue/Saturation adjustment layer is selected so that the layer you're about to create will be added above it.

4 Select the Horizontal Type tool (**T**), and, in the options bar, do the following:

- Choose a bold or heavy typeface from the Font Family pop-up menu. We used Arial Bold.
- Type **55 pt** for the Size, and press Enter or Return.
- Click the Right Align Text button, because you'll soon add a graphic element to the left of the text.
- Click the color swatch and set the text color to white.

5 Drag the Horizontal Type tool to create a text layer across the bottom of the canvas, inset about half an inch away from the sides and bottom. Ours is about 9 inches wide by 1 inch tall.

6 Type **Citrus Lane Farms** to replace the placeholder text, click the Commit button (✓) in the options bar, and leave the text layer selected in the Layers panel.

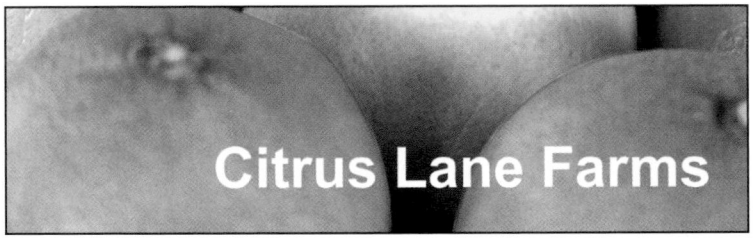

7 This font looks better with tighter letter spacing. With the text selected, in the Character or Properties panel, apply a negative Tracking value; we used **–25**.

8 Select the All Caps button (TT) in the Type Options group in the Properties panel. If you don't see this option, scroll down in the Properties panel.

9 If needed, use the Move tool to reposition the text layer so that it looks better relative to the bottom and right sides. Leave space to the left of the text for a graphic you're about to add.

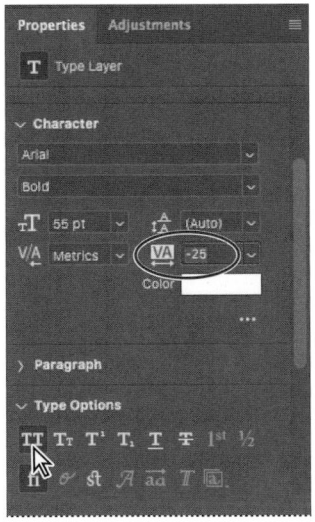

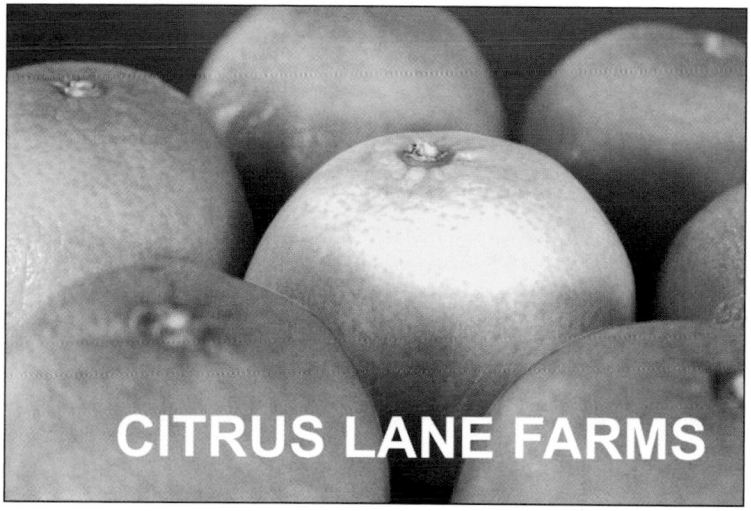

Adding a preset shape

When you need a shape such as a symbol or object, one place you can turn to is the Shapes panel, which contains a wide selection of premade graphics. When you add a shape to a document, it becomes a shape layer.

A shape is a vector object drawn using paths, which has two advantages. You can edit it using the same techniques you used to edit the paths you drew earlier in this chapter. Also, like a text layer, a path is resolution-independent, so it will always be as smooth and detailed as the document resolution allows.

You find shapes in the Shapes panel. It's easy to use, because it works like the other Photoshop panels that contain preset effects, such as the Swatches, Gradients, and Brushes panels: You see small visual previews of each preset, you can organize them in groups (folders), and you can create your own.

1 Choose Window > Shapes to open the Shapes panel. The Shapes panel includes groups of shape presets.

2 Expand the Flowers presets group.

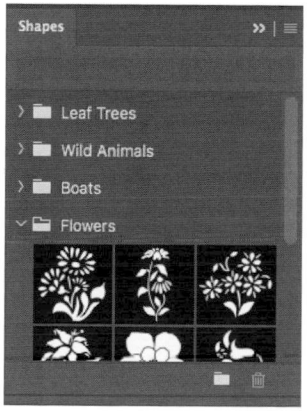

▶ **Tip:** Photoshop includes more preset groups than you see by default in a presets panel list. In the panel menu, choose Legacy Shapes and More to load additional preset groups, including presets that were available in previous versions of Photoshop.

Extra Credit

Using Creative Cloud Libraries with linked Smart Objects

When you organize and share your design assets using Creative Cloud Libraries, you and your team can use those library items in many Creative Cloud desktop and mobile apps. Let's take a look:

1 Open 08End.psd. If the Libraries panel isn't open, choose Window > Libraries.

2 In the Libraries panel menu, choose Create New Library, name it **Citrus Lane Farms**, and click Create.

3 In the Layers panel, select the Flower layer, and then hold down Shift as you click the Citrus Lane Farms text layer so that the two layers are selected.

4 Drag both layers from the Layers panel into the Citrus Lane Farms library.

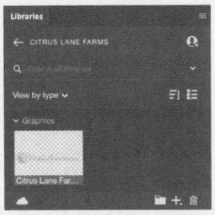

After the Libraries panel finishes syncing the logo to Creative Cloud, it will be available in Creative Cloud applications and mobile apps that use Creative Cloud Libraries.

The appearance of the Citrus Lane Farms text layer was adjusted to look good over the image of the oranges; it should be tested over a wide range of backgrounds and edited as needed for readability. A library item is a Smart Object linked to Creative Cloud, so you can edit it in Photoshop by double-clicking it in the Libraries panel. When you save changes, it updates in all documents that use it.

Adding a color

A library can store colors for use across Adobe applications.

1 With the Eyedropper tool, click the flower in the document window so that its color becomes the foreground swatch in the Tools panel.

2 At the bottom of the Libraries panel, click the Add Elements button (+), and click the Foreground Color swatch, adding it to the current library.

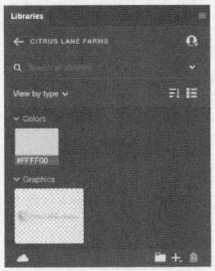

Collaborating

When you share a Creative Cloud Library, your team always has the current version of those assets. In the Libraries panel menu, choose Invite People, and fill in the Invite screen that appears in your web browser. Collaborators will see the library you shared in their Creative Cloud applications (to use this feature, you must have a Creative Cloud account and be signed in).

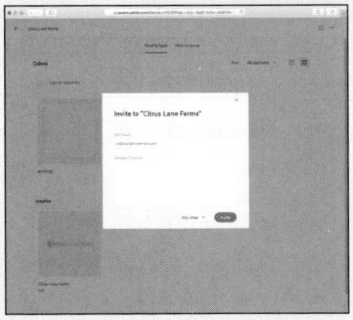

Adding assets to libraries using Adobe mobile apps

Use Adobe mobile apps—such as Adobe Capture—to record color themes, shapes, and brushes from real life and add them to your Creative Cloud libraries. Library assets you add with mobile apps automatically sync to your Creative Cloud account, so you'll see the new assets in your Libraries panel when you return to your computer.

3 Drag the last shape preset, and drop it to the left of the Citrus Lane Farms logo.

The flower shape now appears in the Layers panel. The shape currently has a transform bounding box around it so that you can make adjustments before committing it to the document. And yes, there are some adjustments to be made.

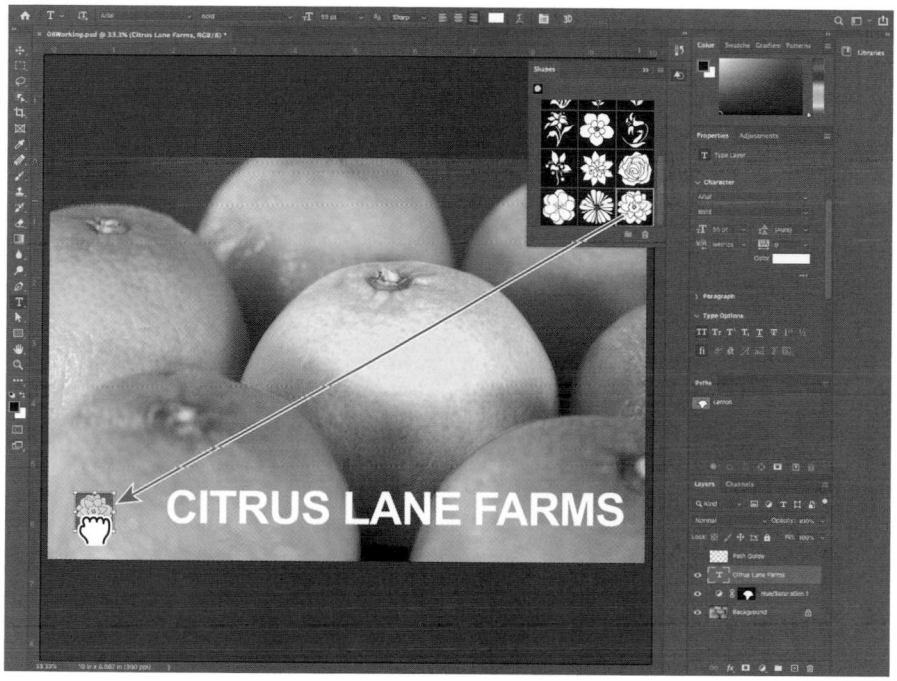

▶ **Tip:** Want to save your own shape preset? Draw a path or shape, select it with the Path Selection tool, choose Edit > Define Custom Shape, name it, and click OK. It's added to the Shapes panel; if a shape group is active, it's added to that group.

4 Drag any handle on the shape to resize it to be about 1.5 inches tall.

5 Drag the flower to position it between the left edge of the document and the Citrus Lane Farms text.

6 Click the Commit Transform button (✓) in the options bar, or press Enter or Return. The transformation bounding box disappears.

▶ **Tip:** If the magenta Smart Guides prevent you from making precise adjustments, hold down the Control key as you drag.

A shape is added using the current fill and stroke settings for shapes, which were the ones set for the practice shape earlier. The flower shape is intended to have a solid yellow fill. That change could not be done while the bounding box was active, but now that it's been committed to the document, the colors can be changed.

7 Make sure the flower shape is still selected in the Layers panel.

8 In the Layers panel, double-click the name of the shape layer, type **Flower**, and press Return or Enter to rename the layer.

9 Select any shape tool, such as the Rectangle tool or any tool grouped with it. The options bar now displays settings for shapes.

▶ **Tip:** Do you wish one of the preset shapes was slightly different? All shapes are paths, so after you add a shape to the document, you can edit it by using the Pen tool or any of the tools grouped with it, or the Direct Selection tool.

10 In the options bar, click the Fill swatch, expand the RGB swatch presets group that appears in the drop-down menu, and click the yellow swatch.

11 In the options bar, click the Stroke swatch, and set it to No Color. Close the pop-up menu by pressing Enter or Return.

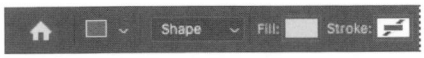

12 Choose Select > Deselect Layers. Now you can see the flower shape without its path being highlighted.

13 If needed, use the Move tool to reposition the flower and text, composing them relative to each other as a logo and relative to the edges of the document.

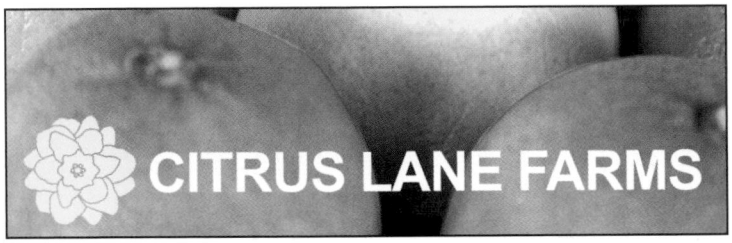

14 Save your file.

You've combined an image, a color adjustment layer masked with the help of a path you drew by hand, a pre-made shape, and a text layer. The postcard is ready to go!

Extra credit

Quickly adding color and effects using presets

You can use presets to quickly enhance the look of both the text and the flower in the logo. The way that you do this is similar to how you added the flower shape with the Shapes panel and changed its color using the Swatches panel.

1 Open 08Working.psd (if it isn't already open), and save it as 08StylePresets.psd.

2 Start by applying a preset to the flower. In the Styles panel (Window > Styles), expand the Basics preset group.

3 Drag the second preset from the Basics group, and drop it on the flower in the document window. The style is applied to the flower shape layer. Then drag the same style and drop it on the text.

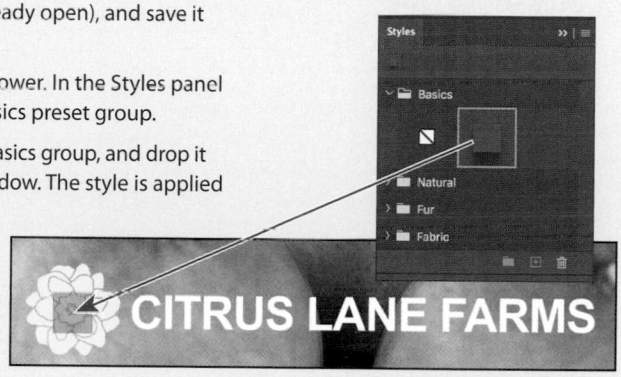

You can apply a preset by dragging and dropping it on a layer or by clicking a preset when the layer is selected. Either way is fine.

In this example, the Basic style applies a simple stroke and drop shadow. But the possibilities are much wider. Explore your design options by freely editing the presets in the Styles, Gradients, Patterns, and Swatches panels and applying them to layers until you get the look you want. And you can add your own presets to those panels.

You can see that the effects have been applied in the Layers panel, and you can fine-tune those effects in different ways:

- Click the eye icon for different layer effects to disable or enable them.
- Double-click an effect name to open the Layer Style dialog box, where you can edit effects.
- If you try to apply a style and it doesn't seem to change the layer, you may first need to delete effects already applied to the layer: In the Layers panel, drag that layer's Effects heading to the Delete (trash can) icon at the bottom of the Layers panel. Note that a preset may also alter a layer's Opacity and Fill Opacity, so you may have to set those back to the default of 100%.
- If you don't see any effects listed after a layer after applying a style, the preset may have been applied as a fill or stroke instead of a layer style. To edit it, double-click the shape layer thumbnail (not the name).
- If you applied a preset to a shape, select any shape tool, such as the Rectangle tool, to display shape options in the options bar. Click the Fill or Stroke swatch to edit the preset.

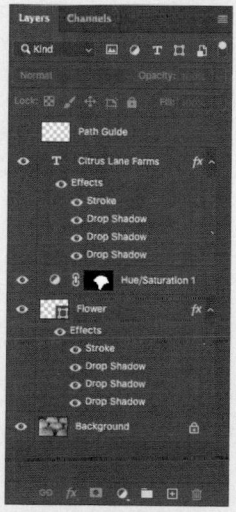

Extra credit

Using Smart Guides to maintain alignment and equal spacing

Let's take this design to the next level. You can use the Citrus Lane Farms logo to make a repeated motif for packaging or other signage. Smart Guides can help you position the images evenly.

1 Open 08End.psd, and save it as 08SmartGuides.psd. Choose View > Show, and make sure there is a check mark next to the Smart Guides command, indicating that it's enabled. If not, select the Smart Guides command to enable it.

2 Select the Flower layer. Then select the Move tool, and hold down the Alt (Windows) or Option (Mac) key as you drag a copy of the Flower layer up about 3 inches, making sure to use the magenta Smart Guides to keep the Flower copy perfectly aligned with the original, and then release the mouse button. Without Smart Guides, you'd have to also press Shift to keep the copy aligned. The Alt or Option key copies the selected layer.

3 In the Layers panel, change the Opacity of the Flower copy layer to 50%.

4 Make sure the Move tool and Flower copy layer are still selected. Hold down the Alt (Windows) or Option (Mac) key as you use the Move tool to drag a copy of the Flower copy layer to the right, until the magenta values indicate that the layer and its copy are about 1 inch apart and still aligned. Then release the mouse button.

5 This time, with the Flower copy 2 layer still selected, hold down Alt or Option as you drag the Flower copy 2 layer to the right; release the mouse when two transformation values boxes appear between the three flower layers across the top. The boxes let you know that the distance between the three flower layers is now equal. Using Smart Guides is a fast and easy way to make sure layers you drag are evenly spaced, without having to do math or use a distribution command.

6 Repeat step 4 so that you have four equally spaced flowers.

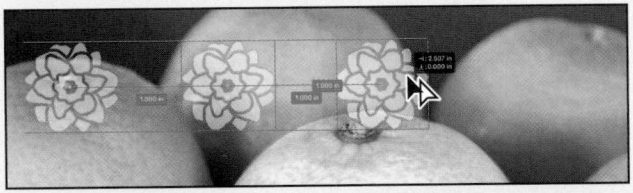

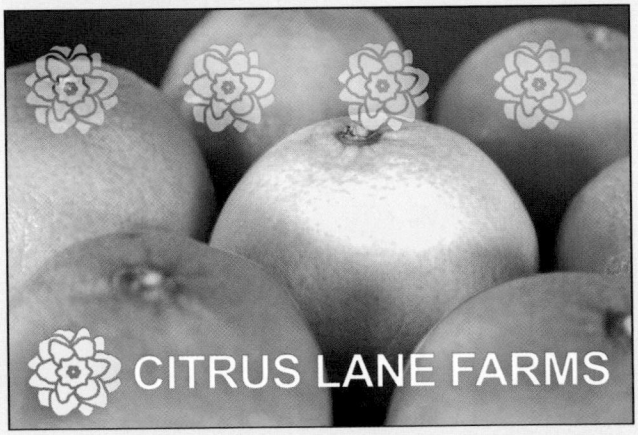

Review questions

1 What is the difference between a bitmap image and a vector graphic?

2 After using the Pen tool to add an anchor point to a path, how do you make sure the next path segment is a curve?

3 How can you add a preset shape to the document?

4 What tool can you use to move and resize paths and shapes?

5 What are some ways to change the shape of a curved path segment?

Review answers

1 Bitmap, or raster, images are based on a grid of pixels and are appropriate for continuous-tone images such as photographs or artwork created in painting programs. Vector graphics are made up of shapes based on mathematical expressions and are appropriate for illustrations, type, and drawings that require clear, smooth lines.

2 Drag the next point with the Pen tool.

3 To add a preset shape, open the Shapes panel, find the shape, and drag it into the document window.

4 You use the Direct Selection tool to move, resize, and edit shapes. You can also modify and scale a selected shape or path by choosing Edit > Free Transform.

5 You can change the shape of a curved path segment by using the Direction Selection tool to drag either of a curved segment's two anchor points, the direction points for either anchor point, or the curved segment itself.

9 ADVANCED COMPOSITING

Lesson overview

In this lesson, you'll learn how to do the following:

- Apply and edit Smart Filters.
- Use the Liquify filter to distort an image.
- Apply color effects to selected areas of an image.
- Apply filters to create various effects.
- Use the History panel to return to a previous state.
- Upscale a low-resolution image for high-resolution printing.

This lesson will take about an hour to complete. To get the lesson files used in this chapter, download them from the web page for this book at www.adobepress.com/PhotoshopCIB2021. For more information, see "Accessing the lesson files and Web Edition" in the Getting Started section at the beginning of this book.

As you work on this lesson, you'll preserve the start files. If you need to restore the start files, download them from your Account page.

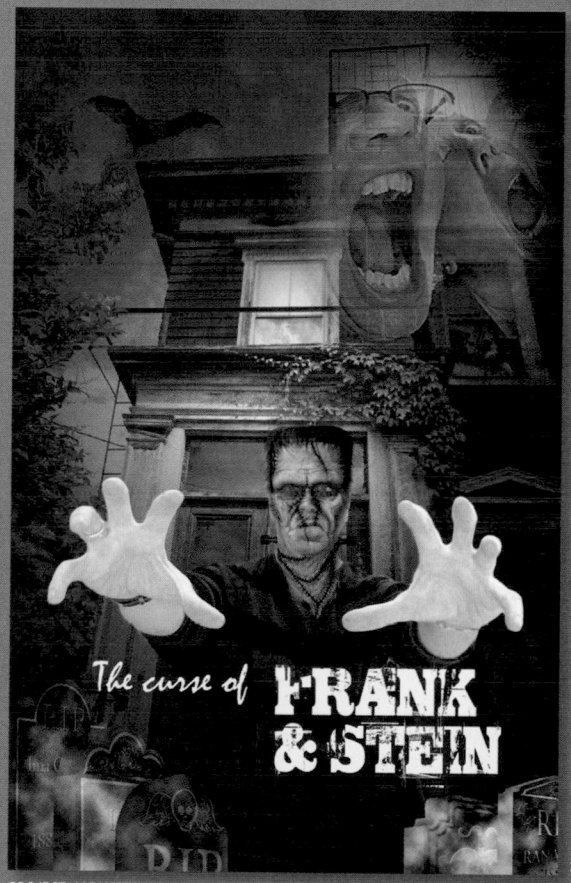

Monster makeup imagery courtesy of Russell Brown

PROJECT: MONSTER MOVIE POSTER DESIGN

Filters can transform ordinary images into extraordinary digital artwork. Smart Filters let you edit those transformations at any time. The wide variety of features in Photoshop lets you be as creative as you want to be.

Getting started

In this lesson, you'll assemble a montage of images for a movie poster as you explore filters in Photoshop. First, look at the final project to see what you'll be creating.

1 Start Photoshop, and then simultaneously hold down Ctrl+Alt+Shift (Windows) or Command+Option+Shift (Mac) to restore the default preferences. (See "Restoring default preferences" on page 5.)

2 When prompted, click Yes to delete the Adobe Photoshop Settings file.

3 Choose File > Browse In Bridge.

4 In Bridge, choose Favorites from the menu on the left, and then click the Lessons folder. Double-click the Lesson09 folder.

5 View the 09_End.psd thumbnail. Move the slider at the bottom of the Bridge window if you need to zoom in to see the thumbnail more clearly.

Note: If Bridge isn't installed, the File > Browse In Bridge command in Photoshop will start the Creative Cloud desktop app, which will download and install Bridge. After installation completes, you can start Bridge.

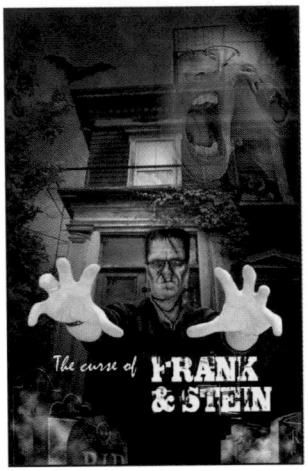

This file is a movie poster that comprises a background, a monster image, and several smaller images. Each image has had one or more filters or effects applied to it.

The monster is composed of an image of a perfectly normal (though slightly threatening) guy with several ghoulish images applied. These monstrous additions are courtesy of Russell Brown, with illustration by John Connell.

6 In Bridge, navigate to the Lesson09/Monster_Makeup folder, and open it.

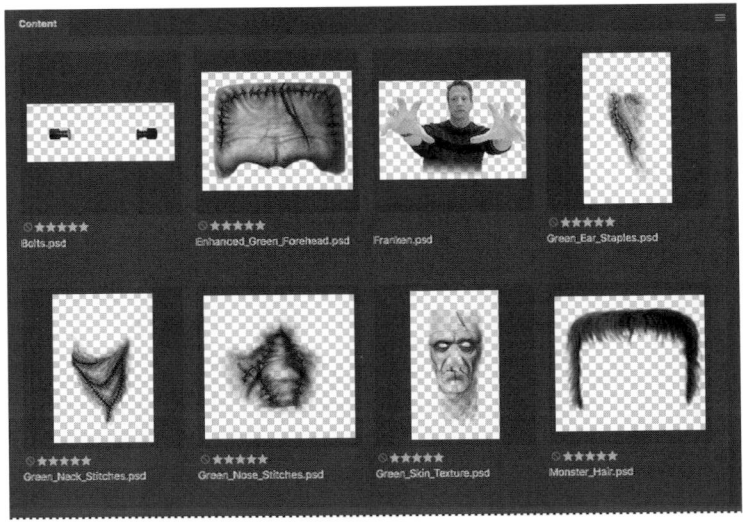

7 Shift-click the first and last items to select all the files in the Monster_Makeup folder, and then choose Tools > Photoshop > Load Files Into Photoshop Layers.

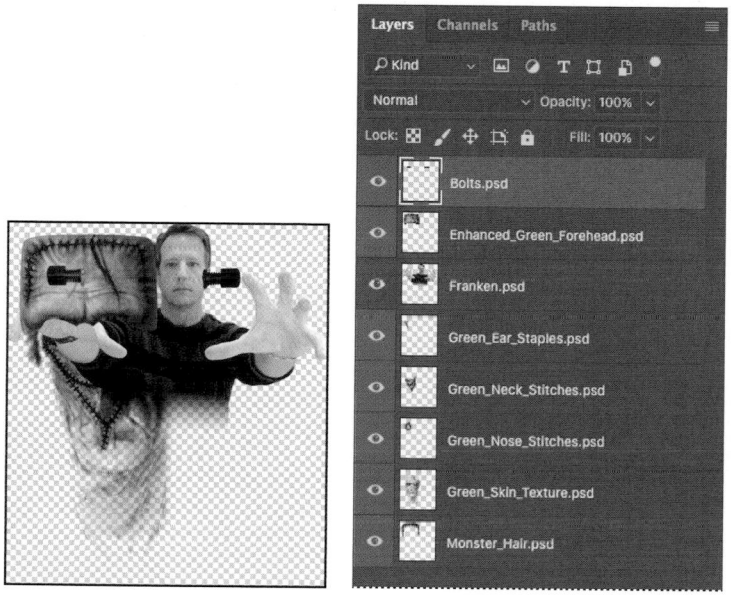

Photoshop imports all the selected files as individual layers in a new Photoshop file. The designer used a red layer color to indicate components of the monster's look.

8 In Photoshop, choose File > Save As. Choose Photoshop for the Format, and name the new file **09Working.psd**. Save it in the Lesson09 folder. Click OK in the Photoshop Format Options dialog box.

Note: If Photoshop displays a dialog box telling you about the difference between saving to Cloud Documents and Your Computer, click Save On Your Computer. You can also select Don't Show Again, but that setting will deselect after you reset Photoshop preferences.

Arranging layers

Your image file contains eight layers, imported in alphabetical order. In their current positions, they don't make a very convincing monster. You'll rearrange the layer order and resize their contents as you start to build your monster.

1 Zoom out or scroll so that you can see all the layers in the document.

2 In the Layers panel, drag the Monster_Hair layer to the top of the layer stack, if it isn't already on top.

3 Drag the Franken layer to the bottom of the layer stack.

4 Select the Move tool (✣), and then drag the Franken layer (the image of the person) to the bottom of the page.

Note: If the wrong layer becomes selected when you try to drag the Franken layer to the bottom of the image, deselect Auto-Select in the options bar.

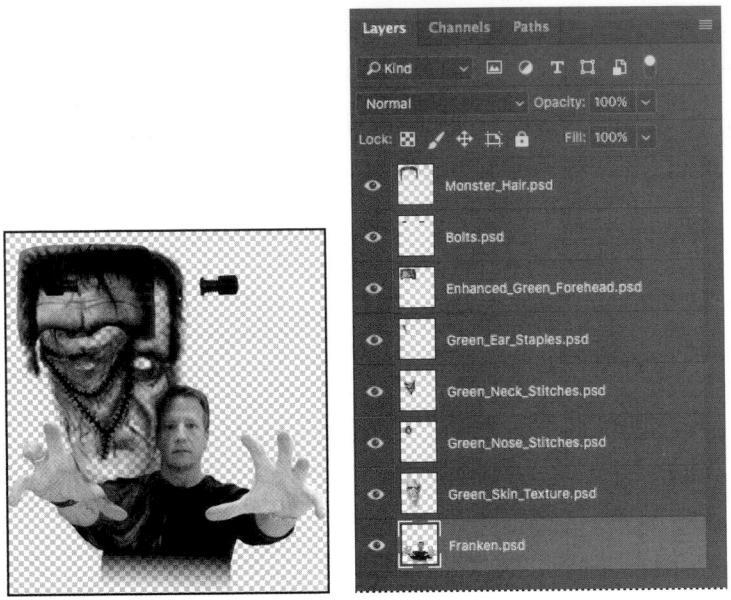

5 In the Layers panel, Shift-select every layer except the Franken layer, and choose Edit > Free Transform.

Tip: The keyboard shortcut for Free Transform is Ctrl+T (Windows) or Command+T (Mac). This is a good all-in-one shortcut to learn because you can use it to move, scale, or rotate selected layers.

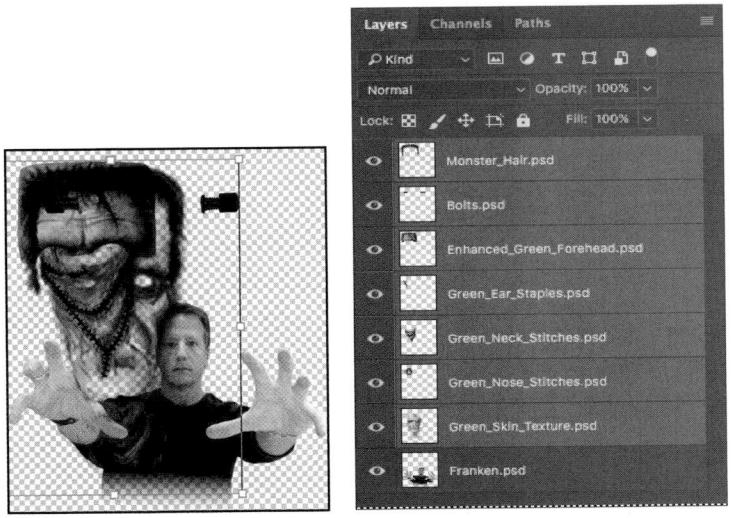

6 Drag down from a corner of the selection to resize all the selected layers to about 50% of their original size. (Watch the width and height percentages in the options bar.)

7 With the Free Transform bounding box still active, position the layers over the head of the Franken layer. Then press Enter or Return to commit the transformation.

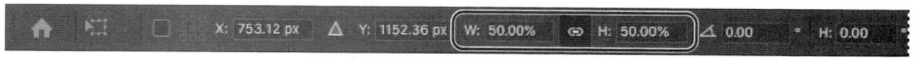

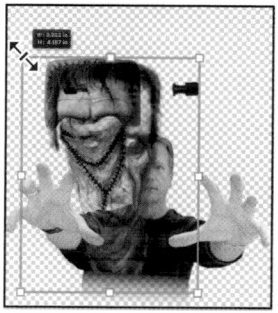

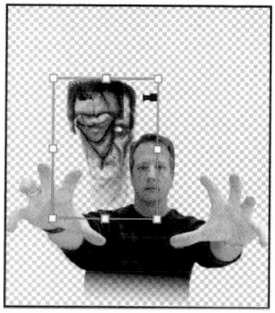

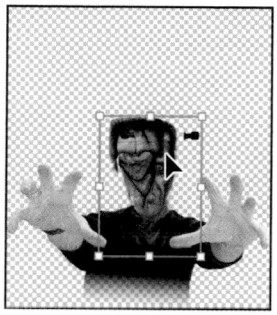

8 Zoom in to see the head area clearly.

9 Hide all layers except the Green_Skin_Texture and Franken layers.

10 Select only the Green_Skin_Texture layer, and use the Move tool to center it over the face.

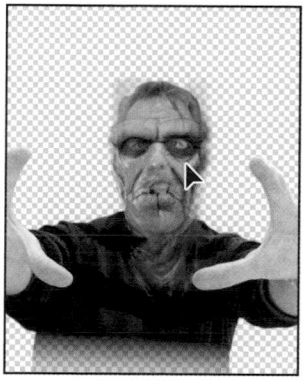

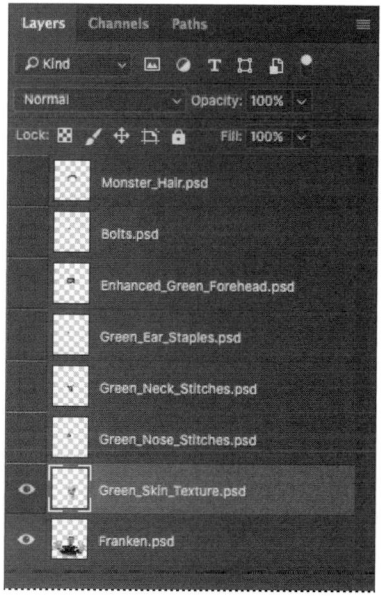

▶ **Tip:** If magenta Smart Guides appear, making it difficult to position the Green_Skin_Texture layer, hold down the Control key to temporarily disable snapping to Smart Guides as you drag. Or permanently disable them by deselecting the View > Show > Smart Guides command.

▶ **Tip:** For more detailed control over how the texture fits the face, choose Edit > Transform > Warp, drag the transform grid or handles, and then press Return or Enter to commit the changes.

11 Choose Edit > Free Transform again to adjust the fit of the texture to the face. Using the eyes and mouth as a guide, press arrow keys to nudge the entire layer into position. Drag handles on the bounding box to adjust the width and height. (To adjust without preserving proportions, Shift-drag a handle.) When you've positioned the skin texture, press Enter or Return to commit the transformation.

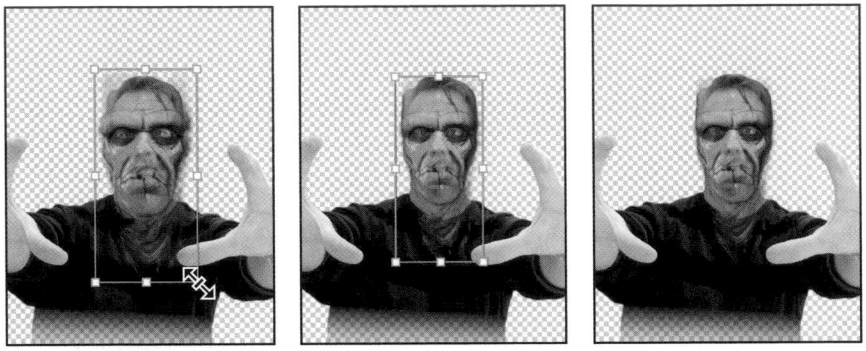

12 Save your file.

Using Smart Filters

Unlike regular filters, which permanently change an image, Smart Filters are nondestructive: They can be adjusted, turned off and on, and deleted. However, you can apply Smart Filters only to a Smart Object.

Applying the Liquify filter

You'll use the Liquify filter to tighten the eye openings and change the shape of the monster's face. Because you want to be able to adjust the filter settings later, you'll use the Liquify filter as a Smart Filter. So you'll first need to convert the Green_Skin_Texture layer to a Smart Object.

▶ **Tip:** In the Layers panel, the thumbnail icon for the Green_Skin_Texture layer now displays a small badge in the bottom-right corner to indicate that it is a Smart Object.

1 Make sure the Green_Skin_Texture layer is selected in the Layers panel, and then choose Filter > Convert for Smart Filters. This creates a Smart Object. Click OK if you're asked to confirm the conversion to a Smart Object.

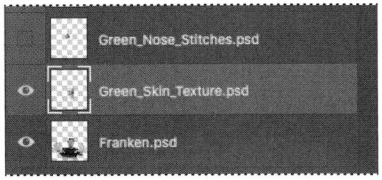

2 Choose Filter > Liquify.

Photoshop displays the layer in the Liquify dialog box.

3 In the Liquify dialog box, click the disclosure triangle next to Face-Aware Liquify to close that group of options.

You already explored Face-Aware Liquify in Lesson 5. While Face-Aware Liquify is a quick and powerful way to modify facial features, the amount of face editing you can do with those options is limited. In this lesson, you'll try some of the more manual Liquify techniques, which you may prefer when you want to create a more expressive face. Hiding the Face-Aware Liquify options makes it easier to concentrate on the other options in the Liquify dialog box.

Note: Step 4 doesn't change the document; it just changes how much you see of other layers while you work on the layer that was selected when you entered the Liquify dialog box.

4 Select Show Backdrop, and then choose Behind from the Mode menu. Set the Opacity to **75**.

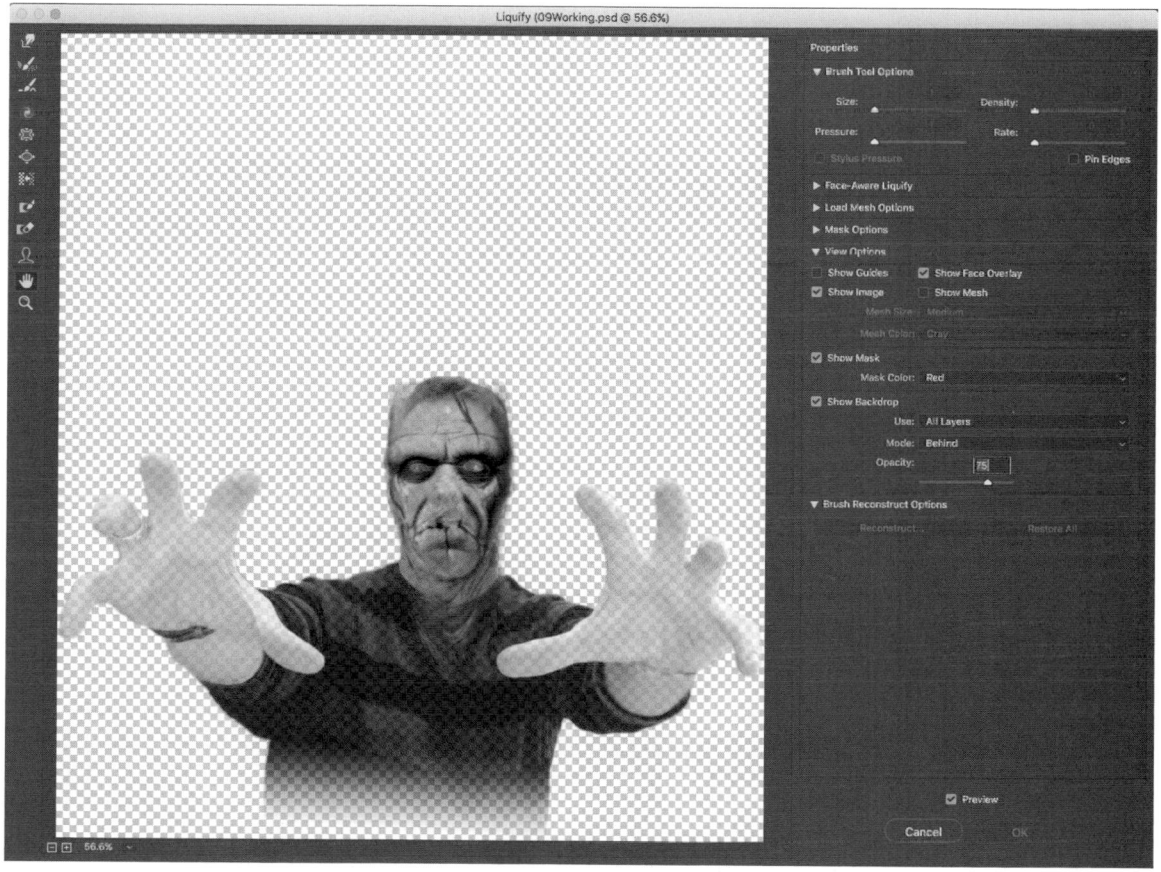

5 Select the Zoom tool (🔍) from the Tools panel on the left side of the dialog box, and zoom in to the eye area.

6 Select the Forward Warp tool (🖌) (the first tool).

The Forward Warp tool pushes pixels forward as you drag.

7 In the Brush Tool Options area, set Size to **150** and Pressure to **75**.

8 With the Forward Warp tool, pull the monster makeup's right eyebrow down to close the eye opening. Then pull up from under the eye.

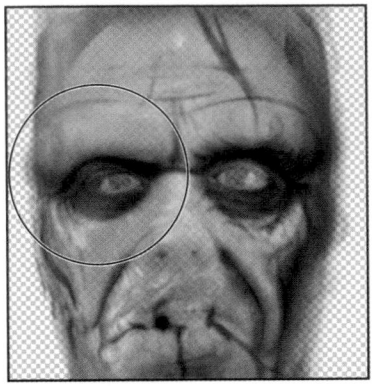

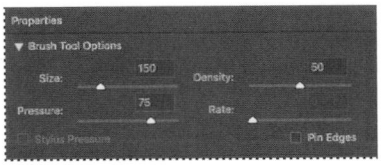

9 Repeat step 8 on the left eyebrow and under-eye area. You might prefer to use the Forward Warp tool differently for each eye, to create an even scarier face.

10 When you've closed the gap around the eyes, click OK.

Because you've applied the Liquify filter as a Smart Filter, you can freely remove or change your Liquify edits later without losing image quality, by double-clicking the Smart Object in the Layers panel.

Positioning other layers

Now that you've got the skin texture in place, you'll move the other layers into position, working up from the lowest layers in the Layers panel.

1 Make the Green_Nose_Stitches layer visible, and select it in the Layers panel.

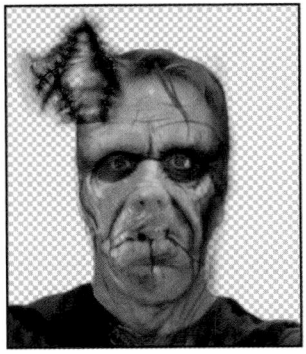

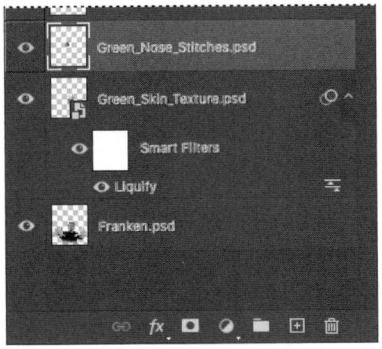

2 Choose Edit > Free Transform, and then position the layer over the nose, resizing it as necessary. Press Enter or Return to commit the transformation.

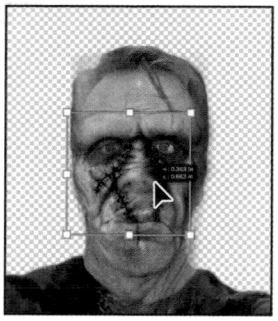

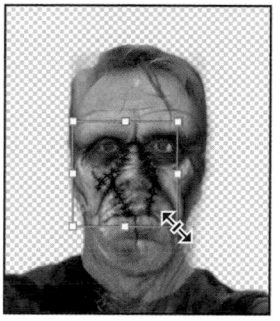

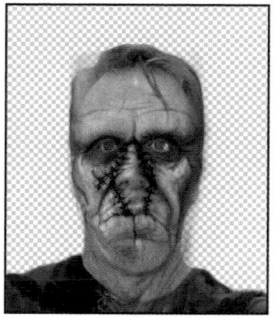

▶ **Tip:** To resize from the center of a selection, hold down Alt (Windows) or Option (Mac) as you drag a bounding box handle.

You'll repeat the process to position the rest of the layers.

3 Make the Green_Neck_Stitches layer visible, and select it. Then move it over the neck. If you need to adjust it, choose Edit > Free Transform, resize it, and press Enter or Return.

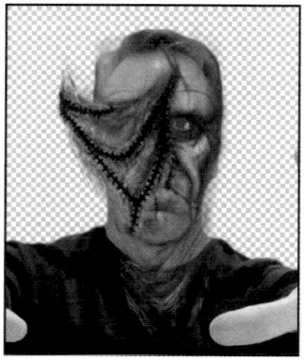

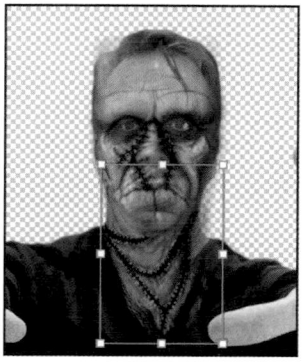

▶ **Tip:** If you only need to move a layer, you can simply drag it with the Move tool. In these steps, choosing Edit > Free Transform lets you both move and resize a layer.

4 Make the Green_Ear_Staples layer visible, and select it. Move the staples over his right ear. Choose Edit > Free Transform, resize and reposition the staples, and then press Enter or Return.

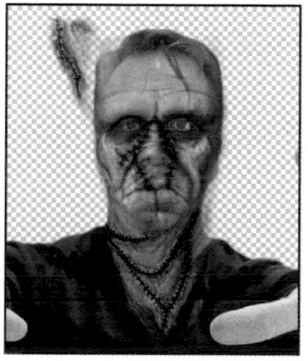

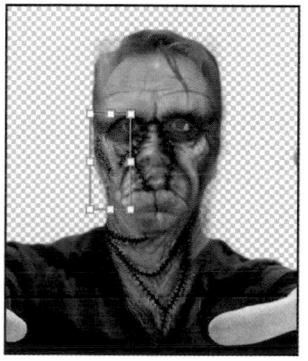

▶ **Tip:** Remember that you can position and size a selected layer using any combination of the Move tool, the Edit > Free Transform command, and nudging by pressing arrow keys. Use whatever tools get the job done!

5 Make the Enhanced_Green_Forehead layer visible, and select it. Move it over the forehead; it's probably a bit large. Choose Edit > Free Transform, resize the forehead to fit his head, and press Enter or Return.

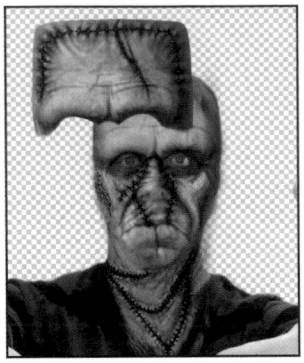

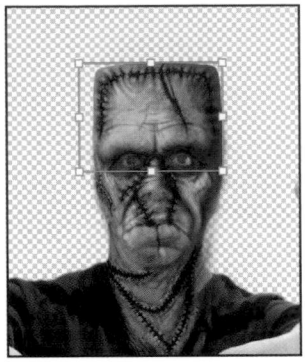

6 Make the Bolts layer visible, and select it. Drag the bolts so they're positioned on both sides of the neck. Choose Edit > Free Transform, and resize them so that they fit snugly against the neck. When you have them in position, press Enter or Return to commit the transformation.

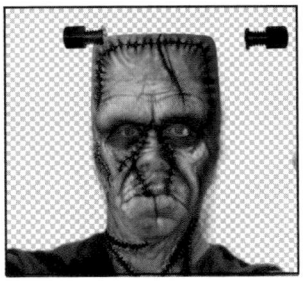

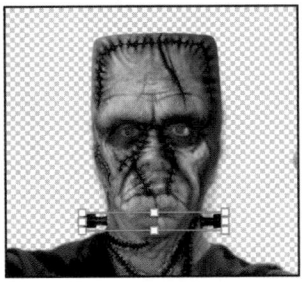

7 Finally, make the Monster_Hair layer visible, and select it. Move it over the forehead. Choose Edit > Free Transform, and then resize the hair so it fits properly against the forehead. Press Enter or Return to commit the change.

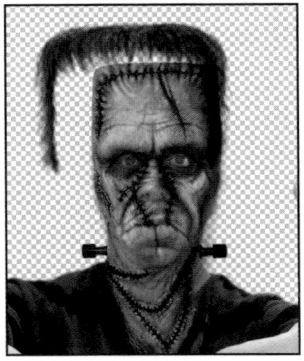

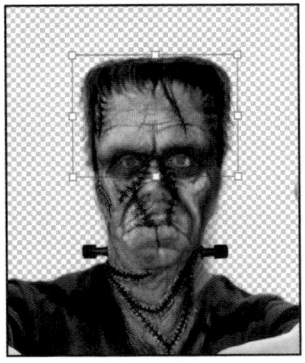

8 Save your work so far.

Editing a Smart Filter

With all the layers in position, you can further refine the eye openings and experiment with the bulges in the eyebrows. You'll return to the Liquify filter to make those adjustments.

1 In the Layers panel, double-click Liquify, listed under Smart Filters in the Green_Skin_Texture layer.

Photoshop opens the Liquify dialog box again. This time, all the layers are visible in Photoshop, so when Show Backdrop is selected, you see them all. Sometimes it's easier to make changes without a backdrop to distract you. Other times, it's useful to see your edits in context.

2 Zoom in to see the eyes more closely.

3 Select the Pucker tool (⊛) in the Tools panel, and click on the outer corner of each eye.

The Pucker tool moves pixels toward the center of the brush as you click or hold the mouse button, or drag.

4 Select the Bloat tool (⊕), and click the outer edge of an eyebrow to expand it; do the same for the other eyebrow.

The Bloat tool moves pixels away from the center of the brush as you click or drag.

5 Experiment with the Pucker, Bloat, and other tools in the Liquify filter to customize the monster's face.

Remember that you can change the brush size and other settings. You can undo individual steps using the Undo keyboard shortcut (Ctrl+Z on Windows and Command+Z on Mac) if the Edit menu isn't available. If you want to discard all current changes and start over, it's easiest to click Cancel and then return to the Liquify dialog box.

6 When you're happy with the monster's face, click OK, and save your work.

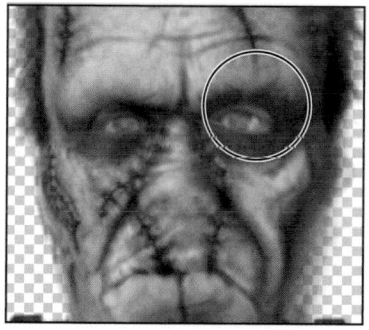

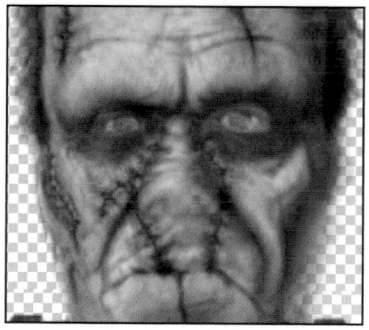

▶ **Tip:** The Pucker, Bloat, and other tools on the left side of the Liquify panel provide more control over Liquify distortions than the Face-Aware Liquify options, and they work on any part of an image. But Face-Aware Liquify is easier for quick and subtle adjustments to facial features.

Painting a layer

There are many ways to paint objects and layers in Photoshop. One of the simplest is to use the Color blending mode and the Brush tool. You'll use this method to paint the exposed skin green on your monster.

1 Select the Franken layer in the Layers panel.

2 Click the Create A New Layer button (⊞) at the bottom of the Layers panel.

Photoshop creates a new layer, named Layer 1.

3 With Layer 1 selected, choose Color from the Blending Mode menu at the top of the Layers panel.

The Color blending mode combines the luminance of the base color (the color already on the layer) with the hue and saturation of the color you're applying. It's a good blending mode to use when you're coloring monochrome images or tinting color images.

4 In the Tools panel, select the Brush tool (🖌). In the options bar, select a **60**-pixel brush with a Hardness of **0**.

5 Hold down Alt or Option to temporarily switch to the Eyedropper tool. Sample a green color from the forehead. Then release the Alt or Option key to return to the Brush tool.

▶ **Tip:** Be sure to distinguish the blending mode of a layer (shown in the Layers panel) from the blending mode of a tool (shown in the options bar). To learn more about blending modes, including a description of each one, see "Blending modes" in Photoshop Help.

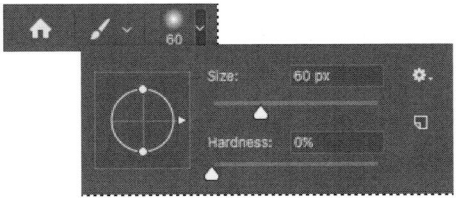

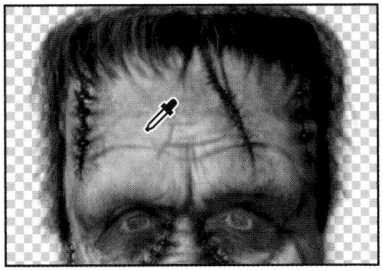

6 Ctrl-click or Command-click the thumbnail in the Franken layer to select its contents. Notice that a selection marquee now appears on the layer.

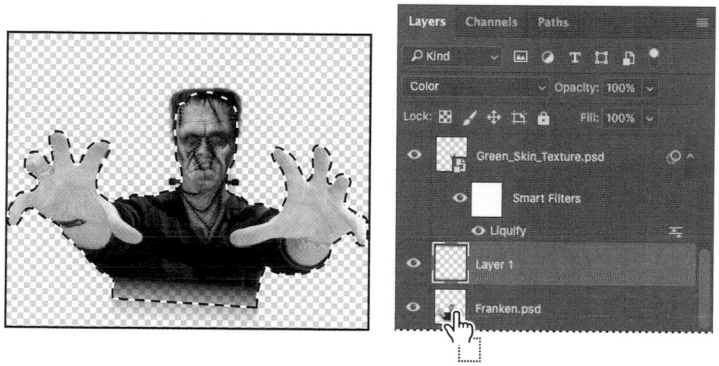

Usually, you select an entire layer in the Layers panel. When you do that, the layer is active, but there isn't actually an active selection. When you Ctrl-click or Command-click the thumbnail of the layer, Photoshop selects the contents of the layer, so you have an active selection. It's a quick way to select all of the contents of a layer—but without the transparent areas.

7 Make sure Layer 1 is still selected in the Layers panel, and then use the Brush tool to paint over the hands and arms. You can paint quickly where the hands are against transparent areas, because painting outside the selection has no effect. However, remember that the shirt is part of the selection, so as you paint the skin close to the shirt color, take care to paint only the skin and not the shirt.

▶ **Tip:** To change the brush size as you paint, press the bracket keys on your keyboard. The Left Bracket key ([) decreases the brush size; the Right Bracket (]) increases it.

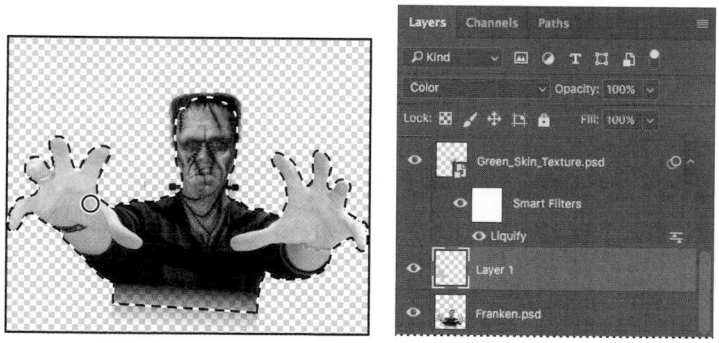

8 Paint any areas of the face or neck where the original flesh color shows through the Green_Skin_Texture layer.

9 When you're happy with the green skin, choose Select > Deselect. Save your work.

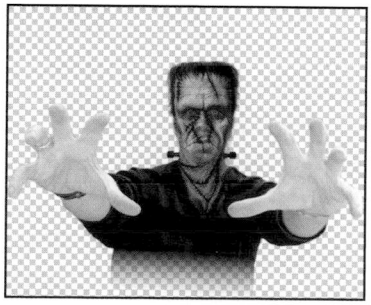

Adding a background

You've got a good-looking monster. Now it's time to put him in his spooky environment. To easily move the monster onto a background, you'll first merge the layers.

▶ **Tip:** Merging or flattening layers permanently combines them into a single layer. That also reduces the file size of the Photoshop document. If you want to preserve the ability to edit the selected layers separately, select layers and choose New Group from Layers instead of Merge Visible in step 1. Then, in step 6, drag that layer group from the Layers panel to the other document.

1 Make sure all the layers are visible. Then choose Merge Visible from the Layers panel menu.

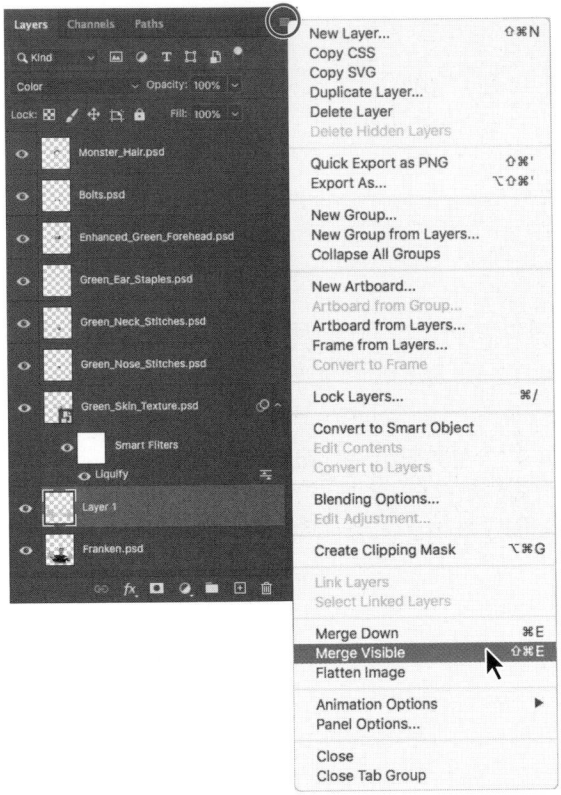

Photoshop merges all the visible layers into one. It's named Layer 1 because that was the selected layer at the time of the merge.

2 Rename Layer 1 **Monster**.

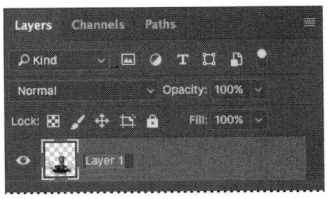

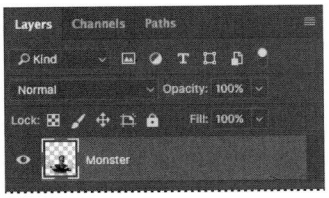

3 Choose File > Open. Navigate to and open the Backdrop.psd file in the Lesson09 folder.

4 Choose Window > Arrange > 2-Up Vertical to display both the monster and backdrop files.

5 Click the 09Working.psd file to make it active.

6 Select the Move tool (✣), drag the Monster layer, and then drop it onto the Backdrop.psd file. Position the monster so his hands are just above the movie title.

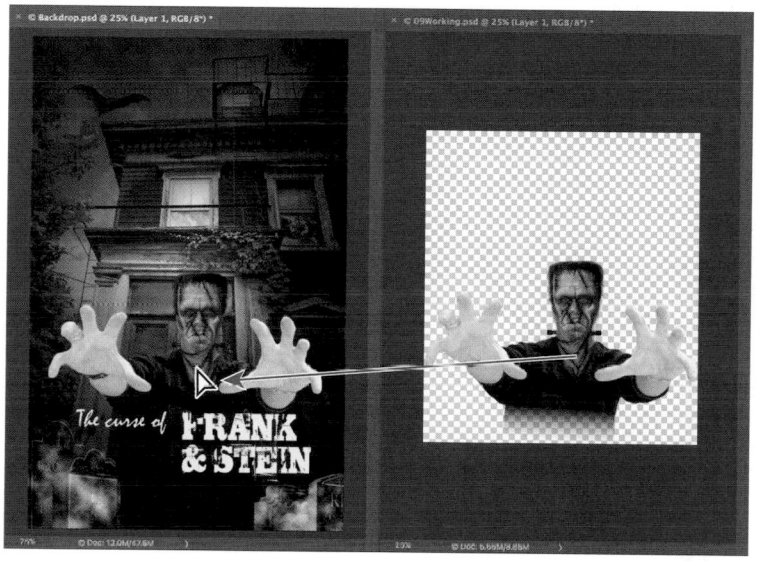

7 Close the 09Working.psd file, saving changes when prompted.

From now on, you'll work on the movie poster file itself.

8 Choose File > Save As, and save the file with the name **Movie-Poster.psd**. Click Save, and then click OK in the Photoshop Format Options dialog box.

Using the History panel to undo edits

You've used the Edit > Undo command to back out of the last change you applied. You can also choose Edit > Redo to reapply a change you just undid. Repeatedly choosing either command steps you back or forward through multiple edits.

You can choose Edit > Toggle Last State to undo and redo only the most recent change. For a quick before/after comparison of your last edit, press the Toggle Last State keyboard shortcut: Ctrl+Alt+Z (Windows) or Command+Option+Z (Mac).

A more visual way to step backward and forward through your changes is to use the History panel; choose Window > History to see it. The History panel shows you a list of your changes. To go back to a certain edit (for example, four steps ago), just select it in the History panel, and continue working from that point.

Applying filters and effects

You'll add a tombstone to the poster, and you'll experiment with filters and effects to see what works, using the History panel to reverse course if necessary.

1 In Photoshop, choose File > Open.

2 Navigate to the Lesson09 folder, and double-click the T1.psd file to open it.

The tombstone image is plain, but you'll add texture and color to it.

3 In the Tools panel, click the Default Foreground And Background Colors icon (◪) to return the default foreground color to black.

▶ **Tip:** A quick way to do step 3 is to press the D key, the keyboard shortcut for setting the foreground color to the default of black and the background color to the default of white.

You'll start by adding a little atmosphere to the tombstone.

4 Choose Filter > Render > Difference Clouds.

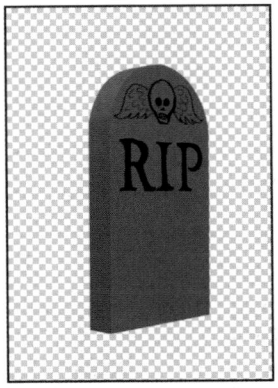

The original is dull.

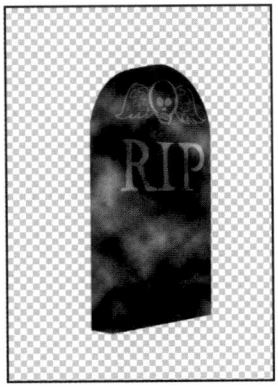

Clouds add drama.

● **Note:** The Difference Clouds you get may not match the figure shown; Difference Clouds renders uniquely each time you run it.

You'll leave the top of the tombstone in focus, but blur the rest using an iris blur.

5 Choose Filter > Blur Gallery > Iris Blur. Photoshop enters the Blur Gallery task space that displays just the tools for certain blur effects.

6 In the document window, drag the Iris Blur ellipse up so that the top of the tombstone is in focus and the rest is not. Then click OK.

▶ **Tip:** If you want to change the shape and area of the blur effect, drag the handles. Dragging the circle near the center is an alternate way to control the Blur Amount option that you see in the Iris Blur options, on the right side of the Blur Gallery task space.

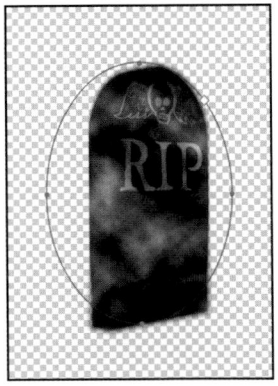

By default, the ellipse is centered.

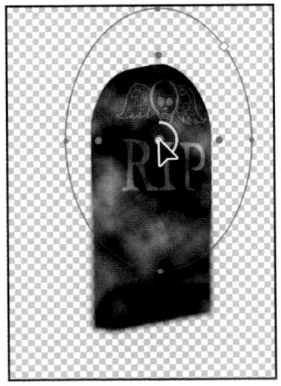

Shift the focus higher.

You'll use adjustment layers to make the image darker and change its color.

7 Click the Brightness/Contrast icon (☀) in the Adjustments panel. Then, in the Properties panel, move the Brightness slider to **70**.

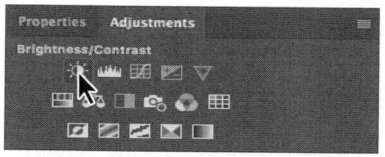

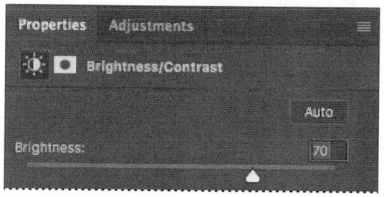

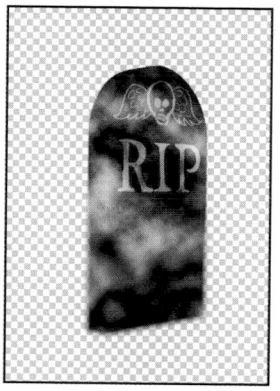

8 Click the Channel Mixer icon (◐) in the Adjustments panel.

9 In the Properties panel, choose Green from the Output Channel menu, and then change the Green value to **+37** and the Blue value to **+108**.

The tombstone takes on a green cast.

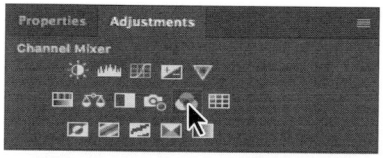

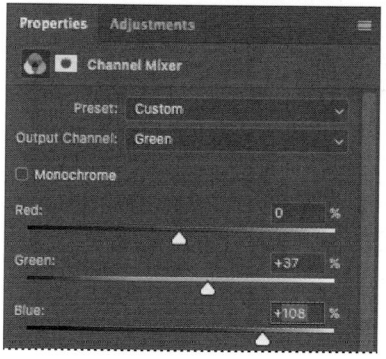

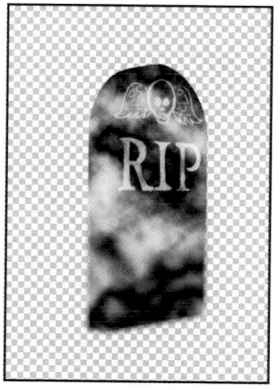

Note: The green channel is set as the Output Channel, so the adjustments changed the green channel to 37% of its original amount while adding 108% of the blue channel to the green channel.

The Channel Mixer is a useful option for correcting color balance, usually by applying much smaller values than you used here. The Channel Mixer is also an alternative to the Black & White adjustment for controlling how colors are converted to grayscale and for tinting effects. In this case, you used Channel Mixer to make a purely creative color adjustment to an image.

▶ **Tip:** The Exposure adjustment is primarily intended for correcting HDR images, but in this lesson it's used as a creative effect.

10 Click the Exposure icon (⊠) in the Adjustments panel. In the Properties panel, move the Exposure slider to **+.90** to brighten the lighter areas of the image.

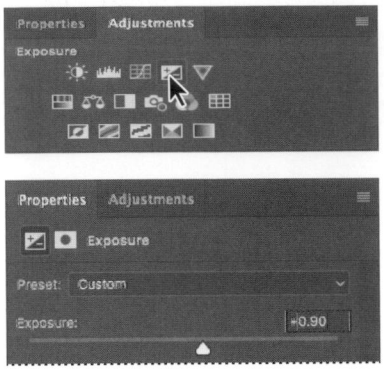

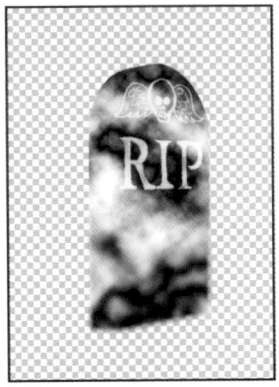

Undoing multiple steps

The tombstone certainly looks different than it did when you started, but it doesn't quite match the tombstones that are already in the poster. You'll use the History panel to revisit the steps you've taken.

1 If the History panel isn't already open, choose Window > History. Drag the bottom of the panel down so that you can see everything in it.

The History panel records the recent steps you've performed on the image. The current state is selected.

2 Click the Blur Gallery state in the History panel.

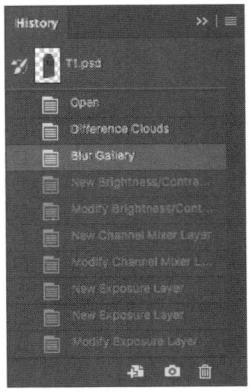

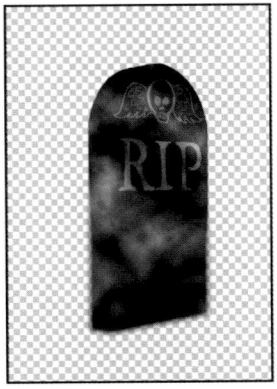

The states below the selected state are dimmed, and the image has changed. The color is gone, as are the Brightness/Contrast settings. At this point, the Difference Clouds filter has been run, and the iris blur has been applied. Everything else has been removed. There are no adjustment layers listed in the Layers panel.

3 Click the Modify Channel Mixer Layer state in the History panel.

Many of the states are restored. The color has returned, along with the brightness and contrast settings. There are two adjustment layers in the Layers panel. However, the states below the one you selected remain dimmed, and the Exposure adjustment layer is not listed in the Layers panel.

You'll return almost to the beginning to apply different effects to the tombstone.

4 Click Difference Clouds in the History panel.

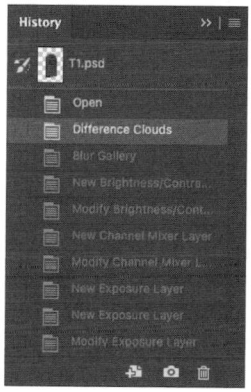

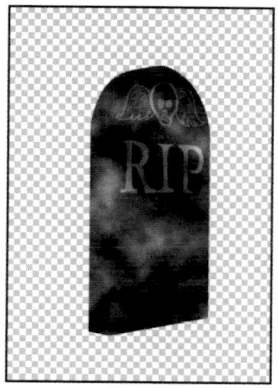

Everything following that state is dimmed.

5 Choose Filter > Noise > Add Noise.

Adding noise will give the tombstone a more stone-like texture.

6 In the Add Noise dialog box, set the Amount to 3%, select Gaussian, and select Monochromatic. Then click OK.

▶ **Tip:** If the Noise adjustments are hard to see, click the magnifying glass icon in the Add Noise dialog box.

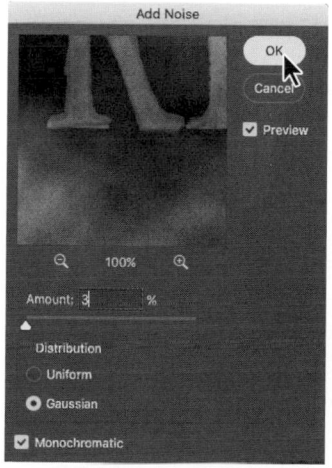

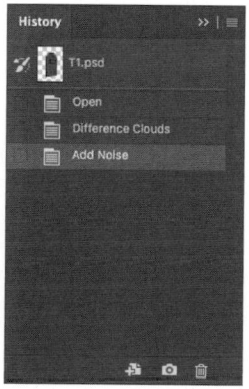

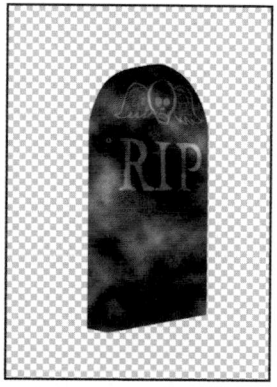

The states that were dimmed after the state you selected (Difference Clouds) are no longer in the History panel. They were replaced by the task you just performed

(Add Noise). You can click any state to return to that point in the process, but as soon as you perform a new task, Photoshop replaces all dimmed states.

Note: The Lighting Effects filter is unavailable if Use Graphics Processor is not selected in the Performance Preferences dialog box. If the graphics hardware in your computer does not support the Use Graphics Processor option, skip steps 7–12.

7 Choose Filter > Render > Lighting Effects.

8 In the options bar, choose Flashlight from the Presets menu.

9 In the Properties panel, click the Color swatch, select a light blue color, and then click OK.

10 In the image window, drag the light source to the upper third of the tombstone, centered over the letters "RIP."

11 In the Properties panel, change the Ambience to **46**.

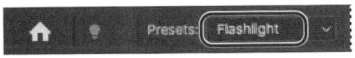

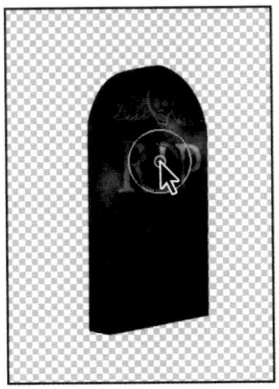

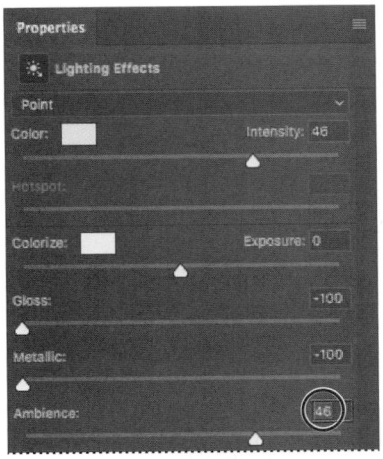

12 Click OK in the options bar to accept the Lighting Effects settings.

The tombstone is ready to join the others in your movie poster.

13 Choose Window > Arrange > Tile All Vertically.

14 With the Move tool, drag the tombstone you just created to the Movie-Poster.psd file. Click OK if you see a color management warning.

15 Drag the tombstone to the bottom-left corner, with the top third of it showing.

16 Choose File > Save to save the Movie-Poster.psd file. Then close the T1.psd file without saving it.

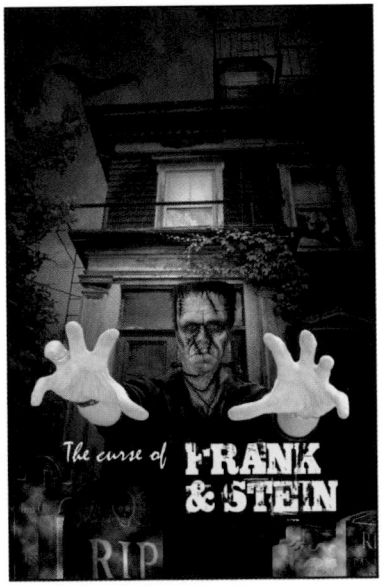

Note: A Paste Profile Mismatch dialog box may appear when you drag a layer between documents with different document color profiles. For this lesson, clicking OK is fine because it will convert the layer colors to match the destination document.

You've had a chance to try some new filters and effects and to use the History panel to backtrack. By default, the History panel retains only the last 50 states. You can change the number of levels in the History panel by choosing Edit > Preferences > Performance (Windows) or Photoshop > Preferences > Performance (Mac) and entering a different value for History States.

Upscaling a low-resolution image

Low-resolution images are fine—even desirable—for web pages and social media. If you need to enlarge them, though, they may not contain enough information for high-quality printing. To scale an image up in size, Photoshop needs to resample it. That is, it needs to create new pixels where none existed, approximating their values. The Preserve Details (Enlargement) algorithm in Photoshop gives the best results when you upscale low-resolution images.

In your movie poster, you want to use a low-resolution image that was posted on a social media site. You'll need to resize it without compromising quality for your printed poster.

1 Choose File > Open, navigate to the Lesson09 folder, and open the Faces.jpg file.

2 Zoom in to 300% or more, so you can see the pixels.

3 Choose Image > Image Size.

4 Make sure the Resample option is selected.

5 Change the width and height measurements to Percent, and then change their values to **400%**.

The width and height are linked by default so that images resize proportionally. If you need to change the width and height separately for a project, click to deselect the link icon to unlink the values.

6 Drag in the preview window to pan so that you can see the glasses.

7 In the Resample menu, choose Bicubic Smoother (Enlargement). The image looks less rough than it did before.

The Resample menu includes options that control how to adjust the image for enlargement or reduction. Automatic is the default, and it picks a method based on whether you're enlarging or reducing, but you may find that another option might look better depending on the image.

8 With the Resample option still selected, choose Preserve Details (Enlargement) from the Resample menu.

The Preserve Details option results in a sharper enlargement than Bicubic Smoother, but this may also make image noise more visible.

Note: Your version of Photoshop may display a Preserve Details 2.0 option in the Resample menu. This is an upgraded version of Preserve Details provided as a Technology Preview for comparison with the older Preserve Details option. Use the option that produces better results for the image you're scaling up.

9 Move the Reduce Noise slider to **50%** to smooth the image.

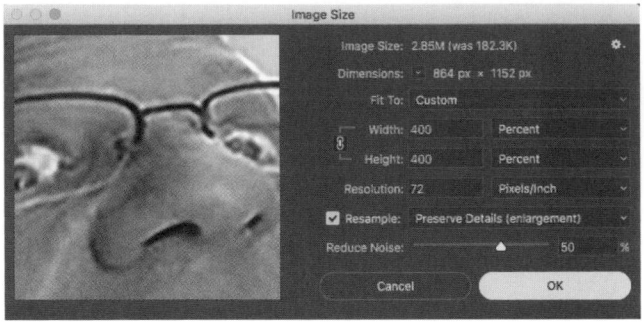

10 Click and hold in the preview window to see the original image so you can compare it to the current settings. You can also compare the current settings to the Bicubic Smoother option by switching between them in the Resample menu. When upscaling or downscaling, choose the Resample method that produces the best balance between preserving details and smoothing pixel jagginess, and then use Reduce Noise to remove noise that remains. If the Reduce Noise value removes too much detail, lower it.

11 Click OK. Now you'll paste the image into a feathered selection on the poster.

12 Choose Select > All, and then choose Edit > Copy.

13 Select the Movie-Poster.psd tab to bring it to the front, and then select the Elliptical Marquee tool (◌), hidden under the Rectangular Marquee tool (⬚).

14 In the options bar, enter **50 px** for Feather to soften the edge of the pasted image.

15 Draw an oval in the upper-right corner of the poster, above the monster's head. The oval should overlap the window and fire escape.

16 Make sure Layer 1 is selected, and then choose Edit > Paste Special > Paste Into. Click OK if you see the Paste Profile Mismatch dialog box.

17 Select the Move tool (✥), and center the pasted image in the feathered area.

18 In the Layers panel, choose Luminosity from the Blending Mode menu, and move the Opacity slider to **50%**.

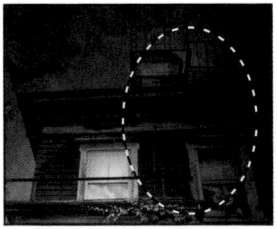
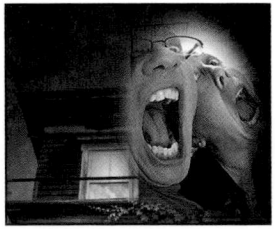
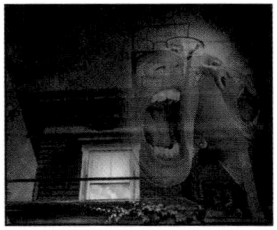

19 You've finished the poster! Close the Movie-Poster.psd document, saving changes. Then close the Faces.jpg file without saving it.

Review questions

1 What are the differences between using a Smart Filter and a regular filter to apply effects to an image?

2 What do the Bloat and Pucker tools in the Liquify filter do?

3 What does the History panel do?

4 What is the relationship of the Undo and Redo commands to the History panel?

Review answers

1 Smart Filters are nondestructive: They can be adjusted, turned off and on, and deleted at any time without altering the pixels of a layer. In contrast, regular filters permanently change a layer or image; once applied, they cannot be removed. A Smart Filter can be applied only to a Smart Object layer.

2 The Bloat tool moves pixels away from the center of the brush; the Pucker tool moves pixels toward the center of the brush.

3 The History panel records recent steps you've performed in Photoshop. You can return to an earlier step by selecting it in the History panel.

4 The Undo and Redo commands move back or forward, respectively, through the steps in the History panel.

10 PAINTING WITH THE MIXER BRUSH

Lesson overview

In this lesson, you'll learn how to do the following:

- Customize brush settings.
- Clean the brush.
- Mix colors.
- Create a custom brush preset.
- Use wet and dry brushes to blend color.

This lesson will take about an hour to complete. To get the lesson files used in this chapter, download them from the web page for this book at www.adobepress.com/PhotoshopCIB2021. For more information, see "Accessing the lesson files and Web Edition" in the Getting Started section at the beginning of this book.

As you work on this lesson, you'll preserve the start files. If you need to restore the start files, download them from your Account page.

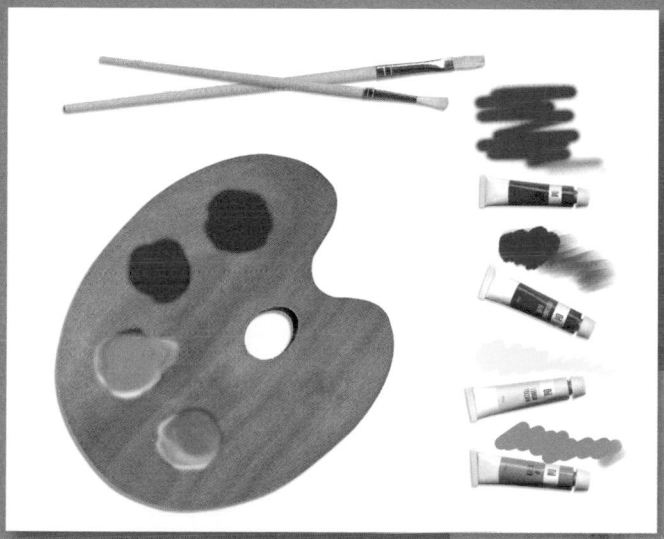

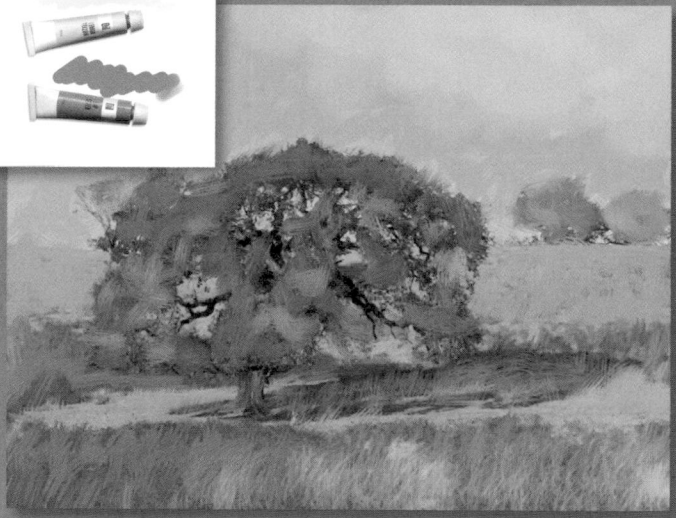

PROJECT: DIGITAL PAINTING

The Mixer Brush tool gives you flexibility, color-mixing abilities, and brush strokes as if you were painting on a physical canvas.

About the Mixer Brush

In previous lessons, you've used brushes in Photoshop to perform various tasks. The Mixer Brush is unlike other brushes in that it lets you mix colors with each other. You can change the wetness of the brush and how it mixes the brush color with the color already on the canvas.

Some Photoshop brush types can have realistic bristles, so you can add textures that resemble those in paintings you might create in the physical world. While this is a great feature in general, it's particularly useful when you're using the Mixer Brush. Combining different bristle settings and brush tips with different wetness, paint-load, and paint-mixing settings gives you opportunities to create exactly the look you want.

Getting started

In this lesson, you'll get acquainted with the Mixer Brush as well as the brush tip and bristle options available in Photoshop. Start by taking a look at the final projects you'll create.

1 Start Photoshop, and then simultaneously hold down Ctrl+Alt+Shift (Windows) or Command+Option+Shift (Mac) to restore the default preferences. (See "Restoring default preferences" on page 5.)

2 When prompted, click Yes to delete the Adobe Photoshop Settings file.

3 Choose File > Browse In Bridge to open Adobe Bridge.

4 In Bridge, click Lessons in the Favorites panel. Double-click the Lesson10 folder in the Content panel.

5 Preview the Lesson10 end files.

Note: If Bridge isn't installed, the File > Browse In Bridge command in Photoshop will start the Creative Cloud desktop app, which will download and install Bridge. After installation completes, you can start Bridge.

You'll use the palette image to explore brush options and learn to mix colors. You'll then apply what you've learned to transform the landscape image into a painting.

6 Double-click 10Palette_Start.psd to open the file in Photoshop.

7 Choose File > Save As, and name the file **10Palette_Working.psd**. Click OK if the Photoshop Format Options dialog box appears.

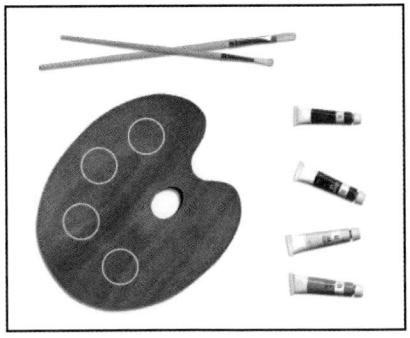

Note: If Photoshop displays a dialog box telling you about the difference between saving to Cloud Documents and Your Computer, click Save On Your Computer. You can also select Don't Show Again, but that setting will deselect after you reset Photoshop preferences.

8 Click the Choose a Workspace icon at the top-right corner of the application frame, and choose the Painting workspace.

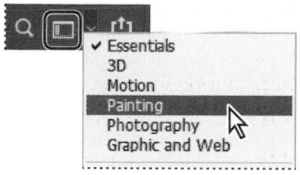

Note: If you use Photoshop for digital painting, consider using a graphics tablet with a pressure-sensitive stylus. If your stylus transmits information such as pressure, angle, and rotation, Photoshop can apply that data to your brush as you paint.

Selecting brush settings

The practice image includes a palette and four tubes of color, which you'll use to sample the colors you're working with. You'll change settings as you paint different colors, exploring brush tip settings and wetness options.

1 Select the Zoom tool (🔍), and zoom in to see the tubes of paint.

2 Select the Eyedropper tool (💉), and click the red tube to sample its color.

The foreground color changes to red.

3 Select the Mixer Brush tool (🖌) in the Tools panel. (When another workspace is selected, you may find the Mixer Brush hidden under the Brush tool [🖌].)

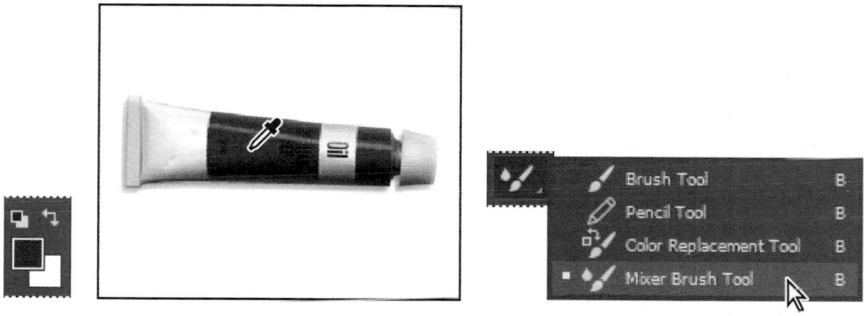

Note: When you hold down the Eyedropper tool on the image, Photoshop displays a sampling ring that previews the color you're selecting. The sampling ring is available if Photoshop can use the graphics processor on your computer (see the Performance panel in Photoshop preferences).

4 Choose Window > Brush Settings to open the Brush Settings panel. Select the first brush.

The Brush Settings panel contains brush presets and several options for customizing brushes.

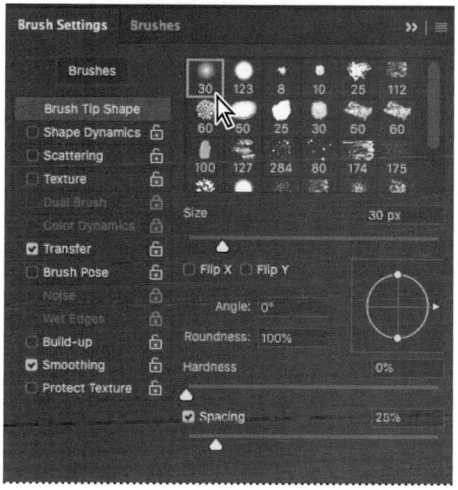

Tip: Looking for a specific brush name in the Brush Settings panel? Hover the pointer over a brush thumbnail, and its name will pop up in a tool tip.

Experimenting with wetness options and brushes

The effect of the brush is determined by the Wet, Load, and Mix fields in the options bar. *Wet* controls how much paint the brush picks up from the canvas. *Load* controls how much paint the brush holds when you begin painting (as with a physical brush, it runs out of paint as you paint with it). *Mix* controls the ratio of paint from the canvas and paint from the brush.

You can change these settings separately. However, it's faster to select a standard combination from the pop-up menu.

1 In the options bar, choose Dry from the pop-up menu of blending brush combinations.

When you select Dry, Wet is set to 0%, Load to 50%, and Mix is not applicable. With the Dry preset, you paint opaque color; you cannot mix colors on a dry canvas.

2 Paint in the area above the red tube. Solid red appears. As you continue painting without releasing the mouse, the paint eventually fades and runs out.

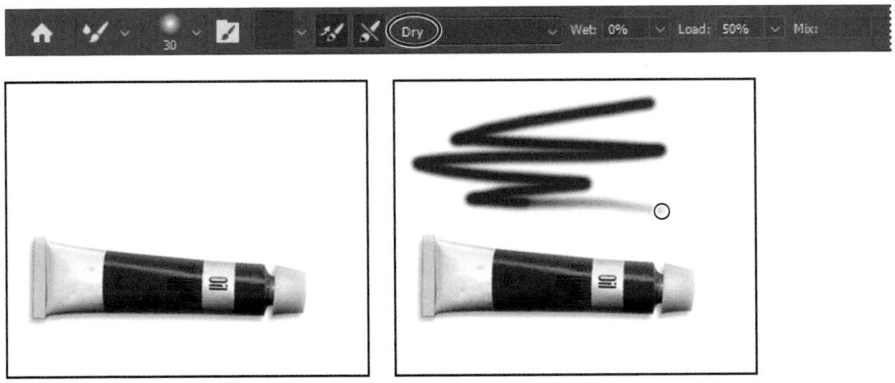

3 With the Eyedropper tool, sample the blue color from the blue tube of paint.

4 Select the Mixer Brush. For the blue paint, in the Brush Settings panel we chose the Round Sketch Ballpoint Pen brush (the first brush in the second row). Choose Wet from the pop-up menu in the options bar.

If the brush you select doesn't match the one shown here, resize the Brush Settings panel so that the brush thumbnails display six columns across.

Note: You can also sample paint by Alt-clicking or Option-clicking the Mixer Brush tool. This samples the area within the brush size as an image, unless you selected Load Solid Colors Only in the Current Brush Load menu in the options bar.

5 Paint above the blue tube. The paint mixes with the white background.

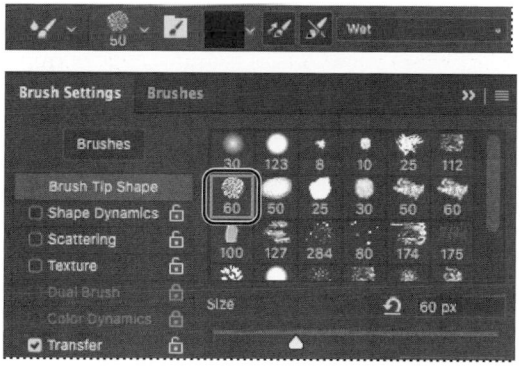

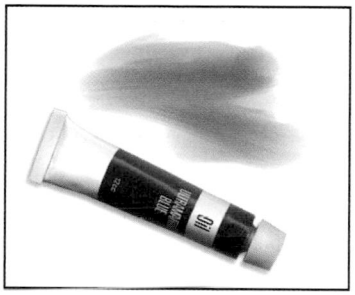

Note: If you aren't getting the same results from the brushes, make sure the Background layer is selected in the Layers panel.

6 Choose Dry from the menu in the options bar, and then paint again above the blue tube. A much darker, more opaque blue appears and doesn't mix with the white background.

7 Sample the yellow color from the yellow paint tube, and then select the Mixer brush. For the yellow paint, in the Brush Settings panel we chose the Pencil KTW 1 brush (the fourth brush in the second row). Choose Dry from the menu in the options bar, and then paint in the area over the yellow paint tube.

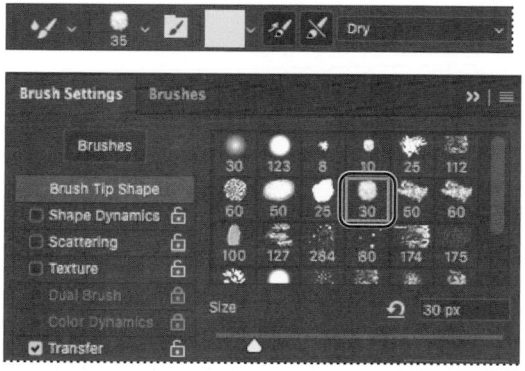

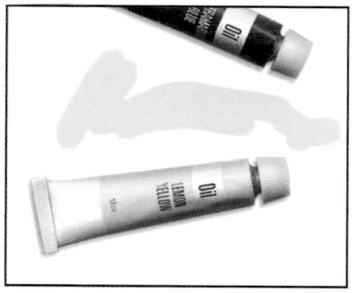

Note: If the brushes in your Brush Settings panel don't match the ones shown in this chapter, open the Brushes panel, Shift-select all brushes and brush folders in the list, click the Delete Brush button (🗑), click OK to confirm, and then choose Restore Default Brushes from the Brushes panel menu.

8 Choose Very Wet from the menu in the options bar, and then paint some more. Now the yellow mixes with the white background.

9 Sample the green color from the green paint tube, and then select the Mixer brush. For the green paint, in the Brush Settings panel we chose the Hard Round 30 brush (the sixth brush in the fifth row). Choose Dry from the menu in the options bar.

10 Draw a zigzag line above the green paint tube.

Mixing colors

Note: Depending on the complexity of your project and the performance of your computer, you may need to be patient. Mixing colors can be an intensive process.

You've used wet and dry brushes, changed brush settings, and mixed the paint with the background color. Now, you'll focus more on mixing colors with each other as you add paint to the painter's palette.

1 Zoom out just enough to see the full palette and the paint tubes.

2 Select the Paint mix layer in the Layers panel so the color you paint won't blend with the brown palette on the Background layer.

The Mixer Brush tool mixes colors only on the active layer unless you select Sample All Layers in the options bar.

3 Use the Eyedropper tool to sample the red color from the red paint tube, and then select the Mixer brush. In the Brush Settings panel, select the Soft Round 30 brush (the first brush in the first row). Then choose Wet from the pop-up menu in the options bar, and paint in the top circle on the palette.

4 Click the Clean The Brush After Each Stroke icon (✕) in the options bar to deselect it.

Tip: If the paint tubes are covered by the Brush Settings panel, feel free to rearrange your workspace to make room. For example, collapse or close panels you aren't using. But make sure you can still see the Layers panel.

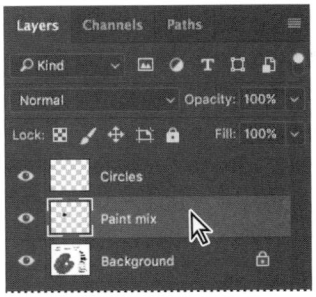

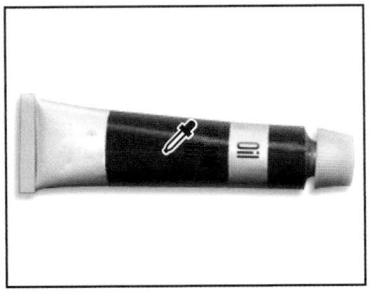

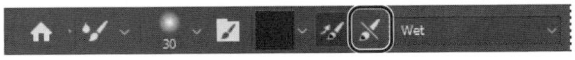

Tip: You can use the Eyedropper tool to sample a color even if the layer that contains the color isn't selected.

5 Use the Eyedropper tool to sample the blue color from the blue paint tube, and then use the Mixer Brush tool to paint in the same circle, mixing the red with the blue until the color becomes purple.

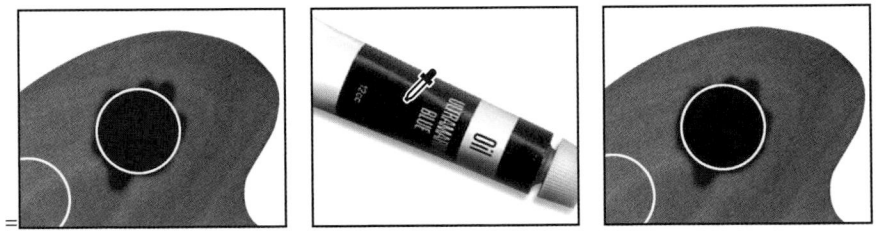

6 Use the Eyedropper tool to sample the purple color from the circle you just painted, and then paint in the next circle.

7 In the options bar, choose Clean Brush from the Current Brush Load pop-up menu. The preview changes to indicate transparency, meaning the brush has no paint loaded.

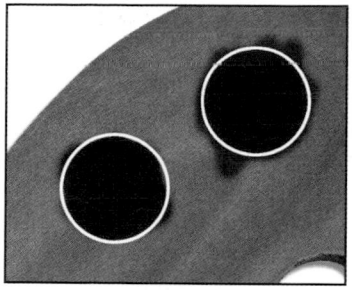

▶ **Tip:** Use the Eyedropper tool to sample the color, since it's on a different layer.

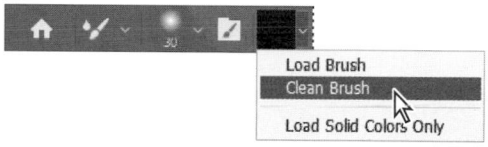

To remove the paint load from a brush, you can choose Clean Brush in the options bar. To replace the paint load in a brush, sample a different color.

If you want Photoshop to clean the brush after each stroke, select the Clean The Brush After Each Stroke icon (✕) in the options bar. To load the brush with the foreground color after each stroke, select the Load The Brush After Each Stroke icon (🖌) in the options bar. By default, both of these options are selected.

8 Use the Eyedropper tool to sample the blue color from the blue paint tube, and then use the Mixer Brush to paint blue in half of the next circle.

9 Sample the yellow color from the yellow paint tube, and slowly paint over the blue with a wet brush to mix the two colors.

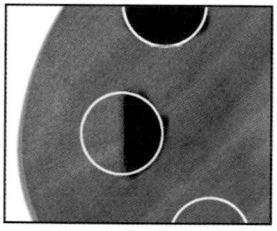

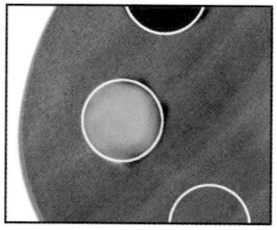

10 Fill the last circle with yellow and red paint, mixing the two with a wet brush to create an orange color.

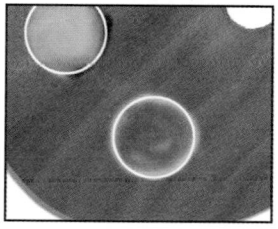

11 Hide the Circles layer in the Layers panel to remove the outlines on the palette. You've mixed paint colors on a digital palette!

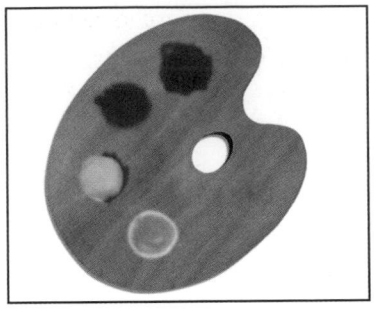

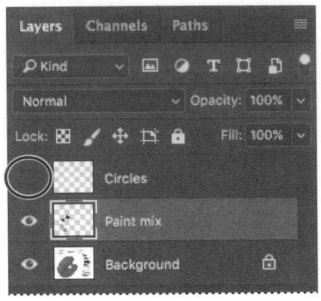

12 Choose File > Save, and close the document.

Julieanne Kost is an official Adobe Photoshop evangelist.

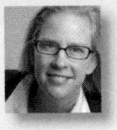

Tool tips from the Photoshop evangelist

Mixer Brush shortcuts

There are no default keyboard shortcuts for the Mixer Brush tool, but you can create your own.

To create custom keyboard shortcuts:

1. Choose Edit > Keyboard Shortcuts.
2. Choose Tools from the Shortcuts For menu.
3. Scroll down to the bottom of the list.
4. Select a command, and then enter a custom shortcut. You can create shortcuts for the following commands:
    - Load Mixer Brush
    - Clean Mixer Brush
    - Toggle Mixer Brush Auto-Load
    - Toggle Mixer Brush Auto-Clean
    - Toggle Mixer Brush Sample All Layers
    - Sharpen Erodible Tips

Mixing colors with a photograph

When you come up with a great brush, you probably want to save all of its settings so that you can use that brush again in a later project. While Photoshop already has a Tool Preset feature that lets you save tool settings, brushes have more options than most tools. For this reason, Photoshop has convenient Brush Presets that can remember everything about a brush.

▶ **Tip:** If you've used earlier versions of Photoshop, you'll find that the Brush Presets in Photoshop CC 2018 or later are simpler and more powerful than in previous versions.

Earlier, you mixed colors with a white background and with each other. Now, you'll use a photograph as your canvas. You'll add colors and mix them with each other and with the background colors to transform a photograph of a landscape into a painting.

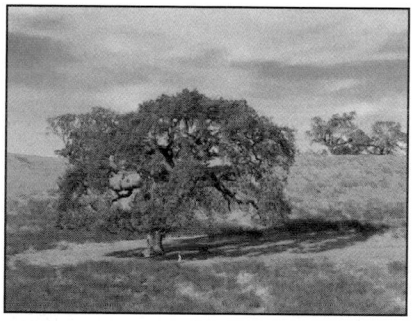

1 Choose File > Open. Double-click the 10Landscape_Start.jpg file in the Lesson10 folder to open it.

2 Choose File > Save As. Rename the file **10Landscape_Working.jpg**, and click Save. Click OK in the JPEG Options dialog box.

Photoshop includes numerous brush presets, which are very handy. But if you need a different brush for your project, you might find it easier to create your own brush preset or download brush presets that another artist has created and shared online. In the following exercises, you'll load, edit, and save custom brush presets.

Loading custom brush presets

The Brushes panel displays visual samples of the strokes created by different brushes. If you already know the name of the brush you want to use, it can be easier to display the brushes by name. You'll list them by name now, so you can find your preset for the next exercise.

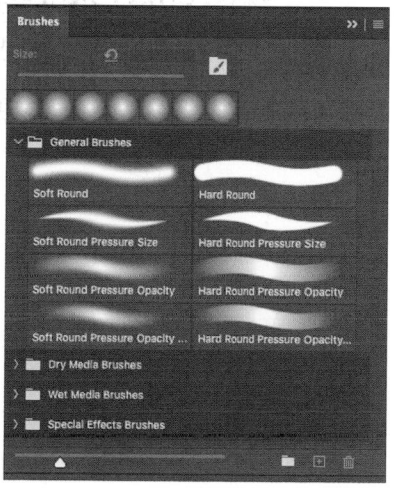

▶ **Tip:** If you have enough space on your screen, you can see more brushes at once by making the Brushes panel wider or taller.

1 In the Brushes panel (choose Window > Brushes if it's not open), expand one of the brush preset groups to see how the brushes are organized.

Now you'll load brush presets that you'll use for this exercise. Loading brush presets is how you use brush presets that you've downloaded or purchased.

▶ **Tip:** If you want to share your custom brushes with others or back them up, select the brushes or brush groups, and choose Export Selected Brushes from the Brushes panel menu.

2 Click the Brushes panel menu, and choose Import Brushes.

3 Navigate to the Lesson10 folder, select CIB Landscape Brushes.abr, and click Open or Load. The CIB Landscape Brushes group appears at the end of the Brushes panel list.

4 Click to expand the CIB Landscape Brushes group, revealing the brushes it contains.

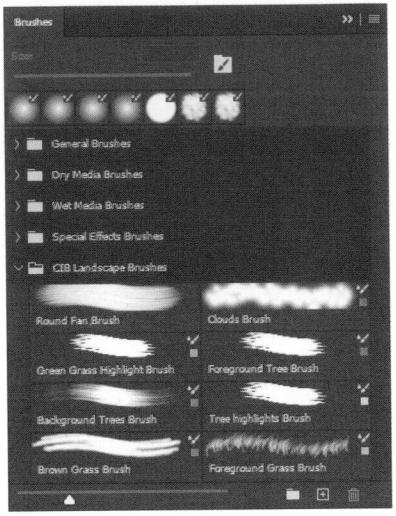

Some of the presets contain not only a stroke preview and a name, but also a color swatch. That's because a color can be part of a brush preset.

Creating a custom brush preset

For the next exercise, you'll create and save a variation on a brush preset that exists in the CIB Landscape Brushes you just imported.

▶ **Tip:** In the Brush Settings panel, the Brush Tip Shape options include the Angle setting, which simulates the rotation angle at which you hold the brush handle. Some graphics tablets can use a stylus that lets you rotate the brush tip as you paint, by rotating the stylus. If you don't have such a stylus, you can rotate the brush tip angle by one degree as you paint, by pressing the Left Arrow or Right Arrow keys. Add the Shift key to rotate in 15-degree increments.

1 Select the Mixer Brush, and then, in the CIB Landscape Brushes group in the Brushes panel, select the Round Fan Brush. You'll use this brush preset as the starting point for the brush preset you'll create.

2 Change the following settings in the Brush Settings panel:

- Size: **36** px
- Shape: Round Fan
- Bristles: **35**%
- Length: **32**%
- Thickness: **2**%
- Stiffness: **75**%
- Angle: **0**°
- Spacing: **2**%

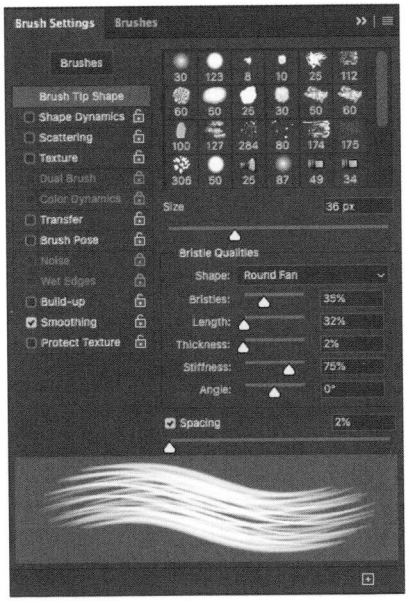

3 Click the Foreground color swatch in the Tools panel. Select a medium-light blue color (we chose R=86, G=201, B=252).

4 Choose Dry from the pop-up menu in the options bar.

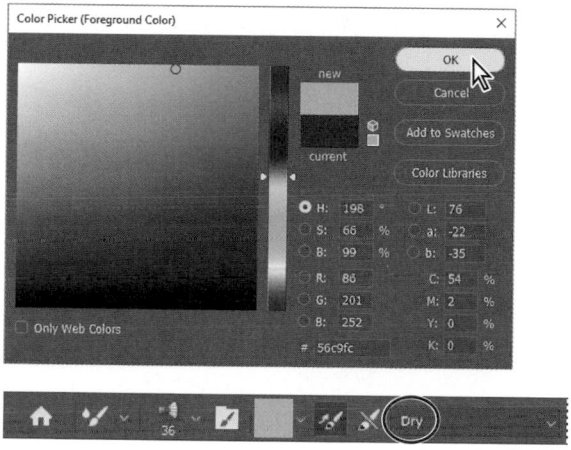

Now it's time to save the settings as a brush preset.

5 Choose New Brush Preset from the Brush Settings panel menu.

6 Name the brush **Sky Brush**, select all of the options in the New Brush dialog box, and then click OK.

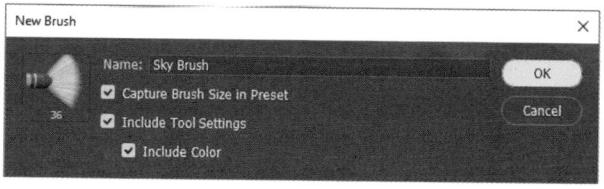

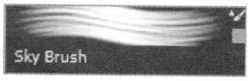

▶ **Tip:** The options in the New Brush dialog box make it possible to save the brush size, the tool settings, and the brush color in the preset.

Your new brush is saved in the CIB Landscape Brushes group because it was based on a brush preset from that group. Feel free to reorganize your brush presets any way you like by dragging and dropping presets into brush preset groups within the Brushes panel. You can create a brush preset group by clicking the Create A New Group button (🗀) at the bottom of the Brushes panel. You can change the order of the Brushes panel list and organize brush preset groups into subgroups.

Painting and mixing colors with brush presets

You'll paint the sky first, using the brush preset you just created.

1 Select the Sky Brush from the Brushes panel.

Presets are saved on your system, so they're available when you work with any image.

2 Paint over the sky, moving in close to the trees. Because you're using a dry brush, the blue paint isn't mixing with the colors beneath it.

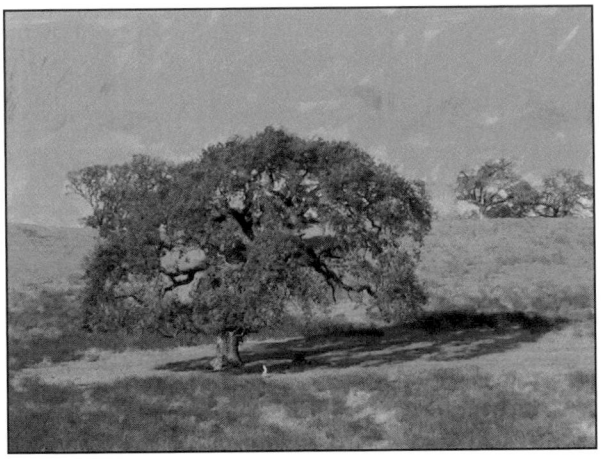

3 Select the Clouds Brush.

4 Use this brush to scrub diagonally in the upper-right corner of the sky, blending the two colors with the background color.

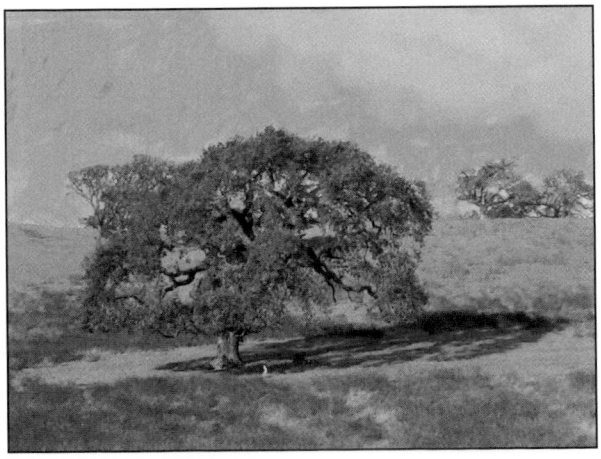

When you're satisfied with the sky, move on to the grass and trees.

5 Select the Green Grass Highlight Brush. Then paint short vertical strokes over the darker grass areas so that they become bright green grass.

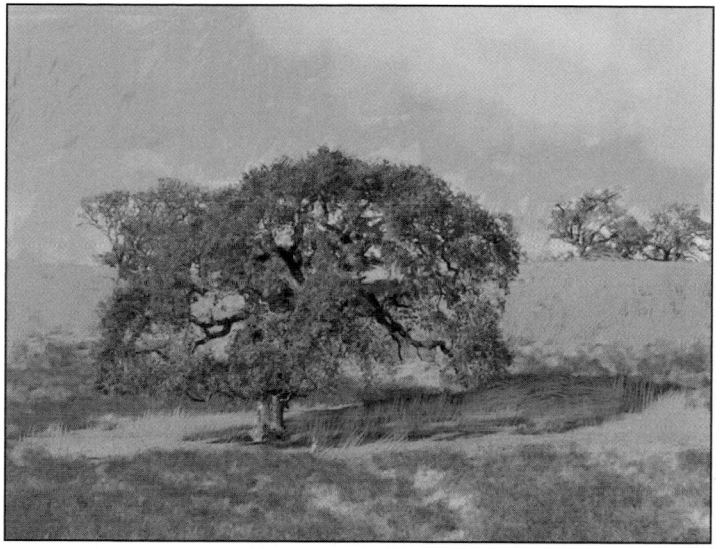

6 Select the Foreground Tree Brush, and then paint the darker areas of the tree. Then select the Background Trees Brush, and paint the two smaller trees on the right side of the painting. Select the Tree Highlights Brush, and paint the lighter areas of the trees. These are Wet brushes so that you can blend colors.

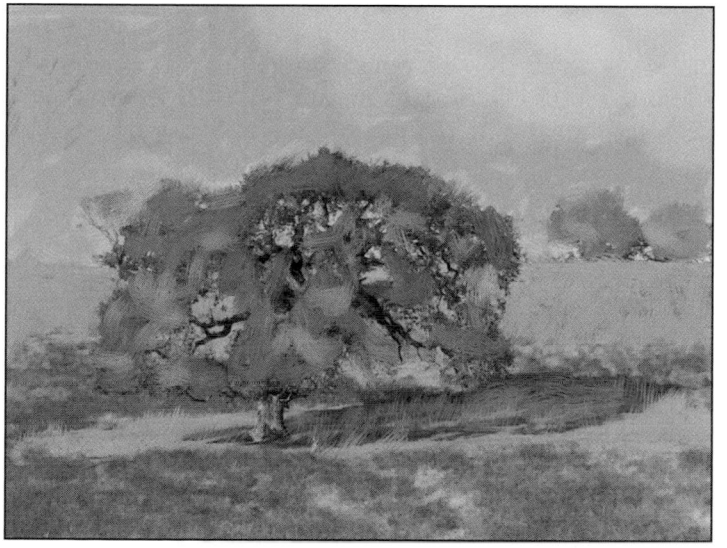

So far, so good. The brown grasses are all that remain to be painted.

▶ **Tip:** If you want to create less jittery strokes with the Mixer Brush, like near the edges of the trees, try increasing the Set Smoothing for Stroke percentage in the options bar.

▶ **Tip:** For different effects, paint in different directions or customize the brush size or other settings. With the Mixer Brush tool, you can go wherever your artistic instincts lead you.

7 Select the Brown Grass Brush. Paint along the brown grass with up-and-down strokes for the look of a field. Use the same brush to paint the trunk of the tree.

8 Select the Foreground Grass Brush. Then paint using diagonal strokes to blend the colors in the grass.

9 Choose File > Save, and close the document.

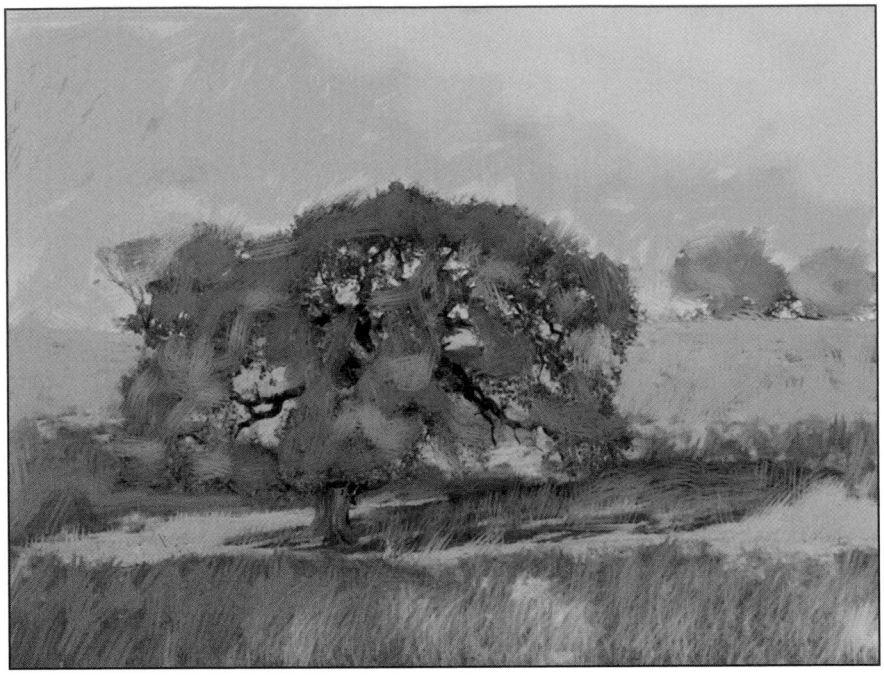

Voilà! You've created a masterpiece with your paints and brushes, and there's no mess to clean up.

Brushes from Kyle T. Webster

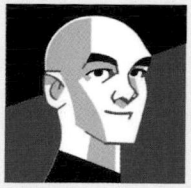

In 2017, award-winning brush designer Kyle T. Webster joined Adobe. At the same time, Adobe acquired the popular brush collections at KyleBrush.com. Kyle has drawn for *The New Yorker*, *TIME*, *The New York Times*, *The Wall Street Journal*, *The Atlantic*, *Entertainment Weekly*, Scholastic, Nike, IDEO, and many other distinguished editorial, advertising, publishing, and institutional clients. His illustration work has been recognized by the Society of Illustrators, Communications Arts, and American Illustration. Kyle now works closely with Adobe product teams on the development of future brushes for Adobe Creative Cloud.

To add the Kyle T. Webster brushes to Photoshop, open the Brushes panel (Window > Brushes), and choose Get More Brushes from the Brushes panel menu. After you download a brush pack and with Photoshop running, double-click the downloaded ABR file to add its brushes as a new group in the Brushes panel.

Painting with Symmetry

If you're painting a design that uses symmetry, try the Paint Symmetry brush option. When a brush type that supports Paint Symmetry is selected, you'll see the Paint Symmetry icon (⊞) in the options bar. Click that icon, and select the type of symmetry axis you want; it appears as a guide object in the document. Move, scale, or rotate the guide if you want, and then press Enter or Return. As you paint with Paint Symmetry, each of your brushstrokes is repeated across the axes you set up.

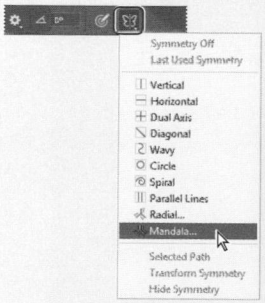

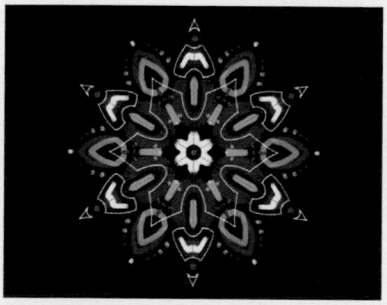

You might use a single axis for simple mirror symmetry, but you can also use multiple axes arranged in different ways. For example, you can use horizontal and vertical axes to design tiles, or radial axes to design mandalas.

The axes are actually paths, so you can see and edit them in the Paths panel. You can even create your own custom axis. Draw with a tool such as the Pen, Curvature Pen, or Custom Shape tool in Path mode (not Shape mode). With the path selected in the Paths panel, choose Make Symmetry Path from the Paths panel menu.

Painting gallery

The painting tools and brush tips in Photoshop let you create all kinds of painting effects.

The following pages show examples of art created with the brush tips and tools in Photoshop.

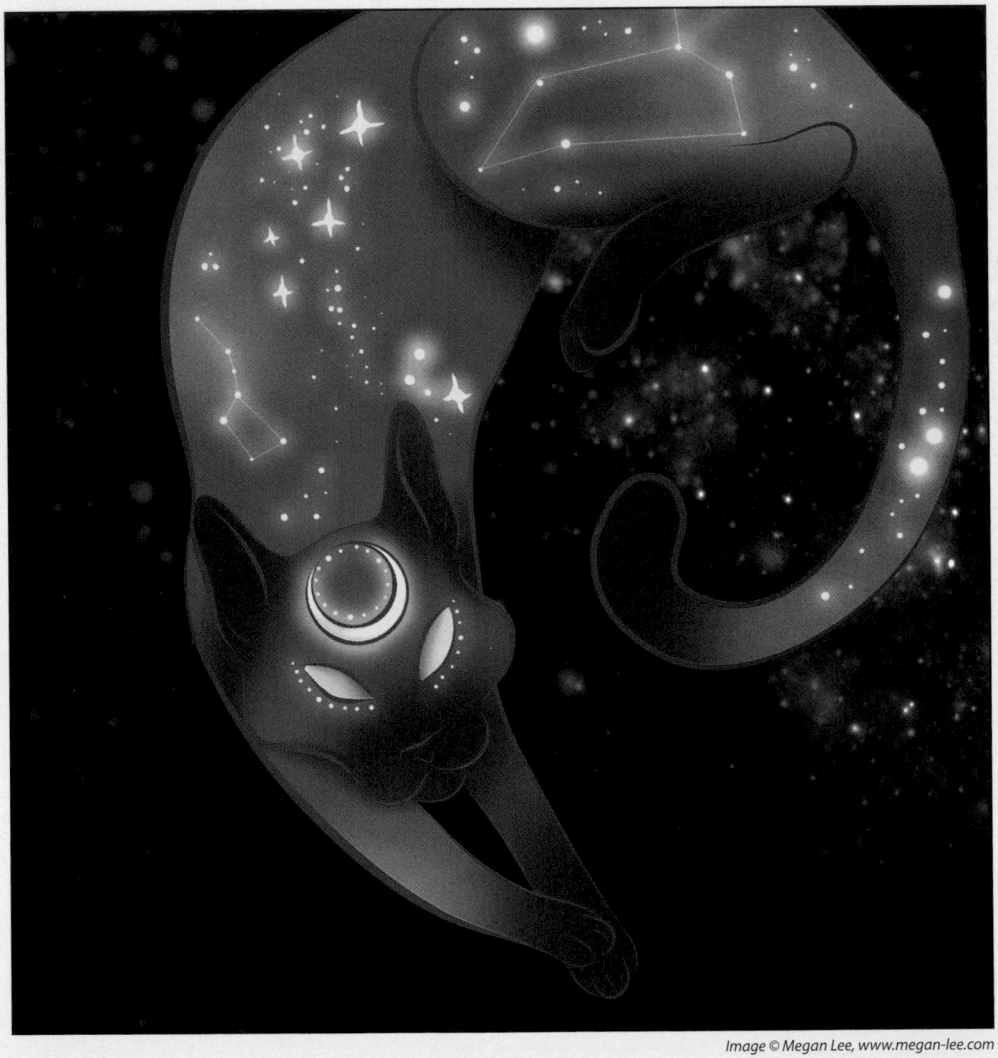

Image © Megan Lee, www.megan-lee.com

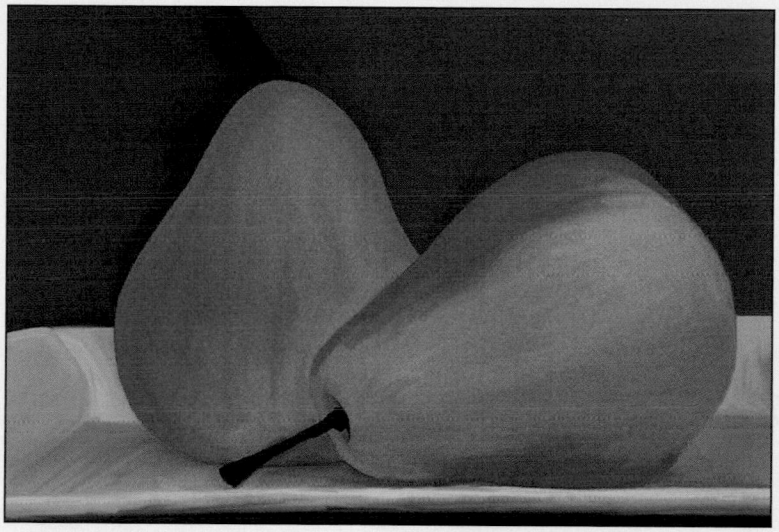

Image © Victoria Pavlov, pavlovphotography.com

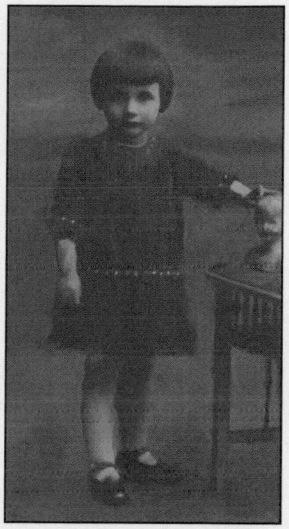

Image © sholby, www.sholby.net

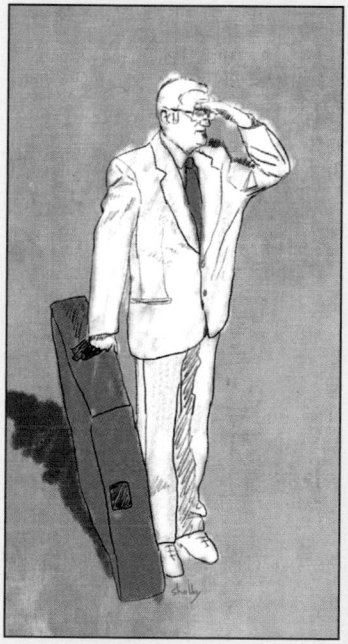

Image © sholby, www.sholby.net

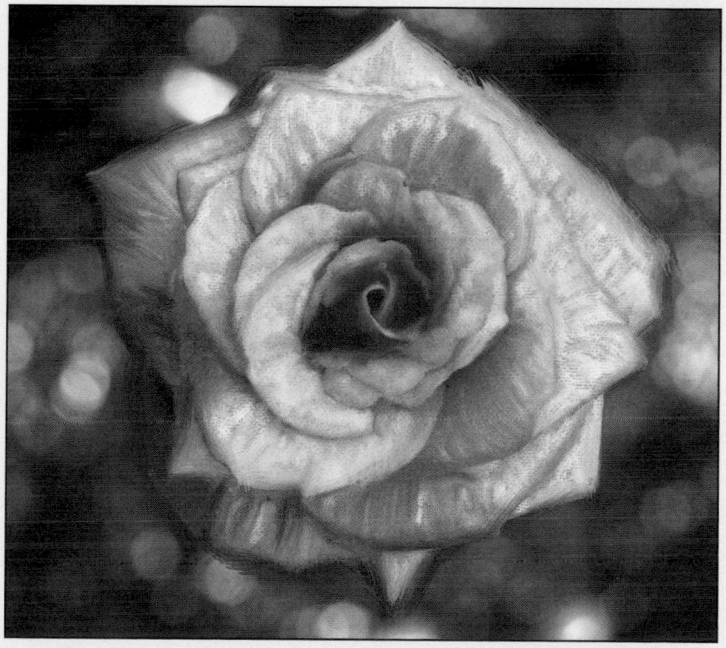

Image © sholby, www.sholby.net

Continues on next page

Painting gallery (continued)

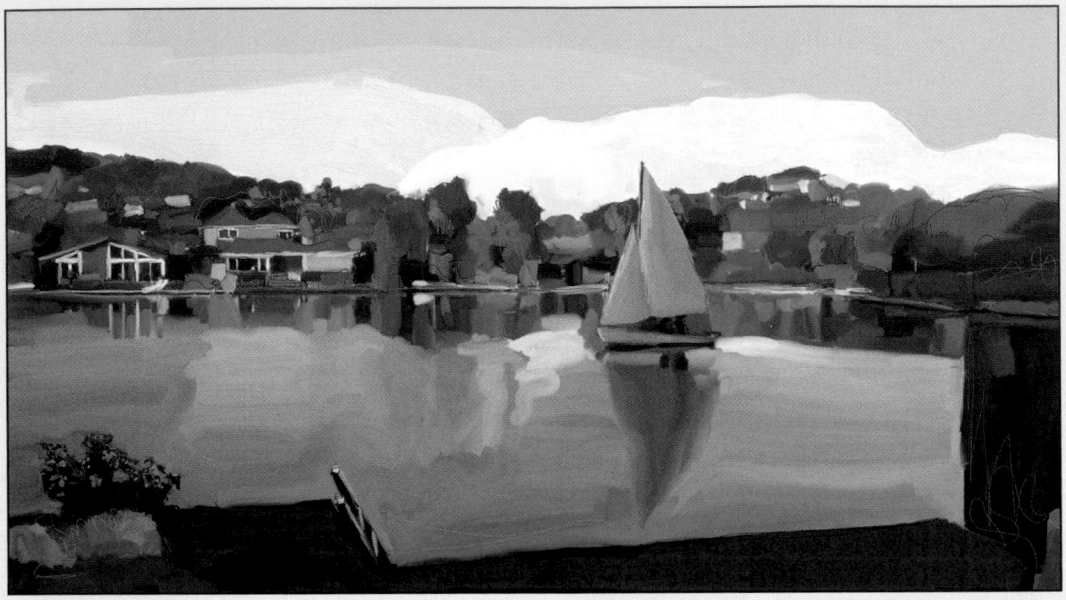

Image © Andrew Faulkner, www.andrew-faulkner.com

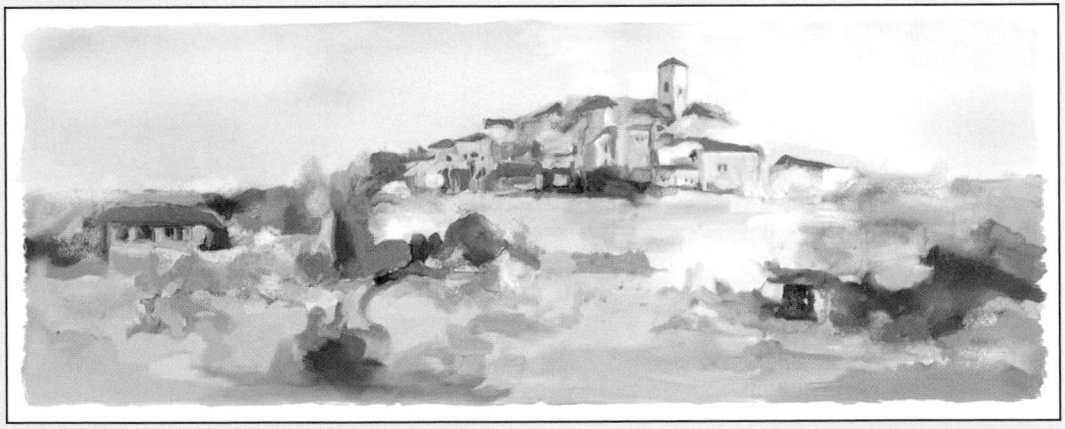

Image © Lynette Kent, www.LynetteKent.com

Review questions

1 What does the Mixer Brush do that other brushes don't?

2 How do you load a mixer brush with color?

3 How do you clean a brush?

4 What is the name of the panel that you use to manage brush presets?

Review answers

1 The Mixer Brush mixes the current brush color with colors on the canvas.

2 You can load color on a mixer brush by sampling a color, either by using the Eyedropper tool or by using keyboard shortcuts (Alt-click or Option-click). Or, you can choose Load Brush from the pop-up menu in the options bar to load the brush with the foreground color.

3 To clean a brush, choose Clean Brush from the pop-up menu in the options bar.

4 You manage brush presets in the Brushes panel.

11 EDITING VIDEO

Lesson overview

In this lesson, you'll learn how to do the following:

- Create a video timeline in Photoshop.
- Add media to a video group in the Timeline panel.
- Add motion to still images.
- Animate type and effects using keyframes.
- Add transitions between video clips.
- Include audio in a video file.
- Render a video.

This lesson will take about 90 minutes to complete. To get the lesson files used in this chapter, download them from the web page for this book at www.adobepress.com/PhotoshopCIB2021. For more information, see "Accessing the lesson files and Web Edition" in the Getting Started section at the beginning of this book.

As you work on this lesson, you'll preserve the start files. If you need to restore the start files, download them from your Account page.

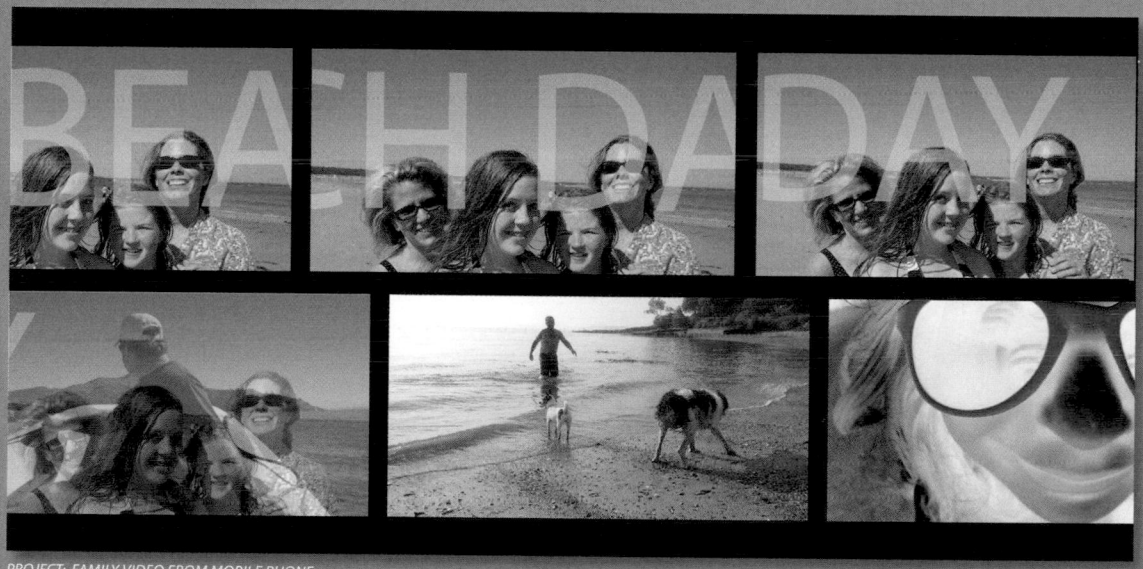

PROJECT: FAMILY VIDEO FROM MOBILE PHONE

You can edit video files in Photoshop using many of the same effects you use to edit image files. You can create a movie from video files, still images, Smart Objects, audio files, and type layers; apply transitions; and animate effects using keyframes.

Getting started

In this lesson, you'll edit a video that was shot using a smartphone. You'll create a video timeline, import clips, add transitions and other video effects, and render the final video. First, look at the final project to see what you'll be creating.

1 Start Photoshop, and then simultaneously hold down Ctrl+Alt+Shift (Windows) or Command+Option+Shift (Mac) to restore the default preferences. (See "Restoring default preferences" on page 5.)

2 When prompted, click Yes to delete the Adobe Photoshop Settings file.

3 Choose File > Browse In Bridge.

4 In Bridge, select the Lessons folder in the Favorites panel. Then, double-click the Lesson11 folder in the Content panel.

5 Double-click the 11End.mp4 file to open it in the default video player for your system, such as QuickTime Player (Mac) or Movies & TV (Windows).

Note: If Bridge isn't installed, the File > Browse In Bridge command in Photoshop will start the Creative Cloud desktop app, which will download and install Bridge. After installation completes, you can start Bridge.

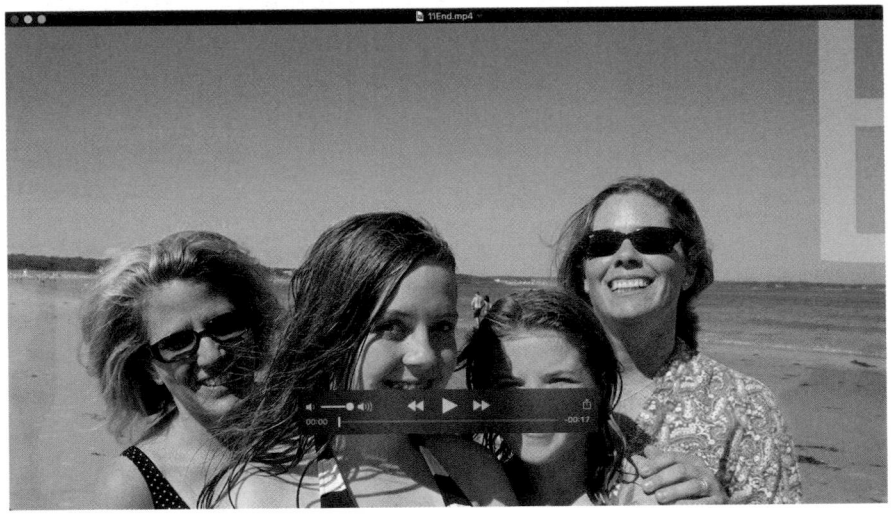

6 Click the Play button to view the final video.

The short video is a compilation of clips from a day at the beach. It includes transitions, layer effects, animated text, and a musical track.

7 Close the video player, and return to Bridge.

8 Double-click the 11End.psd file to open it in Photoshop.

About the Timeline panel

If you've used a video-editing application such as Adobe Premiere® Pro or Adobe After Effects®, the Timeline panel is probably familiar. You use the Timeline panel to assemble and arrange video clips, images, and audio files for a movie file. You can edit the duration of each clip, apply filters and effects, animate attributes such as position and opacity, mute sound, add transitions, and perform other standard video-editing tasks without ever leaving Photoshop.

1 Choose Window > Timeline to open the Timeline panel.

Each video clip or image included in the project is represented in a box in the Timeline panel and as a layer in the Layers panel. Video clips have a blue background in the Timeline panel; image files have a purple background. At the bottom of the Timeline panel is the audio track.

▶ **Tip:** If the Timeline is too short to display both video groups and the audio track all at once, make the Timeline panel taller by dragging its top border up.

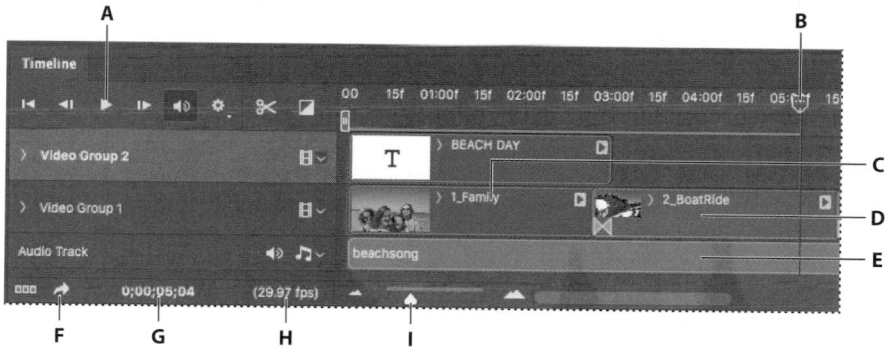

A. *Play button* **B.** *Playhead* **C.** *Image file* **D.** *Video clip* **E.** *Audio track* **F.** *Render Video button* **G.** *Current time* **H.** *Frame rate* **I.** *Control Timeline Magnification slider*

The timeline contents should appear visible as in the figure above. If they're collapsed against the left side so that content titles and previews aren't visible, drag the magnification slider (below the timeline) to the right to see time in more detail.

2 Click the Play button in the Timeline panel to view the movie.

The playhead moves across the time ruler, displaying each frame of the movie.

3 Press the spacebar to pause playback.

4 Drag the playhead to another point in the time ruler.

The playhead's time location determines what appears in the document window.

When you work with video, Photoshop displays guidelines across the document window. To minimize the chance that your content will be cut off along the edges of some televisions, keep important content within the center area marked by the guides.

5 When you've finished exploring the end file, close it, but leave Photoshop open. Don't save any changes you might have made.

Creating a new video project

Working with video is a little different from working with still images in Photoshop. You may find it easiest to create the project first and then import the assets you'll be using. You'll choose the video preset for this project and then add nine video and image files to include in your movie.

Creating a new file

Photoshop includes several film and video presets for you to choose from. You'll create a new file and select an appropriate preset.

1 In the Home screen, click the Create New button, or choose File > New.

2 Name the file **11Working.psd**.

3 Click Film & Video in the document type bar at the top of the dialog box.

4 In the Blank Document Presets section, choose HDV/HDTV 720p.

5 Accept the default settings for the other options, and click Create.

Note: The video in this lesson was shot using an Apple iPhone, so one of the HDV presets is appropriate. The 720p preset provides good quality without providing too much data for smooth online streaming.

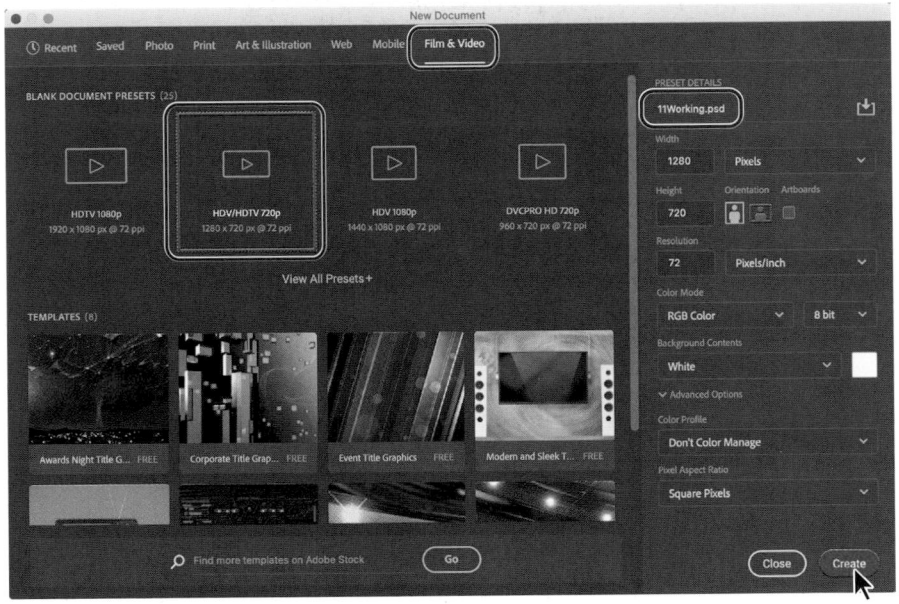

Note: If Photoshop displays a dialog box telling you about the difference between saving to Cloud Documents and Your Computer, click Save On Your Computer. You can also select Don't Show Again, but that setting will deselect after you reset Photoshop preferences.

6 Choose File > Save As. If the dialog box says Cloud Documents, click Your Computer at the bottom, and save the file in the Lesson11 folder.

Importing assets

Photoshop provides tools specifically for working with video, such as the Timeline panel, which may already be open because you previewed the end file. To ensure you have access to the resources you need, you'll select the Motion workspace and organize your panels. Then you'll import the video clips, images, and audio file you need to create the movie.

1 Choose Window > Workspace > Motion.

2 Pull up the top edge of the Timeline panel so that the panel occupies the bottom third of the workspace.

3 Select the Zoom tool (🔍), and then click Fit Screen in the options bar so that you can see the entire canvas within the top half of the screen.

4 In the Timeline panel, click Create Video Timeline. Photoshop creates a new video timeline, including two default tracks: Layer 0 and Audio Track.

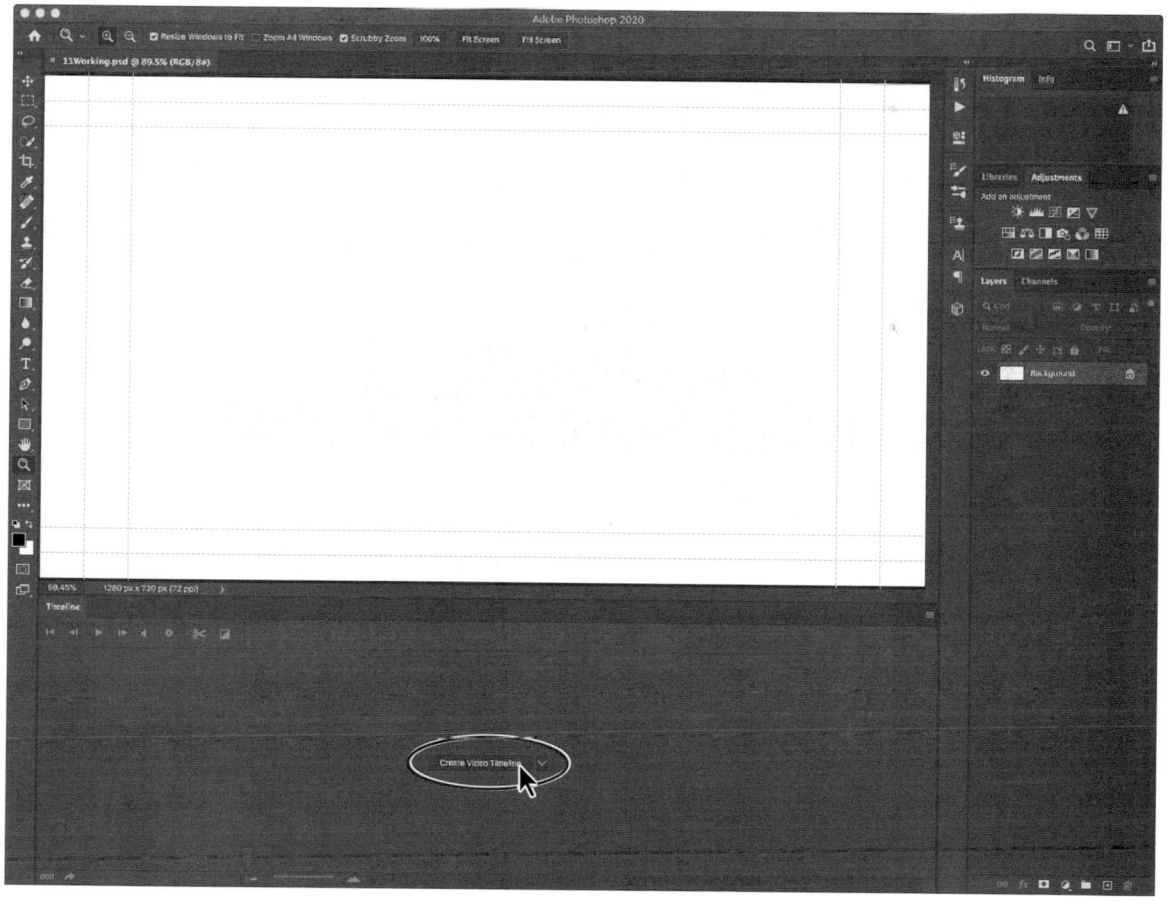

5 Click the Video menu in the Layer 0 track, and choose Add Media.

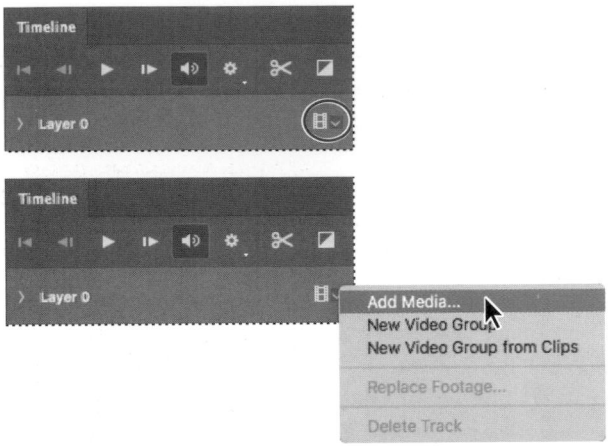

6 Navigate to the Lesson11 folder.

7 Shift-select the video and photo assets numbered 1–6, and click Open.

Note: If the media appear in reverse order in the timeline, choose Edit > Undo, and when you choose Add Media again, make sure you select 1_Family.jpg first and then Shift-select 6_Sunset.jpg. Also, it will be easiest to Shift-select the media if the files are sorted by name. It's normal for the media to appear in reverse order in the Layers panel, where the bottom layer is considered the first.

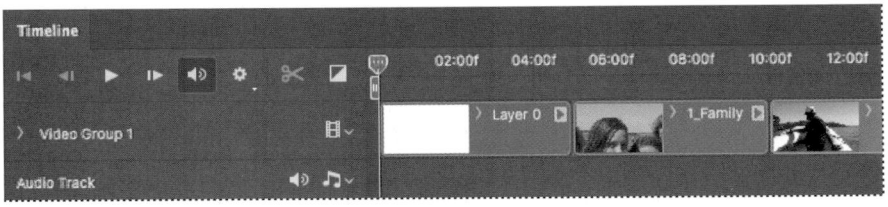

Photoshop imports all six of the assets you selected onto the same track, now named Video Group 1, in the Timeline panel. It displays still images with a purple background and video clips with a blue background. In the Layers panel, the assets appear as individual layers within the layer group named Video Group 1. You don't need the Layer 0 layer, so you'll delete it.

8 Select Layer 0 in the Layers panel, and click the Delete Layer button at the bottom of the panel. Click Yes to confirm the deletion.

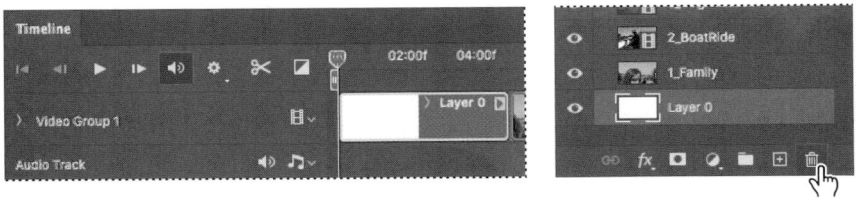

9 Choose File > Save. Click OK in the Photoshop Format Options dialog box.

Changing the duration and size of clips in the timeline

The clips are of very different lengths, meaning they'd play for different amounts of time. For this video, you want all the clips to be the same length, so you'll shorten them all to 3 seconds. The length of a clip (its *duration*) is measured in seconds and frames: 03:00 is 3 seconds; 02:25 is 2 seconds and 25 frames.

1 Drag the Control Timeline Magnification slider to the right at the bottom of the Timeline panel to zoom in on the timeline. You want to be able to see a thumbnail of each clip and enough detail in the time ruler that you can accurately change the duration of each clip.

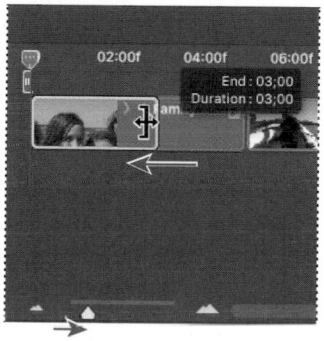

▶ **Tip:** If the Control Timeline Magnification slider is hard to control, click the magnification icons to the left and right of the slider.

2 Drag the right edge of the first clip (1_Family) to 03:00 on the time ruler. Photoshop displays the end point and the duration as you drag so that you can find the right stopping point.

3 Drag the right edge of the second clip (2_BoatRide) to a duration of 03:00.

● **Note:** In this lesson you're shortening each clip to the same duration, but in your own videos it's OK to have clips of different durations, depending on how you want to tell your story.

Shortening a video clip this way doesn't change its speed; it removes part of the clip from the video. In this case, you want to use the first three seconds of each clip. If you wanted to use a different portion of a video clip, you would shorten the clip from each end. As you drag the end point of a video clip, Photoshop displays a preview so you can see exactly what content will appear in the last frame of that clip when you release the mouse button.

4 Repeat step 3 for each of the remaining clips so that each has a duration of 3 seconds.

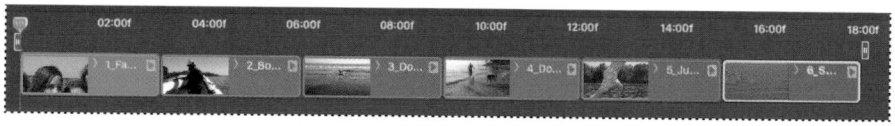

The clips are now the right duration, but some of the images are the wrong size for the canvas. You'll resize the first image before continuing.

5 Make sure the playhead is at the beginning of the timeline, and then in the Layers panel, select the 1_Family layer. That clip also becomes selected in the Timeline panel.

6 Click the triangle in the upper-right corner of the 1_Family clip in the Timeline panel to open the Motion panel.

▶ **Tip:** The arrow on the left side of a clip (next to the clip's thumbnail) reveals the attributes you can animate using keyframes. The arrow on the right side of a clip opens the Motion panel.

7 Choose Pan & Zoom from the menu, and make sure Resize To Fill Canvas is selected. Then click an empty area of the Timeline panel to close the Motion panel.

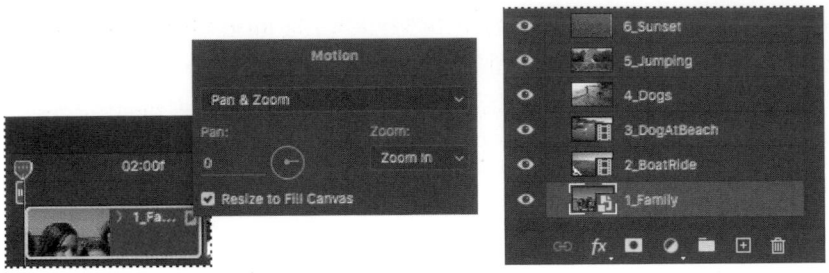

The image resizes to fit the canvas. However, you applied the effect only to quickly resize the image and not to pan and zoom, so you'll remove the effect. That will leave the image at the new size, which is what you want.

8 Open the Motion panel from the 1_Family clip again, and choose No Motion from the menu. Click an empty area of the Timeline panel to close the Motion panel.

9 Save your work.

Animating text with keyframes

Keyframes let you control animation, effects, and other changes that occur over time. A keyframe marks the point in time where you specify a value, such as a position, size, or style. To create a change over time, you must have at least two keyframes: one for the state at the beginning of the change and one for the state at the end. Photoshop interpolates the values for the positions in between so that the change takes effect smoothly over the specified time. You'll use keyframes to animate a movie title (Beach Day) from left to right over the opening image.

Note: All content in the same video group plays in sequence. The reason you create a new video group in step 1 is to add a layer that plays at the same time as other layers. For example, a logo that appears in a corner of the frame for the entire length of a video must be in a different video group than a sequence of clips.

1 Click the Video pop-up menu in the Video Group 1 track, and choose New Video Group. Photoshop adds Video Group 2 to the Timeline panel.

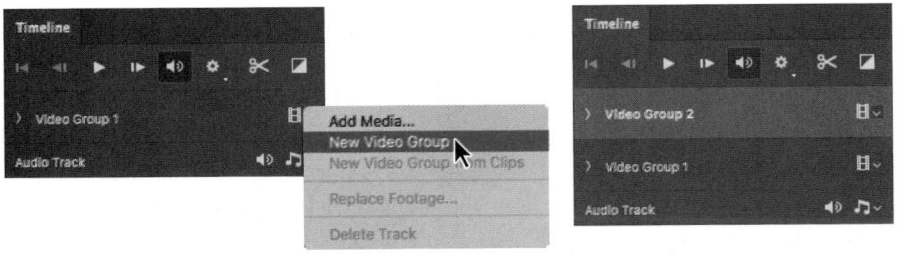

2 Select the Horizontal Type tool (T), and then click on the left edge of the image, about halfway down from the top.

Photoshop creates a new type layer, named Layer 1, in the Video Group 2 track. The type layer initially includes "Lorem Ipsum" placeholder text.

3 Type **BEACH DAY**, replacing the selected placeholder text. Click the check mark (✓) in the options bar to commit the text to the layer.

4 In the options bar, select a sans serif font such as Myriad Pro, set the type size to **600** pt, and select white for the type color.

The text is large enough that it doesn't all fit on the image. That's okay; you'll animate it to move across the image.

5 In the Layers panel, change the opacity for the BEACH DAY layer to **25%**.

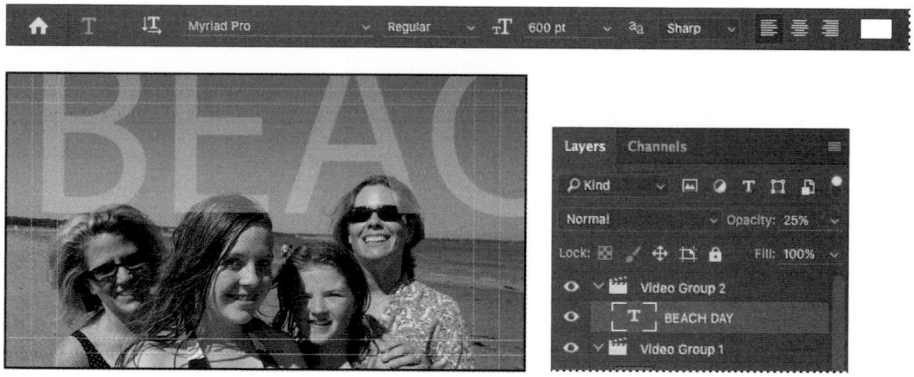

6 In the Timeline panel, drag the end point of the type layer to 03:00 so that it has the same duration as the 1_Family layer.

7 Click the arrow to the left of the BEACH DAY clip title to display the clip's attributes.

8 Make sure the playhead is at the beginning of the time ruler.

9 Click the stopwatch icon (Ö) next to the Transform property to set an initial keyframe for the layer.

The keyframe appears as a yellow diamond in the timeline.

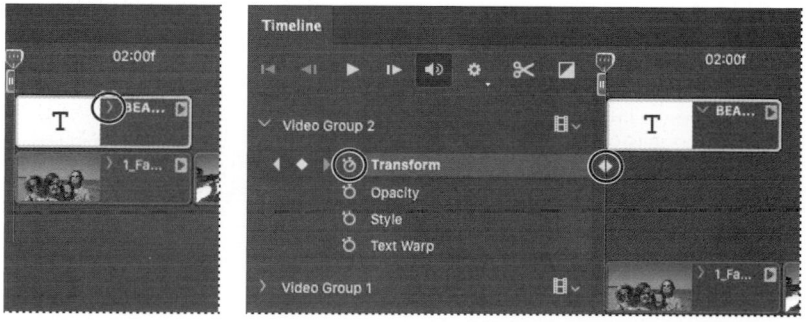

10 Select the Move tool (✣), and use it to drag the type layer up so that the tops of each letter are slightly clipped at the edge of the canvas (if they aren't already). Press the Shift key as you drag the type layer to the right so that only the left edge of the letter "B" in the word "BEACH" is visible on the canvas. The keyframe you set in step 9 ensures that the text will be in this position at the beginning of the movie.

▶ **Tip:** Photoshop displays the playhead's current time in the lower-left corner of the Timeline panel.

11 Move the playhead to the last frame of the first clip (02:29).

12 Press the Shift key as you use the Move tool to drag the type layer to the left over the canvas so that only the right edge of the "Y" in the word "DAY" is visible. Pressing Shift ensures that the type moves straight across as you drag.

Because you've changed the position, Photoshop creates a new keyframe.

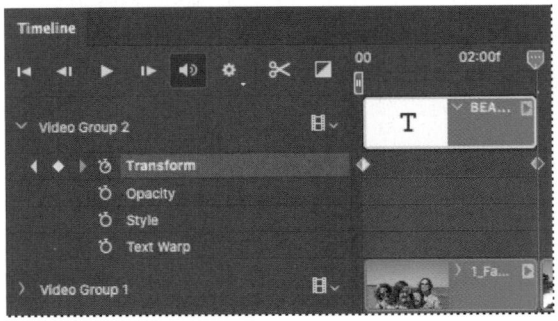

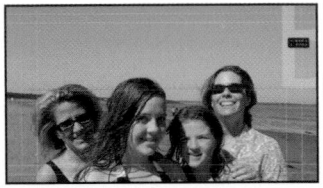

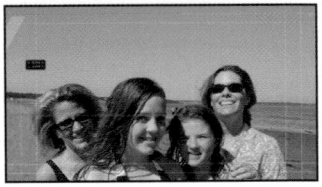

13 Move the playhead across the first three seconds of the time ruler to preview the animation. The title moves across the image.

14 Click the arrow to the left of the title of the BEACH DAY text clip to close the clip's attributes, and then choose File > Save to save your work so far.

Creating effects

One of the benefits of working with video files in Photoshop is that you can create effects using adjustment layers, styles, and simple transformations.

Adding adjustment layers to video clips

You've used adjustment layers with still images throughout this book. They work just as well on video clips. When you apply an adjustment layer in a video group, Photoshop applies it only to the layer immediately below it in the Layers panel.

1 Select the 3_DogAtBeach layer in the Layers panel.

2 In the Timeline panel, move the playhead to the beginning of the 3_DogAtBeach layer so you can see the effect as you apply it.

3 In the Adjustments panel, click the Black & White button (◨).

4 In the Properties panel, leave the default preset, and select Tint. The default tint color creates a sepia effect that works well for this clip. You can experiment with the sliders and the tint color to modify the black-and-white effect to your taste.

▶ **Tip:** To quickly snap the playhead to the first frame of a clip, hold down Shift as you drag the playhead.

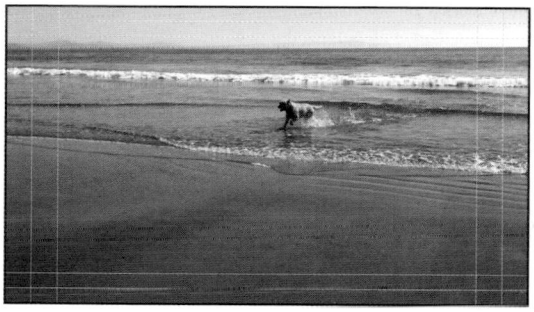

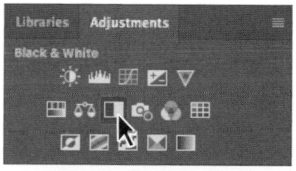

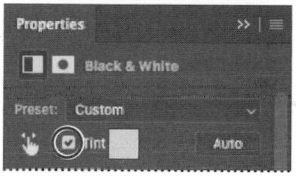

5 Move the playhead across the 3_DogAtBeach clip in the Timeline panel to preview the effect.

Animating a zoom effect

Even simple transformations become interesting effects when you animate them. You'll use animation to zoom in on the 4_Dogs clip.

1 Move the playhead to the beginning of the 4_Dogs clip in the Timeline panel (09:00).

2 Click the arrow at the top-right corner of the 4_Dogs clip to display the Motion panel.

3 Choose Zoom from the pop-up menu, and choose Zoom In from the Zoom menu. On the Zoom From grid, select the upper-left corner to zoom in from that point. Make sure Resize To Fill Canvas is selected, and then click an empty area of the Timeline panel to close the Motion panel.

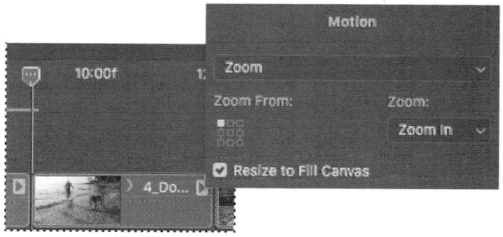

4 Drag the playhead across the clip to preview the effect.

You'll enlarge the image in the last keyframe to make the zoom more dramatic.

5 Click the arrow to the left of the title of the 4_Dogs clip to reveal the attributes for the clip.

There are two keyframes, which appear as yellow diamonds under the clip on the timeline: one for the beginning of the Zoom In effect, and one for the end.

▶ **Tip:** You can move to the next keyframe by clicking the right arrow next to the attribute (in this case, Transform) in the Timeline panel. Click the left arrow to move to the previous keyframe.

6 Click the right triangle next to the Transform attribute (under Video Group 1 on the left side of the Timeline panel) to move the playhead to the last keyframe if it's not already there, and choose Edit > Free Transform. Then enter **120%** for Width and Height in the options bar. Click the Commit Transform button (✓) to confirm the transformation.

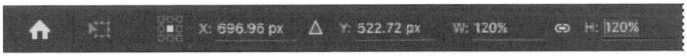

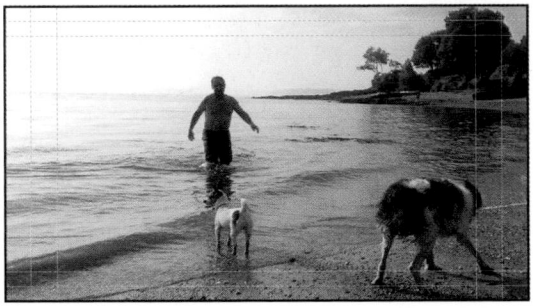

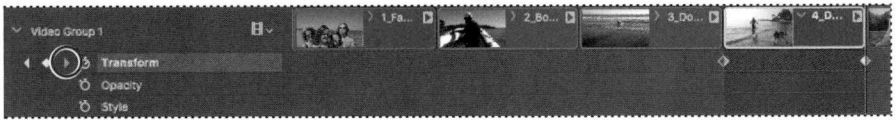

7 Drag the playhead across the 4_Dogs clip in the time ruler to preview the animation again.

8 Choose File > Save.

Animating an image to create a motion effect

You'll animate another transformation to create the appearance of motion. You want the image to begin with the diver's legs and end with his hands.

1 Move the playhead to the end of the 5_Jumping clip (14:29), and select the clip. Using the Move tool, press Shift as you drag the image down in the document window so that the hands are near the top of the canvas, putting the diver in the final position.

2 Click the arrow to the left of the clip title to display the clip's attributes, and click the stopwatch icon for the Position attribute to add a keyframe (a yellow diamond icon) under the clip.

3 Move the playhead to the beginning of the clip (12:00). Using the Move tool, press Shift as you drag the image up so that the feet are near the bottom of the canvas.

Photoshop adds a second keyframe under the clip to complete the animation.

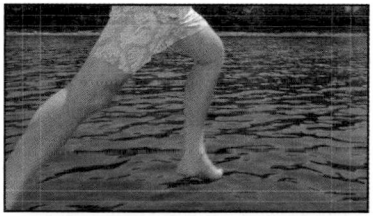

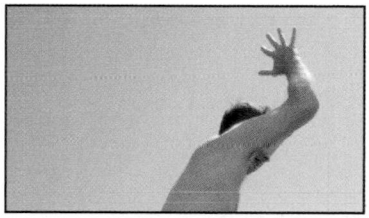

4 Move the playhead across the time ruler to preview the animation.

As you can see, you can build animation keyframes in any order. Sometimes, as in this example, it's easier to start from the final look and then work backwards.

5 Close the clip's attributes. Then choose File > Save to save your work so far.

Adding the Pan & Zoom effect

You can easily add features similar to the pan and zoom effects used in documentaries. You'll add them to the sunset to bring the video to a dramatic close.

1 Move the playhead to the beginning of the 6_Sunset clip.

2 Click the arrow at the top-right corner of the clip to display its Motion panel. Choose Pan & Zoom from the pop-up menu, choose Zoom Out from the Zoom menu, and make sure Resize To Fill Canvas is selected. Then click an empty area of the Timeline panel to close the Motion panel.

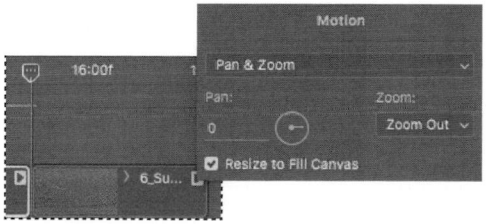

3 Move the playhead across the last clip to preview the effects.

Adding transitions

Simply drag and drop to add transitions, such as fading one clip into another.

1 Click the Go To First Frame button (⏮) in the upper-left corner of the Timeline panel to return the playhead to the beginning of the time ruler.

2 Click the Transition button (◪) near the upper-left corner of the Timeline panel. Select Cross Fade, and change the Duration value to **.25** s (a quarter of a second).

3 Drag the Cross Fade transition and drop it where the 1_Family and 2_BoatRide clips meet.

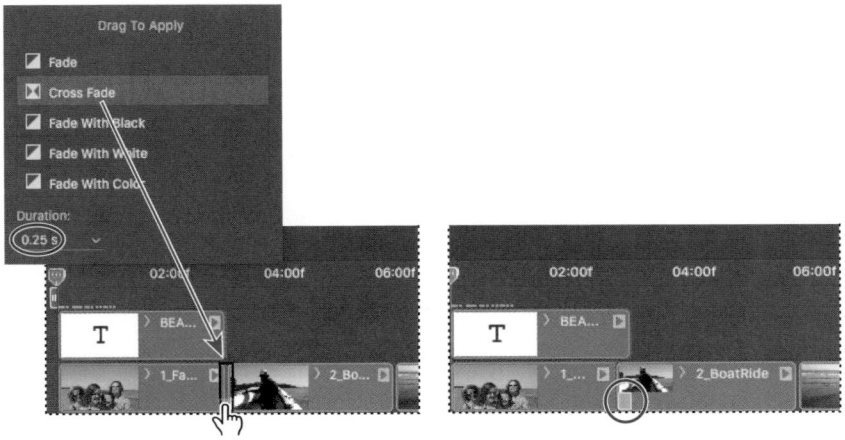

Note: At low Timeline magnifications, transition icons may be condensed into small rectangles. For better visibility and control of transitions, use the Timeline magnification slider to magnify the Timeline.

Photoshop adjusts the ends of the clips to apply the transition and adds a white transition icon in the lower-left corner of the second clip.

4 Drag Cross Fade transitions between each of the other clips.

5 Drag a Fade With Black transition onto the end of the final clip.

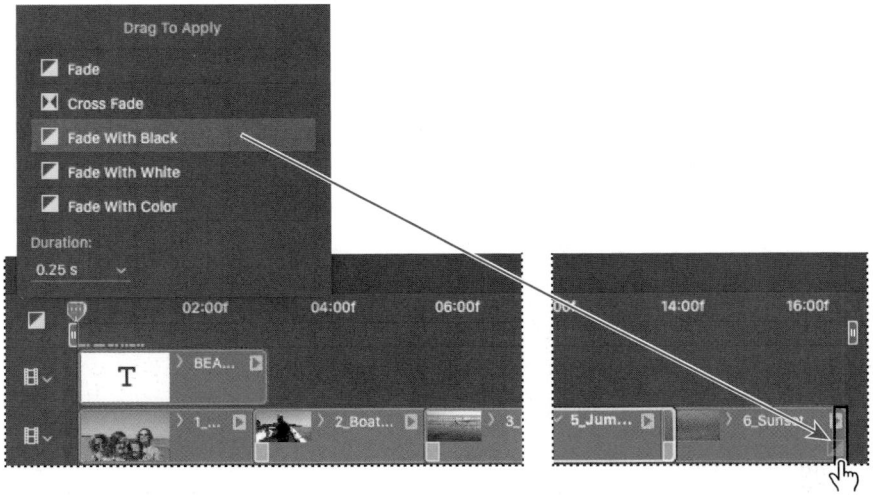

Note: You may notice that adding a transition makes the sequence slightly shorter. That's because adding an 0.25 second cross fade means 0.25 seconds of the clips on both sides of the transition must now overlap, to make the transition possible. Therefore, the second clip shifts earlier in time by the duration of the transition, reducing the duration of the entire sequence.

6 To make the transition smoother, extend the Fade With Black transition by dragging its left edge out to about one-third the total length of the clip.

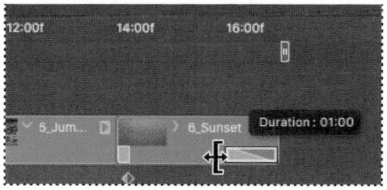

7 Play back the entire sequence; then choose File > Save.

Adding audio

You can add a separate audio track to a video file in Photoshop. In fact, the Timeline panel includes an empty audio track by default. You'll add an MP3 file to play as the soundtrack for this short video.

1 Click the musical-note icon in the Audio Track at the bottom of the Timeline panel, and choose Add Audio from the pop-up menu.

Tip: You can also add an audio track by clicking the + sign at the far-right end of the track in the Timeline panel.

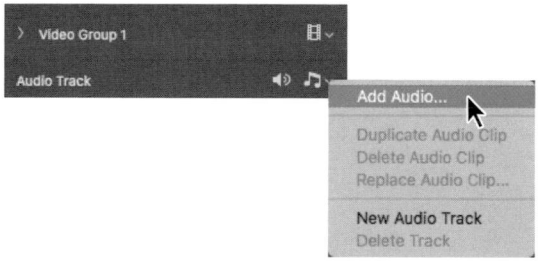

2 Select the beachsong.mp3 file from the Lesson11 folder, and click Open.

The audio file is added to the timeline, but it's much longer than the video. You'll use the Split At Playhead tool to shorten it.

3 Move the playhead to the end of the 6_Sunset clip. With the audio file still selected, click the Split At Playhead tool (✂) in the Timeline panel.

The audio file is clipped at that point, becoming two audio clips.

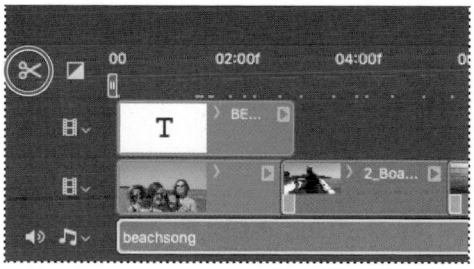

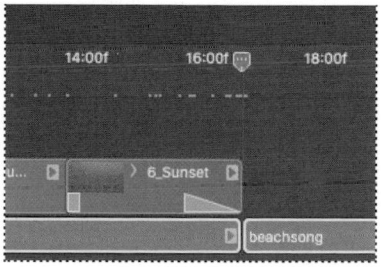

4 Select the second audio file segment, the one that begins after the end of the 6_Sunset clip. Press the Delete key on your keyboard to remove the selected clip.

Now the audio file is the same length as the video. You'll add a fade so that it ends smoothly.

5 Click the small arrow at the right edge of the audio clip to open the Audio panel. Then enter **3** seconds for Fade In and **5** seconds for Fade Out.

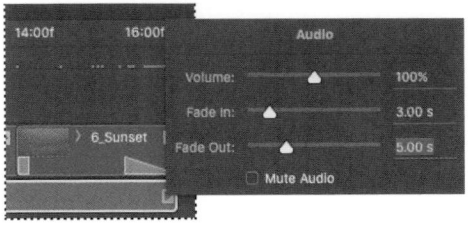

6 Click an empty area of the Timeline panel to close the Audio panel, and save your work so far.

Muting unwanted audio

So far, you've previewed portions of the video by moving the playhead across the time ruler. Now you'll preview the entire video using the Play button in the Timeline panel and then mute any extraneous audio from the video clips.

1 Click the Play button (▶) in the upper-left corner of the Timeline panel to preview the video so far.

It's looking good, but there is some unwanted background noise from the video clips. You'll mute that extra sound.

2 Click the small triangle at the right end of the 2_BoatRide clip.

3 Click the Audio tab to see audio options, and then select Mute Audio. Click an empty area of the Timeline panel to close the Audio/Video panel.

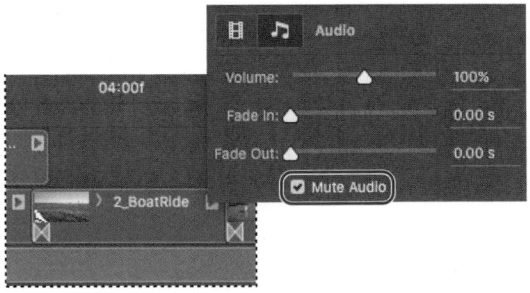

4 Click the small triangle at the right end of the 3_DogAtBeach clip.

5 Click the Audio tab to see audio options, and then select Mute Audio. Click an empty area of the Timeline panel to close the panel.

6 Play the timeline to check your audio changes, and then save your work.

Rendering video

You're ready to render your project to video. Photoshop provides several rendering options. You'll select options appropriate for streaming video to share on the YouTube website. For information about other rendering options, see Photoshop Help.

1 Choose File > Export > Render Video, or click the Render Video button (➦) in the lower-left corner of the Timeline panel.

2 Name the file **11Final.mp4**.

3 Click Select Folder, navigate to the Lesson11 folder, and click OK or Choose.

4 From the Preset menu, choose YouTube HD 720p 29.97.

5 Click Render.

Note: The choices in the Preset menu depend on the selection in the Format menu. For the YouTube options to be available in the Preset menu, the Format menu must be set to H.264.

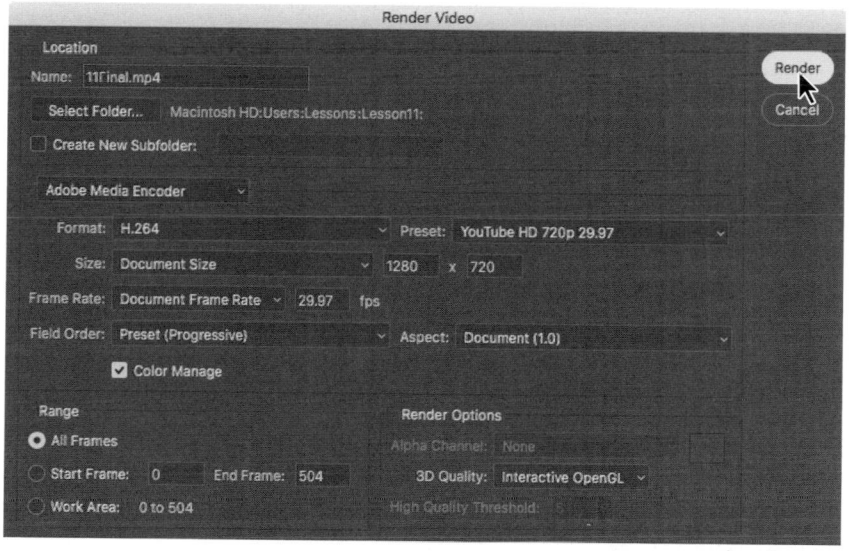

Photoshop displays a progress bar as it exports the video. Depending on your system, the rendering process may take several minutes.

Depending on your system, this may take a while.

6 Save your work.

▶ **Tip:** When a video is selected in Bridge, you can play it inside Bridge by pressing the spacebar on your keyboard. This plays the video in the Preview panel in Bridge. Double-clicking a video opens it in your system's default video player.

7 Locate the 11Working.mp4 file in the Lesson11 folder in Bridge. Double-click it to view the video you made using Photoshop!

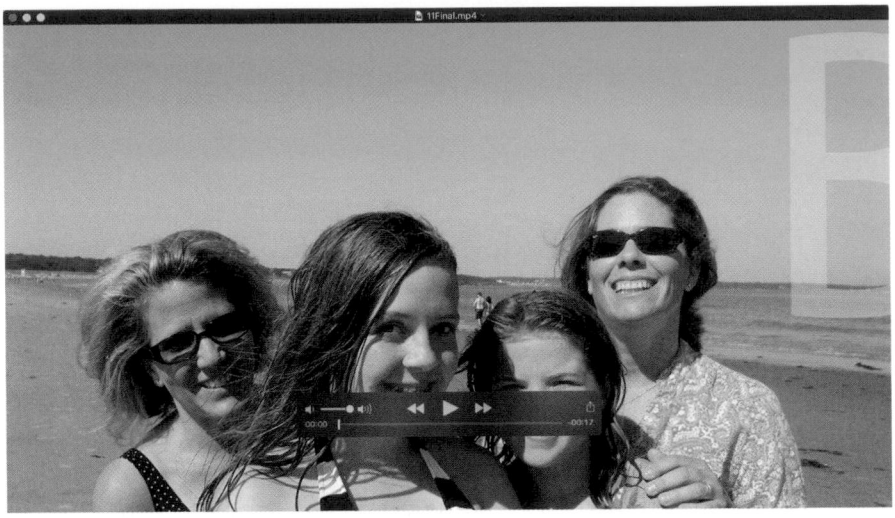

Review questions

1 What are keyframes, and how do you use them to create an animation?

2 How do you add a transition between clips?

3 How do you render a video?

Review answers

1 A keyframe marks the point in time where you specify a value, such as a position, size, or style. To create a change over time, you must have at least two keyframes: one for the state at the beginning of the change and one for the state at the end. To create an initial keyframe, click the stopwatch icon next to the attribute you want to animate for the layer. Photoshop creates additional keyframes each time you change the values of that attribute.

2 To add a transition, click the Transition button near the upper-left corner of the Timeline panel, and then drag a transition onto a clip.

3 To render a video, choose File > Export > Render Video, or click the Render Video button in the lower-left corner of the Timeline panel. Then select the video settings that are appropriate for your intended output.

12 WORKING WITH CAMERA RAW

Lesson overview

In this lesson, you'll learn how to do the following:

- Open a camera raw image in Adobe Camera Raw.
- Adjust tone and color in a raw image.
- Sharpen an image in Camera Raw.
- Synchronize settings across multiple images.
- Open a Camera Raw image as a Smart Object in Photoshop.
- Apply Camera Raw as a filter in Photoshop.

This lesson will take about an hour to complete. To get the lesson files used in this chapter, download them from the web page for this book at www.adobepress.com/PhotoshopCIB2021. For more information, see "Accessing the lesson files and Web Edition" in the Getting Started section at the beginning of this book.

As you work on this lesson, you'll preserve the start files. If you need to restore the start files, download them from your Account page.

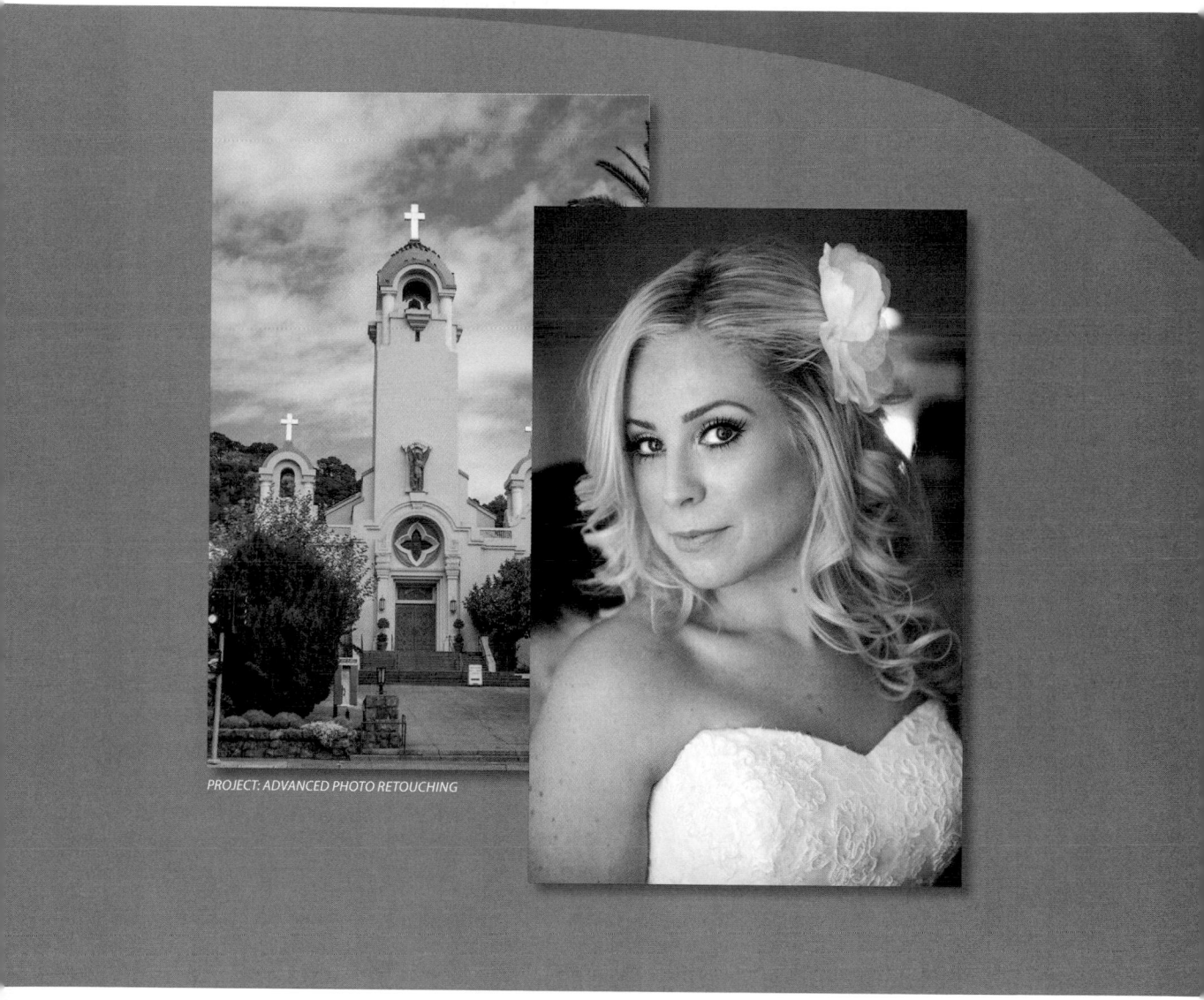

PROJECT: ADVANCED PHOTO RETOUCHING

Camera raw files give you greater flexibility, especially for adjusting color and tone, when compared to editing JPEG format files from a camera. You can tap into that potential by using Adobe Camera Raw, an application integrated with Photoshop and Bridge.

Getting started

In this lesson, you'll edit several digital images using Adobe Camera Raw, a plug-in application you can use from within Photoshop or Bridge. You'll use a variety of techniques to touch up and improve the appearance of digital photographs. You'll start by viewing the before and after images in Adobe Bridge.

1 Start Photoshop, and then simultaneously hold down Ctrl+Alt+Shift (Windows) or Command+Option+Shift (Mac) to restore the default preferences. (See "Restoring default preferences" on page 5.)

2 When prompted, click Yes to delete the Adobe Photoshop Settings file.

3 Choose File > Browse In Bridge to open Adobe Bridge.

4 In the Favorites panel in Bridge, click the Lessons folder. Then, in the Content panel, double-click the Lesson12 folder to open it.

5 Adjust the thumbnail slider, if necessary, so that you can see the thumbnail previews clearly. Then look at the 12A_Start.crw and 12A_End.psd files.

Note: If Bridge isn't installed, the File > Browse In Bridge command in Photoshop will start the Creative Cloud desktop app, which will download and install Bridge. After installation completes, you can start Bridge.

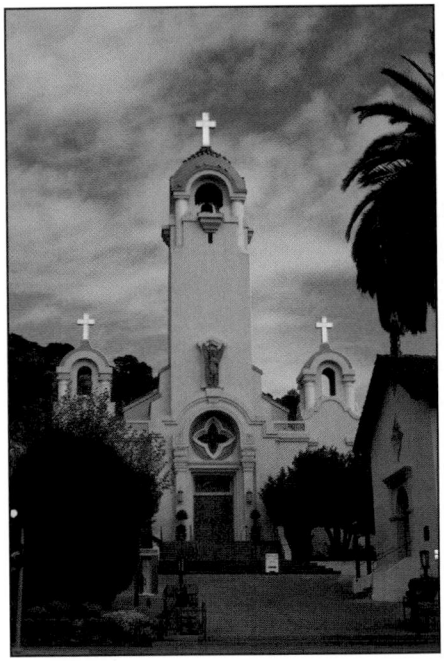

12A_Start.crw

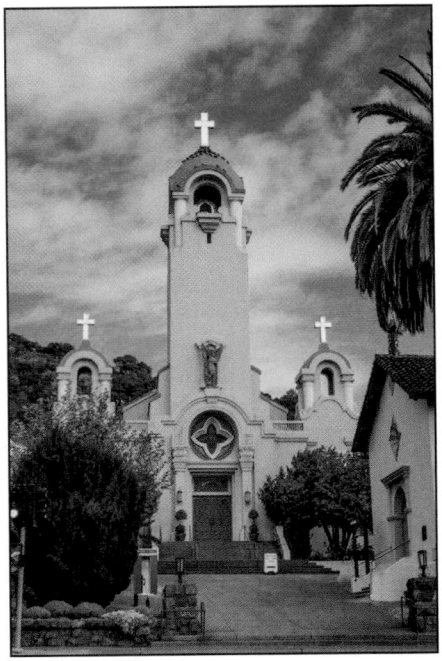

12A_End.psd

Note: We used Adobe Camera Raw 13, which was the current version at the time of publication. Adobe updates Camera Raw frequently; if you're using a later version, some of the steps in this lesson may not match what you see. Also, if you have used an earlier version of Camera Raw, note that the user interface was significantly redesigned in version 12.3.

The original photograph of a Spanish-style church is a camera raw file, so it doesn't have the usual .psd or .jpg file extension you've worked with so far in this book. It was shot with a Canon SLR camera, and its document uses the Canon proprietary .crw file extension. You'll process this camera raw image to make it brighter, sharper, and clearer, and then save it as both a JPEG file for the web and as a PSD file so that you could work on it further in Photoshop.

6 Compare the 12B_Start.nef and 12B_End.psd thumbnail previews.

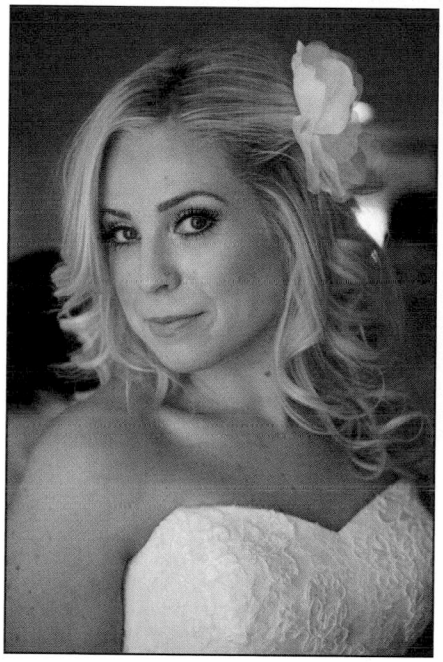

12B_Start.nef

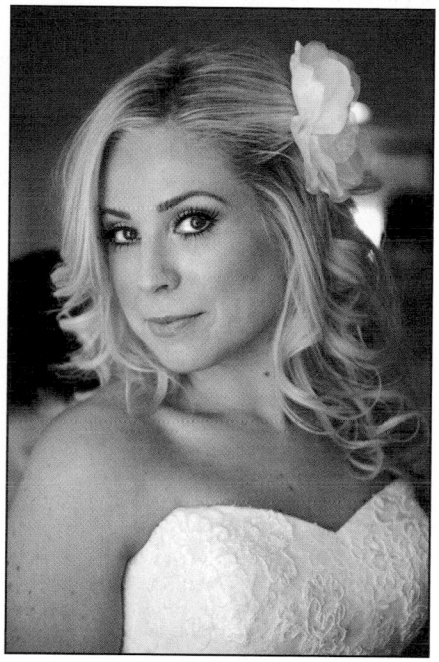

12B_End.psd

This time, the start file was taken with a Nikon camera, and the raw image has an .nef extension. You'll perform color corrections and image enhancements in Camera Raw and Photoshop to achieve the end result.

About camera raw files

Many digital cameras can save images in *camera raw* format. A camera raw file contains unprocessed picture data from a digital camera's image sensor, somewhat like undeveloped film. Raw sensor data has not yet been converted to a standard multiple-channel color image file. It's still one unprocessed channel of sensor data, and in that form, it's unusable as an image. If you were to view the data, it would be gray and dark. You might then wonder: How can you view raw files, such as those included with this lesson, on the back of the camera and on your computer before you open them? The answer is that a camera typically saves a raw file with an embedded preview image that represents the camera's interpretation of the raw data.

Raw processing software such as Adobe Camera Raw interprets the unprocessed raw data into the multiple color channels (such as three RGB channels) that photo editing software such as Photoshop can edit. Camera raw files let you interpret the original image data, giving you more editing flexibility than when you edit a JPEG file saved using the camera's interpretation of the data. You can use Adobe Camera Raw to make wider and deeper changes to white balance, tonal range, contrast, color saturation, noise reduction, and sharpening than you could if the raw data was already converted to RGB. You can reprocess a raw file at any time, without degrading the original image data.

Note: Camera raw files are typically unique to each camera model's sensor. If you have CRW files from three different Canon camera models and NEF files from three Nikon models, chances are those represent six different camera raw formats for Adobe Camera Raw to support. If you buy a new camera, you might need an Adobe Camera Raw update that adds support for its specific raw format.

To create camera raw files, set your digital camera to save files in raw format instead of JPEG format. A raw file has a manufacturer-specific filename extension such as .nef (from Nikon) or .crw (from Canon). In Bridge or Photoshop, you can process camera raw files from a myriad of supported digital cameras from Canon, Fuji, Leica, Nikon, and other makers. You can then export the proprietary camera raw files to DNG, JPEG, TIFF, or PSD file format.

Should you always capture camera raw images instead of JPEG images? If you want maximum editing flexibility, then yes. However, camera raw images require more space to store and more processing power to edit. If your images need little to no editing after the shot, you could decide to capture and edit JPEG images instead.

Processing files in Camera Raw

When you make adjustments to an image in Camera Raw, such as straightening or cropping the image, Photoshop and Bridge store your edits separately from the original file. You can edit the image as you desire, export an edited version, and keep the original intact for different or improved adjustments in the future.

Opening images in Camera Raw

Tip: You can open and edit TIFF and JPEG images in Camera Raw, if those formats are enabled in Camera Raw preferences. However, those formats won't provide the same range of adjustments as a camera raw file.

You can open Camera Raw from either Bridge or Photoshop, and you can edit multiple images in Camera Raw. You can also apply the same edits to multiple files simultaneously. That's useful if you're working with images that were all shot in the same environment and that therefore need similar adjustments.

Camera Raw provides extensive controls for adjusting white balance, exposure, contrast, sharpness, tone curves, and much more. In this exercise, you'll edit one image and then apply the settings to similar images.

1 In Bridge, open the Lessons/Lesson12/Mission folder, which contains three shots of the Spanish church you previewed earlier.

2 Shift-click to select all of the images—Mission01.crw, Mission02.crw, and Mission03.crw—and then choose File > Open In Camera Raw.

3 If the Set Up Camera Raw screen appears, make sure New ACR Default is selected, and click OK.

4 If the Welcome to Camera Raw 13.0 screen appears, click Get Started.

Both the Set Up Camera Raw and Welcome to Camera Raw 13.0 screens appear only the first time you start Camera Raw 13 or the first time after you reset Camera Raw preferences (which are separate from Photoshop preferences).

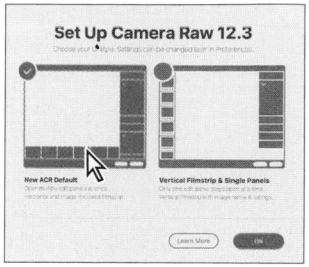

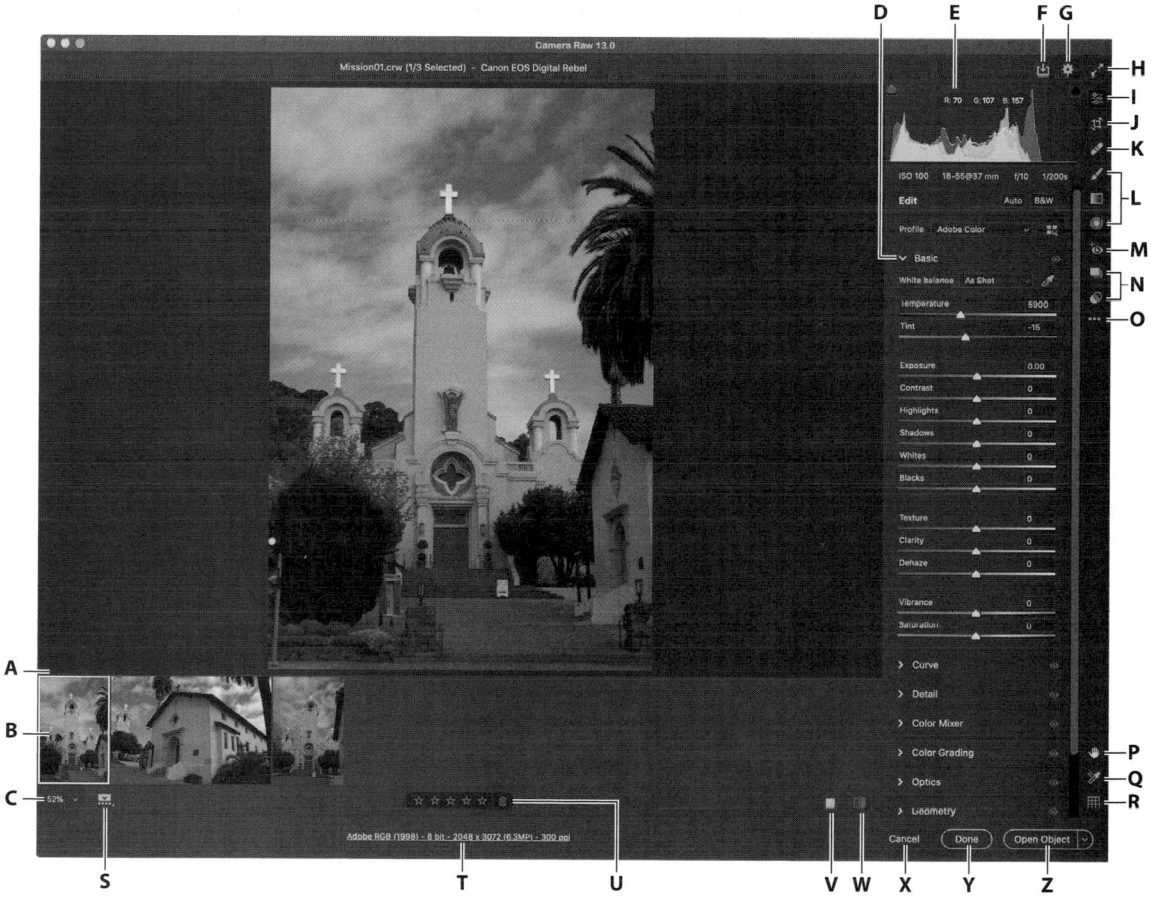

A. *Filmstrip divider (drag to adjust)*
B. *Filmstrip*
C. *Zoom levels menu*
D. *Collapsible adjustments panels (in Edit mode; other modes display other options)*
E. *Histogram with RGB values*
F. *Save selected images*
G. *Camera Raw preference settings*
H. *Toggle Full Screen mode*
I. *Edit (image adjustments)*
J. *Crop & Rotate*
K. *Spot Removal*
L. *Local adjustment tools: Adjustment Brush, Graduated Filter, Radial Filter*
M. *Red Eye Removal*
N. *Snapshots and Presets*
O. *Camera Raw options menu*
P. *Hand tool*
Q. *Toggle Sampler Overlay*
R. *Toggle Grid Overlay*
S. *Filmstrip menu (click to toggle, click and hold for menu)*
T. *Workflow preference settings*
U. *Rate or mark for deletion*
V. *Before/After views (click to toggle, click and hold for options)*
W. *Toggle default settings*
X. *Exit and don't save changes*
Y. *Exit and save changes*
Z. *Exit, save changes, and open in Photoshop*

5 If the photos appear in a vertical strip along the left side of the Adobe Camera Raw window, click and hold the filmstrip menu button (▣) and choose Horizontal from the menu that appears. This is so that the layout matches the figures in this chapter. If you prefer the vertical filmstrip, you may use it for your own work.

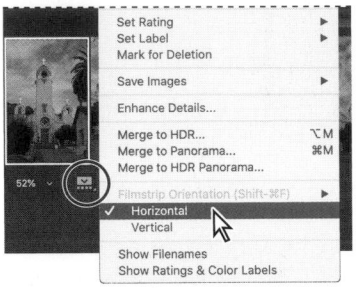

The Camera Raw dialog box displays a large preview of the selected image, and a filmstrip displays all open images. The histogram in the upper-right corner shows the tonal range of the selected image. The workflow options below the preview window control the selected image's color space, bit depth, size, and resolution, which you can click to change. Tools along the right side of the dialog box let you zoom, pan, crop, straighten, and make other adjustments to the image.

In the default mode (Edit), Camera Raw displays a stack of collapsible panels under the histogram. You can expand individual panels to precisely edit the selected image's color, tone, detail (sharpening and noise reduction); correct lens distortions; and more. You can also save settings as a preset so that you can apply them to other images.

Note: When you open a raw format image in Camera Raw, its appearance may appear to change. This is because the preview image created by the camera is replaced by a rendering of the current settings in Camera Raw.

The Camera Raw options within the Edit mode are generally organized for good results by simply using the tabbed panels from top to bottom. But it's OK for you to adjust the options in any order, and you don't have to adjust every option.

You will explore these controls now as you edit the first image file.

6 For this lesson it will be useful to see the filenames for each image. Click and hold the filmstrip menu button (▣), and choose Show Filenames.

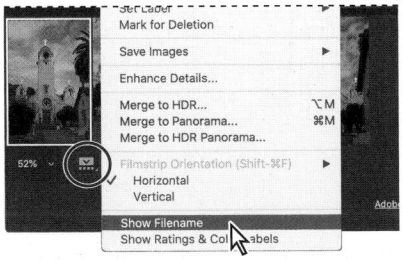

Note: If the filmstrip disappears, it's because you clicked the filmstrip menu button instead of clicking and holding. Click it again to display the filmstrip.

7 Click each thumbnail in the filmstrip to preview all the images before you begin. Or, as a shortcut, you can view each image by pressing the left arrow or right arrow key. When you've seen all three, select the Mission01.crw image.

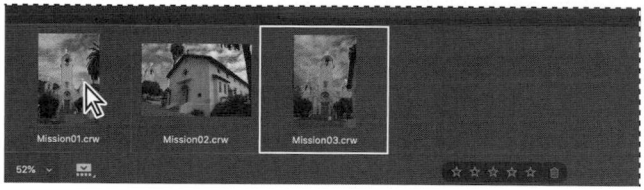

Choosing an Adobe Raw profile

An *Adobe Raw profile* controls the overall color rendering of an image, a separate step combined with the adjustments that you make. You can change the raw profile at any time.

1 If the Profile panel isn't already displayed under the histogram, click the Edit button (⚙). It is at the top of the controls, so if it isn't visible, it might be scrolled out of view; scroll the panel stack down until you can see the top.

2 Choose Adobe Landscape from the Profile menu.

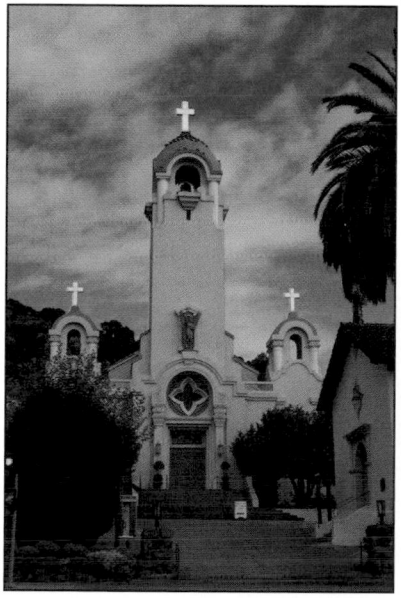

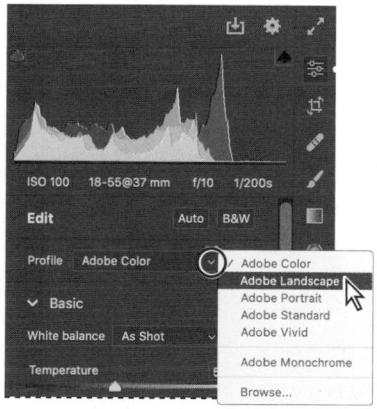

The default profile, Adobe Color, is a general-purpose profile. Adobe Landscape emphasizes colors in nature, like trees and skies, and works well for this image. The goal of Adobe Portrait is natural representation of skin tones, and Adobe Vivid adds punchy color contrast. Adobe Monochrome provides a high-quality conversion to black and white.

▶ **Tip:** If you want the image to look more like the preview generated by the camera, click the Browse Profiles icon to the right of the Profile menu, scroll down to see the list of profile categories, and try a profile from the Camera Matching category.

● **Note:** Adobe Raw profiles are different than the ICC color profiles used by your display or printer. Raw profiles affect only the conversion and processing of a camera raw file into a conventional image.

▶ **Tip:** You can use Creative profiles to apply a visual style to an image. Click the Browse Profiles icon (▦) to the right of the Profile menu, scroll down to see the list of profile categories (such as Artistic, B&W, Modern, and Vintage), select one, and click Done.

A raw profile is capable of a very wide range of changes; the controls you see soon operate within a narrower range for more precision. Choosing a profile lays the foundation for later edits, so it's an important first step in the right direction. Having chosen a profile, you can now move on to more specific edits.

Adjusting white balance

An image's white balance represents the color conditions under which it was captured. A digital camera records the white balance at the time of exposure; this is the value that initially appears in the Camera Raw dialog box image preview.

White balance comprises two components. The first is *temperature*, which is measured in kelvins and determines the level of "coolness" or "warmth" of the image—that is, its cool blue-green tones or warm yellow-red tones. The second component is *tint*, which compensates for magenta or green color casts.

Depending on the settings you're using on your camera and the environment in which you're shooting (for example, with artificial light or mixed light sources), you may want to adjust the white balance for the image.

By default, As Shot is selected in the White Balance menu, applying the white balance settings that were in your camera at the time of exposure. If you think you could improve on the current white balance setting, Camera Raw includes several other White Balance presets that you can try.

1 If you can't see White Balance options under the Profile menu, click the Basic panel heading to expand it.

2 Choose Cloudy from the White Balance menu.

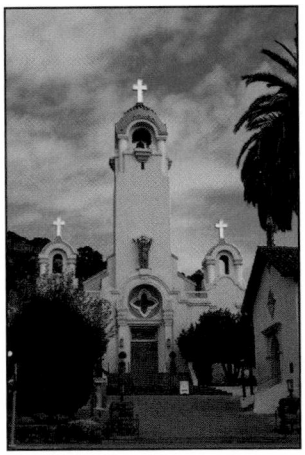

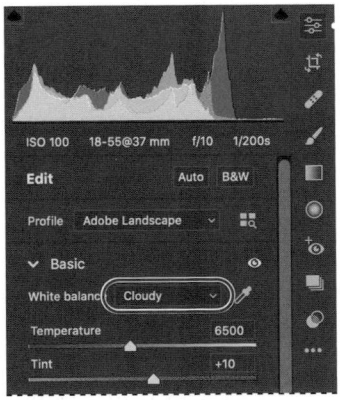

▶ **Tip:** Adjusting white balance is easiest when there is only one light source. When a scene is lit by multiple light sources with different color characteristics, you may have to manually choose a white balance setting and also make local color corrections.

Camera Raw adjusts the temperature and tint for a cloudy day. Sometimes a preset is an instant fix. In this case, though, there's still a blue cast to the image. You'll adjust the white balance manually.

3 Select the White Balance tool (🖉) to the right of the White Balance menu.

To set an accurate white balance, select an object that should be white or gray. The spot where you click becomes a reference for neutral white balance; Camera Raw shifts the image colors accordingly.

4 Click the white clouds in the image. The color balance of the image changes.

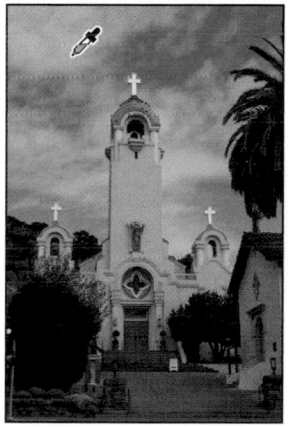

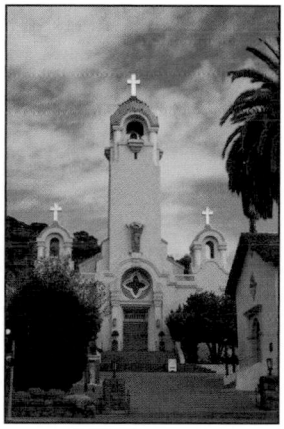

5 Click a different area of the clouds. The color balance shifts again, because that area of the clouds has slightly different color values.

To find the best color balance quickly and easily, click the White Balance tool on an area that should be neutral. Clouds are not always a neutral color, depending on the time of day. In Camera Raw, clicking different areas changes color balance without altering the original image file, so you can experiment freely.

6 Click the white area of the small sign in front of the church. This removes most of the color casts.

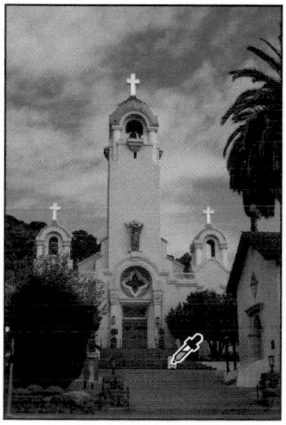

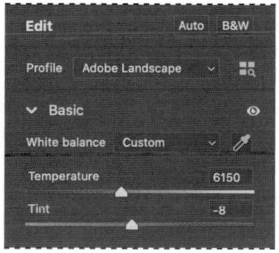

▶ **Tip:** Clicking a known neutral area, such as the sign in step 6, applies White Balance values that result in a neutral image, with unwanted color casts removed. You are then free to use options such as White Balance expressively. For example, apply a higher Temperature value to make a scene appear shot closer to sunset, or simply to evoke a warmer mood.

▶ **Tip:** To expand Camera Raw to fill the screen, click the Toggle Full Screen Mode button (⤢) near the top-right corner of the window, or press F.

7 To see the changes you've made, click and hold the Before/After Views button (■) at the bottom of the window, and choose Before/After Left/Right from the pop-up menu. (If you only click without holding, it cycles to the next option.)

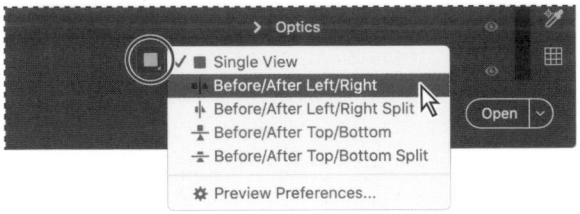

Camera Raw displays the Before image on the left and the After image on the right so you can compare them.

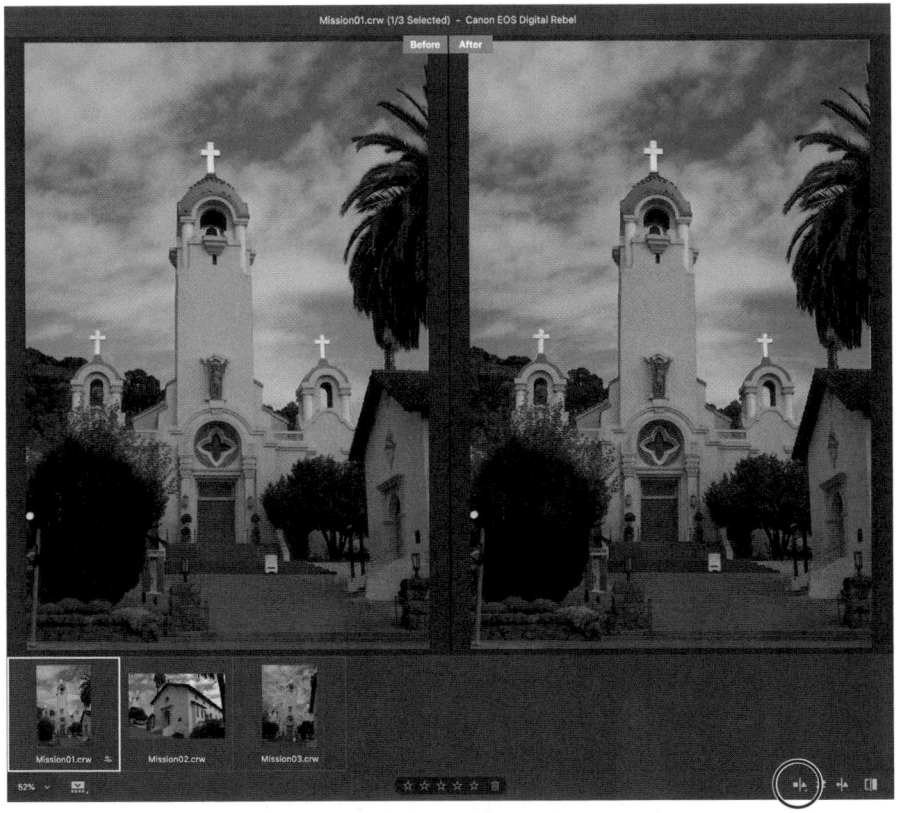

8 To see only the After image again, click and hold the Before/After Views menu and choose Single View. Or, if you prefer, you can leave both views visible so you can see how the image changes as you continue to alter it.

Making tonal adjustments in Camera Raw

The group of options in the middle of the Basic panel (starting with Exposure) affects how tones are distributed from dark to light in the image. Except for Contrast, moving a slider to the right in that group lightens the areas of the image that it affects, and moving it to the left darkens those areas. Exposure sets the overall brightness of the image. The Highlights and Shadows options control detail in the highlights and the shadows, respectively. The Whites option defines the *white point*, or the lightest tone of the image; tones above its value are made white. Conversely, the Blacks option sets the *black point*, or the darkest tone in the image; tones above its value are made black.

Dragging the Contrast slider to the right moves darker and lighter midtones away from the midtone; dragging left moves those tones toward the midtone. For more nuanced contrast adjustments, you can use the Clarity option, which adds depth to an image by increasing local contrast, especially around the midtones.

▶ **Tip:** For the best effect, increase the Clarity slider until you see halos near the edge details, and then reduce the setting until the halos are not distracting.

The Saturation option adjusts the intensity of all colors in the image equally. The Vibrance option is often more useful because it has a greater effect on undersaturated colors. For example, you can use Vibrance to bring life to an image without oversaturating any skin tones in it.

You can use the Auto option to let Camera Raw correct image tone automatically, or you can select your own settings.

1 Click Auto at the top of the Edit mode panel stack.

▶ **Tip:** Clicking Auto again toggles between default settings and Auto settings.

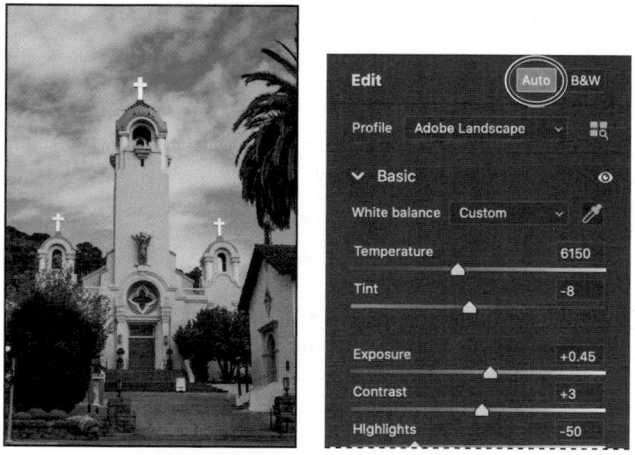

Camera Raw changes several settings in the Basic panel, and the image is greatly improved. The Auto feature often produces a useful image because its corrections are based on advanced Adobe Sensei machine learning technology. This makes Auto a quick way both to reach a good starting point for edits, and, if you like the results, to study and learn from the adjustments made by Auto. However, in this exercise, you'll return to the default settings and adjust them yourself.

▶ **Tip:** Because the Toggle Default Settings button is a toggle, you can use it to compare the current state of the image to how it started. Click it once to see the default settings; then click it again to return to the current settings. However, if you set the image to default settings and then make new changes, those replace the previous non-default settings.

2 Click the Toggle Default Settings button (). All settings are set back to Camera Raw defaults.

3 Set the options as follows (some options are not changed):

- Exposure: +**0.50**
- Contrast: +**0**
- Highlights: -**20**
- Shadows: +**70**
- Whites: +**20**
- Blacks: –**10**
- Clarity: +**20**
- Vibrance: +**20**

These settings brighten the image, especially the dark shadow areas, and boost color without oversaturating it.

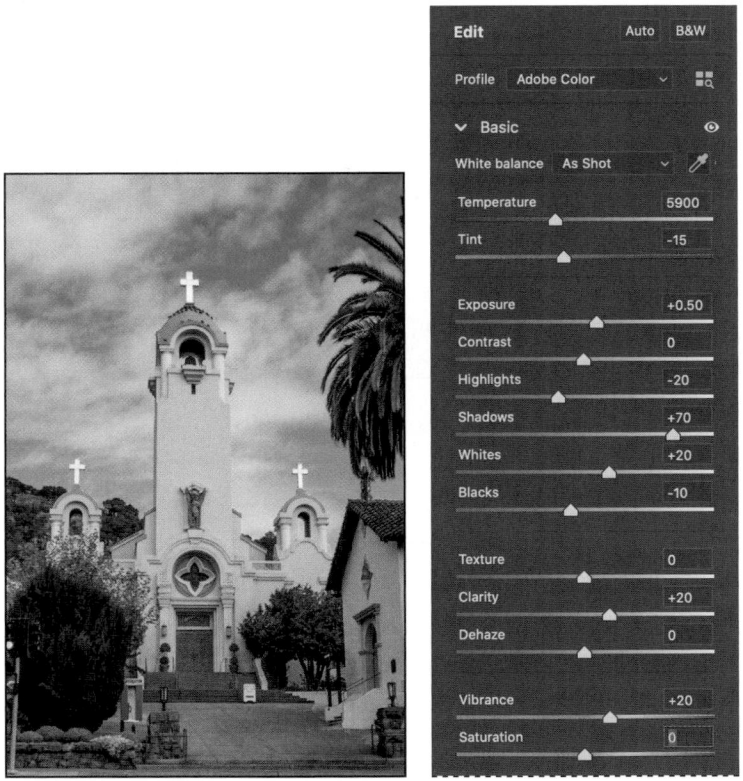

About adjusting color in Adobe Camera Raw

Over time, Adobe Camera Raw has added a number of features that allow multiple approaches to editing camera raw color precisely. This is because many photographers prefer to edit a camera raw image as much as possible before opening it in Photoshop, to take advantage of the greater flexibility and potential for preserving image quality. For many images you may not need to do anything more than apply an appropriate raw profile and White Balance setting; some may also need a Vibrance or Saturation adjustment as covered in this lesson. When you need to solve more complex color issues, you can try the more precise color tools available in Camera Raw:

Local adjustment tools. When you want to apply different color or tone settings to specific areas of an image, you can add a Graduated Filter or Radial Filter, or paint with the Adjustment Brush, and then adjust its color settings. You'll find these tools along the right edge of the Camera Raw window.

Curve panel. Like Curves in Photoshop, you can use the Curve panel in Camera Raw to edit each color channel separately, adjusting the amount of a color channel at any level from black to white. This is one way to compensate for color casts that vary across highlights, midtones, and shadows.

Color Mixer panel. The Color Mixer panel lets you adjust specific ranges of colors by hue, saturation, or luminance. When you click the B&W button at the top of the Edit mode panel stack, you can use the Color Mixer to customize a color to black-and-white conversion similar to how you did in Photoshop at the end of lesson 2.

Color Grading panel. In the Color Grading panel you can use color wheels to adjust the hue, saturation, and luminance separately for midtones, shadows, and highlights. This useful tool is familiar to video editors. Although you can use it for color correction, conventional color grading is typically a step applied after color correction, to create an expressive color palette for an image or for split toning effects.

Custom raw profiles. It's possible to use Photoshop to create custom color lookup tables (CLUTs) that you can use as the basis for your own raw profile that you can apply with one click in Camera Raw.

Calibration panel. The Calibration panel adjusts the fundamental color conversion from camera raw format, which means it affects the range of adjustment that's possible with the rest of the panel. The Calibration panel is used less often today because raw profiles are now a more convenient way to alter that conversion.

Those tools are outside the scope of this book, but when you are in Photoshop (not Camera Raw) you can learn more about them in the Search panel (Edit > Search), which also contains tutorials and help documents.

About the Camera Raw histogram

The histogram in the upper-right corner of the Camera Raw dialog box simultaneously shows the red, green, and blue channels of the selected image and updates interactively as you adjust settings. As you move any tool over the preview image, the RGB values for the area under the pointer appear in the histogram. Selecting the top left or right square highlights where on the image current settings are clipping (losing details) in the shadows or highlights, respectively.

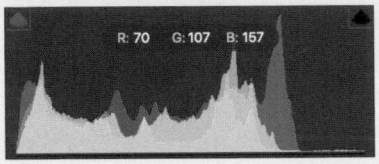

▶ **Tip:** Indications of clipped shadows or highlights don't always mean you've overcorrected an image. For example, a clipped specular highlight (such as a reflection of the sun or a studio light on metal) is acceptable, because a specular highlight has no detail to lose.

Applying sharpening

Photoshop offers several sharpening filters, but when an image is in raw format, it's often a good idea to use the Sharpening controls in Camera Raw. The Sharpening controls are in the Detail panel. To see the effect of sharpening in the preview panel, you must view the image at 100% or greater.

1 Click the Zoom Levels menu (41.6% ⌄) near the bottom-left corner of the window to zoom in to 100%. Then select the Hand tool (✋), and pan the image to see the cross at the top of the mission tower.

2 In the Edit mode panel stack under the histogram, scroll down until you see the Detail panel, and click its heading to expand it.

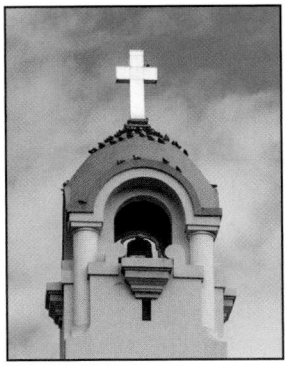

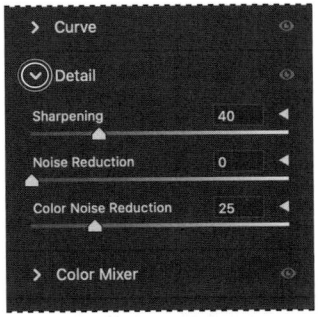

The Amount option determines how much sharpening Camera Raw applies. One approach is to exaggerate the Sharpening value at first to more easily see the effect of other sharpening options, and after those settings are tuned, reduce the Sharpening value back down to a more realistic level.

▶ **Tip:** Sharpening enhances the finest details of an image. The Clarity option in the Basic panel can help emphasize relatively large details. The Texture slider can bring out details that are between the size ranges handled by Sharpening and Clarity, but to avoid making noise more visible, it's often better to apply Texture to specific areas using a tool such as the Adjustment Brush.

▶ **Tip:** You can use keyboard shortcuts to go to each Edit panel directly to avoid scrolling. Press the Ctrl (Windows) or Command (Mac) key along with a number key; the panels are numbered from the Basic panel down. For example, the Detail panel is the third one, so to open it press Ctrl-3 (Windows) or Command-3 (Mac).

3 Change the Sharpening value to **100**.

4 Click the disclosure triangle above the right end of the Sharpening slider to reveal more options.

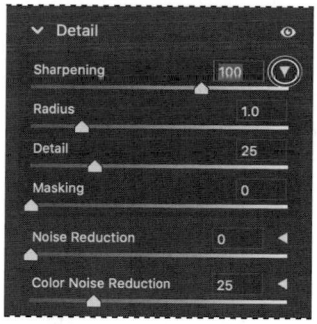

Many Camera Raw features have advanced options that are hidden to save space. If you see a disclosure triangle along the right side, you know there are more options available there if you need them.

5 Change the Radius value to **0.9**.

The Radius option determines how far out from a pixel that sharpening is applied. For properly focused images without motion blur, a Radius value of 1 pixel works well to start. You might decrease the Radius value for images with fine details that are precisely focused or increase Radius to help sharpen blurred details.

6 Change the Detail value to **25**, unless it's already set that way.

The Detail option controls the balance between sharpening edges and textures for images with fine details. Lower values draw sharpening toward edges leaving broad areas smoother; higher values can bring out textures in broad areas.

7 Change the Masking value to **61**.

▶ **Tip:** Press Alt (Windows) or Option (Mac) as you drag the Masking slider; the white areas indicate the areas Camera Raw will sharpen.

The Masking slider is similar to the Detail slider in that it helps keep sharpening constrained along content edges, but Masking is more generally useful because it isn't just for fine details. A higher Masking value makes it easier to increase the Sharpening value without oversharpening noise and textures in broad areas of the image that should look smooth, such as a face or the sky. Lower the Masking value when you want Sharpening to emphasize details in broad areas, such as the weave of threads in fabric.

After you've adjusted the Radius, Detail, and Masking sliders, you can lower the Amount slider to a more reasonable final value.

8 Decrease the Sharpening slider to **70**.

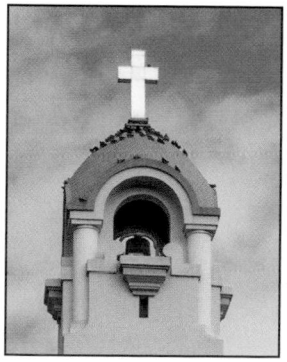

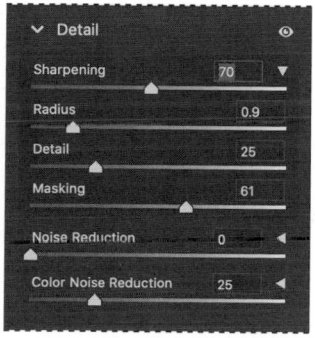

▶ **Tip:** If you have difficulty seeing the effects of sharpening, change the zoom level to 100% or higher.

Your Camera Raw edits are saved in XMP format "sidecar" files that are stored in the same folder as the original file and have the same base filename with an .XMP filename extension. When you move a raw image edited in Adobe Camera Raw to another computer or storage medium, be sure to move its XMP file with it. Camera Raw doesn't save changes into an original raw file, because raw files are intended to be read-only. Adobe Camera Raw can include edits in the same file as the raw image when exporting to the open Adobe DNG raw format.

Synchronizing settings across images

All three of the church images were shot at the same time under the same lighting conditions. Now that you've made the first one look great, you can automatically apply the same settings to the other two images using the Synchronize command.

1 Click and hold the filmstrip menu button (), and choose Select All to select all of the images in the filmstrip.

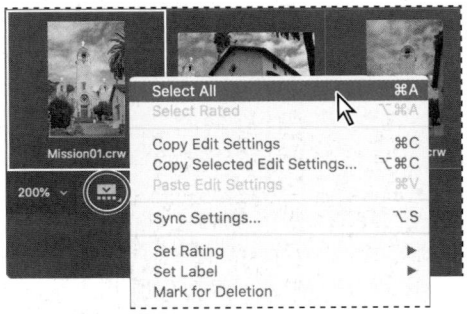

2 Click and hold the filmstrip menu button again, and choose Sync Settings.

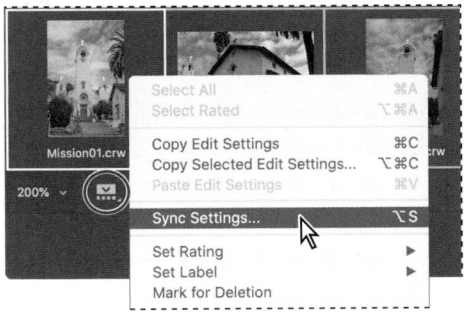

The Synchronize dialog box appears, listing all the settings you can apply to the images. By default, all options except Geometry, Crop, Spot Removal, and Local Adjustments are selected. For this project, you can accept the default selections, even though you didn't change all the settings.

3 Click OK in the Synchronize dialog box.

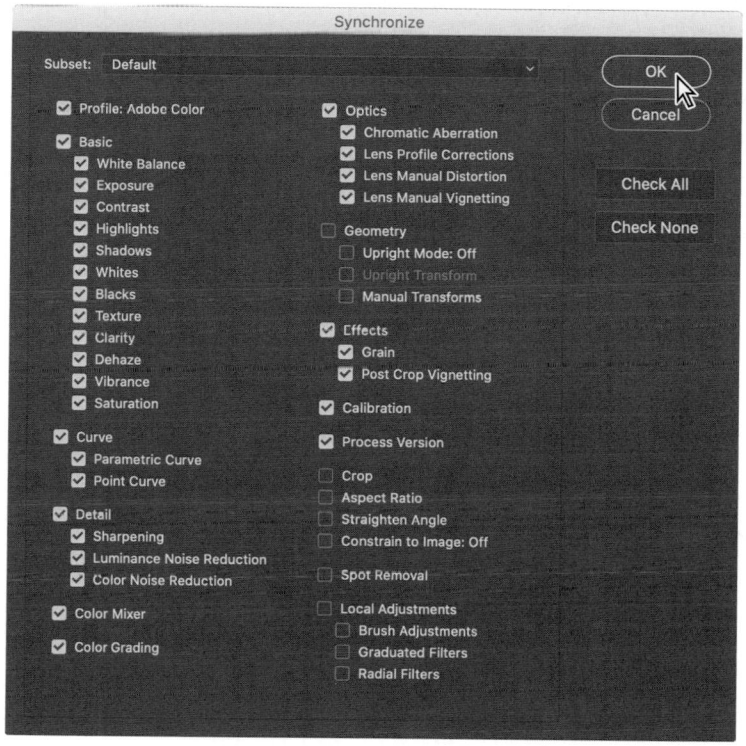

Note: A yellow alert triangle may temporarily appear over a preview or thumbnail image while Camera Raw is synchronizing settings to that image. When the triangle goes away, the preview or thumbnail is up to date.

When you synchronize the settings across all of the selected images, the thumbnails update to reflect the changes you made. To preview the images, click each thumbnail in the filmstrip.

Saving Camera Raw changes as new files

You can save your changes in different ways for different purposes. First, you'll save the images with adjustments as low-resolution JPEG files that you can share on the web. Then, you'll save one image, Mission01, as a Photoshop file that you can open as a Smart Object in Photoshop. When you open an image as a Smart Object in Photoshop, you can return to Camera Raw at any time to make further adjustments.

1 In the Camera Raw dialog box, click the filmstrip menu button, and choose Select All to select all three images.

2 Click the Save Selected Images button (⬇) near the top-right corner of the Camera Raw window.

3 In the Save Options dialog box, do the following:

- Choose Save In Same Location from the Destination menu.
- In the File Naming area, leave "Document Name" in the first box.
- Choose JPEG from the Format menu, and set the Quality level to High (8–9).
- In the Color Space area, choose sRGB IEC61966-2.1 from the Space menu.
- In the Image Sizing area, select Resize To Fit, and then choose Long Side from the Resize To Fit menu.
- Enter **800** pixels. This will set the long side of an image to 800 pixels whether it's a portrait (tall) or landscape (wide) image. When you choose Long Side, the dimension of the short side will automatically be adjusted proportionally.
- Type **72** pixels/inch for the Resolution value.

These settings will save your corrected images as smaller, downsampled JPEG files, which you can share with colleagues on the web. They'll be resized so that most viewers won't need to scroll to see the entire image when it opens. Your files will be named Mission01.jpg, Mission02.jpg, and Mission03.jpg.

4 Click Save.

▶ **Tip:** If your images contain metadata that you consider private, you can restrict what metadata is included when you save copies from Camera Raw. For example, if your images contain camera information, keywords such as names of people, a copyright notice, and other metadata you entered in Bridge, choose Copyright Only from the Metadata menu to include only the copyright notice.

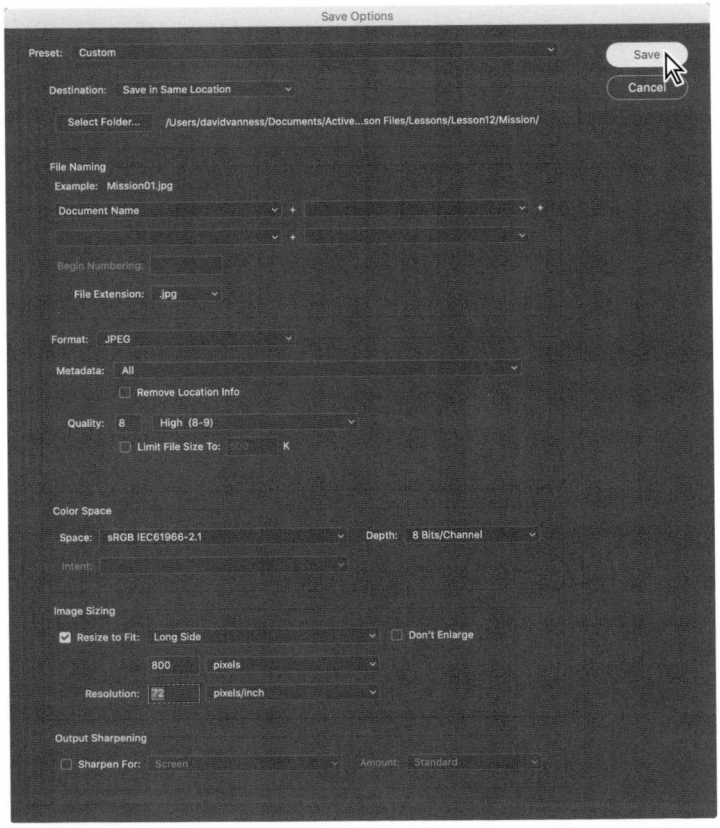

In the Camera Raw dialog box, a readout in the bottom-left corner indicates how many images have been processed until all the images have been saved. The CRW thumbnails still appear in the Camera Raw dialog box. In Bridge, however, you now also have JPEG versions as well as the original raw image files, which you can continue to edit or leave for another time.

Now you'll open a copy of the Mission01 image in Photoshop.

5 Select the Mission01.crw image thumbnail in the filmstrip in the Camera Raw dialog box. Then click the menu of options to the right of the Open button, and choose Open as Object.

Note: If you see a message that says "Skip loading optional and third-party plug-ins?" click No. The message appears if the Shift key is held down when Photoshop starts up.

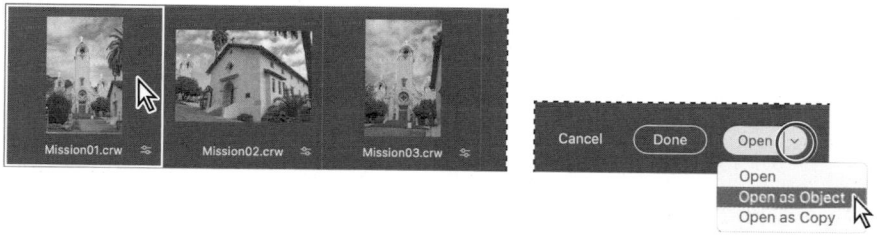

The Open as Object button opens the image as a Smart Object layer in Photoshop: Instead of converting the camera raw file to Photoshop format, it's preserved in camera raw format inside the Photoshop document. This lets you continue making raw-based adjustments at any time, by double-clicking the Smart Object thumbnail in the Layers panel to open Camera Raw. If, instead, you had clicked Open, the image would be permanently converted into a normal Photoshop layer, and no more raw format edits would be possible.

Tip: To change the Open button so that it's always an Open Object button, click the underlined workflow options link at the bottom of the Camera Raw dialog box, select Open In Photoshop As Smart Objects, and click OK.

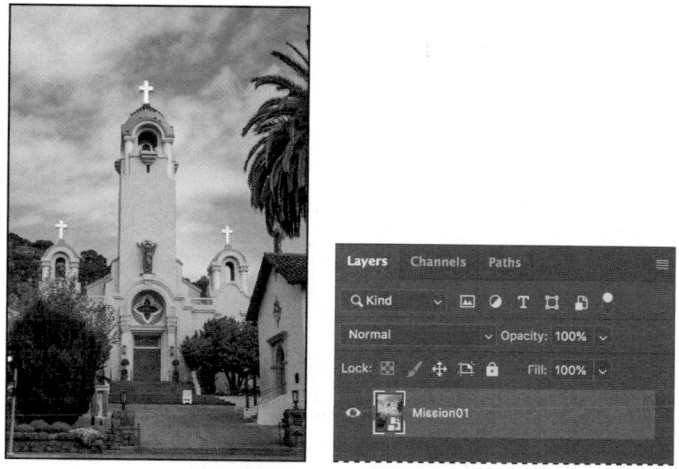

6 In Photoshop, choose File > Save As. In the Save As dialog box, choose Photoshop for the format, rename the file **Mission_Final.psd**, navigate to the Lesson12 folder, and click Save. Click OK if the Photoshop Format Options dialog box appears. Then close the file.

Note: If Photoshop displays a dialog box telling you about the difference between saving to Cloud Documents and Your Computer, click Save On Your Computer. You can also select Don't Show Again, but that setting will deselect after you reset Photoshop preferences.

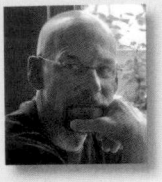

A photographer for more than 25 years, Jay Graham began his career designing and building custom homes. Today, Graham has clients in the advertising, architectural, editorial, and travel industries.

See Jay Graham's portfolio on the web at jaygraham.com.

Pro photo workflow

Good habits make all the difference

A sensible workflow and good work habits will keep you enthused about digital photography, help your images shine, and save you from the night terrors of losing work you never backed up. Here's an outline of the basic workflow for digital images from a professional photographer with more than 25 years' experience. To help you get the most from the images you shoot, Jay Graham offers guidelines for setting up your camera, creating a basic color workflow, selecting file formats, organizing images, and showing off your work.

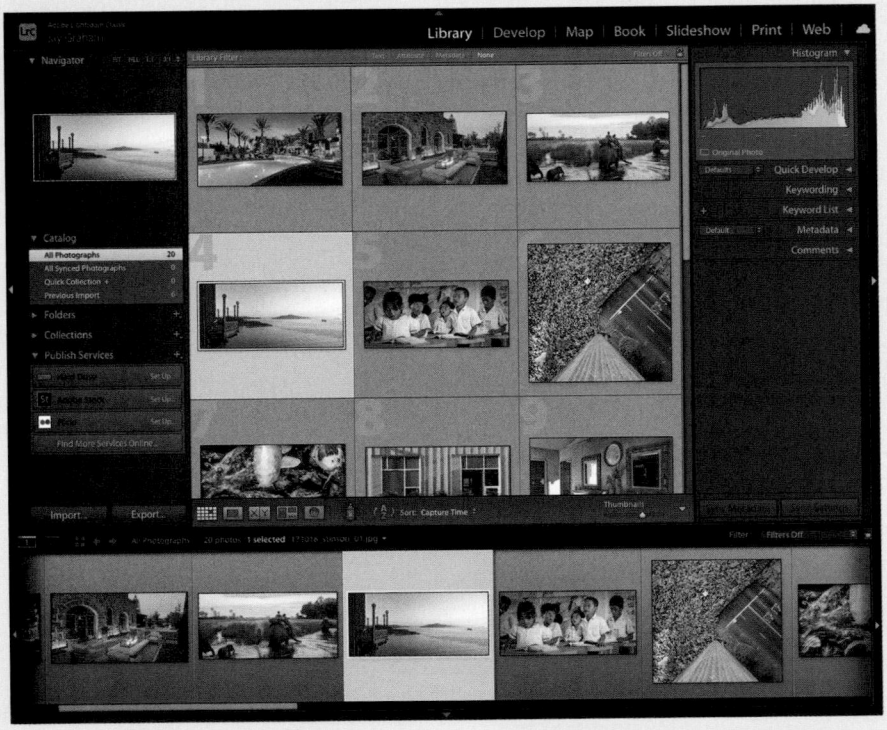

Graham uses Adobe Lightroom® Classic to organize thousands of images.

"The biggest complaint from people is they've lost their image. Where is it? What does it look like?" says Graham. "So naming is important."

Start out right by setting up your camera preferences
If your camera has the option, it's generally best to shoot in its camera raw file format, which captures all the image information you need. With one camera raw photo, says Graham, "you can go from daylight to an indoor tungsten image without degradation" when it's reproduced. If it makes more sense to shoot in JPEG for your project, use fine compression and high resolution.

Start with the best material
Get all the data when you capture—at fine compression and high resolution. You can't go back later.

Organize your files
Name your images as you import them into the Lightroom catalog. "If the camera names files, eventually it resets and produces multiple files with the same name," says Graham. Use Adobe Lightroom Classic to rename, rank, and add metadata to the photos you plan to keep; cull those you don't.

Graham names his files by date (and possibly subject). He would store a series of photos taken October 18, 2017, at Stinson Beach in a folder named "171018_stinson". Within the folder, he names each image incrementally; for example, the first image would be named "171018_stinson_01". This should result in a truly unique filename for each image. "That way, it lines up on the hard drive real easily," he says. Follow Windows naming conventions to keep filenames usable on non-Macintosh platforms (32 characters maximum; only numbers, letters, underscores, and hyphens).

Convert raw images to DNG
Consider converting your camera raw images to the DNG format. Unlike many cameras' proprietary raw formats, the specifications for this format are publicly available so that software developers and device makers can more easily support it.

Keep a master image
Save your master in PSD, TIFF, or DNG format, not JPEG. Each time a JPEG is re-edited and saved, compression is reapplied, and the image quality degrades.

Show off to clients and friends
When you prepare your work for delivery, choose the appropriate color file for the destination. Convert the image to that profile, rather than assigning the profile. sRGB is generally best for viewing electronically or for printing from most online printing services. Adobe 1998 and Colormatch are the best profiles to use for RGB images destined for traditionally printed materials such as brochures. Adobe 1998 and ProPhoto RGB are best for printing with inkjet printers. Use 72 dpi for electronic viewing and 180 dpi or higher for printing.

Back up your images
You've devoted a lot of time and effort to your images: Don't lose them. To protect your photos against a range of potential disasters, it's best to have backups on multiple media such as external storage and a cloud backup service, set to back up automatically. "The question is not if your [internal] hard drive is going to crash," says Graham, reciting a common adage. "It's when."

About saving files in Camera Raw

Every camera model saves raw images in a unique format, but Adobe Camera Raw can process many raw file formats. Camera Raw processes the raw files with default image settings based on built-in camera profiles for supported cameras and on the EXIF (Exchangeable Image File format) data recorded by digital cameras. EXIF data can include exposure and lens information.

You can save the proprietary raw files in DNG format (the format saved by Adobe Camera Raw), JPEG, TIFF, and PSD. All of these formats can be used to save RGB and CMYK continuous-tone, bitmapped images, and all of them except DNG are also available in the Photoshop Save and Save As dialog boxes.

- The **DNG (Adobe Digital Negative)** format contains raw image data from a digital camera along with metadata that defines how the image data should look. DNG is intended to be an industry-wide standard format for raw image data, helping photographers manage the variety of proprietary raw formats and providing a compatible archival format. (You can save this format only from the Camera Raw dialog box.)
- The **JPEG (Joint Photographic Experts Group)** file format is commonly used to display photographs and other continuous-tone RGB images on the web. Higher-resolution JPEG compresses file size by selectively discarding data, starting with the visual information that our eyes are least likely to notice. The greater the compression, the lower the image quality.
- **TIFF (Tagged Image File Format)** is a flexible format supported by virtually all paint, image-editing, and page layout applications. It can save Photoshop layers. TIFF images can also be produced by most applications that control image capture hardware such as scanners.
- **PSD format** is the Photoshop native file format. Because of the tight integration between Adobe products, other Adobe applications such as Adobe Illustrator and Adobe InDesign can directly import PSD files and preserve many Photoshop features.

After you open a file in Photoshop, you can save or export it in many more formats, including Large Document Format (PSB), Photoshop PDF, GIF, or PNG. There's also a Photoshop Raw format (RAW) that you should not confuse with camera raw files; Photoshop Raw is a specialized technical file format that is not commonly used by photographers and designers.

For more information about file formats in Camera Raw and Photoshop, see Photoshop Help.

Applying advanced color correction

You'll use Levels, the Healing Brush tool, and other Photoshop features to enhance the image of this model.

Adjust the white balance in Camera Raw

The original image of the bride has a slight color cast. You'll start your color corrections in Camera Raw, setting the white balance and adjusting the overall tone of the image.

1 In Bridge, navigate to the Lesson12 folder. Select the 12B_Start.nef file, and choose File > Open In Camera Raw.

2 In the Basic panel in Camera Raw, select the White Balance tool (), and then click a white area in the model's dress to remove a green color cast.

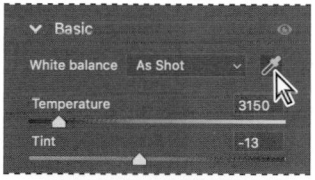

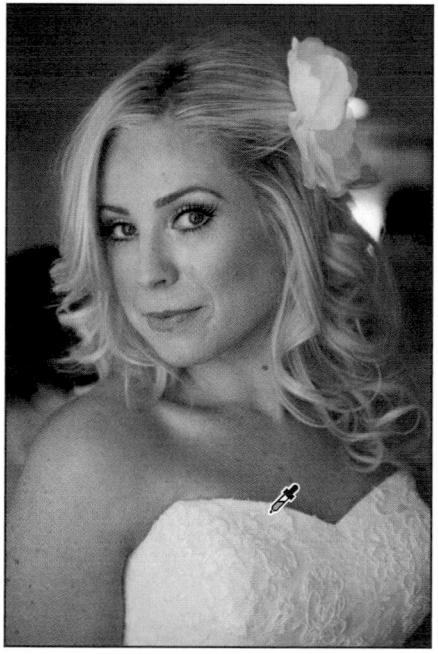

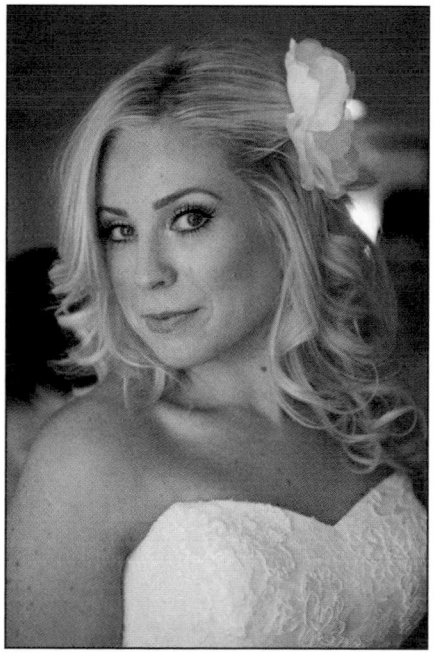

▶ **Tip:** It may work better to click a white area of the dress that is directly lit rather than in shade. The white balance of a neutral area facing the light source is more likely to be consistent with the white balance of the light source. A neutral area in shadow can be shifted by the color of light reflected by nearby surfaces.

▶ **Tip:** Be careful when applying Clarity or Texture to a portrait. Applying too much of either option may emphasize skin texture and surface characteristics such as freckles and wrinkles. Clarity and Texture are often best applied to specific areas with local adjustment tools.

3 Adjust other Basic panel options to make more adjustments at the raw stage:

- Increase Exposure to **+0.30**.
- Increase Contrast to **+15**.
- Increase Clarity to **+8**.

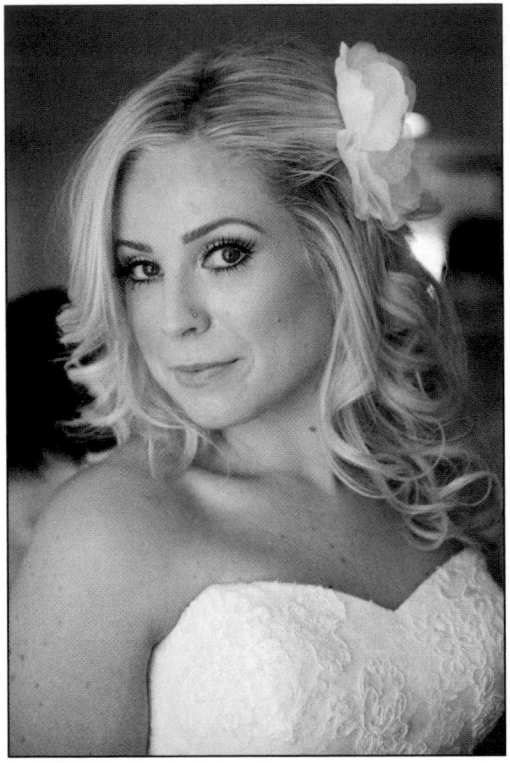

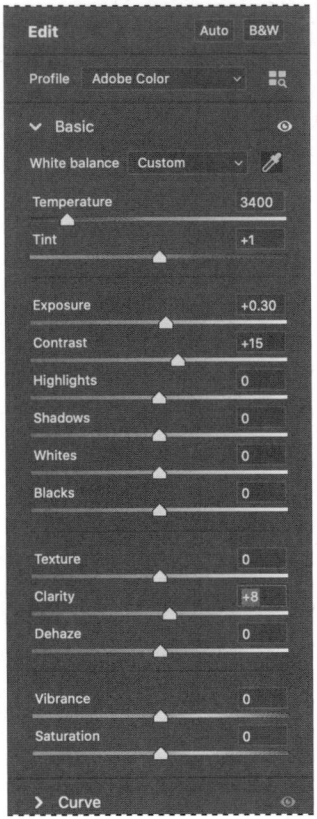

▶ **Tip:** You can try other profiles to see if they work better. For this image, Adobe Color produces a similar result to Adobe Portrait, but other profiles may be too garish or contrasty for skin tones.

4 Click the menu of options to the right of the Open button, and choose Open as Object.

The image opens in Photoshop as a Smart Object.

Adjusting levels

The tonal range of an image represents the amount of contrast, or detail, in the image and is determined by the image's distribution of pixels, ranging from the darkest pixels (black) to the lightest pixels (white). You'll use a Levels adjustment layer to fine-tune the tonal range in this image.

1 In Photoshop, choose File > Save As. Name the file **Model_final.psd**, and click Save. Click OK if you see the Photoshop Format Options dialog box.

2 Click the Levels button in the Adjustments panel.

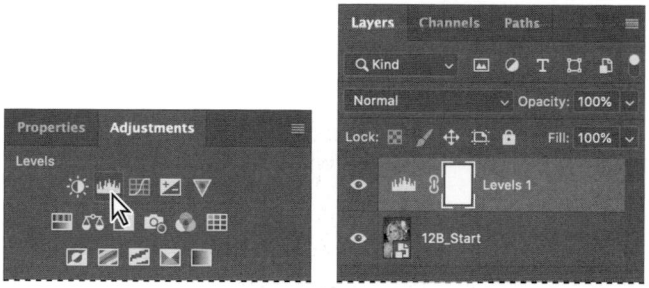

Photoshop adds a Levels adjustment layer to the Layers panel. The Levels controls and a histogram appear in the Properties panel. The histogram displays the range of dark and light values in the image. The left (black) triangle represents the shadows; the right (white) triangle represents the highlights; and the middle (gray) triangle represents the midtones, or gamma. Unless you're aiming for a special effect, the ideal histogram has its black point at the beginning of the data and its white point at the end of the data, and the middle portion has fairly uniform peaks and valleys, representing adequate pixel data in the midtones.

3 Click the Calculate A More Accurate Histogram button (⚠) on the left side of the histogram. Photoshop replaces the histogram.

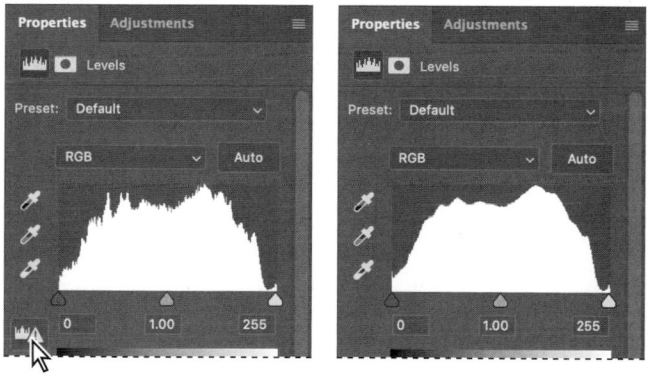

There is a small bump on the far-right side of the histogram, representing the current white point, but the bulk of the data ends further to the left. You want to set the white point closer to where most of the data ends.

4 Drag the right (white) triangle toward the left, where the histogram indicates that significant highlight tones start to appear. We moved it to a value of **242**.

As you drag, the third Input Levels value (beneath the histogram graph) changes, and so does the image itself.

▶ **Tip:** As you drag the white Input Levels triangle to the left, watch carefully to make sure highlight detail is not lost. Never clip skin tones! If you're wondering which highlights on the image are clipped by the white triangle, hold down the Alt/Option key as you drag it. This tip also works with the black Input Levels triangle.

5 Pull the middle (gray) triangle a little bit to the right to slightly darken the midtones. We moved it to a value of **0.9**.

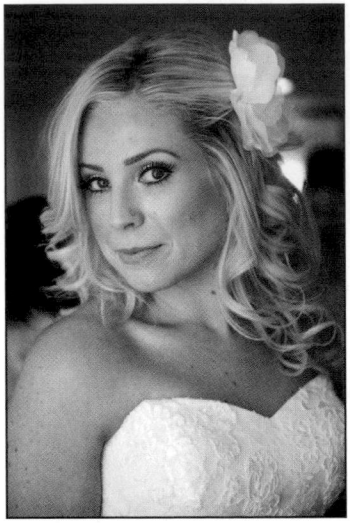

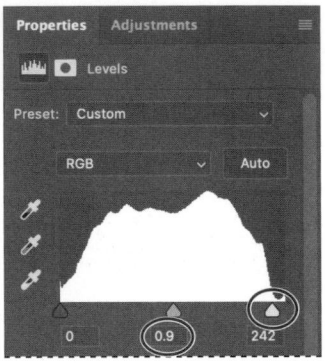

Editing the saturation in Camera Raw

▶ **Tip:** Here you're opening Camera Raw in Photoshop, while earlier you opened Camera Raw in Bridge. It's even possible to have Camera Raw open in both Photoshop and Bridge at the same time, working on different raw images in each.

The Levels adjustments helped significantly, but our bride looks a little sunburned. You'll adjust the saturation in Camera Raw to even out her skin tone.

1 Double-click the 12B_Start layer thumbnail to open the Smart Object in Camera Raw.

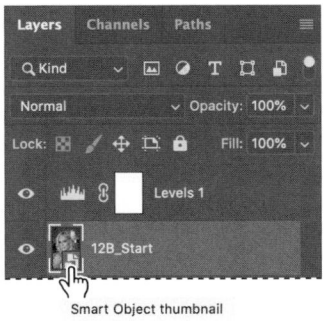

2 In Edit mode, expand the Color Mixer panel, the fourth panel from the top.

3 Click Saturation.

4 Move the following sliders to make the skin look a little less red:

- Reduce Reds to **–2**.
- Reduce Oranges to **–10**.
- Reduce Magentas to **–3**.

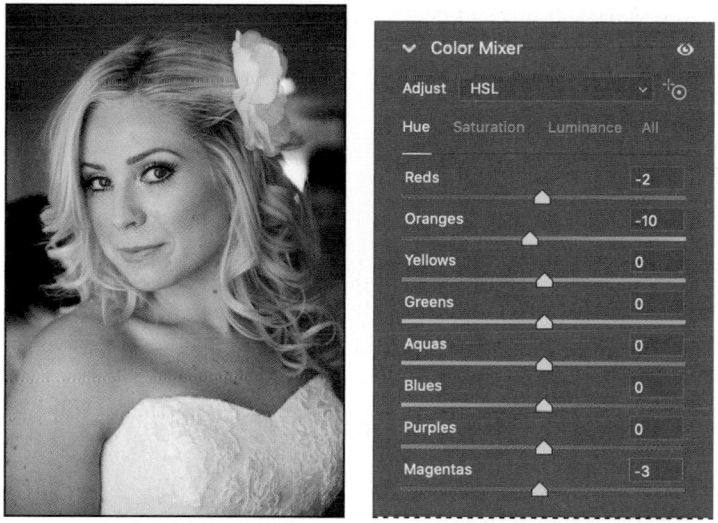

5 See the effect of your changes by clicking and holding the eye icon at the right side of the Color Mixer panel to temporarily disable the changes you made in that panel only; then release the mouse to enable that panel's changes again.

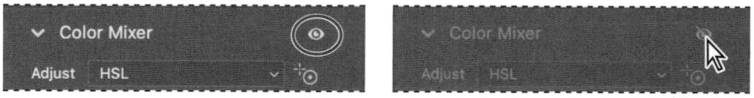

6 Click OK to return to Photoshop.

Using the healing brush tools to remove blemishes

Now you're ready to give the model's face some focused attention. You'll use the Healing Brush and Spot Healing Brush tools to heal blemishes, smooth the skin, remove red veins from the eyes, and even hide the nose jewelry.

1 In the Layers panel, select the 12B_Start layer. Then, choose Duplicate Layer from the Layers panel menu.

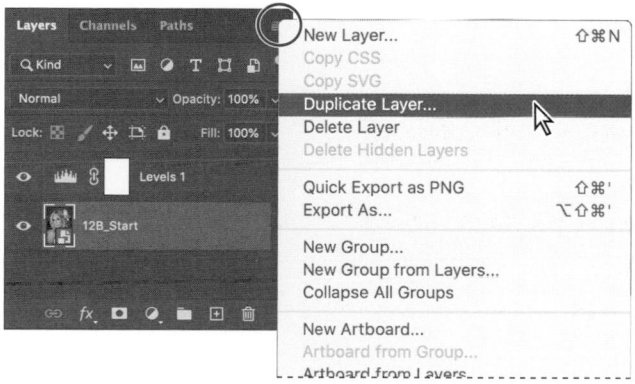

Tip: Camera Raw has its own Spot Removal tool that has the advantage of being adjustable at any time. But Photoshop offers a much wider range of tools and options for healing and patching images, and that's why blemish removal will be done in Photoshop in this lesson.

2 Name the new layer **Corrections**, and click OK.

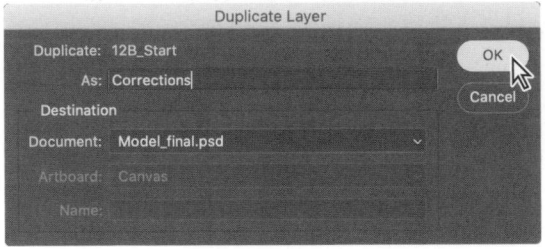

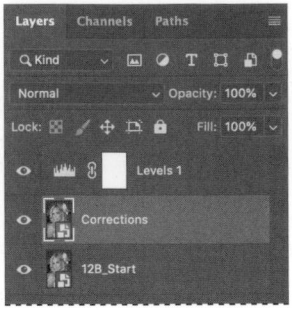

Working on a duplicate layer preserves the original pixels so you can make changes later. You can't make changes using the healing brush tools on a Smart Object, so first you'll rasterize the layer into a normal pixel layer.

3 Choose Layer > Smart Objects > Rasterize.

4 Zoom in on the model's face so that you can see it clearly.

5 Select the Spot Healing Brush tool ( ).

6 In the options bar, select the following settings:

- Brush Size: **35** px
- Mode: Normal
- Type: Content-Aware

7 With the Spot Healing Brush tool, brush out the nose jewelry. A single click may be enough.

Because you've selected Content-Aware in the options bar, the Spot Healing Brush tool replaces the nose stud with skin that is similar to that around it.

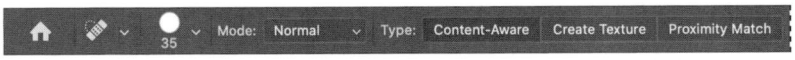

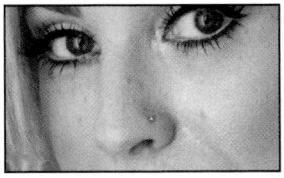

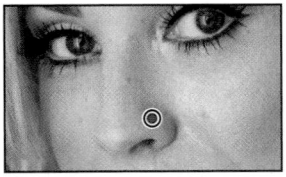

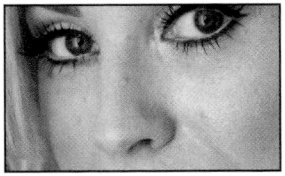

8 Paint over fine lines around the eyes and mouth. You can also brush away freckles and minor blemishes on her face, neck, arms, and chest. Experiment with simply clicking, using very short strokes, and creating longer brush strokes. You can also experiment with different settings. For example, to soften the lines around the mouth, we selected Proximity Match and the Lighten blending

mode in the options bar. Remove obtrusive or distracting lines and blemishes, but leave enough that the face retains its character.

The Healing Brush tool may be a better option for larger blemishes. With the Healing Brush tool, you have more control over the pixels Photoshop samples.

9 Select the Healing Brush tool (), hidden under the Spot Healing Brush tool (). Select a brush with a size of **45** pixels and a Hardness of **100**%.

10 Alt-click (Windows) or Option-click (Mac) an area on her cheek to create the sampling source.

11 Brush over the large mole on her cheek to replace it with the color you sampled. You'll smooth out the texture later.

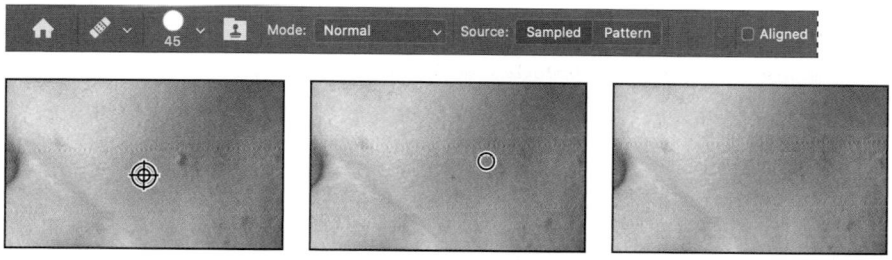

12 Use the Healing Brush tool to heal any larger blemishes that remain.

13 Choose File > Save to save your work so far.

Enhancing an image using the Dodge and Sponge tools

You'll use the Sponge and Dodge tools to brighten the eyes and lips.

1 Select the Sponge tool (), hidden under the Dodge tool (). In the options bar, make sure Vibrance is selected, and then select the following settings:

- Brush Size: **35** px
- Brush Hardness: **0**%
- Mode: Saturate
- Flow: **50**%

2 Drag the Sponge tool over the irises in the eyes to increase their saturation.

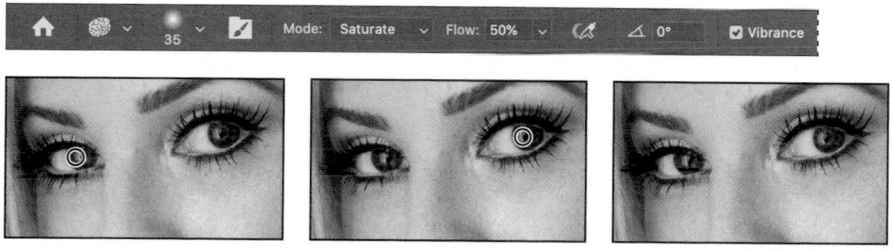

▶ **Tip:** Lowering the Flow value for a tool can give you more control. By lowering the rate at which a tool paints, you have more time to gradually build up an effect by repeating strokes.

3 Change the brush size to **70** px and the flow to **10%**. Then brush the Sponge tool over the lips to saturate them.

You can use the Sponge tool to desaturate color too. You'll reduce the red in the corner of the eye.

4 Change the brush size to **45** px and the flow to **50%**. Then choose Desaturate from the Mode menu in the options bar.

5 Brush over the corner of the eye to reduce the red.

6 Select the Dodge tool (), hidden under the Sponge tool.

7 In the options bar, change the brush size to **60** px and the Exposure to **10%**. Choose Highlights from the Range menu.

8 Brush the Dodge tool over the eyes—the whites and the irises—to brighten them.

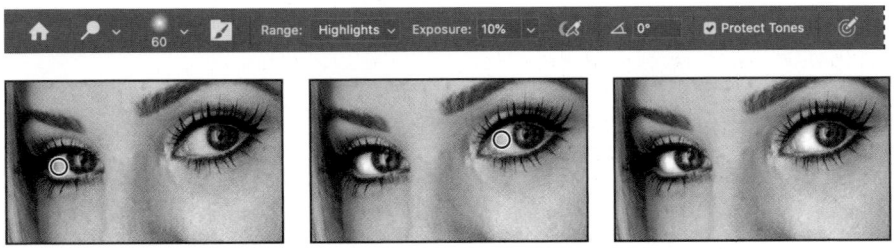

9 With the Dodge tool still selected, select Shadows from the Range menu in the options bar.

10 Use the Dodge tool to lighten the shadow area above the eyes and the areas around the irises to bring out the color.

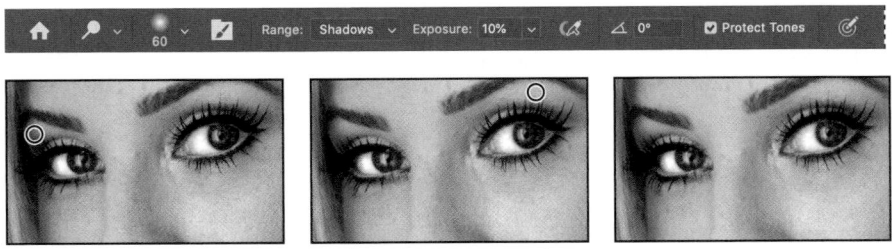

Adjusting skin tones

In Photoshop, you can select a color range that targets skin tones so that it's easier to adjust the levels and color tone of skin without affecting the entire image. The Skin Tones color range selects other areas of the image with similar colors, but if you're making slight adjustments, this is usually acceptable.

1 Choose Select > Color Range.

2 In the Color Range dialog box, choose Skin Tones from the Select menu.

The preview shows that much of the image has been selected.

3 Select Detect Faces.

The preview in the selection changes. Now the face, hair highlights, and lighter areas of the dress are selected.

4 Decrease the Fuzziness slider to **10** to refine the selection. Then click OK.

A lower Fuzziness value tightens up the selection by narrowing the range of colors included in the selection so that less of the hair and dress are included.

▶ **Tip:** Camera Raw offers simple masking, including a Range Mask for local adjustment tools that can be used to select a range of colors or tones. But again, this image was moved to Photoshop to use its more powerful and flexible tools for creating selections based on color or tone.

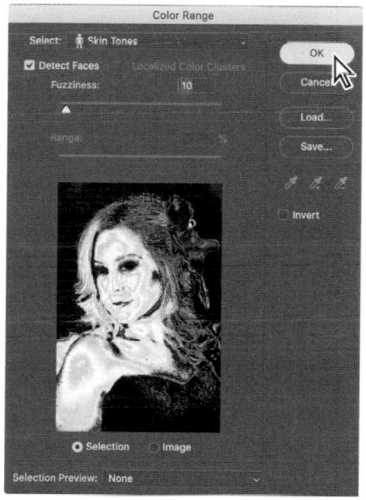

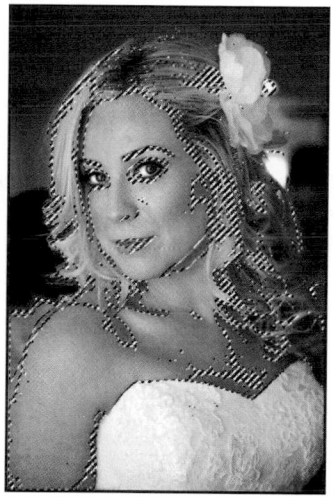

The selection appears on the image itself as animated dotted lines (sometimes called *marching ants).* You'll apply a Curves adjustment layer to the selection to reduce the overall red in the skin tone of the image.

5 Click the Curves icon in the Adjustments panel.

▶ **Tip:** To soften the edges of a selection, such as the selection created by Color Range, choose Select > Modify > Feather. Or, you can wait until the layer mask is created and then blur the mask.

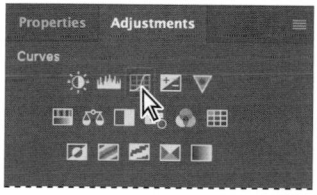

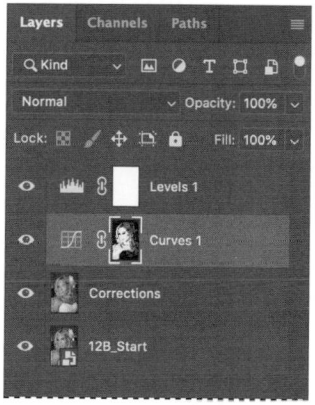

Photoshop adds a Curves adjustment layer above the Corrections layer, and the selection becomes a layer mask for the adjustment layer you just created.

6 Choose Red from the color channel menu in the Properties panel. Then click in the middle of the graph, and pull the curve down very slightly. The selected areas become less red. Be careful not to pull the curve down too far, or a green cast will appear. You can see the difference you've made by clicking the Toggle Layer Visibility button (the eye icon) in the Properties panel or Layers panel.

Because you selected the skin tones before applying the Curves adjustment layer, the skin color shifts, but the background is unchanged. The adjustment affects slightly more of the image than the skin itself, but the effect blends well and is subtle.

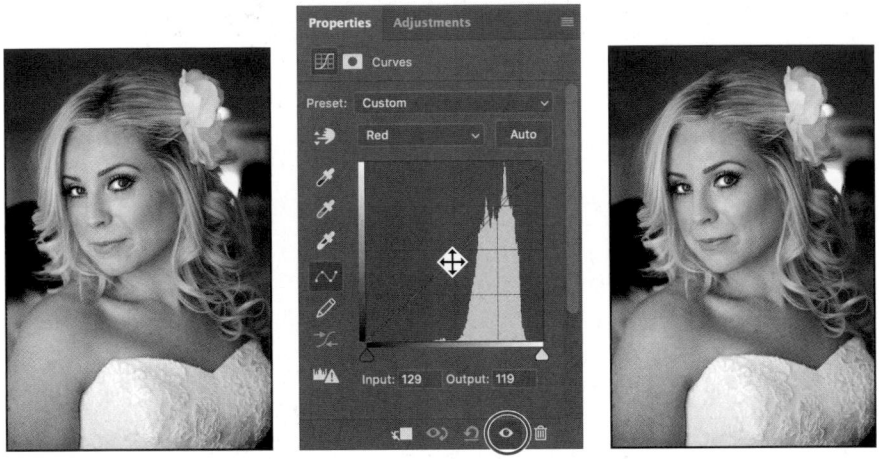

Applying surface blur

You're almost done with the model. As a finishing touch, you'll apply the Surface Blur filter to give her a smooth appearance. Surface Blur confines its blur to areas away from important details and edges.

1 Select the Corrections layer, and choose Layer > Duplicate Layer. Name the layer **Surface Blur**, and click OK in the Duplicate Layer dialog box.

2 With the Surface Blur layer selected, choose Filter > Blur > Surface Blur.

3 In the Surface Blur dialog box, leave the Radius at 5 pixels, and move the Threshold to **10** levels. Then click OK.

The higher the Threshold value, the more distinct a feature needs to be before it will be blurred.

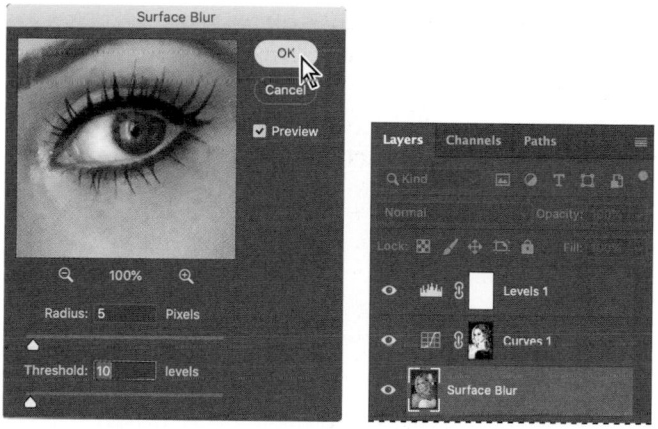

The Surface Blur filter has left the model looking a little glassy. You'll reduce its effect by reducing the opacity of the blur.

4 With the Surface Blur layer selected, change the Opacity to **40%** in the Layers panel.

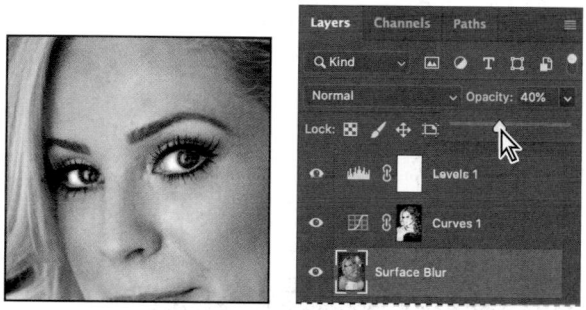

She looks more realistic now, but you can target the surface blur more precisely using the Eraser tool.

5 Select the Eraser tool (). In the options bar, select a brush between **10** and **50** pixels, with **10%** Hardness. Set the Opacity to **90%**.

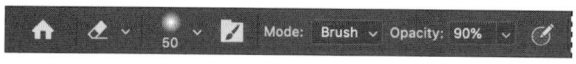

6 Brush over the eyes, eyebrows, the defining lines of the nose, and the detail in the dress. You're erasing part of the blurred layer to let the sharper layer below show through in these areas.

Note: It's normal for a camera raw image to expand to a much larger file size as a Photoshop or TIFF format image. A camera raw image is one channel of sensor data, but after processing it becomes multiple channels (three channels if converted to RGB, four channels for CMYK). If the Photoshop or TIFF file uses a higher bit depth (such as 16 bits per channel) and then you add layers and masks, the file size must increase even more.

7 Zoom out so you can see the entire image.

8 Save your work.

9 Choose Layer > Flatten Image to flatten the layers and reduce file size.

10 Save the image again, and then close it.

You've taken advantage of features in both Camera Raw and Photoshop to help this bride look her best. As you've seen, you can move between Photoshop and Camera Raw to perform different tasks as you enhance and improve an image.

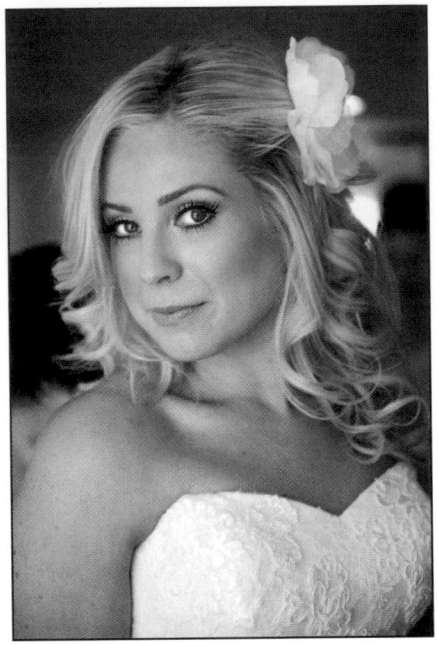

About HDR and panoramas in Camera Raw

When you select more than one image in Camera Raw, you can choose Merge to HDR or Merge to Panorama by clicking and holding the filmstrip menu button. HDR (high dynamic range) requires darker and lighter exposures of the same composition, while a panorama requires multiple exposures as tiles of a larger scene. Photoshop also has HDR or panorama features, but the newer process in Camera Raw is simpler, provides a preview, can process in the background, and produces a DNG file that you can edit in Camera Raw with the flexibility of a raw format image.

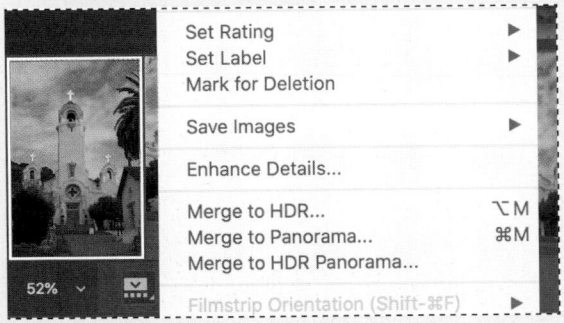

Extra credit

Painting with Light: Using Camera Raw as a Filter

In addition to opening files in Camera Raw to start the editing process, you can apply Camera Raw settings as a filter to any file in Photoshop. You'll use Camera Raw as a filter to make adjustments to this still-life image. First, you'll convert the image to a Smart Object so you can use Camera Raw as a Smart Filter, applying changes without affecting the original file.

1 In Photoshop, choose File > Open. Navigate to the Lessons/Lesson12 folder, and double-click the fruit.jpg file to open it.

2 Choose Filter > Convert For Smart Filters. Click OK in the informational dialog box.

3 Choose Filter > Camera Raw Filter. The image opens in Camera Raw.

The Convert For Smart Filters command converts the image to a Smart Object. You can also apply Camera Raw as a standard filter, but then you can't return to adjust your settings or have the option of hiding the adjustments.

4 Select the Adjustment Brush in the toolbar.

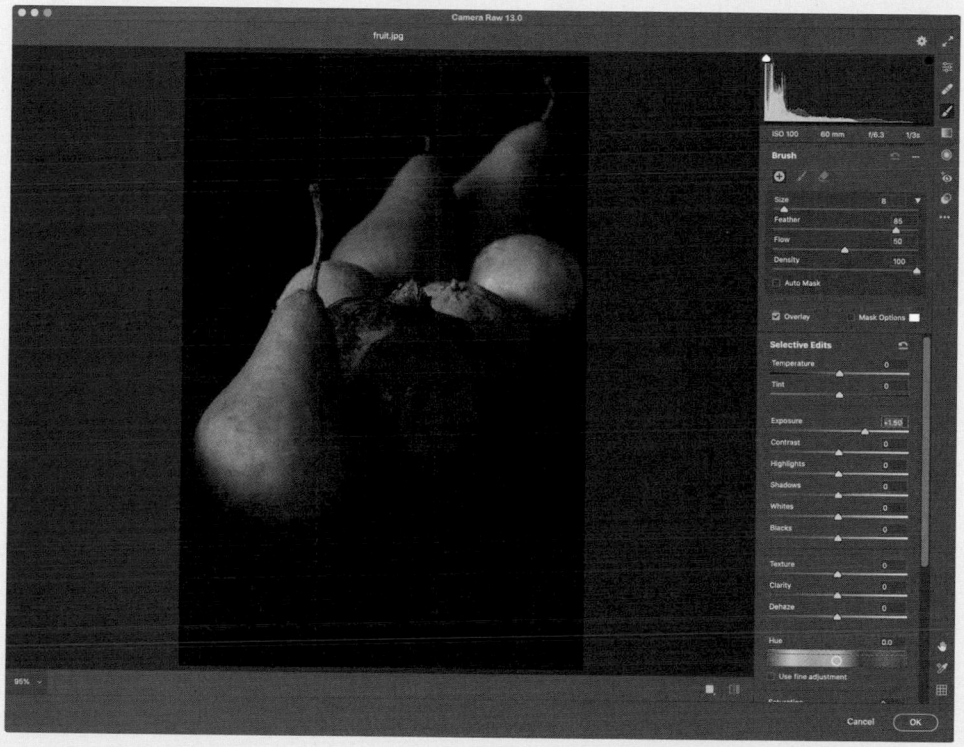

Continues on next page

Extra credit (continued)

With the Adjustment Brush tool in Camera Raw, you can apply Exposure, Brightness, Clarity, and other adjustments to specific areas of a photo by painting them directly onto those areas. The Graduated Filter tool is similar, but it applies the same types of adjustments gradually across a region of the photo that you define.

5 In the Brush panel, change Size to **8**, expand the options below it, and change Feather to **85**. Then in Selective Edits below, change Exposure to **+1.50**. This sets up the brush in advance.

6 Brush the fruit where you want to apply the settings above. Continue until the fruit is too bright.

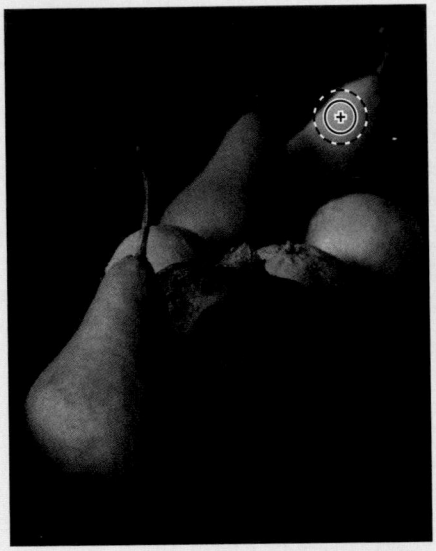

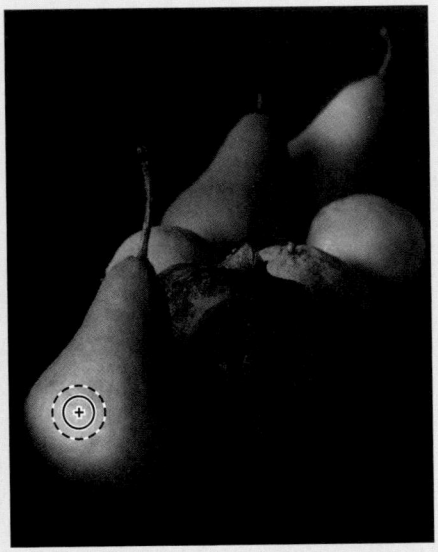

7 Once you've brushed all the fruit, reduce the Exposure setting in the Adjustment Brush panel so the image looks more realistic.

8 To see how your changes affected the image in Camera Raw, click the Before/After Views button at the bottom of the image window, or click the Toggle Default Settings view.

9 When you're satisfied with the changes, click OK.

Photoshop displays the image. In the Layers panel, the Camera Raw filter is listed beneath the layer name. You can toggle the visibility icon for the Camera Raw filter to see the image before and after the adjustment. To edit the Camera Raw smart filter adjustment, double-click Camera Raw Filter in the Layers panel.

You might notice that fewer options are available in Camera Raw when it's applied as a filter to a layer. The full range of Camera Raw options is available when it's editing a true camera raw file.

Review questions

1 How is editing a camera raw image different than editing a photo in a format such as JPEG or Photoshop file format?

2 What is the advantage of the Adobe Digital Negative (DNG) file format?

3 How can you apply the same settings to multiple images in Camera Raw?

4 How can you use Camera Raw as a filter for a non-raw layer in Photoshop?

Review answers

1 A camera raw file contains unprocessed picture data from a digital camera's image sensor. Camera raw files give photographers control over interpreting the image data, rather than letting the camera make the adjustments and conversions. When you edit the image in Camera Raw, it stores the edits separately while leaving the original raw file untouched. This way, you can edit the image as you desire, export it, and keep the original intact for future use or other adjustments.

2 The Adobe Digital Negative (DNG) file format contains the raw image data from a digital camera as well as metadata that defines what the image data means. DNG is an industry-wide standard for camera raw image data. DNG can help photographers manage proprietary camera raw file formats using an openly available standard, and it provides a compatible archival format that includes edits.

3 To apply the same settings to multiple images in Camera Raw, select the images in the filmstrip, click the filmstrip menu button, and choose Sync Settings. Then select the settings you want to apply, and click OK.

4 To apply Camera Raw as a filter, choose Filter > Camera Raw Filter in Photoshop. Make the changes you want to make in Camera Raw, and then click OK. If you want to be able to edit the changes later, apply Camera Raw as a Smart Filter.

13 PREPARING FILES FOR THE WEB

Lesson overview

In this lesson, you'll learn how to do the following:

- Use the Frame tool to create a placeholder for a layout.
- Create and stylize a button for a website.
- Use layer groups and artboards.
- Optimize design assets for the web.
- Record an action to automate a series of steps.
- Play an action to affect multiple images.
- Save entire layouts and individual assets using Export As.
- Design for multiple screen sizes with multiple artboards.

This lesson will take about an hour to complete. To get the lesson files used in this chapter, download them from the web page for this book at www.adobepress.com/PhotoshopCIB2021. For more information, see "Accessing the lesson files and Web Edition" in the Getting Started section at the beginning of this book.

As you work on this lesson, you'll preserve the start files. If you need to restore the start files, download them from your Account page.

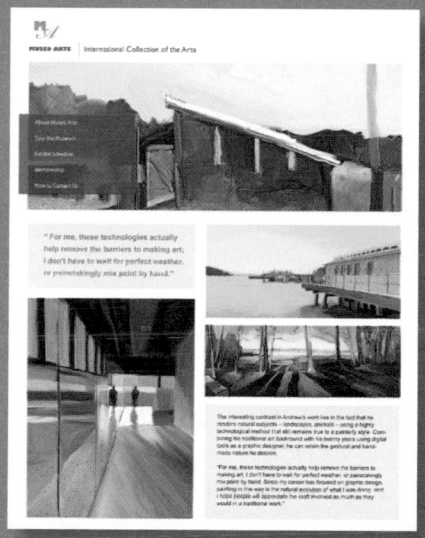

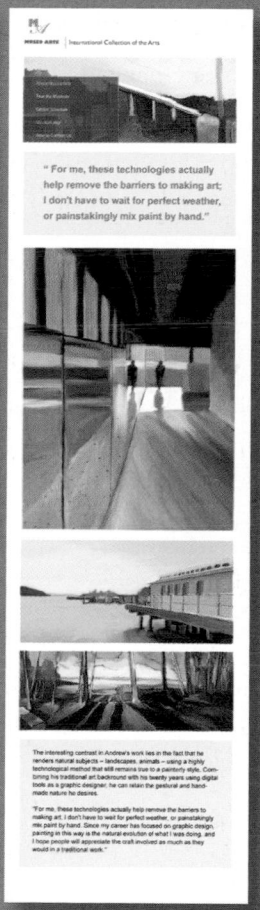

PROJECT: MUSEUM WEBSITE

It's often necessary to create separate images for buttons or other objects in a website. The Export As workflow makes it easy to save layers, layer groups, and artboards as separate image files.

Getting started

In this lesson, you will build buttons for the home page of an art museum's website and then generate appropriate graphics files for each button. You'll use layer groups to assemble the buttons and then create actions to prepare a set of images for use as a second group of buttons. First, you'll view the final web design.

1 Start Photoshop, and then simultaneously hold down Ctrl+Alt+Shift (Windows) or Command+Option+Shift (Mac) to restore the default preferences. (See "Restoring default preferences" on page 5.)

2 When prompted, click Yes to delete the Adobe Photoshop Settings file.

3 Choose File > Browse In Bridge.

4 In Bridge, click Lessons in the Favorites panel. Double-click the Lesson13 folder in the Content panel.

5 View the 13End.psd file in Bridge.

Note: If Bridge isn't installed, the File > Browse In Bridge command in Photoshop will start the Creative Cloud desktop app, which will download and install Bridge. After installation completes, you can start Bridge. For more information, see page 3.

There are eight buttons at the bottom of the page, arranged in two rows. You'll transform images into buttons for the top row and use an action to prepare the buttons for the second row.

6 Double-click the 13Start.psd thumbnail to open the file in Photoshop. Click OK if you see the Missing Profile dialog box.

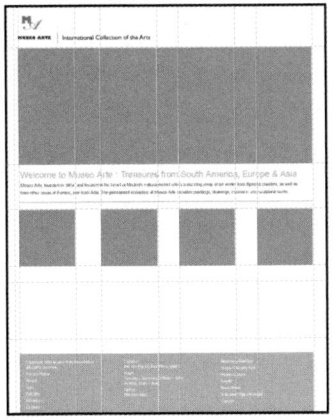

13Start.psd

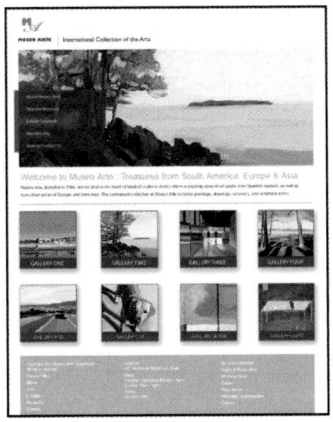

13End.psd

Note: If Photoshop displays a dialog box telling you about the difference between saving to Cloud Documents and Your Computer, click Save On Your Computer. You can also select Don't Show Again, but that setting will deselect after you reset Photoshop preferences.

7 Choose File > Save As, rename the file **13Working.psd**, and click Save. Click OK in the Photoshop Format Options dialog box.

Creating placeholders with the Frame tool

When you lay out objects for a print, web, or mobile device project, it's common to design the layout before you have the final graphics for it. You could add temporary graphics that you plan to replace later with final graphics, but this requires additional file management. You can simplify the design process by creating placeholder shapes, called *frames*, during the early stages of design. As you refine the design and as final graphics become available, it's easy to place graphics directly into a placeholder frame.

You create frames using the Frame tool. A frame can contain an imported graphic, a Smart Object, or a pixel layer. When you create a frame, it appears in the Layers panel, because a frame is like a layer group with a vector mask.

The document 13Working.psd contains empty gray boxes. The gray boxes exist only to help you position new frames that you'll create for this lesson. When you create your own designs, you can design using the Frame tool alone.

1 Choose Edit > Preferences > Units & Rulers (Windows) or Photoshop > Preferences > Units & Rulers (Mac). In the Units area of the dialog box, make sure Pixels is selected in the Rulers menu, and then click OK.

▶ **Tip:** A quick way to change the unit of measure is to right-click (Windows) or Control-click (Mac) the rulers.

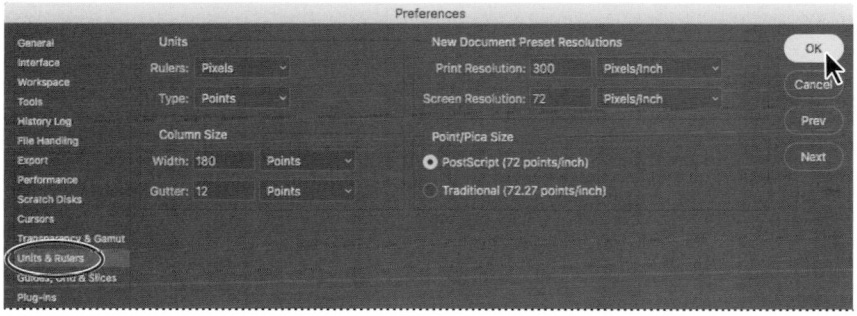

You want to work in pixels because this document is intended to be a web page.

2 Choose Window > Info to open the Info panel.

▶ **Tip:** To customize the Info panel display of the color values under the pointer, click either of the eyedropper icons in the Info panel, and choose the display option you want.

The Info panel displays information dynamically as you move the pointer or make selections. Which information it displays depends on the tool that is selected. You'll use it to determine the position of the ruler guide (based on the Y coordinate) and the size of an area you select (based on the width and height). It's also handy for seeing the values of colors under the pointer.

3 If the rulers aren't visible, choose View > Rulers.

▶ **Tip:** The keyboard shortcut for showing or hiding rulers is Ctrl+R (Windows) or Command+R (Mac).

Adding a frame

Frames are easy to add, because you create them in the same way you'd create a shape such as a rectangle or circle.

▶ **Tip:** You can create an elliptical or circular frame by selecting the Elliptical Frame icon in the options bar for the Frame tool.

1 In the Tools panel, select the Frame tool (⊠).

2 Drag to create a rectangular frame over the large gray rectangle at the top of the document.

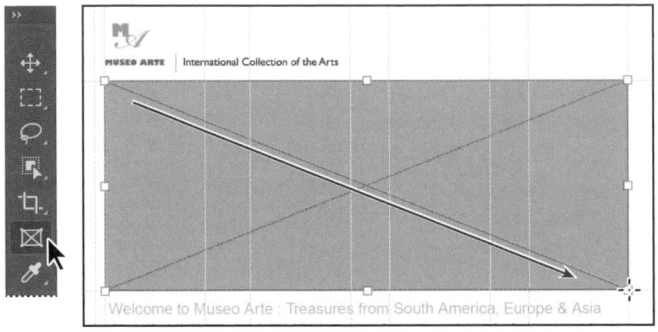

▶ **Tip:** To create a frame of any shape, such as a star, first draw the shape using the Pen tool or a shape tool. Then, with the shape layer selected in the Layers panel, choose Layer > New > Convert To Frame.

The frame appears as a rectangle with an X inside it. The X indicates that it's not just a vector shape, but a placeholder frame. As a placeholder, it's ready to contain a graphic at any time.

Adding a graphic to a frame

When you finalize the images and other graphics that go into a document, you can add them to the placeholder frames you've created.

1 In the Layers panel, make sure the Frame 1 layer is still selected.

2 Choose File > Place Linked.

3 Navigate to the Lesson13/Art folder, select the NorthShore.jpg file, and click Place.

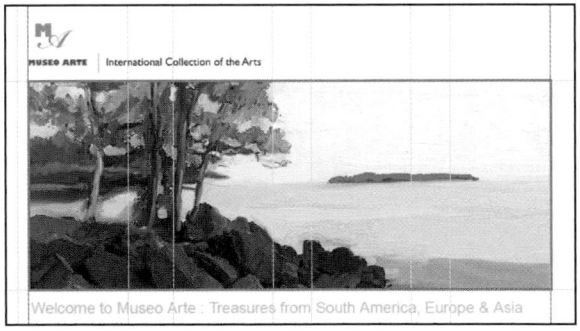

The JPEG image you selected appears inside the selected frame and is automatically sized to fit the frame.

You can also drag an image from Bridge or the desktop and drop it into a frame in a Photoshop document window; this embeds the image. To link an image you drag into a Photoshop document window, hold down Alt or Option as you drag.

Editing frame attributes with the Properties panel

When a frame is selected in the Layers panel, you can see and edit frame attributes in the Properties panel. You can take advantage of this to change a frame after you create it.

1 With the Frame tool, draw a rectangle frame between the row of four gray squares and the bottom of the document. The exact size and position isn't important, because you're about to edit it.

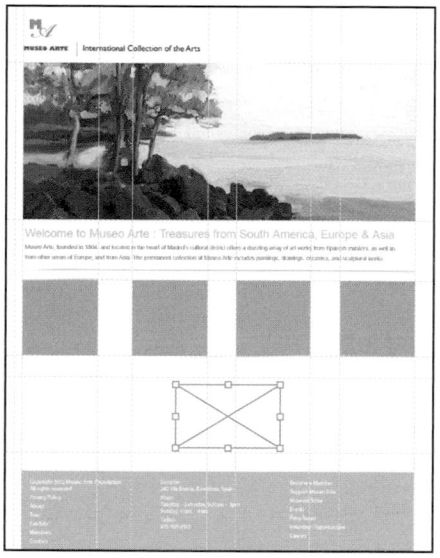

2 With the frame selected, enter the following values in the Properties panel:

- Width: **180**
- Height: **180**
- X: **40**
- Y: **648**

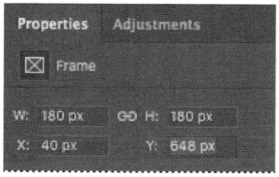

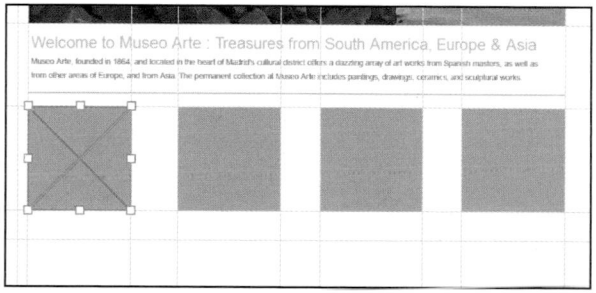

▶ **Tip:** As in the Control panel, you can change the unit of measure in a Properties panel field by right-clicking (Windows) or Control-clicking (Mac) the field. Or you can override a field's unit of measure by typing the unit after the value; for example, **4 in**.

After you apply all of the values, the size and position of the frame should now match the first gray square.

Duplicating frames

The other three squares in the row are the same size, so instead of drawing all four squares manually, you can simply duplicate them. Duplicating a frame is similar to duplicating a layer, because frames appear in the Layers panel.

1 In the Layers panel, drag the Frame 1 layer, and drop it on the Create A New Layer button (⊞). The duplicate layer, Frame 1 Copy, appears in the Layers panel.

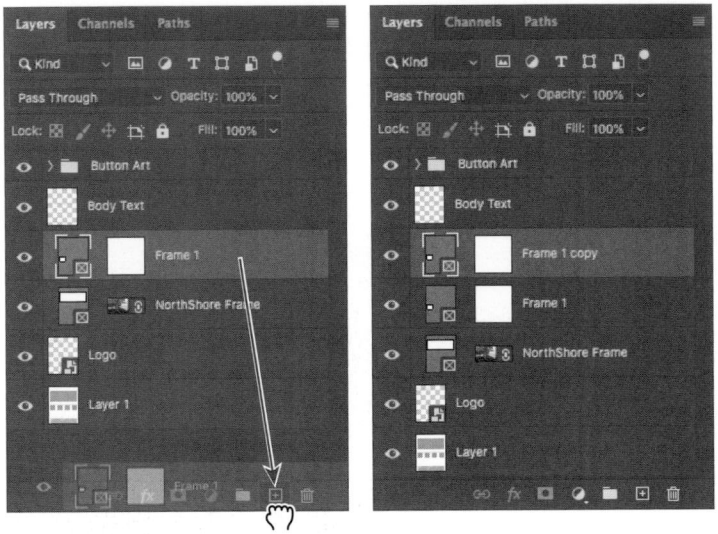

2 With the Frame 1 Copy layer selected, in the Properties panel change the X value to **300**. This makes the duplicate square frame line up with the second gray square.

3 Repeat step 1 to create two more duplicate frames. In the Properties panel, change the X value of the third frame to **550** and the X value of the fourth frame to **800**.

▶ **Tip:** It's always your choice to size and position a selected layer by dragging or by precisely editing values in the Properties panel or options bar.

You've created a complete row of four placeholder frames.

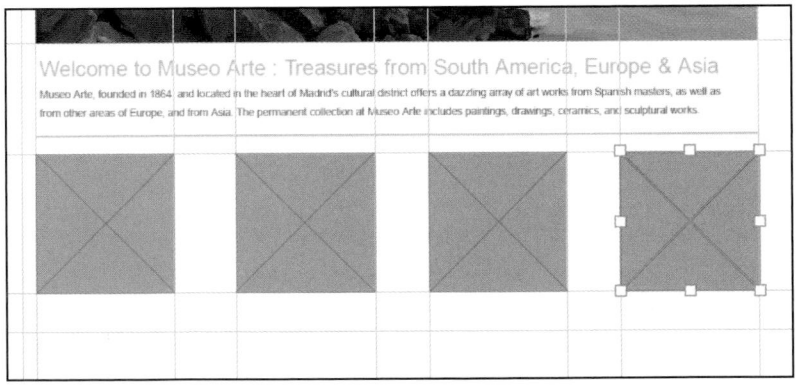

Adding images to frames

When graphics become available to use in the layout, you can quickly add them to each frame. One convenient way is by using the Properties panel.

1 Make sure the first square frame (Frame 1) is selected.

2 In the Properties panel, click the Inset Image menu, and choose Place from Local Disk - Linked.

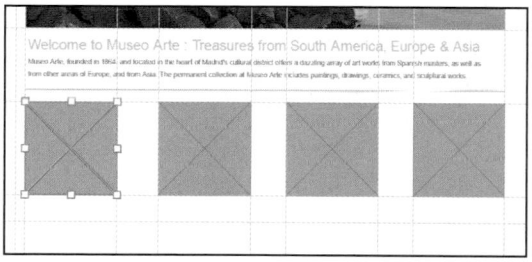

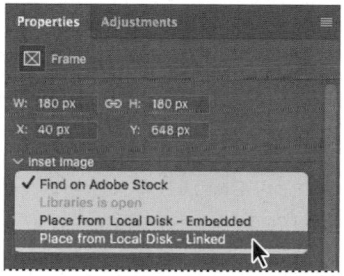

3 Navigate to the Lesson13/Art folder, select the Beach.jpg file, and click Place.

The Beach.jpg file is scaled to fit the frame, the name of the frame changes to Beach Frame, and the Properties panel displays the folder path to the linked document that's placed in the frame.

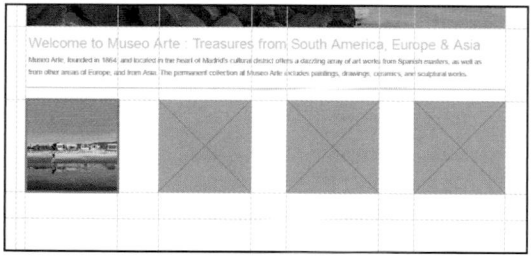

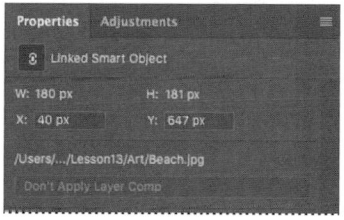

4 Repeat step 2 for the other three square frames, placing the files NorthShore.jpg, DeYoung.jpg, and MaineOne.jpg. Remember that you can also add a linked image to a frame by Alt-dragging (Windows) or Option-dragging (Mac) an image from the desktop and dropping it into a frame.

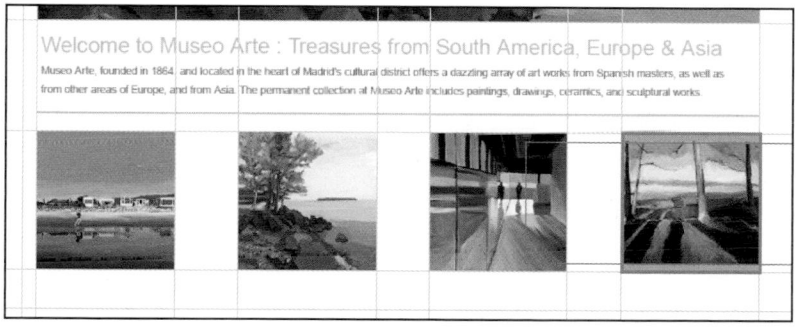

▶ **Tip:** If you want to select just the frame, click the frame edge with the Move tool. This works best when there aren't nearby objects or guides that might become selected instead.

● **Note:** If you can't select a frame or its contents with the Move tool, make sure Auto-Select Layer is enabled in the options bar when the Move tool is selected. When Auto-Select Layer is not enabled, you must click the thumbnail of the frame or the contents in the Layers panel.

5 In the Layers panel, click to select the frame layer thumbnail (the right thumbnail with the link icon) of the MainOne Frame layer. This selects just the contents of the frame. (Clicking the left thumbnail would select the frame.)

6 Choose Edit > Free Transform, drag the image or any of its edge handles to improve the composition of the image within the frame, and press Enter or Return when you're done.

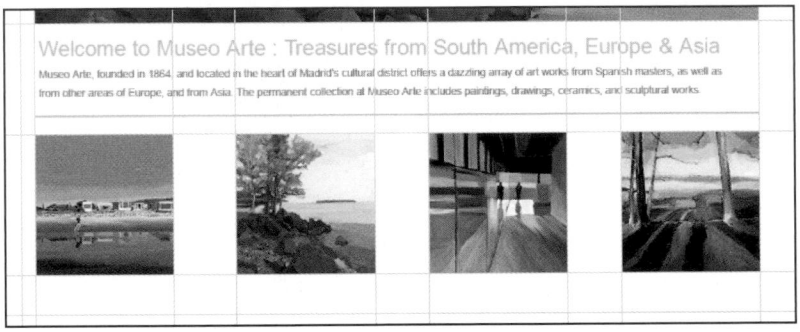

After adding graphics to frames, it's always a good idea to inspect all of the frames to make sure the graphics are well-composed within them. Feel free to adjust any of the other images within their frames.

Using layer groups to create button graphics

Layer groups make it easier to organize and work with layers in complex images, especially when there are sets of layers that work together. You'll use layer groups to assemble the layers that make up each button, and they'll come in handy when you export assets later.

The four frames you created now serve as the basis for buttons. You'll add a label to each, identifying the gallery it represents, and then add a drop shadow and a stroke.

1 Choose Window > Info to open the Info panel, if it isn't already open.

▶ **Tip:** If you have trouble positioning the horizontal ruler guide precisely, zoom in.

2 Position the pointer over the horizontal ruler, and drag a ruler guide down until the Y value in the Info panel is 795 pixels.

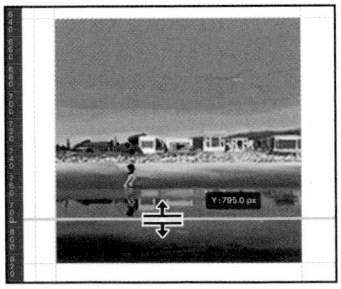

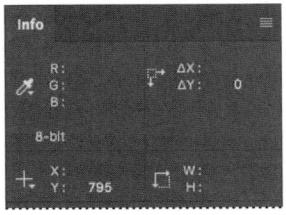

You'll use this guide to draw a band across the bottom of the image for the label.

3 Zoom in on the first square image, of the man on the beach. Then select Beach Frame in the Layers panel.

You'll use this image to design the first button.

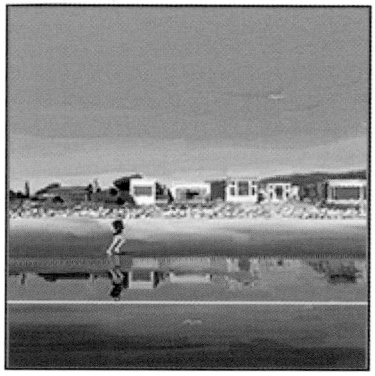

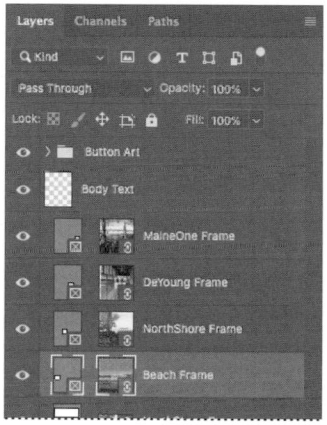

4 Click the Create a New Layer button (⊞) at the bottom of the Layers panel. The new layer is named Layer 2 and appears directly above the Beach Frame layer. Rename it **band**.

5 Select the Rectangular Marquee tool (⬚) in the Tools panel. Then, drag a selection across the bottom of the image, as indicated by the guides. The selection should be 180 pixels wide and 33 pixels high. Make sure the selection lines up with the frame along the sides and bottom.

6 Choose Edit > Fill. In the Fill dialog box, choose Color from the Contents menu, and then, in the Color Picker, select a dark blue (R=**25**, G=**72**, B=**121**). Click OK to close the Color Picker, and then click OK to close the Fill dialog box and apply the fill.

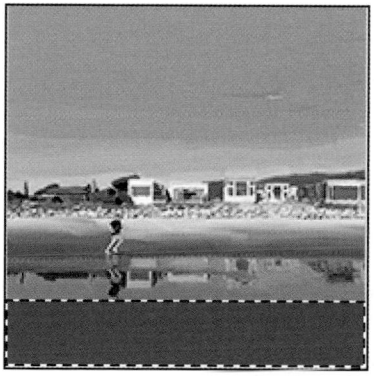

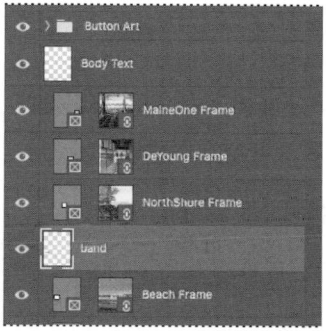

A dark blue band appears at the bottom of the image, where you made your selection. You'll add text to it next.

7 Choose Select > Deselect.

8 Select the Horizontal Type tool, and select the following settings in the options bar:

- Font Family: Myriad Pro
- Font Style: Regular
- Font Size: **18** pt
- Anti-aliasing: Strong
- Alignment: Center
- Color: White

9 Click in the center of the blue band, and type **GALLERY ONE**. Use the Move tool to adjust the position of the type layer if necessary.

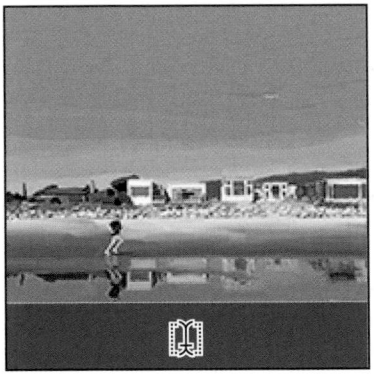

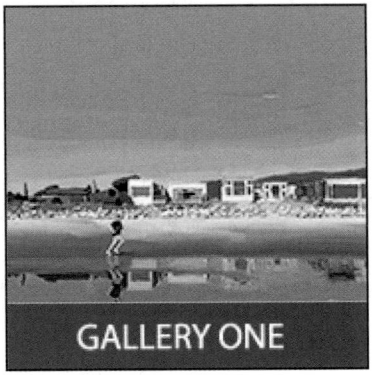

▶ **Tip:** When multiple layers are selected in the Layers panel, you can also create a layer group from them by clicking the New Group button or by pressing the keyboard shortcut Ctrl+G (Windows) or Command+G (Mac).

10 Select both the GALLERY ONE and band layers in the Layers panel, and choose Layer > Group Layers.

Photoshop creates a group named Group 1.

11 Double-click the Group 1 layer group, and rename it **Gallery 1**. Then expand the group. The layers you selected are indented, indicating they're part of that group.

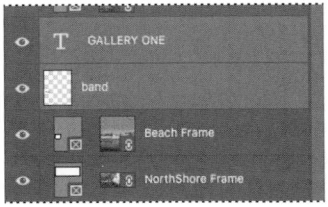

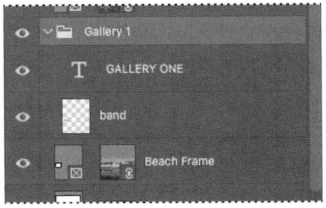

12 Drag the Gallery 1 layer group up so that it's above all of the frame layers.

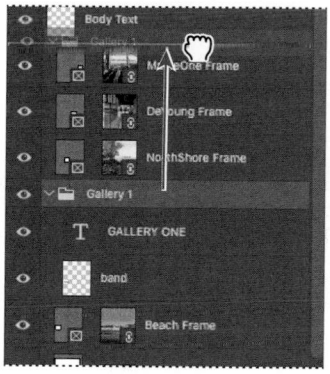

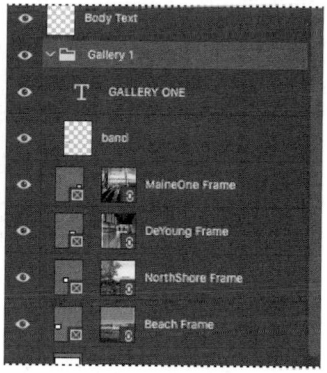

13 Choose File > Save.

Duplicating button bands and text

You've designed the label for one button. You could go through all those steps again to create the band and text for each of the other buttons, but it will be faster to duplicate the layer group you created for the first band and text, and then edit the copies as needed.

1 In the Layers panel, make sure the Gallery 1 layer group is selected.

2 With the Move tool selected, make sure Auto-Select is not selected in the options bar.

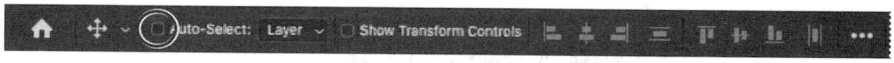

3 With the Move tool, hold down the Alt (Windows) or Option (Mac) key as you drag the Gallery One button to the right, and drop it when it snaps into alignment with the second square frame and its guides.

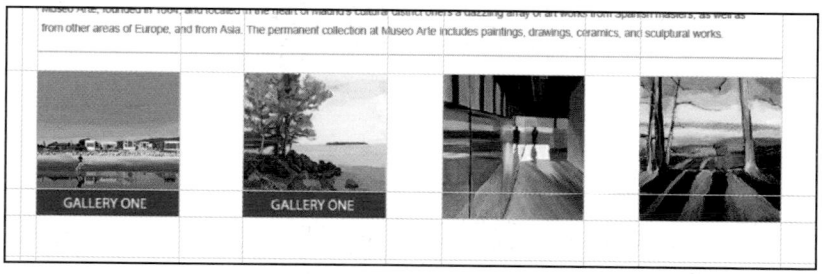

Holding down Alt or Option creates a copy of the selected layer group as you drag it with the Move tool. When you release the mouse button, the copy (Gallery 1 copy) should be selected in the Layers panel.

Note: In the Layers panel, moving a selected layer group moves all layers in it, even if the group's individual layers don't appear selected in the Layers panel. What's important is that the group is selected.

4 Repeat step 3 by Alt-dragging (Windows) or Option-dragging (Mac) a copy of the second button over the third square frame, and then do it one more time to copy the third button over the fourth square frame, completing the row.

Now edit the text in the three copies to match their images.

5 With the Horizontal Text tool, select the ONE text in the second button, and change ONE so that it now says **GALLERY TWO**.

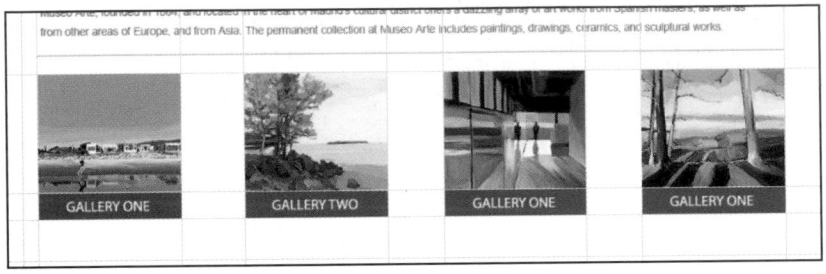

6 Repeat step 5 for the third and fourth buttons so that they say **GALLERY THREE** and **GALLERY FOUR**, respectively.

7 After you finish editing the GALLERY FOUR text, commit the last text edit by selecting the Move tool.

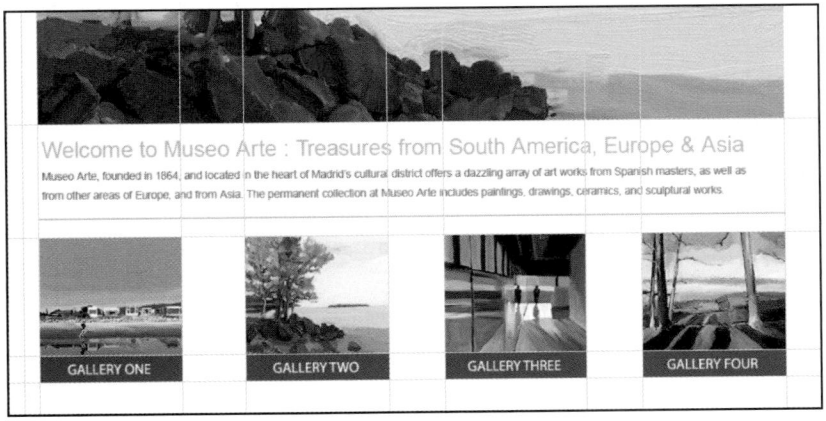

8 In the Layers panel, rename the layer groups to be consistent with their contents:

- Double-click the name of the "Gallery 1 copy" layer group, and name it **Gallery 2**.
- Double-click the name of the "Gallery 1 copy 2" layer group, and name it **Gallery 3**.
- Double-click the name of the "Gallery 1 copy 3" layer group, and name it **Gallery 4**.

▶ **Tip:** These steps are easier if you make the Layers panel taller so that you can see multiple expanded layer groups at once.

Now move each button image into its layer group.

9 In the Layers panel, do the following:

- Drag the Beach Frame layer into the Gallery 1 layer group, below the GALLERY ONE and band layers.

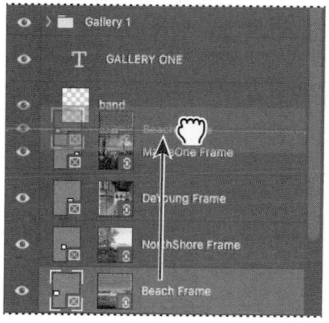

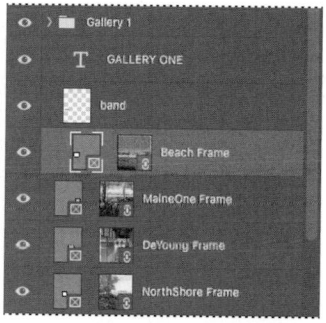

- Drag the upper NorthShore Frame layer into the Gallery 2 layer group, below the GALLERY TWO and band layers.
- Drag the DeYoung Frame layer into the Gallery 3 layer group, below the GALLERY THREE and band layers.
- Drag the MaineOne Frame layer into the Gallery 4 layer group, below the GALLERY FOUR and band layers.

10 Click the arrow next to each of the Gallery layer group icons to collapse them, simplifying the Layers panel display.

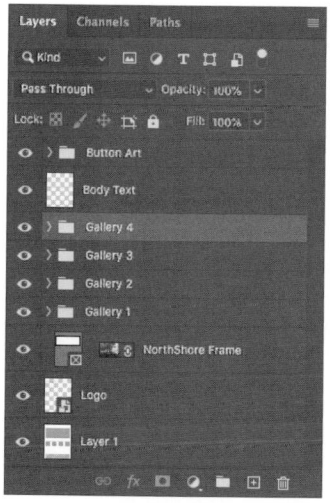

Now you'll add a drop shadow and stroke to improve the appearance of the button.

11 Select the Gallery 1 layer group in the Layers panel. Then, click the Add A Layer Style button (*fx*) at the bottom of the Layers panel, and choose Drop Shadow.

Note: When dragging layers in step 9, position the pointer over the layer name, not the thumbnails, before dragging.

▶ **Tip:** When you apply a layer style to a group, it applies to all layers in that group. In this book you have now tried applying a layer style to one layer and also to a layer group.

12 In the Layer Style dialog box, change the following settings in the Structure area:

- Opacity: **27**%
- Distance: **9** px
- Spread: **19**%
- Size: **18** px

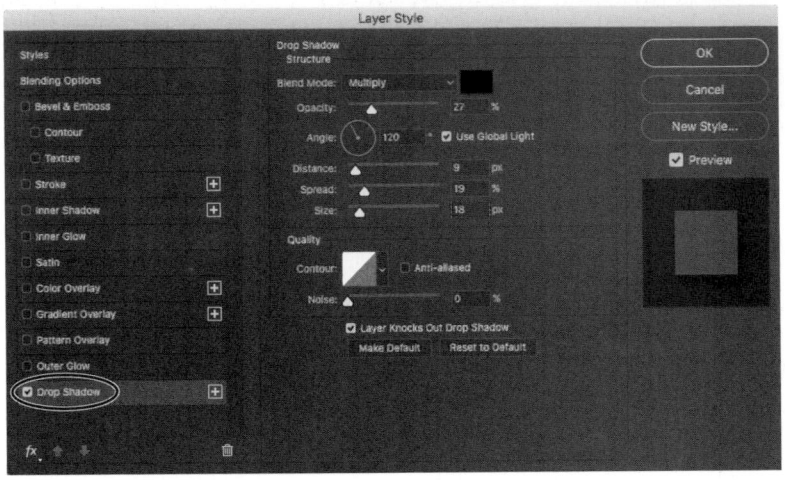

● **Note:** Be sure to click the word Stroke. If you click only the check box, Photoshop applies the layer style with its default settings, but you won't see the options.

13 With the Layer Style dialog box still open, select Stroke on the left, making sure that it's enabled, and apply the following settings:

- Size: **1** px
- Position: Inside
- Color: Click the color swatch to open the Color Picker. Then click the blue band to sample its color, and click OK to select it.

14 Click OK to apply both layer styles.

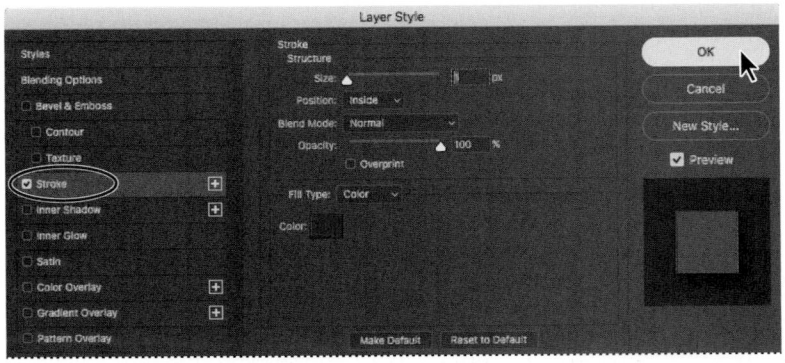

The drop shadow and stroke appear on the button's layer group in the document and also in the Layers panel.

15 In the Layers panel, position the pointer over the fx icon next to the Gallery 1 layer group. Then hold down the Alt (Windows) or Option (Mac) key as you drag the fx icon and drop it on the Gallery 2 layer group. This is a quick way to copy layer effects to another layer or layer group.

▶ **Tip:** Another way to transfer the effects of one layer or layer group to another is to drag its Effects header. That does the same thing as dragging the fx icon.

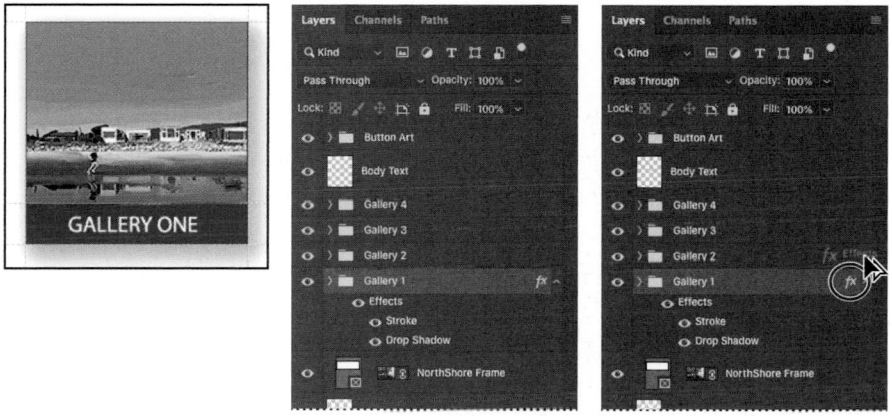

16 Repeat step 15 to copy the layer effects to the Gallery 3 and Gallery 4 layer groups.

17 In the Layers panel, expand the Button Art layer group, and then click the eye icon for the Navigation layer to make it visible. Then collapse the Button Art layer group.

This layer represents the navigation among sections of the museum website.

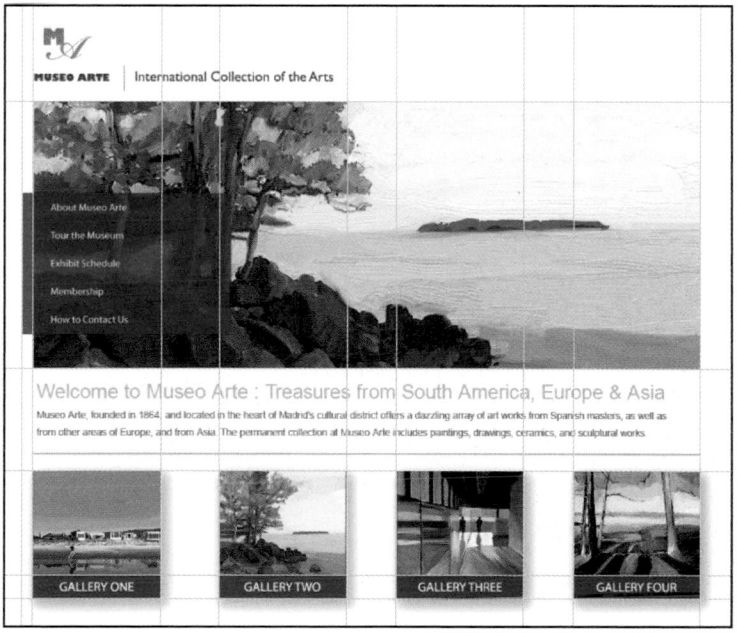

18 Save the file, and then close it.

Automating a multistep task

An *action* is a set of one or more commands that you record and then play back to apply to a single file or a batch of files. In this exercise, you'll create an action to prepare a set of images to serve as buttons for additional galleries on the web page you're designing.

Recording an action

▶ **Tip:** Actions are easy to use, but limited in scope. To automate Photoshop with more control, you can write a script. Photoshop can run scripts written in VBScript (Windows), AppleScript (Mac), or JavaScript (Windows and Mac).

You'll start by recording an action that resizes an image, changes its canvas size, and adds layer styles, so that the additional buttons match the ones you've already created. You use the Actions panel to record, play, edit, and delete individual actions. You also use the Actions panel to save and load action files.

There are four images in the Buttons folder that will serve as the basis for new gallery buttons on your website. The images are large, so the first thing you'll need to do is resize them to match the existing buttons. You'll perform each of the steps on the Gallery5.jpg file as you record the action. You'll then play the action to make the same changes on the other images in the folder automatically.

1 Choose File > Open, and navigate to the Lesson13/Buttons folder. Double-click the Gallery5.jpg file to open it in Photoshop.

2 Choose Window > Actions to open the Actions panel. Close the Default Actions set (folder); you'll create and use your own set for this lesson.

3 Click the Create New Set button (🗀) at the bottom of the Actions panel. In the New Set dialog box, name the set **Buttons**, and click OK.

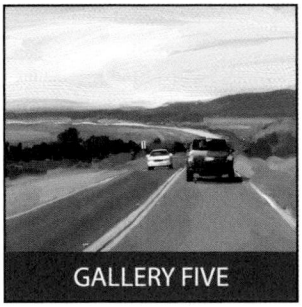

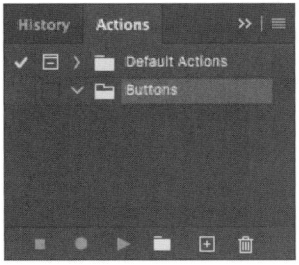

Photoshop comes with several prerecorded actions, all in the Default Actions set. You can use action sets to organize your actions so that it's easier to find the one you want or create.

4 Click the Create New Action button (⊞) at the bottom of the Actions panel. Name the action **Resizing and Styling Images**, and click Record.

It's a good idea to name actions in a way that makes it clear what the actions do, so you can find them easily later.

At the bottom of the Actions panel, the Begin Recording button turns red to let you know that recording is in progress.

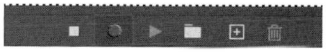

Don't let the fact that you're recording rush you. Take all the time you need to perform the procedure accurately. Actions don't record in real time; they record steps as you complete them, but they play them back as quickly as possible.

You'll start by resizing and sharpening the image.

5 Choose Image > Image Size, and do the following:

- Make sure Resample is selected.
- For Width, choose Pixels from the units menu, and then change the Width to **180**.
- Confirm that the Height has changed to **180** pixels. It should, because original proportions are preserved using the Constrain Aspect Ratio link icon to the left of the Width and Height values, which is selected by default.

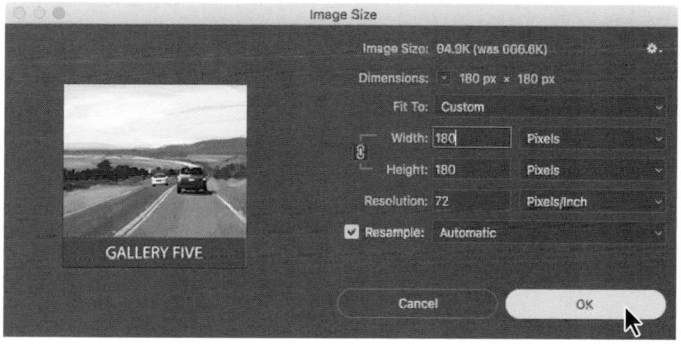

6 Click OK.

7 Choose Filter > Sharpen > Smart Sharpen, apply the following settings, and click OK:

- Amount: **100**%
- Radius: **1.0** px

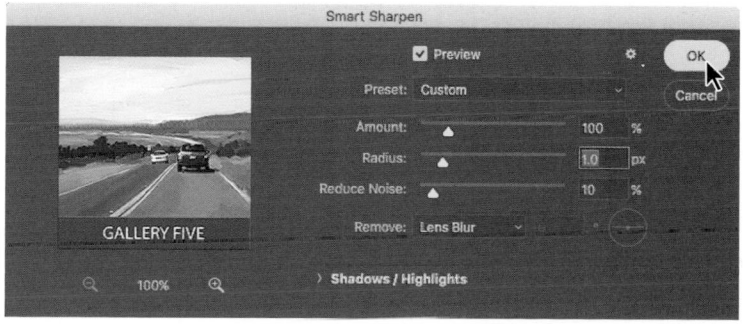

You need to make some additional changes to the image that you can't make as long as the Background layer is locked. You'll convert it to a regular layer.

8 Double-click the Background layer name in the Layers panel. In the New Layer dialog box, name the layer **Button**, and click OK.

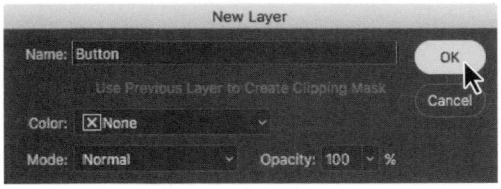

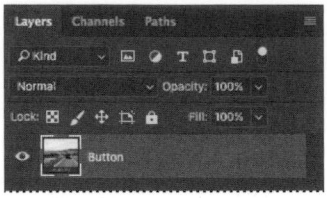

▶ **Tip:** If you want to convert a background layer to a regular layer and you don't need to name it, simply click the Background layer's lock icon in the Layers panel.

When you rename a Background layer, you're converting it to a regular layer, so Photoshop displays the New Layer dialog box. But no layers are added; the Background layer becomes the new layer.

Now that you've converted the Background layer, you can change the canvas size and add layer styles.

▶ **Tip:** Use Canvas Size when you want to add area to or remove area from a document; use Image Size when you want to resample, change the physical dimensions, or change the resolution of a document.

9 Choose Image > Canvas Size, and do the following:

- Make sure the unit of measure is set to Pixels.
- Change the Width to **220** pixels and the Height to **220** pixels.
- Click the center square in the anchor area to ensure the canvas is extended evenly on all sides.
- Click OK.

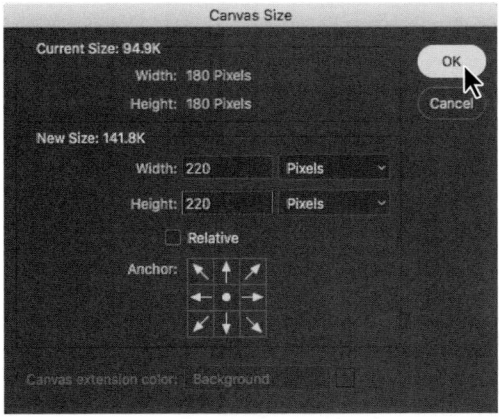

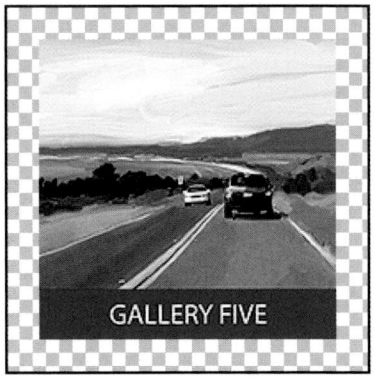

10 Choose Layer > Layer Style > Drop Shadow.

11 In the Layer Style dialog box, apply the following settings:

- Opacity: **27**%
- Angle: **120**°
- Distance: **9** px
- Spread: **19**%
- Size: **18** px

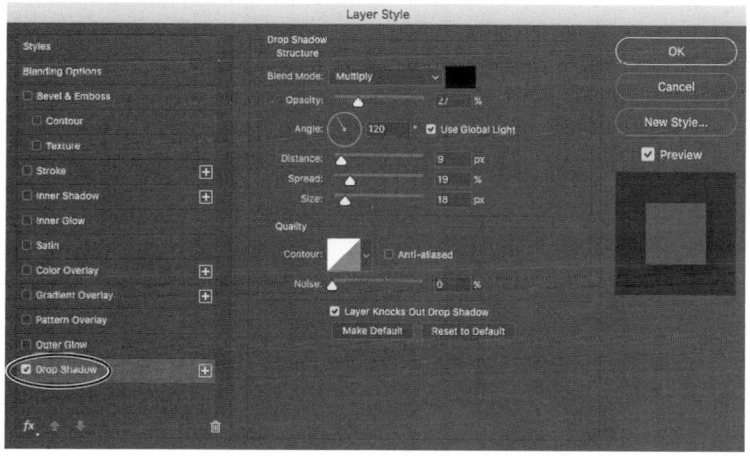

Tip: Stay on task while the Actions panel is recording. It records any Photoshop image edits, so if you record unwanted steps, you'll have to edit them out later. The Actions panel doesn't record view changes such as scrolling and zooming.

12 With the Layer Style dialog box still open, select Stroke on the left, and apply the following settings:

- Size: **1** px
- Position: Inside
- Color: If the color swatch doesn't already match the other blue band you made, click the color swatch and sample the blue band as you did earlier.

13 Click OK to apply both layer styles.

Note: Be sure to click the word Stroke. If you click only the check box, Photoshop applies the layer style with its default settings, but you won't see the options.

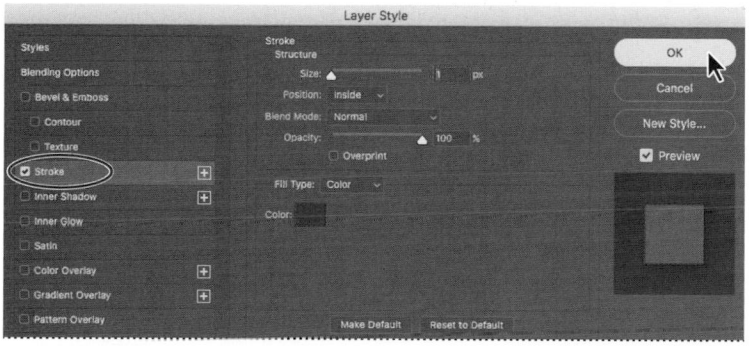

14 Choose File > Save As, choose Photoshop for the Format, and click Save. Click OK if the Photoshop Format Options dialog box appears.

15 Close the file. The Home screen appears, so click the Photoshop icon so that you can see the Actions panel again.

16 Click the Stop Playing/Recording button at the bottom of the Actions panel.

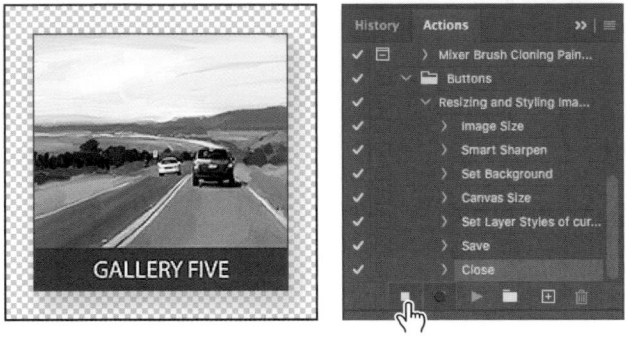

▶ **Tip:** As you review an action, you can edit the sequence by dragging steps, edit steps by double-clicking them (if applicable), or remove unneeded steps by deleting them.

The action you just recorded (Resizing and Styling Images) is now saved in the Buttons set in the Actions panel. Click the arrows to expand different sets of steps. You can examine each recorded step and the specific selections you made.

Batch-playing an action

Applying actions is a timesaving process for performing routine tasks on files, but you can streamline your work even further by applying actions to multiple files at once. You'll apply the action you've created to the three remaining images.

1 Choose File > Open, and navigate to the Lesson13/Buttons folder. Ctrl-select (Windows) or Command-select (Mac) the Gallery6.jpg, Gallery7.jpg, and Gallery8.jpg files, and click Open.

2 Choose File > Automate > Batch.

3 In the Batch dialog box, do the following:

- Confirm that Buttons is chosen in the Set menu and Resizing and Styling Images—the action you just created—is chosen in the Action menu.
- Choose Opened Files from the Source menu.
- Make sure None is chosen for the Destination.
- Click OK.

▶ **Tip:** You can create conditional actions that change their behavior based on criteria you define. To do this, choose Insert Conditional from the Actions panel menu.

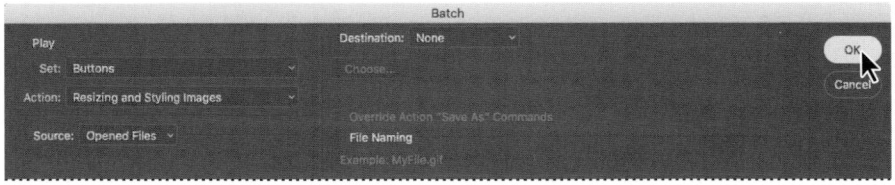

Photoshop plays the action, applying its steps to all the files that are open. You can also apply an action to an entire folder of images without opening them.

Because you saved the file and closed it while you were recording the action, Photoshop saves each of the images as a PSD file in its original folder and then closes the file. After Photoshop closes the last file, Photoshop displays the Home screen.

Note: If you get an error when running an action, click Stop. There may be a problem with the action that was recorded, especially if you had to correct a mistake while recording. Try troubleshooting or re-recording the action.

Placing files in Photoshop

The four additional button images are ready to be placed into the design. You probably noticed that each already has a blue band with its gallery name included in the image, so you don't need to perform those steps. They're ready to go.

1 If the file 13Working.psd is in the Recent list in the Home screen, click its name to reopen it. If not, choose File > Open to open it.

2 In the Layers panel, select the Gallery 4 layer group name. This ensures that the files about to be placed are not added inside any layer groups, because new layers are added above the selected layer.

3 Choose File > Place Embedded.

You'll place these files as embedded Smart Objects. Because they're embedded, the entire image is copied into the Photoshop file.

4 In the Place Embedded dialog box, navigate to the Lesson13/Buttons folder, and double-click the Gallery5.psd file.

Photoshop places the Gallery5.psd file in the center of the 13Working.psd file. But that's not where you want it to go, so you'll move it.

5 Drag the image into position below the Gallery One button. Use the guides to align the image with the one above. When it's in position, commit the change by pressing Enter or Return.

Note: The bounding box of the placed image is larger than the button, because the bounding box includes the complete extent of the drop shadow.

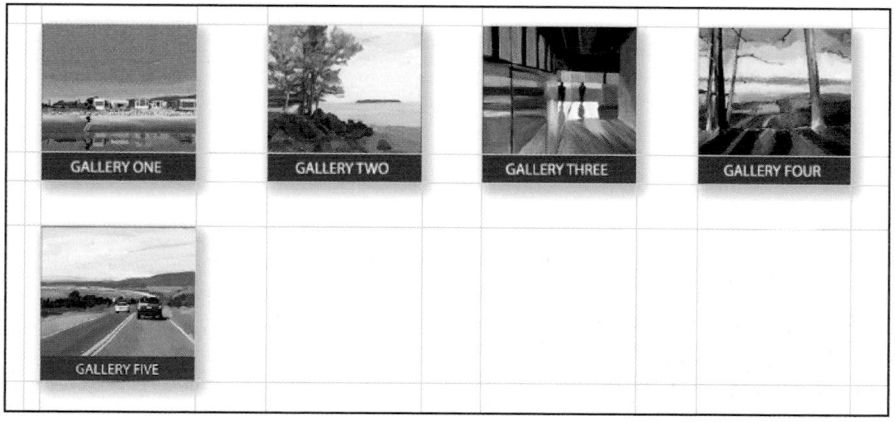

▶ **Tip:** You can also place embedded files by dragging them into the Photoshop document from the desktop or from other applications. You can drag multiple images to place at once; after you commit one image, the next will be placed.

6 Repeat steps 3–5 to place the Gallery6.psd, Gallery7.psd, and Gallery8.psd files so that they line up below the Gallery Two, Gallery Three, and Gallery Four buttons.

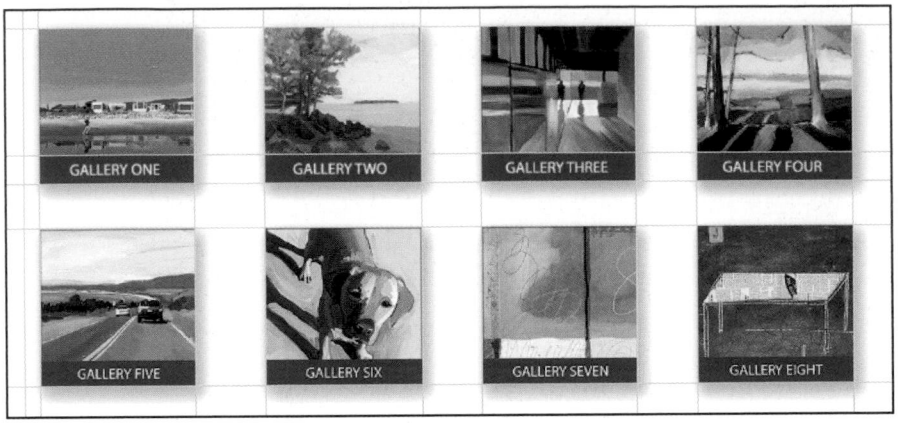

7 Save your work and close the file.

Designing with artboards

▶ **Tip:** If you need advanced control over how layers are exported for web and mobile user interfaces, you may be interested in Adobe Generator. When Adobe Generator is on, Photoshop automatically exports and optimizes layers based on how the layers are named.

▶ **Tip:** You may notice or have been taught to use the older Save For Web command in Photoshop. Although that command is still available under File > Export > Save For Web (Legacy), Save For Web can't export multiple layers, artboards, or scaling factors, while Export As can.

When you're designing websites or user interfaces for mobile devices, you may need to create separate image files for buttons and other content. In Photoshop, you can use the Export As feature to export an entire document or individual layers to web- and mobile-friendly formats including PNG, JPEG, GIF, or SVG. In addition to being able to export multiple layers to individual files at once, Export As makes it possible to export to multiple sizes at once if you need to produce sets of images for low- and high-resolution displays.

You may need to coordinate different ideas for a single design, or design variations for different display sizes. This is easier when you use artboards, which are like multiple canvases in a single Photoshop document. You can also use Export As to export entire artboards.

With Export As, you control what gets exported by selecting artboards or layers in the Layers panel.

Duplicating an artboard

You'll use artboards to adapt the design of the museum website for a different screen size. Later, you'll export both designs at once.

1 In the Photoshop Home screen, click Open. Navigate to the Lesson13 folder, and open the file 13Museo.psd.

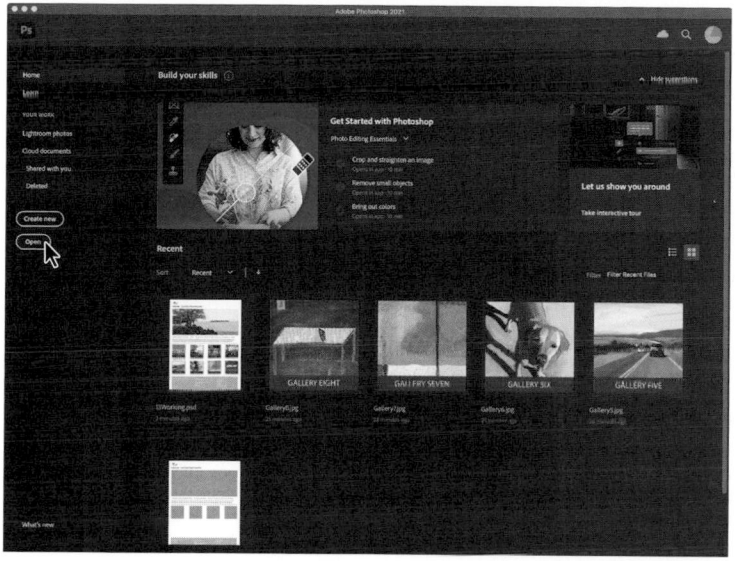

2 Choose File > Save As, rename the file **13Museo_Working.psd**, and click Save. Click OK in the Photoshop Format Options dialog box.

This is a web page that's being adapted for a responsive web design so that it will work well on display sizes from desktops to smartphones.

3 Choose Select > All Layers.

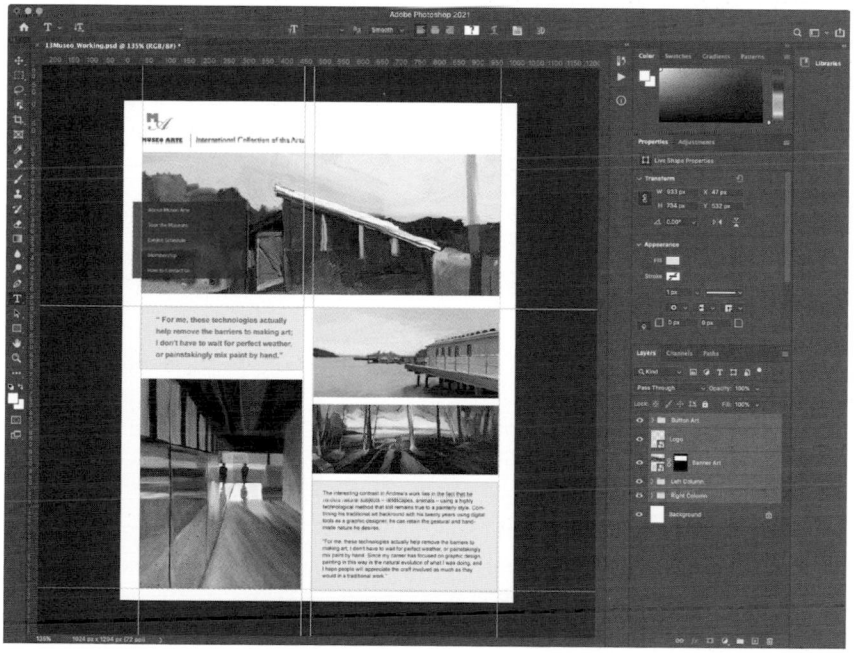

Note: Select > All Layers doesn't select the Background layer, because it's locked by default.

4 Choose Layer > New > Artboard From Layers, name the new artboard **Desktop**, and click OK. The artboard name appears above the new artboard and also on its new artboard group in the Layers panel.

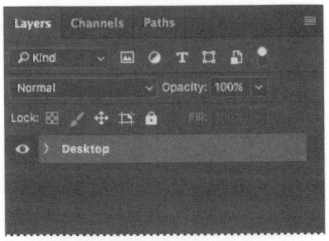

5 Make sure the Artboard tool (⊡) is selected; it's grouped with the Move tool in the Tools panel. Then Alt/Option-click the Add Artboard button to the right of the artboard to duplicate both the Desktop artboard and its contents.

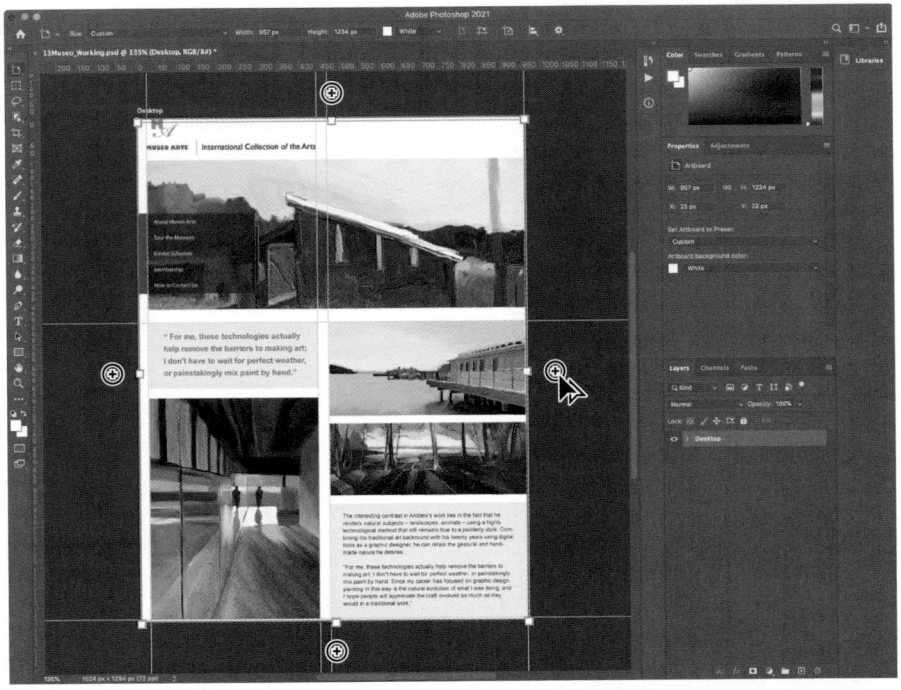

6 In the Layers panel, double-click the name of the Desktop Copy duplicate artboard, and name it **iPhone**.

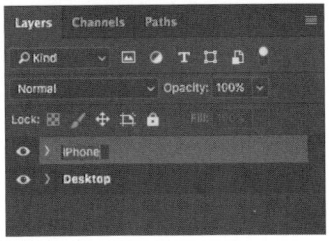

7 In the Properties panel, click the Set Artboard to Preset menu, and choose **iPhone 8/7/6**. That artboard preset applies the pixel dimensions of an iPhone 8, iPhone 7, and iPhone 6 (750 pixels wide by 1334 pixels tall). Now you can develop a design for that iPhone size, using the elements of the Desktop design. It will also be easier to maintain design consistency, since both the desktop and mobile designs are in the same document.

8 Save your work.

▶ **Tip:** You can choose artboard presets from the Size menu in the options bar when the Artboard tool is selected. If none of the artboard presets matches the display you're designing for, such as a newer model, you can enter your own values for Width and Height in the options bar or Properties panel.

Creating a design variation with artboards

You now have different artboards for desktop and smartphone display sizes; the next task is to fit the desktop-sized objects within the width of the smartphone display's pixel dimensions.

1 In the Layers panel, expand the iPhone artboard, and Shift-select the first and last layers in that artboard only. Don't select the artboard name itself.

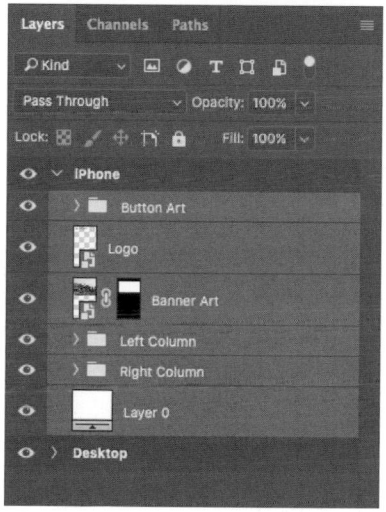

2 Choose Edit > Free Transform.

3 In the options bar, do the following:

- Click the Toggle Reference Point checkbox to select it; this makes the reference point visible in the transformation bounding box and makes it possible for you to reposition the reference point.
- Select the top-left square of the reference point location option. Scaling, rotating, or other transformations will now be performed from the top-left corner of the bounding box (instead of the center) until the transformation is committed.
- Make sure the Maintain Aspect Ratio button (the link icon) is selected so that the selected layers will scale proportionally.
- Enter **726px** for W (Width).

▶ **Tip:** You can position the reference point anywhere inside or outside the transformation bounding box by dragging it.

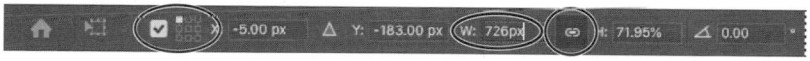

4 Press Enter or Return to apply the new settings to all selected layers as a unit. (Press Enter or Return only once, to apply the value in the options bar. If you press Enter or Return a second time, it will commit the transformation.)

Those settings proportionally scale the selected layers to 726 pixels wide, from the top-left corner of the selection, to better fit the artboard.

5 Position the pointer inside the Free Transform bounding box, and then Shift-drag the selected layers down until you can see the entire Museo Arts logo at the top of the page.

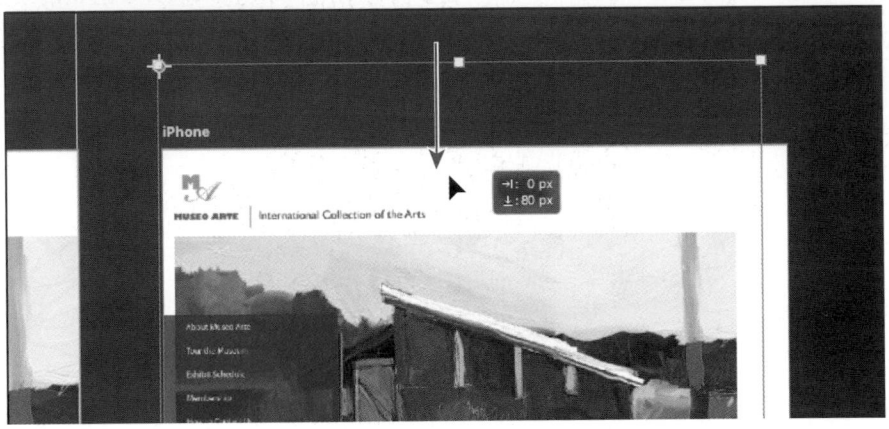

6 Press Enter or Return to exit Free Transform mode, and choose Select > Deselect Layers.

7 In the Layers panel, select the Logo layer, and choose Edit > Free Transform.

8 Drag the bottom-right handle on the Free Transform bounding box until the transformation values next to the pointer indicate that the logo is 672 pixels wide, matching the width of the other elements. Then press Enter or Return. This width makes the logo more readable on a smartphone screen.

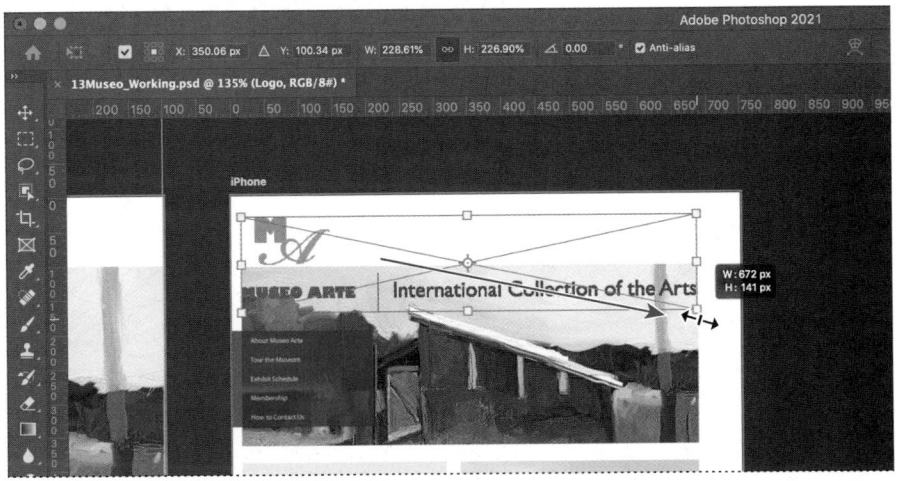

9 In the Layers panel, select the Banner Art, Left Column, and Right Column layers.

10 With the Move tool, Shift-drag the selected layers down until the top is even with the top of the blue button stack on the left.

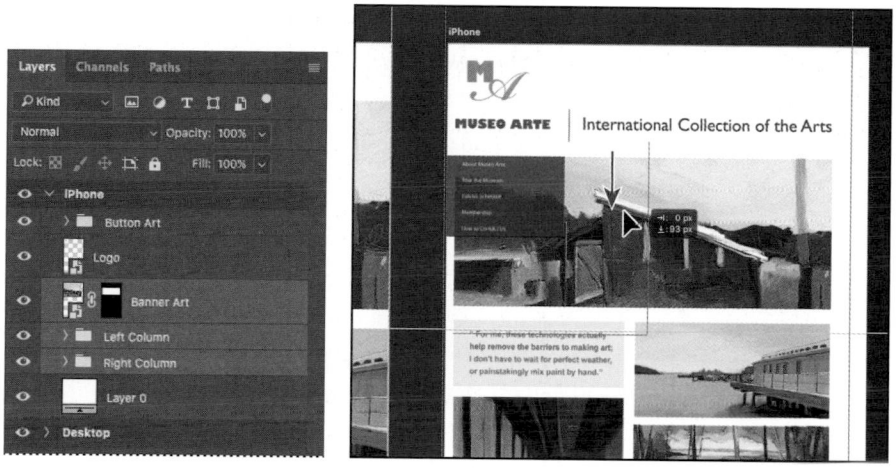

Now you'll take the two-column layout and make each column fill the width of the artboard. But first you'll need to accommodate them by making the artboard taller.

11 Select the iPhone artboard in the Layers panel, and then, with the Artboard tool, drag the bottom handle of the iPhone artboard until the transformation values next to the pointer indicate that it's 2800 px tall.

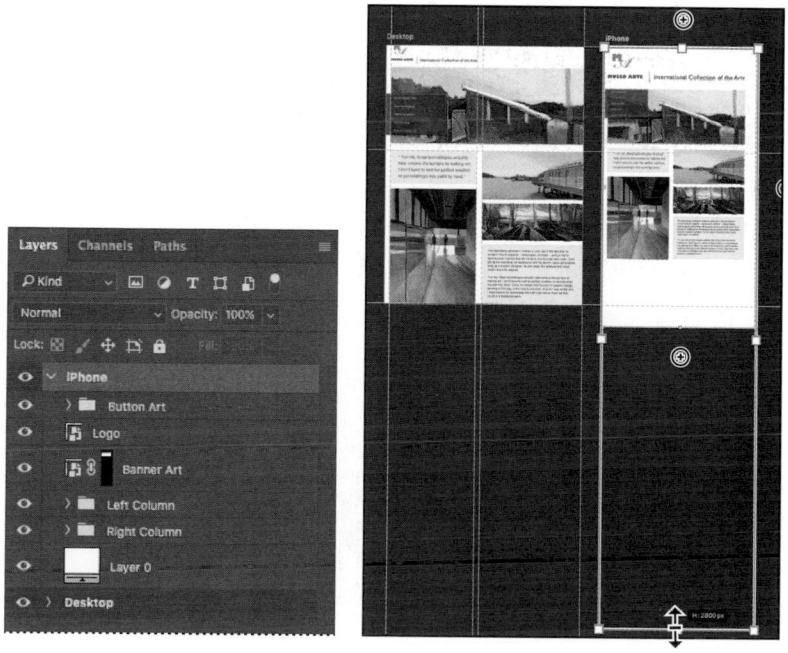

▶ **Tip:** You can also change the height of an artboard by entering a new Height in the Properties panel when an artboard is selected.

● **Note:** If a document uses artboards, resize them only using the Artboard tool. The Image > Image Size and Image > Canvas Size commands work best with a Photoshop document that doesn't use artboards.

12 Select the Right Column layer group in the Layers panel, and then choose Edit > Free Transform.

13 In the options bar, do the following:

- Make sure the Toggle Reference Point checkbox is selected, and then select the top-right square of the reference point location option.
- Make sure the Maintain Aspect Ratio (link) button is selected, and enter **672px** for Width.
- Press Enter or Return to apply the new width.

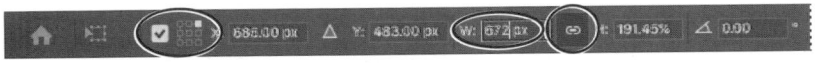

14 Position the pointer inside the Free Transform bounding box, and then Shift-drag the selected layer group down until the transformation values next to the pointer indicate a vertical move of 1200 px (the Y value in the options bar should say about 1680 px when the top-right square of the reference point locator is selected). Press Enter or Return to commit and exit the transformation.

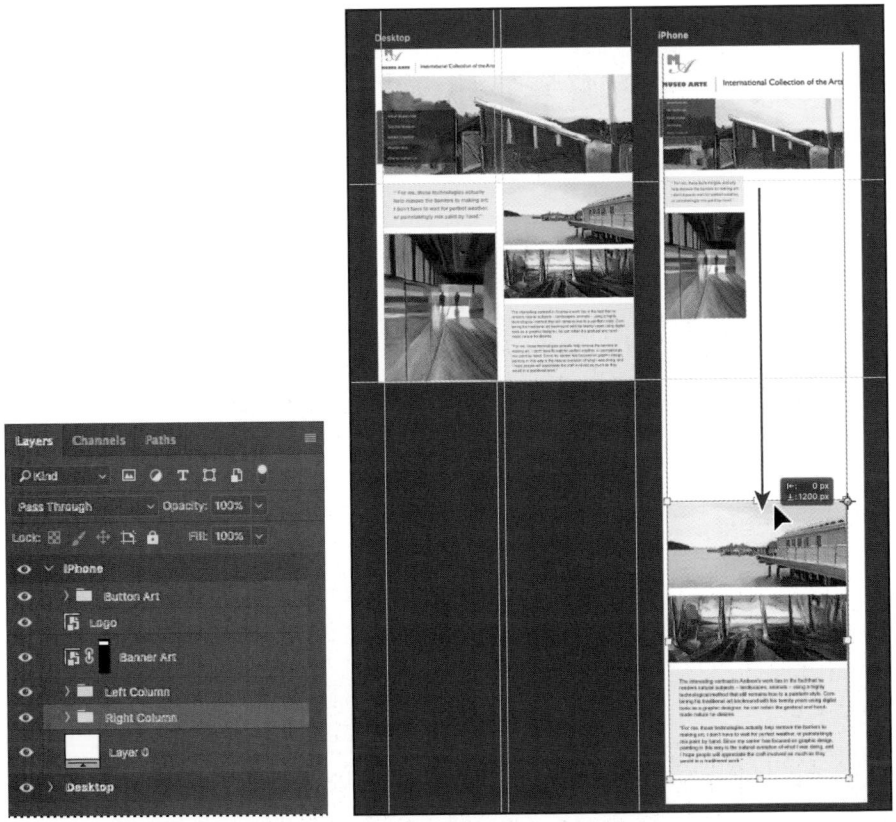

15 Select the Left Column layer group in the Layers panel, and then choose Edit > Free Transform.

16 In the options bar, do the following:

- Make sure the Toggle Reference Point checkbox is selected, and then select the top-left square of the reference point location option.
- Make sure the Maintain Aspect Ratio (link) button is selected, and enter **672px** for Width.
- Press Enter or Return to apply the new width.
- Then press Enter or Return to commit and exit the transformation.

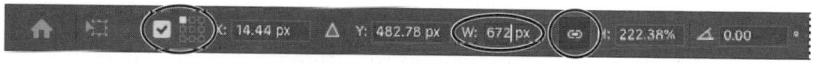

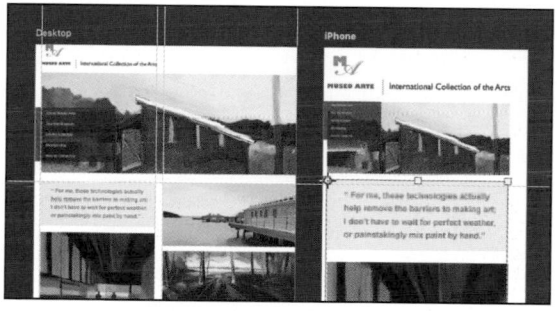

Feel free to adjust the positioning and the vertical spacing among the layer groups and layers.

17 Choose View > Fit On Screen to see both artboards at once, and then save your work.

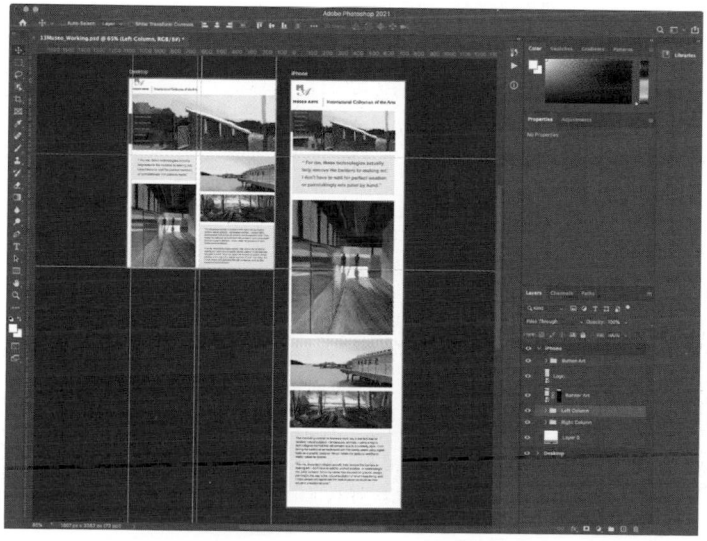

▶ **Tip:** To nudge selected layers or layer groups when the Move tool is active, press the arrow keys. When Free Transform is active, you can also nudge by clicking in a number field and pressing the up arrow or down arrow key.

You've adapted a desktop-sized multicolumn web page layout for a single-column smartphone-sized layout, and both layouts exist on two artboards in one Photoshop document.

Exporting artboards with Export As (File menu)

When it's time to have a client review your designs, you can use the Export As command to easily export any artboard, layer, or layer group into its own file. You'll export the complete desktop and smartphone artboards, and then you'll export the layers of each artboard to their own folder.

1 Choose File > Export > Export As. This command exports each whole artboard, so you see each artboard in the list on the left side of the Export As dialog box.

Note: The Export As dialog box doesn't preview multiple Scale All options. Artboards are previewed at 1x.

You can preview the exported dimensions and file size of each item; the preview is determined by the settings on the right side of the Export As dialog box.

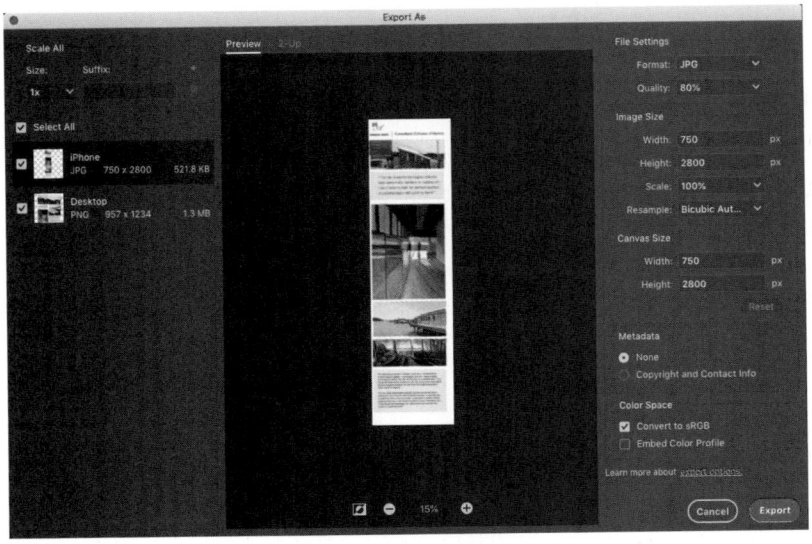

Tip: Not sure about the best combination of format, compression, and visual quality? Click the 2-up tab at the top of the Export As dialog box to see two views. Select one view and change the settings; then select the other view and change its settings. Now you can compare their quality, and you can see the resulting file size below each preview.

2 In the list on the left, click the iPhone artboard to select it, and then set the Export As options to the following:

- In the Scale All section, make sure Size is set to 1x and the Suffix field is empty.
- In the File Settings section, choose JPG from the Format menu, and enter **80%** for Quality.
- In the Color Space section, select Convert to sRGB.
- Other settings can be left at the defaults.

3 In the list on the left, click the Desktop artboard to select it, and apply the same settings as in step 2.

4 Make sure Select All is selected, click Export, navigate to the Lesson13 folder, double-click the Assets folder, and then click Save or Open.

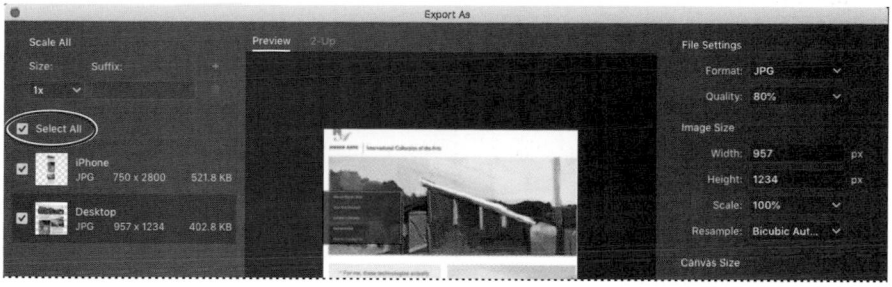

5 Switch to the desktop or Bridge, and open the Assets folder in the Lesson13 folder to see the Desktop.jpg and iPhone.jpg files representing each artboard. The filenames are based on the artboard names. You can send those files for client review.

6 Switch back to Photoshop.

▶ **Tip:** If you frequently use the Export As command with the same settings, choose File > Export > Export Preferences, and specify the settings you use the most. Now you can export to those settings in one step by choosing File > Export > Quick Export As or choosing Quick Export As from the Layers panel menu.

Exporting layers as assets with Export As (Layer menu)

If the client approves the design, you can then use Export As to create separate files for each layer on each artboard, such as images or buttons. Those assets can be used by a web or application developer who executes the design in code.

1 In the Layers panel, Shift-select all layers of the Desktop artboard.

2 Choose Layer > Export As. (Do not choose File > Export As.)

Notice that in the Export As dialog box, each layer is listed separately, because they will export separately.

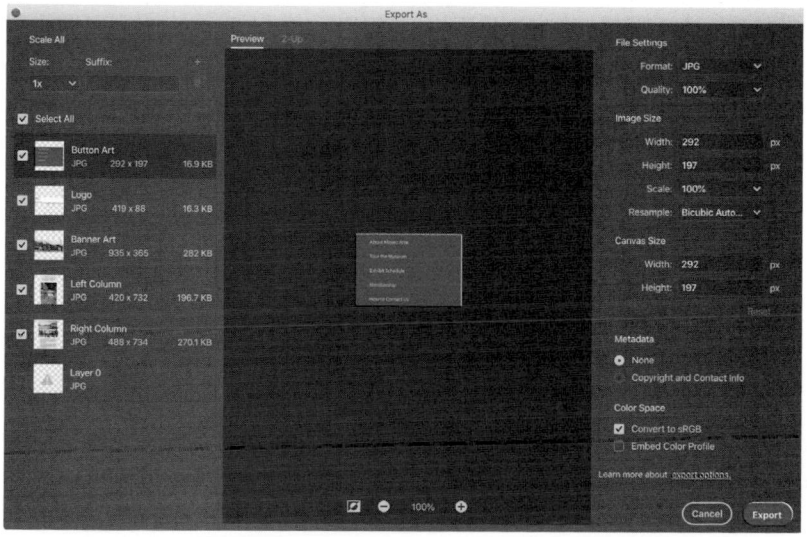

Note: The Layer 0 thumbnail checkbox can't be selected, and its thumbnail displays a checkerboard with a yellow triangle indicating that it won't export. That's because Layer 0 is a Solid Color Fill layer type —it does not contain pixels or shapes to export.

3 Click Button Art to highlight it; then hold down Shift and click Right Column to highlight the five top layers. Now when you adjust settings in the following steps, those changes will affect all highlighted layers.

4 In the Export As dialog box, enter the same settings as you did in step 2 of the previous section (on page 348).

5 Make sure Select All is enabled, click Export, navigate to the Assets_Desktop folder in the Lesson13 folder, and click Open or Save.

You have exported all assets for the Desktop artboard into a single folder.

6 Repeat steps 1–4 for the iPhone artboard.

7 Click Export, navigate to the Assets_iPhone folder in the Lesson13 folder, and click Open or Save.

Tip: If a developer asks for assets at multiple scale factors (for Retina/HiDPI display resolutions), in the Export As dialog box click the plus button in the Scale All section to add and specify additional scale factors (Size) such as 2x or 3x. Those will be exported at the same time. Be sure to specify the proper option in the Suffix field for each scale factor.

8 In Photoshop, choose File > Browse In Bridge.

9 Navigate to the Assets_Desktop folder in the Lesson13 folder, and inspect the images by browsing each folder with the Preview panel open. If you want, you can also inspect the assets you exported to the Assets_iPhone folder.

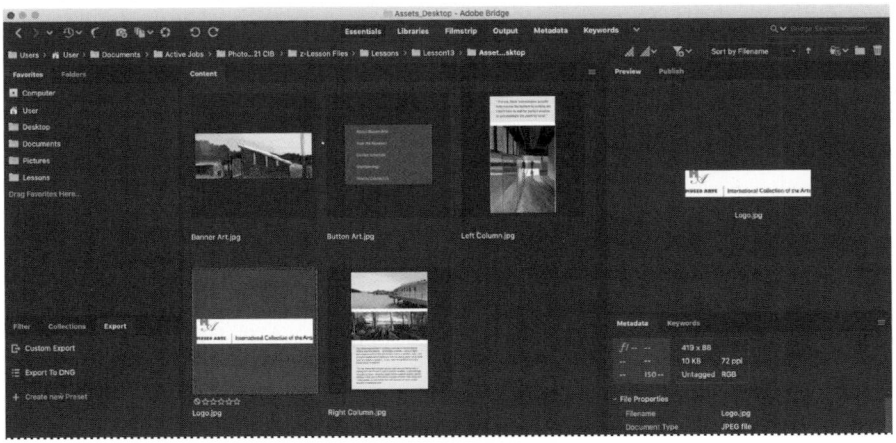

Each layer you exported is in its own file. You were able to quickly produce two different sets of files for two different screen sizes:

- By using the file-based Export As command (File > Export > Export As), you created JPG images of the complete desktop and iPhone artboards.
- By using the layer-based Export As command (on the Layers panel menu or Layer > Export As), you created assets from the individual layers of each artboard.

10 In Photoshop, save your changes, and close the document.

Review questions

1 What is a layer group?

2 What is an action? How do you create one?

3 How can you create assets from layers and layer groups in Photoshop?

Review answers

1 A layer group is a set of layers organized as a unit in the Layers panel. Layer groups make it easier to work with layers in complex images, especially when there are sets of layers that need to stay together when moved or scaled.

2 An action is a set of one or more commands that you record and then play back to apply to a single file or a batch of files. To create one, click the Create New Action button in the Actions panel, name the action, and click Record. Then perform the tasks you want to include in your action. When you've finished, click the Stop Recording button at the bottom of the Actions panel.

3 Use the Export As command to create assets from artboards, layers, and layer groups in Photoshop. To create images of each whole artboard, choose the Export As command on the File menu (File > Export > Export As). To create assets from selected layers and layer groups, choose the Export As on the Layers panel menu or Layer menu (Layer > Export As).

14 PRODUCING AND PRINTING CONSISTENT COLOR

Lesson overview

In this lesson, you'll learn how to do the following:

- Understand how images are prepared for printing on presses.
- Closely examine an image before final output.
- Define RGB, grayscale, and CMYK color spaces for displaying, editing, and printing images.
- Proof an image for printing.
- Prepare an image for printing on a PostScript CMYK printer.
- Save an image as a CMYK EPS file.
- Create and print a four-color separation.

This lesson will take less than an hour to complete. To get the lesson files used in this chapter, download them from the web page for this book at www.adobepress.com/PhotoshopCIB2021. For more information, see "Accessing the lesson files and Web Edition" in the Getting Started section at the beginning of this book.

As you work on this lesson, you'll preserve the start files. If you need to restore the start files, download them from your Account page.

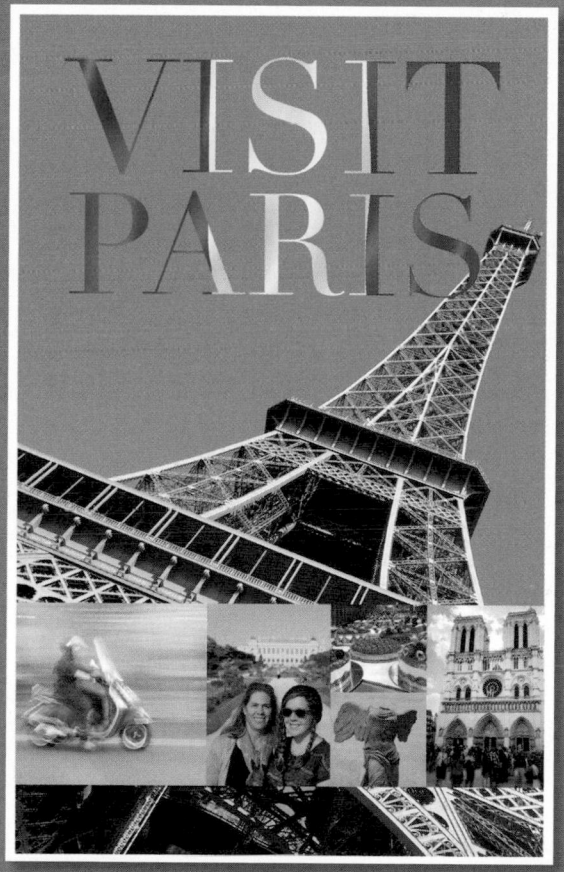

PROJECT: TRAVEL POSTER

To produce consistent color, you define the color space in which to edit and display RGB images and the color space in which to edit, display, and proof CMYK images. This helps ensure a close match between onscreen and printed colors.

Preparing files for printing

Note: One exercise in this lesson requires that your computer be connected to a printer that supports Adobe PostScript. If you don't have access to one, you can do most, but not all, of the exercises. PostScript is not required to print photo-quality images. PostScript is more commonly used in prepress workflows (preparing jobs for printing on a press).

After you've edited an image, you probably want to share or publish it in some way. Ideally, you've been editing with the final output in mind, and you've managed file resolution, colors, file size, and other aspects of the image accordingly. But as you prepare to output the file, you have another opportunity to make sure your image will look its best.

If you plan to print the image—whether you'll print it to your own inkjet printer or send it to a service provider for professional printing—you should perform the following tasks for the best results. (Many of these tasks are described in greater detail later in this lesson.)

- Determine the final destination. Whether you're printing the file yourself or sending it away, identify whether it will be printed to a PostScript desktop printer or platesetter, an inkjet printer, an offset press, or some other device. If you're working with a service provider, ask what format they prefer. In many cases, they may request a file exported to a specific PDF standard or preset.
- Verify that the image resolution is appropriate. For professional printing, 300 ppi is a good starting point. To determine the best print resolution for your project, consult your production team or your printer's user manual, because the optimal resolution can depend on factors such as the halftone screen of a press or the grade of paper.
- Do a "zoom test": Take a close look at the image. Zoom in to check and correct sharpness, color correction, noise, and other issues that can affect the final printed image quality.
- Allow for bleeds if you're sending an image for professional printing: If any color runs to the edge of the image, extend the canvas and the design on all sides (typically by ¼ inch) to ensure that the image goes all the way to the paper edge even if it isn't trimmed precisely. Your service provider can help you determine how to prepare your file to ensure it prints correctly.
- Keep the image in its original color space until your service provider instructs you to convert it. Today, many prepress workflows keep content in its original color space throughout editing to preserve color flexibility as long as possible, converting images and documents to CMYK only at final output time.
- Before flattening large Photoshop documents, always ask your production team first. Some workflows may depend on preserving, not flattening, Photoshop layers so that other applications, such as Adobe InDesign, can control the visibility of imported Photoshop layers from within their documents.
- Soft-proof the image to simulate onscreen how the colors will print.

Getting started

You'll prepare an 11"×17" travel poster for printing on a CMYK press. The Photoshop file is relatively large, because it contains several layers and has a resolution of 300 ppi, which is a typical requirement for high-quality printing.

First, start Photoshop, and restore its default preferences.

1 Start Photoshop, and then simultaneously hold down Ctrl+Alt+Shift (Windows) or Command+Option+Shift (Mac) to restore the default preferences. (See "Restoring default preferences" on page 5.)

2 When prompted, click Yes to delete the Adobe Photoshop Settings file.

3 Choose File > Open, navigate to the Lesson14 folder, and double-click the 14Start.psd file. Because the file is large, it may open slowly, depending on your system.

4 Choose File > Save As, navigate to the Lesson14 folder, and save the file as **14Working.psd**. Click OK if the Photoshop Format Options dialog box appears.

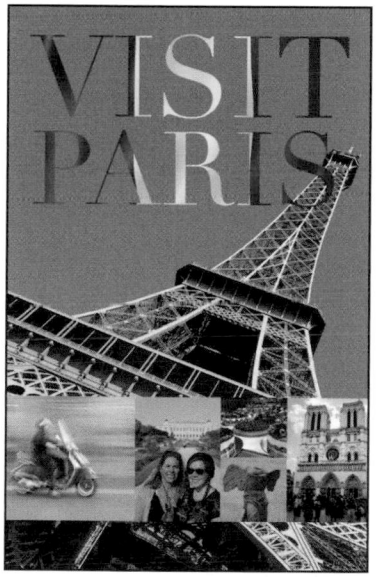

Note: If Photoshop displays a dialog box telling you about the difference between saving to Cloud Documents and Your Computer, click Save On Your Computer. You can also select Don't Show Again, but that setting will deselect after you reset Photoshop preferences.

Performing a "zoom test"

▶ **Tip:** If your keyboard has Page Up, Page Down, Home, and End keys, you can use them to inspect a magnified Photoshop document. Home goes to the top-left corner, and End goes to the bottom-right corner. Add the Ctrl key (Windows) or the Command key (Mac) to make Page Up/Page Down keys navigate horizontally, and add the Shift key to scroll in smaller increments.

It's expensive to redo a big print job, so before you send out an image for final output, take a few minutes to make sure everything is appropriate for your output device and that you haven't overlooked any potentially problematic details. Start with the image resolution.

1 Choose Image > Image Size.

2 Verify that the width and height are the final output size in inches and that the resolution is appropriate. For most printing, 300 ppi produces good results.

This image has a width of 11" and a height of 17", which is the final size of the poster. Its resolution is 300 ppi. The size and resolution are appropriate.

3 Click OK to close the dialog box.

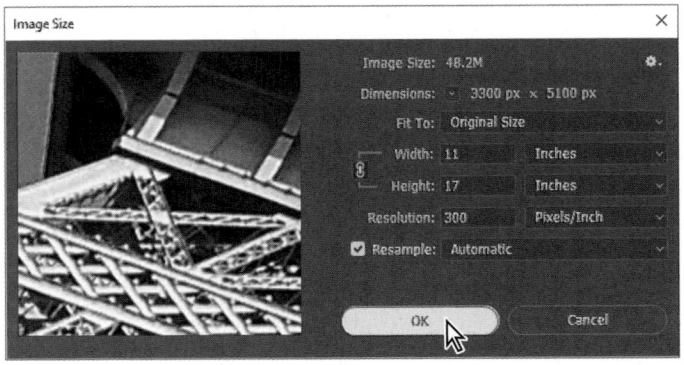

Next, you'll look closely at the image and correct any problems. When you prepare your own images for printing, zoom in and scroll to view the entire image closely.

4 Select the Zoom tool in the Tools panel, and zoom in on the photos in the lower third of the poster.

The photo of tourists is flat and a little muddy-looking.

5 Select the Tourists layer in the Layers panel, and then click the Curves icon in the Adjustments panel to add a Curves adjustment layer.

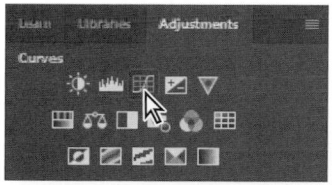

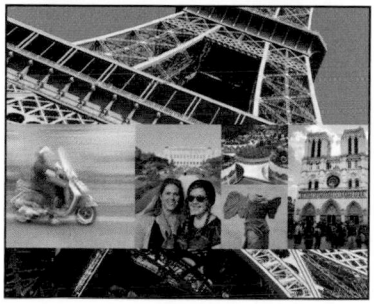

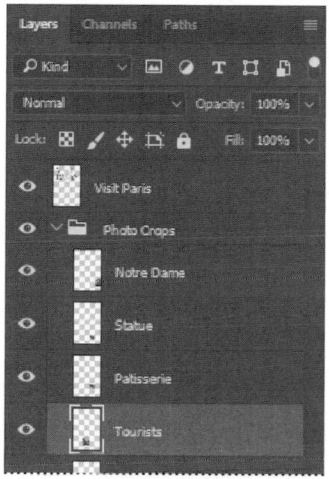

6 Click the Clip To Layer button (↓□) at the bottom of the Properties panel to create a clipping mask.

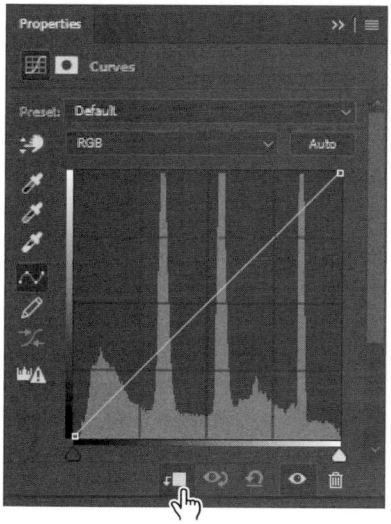

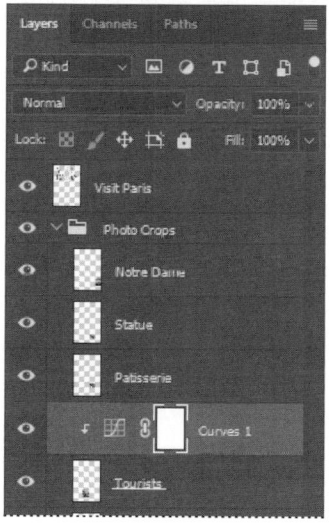

The clipping mask ensures that the adjustment layer affects only the layer directly below it in the Layers panel. If the new adjustment layer was not made into a clipping mask, it would affect all of the layers below it.

▶ **Tip:** It's best to click the White Point eyedropper tool on a spot that is the lightest neutral area of an image that contains detail, not a specular highlight.

7 In the Properties panel, select the White Point eyedropper tool, and then click the white shirt of the person behind the tourists to define that point as the brightest neutral part of the image. (Zoom in as needed to click precisely.) Because the white shirt was not very bright, clicking it as a white point reference brightens it and the rest of the tones in the rest of the image and rebalances the colors in the image.

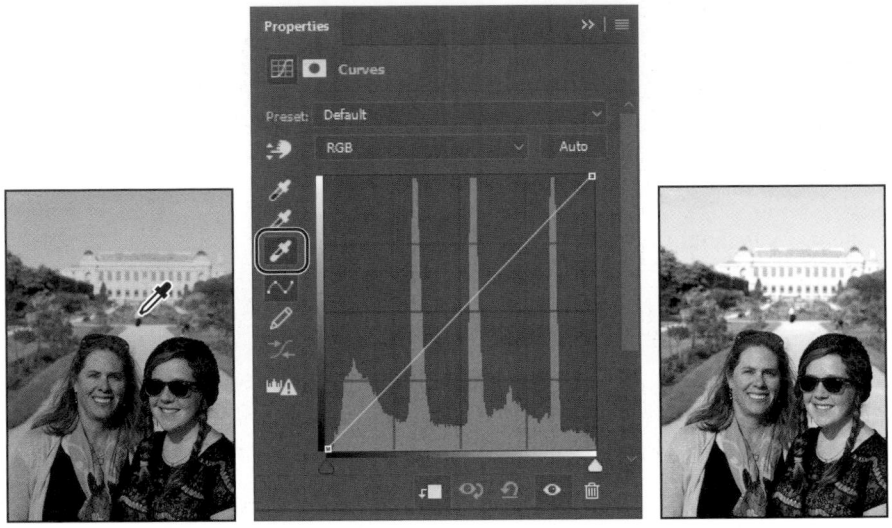

▶ **Tip:** After you click the White Point eyedropper, notice that the curves for the red, green, and blue channels have shifted to define the point you clicked as a neutral color, setting the color balance for the image. That's why it's important to click a spot that should be neutral.

The image of tourists looks better. But the image of the statue appears flat and lacks contrast. You'll fix that with a Levels adjustment layer.

8 Select the Statue layer in the Layers panel, and then click the Levels icon in the Adjustments panel to add a Levels adjustment layer.

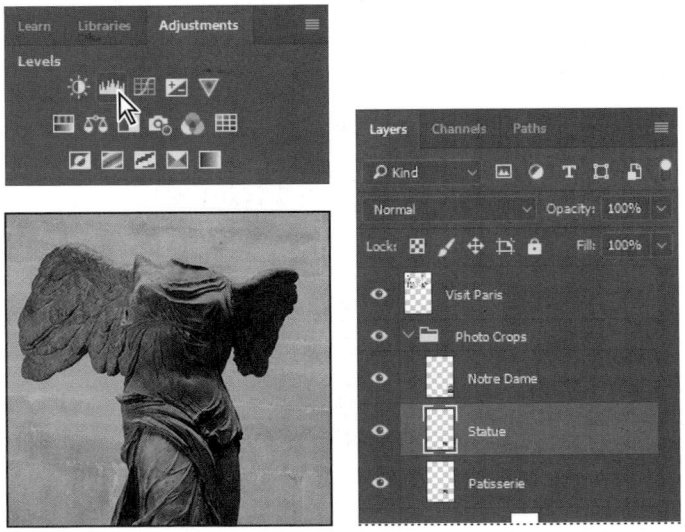

9 Click the Clip To Layer button at the bottom of the Properties panel to create a clipping mask so that the adjustment layer affects only the Statue layer.

10 In the Properties panel, click the Calculate A More Accurate Histogram icon (▲) to refresh the histogram display.

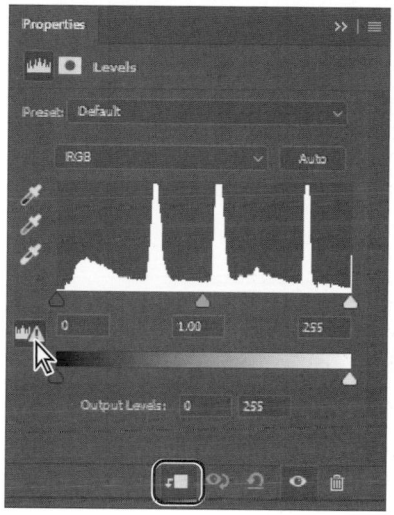

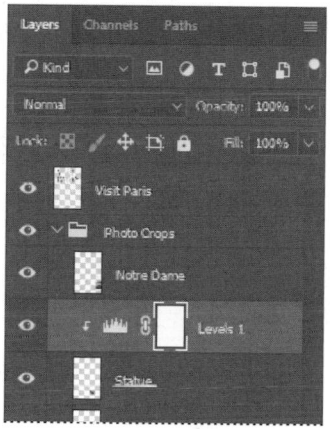

The alert icon next to the initial Calculate a More Accurate Histogram icon indicates that the histogram is based on cached image data. Photoshop first displays the histogram based on cached data because it displays more quickly, but is often less accurate. Refreshing the histogram ensures that it's accurate and up to date before you make edits based on it.

11 Move the input level sliders to punch up the image. We used the values 31, 1.60, 235. Remember that to increase contrast, drag the black point (left) and white point (right) input sliders toward the center, making sure that highlight and shadow detail is still visible, not clipped (excluded).

▶ **Tip:** To see if you're clipping highlight or shadow detail, hold down Alt (Windows) or Option (Mac) as you drag the black or white input level sliders. If pressing that key displays areas that are not solid white (for shadows) or solid black (for highlights), move the slider outward.

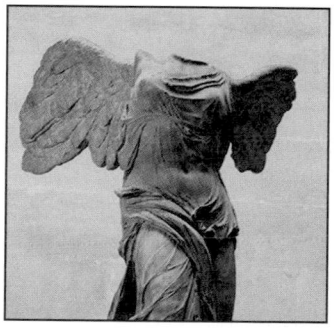

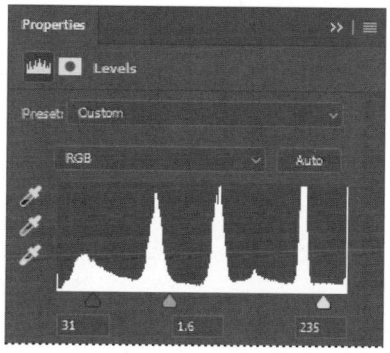

12 Save the file. The whole poster looks better after your improvements to the photos of the tourists and statue.

About color management

Because the RGB and CMYK color models use different methods to display colors, each reproduces a different color *gamut* (color range or color space). For example, RGB uses light to produce color, so its gamut includes neon colors, such as those you'd see in a neon sign. In contrast, printing inks excel at reproducing certain colors that can lie outside the RGB gamut, such as some pastels and pure black.

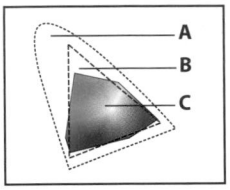

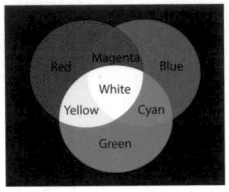

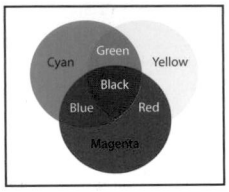

A. *Natural color gamut*
B. *RGB color gamut*
C. *CMYK color gamut*

RGB color model

CMYK color model

But not all RGB and CMYK gamuts are alike. Each monitor and printer model differs, and so each displays a slightly different gamut. For example, one brand of monitor may produce slightly brighter blues than another. The *color space* for a device is defined by the gamut it can reproduce.

The color management system in Photoshop uses International Color Consortium (ICC)–compliant color profiles that work like translators, helping to maintain color appearance when colors are converted from one color space into another. An *ICC color profile* is a description of a device's color space, such as the CMYK color space of a particular printer. You specify which profiles to use to accurately proof and print your images. Once you've selected the profiles, Photoshop can embed them into your image files so that Photoshop and other applications can consistently maintain the colors of your images.

Note: Your monitor may have been factory-calibrated, but you may not know how precisely and to what standard. For example, if your print service provider recommends that your monitor use the common prepress standard of a D65 white point, how do you know how well your monitor meets that standard? To make sure, calibrate and profile your monitor with D65 set as the target standard.

About calibration and profiling

Calibration means adjusting a device to meet a standard, like making sure a monitor displays neutral gray when neutral gray color values are sent to it. A *profile* describes whether the device meets a standard, and if not, how far off it is so that a color management system can correct for the difference and show image colors accurately.

To get the most out of color management, calibrate and profile your monitor so that you evaluate color on a screen using an accurate display profile. You can use calibration/profiling software that drives a color profiling device. The software uses the device to measure the colors produced by your screen and corrects for inaccuracies by creating a customized ICC display profile of your monitor. Your system uses this display profile to show colors accurately in any software that is color-managed, such as Photoshop and most other Adobe graphics software.

RGB color model

Much of the visible color spectrum can be represented by mixing red, green, and blue (RGB) colored light in various proportions and intensities. Where the colors overlap, they create cyan, magenta, yellow, and white.

Because the RGB colors combine to create white, they are also called *additive* colors. Adding all colors together creates white—that is, all light is transmitted back to the eye. Additive colors are used for lighting, video, and monitors. For example, an LCD monitor creates color by emitting its backlight through red, green, and blue filters.

CMYK color model

The CMYK model is based on the light-absorbing quality of ink printed on a substrate (surface) such as paper or packaging. As white light strikes translucent inks, part of the spectrum is absorbed, while other parts are reflected back to your eyes.

In theory, pure cyan (C), magenta (M), and yellow (Y) pigments should combine to absorb all color and produce black. For this reason, these colors are called *subtractive* colors. But because all printing inks contain some impurities, these three inks actually produce a muddy brown and must be combined with black (K) ink to produce a denser black. (K is used instead of B to avoid confusion with blue.) Combining these inks to reproduce color is called four-color process printing.

Specifying color-management settings

Even if your monitor is calibrated and profiled, accurately previewing colors onscreen also depends on correctly setting up the color-management controls in the Color Settings dialog box in Photoshop.

By default, Photoshop is set up for color gamuts that are more appropriate for an RGB-based digital workflow. If you're preparing artwork for printing on a press, as in the document used in this lesson, you'll want to change the settings to be more appropriate for CMYK-based prepress production rather than screen display.

You'll create customized color settings.

1 Choose Edit > Color Settings to open the Color Settings dialog box.

The bottom of the dialog box interactively describes each option.

2 Without clicking (don't change settings), hover the pointer over each part of the dialog box, including the names of sections (such as Working Spaces), the menu names, and the menu options. As you move the pointer, Photoshop displays information about each item in the Description area.

Now, you'll choose a set of options designed for a print workflow.

▶ **Tip:** The Color Settings dialog box can seem complex, so remember that the only thing you usually need to do is pick the Settings preset that matches your workflow most closely. Each Settings preset changes the rest of the options for you.

3 Choose North America Prepress 2 from the Settings menu. The working spaces and color-management policy options change for a prepress workflow. Then click OK.

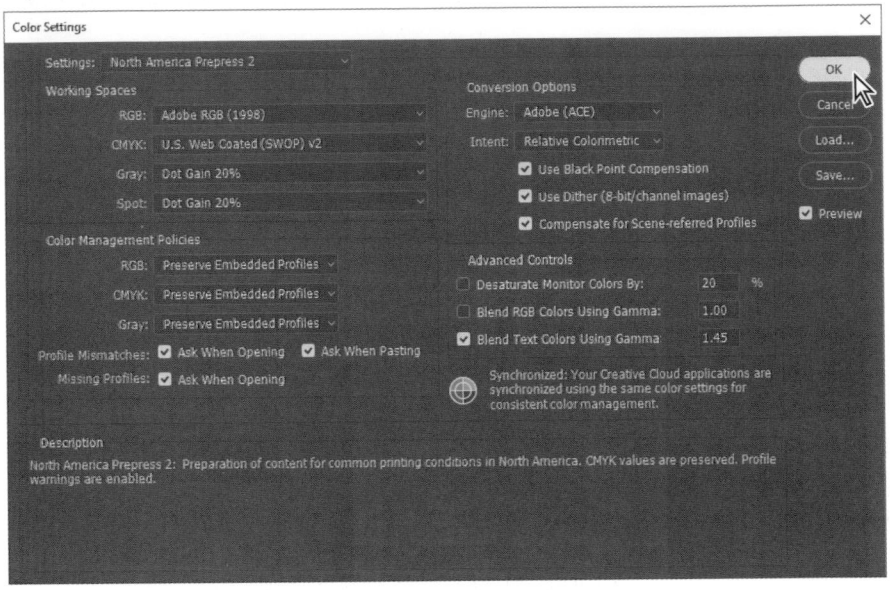

Identifying out-of-gamut colors

Colors on a monitor are displayed using combinations of red, green, and blue light (called RGB), while printed colors are typically created using a combination of four ink colors—cyan, magenta, yellow, and black (called CMYK). These four inks are called *process colors* because they are the standard inks used in the four-color printing process.

The color range covered by typical CMYK printing can reproduce many, but usually not all, of the colors in an RGB image from a digital camera or scanner. For example, colored LED lights or vivid flowers may produce colors that are outside a printer's CMYK gamut. Those colors may print with less detail and saturation than expected. Some intense blue colors in RGB can shift toward purple in CMYK.

Before you convert an image from RGB to CMYK, you can preview which RGB color values are outside the gamut of CMYK.

1 Choose View > Fit On Screen.

2 Choose View > Gamut Warning. Photoshop compares the document colors to the current CMYK color space and displays a neutral gray in the document window to indicate where document colors are outside the CMYK color gamut.

The gray gamut warning covers much of the image, especially the blue areas. A typical CMYK press can reproduce a relatively narrow range of blue compared to most RGB gamuts, so it's not unusual for an image to have RGB blue values that are outside a CMYK printing gamut. In out-of-gamut areas, the printer would end up printing the closest shade of blue its inks can reproduce on a given paper.

Because the gray indicator color can be hard to distinguish in the image, you'll change it to a more visible color.

3 Choose Edit > Preferences > Transparency & Gamut (Windows) or Photoshop > Preferences > Transparency & Gamut (Mac).

4 Click the color sample in the Gamut Warning area at the bottom of the dialog box. Select a vivid color, such as purple or bright green, and click OK.

5 Click OK to close the Preferences dialog box.

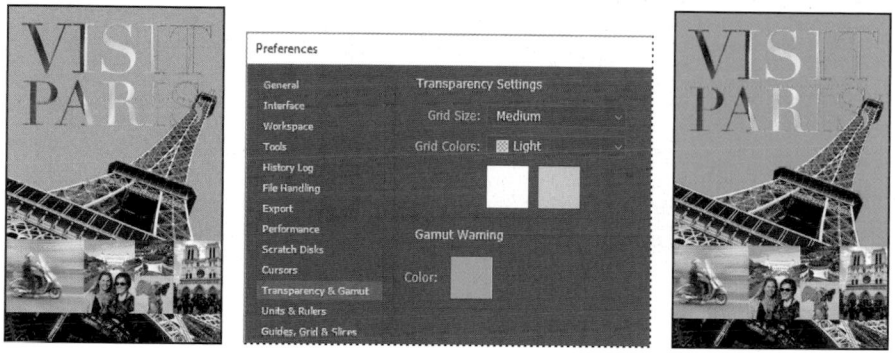

▶ **Tip:** If your gamut warning area looks different, you may be using different settings in the View > Proof Setup > Custom dialog box (see page 364).

The bright new color you chose appears instead of the neutral gray as the gamut warning color; it should be much more obvious which areas are out of gamut. If this was a real job, you might consult your prepress service provider to discuss how their press will reproduce that blue color and whether it's worth editing the color.

▶ **Tip:** When you have concerns about how a color will reproduce on press, you can ask your prepress service provider about seeing a hard proof (test print).

6 Choose View > Gamut Warning to turn off the preview of out-of-gamut colors.

Next, you'll simulate onscreen how the document colors might print, and then you'll bring those colors into the printing gamut.

Proofing document colors on a monitor

You'll select a proof profile so that you can view an onscreen simulation of what document colors will look like when printed. An accurate proof profile lets you proof on the screen (*soft-proof*) for printed output.

That onscreen simulation is based on a *proof setup*, which defines the printing conditions. Photoshop provides a variety of settings that can help you proof images for different uses, including for different printers and devices. For this lesson, you'll create a custom proof setup. You can then save the settings for use on other images that will be output the same way.

1 Choose View > Proof Setup > Custom. The Customize Proof Condition dialog box opens. Make sure Preview is selected.

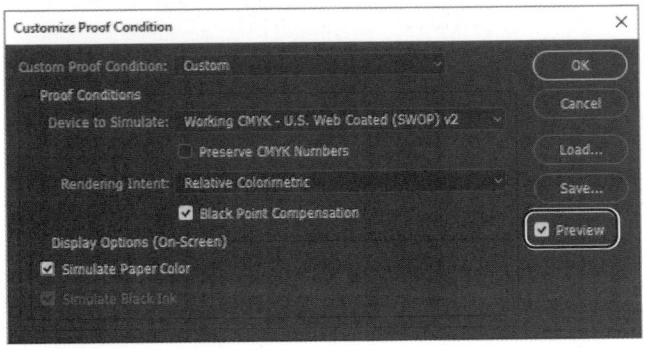

▶ **Tip:** A printer profile represents not only the output device, but also a specific combination of settings, ink, and paper. Changing any of those components can change the color gamut being simulated by the onscreen proof, so choose a profile that's as close as possible to the final printing conditions.

2 From the Device To Simulate menu, choose a profile that represents the final output device, such as that for the printer you'll use to print the image. If you don't have a specific printer, use the profile Working CMYK–U.S. Web Coated (SWOP) v2, the current default.

3 If you've chosen a different profile, make sure Preserve Numbers is *not* selected.

The Preserve Numbers option simulates how colors will appear if they're not converted to the output device color space. This option may be named Preserve CMYK Numbers when you select a CMYK output profile.

4 Make sure Relative Colorimetric is selected for the Rendering Intent.

A rendering intent determines how the color is converted from one color space to another. Relative Colorimetric preserves color relationships without sacrificing color accuracy and is the standard rendering intent for printing in North America and Europe.

5 Select Simulate Black Ink if it's available for the profile you chose. Then deselect it and select Simulate Paper Color; notice that selecting this option automatically selects Simulate Black Ink.

▶ **Tip:** When the Customize Proof Condition dialog box isn't open, you can view the document with or without the current proof settings by selecting or deselecting the View > Proof Colors command.

Notice that the image appears to lose contrast. Most paper is not pure white; Paper Color simulates that. Most black ink is not perfectly solid or neutral black, so Black Ink simulates the actual ink. Both get that information from the output profile, if available.

Don't be alarmed by the loss of contrast and saturation that you may see when you turn on the Display Options. While the image might look worse, the soft-proofing simulation is just being honest about how the image will actually print; paper and ink simply cannot reproduce the same range of tones and colors as a monitor. Choosing higher-quality paper stock and inks can help a printed image match the screen more closely.

6 Toggle the Preview option to see the difference between the image as it is displayed onscreen and as it will print, based on the profile you selected. Then click OK.

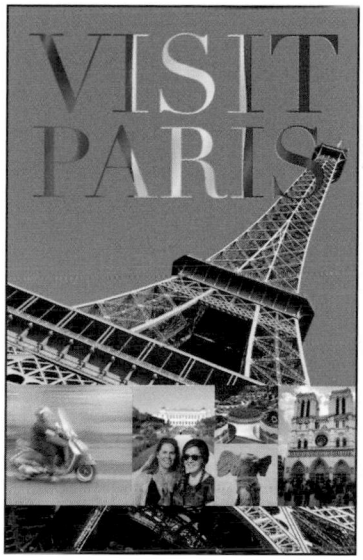

Normal image

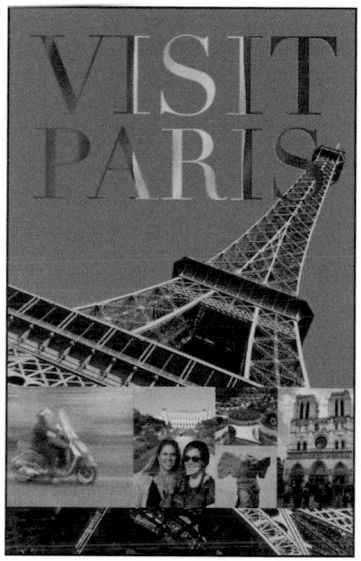

Image with Simulate Paper Color and Simulate Black Ink options selected

7 Click the View menu, and if Proof Colors is enabled, choose Proof Colors to disable it. You can use this command to enable or disable the soft-proof view that you set up in the Customize Proof Condition dialog box.

Bringing colors into the output gamut

The next step in preparing an image for output is to make any necessary color and tonal adjustments based on what you see in the proofs. In this exercise, you'll add some tonal and color adjustments to correct an off-color scan of the original poster.

So that you can compare the image before and after making corrections, you'll start by making a copy.

1 Choose Image > Duplicate, and click OK to duplicate the image.

2 Choose Window > Arrange > 2 Up Vertical so you can compare the images as you work.

You'll adjust the hue and saturation of the image to move all colors into gamut.

3 Select 14Working.psd (the original image) to make it active, and then select the Visit Paris layer in the Layers panel.

4 Choose Select > Color Range.

▶ **Tip:** It isn't always necessary to correct colors that are indicated as out of gamut. The best use of the gamut warning is to know which colors to inspect more closely when you proof document colors. If out-of-gamut colors and details look acceptable when proofing, you may not need to spend time editing them.

Note: In the Color Range dialog box, the color range marked as Out of Gamut depends on the profile selected for the CMYK Working Space in the Edit > Color Settings dialog box. Make sure the correct profile is selected for the press that will print your job.

5 In the Color Range dialog box, choose Out of Gamut from the Select menu, and then click OK.

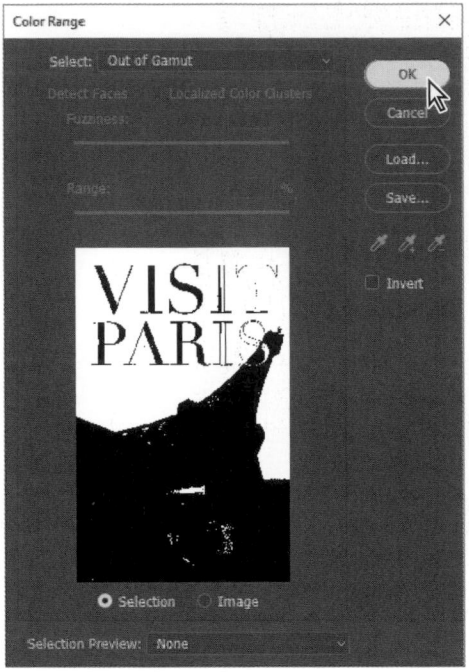

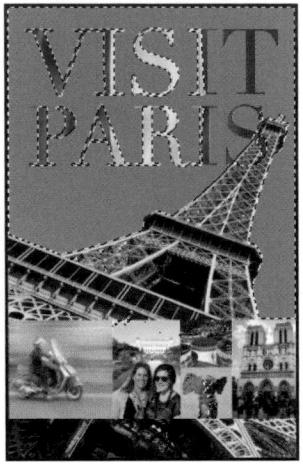

The areas that were marked as out of gamut earlier are now selected, so you can make changes that affect only those areas.

6 Choose View > Extras to hide the selection while you work with it.

The selection border can be distracting. When you hide extras, you no longer see the selection, but it's still in effect.

7 Click the Hue/Saturation button (▤) in the Adjustments panel to create a Hue/Saturation adjustment layer. (Choose Window > Adjustments if the panel isn't open.) The Hue/Saturation adjustment layer includes a layer mask, created from your selection.

8 In the Properties panel, do the following:

- Leave the Hue setting at the default value.
- Drag the Saturation slider to reduce the value (we used –14). Reducing Saturation is one way to bring colors into a target gamut.
- Drag the Lightness to the left to darken the image (we used –2).

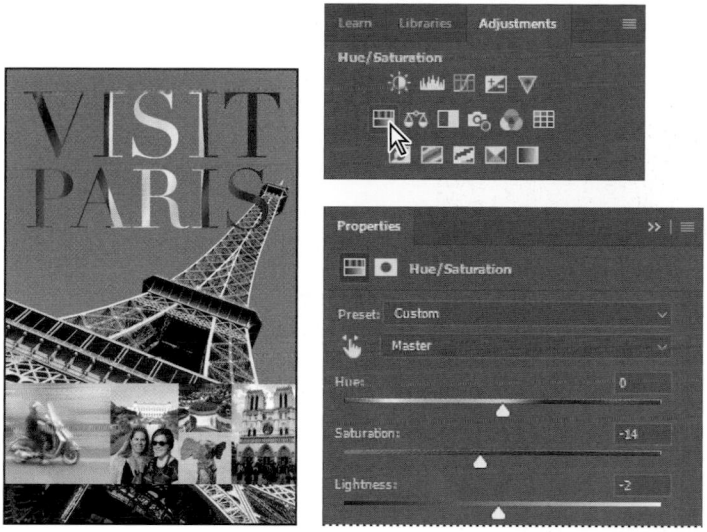

9 Choose View > Gamut Warning. You have shifted most of the out-of-gamut colors so that they're in the target gamut. Choose View > Gamut Warning again to deselect it.

10 Choose View > Extras to enable it so that selection marquees and other non-printing aids will be visible again. In this case, the selection marquee doesn't reappear, because the selection was converted into the layer mask for the Hue/Saturation layer you created in step 7.

11 Close the duplicate image file (the 14Working copy tab) without saving it.

In this exercise, you shifted out-of-gamut colors into the printing gamut mostly by desaturating them. While this is quick and easy, it's considered a basic technique. Skilled image editors use more advanced techniques to preserve color detail while maintaining as much of the original color saturation as possible. Also, when an out-of-gamut color doesn't contain much detail, as in a flat blue sky, it may be acceptable to leave the colors unchanged.

▶ **Tip:** You can also make adjustments with Gamut Warning on so that you know when the colors move into the printing gamut.

Converting an image to CMYK

It's generally a good idea to work in RGB mode as long as possible so that your edits can take place within the larger color gamut of RGB. Also, converting between modes can cause color value rounding errors that may result in unwanted color changes, especially over multiple conversions.

Once you've made final corrections, you're ready to convert the image to CMYK. If you think you might also want to output the image to an inkjet printer or distribute it digitally later, save a copy in RGB mode before converting to CMYK mode.

▶ **Tip:** If you aren't sure if or when you should convert images to CMYK, ask the print service provider that will output your job. They can recommend the image preparation steps that work best with their prepress equipment.

1 Click the Channels tab to bring the Channels panel to the front.

The image is currently in RGB mode, so there are three channels listed: red, green, and blue. The RGB channel is not actually a channel, but a composite of all three. You also see a channel named Hue/Saturation 1 Mask; this channel contains the mask information for the layer currently selected in the Layers panel.

2 Choose Image > Mode > CMYK Color.

3 Click Merge in the message that warns you that you might lose some adjustment layers. Merging the layers helps preserve the appearance of colors.

Another message appears, saying: "You are about to convert to CMYK using the "U.S. Web Coated (SWOP) v2" profile. This may not be what you intend. To choose a different profile, use Edit > Convert To Profile." This message lets you know that the active CMYK profile is U.S. Web Coated (SWOP) v2, the Photoshop default profile for CMYK color. That profile might not represent the actual prepress specification or proofing standard that will be used. In a real-world job, you would ask the print service provider which CMYK profile to use for color conversions; they may be able to provide a custom profile that accurately represents the tonal and color range of their equipment.

4 Click OK in the message about the color profile used in the conversion.

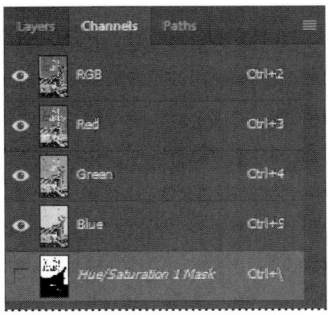

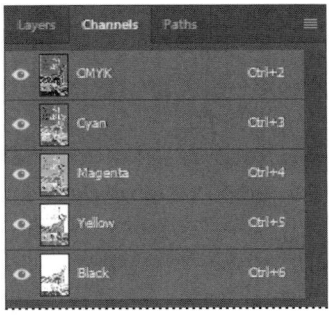

The Channels panel now displays four channels: cyan, magenta, yellow, and black. Additionally, it lists the CMYK composite. The layers were merged during conversion, so there is only one layer in the Layers panel.

Saving the image as a CMYK EPS file

Some print service providers may request that Photoshop images be submitted in EPS format. This format is used less often in newer prepress workflows; it's more common to keep a CMYK image in Photoshop, TIFF, or PDF format. You'll save this image as an EPS file in CMYK mode.

1 Choose File > Save As.

2 In the Save As dialog box, do the following, and then click Save:

- Choose Photoshop EPS from the Format menu.
- Under Color, select Use Proof Setup.
- Accept the filename 14Working.eps.
- If you see a warning, don't be concerned about it in this case. The warning appears when the format you're about to save to, such as EPS, doesn't support all of the features of the current format (such as layers). The document you're saving won't replace the full-featured Photoshop document, as long as Save As a Copy is selected in the lower part of the dialog box and the filename is different than that of the original document.

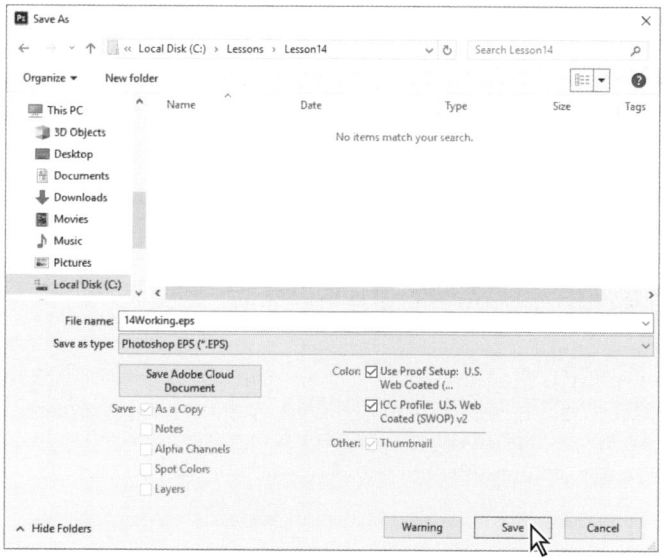

3 Click OK in the EPS Options dialog box that appears.

4 Save and then close the 14Working.psd file.

5 Choose File > Open, navigate to the Lessons/Lesson14 folder, and double-click the 14Working.eps file.

Printing to a desktop inkjet printer

Many color inkjet printers do a good job printing photographs and other image files. The precise settings available vary from printer to printer, and they're different than the best settings for a press. When you're printing images from Photoshop to a desktop inkjet printer, you'll get the best results if you do the following:

- Make sure the appropriate printer driver is installed and that you've selected it. Leaving the printer driver on a generic setting such as "Any Printer" may result in problems such as incorrect page margins.
- Use the appropriate paper for your intended use. Photographic and coated papers are good choices when you're printing photos you want to display.
- Select the correct paper source and media setting in the printer settings. On some printers, those settings adjust ink appropriately. For example, if you're using photo-quality paper, make sure it's selected in the printer settings.
- Select the image quality in the printer settings. Higher print quality is better when viewing is critical, such as for color proofing or framed prints. Lower print quality is useful for speedier printing and for using less ink.
- Don't convert an RGB image to CMYK to print on a desktop inkjet printer, because most are designed to receive RGB color data. The printer or its driver software will do its own conversion from RGB to the ink set specifically used in that printer. Professional quality inkjet printers typically use more inks that reproduce a wider color gamut than the four CMYK inks used on a press.

Printing a CMYK image from Photoshop

▶ **Tip:** Printing color separations on your desktop printer can help verify that colors will appear on the correct plate. But separations from a desktop printer won't match the precision of an actual platesetter. Proofs you create for jobs intended for a press are more accurate on a desktop printer with an Adobe PostScript RIP (raster image processor).

You can proof your image by printing a *color composite*, often called a *color comp*. A color composite is a single print that combines the red, green, and blue channels of an RGB image (or the cyan, magenta, yellow, and black channels of a CMYK image). This indicates what the final printed image will look like.

If you choose to print *color separations*, Photoshop prints a separate sheet, or *plate*, for each ink. For a CMYK image, it prints four plates, one for each process color. In this exercise, you'll print color separations.

If you're printing color separations directly from Photoshop, you will typically use the following workflow:

- Set the parameters for the halftone screen. Consult with your print service provider for recommended settings.
- Print test separations to make sure objects appear on the correct separation.
- Print the final separations to plate or film. This task is typically performed by your print service provider.

1 With the 14Working.eps image open from the previous exercise, choose File > Print.

By default, Photoshop prints any document as a composite image. To print this file as separations, you must set it up accordingly in the Photoshop Print Settings dialog box.

2 In the Photoshop Print Settings dialog box, do the following:

- In the Printer Setup section, make sure the selected Printer is correct.
- In the Color Management area, choose Separations from the Color Handling menu.
- In the Position and Size section, verify the settings. This 11"×17" document may be too large for many desktop printers to print at actual size. You can select Scale To Fit Media to fit the document to the current paper size; to see this option you may need to scroll down or enlarge the dialog box.
- If you're using a printer equipped with Adobe PostScript, scroll down and set PostScript Options such as halftone options. Note that the results on a desktop printer may not be identical to a prepress output device.
- Click Print. (If you don't actually want to print color separations, click Cancel or Done; the difference is that Done saves the current print settings.)

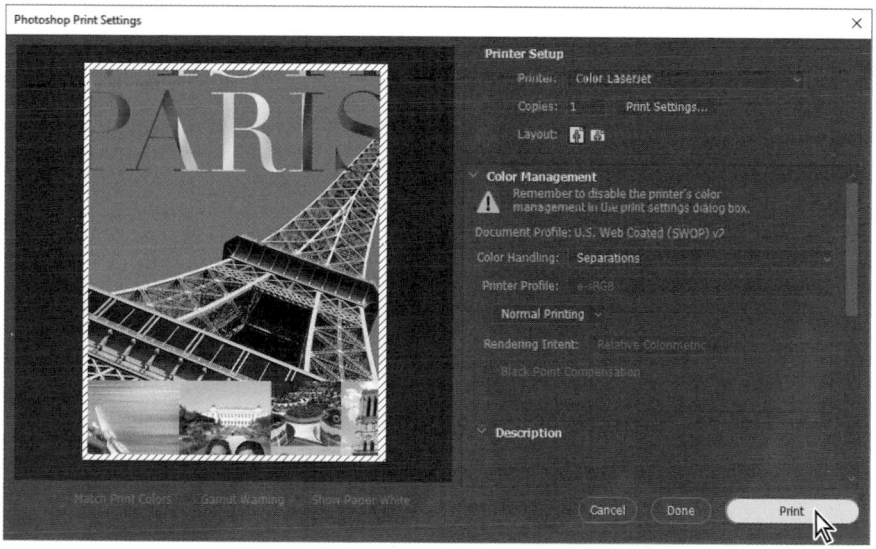

This lesson is an introduction to producing consistent color and printing with Photoshop. If you're printing on a desktop printer, you can experiment with different settings to find the best color and print settings for your system. If you're preparing images for professional printing, consult with your print service provider to determine the best settings to use. For more information about color management, printing options, and color separations, see Photoshop Help.

▶ **Tip:** In the Photoshop Print Settings dialog box, if the Separations option is not available in the Color Handling menu, click Done, and make sure the document is in CMYK mode (Image > Mode > CMYK Color).

▶ **Tip:** The Position and Size section of the Photoshop Print Settings dialog box is two sections below the Color Management section, so if you can't see it, scroll down the right side panel. Also, you can enlarge the Photoshop Print Settings dialog box by dragging a corner or edge so that you can see more options at once.

● **Note:** If you do not normally prepare graphics for a press, when you finish this lesson, go back to page 362, step 3, and choose North American General Purpose 2. Color Settings are not affected when you reset Photoshop preferences.

Extra Credit

Sharing your work on Adobe Portfolio

Integrated into Adobe Creative Cloud is Adobe Portfolio, which you can use to quickly create a well-designed and functional website that showcases your creations, with one-click connections to your social media presence (such as your Instagram, Facebook, and Twitter feeds) and a prebuilt contact form that makes it easy for potential clients and customers to get in touch with you. To test it, you'll first prepare this lesson's image for viewing in a web browser.

1 Open the 14Start.psd file in Photoshop, if it isn't already open. Click OK if the Embedded Profile Mismatch dialog box appears.

   As the original RGB version of the image in this chapter, 14Start.psd contains a wider color gamut than the later version that was converted to CMYK for prepress.

2 Choose File > Export > Export As to prepare the image for display on a website. It's a large, print-resolution image, so it may take a while to display in the Export As dialog box.

3 Choose JPG from the Format menu, and set Quality to **90%**.

4 In the Image Size section, enter a Height in pixels to proportionally resize the exported image. We entered **1000** pixels, enough to show the image with a good amount of detail on many displays.

5 In the Color Space section, select Convert to sRGB and Embed Color Profile to help ensure consistent color in web browsers.

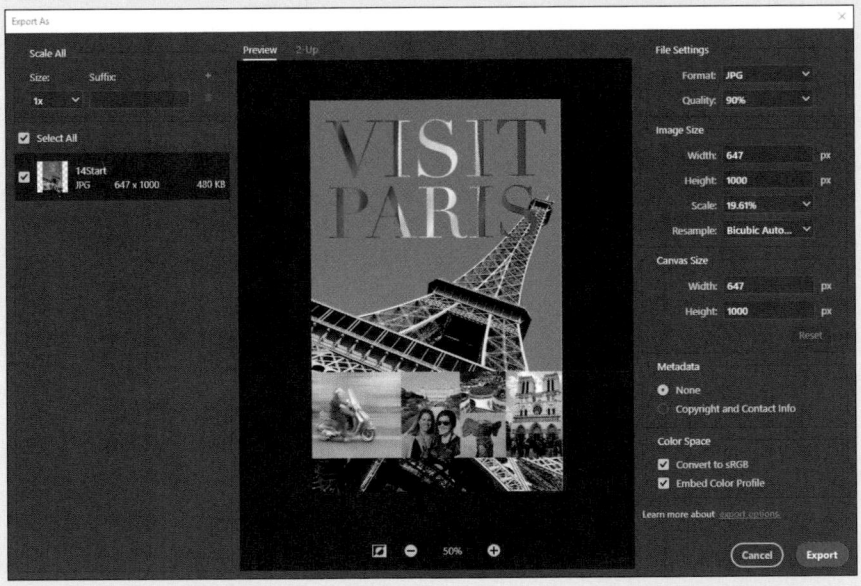

6 Click Export. Navigate to the Lesson14 folder, and click Export or Save.

Now you can start making your website. The Portfolio user interface you see may vary as Adobe updates the service. Some of the following steps may appear only when creating a Portfolio website for the first time.

1 In a web browser, go to myportfolio.com, the web address for Adobe Portfolio.

2 At the top of the Adobe Portfolio home page, click Sign In, enter your Adobe ID email address and password, and click Sign In.

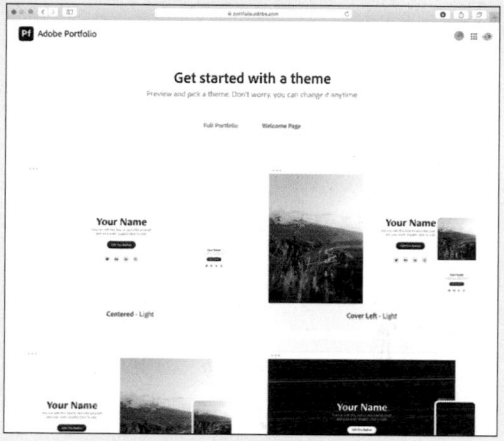

3 On the next screen, click to select the type of site you want to create: Full Portfolio, or Welcome Page. We clicked Welcome Page to make a quick one-page website and scrolled down to pick the Cover Left - Light theme.

4 After the site is created, click the Click To Upload An Image/Video button. Navigate to the Lesson14 folder, select 14Start.jpg, and then click Choose or Open (the button name depends on the web browser you use). Adobe Portfolio processes the image and replaces the left-side placeholder with it.

5 Now edit the text on the splash page. On the right side of the page, double-click in any text object to edit its text. You can add a brief description of you and your work.

6 Click Preview. The buttons at the bottom of the preview show you how the page will look on different device displays and orientations, such as a smartphone held vertically or horizontally.

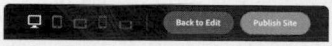

7 Click Back to Edit.

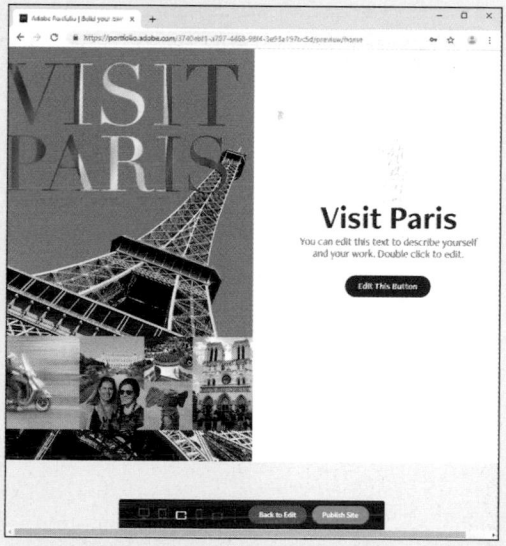

Continues on next page

Extra credit (continued)

As you move the pointer over different page elements, icons appear over them. If you see an edit icon (a circle containing a pencil), click it to edit options for that object. If you see an add icon (a circle containing a plus sign), click it to add new content to a page, such as photos, video, or embedded media.

8 Position the pointer over the button labeled Edit This Button, click the edit icon that appears on the left side of its containing object, and in the menu that appears, click Edit Button. In the Options tab that appears, you can change options such as the button text or the button font, and you can add a link. Other tabs offer options for other button states, such as how it looks when you hover the pointer over it. To exit click the back button (<) at the top-left corner of the Edit Button panel. If you want, edit other sections, such as the social media icons.

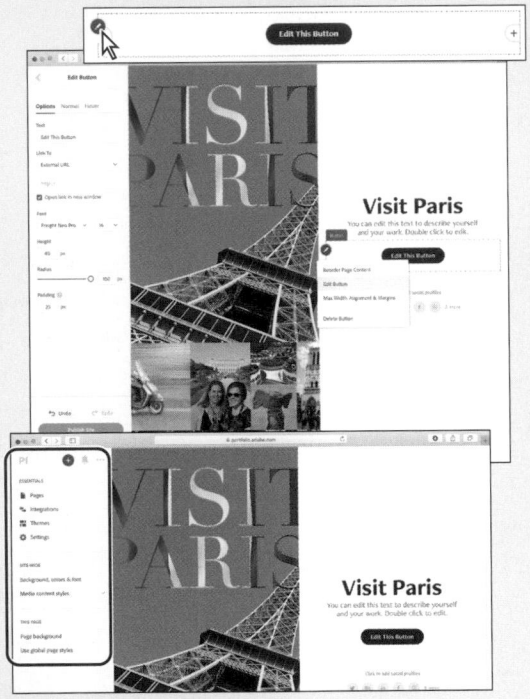

9 Use the options along the left side of the Portfolio editor to add or organize pages, customize the design (including the theme, fonts, and page backgrounds), or set options for the entire website, such as password protection. You can also create and manage multiple websites.

If your site looks good and you want the world to see it, click Publish Site. It's live!

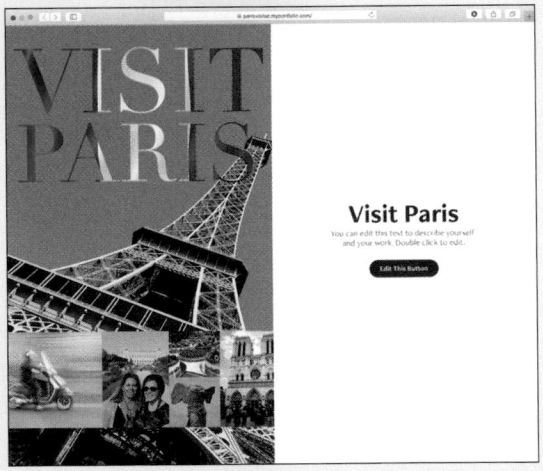

If you have your own Internet domain name, you can easily connect it to Adobe Portfolio so that your website's address is fully consistent with your brand. To do this, click Settings, and then edit settings in the Domain Name panel.

If you don't use a custom domain name, your website address is a subdomain of myportfolio.com. For example, if you name the site "parisvisitor," then parisvisitor.myportfolio.com is the default web address.

Review questions

1 What steps should you follow to reproduce color consistently?

2 What is a gamut?

3 What is a color profile?

4 What are color separations?

Review answers

1 To reproduce color consistently, first calibrate and profile your monitor, and then use the Color Settings dialog box to specify which color spaces to use. For example, you can specify which RGB color space to use for online images and which CMYK color space to use for images that will be printed. You can then proof the image, check for out-of-gamut colors, and adjust colors as needed.

2 A gamut is the range of colors that can be reproduced by a color model or device. For example, the RGB and CMYK color models have different gamuts. Within each color model, various printers, printing standards, and device displays reproduce different gamuts.

3 A color profile is a description of a device's color space, such as the CMYK color space of a particular printer. Applications such as Photoshop can interpret color profiles in an image to maintain consistent color across different applications, platforms, and devices.

4 Color separations are separate plates for each ink used in a document being reproduced on press. Your print service provider will produce color separations of your files for the cyan, magenta, yellow, and black (CMYK) inks.

15 EXPLORING NEURAL FILTERS

Lesson overview

In this lesson, you'll learn how to do the following:

- Understand how Neural Filters are different than other filters and effects in Photoshop.
- Explore the Neural Filters workspace.
- Apply one or more Neural Filters effects to an image.

This lesson will take about 30 minutes to complete. To get the lesson files used in this chapter, download them from the web page for this book at www.adobepress.com/PhotoshopCIB2021. For more information, see "Accessing the lesson files and Web Edition" in the Getting Started section at the beginning of this book.

As you work on this lesson, you'll preserve the start files. If you need to restore the start files, download them from your Account page.

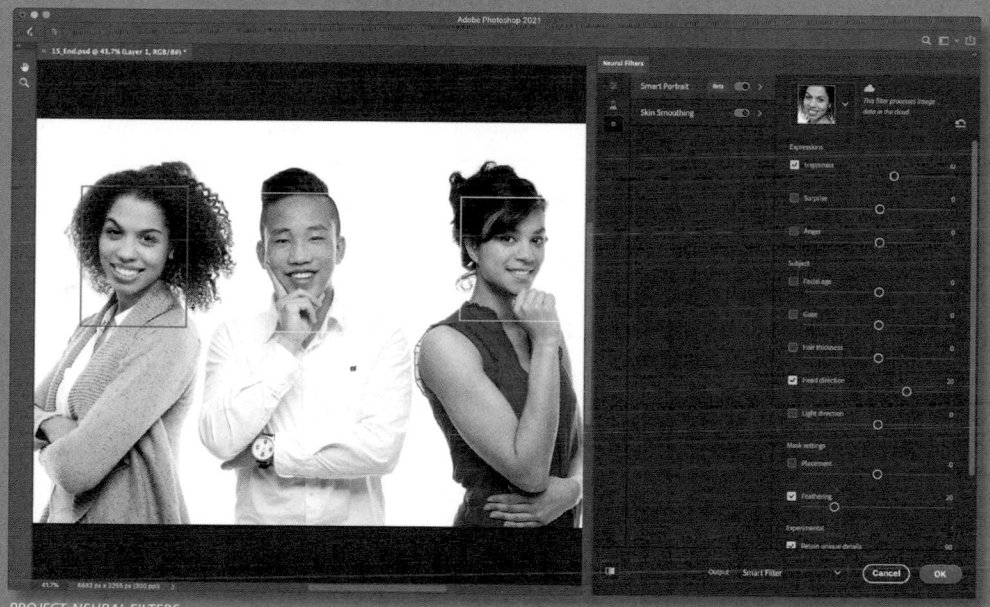

PROJECT: NEURAL FILTERS

Image © Djomas. Shutterstock

Neural Filters are advanced filters trained using machine learning. You can explore ideas that would be more labor-intensive, or sometimes impossible, with conventional digital photo filters and effects.

Understanding Neural Filters

If you worked through the earlier lessons in this book, you've used Photoshop filters such as Surface Blur, Smart Sharpen, Clouds, and Liquify. Those are conventional filters that produce their results with algorithms—procedural programs where the code itself determines the result.

In the newer Neural Filters, effects produce their results in a different way, combining traditional algorithms with *machine learning* and other advanced techniques. Machine learning means that a filter in Neural Filters can be trained using examples of desirable and undesirable outcomes, potentially creating better results than what could be achieved with procedural computer code alone.

Tip: For a quick visual overview of a selection of Neural Filters, see the Neural Filters gallery on pages 384 and 385.

Neural Filters are different from other Photoshop effects in the following ways:

- Neural Filters are trained by machine learning and neural networks.
- Some of the filters need to be downloaded before first use. This is partly to save space on your computer: Large filters you don't use won't take up storage space on your computer. If you need to download a Neural Filter, you can do it with one click inside Neural Filters. This also lets you download new or updated Neural Filters without downloading an entire Photoshop update.
- Some filters process the image on Adobe Creative Cloud servers; those that do display a message to let you know. The rest of the filters process the image locally, on your computer.

It's possible to use some Neural Filters without an Internet connection, but you get the most options when your computer is connected to the Internet.

You can use Neural Filters as long as your computer meets the system requirements for Photoshop, but it generally performs better with a more powerful CPU, more powerful graphics hardware, and in some cases a faster Internet connection.

About beta filters

Some Neural Filters are labeled Beta, which means they function but are still under development. You can use them, but when the finished version is released, those filters may produce different results or some options may be different.

Note: If Bridge isn't installed, the File > Browse In Bridge command in Photoshop will start the Creative Cloud desktop app, which will download and install Bridge. After installation completes, you can start Bridge. For more information, see page 3.

Getting started

Exploring the possibilities of Neural Filters might turn out to be the most fun you have with this book. Let's first take a look at the files you'll work with.

1 Start Photoshop, and then simultaneously hold down Ctrl+Alt+Shift (Windows) or Command+Option+Shift (Mac) to restore the default preferences. (See "Restoring default preferences" on page 5.)

2 When prompted, click Yes to delete the Adobe Photoshop Settings file.

3 Choose File > Browse In Bridge to open Adobe Bridge.

4 In Bridge, click Lessons in the Favorites panel. Double-click the Lesson15 folder in the Content panel.

5 Compare the files 15Start.psd and 15End.psd. If you watch the Preview panel as you select each image, you can more easily see the differences: The head pose changes for the person on the left, and the skin complexion changes for the person on the right.

Note: If Photoshop displays a dialog box telling you about the difference between saving to Cloud Documents and Your Computer, click Save On Your Computer. You can also select Don't Show Again, but that setting will deselect after you reset Photoshop preferences.

Exploring the Neural Filters workspace

1 In Adobe Bridge, double-click the 15Start.psd file to open it in Photoshop.

2 Save the document as **15Working.psd** in the Lesson15 folder.

3 Choose Filter > Neural Filters.

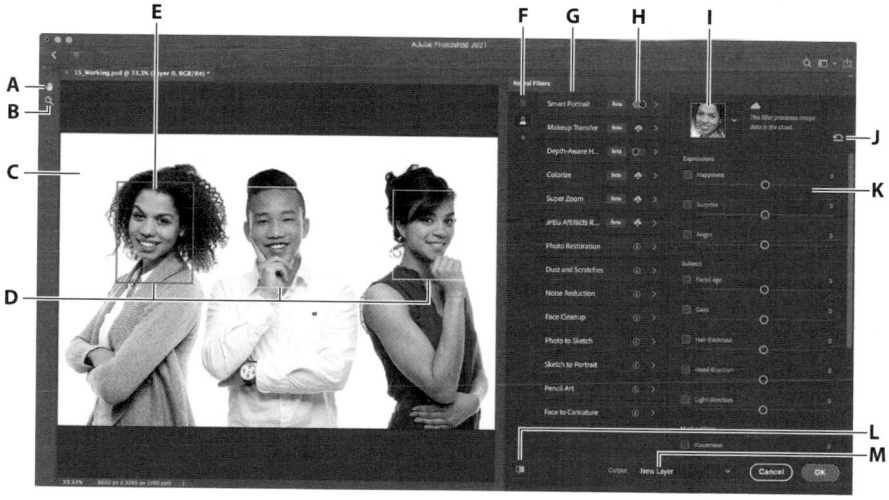

A. *Hand tool*
B. *Zoom tool*
C. *Preview*
D. *Detected faces*
E. *Selected face*
F. *Filter categories*
G. *Filters in the selected category*
H. *Filter toggle, enabled*
I. *Thumbnail menu for selecting a detected subject, such as a face*
J. *Reset filter options to default settings*
K. *Options for the selected Neural Filter*
L. *Preview Changes toggle*
M. *Output options*

In the Neural Filters workspace, the image appears in a large preview area on the left. On the right are Neural Filters controls:

- Filter categories organize the filter list.
- When you select a different category, the filters in the selected category appear to the right.
- To use a filter, it must be enabled. A filter is enabled when its toggle switch is moved to the right position and in color. You can enable multiple filters.
- Options for the currently selected filter appear to the right of the filter list.

- If the current filter can detect multiple potential subjects in the image, such as faces, it lists those candidates in the thumbnail preview menu at the top of the options. You can then choose which one to edit, and it will be outlined in color.
- If a spinning circle icon appears near the top-right corner of the workspace, a filter is processing. When the spinning icon disappears, the filter is done.
- To compare the current filter results with the original image, click the Preview icon at the bottom of the workspace to deselect it, displaying the original layer. Click again to select it, displaying the filter results again.

Note: If the Neural Filters command is not available, make sure a visible layer is selected.

Improving complexion with Skin Smoothing

Note: Adobe may update Neural Filters after this book is published, so the list of categories and filters you see may depend on the version of Photoshop you are using. Also, if Adobe updates how Neural Filters effects are trained, you may see different results than those in this chapter.

To learn more about Neural Filters, let's start by exploring the Skin Smoothing. It can improve skin complexion without significantly altering other facial features.

1 In the Neural Filters workspace, make sure the Featured Filters category is selected, and then click the Skin Smoothing filter toggle switch to enable it. That enables the Skin Smoothing filter options.

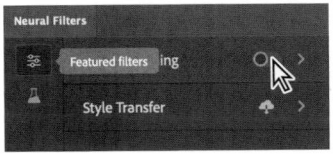

2 If options are not visible but a Download button appears instead, click the Download button because it means the filter is not yet installed. When the download completes, the filter installs itself and will be ready for you to use.

3 Select a face from the thumbnail menu or by clicking the rectangle that marks it in the image. We selected the woman on the right. When a Neural Filter recognizes multiple subjects, it means you can select each detected subject separately (in this case, each face) and apply different filter settings to each one.

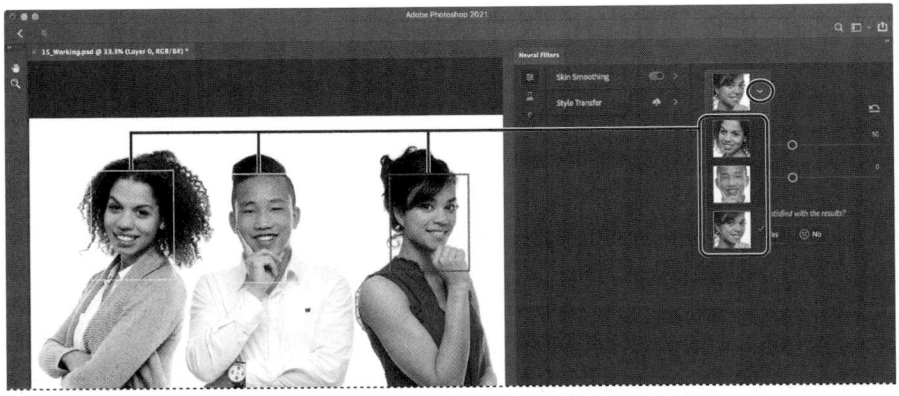

4 Modify the result by adjusting the options. We increased the Blur value to **75** and changed the Smoothness to **10**.

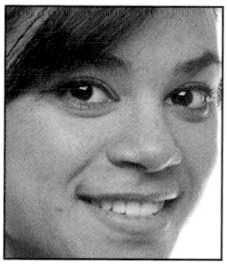

Before

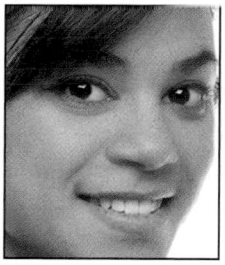

After

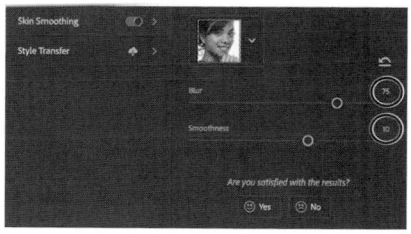

Note: The effect of the Skin Smoothing filter is necessarily subtle so that the changes aren't distracting or artificial.

How is this better than a traditional filter? Skin smoothing typically uses a blur filter and requires additional layers and masking to avoid blurring important face details, such as eyes, teeth, and hair; Lesson 12 includes an example. But Skin Smoothing is trained to recognize which areas should be smoothed and which should be left alone, so it can achieve a good result in fewer steps.

5 To compare the changes with the original, click the Preview Changes button at the bottom of the workspace. Click once to hide the changes and see the original, and click again to show the changes. Make any further adjustments as needed.

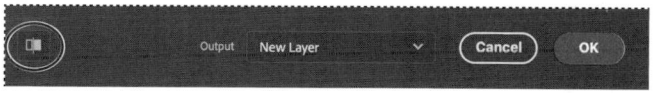

6 If you want, select a different face and modify it using steps 4 and 5.

7 When you're happy with the result, click the Output menu and choose Smart Filter; then click OK. This converts the original layer into a Smart Object with Neural Filters results applied to it so that you can edit the results later by double-clicking Neural Filters. Choosing any option other than Current Layer leaves the selected layer unchanged so that it's always available for you to go back to. You can read about other options in the sidebar "About Output options in Neural Filters."

Note: If a Neural Filter displays the message "Filters applied to this detected face may not work well," something may be making the face difficult to work with, such as a hand, watermark, or other object partially blocking the face. Also, Neural Filters face detection works best with subjects that face the camera; face detection and editing is less effective for faces turned away from the camera or in profile.

Combining Neural Filters

When you apply multiple Neural Filters, the Applied Filters list displays only the filters you applied, making it easier to work with just those filters.

1 Apply any combination of different filters in the Neural Filters workspace. Remember, a filter is applied if its toggle switch is enabled.

2 Click Applied Filters to see a list of just the filters you applied. All of the other filters you didn't use are conveniently hidden, so you can concentrate on the specific combination of filters you used.

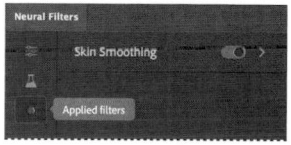

3 Explore how the image looks with some of the filters disabled by clicking the toggle switches. Or adjust how each filter contributes to the final result.

4 Click OK. Save your changes and close the document.

You learned the basics of using Neural Filters. Neural Filters results might not always be perfect, but because you can output the results to a separate masked layer, you can blend them with the original layer to achieve a more convincing result and still save steps over more labor-intensive methods.

You're ready to explore the possibilities of the Neural Filters with your own images!

About Output options in Neural Filters

In other lessons in this book, you explore features such as Content-Aware Fill that let you control how the final result is applied to document layers. Neural Filters provide this option too. Your choice affects the amount of editing flexibility you have later.

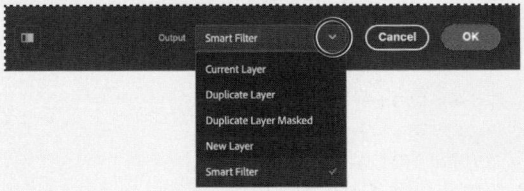

Current Layer applies the result to the selected layer. This permanently alters the original layer. The only way to back out of it is to undo it before you close and save the document. We recommend using one of the following options instead, because they leave the current layer intact.

Duplicate Layer applies the result to a full copy of the selected layer, which itself is left unchanged.

Duplicate Layer Masked applies the result to a copy of the selected layer with the changed areas showing through a layer mask. This helps ensure that areas of the image that were not supposed to be changed remain as they are on the original layer.

New Layer applies the result to a new layer that contains only the pixels that were changed by Neural Filters. Unchanged areas are transparent, letting the original layer show through.

Smart Filter applies the result to a copy of the selected layer as a Smart Object layer with Neural Filters results applied to it. As a Smart Filter, you'll be able to change the result at any time by double-clicking the Smart Object layer.

The choice you make can depend on the balance you want between flexibility and file size. Duplicate layers and Smart Objects provide more editing freedom but tend to create larger file sizes.

When you make multiple edits within a filter, such as changing multiple faces differently in a group portrait, all changes are included in the output. For example, if you use Smart Portrait on two faces and then apply Style Transfer, all of those results are applied to a single layer or Smart Filter.

Finding the filter or effect you want

The wide range of filters and effects in Photoshop appear in multiple places in the workspace and menus, and there can be multiple types of the same filter. That can make it difficult to find the filter you need.

One way to distinguish types of filters and effects is if they are destructive. A *destructive* edit permanently alters the pixels of a layer. A *nondestructive* edit is easy to change at any time, and removing it restores the unchanged original layer; this is obviously a better way to keep your options open.

Here is a quick guide to the places where you can find filters and effects in Photoshop:

General filters are on the Filter menu and its submenus. Not every filter is visible on the submenus, so also remember to look inside the next two filter galleries.

Filter Gallery (Filter > Filter Gallery) offers a large number of conventional (algorithmic) filters, such as Diffuse Glow and Mosaic Tiles. These are mostly intended for creative effects.

Neural Filters (Filter > Neural Filters) offer the newest and most advanced filters, trained by machine learning. They can produce results that are better than, or not possible with, conventional filters. Neural Filters are also capable of more intelligent radical edits, such as changing which way eyes are looking.

To explore all your options, keep those multiple filter locations in mind. For example, if you want to improve skin complexion, you can use the more traditional multistep technique in Lesson 12 that uses the Surface Blur filter, compare that to the results you get from using the one-step Skin Smoothing filter in Neural Filters, and use the result you think is better for a specific image.

Layer styles are nondestructive, easy ways to apply drop shadows, glows, and other effects you have tried in this book. You can find them by clicking the fx button at the bottom of the Layers panel or on the Layer > Layer Style submenu.

As you have done in this book, even a destructive filter or effect can be applied nondestructively if the layer is a Smart Object. When you do this, the filter is applied as a Smart Filter so that you can edit the results.

If you want to combine filters on a layer, with most filters you simply apply each filter in turn. For filters in a filter gallery dialog box or workspace (Filter Gallery, Neural Filters, and Blur Gallery), you can combine multiple filters in that gallery before you exit the dialog box or workspace.

Neural Filters gallery

These are examples of some of the Neural Filters included in the 2021 release of Photoshop. Some are useful for restoring and correcting images, others are fun ways to explore creatively. Adobe may update, add to, or change the filters in Neural Filters, so the exact list of Neural Filters in Photoshop may depend on the version that you have installed.

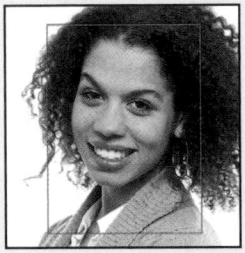

Before

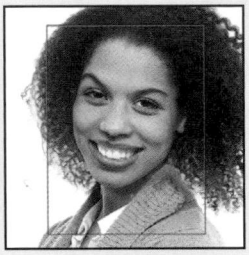

After

Smart Portrait lets you tune details of portraits such as emotions, facial expressions, facial age, and gestures such as which way the eyes are looking.

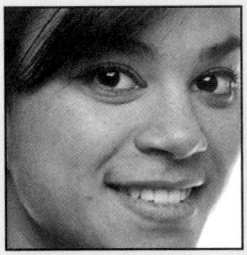

Before

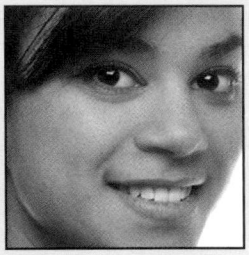

After

Skin Smoothing can reduce acne, blemishes, and other skin irregularities in portraits, while preserving the overall character of the skin.

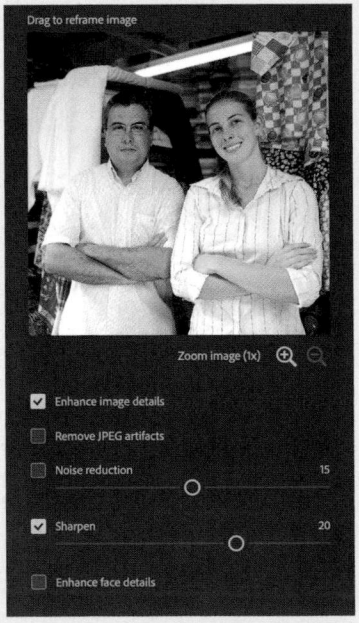

Image © mangostock. Shutterstock

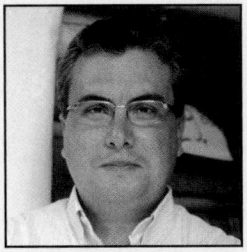

Super Zoom, 3x

Super Zoom is a convenient way to enlarge part of an photo to use as a portrait. For example, you can pick out one person in a group photo and create an enhanced, sharpened enlargement for a profile picture. Or, if a person's face is too small in the middle of a smartphone photo, you can fill more of the frame with their face. Unlike many scaling methods, Super Zoom offers detail enhancement, noise reduction, and JPEG artifact removal powered by machine learning. Super Zoom is optimized for portraits, but you can try it with other types of subjects.

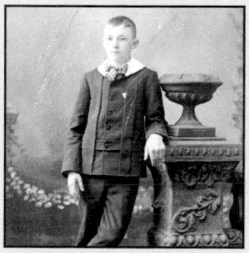

Before

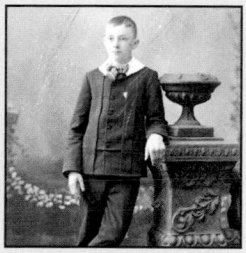

After

Colorize lets you quickly add color to a black-and-white image. You simply position dots of color over distinct content areas. The filter detects the content edges and colorizes within those edges. For example, placing a blue dot over a jacket colors the jacket but not the background or skin.

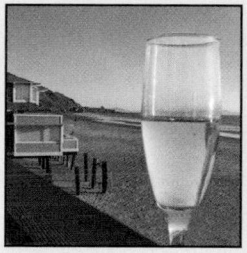

Before

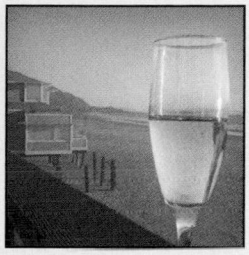

After

Depth-Aware Haze is a way to help isolate a subject by detecting background depth and adding haze to it. You can also make the haze cooler or warmer.

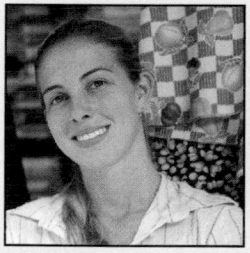

Before

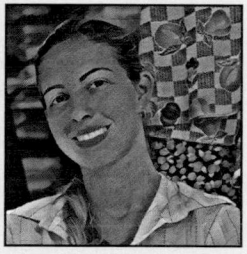

After

Style Transfer lets you apply the artistic style of one image to another image. You can choose from a range of styles and then customize the look further using filter options.

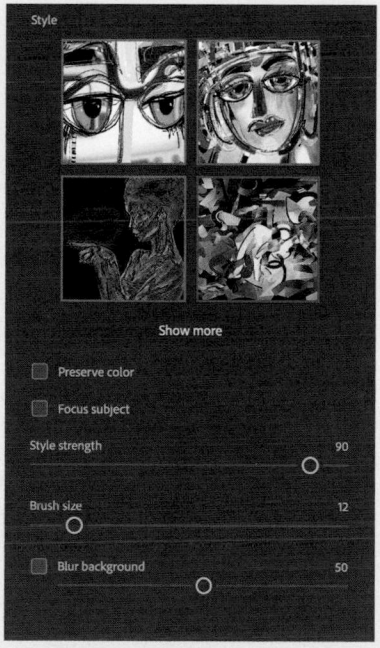

Improving Photoshop with your usage data and images

An important way that software developers improve features based on machine learning is to train them using examples of good results and bad results. Any company that uses machine learning needs a way to train the models that their software uses, ideally using examples that represent the interests of the customers of the software. But many software developers don't have very large data sets of actual customer files, and even if they store customer files in the cloud, they typically do not have customers' permission to use their files to train software.

To make it easier to improve Photoshop, Adobe added a Product Improvement pane to the Preferences dialog box in Photoshop. The purpose of the Photoshop Improvement Program is to request permission to use your images and usage data to help improve Photoshop features; this is not necessarily limited to machine learning. The "Yes, I'd like to participate" option is disabled by default, but if you want to participate, you can enable it. When it's enabled, Adobe researchers may collect usage data, Cloud Documents, and other images you edit in Photoshop.

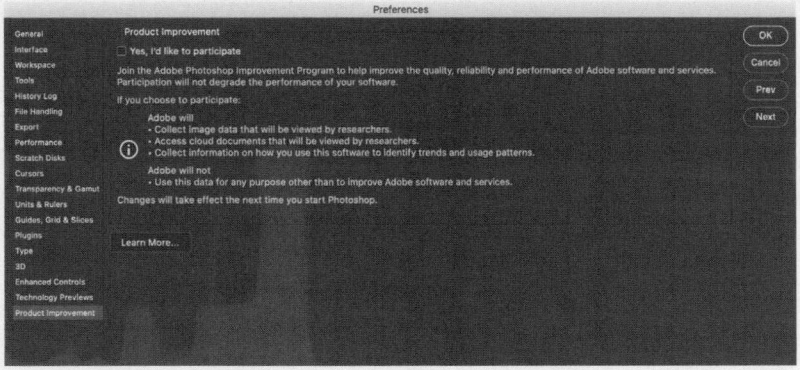

Whether or not you participate in the Photoshop Improvement Program is partly a personal decision. You may want to participate if you think your usage data might help improve how Photoshop handles the specific kinds of image editing that you do.

However, if you work for a company or organization that handles confidential documents, if you need to protect the privacy or proprietary data of your clients, or if you are legally bound by nondisclosure agreements, you should be aware of the potential consequences of participating in the Photoshop Improvement Program.

For more information about how your usage information is handled, see the Adobe Product Improvement Program web page at www.adobe.com/privacy/apip.html.

Review questions

1 How does a filter in Neural Filters differ from other filters in Photoshop?

2 How does an Internet connection affect how you use Neural Filters?

3 How can you easily control the combination of filters you apply in the Neural Filters workspace?

4 Why is it typically best to choose any Neural Filters output option except Current Layer?

Review answers

1 Neural Filters are trained using machine learning, so they are capable of results that are not attainable using conventional algorithmic filters.

2 If you are connected to the Internet, you can download Neural Filters and use Neural Filters that process image data in the cloud. If you choose to participate in the Photoshop Improvement Program, an Internet connection allows your usage data and images to be sent to Adobe for use by researchers.

3 Select the Applied Filters category in the Neural Filters workspace. It lists only the filters you applied, and you can enable or disable any of them there.

4 The Current Layer option applies the results of Neural Filters to the selected layer, permanently changing it. The other Output options apply the results of Neural Filters to a separate layer or as a Smart Filter so that you can easily start over from the original layer at any time.

Appendix: Tools panel overview

Photoshop 2021 Tools Panel

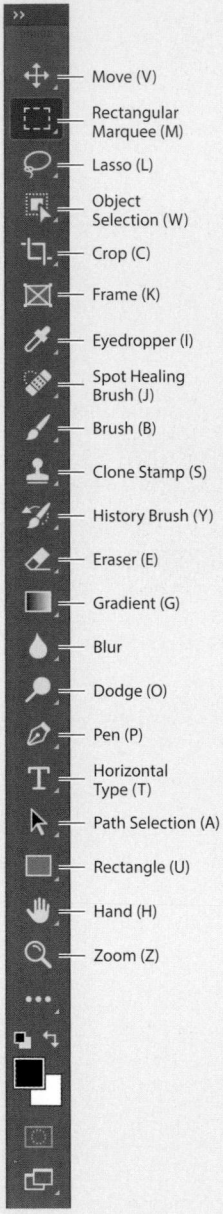

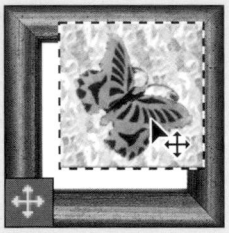

The Move tool moves selections, layers, and guides.

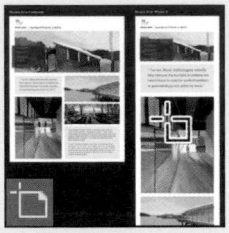

The Artboard tool moves, resizes, and adds artboards.

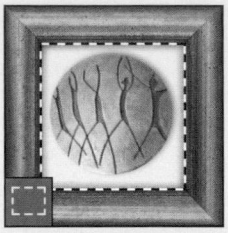

The marquee tools make rectangular, elliptical, single row, and single column selections.

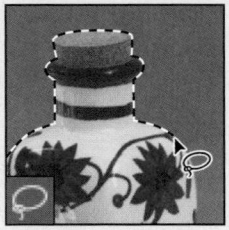

The lasso tools make free-hand, polygonal (straight-edged), and magnetic (snap-to) selections.

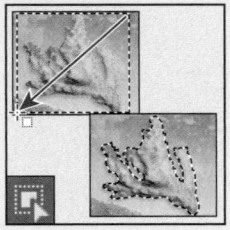

The Object Selection tool precisely selects an irregularly shaped object after you draw a loose selection marquee.

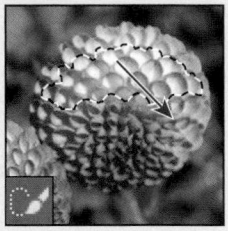

The Quick Selection tool lets you quickly "paint" a selection using an adjustable round brush tip.

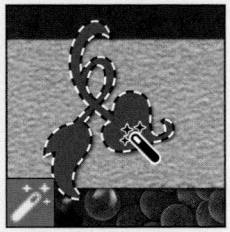

The Magic Wand tool selects similarly colored areas.

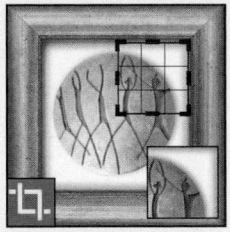

The crop tools trim, straighten, and change the perspective of images.

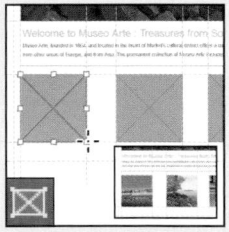

The Frame tool creates placeholder rectangles, so you can design now and drop in final artwork later.

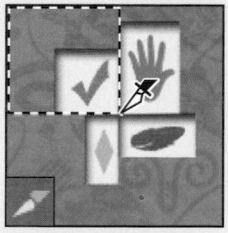

The Slice tool creates slices that can be exported as separate images.

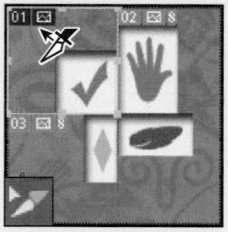

The Slice Select tool selects slices.

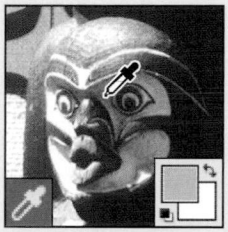

The Eyedropper tool samples colors in an image.

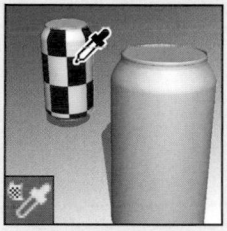

The 3D Material Eyedropper tool loads selected material from a 3D object.

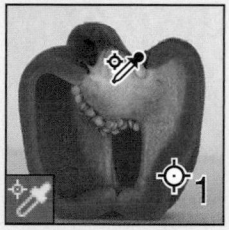

The Color Sampler tool samples up to four areas of an image.

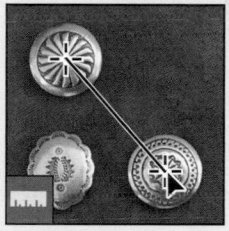

The Ruler tool measures distances, locations, and angles.

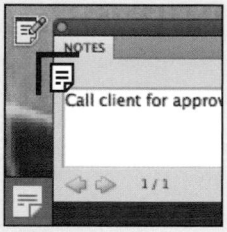

The Note tool makes text notes that can be included with a document.

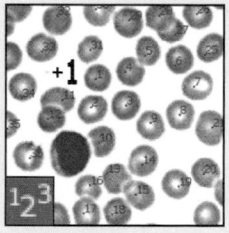

The Count tool counts objects in an image, for statistical image analysis.

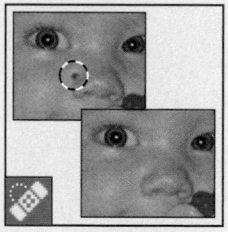

The Spot Healing Brush tool quickly removes blemishes and imperfections from photographs that have a uniform background.

Continues on next page

Appendix: Tools panel overview (continued)

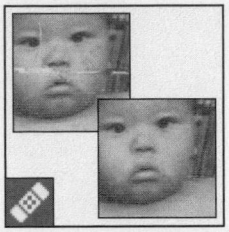

The Healing Brush tool paints with a sample or pattern to repair imperfections in an image.

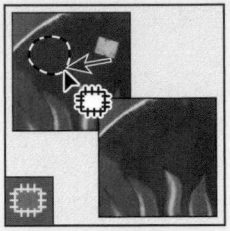

The Patch tool repairs imperfections in a selected area of an image, using a sample or pattern.

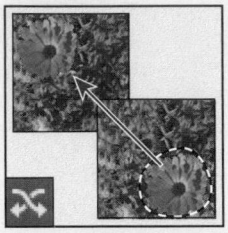

The Content-Aware Move tool recomposes and blends pixels to accommodate a moved object.

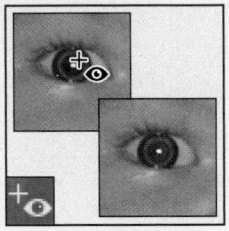

The Red Eye tool removes red eye in flash photos with one click.

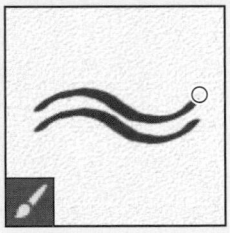

The Brush tool paints strokes using the current Brush Settings.

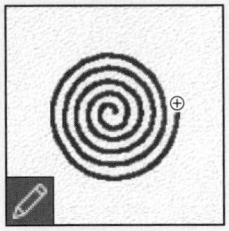

The Pencil tool paints hard-edged strokes.

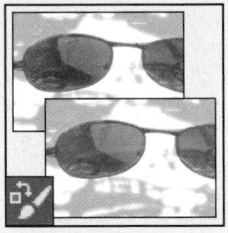

The Color Replacement tool substitutes one color for another.

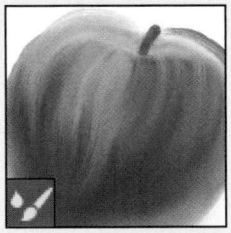

The Mixer Brush tool blends a sampled color with an existing color.

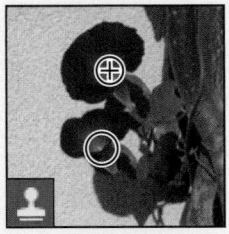

The Clone Stamp tool paints with a sample of an image.

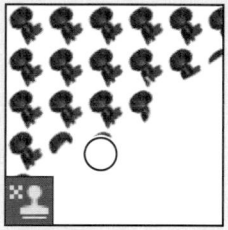

The Pattern Stamp tool paints with a part of an image as a pattern.

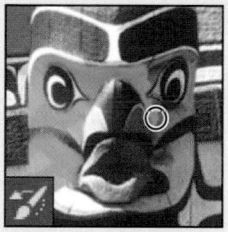

The History Brush tool paints a copy of the selected state or snapshot into the current image window.

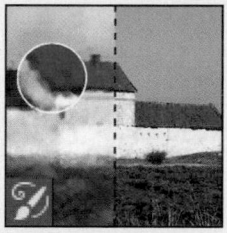

The Art History Brush tool paints stylized strokes that simulate the look of different paint styles.

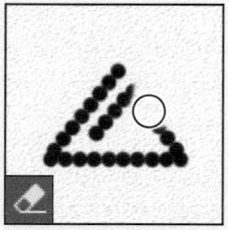

The Eraser tool erases pixels and restores parts of an image to a previously saved state.

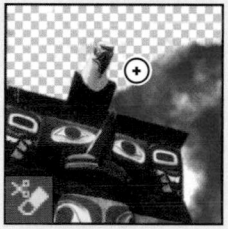

The Background Eraser tool erases areas to transparency by dragging.

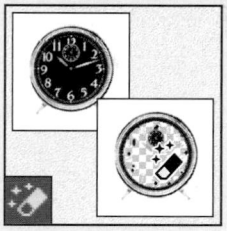

The Magic Eraser tool erases solid-colored areas to transparency in a single click.

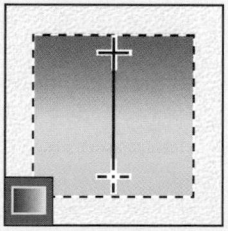

The Gradient tool creates straight-line, radial, angle, reflected, and diamond blends between colors.

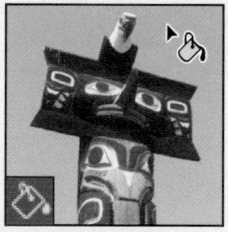

The Paint Bucket tool fills similarly colored areas with the foreground color.

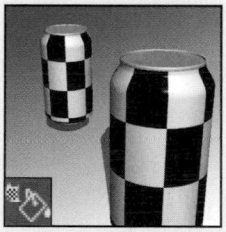

The 3D Material Drop tool drops the material loaded in the 3D Material Eyedropper tool onto the targeted area of a 3D object.

Continues on next page

Appendix: Tools panel overview (continued)

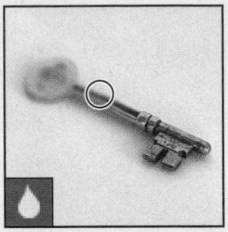

The Blur tool blurs hard edges in an image.

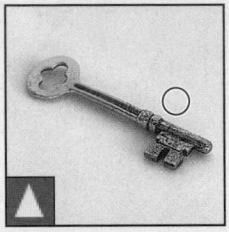

The Sharpen tool sharpens soft edges in an image.

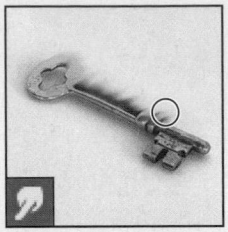

The Smudge tool smudges data in an image.

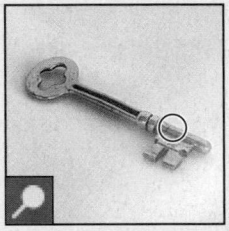

The Dodge tool lightens areas in an image.

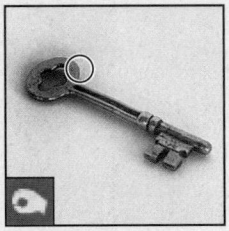

The Burn tool darkens areas in an image.

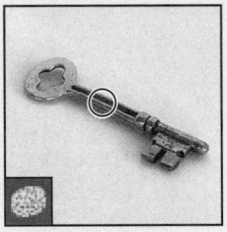

The Sponge tool changes the color saturation of an area.

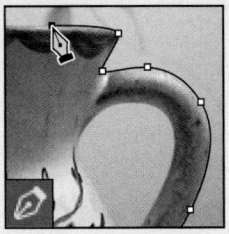

The pen tools draw and modify smooth-edged vector paths.

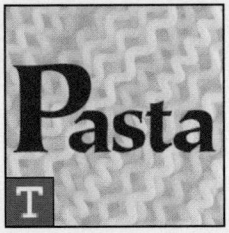

The type tools create type on an image.

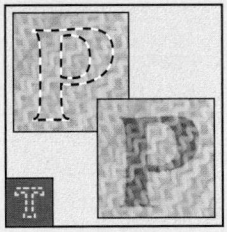

The type mask tools create a selection in the shape of type.

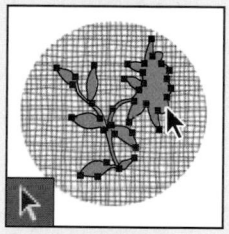

The path selection tools make shape or segment selections showing anchor points, direction lines, and direction points.

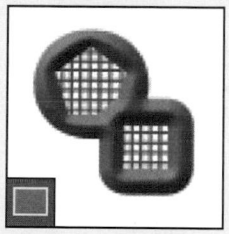

The shape tools and Line tool draw shapes and lines in a normal layer or shape layer.

The Custom Shape tool makes customized shapes selected from a custom shape list.

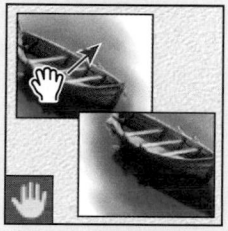

The Hand tool moves an image within its window.

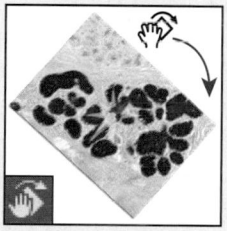

The Rotate View tool turns the canvas for stylus painting and drawing.

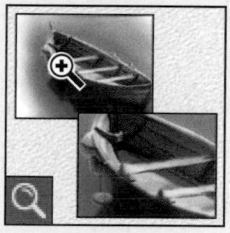

The Zoom tool magnifies and reduces the view of an image.

Appendix: Keyboard shortcuts

Learning the shortcuts for tools and commands you use most often can save you time. Want to customize them? Choose Edit > Keyboard Shortcuts. While there, click Summarize to export a list updated with your own shortcuts.

Tools *Each group of tools in the Tools panel shares a shortcut. Press Shift+ the letter key repeatedly to cycle through hidden tools. This list is based on the Essentials workspace. Other workspaces may change tool groupings and keyboard shortcuts, so if a shortcut isn't working for you, check which workspace is active.*

Move tool	V
Artboard tool	V
Rectangular Marquee tool	M
Elliptical Marquee tool	M
Lasso tool	L
Polygonal Lasso tool	L
Magnetic Lasso tool	L
Object Selection tool	W
Quick Selection tool	W
Magic Wand tool	W
Eyedropper tool	I
3D Material Eyedropper tool	I
Color Sampler tool	I
Ruler tool	I
Note tool	I
Count tool	I
Crop tool	C
Perspective Crop tool	C
Slice tool	C
Slice Select tool	C
Frame tool	K
Spot Healing Brush tool	J
Healing Brush tool	J
Patch tool	J
Content-Aware Move tool	J
Red Eye tool	J
Brush tool	B
Pencil tool	B
Color Replacement tool	B
Mixer Brush tool	B
Clone Stamp tool	S
Pattern Stamp tool	S
History Brush tool	Y
Art History Brush tool	Y
Eraser tool	E
Background Eraser tool	E
Magic Eraser tool	E
Gradient tool	G
Paint Bucket tool	G
3D Material Drop tool	G
Dodge tool	O
Burn tool	O
Sponge tool	O
Pen tool	P
Freeform Pen tool	P
Curvature Pen tool	P
Horizontal Type tool	T
Vertical Type tool	T
Horizontal Type Mask tool	T
Vertical Type Mask tool	T
Path Selection tool	A
Direct Selection tool	A
Rectangle tool	U
Rounded Rectangle tool	U
Ellipse tool	U
Triangle Tool	U
Polygon tool	U
Line tool	U
Custom Shape tool	U
Hand tool	H
Rotate View tool	R
Zoom tool	Z
Default Foreground/Background Colors	D
Swap Foreground/Background Colors	X
Toggle Standard/Quick Mask Modes	Q
Toggle Screen Modes	F
Toggle Lock Transparent Pixels	/
Decrease Brush Size	[
Increase Brush Size	]
Decrease Brush Hardness	{
Increase Brush Hardness	}
Previous Brush	,
Next Brush	.
First Brush	<
Last Brush	>

Application menus *These shortcuts are for Windows. For Mac, substitute Command for Ctrl and Option for Alt.*

File

New . . . **Ctrl+N**
Open . . . **Ctrl+O**
Browse in Bridge . . . **Alt+Ctrl+O**
Close . . . **Ctrl+W**
Close All . . . **Alt+Ctrl+W**
Close and Go to Bridge . . . **Shift+Ctrl+W**
Save . . . **Ctrl+S**
Save As . . . **Shift+Ctrl+S** or **Alt+Ctrl+S**
Export As (entire document) . . . **Alt+Shift+Ctrl+W**
Save for Web (Legacy) . . . **Alt+Shift+Ctrl+S**
Revert . . . **F12**
File Info . . . **Alt+Shift+Ctrl+I**
Print . . . **Ctrl+P**
Print One Copy . . . **Alt+Shift+Ctrl+P**
Exit/Quit . . . **Ctrl+Q**

Edit

Undo . . . **Ctrl+Z**
Redo . . . **Shift+Ctrl+Z**
Toggle Last State (of undo/redo) . . . **Alt+Ctrl+Z**
Fade . . . **Shift+Ctrl+F**
Cut . . . **Ctrl+X** or **F2**
Copy . . . **Ctrl+C** or **F3**
Copy Merged . . . **Shift+Ctrl+C**
Paste . . . **Ctrl+V** or **F4**
Paste Special > Paste in Place . . . **Shift+Ctrl+V**
Paste Special > Paste Into . . . **Alt+Shift+Ctrl+V**
Search . . . **Ctrl+F**
Fill . . . **Shift+F5**
Content-Aware Scale . . . **Alt+Shift+Ctrl+C**
Free Transform . . . **Ctrl+T**
Transform > Again . . . **Shift+Ctrl+T**
Color Settings . . . **Shift+Ctrl+K**
Keyboard Shortcuts . . . **Alt+Shift+Ctrl+K**
Menus . . . **Alt+Shift+Ctrl+M**
Preferences > General . . . **Ctrl+K**

Image

Adjustments >
- Levels . . . **Ctrl+L**
- Curves . . . **Ctrl+M**
- Hue/Saturation . . . **Ctrl+U**
- Color Balance . . . **Ctrl+B**
- Black & White . . . **Alt+Shift+Ctrl+B**
- Invert . . . **Ctrl+I**

Desaturate . . . **Shift+Ctrl+U**
Auto Tone . . . **Shift+Ctrl+L**
Auto Contrast . . . **Alt+Shift+Ctrl+L**
Auto Color . . . **Shift+Ctrl+B**
Image Size . . . **Alt+Ctrl+I**
Canvas Size . . . **Alt+Ctrl+C**
Record Measurements . . . **Shift+Ctrl+M**

Layer

New > Layer . . . **Shift+Ctrl+N**
New > Layer via Copy . . . **Ctrl+J**
New > Layer via Cut . . . **Shift+Ctrl+J**
Quick Export . . . **Shift+Ctrl+'**
Export As (selected layers) . . . **Alt-Shift+Ctrl+'**
Create/Release Clipping Mask . . . **Alt+Ctrl+G**
Group Layers . . . **Ctrl+G**
Ungroup Layers . . . **Shift+Ctrl+G**
Hide Layers . . . **Ctrl+,**
Arrange >
- Bring to Front . . . **Shift+Ctrl+]**
- Bring Forward . . . **Ctrl+]**
- Send Backward . . . **Ctrl+[**
- Send to Back . . . **Shift+Ctrl+[**

Lock Layers . . . **Ctrl+/**
Merge Down/Merge Layers . . . **Ctrl+E**
Merge Visible . . . **Shift+Ctrl+E**

Select

All . . . **Ctrl+A**
Deselect . . . **Ctrl+D**
Reselect . . . **Shift+Ctrl+D**
Inverse . . . **Shift+Ctrl+I** or **Shift+F7**
All Layers . . . **Alt+Ctrl+A**
Find Layers . . . **Alt+Shift+Ctrl+F**
Select and Mask . . . **Alt+Ctrl+R**
Modify > Feather . . . **Shift+F6**

Filter

Last Filter . . . **Alt+Ctrl+F (Windows), Control+Command+F (Mac)**
Adaptive Wide Angle . . . **Alt+Shift+Ctrl+A**
Camera Raw Filter . . . **Shift+Ctrl+A**
Lens Correction . . . **Shift+Ctrl+R**
Liquify . . . **Shift+Ctrl+X**
Vanishing Point . . . **Alt+Ctrl+V**

3D

Show/Hide Polygons > Within Selection . . . **Alt+Ctrl+X**
Show/Hide Polygons > Reveal All . . . **Alt+Shift+Ctrl+X**
Render 3D Layer . . . **Alt+Shift+Ctrl+R**

View

Proof Colors . . . **Ctrl+Y**
Gamut Warning . . . **Shift+Ctrl+Y**
Zoom In . . . **Ctrl++** or **Ctrl+=**
Zoom Out . . . **Ctrl+-**
Fit on Screen . . . **Ctrl+0**
100% . . . **Ctrl+1** or **Alt+Ctrl+0**
Extras . . . **Ctrl+H**
Show > Target Path . . . **Shift+Ctrl+H**
Show > Grid . . . **Ctrl+'**
Show > Guides . . . **Ctrl+;**
Rulers . . . **Ctrl+R**
Snap . . . **Shift+Ctrl+;**
Lock Guides . . . **Alt+Ctrl+;**

Window

Actions . . . **Alt+F9** or **F9**
Brush Settings . . . **F5**
Color . . . **F6**
Info . . . **F8**
Layers . . . **F7**

Help

Photoshop Help . . . **Ctrl+F**

INDEX

SYMBOLS

3D Material Drop tool 391
3D Material Eyedropper tool 389

A

actions
- batch 338
- playing 338
- recording 334–339
- sets 334
- stopping recording 338

Actions panel 334
Add Artboard button 342
Add Audio option 275
Add Layer Mask button 108
Add Media button 266
Add Noise filter 235
Adjustment Brush tool. *See* Adobe Camera Raw: Adjustment Brush tool
adjustment layers
- about 99–100
- Black & White 50, 271
- Brightness/Contrast 233
- Channel Mixer 233
- Curves 17, 114–115, 311
- defined 17
- Exposure 234
- Hue/Saturation 99, 206
- Levels 124, 304
- using in video 270

Adobe Bridge
- installing 3
- Load Files into Photoshop Layers command 219
- opening files in Camera Raw from 284
- opening files in Photoshop from 36
- previewing a file 122

Adobe Camera Raw
- about 283
- adjusting white balance in 288
- Adjustment Brush tool 285, 293, 315
- Basic panel 291
- cameras supported by 284
- Detail panel 294
- file formats for saving changes 302
- histogram 294
- Open as Object button 299
- opening images in 284
- profiles 287
- saving files from 297–298, 302
- synchronizing settings across images 296
- using as a filter 315–316
- version 282
- workflow 286
- workspace 286

Adobe Capture 210
Adobe Creative Cloud
- mobile apps 210
- portfolio online 372

Adobe Creative Cloud desktop application 3, 7
Adobe DNG (Digital Negative) file format 284, 301, 302, 314, 317
Adobe Fonts 188, 190
Adobe Generator 340
Adobe Illustrator 196, 302
Adobe InDesign 177, 302
Adobe Lightroom 11
Adobe Lightroom Classic 300–301

Adobe PDF (Portable Document Format)
Photoshop PDF format 188
printing on press 354
Adobe Photoshop
installing 3
new features 2
resetting default preferences 10
starting 4, 10
work area 10–31
Adobe Photoshop Classroom in a Book (2021 release)
about 1
lesson files and Web Edition 5
prerequisites 2
Adobe Portfolio 372–374
Adobe Raw profile 287
Adobe Stock 11
designing with 108
Libraries panel import 89
licensing 108
Search Adobe Stock command 80
Aligned option 47
alpha channels 148, 149, 163, 164
anchor points 197, 200
animating
Pan & Zoom effect 273
position 272–273
text 268–270
zoom 271–272
anti-aliasing 64
application frame, Mac 13
applying an edit 25
arrow keys, nudging with 63–64
artboards
about 340
adding 342
duplicating 340
exporting 348
mobile devices and 343
presets for sizes 342
resizing 345
Artboard tool 342, 345, 388
Art History Brush tool 391
audio
adding to a video timeline 275
fading 276
muting 276–277
shortening clips 275
Audio track 275
Auto-Align Layers 134
automating tasks 334–340
Auto-Select option 103

B

Background Eraser tool 391
background layer
about 76, 78
converting to a regular layer 78, 336
erasing 81
background, removing 149
barrel distortion, correcting 129
Basic panel (in Camera Raw) 291
Before/After views, Adobe Camera Raw 285
bitmap images
overview 10
vector graphics vs. 194–195
black and white, converting color images in Photoshop 50
black point 291
Black & White adjustment layer 50, 271
blemishes, removing 44, 380
Blend Images Together option 123
blending colors with a photograph 249
blending modes
applying to layers 85
deciding which to use 86
definition 84
previewing 85, 86
Bloat tool in the Liquify filter 227
blog, Photoshop tips and info 7
blur
camera shake, removing 144
Field Blur 120
Iris Blur 118–119, 120, 232
Path Blur 120, 121
restore noise 121
Spin Blur 120
surface blur 312–314
Tilt-Shift 120
Blur Effects panel 121
Blur Gallery 118–121
Blur tool 392
borders, adding 81, 103
Bridge. *See* Adobe Bridge
brightening an image 114–115, 124
Brightness/Contrast adjustment layer 233
bristle tips 242
Browse In Bridge command 36
brushes
loading with color 247
presets. *See* brush presets
rotation angle 250
settings 243
Brushes panel 249
brush presets
exporting 250
loading 249–251
painting with 252–254
Brush Settings panel 243
Brush tool 390
about 20
Paint Symmetry 255
setting options 160
Burn tool 392
buttons
creating 321–340
duplicating 329

C

calibration, monitor 360
Calibration panel, in Adobe Camera Raw 293
Camera Raw. *See* Adobe Camera Raw
camera raw images
creating 284
opening 284–285
sharpening 294

Camera Shake Reduction filter 144
Canvas Size command 336
CC Libraries. *See* Libraries, Creative Cloud
centering during drag-and-drop import 174
center point, selecting from 68
channel masks 149
Channel Mixer adjustment layer 233
channels
  about 148
  alpha channels 163, 164
  shadow created with 163
Character panel 91, 185
character styles 177
checkerboard transparency indicator 81
chromatic aberration 129
Clarity option 304
Classroom in a Book. *See* Adobe Photoshop Classroom in a Book (2021 release)
Clean Brush After Every Stroke icon 246
Clean Brush option (Mixer Brush tool) 247
clipping masks
  about 149, 171
  creating 100, 174–176, 357
  indicator 176
  shortcut 176
Clone Stamp tool 390
closed paths 195, 197
closing a Photoshop file 13
Cloud Documents
  about 55
  dialog box 18
  opening 11, 56
  saving 56
Clouds filter 89
CMYK color mode, converting to 362
CMYK color model 360, 361
collaborating with libraries 210
color
  additive 361
  adjusting overall 40
  changing foreground 18
  converting to black and white 50
  default foreground and background 232
  default text 174
  fonts 185
  management. *See* color management
  mixing with the Mixer Brush 246
  out-of-gamut 362
  previewing gamut clipping 362
  sampling 18, 243
  selecting by 54
  softening edge transitions 64
Color blending mode 86, 228
Color Burn blending mode 86
color casts, removing 40
color channels 149
color comp 370
Color Dodge blending mode 86
color gamut. *See* gamut
Color Grading panel, in Adobe Camera Raw 293
Colorize 385
color management 360–363, 361
Color Mixer panel, in Adobe Camera Raw 293
Color panel 28
color profile. *See* profiles, color
Color Range command 310
Color Replacement tool 390
color samplers
  in Adobe Camera Raw 285
Color Sampler tool 389
color separations 370
Color Settings dialog box 361–362
color settings, saving and restoring 6
color space 360
color theme, for user interface 30
combining images
  by dragging layers 79–82
  in a panorama 122–125
  with different perspectives 141–144
Commit Any Current Edits button 102
committing (applying) an edit 25
compositing. *See* combining images
Content-Aware Crop 126
Content-Aware Fill 135
Content-Aware Fill for panoramas 122, 123
Content-Aware Move tool 139, 390
Content-Aware Patch tool 45
Content panel, in Bridge 37
context menus
  annotations 188
  type 178, 181
  using 20
Contrast slider in Camera Raw 291
Control Timeline Magnification slider 267
Convert for Smart Filters 315
converting images to black and white 50
Copy command 79
copying
  anti-aliasing edges 64
  commands 71
  images 105, 365
  images, and centering 79
  layers 79, 79–81
  selections 70, 71
  settings in Camera Raw 296
Copy Merged command 71
corner points 197
Count tool 389
creases, repairing 44
Create Video Timeline 265
Creative Cloud. *See* Adobe Creative Cloud
Crop and Straighten Photos command 39

Crop tool 38–39, 72–73, 388
in Adobe Camera Raw 285
clearing settings 39
crop shield 38
leveling 38
Cross Fade transition 274
Curvature Pen tool 195, 196, 199, 392
curved paths 197
Curve panel, in Adobe Camera Raw 293
Curves adjustment layers 17–18, 114, 311
customizing the user interface 30
Custom Shape tool 393

D

Darken blending mode 86
Darker Color blending mode 86
Decontaminate Colors option 159
Default Foreground And Background Colors 232
defaults, resetting 5, 10
Define Custom Shape command 211
Delete Cropped Pixels option 38
deleting documents
from Adobe Camera Raw 285
from Cloud Documents 57
Depth-Aware Haze 385
depth map 119
depth of field, extending 132
Deselect command 23, 60
Deselect Layers command 23
Detail panel in Camera Raw 294
Difference blending mode 86
Difference Clouds filter 232
Direct Selection tool 197, 205, 393
Discover panel 6
discretionary ligatures 185
distortions, correcting 141
DNG. *See* Adobe DNG (Digital Negative) file format
docking panels 27
document size, displaying 105
document window
fitting image to 69
scrolling 16
status bar 14
Dodge tool 309–310, 392
dots per inch (dpi) 36
drag-and-drop importing 89
Drop Shadow layer style 331, 336
drop shadows 94–95, 96
duplicating
areas of a scene 135
buttons 329–333
images 105, 365
layers 329
duration of video clips, changing 267
Dust & Scratches filter 48

E

Edit In Quick Mask Mode button 160
educators, resources for 7
Ellipse tool 393
Elliptical Marquee tool 388
centering selection 68
circular selections with 62
in Tools panel 54
emoji fonts 185
Enhance Edge option 59
enlargement 384
EPS file format 369
Eraser tool 391
Exclusion blending mode 86
Export As command
exporting artboards 348
exporting layers 349
exporting
artboards 340, 348
brushes 250
Camera Raw files 284, 297–302
image files from layers 340, 349
layer visibility 167
video 277
web assets from layers 349
Exposure adjustment layer 234
Eyedropper tool 18, 19, 243, 389
eye icon, in the Layers panel 77

F

face adjustments
with healing tools 307
with Liquify filter 116, 222
with Skin Smoothing filter 380
with Smart Portrait filter 384
Face-Aware Liquify filter 116
Fade With Black transitions 274
fading audio 276
Feather command 64
feathering 64
Field Blur 120
file formats. *See* name of format
file sizes, differing among formats 313
fills
foreground color 103
gradient 93
filmstrip, Adobe Camera Raw 285
filters 383
adding clouds with 88
Add Noise 235
Camera Raw Filter 315
Camera Shake Reduction 144
Difference Clouds 232
Dust & Scratches 48
Lighting Effects 236
Liquify 222–223
Neural Filters 378
Smart Sharpen 48, 335
Find. *See* Search command
Fit On Screen command 69
fitting image in window 68
Flatten Image command. *See* flattening
flattening 41, 105, 189, 354
focus, adjusting 132
fonts
alternates 185
changing in the options bar 23

fonts (*continued*)
color 185
emoji 185
Font Similarity 188
OpenType 185
PostScript 170, 185
previewing in context 173
selecting 172
special characters 189
variable 185
Font Similarity option 188
Foreground color swatch 89
forum, Photoshop community 7
four-color printing 362
fractions 185
frames 321
Frame tool 321, 388
Freeform Pen tool 195, 392
freehand selections 65–66
Free Transform command 220, 222
moving with 225
options bar settings 343
resizing with 87
rotating with 180
Full Screen mode, Adobe Camera Raw 285

G

gamut
colors outside of 362–363
defined 360
Gamut Warning 362–363
Generator. *See* Adobe Generator
Geometric Distortion Correction option 123
GIF (Graphics Interchange Format) file format 340
Global Light option 94
glyph alternates 180
Glyphs panel 185, 189
Go To First Frame button 274
Gradient Picker 93
gradients, listing by name 93
Gradients panel 97
Gradient tool 93, 391
Graduated Filter, Adobe Camera Raw 285, 293
graphics hardware 3
grid
in Adobe Camera Raw 285
in Lens Correction filter 130
guides
adding 171
ruler 326
Smart Guides 214

H

Hand tool 68, 393
in Adobe Camera Raw 285
Hard Light blending mode 86
Hard Mix blending mode 86
HDR in Camera Raw 314
Healing Brush 390
Healing Brush tool 44, 307
HEIF format 119
Help, Photoshop 7
hiding
layers 80
selection edges 64–65
HiDPI
graphics export 350
resolution 35
high-resolution images 35
histogram
Camera Raw 285, 294
Levels adjustment layer 41, 305, 359
History Brush tool 391
History panel 231–237
Home screen 10
Horizontal Type Mask tool 392
Horizontal Type tool 23, 91, 172, 392
hue, adjusting for printing 365
Hue blending mode 86
Hue/Saturation adjustment layers 17, 161, 206

I

Illustrator. *See* Adobe Illustrator
importing
audio 275
embedded Smart Objects 339
multiple files from Bridge 219
video 265
InDesign. *See* Adobe InDesign
Info panel 321, 326
inkjet printers 370
Inner Shadow layer style 176
interface. *See* user interface
International Color Consortium (ICC) 360
iPad, Apple 55
iPhone, designing for 342
Iris Blur 118–119, 120, 232
Isolate Layers command 102

J

JPEG (Joint Photographic Experts Group) file format
Camera Raw and 284, 297, 302
compared to other formats 302
Export As 348
image quality degradation 301
type quality 188
web design 340

K

keyboard shortcuts
customizing 248
duplicating 70
list of 394–395
keyframes
appearance of 269
moving to the next or previous 272
using to animate text 268

L

Large Document Format 302
Lasso tool 388
Lasso tools 54, 65–66

layer comps 104
layer effects
adding 94–99
updating 102
layers
about 76
adding 88–89
aligning 80
Background 78
blending modes 84–85
converting Background to regular 336
converting to Background 78
copying 79–81
copying and centering 79, 83
copying and merging 71
copying and pasting 79
copying to other 79
duplicating 84, 329
effects. *See* layer effects; *See also* layer styles
erasing 81–83
exporting individually 349
flattening 105, 106
generating images from 340
groups 326
hiding and showing 77, 80, 81
linking 87–89
locking 77
masks 149
merging visible 105
opacity 84
overview 76
painting 228
rearranging 82–84
removing pixels from 81–83
renaming 79
resizing 87–89
rotating 87
saving in GIF or JPEG formats 76
selecting 18
showing and hiding 80
styles. *See* layer styles
thumbnail icons 77
transforming 87
transparency 84–85
type 91
Layers panel
overview 77–78
Quick Mask mode indicator 160
searching within 102
layer styles 383
adding to type 176
applying 92–95, 94–97
in Creative Cloud Libraries 95
Drop Shadow 94, 98, 331, 336
multiple instances of effects 101
overview 92, 94
presets 213
Satin 98
Stroke 96, 332
leading 183
learning resources for Adobe Photoshop 6
Learn tutorials 11
length of video clips, changing 267
Lens Correction filter 129–131
lens flaws, correcting 129–131
lesson files, accessing 3
Levels adjustment layers 41–42, 124, 304
Libraries, Creative Cloud
Adobe Stock 89
color swatches 89
images 89
layer styles 95
linked Smart Objects 210
mobile apps 210
Libraries panel 108
licensing, Adobe Stock 108
ligatures 185
Lighten blending mode 86
lightening an image 114–115, 124
Lighter Color blending mode 86
Lighting Effects filter 236
Lightroom. *See* Adobe Lightroom Classic
Lightroom photos online storage 11, 31
Linear Burn blending mode 86
Linear Dodge blending mode 86
linear gradients 88–90
Linear Light blending mode 86
Line tool 393
Liquify, Face-Aware filter 116
Liquify filter 222–223
Load Files Into Photoshop Layers command 219
loading brushes with color 247
Load Selection command 164
low resolution images
about 35
upscaling 237
Luminosity blending mode 86

M

Mac, differences in work area 13
machine learning 378
Magic Eraser tool 391
Magic Wand tool 54, 57–58, 61–62, 388
Magnetic Lasso tool 54, 67–68, 388
magnification. *See* Zoom tool
document 14–16
Timeline panel 267
magnifying glass. *See* Zoom tool
mandalas, painting 255
marching ants. *See* selection marquee
marquee tools 54
masks 148
creating 149–152
inverting 161
overview 148
refining 153–159
terminology 149
vector 149
Match Font command 190
megapixels 35
Merge Visible command 106
merging
images 132
images into a panorama 122

merging (*continued*)
images with different perspectives 141–144
layers 105
multiple Photoshop files 219
mistakes, correcting 25–31
Mixer Brush tool 390
about 242
cleaning the brush 247
mixing colors
with a photograph 249
with Mixer Brush tool 246
mobile devices
designing for, with artboards 343
using with libraries 210
monitor calibration 360
motion blur effects 121
Motion dialog box 268, 271
Motion workspace 265
Move tool 388
Auto-Select option 103
moving selections 60
scissors icon 69
using 26
moving
panels 27
selections 60–61
Multiply blending mode 86
muting audio 276–277

N

navigating
using the Navigator panel 16
with the Zoom tool 13–14
Navigator panel 16
Neural Filters 117, 378, 383
compared to other filters 383
downloading filters 380
output options 382
previewing changes 381
using 379
noise, reducing 48
nondestructive filters 222
notes, deleting 188
Notes panel 183
Note tool 389
nudging layers 347
nudging selections 63

O

Object Selection tool 61, 388
on-image adjustment tool. *See* targeted adjustment tool
opacity, changing 84–85
opening images in Camera Raw 284
Open Object button (in Camera Raw) 299
open paths 195, 197
OpenType file format 170, 185
OpenType SVG 185
options bar
compared to panels 29–30
overview 23–24
reference point icon 343
setting type options in 23
organizing photos 300–301
out-of-gamut color 362–363
output options, Neural Filters 382
output resolution, determining 35
Overlay blending mode 85, 86

P

Paint Bucket tool 391
painting
layers 228
wetness options 244
with the Mixer Brush tool 240–254
painting gallery 256
Paint Symmetry option 255
panels
compared to options bar 29
docking 27
expanding and collapsing 28–29
moving to another group 27
overview 27–28
resizing 28
reveal hidden side panels 27
undocking 27
panning
with the Hand tool 393
with the Navigator panel 16
panoramas
in Adobe Camera Raw 314
in Photoshop 122–125
Pan & Zoom option 268, 273, 273–274
Paper Color option 364
paper, simulating white 364
Paragraph panel 28
paragraph styles 177
paragraph type 172
Paste command 79
Paste in Place command 71
Paste Into command 71, 238
Paste Outside command 71
Paste Profile Mismatch dialog box 236
Paste Without Formatting command 71, 183
pasting layers 79
Patch tool 45, 390
Path Blur 120–121, 121
paths
about 195
adding type to 178–179
closing 197
compared to shapes 203
converting to selection 206
creating from selection 206
drawing 196–201
drawing curved segments 197
drawing straight segments 197
editing 205
guidelines for drawing 200
moving 205
saving 197
Path Selection tool 205, 393
Paths panel
using 198
work path 197
Patterns panel 213

Pattern Stamp tool 391
Pencil tool 195, 390
Pen tool 392. *See also* paths
as selection tool 196
drawing paths 196–200
keyboard shortcut 195
overview 195–196, 197
setting options 198–199
Perspective Crop tool 388
Perspective Warp command 141
Photomerge 122–125
photo restoration, manual 42–43
Photoshop PDF file format 188
pincushion distortion 129
Pin Light blending mode 86
pixel dimensions 35
pixels
compared to vector graphics 194
defined 10
path tools option 203
resolution and 35
pixels per inch 35
Place Embedded command 339, 340
placeholders 321
planes, Perspective Warp 142
playhead, in the Timeline panel 270
plug-ins 10
PNG (Portable Network Graphics) file format 302, 340
point type
defined 172
distorting 181–182
paragraphs vs. 182
Polygonal Lasso tool 22, 54, 388
Polygon tool 393
portfolio. *See* Adobe Portfolio
position, animating in video 272
PostScript fonts 170, 185
ppi (pixels per inch) 35
preferences
Export 349
gamut-warning color 363
History States 237
restoring defaults 5, 10
Units & Rulers 321
Use Graphics Processor 236
user interface lightness 30
preferences, Adobe Camera Raw 285
Preserve Details 2.0 option 237
Preserve Details (Enlargement) option 237
Preserve Numbers option 364
presets
in Adobe Camera Raw 285
artboard 342
brush 249–251
Curves panel 114
Gradients panel 97
Lighting Effects 236
shapes 209
Styles panel 213
White Balance (Camera Raw) 288
previewing
colors for printing 363
edits in dialog boxes 49
files in Adobe Bridge 37
fonts in context 173
Print dialog box 371
printing
CMYK model and 360–361
for press 353–375
guidelines 370
identifying out-of-gamut color 362–363
for inkjet printers 370
preparing images for 354
preparing text and vector shapes for 189
proofing images onscreen 363–366
saving image as separations 369
printing inks, simulating onscreen 364
process colors 34, 362
profiles, Adobe Raw 287, 304
profiles, color
CMYK 368
ICC 360
printer 364
proofing images 363–366
Properties panel 29 30
artboard editing 342
Brightness and Contrast adjustment 17
clipping masks 357
Curves adjustment 40
Levels adjustment 305
targeted adjustment tool 50
type settings 173
proxy icon 343
PSB (Large Document Format) 302
PSD (Photoshop) format 284, 302
Pucker tool in the Liquify filter 227
Puppet Warp command 162

Q

quick mask 149
Quick Mask mode 160, 161
Quick Selection tool 54, 59, 151, 388

R

Radial Filter, in Adobe Camera Raw 285, 293
radial symmetry 255
raster images, overview 194
rate images, in Adobe Camera Raw 285
raw profiles 293
recording actions 334–338
rectangles, rounded 186
Rectangle tool 393
Rectangular Marquee tool 20, 54, 327, 388
red eye, correcting 112–114
Red Eye Removal, Adobe Camera Raw 285
Red Eye tool 113–114, 390
Redo command 26
reference point 343
Refine Edge. *See* Select and Mask
Refine Edge Brush tool 153
rendering video 277
repositioning selections 62

Resize To Fill Canvas option 268
resizing. *See also* scaling
from center 225
layers 87
panels 28
proportionally 70
video assets 268
resolution
about 35–36
Adobe Stock images 80, 108
best practices 301
bitmap images vs. vector graphics 194
Camera Raw 286, 298
Crop tool option 38
defined 34
increasing 237
professional printing 354, 356
screens of high and low 340, 350
sharpening and 49
text 191
responsive design 341
Retina resolution 35, 350
retouching/repairing
removing blemishes 44–45
strategy 34
with the Healing Brush tool 307
with the Spot Healing Brush tool 44, 307–309
Return To Adobe Photoshop command 118
RGB color mode, converting to CMYK 362
RGB color model 360, 361, 362–364
right-click menus 20
Rotate View 393
rotating
constraining 66
images 129
layers 87
paths 180
in Puppet Warp 163
selections 66
stylus 243, 250
Rounded Rectangle tool 186–187, 393
ruler guides 171, 326
rulers 19, 172
Ruler tool 389

S

Sampling Brush tool 137
sampling colors 18, 243
Satin layer style 98
saturation
in Camera Raw 291
in Photoshop 309–310
Saturation blending mode 86
Save for Web (Legacy) command 340. *See also* Export As command
saving documents 18. *See also* exporting
as Cloud Documents 56
flattening and 105–108
as Photoshop format 18
as Photoshop PDF format 188
as CMYK EPS format 369
scale factors, exporting for Retina/HiDPI 350
scaling
enlarging 237
layers 175
proportionally 70
Screen blending mode 86
scrubbing numeric values 23–24
Search command 6
Search icon 11, 12
searching
Adobe Stock 108
within Layers panel 102
within Photoshop 11
Select and Mask command 149
selecting. *See also* selections
about 54
center point, from 68–69
by color 54
creating from a path 206
high-contrast edges 67–68
layers 18
skin tones 310
a subject automatically 151
text 102
selection marquee 20
selections. *See also* selecting
circular 69
converting into path 206
copying 71
duplicating 70
elliptical 61–69
feathering 64
freehand 54
geometric 54
hiding edges of 64
inverting 161
marquee 20
moving 60–61, 63, 69–70, 70
rotating 66–67
saving 161
showing edges of 64
softening 64
selection tools 54–55
Select Subject command 151
separations. *See* color separations
sepia effect, creating 271
shadows, creating 163
shapes
creating your own 211
defined 203
editing 211
presets 207–210
Share an Image button 12
sharpening
in Camera Raw 294–295
in Photoshop 48–49
Sharpen tool 392
shortcut menus 20
shortcuts. *See* keyboard shortcuts
shortening video clips 267
Show/Hide Visibility column 81
side by side documents 79
sidecar XMP files 296
Single Column Marquee tool 54, 388

Single Row Marquee tool 54, 388
skewing an object 166
Skin Smoothing 380, 384
skin tones, selecting 310
Slice Select tool 389
Slice tool 389
Smart Filters 118, 222–225, 227
Smart Guides 214
Smart Objects
  converting layers to 222
  editing 119, 224
  embedded 339
  icon badge 222
  linked 210
  Smart Filters and 222
Smart Portrait 384
Smart Sharpen filter 48, 335
smooth points 197
Smudge tool 392
snapshots, in Adobe Camera Raw 285
Soft Light blending mode 86
soft-proofing 363–366
special characters 189
spell checking 178
Spin Blur 120
Split at Playhead button 275
Sponge tool 309–310, 392
Spot Healing Brush tool 44–45, 307–309, 389
Spot Removal tool, in Adobe Camera Raw 285
stacking order, changing 82–84
Standard mode 160
starting Photoshop 10
status bar 14
sticky notes 183
Stop Recording button 338
stopwatch icon in the Timeline panel 269
Straighten button 126
Straighten button for Crop tool 38
strobe effect 121
Stroke layer style 96, 332
Structure option 139
Styles panel 213
Style Transfer 385
Super Zoom 384
Surface Blur filter 312
SVG (Scalable Vector Graphics) file format 185, 340
swashes 185
Swatches panel 24–25, 25
swatches, selecting 24
symmetry, painting with 255
synchronizing settings in Camera Raw 296

T

targeted adjustment tool 50
teachers, resources for 7
temperature, image color 288
text. *See also* type
  adding 172
  animating 268
  applying edits 173
  creating 23, 91–92
  default color 174
  moving 92
  selecting 102, 173
Texture option 304
thumbnail icons, layer 77
TIFF (Tagged Image File Format)
  camera raw images and 284–285, 302
  compared to other formats 301, 302
  type quality 188
Tilt-Shift Blur 120
timeline, creating 265
Timeline panel
  changing the magnification 267
  returning to the first frame 274
Tint
  in Black & White adjustment layers 50, 271
  in white balance (Camera Raw) 288
Toggle Last State command 26, 231
Toggle Reference Point option 343
Tolerance option for the Magic Wand tool 58
tone, adjusting 40–41
tools
  Brush tool 20
  Content-Aware Move 135, 139
  Crop tool 38
  Elliptical Marquee 238
  Eyedropper 18, 243
  Healing Brush tool 44
  Horizontal Type tool 23
  keyboard shortcuts 195, 394
  Lasso tool 65
  Magic Wand tool 57, 61
  Magnetic Lasso tool 65, 67
  Move tool 26
  Object Selection tool 61
  overview 388–391
  Patch tool 45
  Polygonal Lasso tool 22, 65
  Quick Selection tool 59, 151
  Rectangular Marquee tool 20, 327
  Rounded Rectangle tool 186–187
  selecting hidden 21–22
  selection 54–55
  Spot Healing Brush tool 44
  using 13–19
Tools panel. *See also* tools
  compared to other panels 29–30
  double-column view 14
  overview 388–391
  selecting and using tools from 13–19
tool tips, displaying 14
tracing a photo 202
tracks, in a timeline 265
transforming 87. *See also* Free Transform command
transitions
  adding to video 274
  changing the length of 275

transparency
adjusting 84–85
blending modes and 86
recognizing (checkerboard) 81
Transparency & Gamut preference 363
TrueType fonts 185
tutorials built into Photoshop 11
type. *See also* text
aligning 172
clipping mask 171, 174–176
creating 172–173
on a path 178–179
overview 170
resizing 170
setting options 172
swashes 185
tricks 178
true fractions 185
vertical 187–188
warping 181–182
typefaces. *See* fonts
formats 170
selecting 172
Typekit. *See* Adobe Fonts
type layers
creating new 91, 178
selecting contents 178
Type tool 23–24

U

undocking panels 27
Undo command 25
undoing actions
with commands 25–26
with the History panel 231–237
unit of measure 19
Units & Rulers command 19
Units & Rulers preferences 321
upscaling images 237, 384
Use Global Light command 94
user interface
Adobe Camera Raw 286
changing settings for 30
overview 10–13

V

Variable Fonts 185
vector graphics
bitmap images vs. 194
defined 10
overview 194
vector masks 149
version, Photoshop 2
Vertical Type Mask tool 392
Vertical Type tool 187, 392
video
adding audio to 275
adding pan and zoom effects 273–274
adding transitions 274–275
exporting 277
groups 266
importing assets for 265
Motion workspace 265
overview 264
rendering 277
resizing assets for 268
using adjustment layers in 270
vignetting 129
visibility icon. *See* eye icon
Vivid Light blending mode 86

W

warping
images with the Liquify filter 222
perspective 141–144
Puppet Warp 162–163
type 181–189
watermark, Adobe Stock 108
web design
HiDPI 350
responsive 341
Retina 350
workflow 318
Web Edition 5
wetness options, in painting 244
White Balance tool (in Camera Raw) 289–290
white point 291
White Point eyedropper tool 358
Windows, differences in work area 13
work area 10–31
workflow preferences, Adobe Camera Raw 285
workflows
color-managed 361–363
compositing 76
organizing photos 300–301
prepress 354, 362
professional photography 300–301
retouching 34
video 260
web design 319
work path 197
workspaces
default 13
Essentials 29, 394
Graphics and Web 171
Motion 265
Painting 243
Workspaces menu 12

X

XMP files 296

Y

YouTube 277

Z

Zoom option in video 271
zoom test, before printing 356
Zoom tool 393. *See also* magnification
shortcuts 155
using 13–16

Production Notes

Adobe Photoshop Classroom in a Book (2021 release) was created electronically using Adobe InDesign. Art was produced using Adobe InDesign, Adobe Illustrator, and Adobe Photoshop. The Myriad Pro and Warnock Pro OpenType families of typefaces were used throughout this book. For information about OpenType and Adobe fonts, visit www.adobe.com/type/opentype/.

References to company names in the lessons are for demonstration purposes only and are not intended to refer to any actual organization or person.

Images

Photographic images and illustrations are intended for use with this book's lessons only.

Lesson 4 pineapple and flower photography © Image Source, www.imagesource.com; ukulele image from Adobe Stock, stock.adobe.com

Lesson 15 group photo: © Djomas. Shutterstock; photo of pair in fabric shop: © mangostock. Shutterstock

Team credits

The following individuals contributed to the development of *Adobe Photoshop Classroom in a Book (2021 release)*:

Project Manager: Anne-Marie Praetzel

Writer: Conrad Chavez

Illustrator and Compositor: David Van Ness

Copyeditor and Proofreader: Kim Wimpsett

Indexer: Conrad Chavez

Technical Reviewer: David Van Ness

Production Assistant: Caroline Praetzel

Interior design: Mimi Heft

Art Director: Andrew Faulkner

Designer: Anne-Marie Praetzel

Adobe Press Executive Editor: Laura Norman

Adobe Press Production Editor: Tracey Croom

Contributors

Jay Graham began his career designing and building custom homes. He has been a professional photographer for more than 25 years, with clients in the advertising, architectural, editorial, and travel industries. He contributed the "Pro photo workflow" tips in Lesson 12. www.jaygraham.com

Lisa Farrer is a photographer based in Marin County, CA. She contributed photography for Lesson 5.

Gawain Weaver has conserved and restored original works by artists ranging from Eadweard Muybridge to Man Ray, and from Ansel Adams to Cindy Sherman. He contributed to "Real-world photo restoration" in Lesson 2. www.gawainweaver.com

Special Thanks

We offer our sincere thanks to Stephen Nielson, Joel Baer, Russell Brown, Pete Falco, Rikk Flohr, Steve Guilhamet, Meredith Payne Stotzner, Jeff Tranberry, and Casey Atud for their support and help with this project. We couldn't have done it without you!

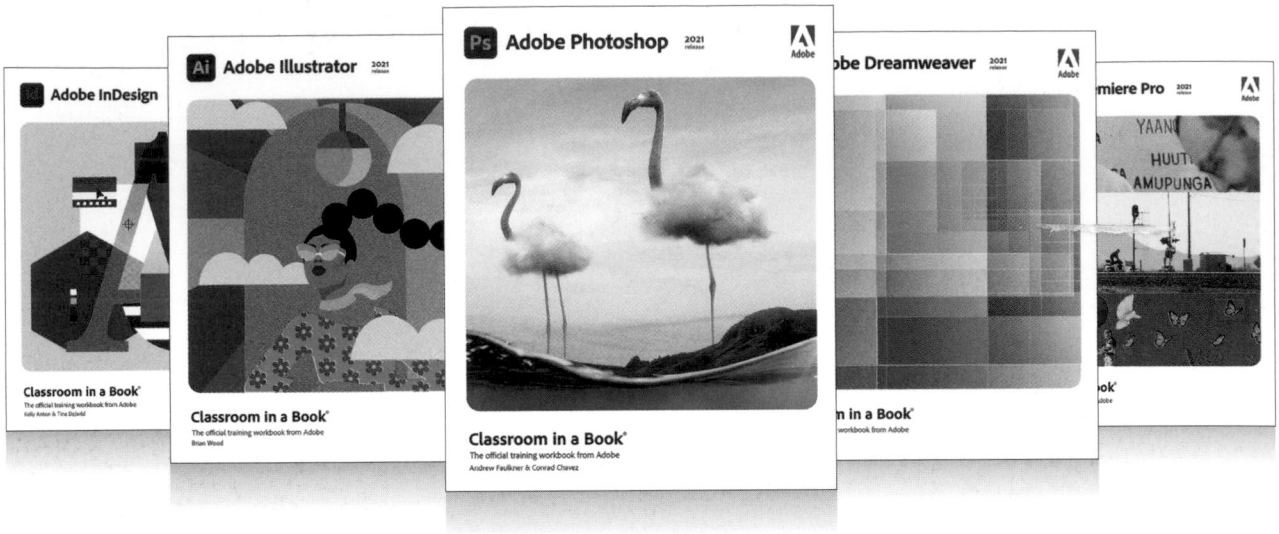

The fastest, easiest, most comprehensive way to learn **Adobe Creative Cloud**

Classroom in a Book®, the best-selling series of hands-on software training books, helps you learn the features of Adobe software quickly and easily.

The **Classroom in a Book** series offers what no other book or training program does—an official training series from Adobe Systems, developed with the support of Adobe product experts.

To see a complete list of our Classroom in a Book titles covering the 2021 release of Adobe Creative Cloud go to: www.adobepress.com/CC2021

Adobe Photoshop Classroom in a Book (2021 release)
ISBN: 9780136904731

Adobe Illustrator Classroom in a Book (2021 release)
ISBN: 9780136805533

Adobe InDesign Classroom in a Book (2021 release)
ISBN: 9780136870289

Adobe Dreamweaver Classroom in a Book (2021 release)
ISBN: 9780136875239

Adobe Premiere Pro Classroom in a Book (2021 release)
ISBN: 9780137280926

Adobe Dimension Classroom in a Book (2021 release)
ISBN: 9780136870104

Adobe After Effects Classroom in a Book (2021 release)
ISBN: 9780136815648

Adobe Animate Classroom in a Book (2021 release)
ISBN: 9780136887423

Adobe Photoshop Lightroom Classic Classroom in a Book (2021 release)
ISBN: 9780136885382

Adobe Press